D0563815

WITHDRAWN
FROM
UNIVERSITY OF PENNSYLVANIA
LIBRARIES

THE PSYCHOLOGY OF MENTAL RETARDATION:

Issues and Approaches

Contributors

John M. Belmont, Ph.D.
University of Kansas Medical
Center
Kansas City, Kansas

Irv Bialer, Ph.D.
Child Psychiatric Evaluation
Research Unit
State of New York Department of
Mental Hygiene
Brooklyn, N.Y.

Leonard S. Blackman, Ph.D.
Teachers College, Columbia
University
New York, N.Y.

Diane D. Bricker, Ph.D.
Debbie School
Mailman Center for Child
Development
Miami, Florida

William A. Bricker, Ph.D.
Kent State University
Kent, Ohio

Earl C. Butterfield, Ph.D.
University of Kansas Medical
Center
Kansas City, Kansas

Robert J. Gaylord-Ross, Ph.D.
Ferkauf Graduate School
Yeshiva University
New York, N.Y.

John E. Gordon, Ph.D.
Temple University
Philadelphia, Pa.

Paul Heintz, Ed.D.
New York University
New York, N.Y.

Reuben M. Schonebaum, Ph.D.
The Shield Institute
Flushing, N.Y.

Manny Sternlicht, Ph.D.
Yeshiva University and
Willowbrook Developmental
Center
New York, N.Y.

Harvey N. Switzky, Ph.D.
Northern Illinois University
Dekalb, Illinois

Luke S. Watson, Jr., Ph.D.
Behavior Modification Technology
Tuscaloosa, Alabama

Bertrand G. Winsberg, M.D.
State of New York Department of
Mental Hygiene
Brooklyn, N.Y.

John J. Winters, Jr., Ph.D.
Edward R. Johnstone Training and
Research Center
Bordentown, N.J.

Joan Wagner Zinober, Ph.D.
Hillsborough Community Mental
Health Center Inc.
Tampa, Florida

THE PSYCHOLOGY

OF

MENTAL RETARDATION:

ISSUES AND APPROACHES

EDITED BY

IRV BIALER

Child Psychiatric Evaluation Research Unit
New York Department of Mental Hygiene

MANNY STERNLICHT

Yeshiva University and
Willowbrook Developmental Center

PSYCHOLOGICAL DIMENSIONS, INC.

500 Fifth Avenue, New York, N.Y. 10036

Copyright 1977 by Psychological Dimensions, Inc.

All rights reserved.

RC
570
P79

Printed in the United States of America
1987654321

Library of Congress Cataloging in Publication Data

Main entry under title:

The Psychology of mental retardation.

    Bibliography: p.
    Includes indexes.
    1. Mental deficiency. 2. Psychological research.
3. Clinical psychology. I. Bialer, Irv, 1919-
II. Sternlicht, Manny. [DNLM: 1. Mental retardation.
WM300 P974]
RC570.P79   616.8'588   77-4130
ISBN 0-88437-013-5

UNIVERSITY
OF
PENNSYLVANIA
LIBRARIES

Psychology of

(3

Res. pur.

This book is dedicated
to our wives, Judy and Madeline,
to our children, and
to the memory of Mrs. Blanche Sternlicht.

Contents

Preface

Some years ago, we conducted a survey to determine what psychologists in and outside of mental retardation considered as the most cogent issues in the field (Bailer & Sternlicht. Psychological issues in mental retardation: Report of a survey. *Mental Retardation,* 1969, 7(4), 35-37). The findings indicated strong agreement among psychologists of various subspecialties as to important extant and emerging concerns among those professionals with regard to the psychology of mental retardation. That survey made obvious the need for a book such as this, which goes beyond comprehensive reviews of relevant literature to definitive discussions aimed at clarifying crucial issues and delineating their theoretical and practical implications for the field.

For purposes of this work, an (crucial) issue is defined as:

> A major area of concern or controversy around which may hinge (or which may determine) the direction of development or implementation of research, theory, and/or practice in a given field.

In essence, the work was designed to provide a forum in which selected experts with strong biases and opinions regarding certain critical psychological issues could document and discuss the rationale for their standpoints and the implications of their views for the area as a whole. Given the license of such a forum, the contributors were encouraged to express clearly considered and clearly stated (sometimes controversial) viewpoints designed to stimulate thinking and discussion with regard to prevention, control, diagnosis, and treatment in the field of mental retardation—extending beyond the realm of psychology per se.

The 14 chapters are grouped according to an informal arrangement which reflects the fact that their contents fall under the general rubrics of: overviews of psychological issues and the role of the psychologist in mental retardation (Chapters 1 and 2); definition, classification, and etiology (Chapters 3 and 4); research and theory (Chapters 5-7); assessment and diagnosis (Chapters 8-10); and treatment and programming (Chapters 11-14).

The book should serve not only as a text in its own right, but also as a useful adjunct to more wide-ranging works dealing with the psychology of mentally retarded people. Nevertheless, the theoretical and practical issues and approaches covered in the text—while emphasizing the *psychological* aspects of mental retardation—are relevant to the concerns of all disciplines in this field, in which all aspects are interrelated. Thus, it may be prescribed as either a basic or auxiliary text for a variety of graduate-level courses designed to train professional workers in mental retardation, regardless of the specialty involved. It also can serve as a supplementary text in undergraduate courses covering the psychology of mental retardation in particular, or of exceptional children in general. In addition, it is hoped that this volume will provide a useful reference source for practicing clinicians, researchers, and allied personnel in the field of mental retardation and developmental disabilities.

We wish to thank Marian Castellano, Janet Sigel, and Shaindy Soskin Applegrad for their dedicated secretarial assistance in the preparation of this volume.

Irv Bialer
Manny Sternlicht

THE PSYCHOLOGY OF MENTAL RETARDATION:

Issues and Approaches

Irv Bialer, a graduate of Brooklyn College (B.A., 1943), received his Ph.D. degree in clinical psychocology from George Peabody College in 1960, with a minor in education of exceptional children. At Peabody, he was a Fellow in the NIMH-sponsored Mental Deficiency Training Program; and from 1959-1960, he served his clinical psychology internship at Southbury (Conn.) Training School. Currently, he is licensed in Tennessee and certified in New York State.

He has been Chief Clinical Psychologist and Director of Human Development Services at Clover Bottom Hospital and School, in Nashville (1960-1964), and Director of Research at the Kennedy Child Study Center in New York City (1964-1970). At present, he is Principal Research Scientist with the Child Psychiatric Evaluation Research Unit of the New York State Department of Mental Hygiene, and is also a clinical consultant to the Kennedy Learning Clinic in Brooklyn, N.Y.

Dr. Bialer has held academic positions in Psychology and Special Education at a number of universities, and is currently on the adjunct faculty of Brooklyn College, New York University, and Downstate Medical Center of the State University of New York. He is a Fellow of the American Psychological Association and of the American Association on Mental Deficiency (AAMD), serving as chairman of the AAMD Awards Committee for 1976-1977. He has also been a consulting editor to the American Journal of Mental Deficiency, *and has served as that journal's book review editor since 1971.*

Dr. Bialer's publications have dealt with motivational and personality development in retarded individuals, issues of assessment and diagnosis in the areas of mental retardation and neurological impairment, and pharmacological treatment of behavior problems in neuropsychiatrically impaired children. He has over 30 publications to his credit, including three book chapters.

Dr. Bialer is married to the former Judith R. Levine, and they have three children, Cheryl Anne, Robin Sue, and Jeffrey Stewart.

Manny Sternlicht is a clinical psychologist whose views are an amalgam derived from his academic background and an active research orientation. He is currently serving as Professor of Psychology at Yeshiva University and as Chief of Psychological Services at Willowbrook Developmental Center in New York. He is a certified practitioner in the states of New York and New Jersey.

Dr. Sternlicht earned his Master's degrees in school psychology and experimental psychology, and completed his doctoral studies at Yeshiva University, receiving the Ph.D. degree in 1960. He interned in clinical psychology at Kings County Hospital, Brooklyn, N.Y., and served as a clinical psychologist at the Illinois Institute for Juvenile Research, as well as Chairman of the Psychology Department at Rockford College in Illinois.

Dr. Sternlicht has made and continues to make important contributions in the area of mental retardation. He has presented a great many professional papers at scientific conventions, and has published widely in this sphere, having more than a hundred publications to his credit. He is the senior author of an earlier book, Personality Development and Social Behavior in the Mentally Retarded, *and has contributed chapters to several other books. He is an acknowledged authority on psychotherapy and novel therapeutic modalities for the retarded client, and has pioneered in the development of new techniques of evaluation with retarded and nonretarded children. In addition, he has made innovations in methods of programming for mentally retarded individuals of all ages.*

Dr. Sternlicht is a Fellow of the American Psychological Association and of the American Association on Mental Deficiency, and he is a Diplomate in clinical psychology, American Board of Professional Psychology.

He is married to the former Madeline Goldstein, and has four children, Elliot, Harold, Jeffrey and Riva.

1

Psychological issues in mental retardation: An overview

Manny Sternlicht and Irv Bialer

Many of the issues relating to the work of the psychologist in mental retardation, or to the training of individuals for such work, are deeply rooted in the early history of psychology as a science and as a profession. Other psychological issues are tied to the development of the field of mental retardation itself as a multidisciplinary arena in which individuals with various professional specialties and areas of expertise are striving to meet the needs of this particular segment of the population.

As a member of a particular profession, the psychologist holds himself forth, on the one hand, as a provider of services which are necessary to meet the various responsibilities he has been asked to assume. In this role, he fulfills clinical, consulting, administrative, training, and research functions— the last often designed to provide supporting information for the clinician, the educator, or the administrator. On the other hand, as a behavioral scientist, the psychologist purports to be a trained experimentalist who is concerned with the scientific analysis of retarded behavior as it relates to solving practical problems ("applied" research) or to the general laws of human behavior ("pure" or "basic" research). While some psychologists in the field think of themselves primarily as either providers of services or behavioral scientists, these aspects of the psychologist's image are often inseparable, and the issues relevant to both aspects overlap considerably.

In this chapter, we present an overview of the many psychological issues in mental retardation, together with indications as to how they are covered in the various contributions to this volume. To that end, a brief consideration of the historical foundations of the psychologist's involvement in the field is followed by discussions of (a) the training of psychologists as it relates to the roles they are expected to play (training and role issues); (b)

3

actual provision of services by the mental retardation psychologist (service issues); and (c) his special function as an experimentalist (research issues).

HISTORICAL FOUNDATIONS

It has been noted (Seeman, 1968) that whether you date the birth of psychology as a distinct scientific discipline from 1875-1876 (when William James began his demonstration experiments at Harvard) or from 1879 (when Wundt established his laboratory at Leipzig), modern psychology is less than a century old. These same roots from which modern psychology sprang (i.e., a concern with the quantification and measurement of human behavior by utilizing the scientific method) served also to generate psychology's involvement with mental subnormality. Thus, formal contributions to mental retardation by psychologists also date back less than a century. The initial stimulus for these contributions was the advent of the mental testing movement. Emerging from the realm of philosophy, via psychophysics, into measurement of mental phenomena in the laboratory, psychology branched into issues of tremendous social import with the development of psychometrics.

First to bridge the gap was J. McKeen Cattell (Herrnstein & Boring, 1966c), who had received his degree from Wundt. Cattell held to the credo that psychology could not attain the exactness of the physical sciences unless it rested on the foundations of experiment and measurement, and he advocated that a major step toward helping psychology achieve the status of an exact science was the application of a series of mental measurements to large numbers of individuals. Consequently, in 1890, Cattell devised a series of what he called "mental tests" in order to assess human capacity and, following the lead of Galton, applied statistical techniques to the data he collected. This was the beginning of a psychology of individual differences.

The concern with individual differences was basic to the subsequent work of Binet and his collaborators (Herrnstein & Boring, 1966a). Yet, in point of time, Binet's contribution was preceded by that of another important psychologist, Hermann Ebbinghaus.

Ebbinghaus is principally known for his work on memory. A less well-known but extremely important product of his concern with psychological measurement was his contribution to the field of intelligence testing (Postman, 1968). It is of interest to note that the circumstances were analogous to those which led to Binet's investigations into quantification of higher mental processes.

In 1895, the municipal authorities of the city of Breslau, Germany, asked Ebbinghaus to serve on a committee appointed to consider the effects of mental fatigue on school performance among children. He felt that the work of the commission would be facilitated if its members had a means of measuring the mental capacity of school children, and he set about to find a suitable technique. In this connection, Ebbinghaus tried three different kinds of tests: computation, memory span, and sentence completion. He found that only the latter seemed related to school grades (Guilford, 1967). Consequently, Ebbinghaus argued that the completion test came closer to testing mental capacity than did other tests in general use at the time. In Ebbinghaus' sentence completion method, the child was given a sample of written text in which words or parts of words were omitted, and he was asked to fill in the blanks. This technique is used in many current intelligence tests, appearing, for example, in the form of the "Minkus Completion" subtest in the Stanford-Binet Intelligence Scale. Most notably, however, this contribution by Ebbinghaus played a significant role in favoring Binet's belief that mental tests should deal directly with the higher mental process, in contrast to Cattell's stand that such tests should primarily tap sensory processes (Herrnstein & Boring, 1966b).

Binet's contribution to the field of mental retardation is too well known to require detailed exposition here. However, it is of note that the origins of the psychologist's role as a psychometrician and, in a much broader sense, as a clinician lies in the concern with intellectual subnormality by early psychologists. In fact, dating from the earliest beginnings, these roles could not be divorced from the psychologist's self-image as an experimentalist.

Alfred Binet, the leading experimental psychologist of his time in France (Pollack & Brenner, 1969), had a long-standing interest in the quantification of human behavior well before 1905, when he and Simon published their first metric scale of intelligence. So entrenched was Binet's philosophy in the scientific method that, in concluding a paper published in 1915, which described the appropriate techniques for administering the Binet-Simon tests (which by then had gone through two successive revisions), those authors cautioned ". . . for the results of this method to have a scientific value, it is absolutely necessary that the individual who uses it should have served an apprenticeship in a laboratory of pedagogy or possess a thorough knowledge of psychological experimentation" (Beck & Molish, 1959, p. 151).

The work of three other pioneers—Goddard, Doll, and Witmer—demonstrate the early intermingling of research and clinical roles among psychologists concerned with mental retardation in the United States.

Henry H. Goddard was appointed director of research at The Training School at Vineland, New Jersey, in 1906 and served in that capacity for 12 years (Irvine, 1971b). Having received his doctorate in 1899 from Clark University, where G. Stanley Hall had been conducting research in child and adolescent psychology, Goddard was apparently primed for the study of

deviant children. At Vineland, he established the first psychological laboratory to be devoted principally to research with retarded individuals (Irvine,
1971b). Beginning in 1908, when Goddard translated the 1905 version of the
Binet-Simon Scale (he later translated their 1908 version as well), that device
was a primary tool in his investigations. Not only did, Goddard use of the
Binet tests serve to inaugurate their employment in the United States as
clinical instruments, but the mental age scores derived from those tests also
served as the basis for Goddard's formulation of the first system for
classifying "feebleminded" individuals at different levels of deviation from
the norm. It was in connection with this first classificatory effort that
Goddard coined the word "moron" to designate the highest level of
feeblemindedness. The classification system suggested by Goddard was
adopted in 1910 by the then Association for the Study of the Feeble-Minded
(now the American Association on Mental Deficiency); and it helped
introduce uniformity in the classification of intellectually deviant individuals.
(Pertinent issues with regard to such classification are discussed at length by
Bialer in Chapter 3.)

Edgar A. Doll was introduced to the field of mental retardation in
1913, when he was appointed as a research and clinical psychologist under
Goddard at the Training School at Vineland. In that position, Doll became
involved in early work with the Binet-Simon Scale, devising a brief form as a
screening instrument (E. E. Doll, 1969; Irvine, 1970). Subsequent to
Terman's introduction of the intelligence quotient into the field of mental
measurement in 1916, it soon became common practice to use the IQ as the
major basis for classifying individuals as "feebleminded." However, stimulated by his experiences in the Vineland laboratory, Doll, as early as 1917,
began to posit the notion that level of social behavior was an important
diagnostic consideration. In 1925, Doll became director of research at the
Training School, and his insistence on full clinical diagnosis of mental
deficiency—taking into account the variable of social competence—led, in
1935, to the development of the Vineland Social Maturity Scale. That
instrument opened another area of human development for comparative
measurement (Luckey, 1967) as well as for fruitful research among mentally
retarded populations.

Lightner Witmer, who as a student of Wundt received his doctorate
from the University of Leipzig in 1892, was one of the most important
precursors—albeit probably the most neglected one (J.M. Gardner, 1968a)—
with reference to the contribution of psychologists to the field of mental
retardation. Witmer's pioneering efforts revolved around the evolution of
clinical psychology (which he in effect founded) out of the psychological
laboratory which Cattell had established at the University of Pennsylvania.

In 1892, Witmer succeeded Cattell as director of the laboratory.

Despite his earlier training with Cattell (to whom he had been an undergraduate assistant) and with Wundt, Witmer was unwilling to limit his research to the then-current theoretical concerns of psychology; instead, he turned to the study of learning and behavior problems in children (Irvine, 1969). While, as Seeman (1968) pointed out, Witmer's ideas bore the clear stamp of the behavioral science he had learned at Leipzig, he believed that there was no valid distinction between "pure" and "applied" science and that "... in the final analysis the progress of psychology, as of every other science, will be determined by ... its contributions to the advancement of the human race" (Beck & Molish, 1959b, p. 152). Witmer further argued that such advancement could only be achieved through psychological research that went beyond the traditional laboratory setting for material to study and that: "The school room, the juvenile courts, and the streets are a larger laboratory of psychology" (Beck & Molish, 1959b, p. 153). Thus, over a 4-year period, Witmer developed what he called the "clinical method in psychology and the diagnostic method of teaching" (Irvine, 1969), and in 1896 he established a psychological clinic, which was thereafter regularly conducted in connection with the laboratory. The clinic was organized to carry out "... the purpose of the clinical psychologist, as a contributor to science ... to discover the relation between cause and effect in applying ... various pedagogical remedies to a child who is suffering from general or special retardation" (Beck & Molish, 1959b, p. 154). Thus, from the beginning, the subject matter with which Witmer was concerned was mental and educational retardation.

The establishment of Witmer's clinic marked more than the formal beginning of clinical psychology. It might well have laid the conceptual and procedural groundwork for practically every role the psychologist plays today in the field of mental retardation. These roles were outlined in his 1896 address before the American Psychological Association, when he presented "a scheme of practical work in psychology" along four major dimensions (Beck & Molish, 1959b): (a) investigation and assessment of mental development in retarded children—utilizing statistical and clinical methods; (b) providing diagnostic and other clinical services in a special education setting as consultant to special teachers; (c) training other professionals (e.g., teachers, physicians, social workers) to work with retarded children; and (d) preparing a new profession of psychological experts for the evaluation and treatment of mentally retarded children. The current and emerging roles of the mental retardation psychologist (see Chapter 2) can be seen clearly to stem from this early schema.

It is of particular interest that Witmer conceptualized an interdisciplinary approach to mental retardation and that he saw the new type of psychological expert he proposed to train as one who would work primarily within the school system. Consequently, in operationalizing his plan, Witmer may have founded not only clinical psychology, but school psychology as well. Nevertheless, one of the truly overlooked and underemphasized contributions of Witmer was his insistence from the very beginning that the academic preparation psychologists were then receiving (while it was essential to their work among children with educational problems) was not adequate for effective work with deviant children, and that psychologists had to receive special training in the "new profession." Unfortunately in this, as in many of his other notions, he was in advance of his time, and as Beck and Molish (1959c) noted: "A whole generation of psychology had to be lived before his vision materialized . . ." (p. 144).

TRAINING AND ROLE ISSUES

Innovative Programs

Some 20 years ago, and more than 50 years after Witmer formulated his plan for training psychologists in "the new profession," Sarason (1953) felt called upon to make the following observation regarding preparation of psychologists to work with mentally retarded individuals:

> Although clinical psychology as a discipline grew out of attempts to identify, educate, and train the mentally defective child, the clinical student today gets very little experience with the defective child. . . . It is the rare graduate department of psychology which has as a requirement course instruction in or clinical experience with the psychological problems in mental deficiency" (p. 367).

Sarason (1953) went on to make the point that in order to effect any change in what he characterized as a general professional disinterest in the psychological aspects of mental retardation, it would be necessary to combat attitudes such as (a) working with retarded individuals is dull and unrewarding—in effect, a professional "dead end"; (b) from the psychological standpoint, mental deficiency presents no major or intriguing research problems; and (c) no special knowledge or training is required to handle a case of mental deficiency adequately.

Further, in decrying the fact that research was generally not encouraged in institutional facilities for retarded people, Sarason (1953) concluded:

> One of the most serious consequences . . . has been the absent of basic research concerning psychological aspects of the problem. Without such research practice becomes routinized and superficial, innovation and experimentation meet with resistance, and the field more and more becomes divorced from the mainstream of scientific advance. (p. 369)

By a fortuitous congruence of circumstances, just about the time those observations appeared in print, a major pioneering effort was getting under way at George Peabody College, in Nashville, Tennessee, a center of learning which was then relatively obscure with respect to the area of mental retardation. This was to launch a new era in the training of psychologists for the field.

Early in 1953, Peabody College applied to the National Institute of Mental Health for a grant to establish a doctoral training program in mental deficiency within its Department of Human Development. The proposal followed from the dual conviction that there existed a critical need for well-trained psychologists capable of attacking many of the problems posed by the condition of mental retardation, and that the field presented numerous research and clinical problems of an interesting and challenging nature for psychologists. Consequently, the proposed fellowship program was designed to provide doctoral students in psychology with research and clinical skills which would give them specific expertise for working with mentally retarded populations (Cantor & Cromwell, 1959).

Fellowship students in the mental deficiency program received the broad training which characterized any graduate program leading to a Ph.D. degree in psychology—with the incoming Fellow electing to major either in experimental or clinical psychology. The specific mental retardation training was incorporated as a minor area within the Department of Education of Exceptional Children. The prescribed minor concentrated heavily on the medical,[1] psychological, and sociological aspects of mental retardation. In addition, all trainees carried out supervised research with retarded subjects; and each completed a 9-month predoctoral internship in a facility for mentally retarded clients. During the internship, research was heavily emphasized.

---

[1] One of the most unique characteristics of this *avant-garde* training program was the inclusion of lectures, demonstrations, consultations, and projects relevant to medical aspects of mental retardation. This was designed to orient and sensitize the psychology trainee toward the etiological, diagnostic, and treatment problems as encountered by the physician, and to facilitate eventual interdisciplinary communication and collaboration.

With minor modifications, the Peabody Mental Retardation Program has been in operation for some 20 years at this writing, during which time, Peabody College has emerged from relative obscurity in the field to a position of prominence. Peabody's pioneer efforts set the stage for similar programs, of which that at the University of Alabama is an outstanding example. The objective of the Alabama program is to train research and/or academic psychologists who will make major work commitments to the field of mental retardation, either as teachers in graduate programs or as researchers in universities and/or other training facilities.

As with the Peabody program, the Alabama Fellows receive the core curriculum required of all psychology majors. Master's theses and/or doctoral dissertations completed under this program must relate directly to mental retardation, and all Fellows work directly with a major advisor who is continually involved in mental retardation research. A predoctoral internship is not required. However, all trainees are encouraged to gain teaching experience prior to graduation and to complete a year of postdoctoral study and research at another university.

While the Peabody and Alabama programs seem to be successful in accomplishing their intended purposes, there has been and still is a lack of concensus as to what constitutes adequate and appropriate training for psychological work in mental retardation, and as to the subsequent role of the psychologist in that field. Various attempts to clarify the issues and to resolve the disagreements have been made by diverse groups over the past 15 years through conferences, committees, symposia, and workshops. In this chapter we shall look briefly at some of the more notable efforts.

Involvement of Professional Associations

The 1958 AAMD–APA conference. The American Association on Mental Deficiency (AAMD) was an early leader in exploring means of effective recruitment and training of psychologists for research and service with retarded individuals. In November 1958, as one of its first efforts, the AAMD Technical Planning Project—with the cooperation and participation of the American Psychological Association (APA)—organized a conference to stimulate psychologists' interest in research, program development, and training in the area of mental retardation, and to make appropriate recommendations (AAMD Committee on Psychology, 1961).

The conference recognized the vital historical role of psychology in the area, with concomitant acknowledgment that despite past contributions of the profession and the fact that both public and professional interest in mental retardation was then developing, there was considerable disinterest and disregard of the field on the part of most psychologists. It was pointed out that, by and large, psychologists were ignoring the challenges of the mentally retarded population and that failure to recognize the relationships among problems involving the latter and more general psychological issues had resulted in extremely limited impact of the many theoretical and practical advances in psychology on the field of mental retardation. Participants agreed that in the period since World War II the emphasis in clinical and counseling psychology had shifted from deviant children to emotionally disturbed adults; consequently, training programs—by under-emphasizing methods and content courses related to developmental psychol-ogy—lacked a general, comprehensive model for conceptualizing deviant development. With regard to the role of institutions, it was emphasized that residential facilities in general were interested only in the service function provided by psychologists (primarily in the form of psychometric evalua-tions), and not in encouraging training and research developments.

Conclusions and recommendations which sprang from this seminal conference included the following:

1. With the provision of jobs carrying appropriate prestige and remuneration, psychologists would be attracted to the field. Salary schedules of psychologists in mental retardation should be reviewed and reevaluated.

2. Interest in the field would be developed and fostered by the organization of both specialized and interdisciplinary symposia and workshops.

3. Graduate training programs, particularly in clinical, counseling, and school psychology, should increase emphasis on normal and deviant human development and on appropriate assessment techniques, especially at early developmental stages. Expanded interest in mental retardation would hopefully also reinforce the weakened ties between the professions of psychology and educa-tion.

4. Psychology departments should begin to introduce students to the field of mental retardation at the undergraduate level. Collaterally, student psychologists should be encouraged to participate in research projects related to mental retardation which are conducted by their professors.

5. There is a need to conduct better and more adequate research on the personal, emotional, and social development of the mentally retarded child. As a deviant group, such individuals could provide stimulating challenges to theories of learning and personality.

6. Institutions should be encouraged to set up remunerative and

attractive research internships, and they must see themselves as having responsibilities for cooperating in and developing research and training programs for psychologists.

7.   The Education and Training Board of the American Psychological Association should reexamine its policies regarding the approval of clinical internship programs in schools and institutions for the mentally retarded person.

8.   AAMD should develop close liaison with APA, and a recommendation should be sent to the latter organization to establish a general APA Committee on Mental Retardation.

9.   Psychologists should help develop and teach in-service training programs for subprofessional personnel performing services for the mentally retarded client.

10. The confusion and disagreement as to what might constitute adequate and appropriate training for psychological work in mental retardation was expected to result in various approaches to setting up such training programs. In order to provide the most relevant experiences to psychology students, it would be necessary to have knowledge of the minimal requirements, by way of staff and program, which must be met by a specialized community or residential facility for the mentally retarded citizen. In other words, training programs should be geared to the kinds of services psychologists may be expected to be called upon to provide (i.e., to the contemplated role of psychologists in mental retardation) and to the expected magnitude of the demand for such services.

Meanwhile, other currents were stirring up active participation by psychology as a profession with concerns relevant to the field.

APA committees. Early in 1958, a committee on mental retardation—headed by William Sloan, then editor of the *American Journal of Mental Deficiency*—was established within the Division of Clinical Psychology (Division 12) of APA. The meetings of this divisional body soon drew the attention of professionals in other areas such as school counseling and developmental psychology, some of whom evidently also were affiliated with rudimentary mental retardation committees (Cromwell, 1961).

Consequently, pursuant to the recommendation of the Division 12 committee, the Board of Professional Affairs of APA appointed an association-wide body to coordinate the various elements. The resultant ad hoc Committee on Mental Retardation of the American Psychological Association began operation in 1960, under the chairmanship of Rue L.

Cromwell. This committee took unto itself the task of serving as a clearing house and focal point for consideration of issues which were of concern to all psychologists serving the area of mental retardation (Cromwell, 1961), while Sloan's group relegated its activities to the larger divisional body.

Among the issues of concern to Cromwell's committee were the need to improve the attitude of psychologists toward work in mental retardation, and the need to explore feasible approaches to training psychologists for knowledgeable and skillful involvement in this special area. On behalf of improving professional attitudes and attracting psychologists to mental retardation, the ad hoc committee suggested (a) forming liaisons with the APA divisions of clinical, counseling, and school psychology, and motivating them to plan relevant symposia and paper sessions at their meetings and conventions; (b) utilizing various divisional newsletters to disseminate information regarding activities of psychologists with retarded persons and to urge qualified professionals to join the Psychology Section of the American Association on Mental Deficiency; and (c) encouraging journal editors to consider publication of papers on mental retardation so as to inhibit the fractionation of reports of research in that area from those of other child development research (Cromwell, 1961).

With regard to training, the APA committee outlined a program of (a) instigating (at cooperating institutes) short-term introductory, refresher, and advanced training institutes or courses in the diagnosis, management, and treatment of retarded persons; (b) developing interdisciplinary symposia and conferences on specific topics (e.g., a joint conference with social work professionals on parent counseling); (c) encouraging development of formal postdoctoral study and resident programs at various clinical and academic facilities; and (d) investigating the problems inherent in lack of APA accreditation of mental retardation agencies as internship facilities (Cromwell, 1961).

The Section 1 committee. The efforts of the ad hoc APA committee to implement its suggested program, which was oriented toward psychologists in general, bore fruit very slowly over the succeeding years. Eventually, under Lewis Klebanoff, that group was elevated to the status of an APA "Task Force on Mental Retardation," although it was still oriented toward the broad aspects of the condition as it is related to all ages, and cut across various psychological disciplines. Consequently, late in 1966, in an effort to complement the activities of the Task Force and to provide a more specific clinical emphasis, the Section on Clinical Child Psychology (Section 1) of Division 12, APA, formed the standing Committee on Mental Retardation, under the chairmanship of Henry Leland.

From its inception, the Section 1 committee was charged with exploring the relationship between the problems of mentally retarded children and those of children in general—as these problems are reflected in the work of the clinical child psychologist (Leland, Smith, Warren, & Bialer, 1968). Such exploration was to involve not only a concern for specifically defining the role of the clinician in this realm, but also an emphasis on the almost gratuitous concept that the problems of the retarded child are significantly different from other child clinical problems.

With a view toward fostering a major expansion in all facets of professional training for clinical psychologists to include special emphasis on mental retardation, the committee urged that major training programs in academic and service settings be modified to include course work, practicum experience, and internships in mental retardation, both as part of the requirements for the doctoral degree and as an integral facet of postdoctoral experience.

APA workshops. By way of operationalizing the latter suggestions, a 2-day workshop was held prior to the 1968 APA convention in San Francisco (Leland, Smith, & Barclay, 1969, 1970). The participants oriented their discussion around three major questions, of which we are here concerned principally with the third: "(a) What is unique about clinical child psychology in mental retardation? (b) What are the relative merits of a person trained as a generalist versus a person trained as a specialist? (c) What are some of the prospective training models to be examined?" (Leland et al., 1970, p. 24).

With regard to mental retardation as a unique area for the clinician, it was observed that the emergence of intelligence testing in the early part of the 20th century led to the identification of psychology with the diagnostic process in that area. Individuals performing the work we now consider "clinical psychology" found that, on the basis of intelligence data, they were responsible for the ultimate diagnosis of the individual and that they were often the professionals *solely* responsible for that diagnosis. In addition, since the mentally retarded groups were typically isolated from the community, the psychologist working with such a population tended to find himself isolated from other psychologists. By the same token, these clinicians found themselves working in multidisciplinary teams more frequently than did other clinical psychologists. As Leland et al. (1970) put it, "the history of diagnosis in mental retardation plus the isolated institutional history tended to produce a group of psychologists who had tradition, practices and knowledge which existed in no other area" (p. 25). Further, the latter report pointed out that since clinicians working with mentally retarded clients are largely concerned with children who present medical, educational, and habilitative problems which require long-term and often lifetime planning, the special role of the clinical psychologist here springs from an "orientation [which] is a mixture of psychological, educational, rehabilitative and . . . biomedical processes" (p. 25)

Discussion of the generalist versus specialist issue led to the conclusion that "the emphasis . . . is not one of establishing a group of specialists who continue to be isolated from the mainstream of the psychological community, but rather a group of individuals who, having training in clinical psychology, have elected . . . [mental retardation] as a unique interest area where they want to further their training and careers" (Leland et al., 1970, p. 26).

Consideration of alternative models for training clinical child psychologists in mental retardation was linked to the notion that such training had to take three kinds of "consumer" groups into account: (a) the mentally retarded persons themselves—who "used" diagnostic, therapeutic, and rehabilitative services; (b) other professional groups, such as special therapists, educators, and physicians who sought psychological services and/or consultation as an adjunct to their own efforts with retarded children and adults; and (c) psychologists in other specialties, including school psychologists, developmental psychologists, and child guidance specialists who might call upon a colleague trained in the area of mental retardation to help solve special problems or set up specific programs.

To meet the needs of such potential "consumers," as well as to prepare the clinician for such anticipated roles as researcher, administrator, and trainer of other professionals, the workshop participants examined four possible training models:

1. A doctorate in mental retardation, with a clinical internship in a relevant institutional or community setting.
2. A general doctorate in clinical psychology, with an identified specialty in mental retardation, and an internship as in model 1.
3. A general doctorate in clinical psychology, with extensive course work in mental retardation, and a specialized internship in an appropriate facility.
4. A doctorate in clinical child psychology with broad-ranging course work in mental retardation, and an internship rotating between facilities for retarded and for other deviant children.

It was also proposed that models 3 and 4 could include postdoctoral mental retardation programs for those who wished additional training.

The training pattern which received the strongest recommendation of the group was a slight modification of model 3: *General training in clinical child psychology—in an academic setting which allowed for interaction with a variety of other psychological disciplines—and with an internship in mental retardation to be served in a university-affiliated center or its equivalent* (Leland et al., 1970). It was also recommended in this model that "while some of the course work during the initial training would include mental retardation, the major didactic material in mental retardation be obtained either through the practicum internship or through postdoctoral studies" (Leland et al., 1969, p. 28).

The workshop group further pursued the notion that many demands made on the professional psychologist by the "consumer" could be met by subprofessional individuals such as psychological assistants and technicians, thereby freeing the psychologist for those duties which required intensive training and extensive experience. They also felt that the field of mental retardation would be more attractive to the doctoral student if some tasks traditionally assigned to the graduate psychologist could be relegated to technicians, assistants, or other subprofessional personnel inside or outside the discipline of psychology. It was consequently recommended that a future workshop be organized to discuss the issues and to consider programs for training such supportive personnel. This recommendation was implemented the following year, but the results were inconclusive (Sutter, Leland, & Barclay, 1969). A more recent workshop on issues concerning roles and training of paraprofessionals in mental retardation raised some important issues, but was likewise inconclusive (Crawford, Dervin, Golden, Leland, & Van Overloop, 1975). (In Chapter 2, we provide in-depth discussions of the training and utilization of paraprofessional psychological personnel in this field.)

APA division on mental retardation. As a further result of the strenuous and fairly dedicated efforts of the Section 1 committee and of the Psychology Division of AAMD, a Division on Mental Retardation (Division 33) was officially constituted within the American Psychological Association in September 1972. The establishment of this new APA unit seems to augur a general climate of acceptance (among psychologists in general) of professional involvement in mental retardation, and it seems bound to stimulate increasing interest in academic and nonacademic circles toward the training of psychological personnel for research and service in that area.

University Affiliated Facilities

A comparatively recent development, which has added tremendous thrust and scope to training programs for psychologists in the field, was the establishment by the Federal government of the University Affiliated Facilities (UAF) program. This program, authorized under Part B, Title I, of the Mental Retardation Facilities and Community Mental Health Centers Construction Act of 1963 (P.L. 88-164), was intended to provide matching Federal funds to help qualified establishments build facilities for training professional and technical personnel in the special area of mental retardation.

Construction projects funded under P.L. 88-164 had to provide for a public or other nonprofit clinical facility which would (a) make available comprehensive (multidisciplinary) inpatient and outpatient services for mentally retarded persons; (b) train specialized personnel in various biomedical, behavioral, and special educational disciplines for the field of mental retardation; and (c) demonstrate new techniques of specialized services for retarded clients. While the UAF program was originally committed to construction, the Developmental Disabilities Services and Facilities Construction Act of 1970 (P.L. 91-517), authorized grants for the administration and operation of UAFs, and it expanded their focus to involve other developmental disabilities along with mental retardation.

Routh (1973), in describing the advantages offered to psychologists by the UAF as both an employment facility and a training site, noted that such facilities were essentially expanded versions of the developmental clinic which "had its historical origin in the work of Arnold Gesell, who in addition to studying the biological and psychological aspects of development, made his services and those of his colleagues available for the clinical examination of children who were not developing at a normal rate, in whatever sphere" (p. 5). It is also of historical interest that Gesell was both a developmental psychologist (having received his doctorate in 1906 from Clark University, where he was a student of G. Stanley Hall), and a pediatrician, having received his medical degree from Yale in 1915 (Irvine, 1971a). Thus, not only did Gesell's early work provide a training model for psychologists in mental retardation, but his concern with developmental diagnosis also served as a bridge for the clinical interaction of psychology and medicine as professions. (An expanded discussion of relevant issues is provided by Winsberg in Chapter 10.)

Comparative perspectives on training and roles. In order to assess the significance of the UAF in defining both the training model and role of psychologists in mental retardation, Forehand and Gordon (1971) conducted a questionnaire survey among the psychology program directors of the University Affiliated Facilities then in operation. Asked to rank from "best" to "worst" the four training models presented by the 1968 APA workshop (Leland et al., 1969, 1970), the respondents chose as most adequate that which called for a general doctoral degree in clinical psychology with an extensive number of mental retardation courses and a specialized mental retardation internship. Respondents also considered an internship in a facility serving retarded individuals as the most important type of training for clinical psychologists in the field (two-thirds of the facilities were offering such internships). Thus, UAF psychology program directors agreed with the participants of the APA workshop, both with respect to the format of the most highly recommended training model and in seeing the mental retardation clinician "primarily as a clinical psychologist who, in addition, has a specialization in MR" (Forehand & Gordon, 1971, p. 25).

With regard to defining the role of the mental retardation psychologist, respondents ranked the training of students as his most important function, while research was ranked as second in importance, with therapy a very close third. Testing brought up the rear, being viewed as the least important responsibility of the clinical psychologist. These relative rankings of research, therapy, and testing functions by UAF psychology program directors have important implications for the differential utilization of such facilities, as opposed to residential sites, for practicum and internship training. The implications derive from the contrasting conceptualizations among administrators as to both the role of psychologists in mental retardation and the contributions the latter can make to the field, as well as from the distinctive roles which psychologists perceive for themselves.

In sharp contrast to research being ranked as second in importance among directors of psychology programs in university affiliated facilities, surveys among administrators of state institutions for mentally retarded residents have revealed that superintendents, particularly those who were physicians, generally regarded research as the least important activity of psychologists (Baumeister, 1967) and that even if they were "for research," few administrators were committed to providing a facilitating climate (Wolfensberger, 1965). Obviously, the latter findings do not imply that research is not being conducted in institutions. The whole history of research in the field, as well as a perusal of the *American Journal of Mental Deficiency* and other publications (including Chapter 14 in the present volume), belies this notion. Just as obviously, many institutional administrators actively encourage both ongoing psychological research and the training of interns in such activities (see Sternlicht, 1966b; Sternlicht & Bialer, Chapter 2, herein). Consequently, the above comparison only serves to emphasize the greater *probability* of freedom for, encouragement of, and facilitation of research and research training in settings like the UAFs. Such a state of affairs is greatly in keeping with the investment in research training represented by such mental retardation programs as those at Peabody College and at the University of Alabama, as well as being congruent with the clinical psychologist's conception of his role as that of both a researcher and a clinician (i.e., the so-called scientist-professional role model).

Probably the most notable disparity of the conceptualization of roles and of service functions is that with regard to psychometrics. Thus, Forehand and Gordon (1971) noted: "Perhaps the most important finding of this survey was that U.A.F. psychology program directors did not view testing as a psychologist's primary function. Rather, testing was seen as . . . a duty that for the most part could be handled by subprofessionals. This de-emphasis of assessment represents a trend seen throughout clinical psychology" (p. 24). This stands in stark contrast to Baumeister's conclusion that "it is very clear that [among institution superintendents] the psychologist's primary role is viewed as that of psychometrician. . . . This has been the traditional role of psychologists working in residential facilities and there is little in the present survey to suggest that this characterization, on the whole, has changed" (1967, p. 4). Again, we cannot come away with the notion that testing is the *only* function sanctioned among psychologists and trainees in institutions serving mentally retarded residents. Not only does our everyday experience (and published reports, such as Sternlicht, 1966a, 1966b) run counter to that idea, but Baumeister (1967) also found that his sample rated psychotherapeutic functions and training responsibilities of psychologists second and third, respectively, in order of importance. So the issue at point is the question of relative probabilities as to which situation would offer the greatest opportunity for the psychologist in mental retardation to function in accordance with his role image and to provide the services for which his professional training has best prepared him.

In Chapter 2, we discuss the numerous facets of the mental retardation psychologist's role as it is carried out in various settings and from the standpoint of the multiplicity of services provided. The sections below are intended to introduce some issues pertaining to given aspects of those services.

SERVICE ISSUES

Assessment

Whether or not the mental retardation psychologist wishes to be identified primarily with clinical psychometrics, it is a fact that he is the only professional in the field whose training and experience qualify him to provide those services which, by dint of tradition and his unique training, he is most often called upon to perform. Psychodiagnostic services cover assessment of intellectual and social skills, emotional status, personality and motivational development, motor skills, psycholinguistic development, academic achievement, vocational abilities, and neurological integrity. Such services play an important role in defining mental retardation and in the behavioral classification of retarded individuals (see Chapter 3).

In recent years, there has been growing dissatisfaction among psychologists, as well as among other professionals in the field concerning the adequacy of traditional psychometric procedures in providing a useful data base for educational and social programs for retarded individuals. In the present volume, the contributions by Bialer (Chaper 3), Gordon (Chapter 9), and Winsberg (Chapter 10) reflect some of these concerns. More specifically, in response to this dissatisfaction, there is a proliferating literature on emerging and innovative approaches to psychological assessment. Some examples follow.

Heintz and Blackman (Chapter 8) suggest an evaluative procedure which would identify the "school-relevant psycho-educational charac-teristics" of given children. This approach would be based on an a priori determination of the psychological processes which enter into acquiring given academic skills and of assessing the extent to which these processes are available in specific children, thus yielding a data base for a technology of individualized academic programming. Psychoeducational considerations in mental retardation also include issues concerning assessment of learning strategies and learning characteristics of retarded individuals. Schonebaum and Zinober (Chapter 6) and Butterfield and Belmont (Chapter 7) discuss these issues and their current status.

In a chapter devoted to a consideration of behavioral assessment of retarded children via measurement of the learning *process,* as opposed to that of *products* of prior learning, Haywood, Filler, Shifman, and Chatelanat (1975) delineate, evaluate, and advocate the employment of "Learning Potential" assessment strategies. Such approaches, which have been developed principally by Budoff (1969) and Feuerstein(1970), are designed to replace traditional IQ testing with purportedly more valid procedures for measuring the retarded child's ability to reason and to profit from learning experiences. Essentially, the given procedures involve systematic training in problem solving with nonverbal materials.

"Radical Behaviorist" approaches to assessment, based on operant conditioning paradigms, and having direct relevance to treatment strategies, have been suggested by Lindsley (1964) and by Throne (1972). Lindsley (1964) describes the use of free-operant conditioning methods for direct measurement of human behavioral deficits and suggests that for individual cases, prosthetic environments can then be designed "to decrease the debilitation resulting from the behavioral deficit" (p. 74). Throne (1972) advocates forgoing the use of standardized intelligence test scores altogether in favor of measuring intelligent behavior under conditions which facilitate the production of such behavior. In that procedure, according to Throne, "an assessment strategy requiring treatment is substituted for one debarring it" (1972, p. 9), and the psychologist "assesses intelligent behavior through its improvement" (1972, p. 11). Berkson (1973), in arguing for a "process analysis" approach to behavioral measurement in mental retardation, does not identify himself as a radical behaviorist. However, his position seems to be similar to that of both Lindsley and Throne when he concludes that "close attention to behavioral processes and modification of environments to improve their functioning tends to be an active strategy since it rejects a concept of mental deficiency as an immutable condition" (Berkson, 1973, p. 68). Finally, Meyers (1973) notes that a behavioral approach to measurement "designed to serve treatment or education rather than nosology and prediction, is an increasing function of the psychologist" (p. 39). In-depth discussions of the *functional analysis of behavior* approach to diagnosis and assessment of retarded individuals are presented by W. I. Gardner (1971) and by Bricker and Bricker (Chapter 13) and Watson (Chapter 12).

With the burgeoning of interest in applying Piaget's theory of cognitive development to mental measurement, it is noteworthy that the Piaget-based Infant Psychological Developmental Scale (Uzgiris & Hunt, 1966, 1975), which provides an ordinal measurement of cognitive growth in seven areas, has been found to have potential applicability to older, preschool retarded children (Wachs, 1970).

The employment of psychological test data in the detection and location of possible cerebral pathology has long been the province of clinical psychologists. Of more recent vintage is the philosophy that information derived through neuropsychological assessment can be of service for educational and social programming among children with learning disorders, including those who are mentally retarded. This philosophy and its ramifications have been discussed by Gaddes (1968) and by Haywood and Gordon (1970). Spreen and Gaddes (1969) have compiled developmental norms (covering ages 6 to 15) for 15 neuropsychological tests. In the present volume, Gordon (Chapter 9) elaborates upon the issues which are particularly relevant to the field of mental retardation, and Winsberg (Chapter 10) discusses the validity of neuropsychiatric data gathered in infancy for predicting later intellectual status.

While the field of genetics per se is not within the immediate purview of the psychologist, the issue of the relative roles played by heredity and environment as determinants of human behavior (the so-called "nature-nurture" controversy) has been of major concern to many psychologists over the past 50 years. The recent synthesis of the fields of psychology and genetics into the interdisciplinary area of behavior genetics, and the attendant techniques of behavior-genetic analysis, seem to offer the promise of unraveling the complexities of the interaction between biogenetic and environmentalistic factors in human development. Behavior genetics deals with the relationship of heredity (the genotype) to individual differences in behavior (the phenotype). Hirsch (1967) defines behavior-genetic analysis (which employs the methods of both the behavioral sciences and genetics) as "the experimental analysis of well-defined behaviors into their sensory and response components, the . . . measurement of individual differences in the behaviors and in their component responses, *then* subsequent . . . pedigree analysis by the methods of genetics over a specified set of generations in the history of a given population under known ecological conditions" (p. 121). In Chapter 4, Switzky and Gaylord-Ross discuss specific aspects of behavioral genetics as they relate especially to mental retardation.

Treatment

Many workers in the field have been concerned with the appropriateness, feasibility, and effectiveness of traditional methods for psychological treatment of retarded persons. The issues related to psychotherapy and counseling with the mentally retarded person have been elaborated upon by Bialer (1967) and by Sternlicht (1966a). In Chapter 11, herein, Sternlicht discusses current issues relative to those treatment approaches with the mentally retarded client, devoting special attention to novel techniques requiring little verbal ability and which have been shown to be particularly effective or useful with such clients.

Other approaches that seem to present exciting new avenues to modifying maladaptive behavior in mentally retarded persons are those using conditioning techniques. Issues of interest to the psychologist employing behavior-shaping procedures with retarded individuals have been clearly delineated by W. I. Gardner (1971) and by Watson (1970). In the present book, Watson (Chapter 12) addresses himself to some of the current concerns in utilizing behavior modification with retarded populations. Following is a brief discussion of background issues in the various treatments.

Counseling and psychotherapy. The psychologist who is called upon to provide psychological treatment to retarded individuals and their families does not have much of a "tradition" to look back upon when it comes to applying therapeutic techniques to his client's behavioral or emotional problems. On the contrary, as Stacey and DeMartino (1957) noted in their first-of-its-kind compendium of relevant papers: "Up to the present time *psychotherapy* with the mentally retarded has received relatively little attention from psychologists, psychiatrists and therapists in general. In part this has been due to the belief that psychotherapy, as well as other forms of therapy, is ineffectual with the mentally retarded" (p. 9). Even as recently as 1965, Robinson and Robinson felt called upon to note that "for whatever reasons, psychologists who have chosen to work with this group have not tended to be interested in or trained to carry out psychotherapy" (1965, p. 481).

A major reason for the relative disinterest among psychologists, whether as trainers or practitioners, in applying psychological treatment to the intellectually subnormal client is suggested by Sternlicht (1966a) as lying "in the conceptual frameworks of various theories of personality which have militated against . . . [using] psychotherapy with the mentally retarded" (p. 279). By way of example, Sternlicht pointed out that Freud and his adherents ruled out psychoanalysis with such clients on the grounds that normal intelligence was a prerequisite to accepting analytical interpretations; neo-Freudians maintained that only a normal intellect could experience the insights necessary for personality change; and Rogerians held that retarded persons lacked the ability to verbalize and to deal cognitively with one's impulses—abilities deemed necessary for effective therapy.

Another cogent factor was the one-time prevalent notion of mental retardation as being an incurable condition since it was presumably based on neuropathology. As Sternlicht (1966a) put it, "their [retarded persons'] doom was considered sealed, since neurological tissue does not regenerate and cerebral defects are essentially irreversible. Furthermore, psychological treatment which is functional has never proposed, except in psychosomatic instances, to effect structural changes" (p. 280).

Despite these historic drawbacks, the accumulated evidence has clearly demonstrated that retarded individuals can engage in and profit from a psychotherapeutic regimen (Bialer, 1967). As noted, Sternlicht brings the state of the art up to date in Chapter 11. In additon, issues and approaches bearing on counseling and psychotherapy with parents of retarded children—and with other members of their families—are reviewed and discussed in Chapter 2.

Behavior modification. A foremost early advocate for employing behavior-shaping principles to train retarded persons, particularly those who are profoundly and severely retarded, was Ellis (1963c), whose suggestion that mental retardation psychologists should become "behavior engineers" immediately preceded an upsurge of activity apparently aimed in that direction. Thus, in a very brief overview paper, J. M. Gardner (1968b) pointed to the positive accomplishments of behavior modification programs in developing personal and social skills among institutionalized children and to programs for training various professional and nonprofessional personnel as "behavior modification engineers." That writer came to the very optimistic conclusion that research to that date had "clearly established . . . [behavior modification] as a primary therapeutic tool . . . particularly . . . for the severely and profoundly retarded . . . " (J. M. Gardner, 1968b, p. 54).

In an early burst of enthusiasm, Baumeister (1967) suggested that psychologists trained in the modification and control of retarded behavior could play a unique role in institutional programs, and he warned that "unless residential psychologists more universally adopt the role of 'behavioral engineer' and become more directly and actively involved in the manipulation of behavior they may not be needed" (p. 5). However, in a later publication, Baumeister (1969) cautioned that perhaps operant conditioning had become something of a fad among some professionals, and that it still remained to be shown that such procedures are more successful and/or more efficient than "conventional" techniques for effecting behavior change. Halpern (1968) also addressed himself to the latter point, challenging W. I. Gardner's (1967) notion of having psychologists completely abandon traditional psychotherapeutic approaches with the mentally retarded client in favor of a strict behavioral orientation toward treatment. The later chapters herein by Sternlicht and by Watson make it clear that procedures based on both orientations have a place in the mental retardation psychologist's armamentarium.

Institutional programming. While the majority of individuals identified as mentally retarded do not reside in institutions, the 200,000 retarded children, adolescents, and adults who now live in residential facilities (Butterfield, 1969) comprise a substantial clientele for psychological services within the scheme of institutional treatment. Nevertheless, the psychologist must be concerned not only with the service functions he fulfills in residential programs, but also with the psychological aspects of such programs from the standpoint of the individual, his family, and the community.

Throughout earlier sections of this chapter we have referred to issues relevant to the provision of services by the psychologist in the institution; and these issues (covering clinical, consultative, training, and research services) are explored in much greater depth in Chapter 2 and in other contributions (e.g., Chapters 11 and 12). However, in response to the genuine fear in some quarters that all forms of long-term residential living inevitably place the retarded client at a disadvantage with regard to cognitive, emotional, social, and vocational development and behavior, Chapter 14 explores in depth the pertinent issues touching on all these variables. Also considered therein are alternatives to residential care as presently administered.

In a brief review of the institutional aspects of the so-called mental retardation system, Edgerton, Eyman, and Silverstein (1975) advised against precipitously shutting down all institutions pending conclusive research evidence as to their ill effects. Some of the research findings delineated in Chapter 14 already seem to (a) at least contraindicate the inevitability of such effects, and (b) at most indicate facilitation of some behaviors. In addition, the programming alternatives point the way toward avoiding what Edgerton and his associates feel may be "the danger that bad large institutions may be replaced by small ones that are even worse" (1975, p. 80)

RESEARCH ISSUES

It was noted above that Sarason (1953) pointed to earlier professional disinterest in the psychological aspects of mental retardation as partially being due to the attitude that the field presented no major or interesting research problems. Fortunately, that attitude was then already about to undergo a drastic change. No doubt the change was in part inspired by new university training programs which emphasized research in mental retardation (e.g., Peabody College). Be that as it may, convincing evidence that psychologists were finding the field to offer many challenging and intriguing research opportunities appeared in 1963, in the form of a seminal publication, whose editor noted: "Most of the research upon which this book is based has been conducted within the past decade or so. . . . The systematic study of mental deficiency by the behavioral sciences is still in an embryonic state. However, there is clear evidence of rapid, healthy growth" (Ellis, 1963b, pp. xi-xii).

The rapid proliferation of pscychological research in mental retardation within a relatively brief period of time is attested to by the seven volumes (to date) of more-or-less annual reviews which Ellis has also edited. In the preface to the first volume, he commented: "Behavioral research pertaining to mental retardation has suddenly burgeoned. A decade ago, an investigator could, with little effort, familiarize himself with all the research literature . . .; now he can hardly keep abreast of a particular problem area within the field" (Ellis, 1966, p. vii). This statement is even more cogent today. Over the years, given problem areas have been investigated by behavioral scientists whose professional orientations have been in such subspecialities as clinical, experimental, social, school, educational, developmental, and physiological psychology, and whose theoretical leanings have covered the gamut from classical psychoanalysis to radical behaviorism.

The psychological researcher in mental retardation faces many practical, conceptual, theoretical, and methodological problems. A number of issues pertaining to research as it impinges upon given aspects of the psychologist's role in the field have already been mentioned. Many more are covered in Chapter 2 and throughout the rest of this volume. However, as Ellis noted, primary pervasive issues revolve around the following questions: "Did . . . [the investigator] have a clear objective for his research; i.e., did he ask a question pertaining to a significant source of behavioral variability? Was his methodology such that his results can be viewed with confidence?"

(1963a, p. 3). In Chapter 5, Winters addresses himself to many facets of the methodological issues (together with their theoretical and conceptual underpinnings) to be considered in psychological research with retarded individuals and to the need for methodological acumen in deriving laws of human behavior. In the same vein, the contributions by Schonebaum and Zinober (Chapter 6) and Butterfield and Belmont (Chapter 7)—which complement each other as well as that of Winters—focus specifically on procedures designed to elicit cogent information with regard to what must be considered of prime concern from the standpoint of questions to be addressed in the field: cognitive functioning and cognitive efficiency, both in retarded individuals themselves and in comparison to nonretarded persons.

SUMMARY

This chapter presents an overview of the issues which are of major concern to the mental retardation psychologist. It is noted that many issues stem from the early history of psychology as a science and a profession as well as from the peculiar development of the field of mental retardation itself. Historical foundations of psychology's involvement are outlined, followed by discussions of primary issues relating to (a) the training and perceived role of the psychologist in mental retardation, (b) the actual services he is called upon or is trained to provide, and (c) his special function as a behavioral scientist-researcher.

REFERENCES

AAMD Committee on Psychology. Training of psychologists in mental retardation. *American Journal of Mental Deficiency,* 1961, *65,* 634-651.

Baumeister, A. A. A survey of the role of psychologists in public institutions for the mentally retarded. *Mental Retardation,* 1967, *5*(1), 2-5.

Baumeister, A. A. More ado about operant conditioning—or nothing? *Mental Retardation,* 1969, *7*(5), 49-51.

Beck, S. J., & Molish, H. B. Alfred Binet and Th. Simon: The child is an X. In S. J. Beck and H. B. Molish (Eds.), *Reflexes to intelligence.* Glencoe, Ill.: Free Press, 1959, pp. 146-151. (a)

Beck, S. J., & Molish, H. B. Lightner Witmer: Clinical psychology is born. In S. J. Beck and H. B. Molish (Eds.), *Reflexes to intelligence.* Glencoe, Ill.: Free Press, 1959, pp. 151-155. (b)

Beck, S. J., & Molish, H. B. (Eds.) *Reflexes to intelligence.* Glencoe, Ill.: Free Press, 1959. (c)

Berkson, G. Behavior. In J. Wortis (Ed.), *Mental retardation and developmental disabilities.* (Vol. 5). New York: Brunner/Mazel, 1973, pp. 55-71.

Bialer, I. Psychotherapy and other adjustment techniques with the mentally retarded. In A. A. Baumeister (Ed.), *Mental retardation: Appraisal, education, and rehabilitation.* Chicago: Aldine, 1967, pp. 138-180.

Budoff, M. Learning potential: A supplementary procedure for assessing the ability to learn. *Seminars in Psychiatry,* 1969, *1*(3), 278-290.

Butterfield, E. C. Basic facts about public residential facilities for the mentally retarded. In R. B. Kugel and W. Wolfensberger (Eds.). *Changing patterns in residential services for the mentally retarded.* Washington, D. C.: President's Committee on Mental Retardation, 1969, pp. 15-33.

Cantor, G. N., & Cromwell, R. L. Training and research program in the psychology of mental deficiency. *The Peabody Reflector,* 1959, *32*(1), 26-29.

Crawford, C., Dervin, D., Golden, D., Leland, H., & Van Overloop, D. The 1974 APA workshop on paraprofessionals—Summary of the preliminary report. *Division 33 (APA) Newsletter,* 1975, *2*(1), 3-6.

Cromwell, R. L. Mental retardation and some current dilemmas in the profession of psychology. *Training School Bulletin,* 1961, *58,* 83-91.

Doll, E. E. Edgar Arnold Doll, 1889-1968. *American Journal of Mental Deficiency,* 1969, *73,* 681-682.

Edgerton, R. B., Eyman, R. K., & Silverstein, A. B. Mental retardation system. In N. Hobbs (Ed.). *Issues in the classification of children* (Vol. 2). San Francisco: Jossey-Bass, 1975, pp. 62-87.

Ellis, N. R. Introduction. In N. R. Ellis (Ed.), *Handbook of mental deficiency: Psychological theory and research.* New York: McGraw-Hill, 1963, pp. 1-7. (a)

Ellis, N. R. Preface. In N. R. Ellis (Ed.), *Handbook of mental deficiency: Psychological theory and research* New York: McGraw-Hill, 1963, pp. xi-xii. (b)

Ellis, N. R. Toilet training the severely defective patient: An S-R reinforcement analysis. *American Journal of Mental deficiency, 1963, 68, 98-103. (c)*

Ellis, N. R. Preface. In N. R. Ellis (Ed.), *International review of research in mental retardation* (Vol. 1). New York: Academic Press, 1966, p. vii.

Feuerstein, R. A dynamic approach to causation, prevention, and alleviation of mental retardation. In H. C. Haywood (Ed.), *Social-cultural aspects of mental retardation.* New York: Appleton-Century-Crofts, 1970, pp. 341-377.

Forehand, R., & Gordon, D. A. A survey of U.A.F.'s regarding the role and training of clinical psychologists in mental retardation. *Mental Retardation,* 1971, *9*(6), 22-25.

Gaddes, W. H. A neuropsychological approach to learning disorders. *Journal of Learning Disabilities,* 1968, *1*, 523-534.

Gardner, J. M. Lightner Witmer—a neglected pioneer. *American Journal of Mental Deficiency,* 1968, *72*, 719-720. (a)

Gardner, J. M. The behavior modification model. *Mental Retardation,* 1968, *6*(4), 54-55. (b)

Gardner, W. I. What should be the psychologist's role? *Mental Retardation,* 1967, *5*(5), 29-31.

Gardner, W. I. *Behavior modification in mental retardation: The education and rehabilitation of the mentally retarded adolescent and adult.* Chicago: Aldine-Atherton, 1971.

Guilford, J. P. *The nature of human intelligence.* New York: McGraw-Hill, 1967.

Halpern, A. S. Why not psychotherapy? *Mental Retardation,* 1968, *6*(6), 48-50.

Haywood, H. C., Filler, J. W., Jr., Shifman, M. A., & Chatelanat, G. Behavioral assessment in mental retardation. In P. McReynolds (Ed.), *Advances in psychological assessment* (Vol. 3). San Francisco: Jossey-Bass, 1975, pp. 96-136.

Haywood, H. C., & Gordon, J. E. Neuropsychology and learning disorders. *Pediatric Clinics of North America,* 1970, *17*, 337-346.

Herrnstein, R. J., & Boring, E. G. Alfred Binet (1857-1911) and Victor Henri (1872-1940) on the psychology of individual differences, 1895. In R. J. Herrnstein and E. G. Boring (Eds.), *A source book in the history of psychology.* Cambridge: Harvard University Press, 1966, pp. 428-433. (a)

Herrnstein, R. J., & Boring E. G. Hermann Ebbinghaus (1850-1909) on the completion test. In R. J. Herrnstein and E. G. Boring (Eds.), *A source book in the history of psychology.* Cambridge: Harvard University Press, 1966, pp. 433-437. (b)

Herrnstein, R. J., & Boring, E. G. James McKeen Cattell (1860-1944) on mental testing, 1890. In R. J. Herrnstein and E. G. Boring (Eds.), *A source book in the history of psychology.* Cambridge: Harvard University Press, 1966, pp. 423-427. (c)

Hirsch, J. Behavior-genetic, or "experimental," analysis: The challenge of science versus the lure of technology. *American Psychologist,* 1967, *22* 118-130.

Irvine, P. Lightner Witmer (1867-1956). *Journal of Special Education,* 1969, *3,* 229.

Irvine, P. Edgar Arnold Doll (1889-1968). *Journal of Special Education,* 1970, *4,* 126.

Irvine, P. Arnold Lucius Gesell (1880-1961): A biographical sketch. *Journal of Special Education,* 1971, *5,* 308. (a)

Irvine, P. Henry Herbert Goddard (1866-1957): A biographical sketch. *Journal of Special Education,* 1971, *5,* 210. (b)

Leland, H., Smith, D. E., & Barclay, A. (Eds.) *Report of the workshop on the training of clinical child psychologists in mental retardation, San Francisco, California, August 27-28, 1968.* Washington, D.C.: Section 1, Division 12, American Psychological Association, 1969.

Leland, H., Smith, D. E., & Barclay, A. Report of the workshop on the training of clinical child psychologists in mental retardation. *Mental Retardation,* 1970, *8*(4), 24-28.

Leland, H., Smith, D. E., Warren, S. A., & Bialer, I. Report of the committee on mental retardation. *Newsletter, Section on Clinical Child Psychology (APA),* 1968, *7*(1), 4-7.

Lindsley, O. R. Direct measurement and prosthesis of retarded behavior. *Journal of Education,* 1964, *147,* 62-81.

Luckey, B. M. The contributions of psychology to the problems of mental retardation with some implications for the future. *American Journal of Mental Deficiency,* 1967, *72,* 170-175.

Meyers, C. E. Psychometrics. In J. Wortis (Ed.), *Mental retardation and developmental disabilities* (Vol. 5). New York: Brunner/Mazel, 1973, pp. 25-54.

Pollack, R. H., & Brenner, M. J. *The experimental psychology of Alfred Binet.* New York: Springer, 1969.

Postman, L. Hermann Ebbinghaus. *American Psychologist,* 1968, *23,* 149-157.

Robinson, H. B., & Robinson, N. M. *The mentally retarded child: A psychological approach.* New York: McGraw-Hill, 1965.

Routh, D. K. The psychologist in the university affiliated facility. *Newsletter of the Society of Pediatric Psychology (APA),* 1973, *2*(1), 5-7

Sarason, S. B. *Psychological problems in mental deficiency* (2nd ed.). New York: Harper & Row, 1953.

Seeman, J. The psychological center: A historical note. *American Psychologist,* 1968, *23,* 522-523.

Spreen, O., & Gaddes, W. H. Developmental norms for 15 neuropsychological tests age 6 to 15. *Cortex,* 1969, *5,* 171-191.

Stacey, C. L., & DeMartino, M. F. (Eds.) *Counseling and psychotherapy with the mentally retarded: A book of readings.* Glencoe, Ill.: Free Press, 1957.

Sternlicht, M. Psychotherapeutic procedures with the retarded. In N. R. Ellis (Ed.), *International review of research in mental retardation* (Vol. 2). New York: Academic Press, 1966, pp. 279-354. (a)

Sternlicht, M. The clinical psychology internship. *Mental Retardation,* 1966, *4*(6), 39-41. (b)

Sutter, E., Leland, H., & Barclay, A. (Eds.) *Report of the workshop on the role of subprofessionals in clinical child psychology and mental retardation, Washington, D. C., August 31, 1969.* Washington, D. C.: Section 1, Division 12, American Psychological Association, 1969.

Throne, J. M. The assessment of intelligence: Toward what end? *Mental Retardation,* 1972, *10*(5), 9-11.

Uzgiris, I. C., & Hunt, J. McV. *An instrument for assessing psychological development.* Urbana, Ill.: University of Illinois, Psychological Development Laboratory, 1966. (Mimeo)

Uzgiris, I. C., & Hunt, J. McV. *Assessment in infancy: Ordinal scales of psychological development.* Urbana, Ill.: University of Illinois Press, 1975.

Wachs, T. D. Report on the utility of a Piaget-based infant scale with older retarded children. *Developmental Psychology,* 1970, *2,* 449.

Watson, L. S., Jr. Behavior modification of residents and personnel in institutions for the mentally retarded. In A. A. Baumeister and E. C. Butterfield (Eds.), *Residential facilities for the mentally retarded.* Chicago: Aldine, 1970, pp. 201-245.

Wolfensberger, W. Administrative obstacles to behavioral research as perceived by administrators and research psychologists. *Mental Retardation,* 1965, *3*(6), 7-12.

Manny Sternlicht and Irv Bialer biographical information: see page 2.

2

The role of the psychologist in mental retardation

Manny Sternlicht and Irv Bialer

The psychologist in mental retardation will probably continue to maintain a goodly portion of his traditional roles for some time to come. Nevertheless, his role image, both as he perceives himself and as he is perceived by other disciplines, has been, and is, changing considerably. The notion of the psychologist as primarily a "mental tester," who also administers psychological treatment, is available for occasional consultation, and indulges in research when he has time, is giving way to that of an innovator, planner, programmer, and evaluator, one with clinical, administrative, and research skills. The expertise of the mental retardation psychologist also is increasingly being called upon by law-making bodies at the local, state, and national levels as they consider legislation affecting the mentally retarded citizen, and by the legal profession in behalf of retarded clients. Thus, the mental retardation psychologist is assuming increasing recognition as a citizen-professional advocate in the field (see Leland & Smith, 1974; Wolfensberger & Zauha, 1973).

The clinical psychologist in mental retardation can never ignore or be rid of his service responsibilities, and formal training programs to prepare such professionals for delivery of clinical services cannot be neglected, with the proviso that such programs also prepare the clinician for the consultative, administrative, training, and research responsibilities he will be called upon to assume. By the same token, many other professional personnel are assuming some of the service functions traditionally carried by the psychologist, including assessment and treatment, and the clinician has taken upon himself the responsibility of training paraprofessional personnel for the performance of psychological services under his supervision. Perhaps, eventually, as Haywood (1966) put it, "the cause of the mentally retarded will ultimately be best served [by psychologists, not by emphasizing their service functions, but] by applying highly trained manpower to research and innovative functions, through discovery and development relating to the nature of intelligence, developmental processes, strategies of learning, personality, and motivation in retarded populations" (p. 4). For the present, the psychologist's role in the field is shaped by the varied responsibilities (including various "research and innovative functions") which he is called upon to assume.

The role of the psychologist with regard to mentally retarded individuals and their families is played out directly or indirectly in a variety of settings, which include the institution (public and private residential facilities), the community (day schools, clinics, vocational settings, counseling centers, consultation rooms), and academia (colleges, universities, and university-affiliated facilities). In the following sections we briefly discuss the roles and services (traditional as well as emerging and innovative) of the mental retardation psychologist—sometimes without specific regard to the sites in which these are fulfilled—from the standpoint of (a) clinical services, (b) consultative services, (c) administrative, supervisory, and training services, and (d) research services.

ROLES AND SERVICES

Clinical Services

The psychologist working in the field of mental retardation has been called upon to provide clinical services for a variety of purposes, which include diagnosis and classification, educational placement, vocational planning, treatment programming, and emotional adjustment. Such activities fall into the major categories of psychodiagnostic evaluation and assessment, counseling and psychotherapy, and behavior modification—behavior therapy.

Psychodiagnostic evaluation and assessment. In apparent keeping with the traditional role image of the psychologist as a "giver of tests," Robinson and Robinson (1965) stated: "One of the areas in which the psychologist is best equipped to make a unique contribution is in the administration and interpretation of standardized tests" (p. 375). They went on to note: "Because so great an emphasis has been placed on testing the retarded, it has principally been psychologists skilled in this aspect who have been attracted to the field . . ." (p. 481). In this same vein, Fishler (1971), in an excellent overview of the psychologist's participation as a member of a multidisciplinary team in the clinical assessment of mental retardation, emphasized that "the psychologist's chief contribution to the team often involves the use of psychometric and psychological tests in the assessment of the child's strengths and liabilities" (p. 157).

Meyers (1973a), in a succinct account of the theory and practice of psychological measurement as applied to mental retardation, observed: "Psychometrics refers to the measurement of behavioral characteristics and of inferred mental and feeling states and dynamics, as well as interpersonal or social behavior. . . . Such measurement is performed by properly certified psychologists or those with similar readiness to use and interpret the assessment measures employed" (p. 25).

It has been noted (see Chapter 1) that the psychologist's role as a psychometrician—indeed, as a clinician—stems from concern among early practitioners and researchers with identifying intellectual subnormality. An important function of the psychologist is still to help determine whether given individuals meet two of the major criteria (i.e., impaired intellectual and social behavior) imposed by the AAMD definition of "mental retardation" (Grossman, 1973). (Issues pertinent to this aspect of the psychologist's contribution are fully explored by Bialer in Chapter 3.) However, the involvement of the mental retardation psychologist obviously extends— beyond the assessment of intellectual and social competence for such diagnostic/classification purposes—to the evaluation of a variety of behaviors for purposes of deriving useful data for educational, vocational, and social programming on behalf of retarded individuals. Thus, information regarding emotional status, motor and perceptual-motor skills, psycholinguistic development, vocational skills, learning characteristics and strategies, and central nervous system pathology (if present) could be of enormous assistance in program planning and implementation. The more-or-less traditional approaches to assessment of many of these variables in retarded populations have largely involved standardized tests such as those described by Robinson and Robinson (1965) and Fishler (1971).

However, in response to an increasing uneasiness among various professionals as to the appropriateness of traditional procedures for programming purposes, a number of potentially fruitful innovative approaches to psychometric and psychoeducational assessment are under consideration. These procedures, which are discussed in more detail in Chapter 1 and in various other sources—including contributions to the present volume—involve (a) derivation of "school relevant psychoeducational characteristics" of children (Heintz & Blackman, Chapter 8); (b) measurement of "learning potential" (Haywood, Filler, Shifman, & Chatelanat, 1975); (c) methods based on learning and behavior theory (Berkson, 1973; Bricker & Bricker, Chapter 13; W. I. Gardner, 1971; Lindsley, 1964; Meyers, 1973a; Throne, 1972; Watson, Chapter 12); (d) measuring scales based on Piagetian theory

(Uzgiris & Hunt, 1966, 1975; Wachs, 1970; (e) novel applications of data from neuropsychological assessment (Gaddes, 1968; Gordon, Chapter 9; Haywood & Gordon, 1970: Spreen & Gaddes, 1969); (f) neuropsychiatric approaches (Winsberg, Chapter 10); and (g) behavior-genetics (Hirsch, 1967).

Counseling and psychotherapy. In spite of the early (and, to some extent, continuing) pessimism regarding the practicality and utility of psychological treatment in general—and of specific techniques in particular—for emotional and adjustment problems of retarded clients, there can be no question but that the role of the psychologist in mental retardation clearly includes the practice of counseling and psychotherapy. Not only do some clinical psychologists prefer being thought of as therapists rather than as "testers" or diagnosticians (Forehand & Gordon, 1971), but the literature collated and reviewed in a number of sources (e.g., Bialer, 1967; Leland & Smith, 1965; Stacey & DeMartino, 1957; Sternlicht, 1966a; Sternlicht, Chapter 11) indicates that clinicians and researchers have applied traditional (if slightly modified) psychoanalytic and client-centered approaches (among others) to retarded populations, and that such methods have been found both feasible and effective with given individuals, under given conditions, and with given therapists. In addition to personal counseling (usually subsumed under the rubric of "psychotherapy") in individual and group settings, the psychologist may be called upon to serve as a vocational, educational, or recreational counselor to retarded individuals.

The role of the psychologist in helping the members of the retarded person's family (particularly the parents) recognize, accept, and cope with the many problems inherent in the situation has been amply discussed elsewhere (Sternlicht, 1966a; Wolfensberger, 1967; Wolfensberger & Menolascino, 1970).

In his review of research on psychotherapy with parents, Sternlicht (1966a) emphasized that the client-psychologist relationship can take any one or all of three forms: (a) didactic-like imparting of information and advice (educational counseling); (b) exploration of feelings and attitudes relating to the child (personal counseling); and (c) focus on the parents' own emotional problems rather than on the problem of mental retardation (psychotherapy).

Wolfensberger (1967) provides a most comprehensive and critical exposition of the issues in counseling parents of the retarded child, and covers (a) impact of the child on the parent, including initial and continuing reactions; (b) impact of the child on the cohesiveness of the family unit and the adjustment of siblings; (c) parental dynamics, such as the nature of attitudes toward the child, maternal versus paternal dynamics, and perception of the child's level of functioning; (d) parental coping mechanisms, including the degree of acceptance of the problem and the role of religion; (e) parent-professional relationships, such as the professional worker's responsibilities at time of initial disclosure regarding the child's condition, as a source of referral, and as a provider of services; (f) handling special problems—such as the decision to institutionalize, or the needs of special groups—for example, parents of children with Down's syndrome; (g) genetic counseling; and (h) the parent's perception of professional services.

The general tenor of the benefits attending the provision of management services (including counseling and psychotherapy) to families of the mentally retarded individual has been succinctly stated by Wolfensberger and Menolascino (1970) as follows:

> First, there is the retarded person himself. . . . Often, the only way to help him and to insure that services rendered to him are not wasted is by working with and through the family. Second, services may provide significant . . . assistance to . . . the family so that they . . . can function in a relatively normal . . . fashion. Third, society itself benefits by preventing individual and family disorganization or the need for even more costly services later. (p. 490)

The demonstrated value of personal counseling and psychotherapy as adjustment techniques for retarded clients and their families, together with the relatively positive attitude on the part of administrators toward psychologists providing such services (Baumeister, 1967; Forehand & Gordon, 1971), seems to call for appropriate modification in training programs for clinical psychologists along the lines proposed by Leland (1969), who insists that the training setting must make provisions for the trainee to receive psychotherapy experiences.

Within the general realm of family counseling, another facet may eventually be added to the mental retardation psychologist's role. It has been pointed out (Forehand, Mulhern, & Gordon, 1970; Wolfensberger, 1967) that the psychologst's contacts with parents of retarded children frequently oblige him to discuss with them the role of genetics in their child's condition, and/or to communicate to them the probability of their having another retarded child. While genetic counseling has traditionally been seen as being within the domain of the physician or the medical geneticist, it may eventually emerge as an important activity for the psychologist, in view of the potential contribution the science of behavior genetics can make to the field of mental retardation (Gottesman, 1971). (In Chapter 4, Switzky and Gaylord-Ross discuss the relevance of behavior genetics to genetic counseling in this field.)

Behavior therapy. In an earlier discussion of approaches to psychological treatment in mental retardation, Bialer (1967) noted that at that time clinical psychologists were showing increasing interest and concern with the techniques of behavior therapy, which he defined as: "the application of behavior-shaping strategies and techniques (i.e., classical and operant conditioning principles) to psychotherapeutic goals" (p. 158). Bialer (1967) also made the point that while the then-extant literature scarcely mentioned the application of such reinforcement principles to *therapeutic* goals with the mentally retarded client, there were strong beginnings of a movement toward effective application of conditioning procedures in teaching and training programs for retarded individuals.

Chapter 1 outlined some pioneer and optimistic viewpoints regarding the mental retardation psychologist's role as a "behavioral engineer" (Baumeister, 1967; Ellis, 1963; J. M. Gardner, 1968; W. I. Gardner, 1967), along with early cautions regarding the superiority of conditioning approaches over more traditional psychotherapeutic procedures with retarded clients (Baumeister, 1969; Halpern, 1968). In recent years, there has been a great upsurge of interest and activity in behavior modification programs with mentally retarded groups; and many psychologists are incorporating the concept of "behavior modification engineer" into their roles.

Major discussions of behavior-shaping methodology, as employed in both treatment and training of retarded persons, have been presented by W. I. Gardner (1971), Thompson and Grabowski (1972), and Watson (1970). In the present volume, Bricker and Bricker (Chapter 13) describe a language-training program based on reinforcement principles, and Watson (Chapter 12) delineates a comprehensive treatment plan based on the use of behavior modification with retarded populations. It seems clear that these approaches offer fruitful alternatives to the more traditional methods of treating emotional and behavioral problems in retarded clients.

Consultative Services

The psychologist involved in programs for mentally retarded persons, whether in residential or community settings, serves as a consultant under various circumstances which call for different commitments, such as (a) a collaborative member of an interdisciplinary clinic team, (b) a professional with unique research skills, and (c) a representative of his profession and/or his employment setting to the community at large.

As a clinician, the mental retardation psychologist not only provides data and recommendations pertaining to diagnosis, classification, program planning, and referral, but is also available for consultation with staff members of other professions regarding pertinent problems in inpatient or outpatient case management; and he may be available to the administration for aid in screening job applicants and other administrative tasks.

Since the psychologist is often the staff member with the strongest background in research methodology and statistics, he may be approached by his colleagues for help in devising research to solve specific problems, in operationalizing their own research ideas, in analyzing experimental data, and/or in the preparation of manuscripts for publication.

In the area of community relations, the mental retardation psychologist often is called upon to consult with parent and civic groups who have an interest or involvement in the field, or he may be asked to address such groups more formally on the topic of psychological aspects of mental retardation. He may also be called upon to help devise agency programs which will facilitate the retarded client's participation in community life. In addition, he can assist in strengthening the public image of the institution or agency by active involvement in local community programs for mental health and mental retardation.

The consultative role of the psychologist may often combine all three of the above aspects of that role. Thus, a major innovation in the use of the psychologist as a consultant has been with regard to program development in the institution. In this capacity, he may assume responsibility for the design and assessment of new programs and for training those individuals who would appropriately carry them out, as well as responsibility for ongoing maintenance and effective operation of these programs. Following are examples of the kinds of programming that can result from the consultation function of the psychologist in a residential facility.

Research-inspired programs. Studies of the retarded residents and of programs designed to serve them are an essential component in the systematic development of services to retarded clients and of the organization itself as they bear on total planning efforts. The ongoing research efforts of the psychologist in a facility serving retarded individuals can have powerful impact on stimulation of new programs and on continuation and expansion of ongoing or experimental programs.

An example of the latter is a behavior modification program established at one of the large residential schools in New York State. The paraprofessionals and professionals on the psychology staff use operant conditioning techniques for the purpose of decelerating negative and undesirable behaviors and of accelerating social-adaptable behavior and self-help skills among their retarded charges. The goal is to extinguish aggressive acting out so that eventual return to the community can be accomplished. A one-to-one staff-resident ratio is utilized, with planning for individual programs done by supervisors and consultants, and carried out with the help of students and therapy aides. As a result of these efforts, many of the profoundly and severely retarded participants have able to take on new behaviors, such as eating with utensils, doing simple jobs, and generally showing more sociability.

The systematic analysis of research data bearing on psychological assessment can also have an impact (albeit an indirect one) on program implementation by helping the institutional staff gain insights into resident behavior. Such studies have concerned teacher assessments of institution-alized residents (Sternlicht, Deutsch, & Alperin, 1970); comparison of "organic" and "cultural-familial" retarded individuals (Sternlicht, Pustel, & Siegel, 1968); consideration of emotional needs and socialization patterns, such as time orientation and friendship patterns, of retarded residents (Sternlicht & Siegel, 1968); and general personality development and social behavior of retarded individuals (Sternlicht & Deutsch, 1972). Other research efforts covering therapy techniques and the monitoring of programs in the residential institution can encourage further movement in fruitful directions. Examples are research into: the effects of musical stimulation on the functioning of residents (Sternlicht, Deutsch, & Siegel, 1967), the variety of therapy techniques which could be employed with a retarded population (Sternlicht, 1966a), and programmatic attempts to reduce headbanging behavior in the profoundly retarded child (Sternlicht, Brandwein, & Alperin, 1972).

In carrying out such intramural research studies, the psychologist-researcher must be aware of the interactional as well as the analytical aspects of data collection and analysis, and of their implications for other personnel in the organization. Intra-institutional research requires contact with many levels of personnel and depends for its validity on the cooperation of staff in giving accurate representation of research problems along with access to data sources. Often the success of the research effort will depend entirely on the willingness of line staff to accurately complete data source documents. A helpful chart (Sullivan, 1972) outlining the interactional as well as the analytical tasks in conducting intra-organizational research is contained in Table 2.1.

Cooperative programs. These programs essentially involve large-scale commit-ment of other disciplines and levels of personnel in the organization as well as the psychological staff. Some examples follow.

Training Adults for Community Living (TACL) is a typical program—developed in a large residential facility in New York State—which requires the cooperation of psychologists, educators, social workers, vocational rehabilita-tion specialists, and facility administrators and attendants (Sternlicht,

Hammond, & Siegel, 1972). The TACL program is viewed as that part of the continuum of services which comes into play prior to the termination of the retarded adult's institutional experience, and which bridges the gap between institutional dependence and ultimate self-care. Broadly designed to assist insitutionalized retarded young adults to realize all of their capability and to provide them with experiential preparation for community living, TACL specifically is focused upon a therapeutically oriented, student-governing milieu devised to enhance each resident's self-concept and sense of self-sufficiency and vocational ability. To accomplish this, maximum utilization is made of all available institutional resources, such as counseling, recreational, religious, child-caring services, adult education, speech and grooming programs, and prevocational and vocational training experiences.

Another such program in the same facility is the Infant Toddler Training program, which again utilizes personnel from education, occupational therapy, recreational therapy, pediatrics, psychiatry, psychology, and nursing service to accomplish the overall goals of the program of intensive training in self-care and primary stimulation for profoundly retarded youngsters.

Another cooperative program stimulated by the psychology department's innovative stance in the New York institution is an Infant Therapy Center, focusing on profoundly retarded infants, and introducing interpersonal relationships and emotional development, as well as expressive communication (Sternlicht, 1968).

Occasionally, the psychologist, alerted to the opportunities available in private industry for training the retarded adolescent and adult in very specific, suitable occupations, can develop such programs by involving the private sector to the fullest extent possible. An example is the Ware-Washing Program, in that same residential school. This program evolved out of that for Training Adults for Community Living and was originated by the Laboratory for Economic Development (a private corporation) to train young retarded males in restaurant kitchen duties.

Plant design and utilization. An innovative use of the psychologist as consultant is to involve him in the architectural design of facilities housing and/or serving the retarded client. In this collaborative effort, he could bring to bear all resources that he has available, not only in the psychology of the individual mentally retarded person, but also in the social psychology of mentally retarded individuals in groups, and indeed of all individuals interacting in group situations. For example, he could contribute information about the psychological effect of noise levels and about lighting that would prevent creation of shadowy, potentially fear-producing rooms and halls. His knowledge of the limits on mobility of some members of the retarded

Table 2.1

Analytical and Interactional Tasks by Stages of Program Evaluation in Social Agencies

Stages	Analytical Tasks	Interactional Tasks
Planning the Study	Ascertaining levels of objectives of the program to be studied and the assumptions underlying them. Specifying the questions to be answered by the study and usefulness of the answers to the agency. Studying procedural information about the program to be studied in terms of its operation and its tracking devices. Planning deployment of research personnel and time resources. Integrating the study demands into ongoing unit activities; building a time frame for the study stages.	Eliciting information from affected personnel. Assessing administrative concerns in the study, including administrative feasibility of the project. Establishing legitimacy of the research activity and its usefulness for staff. Determining accessibility to possible data sources; assessing reliability of data sources; establishing formal and informal communications with affected personnel and with data sources.
Building the Research Design	Designing the study method; specifying the target population, the control group, the sampling procedures. Specifying variables to be measured and their possible relationships; illustrating expected relationships in dummy tables. Choosing valid indicants of variables to be measured; testing their reliability. Specifying the statistical analyses to be used and tests of significance, if appropriate. Planning contingency procedures for data collection and analysis.	Eliciting information from appropriate agency personnel as to program client selection procedures and feasibility of measuring specified variables. Locating relevant data sources; becoming familiar with record-keeping idiosyncracies of the program to be studied. Locating and obtaining access to agency records. Involving program staff in formulation of the study design and its development and modification.

Implementing the Research Design	Anticipating possible barriers to data collection. Designing a data coding system for computer analysis; specifying and writing the appropriate program for computer summary; analyzing the data from the computer printout. Drawing conclusions from the analysis related to questions posed in the study; performing tests of significance, if appropriate. Conceptualizing and relating to relevant policy issues the implications in the study findings and their usefulness to the agency.	Arranging access of research staff to data sources. Establishing interoffice or interagency liaison; if appropriate, ensuring cooperation of program personal with research staff. Obtaining cooperation in testing research instruments. Conducting interviews.
Interpretation and Application of Study Results	Translating the study results into concrete implications for practice; specifying application to the agency and for the program staff. Writing up the study results for administration and staff with specific recommendations for program modification, if appropriate. Planning procedures to establish ongoing evaluation into the program operation; integrating them into the agency's ongoing record-keeping procedures. Building a process for obtaining feedback from affected personnel.	Assisting decision makers in interpreting findings and recommendations. Eliciting interpretation by affected staff of study results and suggestions for application. Securing commitment of relevant staff to propose modifications. Eliciting ongoing feedback on program modifications; assisting decision makers in making progressive adjustments in the program. Communicating findings to public relations staff; coordinating the use of study findings internally and externally.

43

population could help in designing the actual physical layout of the buildings, thus reducing the necessity for sometimes difficult movement around the facility.

Administrative, Supervisory, and Training Services

With increasing frequency, psychologists are being called upon to assume management and training positions in mental retardation settings; as his role more and more incorporates such responsibilities. The impact of the psychologist as administrator, supervisor, and trainer in the field continues to grow. Following is an overview and discussion of the multifaceted involvement of the mental retardation psychologist in these aspects of his role.

Director of psychological services. Any psychology department stands in an interdependent relationship to other service components and departments of a given facility. The status of the psychology department in a state institution, for example, usually depends to a large extent upon the chief administrator's (i.e., the institution director's) conception of administration and of the role and contribution of psychology in the organization. Nevertheless, there exists a minimum triadic cornerstone of functions to be performed by the psychology department, under the aegis of the chief psychologist, regardless of the specific frame of reference within which it operates. The triad consists of assessment and evaluation, psychotherapeutic programs, and research activities.

Within realistic limits, the director of psychological services will determine the number and nature of psychological evaluations to be performed. He also will have to ascertain that these evaluations result in a complete and viable analysis and synthesis of the client's current level of overall behavioral functioning, that any referral questions have been answered appropriately, and that any specific recommendations are clearly detailed.

New evaluative procedures will have to be introduced to staff, with their advantages and limitations clearly spelled out. Thus, it will be necessary to maintain intensive and continuing inservice education and training programs with regard to psychological assessment. New interns also will need to be trained in this area.

Appropriate and suitable psychotherapeutic programs must be designed and implemented for the retarded clients as well as for their parents. These programs may be of two types: (a) those that will be carried out directly by the psychology staff, and (b) those that will be performed directly by the child care personnel under minimal direction of the staff psychologist. Behavior modification techniques and group psychotherapeutic approaches may need to be emphasized. Although it is likely that these kinds of decisions will be made by the entire psychology department, the director will need to have especial expertise in these spheres.

Research activities of the department would include evaluation of existing and proposed programs, research consultation with other disciplines, and the execution of applied research efforts which would be designed to answer specific, practical, service-oriented questions. The chief psychologist, in particular, usually has special research skills the should be offered, indeed advertised, for consultation to other departments which may be interested in finding scientific answers to questions generated in the everyday life of the organization.

The director of the psychology department must be cognizant of the organizational dynamics of his agency, since his professional role and that of his staff can only be effectuated with maximum cooperation of both other incumbents in key positions and the line staff. Of major importance is consideration of the demands made on those colleagues by their own roles so that requests for cooperation are more likely to be met. It is also important that the chief psychologist be easily visible and accessible. This will maximize the chances of his being called upon to take a role in organizational development and in contributing to planning on a facility-wide basis.

As he progresses up the ladder of responsibility and authority in the community agency or residential facility in which he is employed, the psychologist may also find himself working in areas for which he has not been specifically prepared. For example, he may be asked to assume the role of head (chief) of a multidisciplinary team or that of participant in management-labor contract negotiations. Or, he may progress to the position of director of a facility.

Director of multidisciplinary work force. In this role, the psychologist must have sensitivity in directing the work of members of separate disciplines who identify strongly with their own point of professional reference. The team chief must take care to preserve those professional reference-group identifications, but he also must foster individual identification with the team and its goals as they relate to overall organization goals. This is an important component in multidisciplinary team process. If left undone, at the least, harmful professional isolation can result; at the most, it may lead to fragmentation of services to the retarded client with little chance of that individual's being seen and responded to as a whole person. This role requires a well-developed appreciation of the areas of expertise of all disciplines represented as well as an equal consideration of all points of view, including those of the psychologist-head's own profession.

When this multidisciplinary team operates in a large bureaucracy, as it is likely to do in services for the retarded child, the chief must be conscious of the possible opposition that can occur between the professional and the bureaucratic mode of operation. Some sources of possible conflict between these modes follow:

1.   The professional mode of operation calls for specialized expertise with practice limited to that field of training and experience; the bureaucratic mode may require and assume administrative expertise as well.

2.   The professional mode calls for a universalistic set of criteria, applied with knowledge and skill to a particular case under consideration; the bureaucratic mode may be set up to meet the organization's needs for group processes, with little inclination to individualize residents or clients.

3.   The professional mode calls for neutral affect, no conflict; the bureaucratic mode does so also, but the effect of neutrality may be dehumanizing in a residential institution.

4.   The professional mode calls for protection of the vulnerability of clients; the bureaucratic mode may exploit clients in order to serve system-maintenance goals.

5.   The professional mode dictates that status derives from job performance; the bureaucratic mode dictates that status and reward are given for loyalty to the system.

The possible conflicts, as presented, are very real and must be recognized, anticipated, and dealt with effectively by the head of any multidisciplinary team.

Participant in management-labor negotiations. Conflict can be looked upon as either a pathological or a healthy state. In the latter case, conflict behavior is to the clinical psychologist rational, conscious, artful behavior which sometimes comes to be known as "strategy." Psychological conflict is difficult to measure in its quantitative aspects, but qualitatively, it can be either bitter and destructive or fruitful and constructive. It is the process of moving the conflict toward some kind of resolution which gives it meaning and makes it adaptive, and this too is a familiar and accepted concept to the psychologist.

In contract negotiations, conflict as an essential ingredient is taken for granted, but it also assumes some common interest between adversaries. It focuses on the fact that each participant's "best" choice of action depends on what he expects the other to do, and that strategic behavior is concerned with influencing another's choice by working on his expectation of how one's own behavior is related to that of the other party. In simpler terms, how does one act in order to elicit the most desirable reaction from among a range of possible reactions on the part of one's adversary?

In negotiating contracts, whatever procedural resolution he opts for—whether reconciliation, compromise, or award—the psychologist-negotiator is faced in a given situation with a certain number of alternative courses of action, each of which is likely to lead to one of several possible consequences. He acts rationally if he takes into account the possible consequences of each course of action, has a preference order among the consequences, and accordingly chooses the course of action which is likely to lead to the most preferred consequence. In doing so, the psychologist-negotiator is not using strategy as an application of force, but rather as an exploitation of potential force.

Sometimes during the conduct of labor-management relations in an organization, an issue or problem arises which is of such a complex and emotional nature that it is extremely difficult to settle in the course of normal negotiations. Many of these problems arise because of tremendous pressure on management, which causes it to seek changes in performance or work practices in a short period of time. This can easily happen in a public bureaucracy serving the retarded individual when it commences a change process in response to sudden societal pressures for more efficient service to its residents or clients. Bargaining in such a case is difficult because neither party is certain as to what the implications are. Tension at the bargaining table may prevent a free exploration of the issues, and each side has a constituency which demands a "win."

Most bargaining situations ultimately involve some range of possible outcomes within which each party would rather make a concession than fail to reach a decision at all. The final outcome must be a point from which neither expects the other to retreat. In a game of strategy, there is an interdependence of expectations, and each person's course of action is determined by what he expects the other to do. A strategic move is one that influences the other person's choice in a manner favorable to one's self, by affecting the other person's expectations on how one will behave. One constrains and/or facilitates the other party's choice by constraining his own behavior. The main ingredient in bargaining, then, is to set up for one's self (and communicate persuasively to the other party) a mode of behavior that leaves the other party with a simple maximization problem whose solution for him is the optimum choice for you and at the same time to impede his ability to do the same to you. The psychologist would seem to be uniquely prepared for such strategy.

Director of facility. If we can view the facility director's mandate as one of guiding and directing the efforts of a large group of employees toward a common goal, then the psychologist is well suited for the role of director. Because he has been trained in understanding the importance of personal and social variables, he should have a very broad awareness of social and psychological factors, especially as they enter into decision-making processes. The psychologist's sensitivity to individual differences would enable him to utilize each employee to his best capacity, and to be objective in dealing with personnel problems. The clinical psychologist also is very closely attuned to the need to listen to a person with his "third ear," to clarify confusing emotions. Thus, he often can prevent explosive situations from occurring, thereby forestalling any possible drainage of work capacities. His background and training in the spheres of human relations and problem solving can also facilitate the psychologist-manager's ability to smooth out any potential management-labor frictions, and to establish a true "team approach" to the problems besetting his charges.

The ability to understand and appreciate the principles of human behavior certainly will hold the director of any service facility in good stead, if not in understanding the people who work with him, at least in understanding himself. And what more, in a sense, can one ask of a top-level administrator, a handler of people and resources, than that he always be conscious of his own weaknesses and limitations?

In this role, however, the psychologist becomes more than a psychologist. He becomes a psychologist-administrator-manager, responsible for policies and decisions that affect the total system, as well as for motivating enactment of those policies and decisions by all levels of personnel in the organization. His identification with the organization must, of necessity, be central; identification with his profession may become peripheral—hence a new role.

His administrative role will be carried out more often than not in a large public bureaucracy. He will need to be conscious of the characteristics of bureaucracies, both those that are functional and those that are dysfunctional, so that he can use structure and process within the organization to best advantage. A bureaucracy is, after all, a form of cooperation created by society for efficiently accomplishing some stated purpose through group means. But the psychologist-administrator will need to be aware of some of the common dysfunctions of large bureaucracies so that he can guard against them. He will need to ask himself if there is an atmosphere of conformity in the organization which militates against creative innovation and independent, rational judgment. Is upward-flowing information limited to reports of achievement and is it based on subjective judgments rather than on facts? Are promotions based on a scheme which discourages excellence among staff? Does the factor of impersonality or neutral affect between staff members, and between staff and client-residents, discourage a spirit of shared experience? Is the informal structure allowed, even nurtured, to the extent that it produces greater efficiency?

As the director of a facility, the psychologist will need a total system perspective and the ability to analyze and balance the demands of various subsystems in the allocation of resources—always scarce—in order to meet overall organizational goals. He knows the bureaucratic organization has a built-in preference for self-maintenance, often at the expense of goal achievement. The director is the one person in the entire organization charged with meeting the needs of all subsystems, those concerned with production or goal achievement as well as those concerned with system maintenance.

The psychologist also must know that organizations do not remain static for long, but are ever-changing, organic entities which strive to maintain a state of dynamic equilibrium at all times. Organizations which serve vulnerable groups in society, such as retarded children, often will be inactive about change too long; and then, in response to sudden societal concern, they will move too rapidly on a single dimension of change. The psychologist-administrator is presumably well qualified to develop, modify, and evaluate programs which will enhance and maximize all of the retarded client's capabilities for effectively relating with his environment, both external and internal. However, like any administrator, he will need to ensure that changes that are made incorporate the goals of service to the retarded individuals served by the system he governs. He must satisfy himself that change is not occurring for change's sake, but that real benefit will result for the vulnerable clients served by his organization.

Internship training and supervision. It is the responsibility of every psychologist constantly to update his knowledge of the field in which he practices. One effective way to do this is through the supervision of professional internships in the organization. This activity offers to the practicing psychologist in mental retardation the opportunity to introduce experience in the field—as noted, an often-neglected one within psychology— to newcomers to the discipline and to prepare them for an appropriate professional role.

The program for psychology internships in residential facilities, for example, can be roughly divided into several major areas of learning experience, many of which can go forward simultaneously (Sternlicht, 1966b). The first is that of initial orientation and observation. Here, the intern is provided with an overall "feel" for the field in general and for practice in a "total institution." This is done through his working as an attendant for a short period of time, preferably in a variety of living units, during which he absorbs the institution's structure and pattern of activities, learns something about interdisciplinary relationships, and gets some feel for the overall field of retardation. The second learning experience is that of regular didactic sessions with content relating to his ongoing clinical and reading assignments. Teaching takes place around clinical assessment of the retarded resident and effective report writing. The intern also will become familiar with research needs, research methodology, and the researchability of practical problems in mental retardation. A large portion of the intern's training is devoted to acquiring skills in assessment of both intellectual functioning and emotional behavior in overall diagnosis. It is here that the trainee is permitted as much freedom as possible to practice independently with the broadest possible range of clients so as to develop the scope of his knowledge about retarded people.

Based on this foundation in evaluation and diagnosis, the intern begins to learn firsthand about treatment through review of ongoing psychotherapy and observation of treatment sessions with retarded clients. Eventually, the intern is assigned a prognostically favorable case to work with individually, albeit with intensive ongoing supervision. At the same time, he will be expected to develop an individual research project in a topic area of his choice in the field of mental retardation. Supervision would then focus around development of sound research methodology and the implementation of the study.

During the course of his training, the intern is expected to participate in staff symposia, taking responsibility for at least two discussion topics himself over the duration of his internship. He will also attend interdisciplinary conferences during which plans are made for the care and treatment of the residents, both those remaining in the institution and those preparing for discharge to a community setting. During the entire internship, stress is placed on the psychology trainee's professional growth and development. He is encouraged to attend professional meetings, to take part in workshops and conferences, and to take membership in professional associations.

Preparation for clinical practice in a community-oriented facility can also be incorporated into the psychology internship to produce a professional flexibility responsive to variations in traditional clinical methods necessitated by the community orientation. This approach to training emphasizes breadth of exposure rather than in-depth experience in testing, assessment, or a specific treatment modality. Training is centered initially on workshops in diagnostic techniques—using a broad range of materials, including case history, observation, interview, and diagnostic testing. Introduction to professional roles, to interdisciplinary relationships, and to the community setting in which he practices is given the intern during this time. Deficiencies in theoretical background are also identified and remedied. Following this basic training, the trainee moves on to therapeutic work with focus on broad sharing of supervision and consultation among several interns and, again, with the community seen as the social milieu within which the client interacts multidimensionally to pressures of social circumstance as much as to pressures of intrapsychic distress. The intern is encouraged to follow up the community setting (e.g., home, school) in the context in which the client's difficulties occur.

Within the purview of an institution for mentally retarded persons, this training has particular applicability in the successful return of the residents to homes of family or of foster parents. The psychologist thus trained can take an active part in maintaining the retarded client in community placement by helping various components of society (i.e., local neighborhoods, commercial areas, transportation facilities, schools, libraries) to understand and to have realistic expectations for the retarded person living among them.

Inservice training and supervision. In facilities serving mentally retarded clients, inservice training of the psychological staff is important and needs to be conducted on a regular, programmed basis. Important elements of inservice training and supervision are built into the concept of career ladders in some state civil service programs. An example of a typical career ladder for psychologists in state civil service is provided by the New York State model, as follows: The position of Psychology Trainee I, which calls for 2 years of college or 2 years of mental retardation experience, is the lowest step on the ladder, which then advances to Psychology Assistant I, requiring 2 years of college plus 1 year of experience. The B.A. degree level is next, with the Psychology Trainee II designation, followed by Psychology Assistant II, needing an additional year of experience in psychology. The fifth level requires either the M.S. degree or the B.A. degree with 2 years of experience. Staff members at all of these five levels—which carry subprofessional status—perform duties (based on their level of training) in the following areas: assisting in research and in test administration, counseling with parents and residents, assisting with techniques of individual and group therapies, and general preparation for professional-level assignments.

The sixth and higher levels are those of professional status, beginning with the Psychologist I position, requiring the M.S. degree and 2 years of experience, one of which follows acquisition of the graduate degree. Psychologist II follows, with the requirement of an additional year of experience. The Associate Psychologist level requires the Ph.D. degree and completion of the internship. Individuals at these professional levels perform evaluations, prepare and administer tests, guide and counsel parents, conduct research, and engage in psychological therapy. Normally, the work is done within the framework of an interdisciplinary team.

The two top levels of the career ladder are administrative positions, in which psychologists plan, develop, and implement programs, act on a consulting basis to their organization on staffing, treatment, and policy questions, plan and carry out research studies, and train psychology personnnel in the organization. These last two positions are designated Principal Psychologist and Chief Psychologist, in ascending order.

Paraprofessional training and supervision. A large portion of the psychologist's training efforts will be in the area of supervision of paraprofessional personnel who can provide psychological services not heretofore relegated routinely to subprofessional personnel. Such a trainee (who may have college training and/or experience in the field of psychology) may engage in a variety of assisting roles in any facility serving the retarded individual. Though these trainees by no means substitute for fully trained psychologists, paraprofessionals can assist in gathering research data and in standardized testing procedures, leaving interpretation and diagnosis to the professional staff. They can be trained also to aid the psychology staff in the preparation of reports and staff presentations. Yen (undated) suggested that the work assignment at this level could include in-depth interviews, for purposes of ascertaining the client's level of intellectual functioning, language and communication ability, and emotional development. (Such interviews could also facilitate an understanding of the integrative patterns of the client.) In addition, the psychology paraprofessional could follow up on the outcome of recommendations made by the staff by gathering information about client progress after appropriate assessment and referral.

Another role could be that of behavior modification aide or counselor-therapist, both under supervision. The need for a directive approach with retarded clients in psychotherapy precludes the need for a high level of skill in insight therapy; and in taking a consulting role with other disciplines, the psychologist-paraprofessional has the advantage of not having yet acquired a narrow technical jargon.

Another extremely important need which could be filled by the paraprofessional psychology worker would be that of retardation specialist in agencies set up primarily to service other problem areas, such as mental health clinics, hospitals, child foster care or adoption services, child guidance clinics, day-care centers, and employment counseling agencies. The retardation specialist would be a source of information and referral, and would fulfill a coordinative function in service, thereby preventing overlap and fragmentation of services to the retarded clients and their families.

The psychologist also may become involved in the training of paraprofessionals in other than psychological services. An example might be preparing child care workers for assuming supportive roles with the retarded child. Psychologists can be of help in developing mature capacities in such paraprofessionals for sharing the life of a child. With direct child caring staff, the training expertise of the psychologist can have greatest impact, as this is the level which has the most direct influence in many ways upon the quality of life for retarded residents in any institution. Child care personnel can be urged to recognize the fears that children have, the emotional needs of retarded children, their "normal" qualities—which tend to be obscured by their abnormalities, which are far more visible—their need for normalized group interaction, and their ability to improve in every way, given sympathetic understanding and stimulation.

Professionals should approach the division of labor in terms of reserving to themselves only those performance aspects which cannot be carried out by persons with less than professional training, and by delegating responsibilities to such persons to the fullest extent possible. To reiterate, planning for the effective utilization of personnel in psychology should include a shift in the total workload from highly trained professionals to less highly trained paraprofessionals, who could carry out a large portion of the work under close supervision and on-the-job training by the professionals. Paraprofessionals drawn from particular socioeconomic or ethnic groups are in a unique position to be effective with clients from similar backgrounds, often the hard-to-reach clients, which represent a gap in service to the total community.

Inservice training of other disciplines. The psychologist can be of great help in the training of educational personnel by assisting them to use information derived from psychological assessment in understanding the developmental capacities and progress of retarded youngsters. Evidence of central nervous system pathology and of learning disabilities, as may be elicited in the testing performed by the psychologist, can help the educators to gear programs of instruction on an individualized basis to the capacities of their retarded students. Psychologists also can help teachers guard against the phenomenon of the self-fulfilling prophecy by encouraging them to expect more, rather than less, than the test results indicate, but not to feel personally chagrined when high expectations are not realized. The psychologist could even admit to the possibility of one-shot testing results being inconclusive, and could encourage the teacher to start fresh with the pupils each day rather than going along day by day expecting little from the students and having them live down to these expectations.

In the training of nursing personnel, the psychologist can add to their diagnostic and treatment armamentarium by encouraging recognition and consideration of the emotional components of mental retardation and of the important part emotional well-being can play in the maintenance of physical health.

Extramural and academic training and supervision. The psychologist can become involved in supervising the training of university or college students—candidates for all degree levels and in all disciplines—who are fulfilling field work requirements by their institutional or agency assignment. The psychologist can design an on-the-job learning experience for them in which they can first become familiar with total operations in breadth and then take on an in-depth project in their area of interest and special course work. For instance, students in special education courses can spend the first week or so of their field work becoming familiar with the institution or agency, with particular emphasis on its broad range of educational programs, and then delve more deeply into work in a more specific area—such as education of severely retarded children—taking on an individual or group treatment project or a relevant research assignment.

Social work students could take on an in-depth project in social service—such as investigating community resources, counseling groups of parents (or of current and prospective foster parents) of retarded children, or engaging in case work with retarded clients. They might also become involved in volunteer service, developing approaches for mobilizing and effectively utilizing volunteer workers. The community organization social worker could take an interest in development of placements in the community for retarded clients, conducting community education programs, and mobilizing community resources for supportive functions to the retarded person in placement.

There is a mutuality of interests in the assignment of all students in that their need for training is being met in an area of their particular interest and choice, and the institution or agency is in a position to benefit from the additional man-hours of work provided to it in this manner. For both to be possible, careful planning will need to be done by the psychologist-supervisor in assigning a reasonable workload to the student, yet which is not busywork that results in little benefit to either the trainee or the organization. The psychologist-supervisor may want to have regular ongoing contact with a school representative to coordinate field training with course work in order to produce a blend of knowledge and skill in the student.

Many employment settings make provision for joint academic appointments of staff psychologists to departments of psychology, special education, or medicine (among others) in area universities. These arrangements allow the mental retardation psychologist to take a direct hand in academic instruction of future professionals in his own and related areas. Needless to say, the psychologist in this training sphere will have to gear his discussions to the specific audience that he is trying to reach. With all, however, he will need to stress that the retarded individual's total environment must be continuously evaluated in an attempt to distinguish those positive and negative factors which will affect development.

Research Services

The preceding discussion has made it quite clear that the mental retardation psychologist is involved in research at various levels, including intramural projects, cooperative studies, and research training and supervision. This involvement is summarized briefly below.

As noted, within the confines of his own operating base or place of employment, the psychologist conducts individual or group psychological research, or he serves as a collaborator in interdisciplinary projects.

Cooperative research activities may involve the interaction between residential or community facilities and area colleges or universities, with the former providing space and subjects for studies conducted by the latter. Within the experience of the present authors, for example, Clover Bottom Developmental Center in Nashville, Tennessee (a state residential facility), maintains an on-grounds behavioral laboratory which is operated by the psychology faculty and students of Peabody College. Utilization of residents and other institutional resources for projects conducted in this laboratory is coordinated by Clover Bottom's chief psychologist. As another example, cooperative research between the Kennedy Child Study Center—a day school for young retarded children in New York City—and various local universities has been regulated by the Center's Director of Research, a clinical psychologist.

In his role as trainer, research supervisor, and director of research, the psychologist works with psychological interns and other trainees who find their way to his bailiwick. He may also train students of other disciplines—such as social work, education, and medicine—to plan and conduct experiments, and to analyze and interpret research findings involving retarded individuals.

Research trends. Among the many areas that have been the concern of the mental retardation psychologist, some stand out more than others in delineating the direction toward which he is increasingly turning his research interests and responsibilities. These may be enumerated as follows:

1. In the area of psychoeducational assessment, research is moving away from concern with deriving and validating predictive data (e.g., standardized intelligence test scores) toward devising techniques for what Meyers (1973a) calls "measurement for behavioral improvement," a class of procedures that "makes no etiological inferences, ignores categorical diagnoses, implies no underlying dynamics ... [but whose] purposes are to be objectively descriptive of relevant behaviors at some starting time, and to provide repeated behavior measures for noting change due to treatment" (Meyers, 1973a, p.

38). Undoubtedly, the testing procedures advocated by the radical behaviorists (Lindsley, 1964; Throne, 1972) and by Berkson (1973), as well as by "learning potential" advocates (Haywood et al., 1975) and by Heintz and Blackman (Chapter 8) may all be subsumed under the rubric of "measurement for behavioral improvement." This all points to the emergence of a much stronger role for the mental retardation psychologist in psychoeducational concerns; and it could provide strong direction to the role of the school psychologist in mental retardation. The latter contingency is certainly in keeping with Meyers' (1973b) call for reconceptualization of the role of the school psychologist in educational programming for the retarded child.

2. An area of research which is directly relevant to psychoeducational approaches with retarded students concerns their learning characteristics and learning strategies. Interesting new directions such research might take are exemplified by the work of Butterfield and Belmont (Chapter 7) and the research reviewed by Heintz and Blackman (Chapter 8).

3. In psychological treatment, it is obviously the general area of behavior therapy/modification which is of prime research concern at present. The directions in which such research seem to be heading are toward a clear delineation of the process variables which go into the effectiveness of such approaches with retarded clients, and toward obtaining data as to the relative effectiveness of such treatment over more traditional approaches.

4. As noted, the psychologist in mental retardation is in an increasingly strong position to initiate and/or participate in evaluative and administrative research. Program evaluation, in particular, is coming more to be within his purview. A relatively neglected area of evaluative research has been that of programs in special education. In that connection, Miller (1966) has made the cogent suggestion that the school psychologist, in view of his training in research methodology, his familiarity with educational practice, and his sensitivity to behavioral nuance, would make an ideal communications link between the program designer and the program evaluator. Of course those same attributes qualify the school psychologist in a mental retardation setting to carry out evaluative research in his own right. Table 1 presents useful guidelines for conducting such research in any setting.

5. Finally, in view of their theoretical and practical concerns regarding the nature of "intelligence," an inevitable research interest among mental retardation psychologists promises to be that of behavior genetics. Unquestionably, there are, and will be in larger numbers, those who see in that science the source of answers to the perplexing questions regarding not only the heritability of intelligent behavior, but the relative influence of environmental conditions on intellectual development.

FUTURE DIRECTIONS

The future of habilitation in mental retardation will be concentrated on the prevention of retardation, on normalization and community living for retarded residents now in institutions, and on prevention of institutionalization of retarded citizens now in the community. In line with these foci, psychology as a profession would have important functions, all of which could be carried out in community psychological services centers.

A Psychological Services Center for the Mentally Retarded Client

As we envision it, a psychological services center for the mentally retarded citizen would be a community-based, community-oriented facility, offering a maximal variety of services for individuals of all ages and all degrees of retardation. This center would be staffed by psychologists filling a wide span of roles, limited only by imagination and available man-hours, with adjunctive professional persons being on call and utilized on an as-needed, when-needed basis. Such a center can be visualized as providing a continuum of comprehensive services, ranging from prevention of retardation by public education, evaluative assessments, case finding, and referral, through normalization efforts via crisis counseling, psychotherapy and behavior modification, and community education, to job development and continuing follow-up for retarded workers. Outreach satellite centers also may have to be developed.

In addition to outpatient services, the center would have to provide a full complement of temporary or transitional inpatient services. The latter would be varied according to the characteristics and needs of the particular individuals involved. Thus, some clients might require some form of residential treatment during the daytime hours only, others during the evening hours, and still others for weekends only. This obviously would require considerable flexibility in programming, since the types of retarded clients to be served at any given time might vary.

Any such psychological services center also should be a key facility for the training of professional and paraprofessional persons, as well as a hub for research activities, particularly in terms of applied research in the programming sphere. In this regard, center policy would have to encourage broad-based innovative roles for the psychologist to equip him for meeting significant social needs.

Information-giving and referral would be an integral part of this center's functioning. Necessary follow-up also would need to be performed. Public information on prevention and early diagnosis of retardation would reach into the media and into the social and professional life of the community. Case finding would rely to great extent on the success of these public information efforts. Consultation to community schools would be of great help in developing learning experiences which would maximize the capabilities of the retarded students in special classes, and it would secure the parents' cooperation in the development of needed special programs. Parent counseling would be an important part of this service, both for natural parents and for current and prospective foster parents of the mentally retarded individual.

Maintenance of the retarded person in society often depends on his ability to walk unnoticed among the "normal" citizens and to take part, inconspicuously, in the usual life of the community. Therefore, the psychologist would concern himself with helping the community to understand and accept the retarded person in the use of the transportation system, in public buildings, and in facilities such as theaters, libraries, schools, and shopping centers, so that normalization would be enhanced. Another very important and related function would be that of job development for the retarded client. The inhabitants of the community, and the commercial and industrial establishments within it, have a mutually dependent relationship, one which can be utilized by the psychologist to apply pressure for development of appropriate job opportunities for the community-based retarded citizen. The psychologist would take an active role in developing the job placement and in ensuring the successful employment of the retarded worker via continuing follow-through procedures.

By the same token, psychologists involved in community mental retardation programs should place a very high priority indeed upon collaborative, self-modifying, social interventions—with a focus on prevention via facilitating the retarded child's accomplishment of developmental tasks. This is necessary because, as research in human development has found repeatedly, failures to accomplish the psychosocial tasks of an earlier stage of development increase the individual's vulnerability to failure in accomplishing those tasks required at later developmental stages.

The psychologist in such a setting also could very well find himself taking an advocacy role on behalf of any retarded individual who may be at risk of ejection from the community for aberrant behavior. In another aspect of the advocacy role, the center might have to act as a lobbyist, helping to develop public policy and to promote suitable legislation on behalf of the mentally retarded individual. The facility would also provide ongoing organizational and programmatic consultation with regard to dealing with the retarded offender—especially to social caretaking agencies and institutions, but also to other appropriate facilities (e.g., to police units).

CONCLUSIONS

The saliency of the changing role of the psychologist in mental retardation can be conceptualized on three levels: that of technician, that of manager or middle manager, and that of administrator. His role has been and continues to be changing on all three levels. As a technician, novel modalities of treatment, of training, and of assessment, as well as innovative research horizons, require new awarenesses and skills. On the manager and middle-manager level, all issues in the management of organizational work are his concern, including task accomplishment, employee skill development, and morale. On the administrative level, issues of consumerism and of environmental pressures toward change, together with the problem of gaining support and legitimation for emerging policy issues—such as community living for the retarded citizen—are in his purview. Each of these levels makes unique demands on the skills, the imagination, and the willingness to grow on the part of mental retardation psychologists.

The stimulus to change is a given in our transitional society. The social fabric is woven with modification, and organizational life is ever-changing as well. The psychologist has learned to respond and to modify his behavior. His future is even more likely to reflect change, but at an accelerating rate.

Most psychologists see themselves as providers of service first and foremost, with responsibilities at other levels (i.e., administration) coming later in one's self-image. As a psychometrician, the psychologist is a technician who brings his assessment skills to bear in very specific techniques limited to a given time-structured situation and a given population of clientele. As a clinician, his psychodiagnostic, psychotherapeutic, and research activities all demand currency and awareness of change and innovation. He uses very specific and variously developed technical skills in his role of behavioral scientist-researcher as well.

In his clinical work, the psychologist in mental retardation has never been far from the laboratory. However, the importance of research is paramount at all levels of responsibility. For example, the middle- and top-level administrative roles of the psychologist permit problems from the clinical practice level to become researchable areas. Research-derived programming innovations at the practice level are likely to be fostered and encouraged as well by psychologists in the administrative ranks.

Also, at the manager or middle-manager level, the mental retardation psychologist is required to be a programmer, trainer, motivator of personnel, and problem solver. This is the administrative level that is attuned both to internal procedures and to the policy choices that limit and constrain the upper levels in the organization. He often is the mediator between demands from the top for performance and factors on the lower level that either constrain or facilitate performance. In his manager- or middle-manager role, human understanding is most importnat, especially with regard to motivation and to the managerial controls that produce efficient performance.

At the top administrative level, the psychologist's role is even more varied. Quite different from one-to-one technical application of skills which typifies the clinical role, this top level requires an ability to relate effectively with many persons simultaneously in the organization and with the external environment in obtaining legitimation and support. Most importantly, it requires the ability to assess changing trends in the field of mental retardation that will affect organizational operations. In these days of consumerism, the external environment is especially important to organizations. Increasingly vulnerable to examination of policies and procedures, service facilities for the mentally retarded individual are under critical scrutiny by a number of publics who expect these facilities to produce effective services efficiently.

The properly trained mental retardation psychologist comes equipped to grow, to change, to mold himself in accordance with the demands of new roles and images. The credo of individual differences has been the cornerstone of his development as a clinician, and he is served by it at all levels. The field has evolved from step-child status in the profession of psychology to one recognized as demanding very special theoretically based training and support. The educational requirements have correspondingly kept pace, with concentrations in coursework and internship expanding. Concomitantly, the various professional associations have devoted their interests and their conference time to problems in the field of retardation, recognizing the growing needs of a large body of practitioners and researchers.

As interest in the field within psychology has enlarged, salaries and perquisites for various positions have been raised, attracting more and better psychologists to this area. The field is expanding dramatically, and mental retardation as a unique area of interest, is attracting more qualified professionals in many related disciplines. The psychologist's ability to relate to other professionals is obviously crucial to achieving the kind of teamwork on which coordinated services depend.

The emerging roles of the mental retardation psychologist can be seen as incorporating several new responsibilities heretofore reserved to other professions. Yet, his professional identity may stress the more traditional activities of tester, therapist, and researcher. His role is therefore not just an emerging and changing approach to retardation, but also to his profession—and in organizational and social life as well. His negotiation of these new roles offers personal and professional growth in an especially needful field of psychology.

SUMMARY

In this chapter, the psychologist's traditional roles of clinician, therapist, and consultant are explored, as are his services as administrator-trainer and researcher. New roles are delineated, including: innovator in assessment and treatment techniques, programmer and supervisor, coordinator of new uses of manpower, and program evaluator.

Future trends identified with regard to the role of the psychologist in mental retardation include community-based comprehensive services, and organizational and legislative advocacy for mentally retarded citizens.

REFERENCES

Baumeister, A. A. A survey of the role of psychologists in public institutions for the mentally retarded. *Mental Retardation,* 1967, *5*(1), 2-5.

Baumeister, A. A. More ado about operant conditioning—or nothing? *Mental Retardation,* 1969, *7*(5), 49-51.

Berkson, G. Behavior. In J. Wortis (Ed.), *Mental retardation and developmental disabilities* (Vol. 5). New York: Brunner/Mazel, 1973, pp. 55-71.

Bialer, I. Psychotherapy and other adjustment techniques with the mentally retarded. In A. A. Baumeister (Ed.), *Mental retardation: Appraisal, education, and rehabilitation.* Chicago: Aldine, 1967, pp. 138-180.

Ellis, N. R. Toilet training the severely defective patient: An S-R reinforcement analysis. *American Journal of Mental Deficiency,* 1963, *68,* 98-103.

Fishler, K. Psychological assessment services. In R. Koch and J.C. Dobson (Eds.), *The mentally retarded child and his family: A multidisciplinary handbook.* New York: Brunner/Mazel, 1971, pp. 156-196.

Forehand, R., & Gordon, D. A. A survey of U.A.F.'s regarding the role and training of clinical psychologists in mental retardation. *Mental Retardation,* 1971, *9*(6), 22-25.

Forehand, R. L., Mulhern, T., & Gordon, D. A. Psychological services in the institution. In A.A. Baumeister and E.C. Butterfield (Eds.), *Residential facilities for the mentally retarded.* Chicago: Aldine, 1970, pp. 372-396.

Gaddes, W. H. A neuropsychological approach to learning disorders. *Journal of Learning Disabilities,* 1968, *1,* 523-534.

Gardner, J. M. The behavior modification model. *Mental Retardation,* 1968, *6*(4), 54-55.

Gardner, W. I. What should be the psychologist's role? *Mental Retardation,* 1967, *5*(5), 29-31.

Gardner, W. I. *Behavior modification in mental retardation: The education and rehabilitation of the mentally retarded adolescent and adult.* Chicago: Aldine-Atherton, 1971.

Gottesman, I. I. An introduction to the behavioral genetics of mental retardation. In R. M. Allen, A. D. Cortazzo, and R. P. Toister (Eds.), *The role of genetics in mental retardation.* Coral Gables, Fla.: University of Miami Press, 1971, pp. 49-69.

Grossman, H. J. (Ed.) *Manual on terminology and classification in mental retardation.* (1973 rev.) Washington, D.C.: American Association on Mental Deficiency, 1973.

Halpern, A. S. Why not psychotherapy? *Mental Retardation,* 1968, *6*(6), 48-50.

Haywood, H. C. The changing role of the psychologist in mental retardation. Paper presented at the meeting of the American Association on Mental Deficiency, Chicago, May 1966.

Haywood, H. C., Filler, J. W., Jr., Shifman, M. A., & Chatelanat, G. Behavioral assessment in mental retardation. In P. McReynolds (Ed.), *Advances in psychological assessment* (Vol. 3). San Francisco: Jossey-Bass, 1975, pp. 96-136.

Haywood, H. C., & Gordon, J. E. Neuropsychology and learning disorders. *Pediatric Clinics of North America,* 1970, *17,* 337-346.

Hirsch, J. Behavior-genetic, or "experimental," analysis: The challenge of science versus the lure of technology. *American Psychologist,* 1967, *22,* 118-130.

Leland, H. Responsibilities of a training program. In H. Leland, D. E. Smith, and A. Barclay (Eds.), *Report of the workshop on the training of clinical child psychologists in mental retardation, San Francisco, California, August 27-28, 1968.* Washington, D.C.: Section 1, Division 12, American Psychological Association, 1969, pp. 10-13.

Leland, H., & Smith, D. E. *Play therapy with mentally subnormal children.* New York: Grune & Stratton, 1965.

Leland, H., & Smith, D. E. *Mental retardation: Present and future perspectives.* Belmont, Calif.: Wadsworth, 1974.

Lindsley, O. R. Direct measurement and prosthesis of retarded behavior. *Journal of Education,* 1964, *147,* 62-81.

Meyers, C. E. Psychometrics. In J. Wortis (Ed.), *Mental retardation and developmental disabilities* (Vol. 5). New York: Brunner/Mazel 1973, pp. 25-54. (a)

Meyers, C. E. The school psychologist and mild retardation. Report of an ad hoc committee. *Mental Retardation,* 1973, *11*(1), 15-20. (b)

Miller, M. B. Evaluation and quality control in special programs. Paper presented at the meeting of the American Psychological Association, New York, September 1966.

Robinson, H. B., & Robinson, N. M. *The mentally retarded child: A psychological approach.* New York: McGraw-Hill, 1965.

Spreen, O., & Gaddes, W. H. Developmental norms for 15 neuropsychological tests age 6 to 15. *Cortex,* 1969, *5,* 171-191.

Stacey, C. L., & DeMartino, M. F. (Eds.) *Counseling and psychotherapy with the mentally retarded: A book of readings.* Glencoe, Ill.: Free Press, 1957.

Sternlicht, M. Psychotherapeutic procedures with the retarded. In N. R. Ellis (Ed.), *International review of research in mental retardation* (Vol. 2). New York: Academic Press, 1966, pp. 279-354. (a)

Sternlicht, M. The clinical psychology internship. *Mental Retardation,* 1966, *4*(6), 39-41. (b)

Sternlicht, M. Toddler training and stimulation for maximum potential. Paper presented at the annual meeting of the American Association on Mental Deficiency, Boston, April 1968.

Sternlicht, M., Brandwein, H., & Alperin, N. Reduction of headbanging in profoundly retarded institutionalized boys: Application of behavior therapy and motivation therapy. Paper presented at the meeting of the American Association on Mental Deficiency, Minneapolis, May 1972.

Sternlicht, M., & Deutsch, M. R. *Personality development and social behavior in the mentally retarded.* Lexington, Mass.: D.C. Heath, 1972.

Sternlicht, M., Deutsch, M., & Alperin, N. Psychological evaluations and teacher assessments of institutionalized retardates. *Psychology in the School,* 1970, *7,* 164-167.

Sternlicht, M., Deutsch, M. R., & Siegel, L. Influence of musical stimulation upon the functioning of institutionalized retardates. *Psychiatric Quarterly Supplement,* 1967, *41* (Part 2), 323-329.

Sternlicht, M., Hammond, J., & Siegel, L. Mental retardates prepare for community living. *Hospital & Community Psychiatry,* 1972, *23*(8), 15.

Sternlicht, M., Pustel, G., & Siegel, L. Comparison of organic and cultural-familial retardates on two visual-motor tasks. *American Journal of Mental Deficiency,* 1968, *72,* 887-889.

Sternlicht, M., & Siegel, L. Time orientation and friendship patterns of institutionalized retardates. *Journal of Clinical Psychology,* 1968, *24,* 26-27.

Sullivan, I. Analytical and interactional tasks by stages of program evaluation in social agencies. Unpublished chart, April 1972.

Thompson, T., & Grabowski, J. (Eds.) *Behavior modification of the mentally retarded.* New York: Oxford Univeristy Press, 1972.

Throne, J. M. The assessment of intelligence: Toward what end? *Mental Retardation,* 1972, *10*(5), 9-11.

Uzgiris, I. C., & Hunt. J. McV. *An instrument for assessing psychological development.* Urbana, Ill.: University of Illinois, Psychological Development Laboratory, 1966. (Mimeo.)

Uzgiris, I. C., & Hunt, J. McV. *Assessment in infancy: Ordinal scales of psychological development.* Urbana, Ill.: University of Illinois Press, 1975.

Wachs, T. D. Report on the utility of a Piaget-based infant scale with older retarded children. *Developmental Psychology,* 1970, *2,* 449.

Watson, L. S., Jr. Behavior modification of residents and personnel in institutions for the mentally retarded. In A. A. Baumeister and E. C. Butterfield (Eds.), *Residential facilities for the mentally retarded.* Chicago: Aldine, 1970, pp. 201-245.

Wolfensberger, W. Counseling the parents of the retarded. In A. A. Baumeister (Ed.), *Mental retardation: Appraisal, education, and rehabilitation.* Chicago: Aldine, 1967, pp. 329-400.

Wolfensberger, W., & Menolascino, F. J. A theoretical framework for the management of parents of the mentally retarded. In F. J. Menolascino (Ed.), *Psychiatric approaches to mental retardation.* New York: Basic Books, 1970, pp. 475-493.

Wolfensberger, W., & Zauha, H (Eds.) *Citizen advocacy and protective services for the impaired and handicapped.* Downsview, Canada; National Institute on Mental Retardation, 1973.

Yen, S. The mental health technician (associate) in the psychological service. (Unpublished manuscript, undated)

Manny Sternlicht and Irv Bialer biographical information: see page 2.

3

Mental retardation as a diagnostic construct

Irv Bialer

The issues which bear most closely on the concept of mental retardation as a diagnostic construct pertain to the *definition* of the term and its use in the *classification* and *labeling* of children. While no one of these variables would have any meaning without the others, each may be conceptualized as subtending somewhat different subissues. In this chapter, therefore, the problems encountered in defining, classifying, and labeling mentally retarded individuals will be considered as separate but intimately related issues.

DEFINITIONAL ISSUES

Children typically call attention to themselves by deviant behavior before the identification and labeling process begins. Consequently, the need for and utility of a definition—which lays the basis for a given label—are socially determined.[1] A definition is useful only if it helps us meaningfully to group individuals with common characteristics to the end that effective treatment and/or programming may be based on such grouping. This is the rationale for a classification system. Thus, we need to define certain aspects of deviant behavior consistently, so that (a) we may recognize the class in which they are to be grouped for treatment purposes, and (b) it is possible to communicate unequivocally across the several disciplines which may be involved in the treatment. In a broader sense, too, a diagnostic label reflects

---

The writer is indebted to Martin B. Miller for his role in the development of the ideas expressed in this paragraph.

the expectations of the culture regarding persons so labeled; and these cultural expectations are build into definitional statements in the form of specific criteria. These criteria help us to identify those individuals who, because of a core of common characteristics, are considered sufficiently deviant from the general population so as to require special attention from society. Since a label is a shorthand way of describing the relationship among a number of characteristics, it must be based upon clear-cut and invariable definitional criterial which distinguish that particular brand of deviancy from other forms of deviancy and which help us to identify not only special individuals but also their special needs. Therein lies the practical need for defining diagnostic constructs in unequivocal terms.

CRITERIA FOR DIAGNOSTIC CONSTRUCTS

Cromwell, Blashfield, and Strauss (1975) emphasized that diagnostic constructs may be viewed as specialized types of scientific constructs and, accordingly, that they must meet the criteria which philosophers of science apply to scientific constructs in an effort "to guide the establishment of meanings of given constructs and to clarify the relationships between constructs in a way that . . . [is] empirically based" (p. 6). Thus, the prime (dual) criteria which a diagnostic construct must satisfy are that it be *clear and useful.* These criteria should tend to preserve the uniformity of the given concept and to reduce change over time. Cromwell et al. went on to point out that the criterion of *clarity* demands that "the definition of a construct must lend itself to publicly observable assessment (people must be able to determine whether and to what extent the construct describes a given observable event" (p. 6); and in order for the criterion of *utility* to be satisfied, "the construct must bear a relationship to another set of events (to other constructs)" (p. 6).

However, as was also made clear by Cromwell et al., in addition to meeting the basic criteria, diagnostic constructs should display specialized characteristics which are germane to specific conditions. Clarity is enhanced when their definitions are restricted to historical-etiological and/or currently observable and assessable characteristics. The utility of diagnostic constructs in individual clinical, educational, or social treatment depends on the extent to which given intervention approaches (or no intervention at all) that follow from the diagnosis allow for the prediction of some outcome (prognosis). In other situations, the utility of a diagnostic construct may be gauged by the extent to which it facilitates (a) prevention of a given condition in others, (b) communicability of research procedures and findings, and/or (c) gathering and interpretation of epidemiological data.

The concepts of clarity and utility are closely related to those of reliability and validity, respectively. To the extent that a construct is defined in clear, communicable, unambiguous terms, with a consistent set of referents, that construct may be said to possess reliability. That is, whatever the definition refers to, it does so consistently, and one knows what it means whenever it is used and whoever uses it. Also, since from a clinical standpoint the primary purpose of a diagnostic construct is to facilitate treatment and programming, and from a scientific standpoint the purpose is to facilitate basic and applied research, the extent to which a definition helps accomplish these aims is a measure of its validity (i.e., it does what it was designed to do). However, the ability to generate prognostic statements or to predict outcome is also an indicator of validity. Consequently, clear diagnostic constructs which combine historical-etiological and/or assessment data with the capability of facilitating interventive approaches, prognostic statements, and meaningful research are most reliable and valid.

The present writer holds that the recent definitions promulgated by the American Association on Mental Deficiency (AAMD) (Grossman, 1973; Heber, 1959, 1961) lay the basis for establishing the term "mental retardation" as a reliable and valid diagnostic construct with respect to the foregoing requirements. Before going on to give those definitions and to discuss their merits, a historical overview of definitional approaches is in order.

Early Definitions

An examination of recorded histoy reveals descriptions and references reaching back into antiquity about individuals who deviated so markedly from the "norm" in both intellectual and social behavior as to require social, legal, or administrative action on their behalf. As far as is known, the problem has existed since the beginning of humanity, and it has been associated with a variety of referents (E. E. Doll, 1962; Kanner, 1964). Over the centuries, however, the criteria by which such individuals—who were variously given such labels as "fool," "idiot," "imbecile," "feebleminded," "ament," "mentally defective," "mentally subnormal," and "mentally retarded"—were recognized as deviant has changed with differing social, administrative, and educational needs.

Acccording to Hilliard (1965), an early attempt to understand and cope with the problems of intellectual and social inadequacy consisted of legislative efforts in 14th century England to differentiate between mental *subnormality* (i.e., "idiocy") and mental *abnormality* (i.e., "lunacy") so as to facilitate the legal disposition of the estates of idiots and lunatics. Thus, the "King's Prerogative" of 1325 declared that the land of idiots ("natural fools") was to be protected during their lifetime and given to their rightful heirs after their death; but the land of lunatics ("persons of unsound mind") was to be kept safe and restored to them on recovery. This gross differentiation saw the idiot as suffering from a permanent lack of mental capacity and the lunatic as potentially recoverable of normal facilities.

Clearly, such early legislation was concerned more with property rights than with the rights and welfare of individuals. It therefore did not affect the lives of the population at large and carried no implication for care or treatment of persons unable to care for their own needs. Some 300 years later, in 1534, the first known indication of modern concepts appeared in England in a legal definition of "idiocy," which combined the developmental, intellectual, and social aspects of current terminology (E. E. Doll, 1962). According to this definition, the test of "natural" or "born idiocy" included the ability of the individual to count 20 pence, to tell who his parents were, to know his age, and to have "understanding of reason what shall be to his profit . . . and what for his loss . . ., and that he know and understand his letters, and do read by teaching or information of another man . . . " (E. E. Doll, 1962, p. 23). While these definitional criteria were considerably more refined, they were apparently still designed to clarify legal rights and duties with regard to property. Hilliard (1965) noted that it was only toward the middle of the 19th century that society realized the need to make special provisions for the care and treatment of persons who might be designated as "mentally subnormal."

In all countries in which such provision was begun in the middle 1800s, it took the initial form of institutional services (Baumeister, 1970; E. E. Doll, 1962; Hilliard, 1965). In these early institutional programs, the avowed aim was schooling, with a view toward returning the residents to the community, and the educational approaches were originated and administered by physicians (Kanner, 1960). Kirk and Johnson (1951) also made the extremely important point that most of the major contributions to the 19th century movement for education of mentally subnormal children—in and out of institutions—were made by physicians. Chief among these was Seguin in France.

E. E. Doll (1962) pointed out that the basis for American work with individuals we now designate as "mentally retarded" was laid in France in the late 18th and early 19th centuries. There, from 1799 to 1804 (Itard, 1894/1962), demonstrated the educability of even severely subnormal children; and Esquirol in 1838 (as cited in Doll, 1962), addressing himself to the psychiatric aspects of the problem of providing more adequate services to such children, felt it important to differentiate "idiocy" from a somewhat less debilitating condition, "imbecility—and both pathological states from "insanity." In contrast to similar efforts in medieval England, as noted by

Itard, Esquirol's definition carried educational and treatment implications. The following passage from E. E. Doll (1962) makes this apparent:

> Esquirol defined idiocy, in contrast to insanity, as arrested or imperfect development, incurable, and based upon defects in structure visible at autopsy. He added that it was a condition not an illness. Imbecility he defined as a similar affliction, but less severe. Esquirol described imbeciles as endowed with feeble intellectual and affective capabilities. . . . Positively, he noted their ability to do rough . . . work, and to learn reading, writing and a little music. . . . Among idiots, on the other hand [he posited that], instinct dominates all facilities, speech scarcely exists, . . . and emotions [are] nonexistent. . . . Esquirol [has been credited] with being the first to recognize that the basic lack of both classes was primarily intellectual. (p. 26)

Despite Esquirol's attempt to make a meaningful (if not completely operational) distinction between terms which described individuals functioning at different intellectual levels—and despite his pronouncement that idiots (as opposed to imbeciles) could never be educated because "idiocy is . . . a condition in which the intellectual facilities . . . have never been developed sufficiently to enable the idiot to acquire . . . knowledge, . . . " (Sarason & Doris, 1969, p. 214) —the term "idiot" continued to be employed in a generic sense by his colleague, Seguin, who had been a student of Itard.

Seguin (1866/1971), proposing a definition of the term "idiocy" which would "express the [underlying] physiological infirmity . . . [p. 39]," showed strong dissatisfaction with previous definitions in words which have a contemporary ring:

> Its definitions have been . . . numerous, they are . . . different one from the other, and they have . . . little bearing on the treatment. . . . Our own, . . . will be found at least to correspond to a plan of treatment, both supporting each other; and it may suffice until a better definition and a better treatment can be devised. (p.39)

Thus, Seguin defined idiocy as *"a specific infirmity of the cranio-spinal axis, produced by deficiency of nutrition in utero and in neo-nati"* (1866/1971, p. 39). To support this definition and its ramifications, Seguin propounded a "physiological method" of training "idiotic" children. In promulgating his teaching method, which was based on a neurophysiological hypothesis, Seguin suggested that "idiocy" could be classified into two etiological types (both of which, he declared, could derive equal benefit from his method): *superficial idiocy,* in which the peripheral nervous system was damaged, and *profound idiocy,* characterized by defects in the central nervous system.

Clarke and Clarke (1975) noted that Seguin's classic work perpetuated the use of "idiocy" as a generic term in British legal and administrative usage until the Idiots Act of 1886 specifically distinguished "lunacy" from "imbecility," and "in using the term imbecile . . . [Seguin's work] clearly indicated that a class of subnormals existed, less defective than the idiot. It also recognized that the idiot could be trained" (p. 15).

With the passage of the British Mental Deficiency Act of 1913 and its amendment in 1927, "mental defectiveness" became the generic term in British usage, subtending various (further defined) classes of "mentally defective" persons, including "idiots," "imbeciles," "feebleminded persons," and "moral defectives" (Hilliard, 1965). *Mental defectiveness* was here defined in essentially biological terms (combining congenital and acquired aspects of etiology) as "a condition of arrested or incomplete development of mind existing before the age of 18 years, whether arising from inherent causes or induced by disease or injury" (Hilliard, 1965, p. 7). The various subconditions, however, were very loosely defined in terms of social competency. Thus, *idiots* were seen as persons "in whose case there exists mental defectiveness of such a degree that they are unable to guard themselves against common physical dangers" (Hilliard, 1965, p. 7). In parallel definitions, *imbeciles* were delineated as persons whose mental deficiency, while not amounting to idiocy, was pronounced enough to render them incapable of managing themselves or their affairs, or if they were children, of being educated to do so. *Feebleminded* individuals, in general—functioning at a higher level than imbeciles—were described as requiring care, supervision, and control for their protection and that of others, while children were to be designated as feebleminded if they showed a "disability of mind" severe enough to render them incapable of receiving an education at school (i.e., were ineducable). *Moral defectives* were defined as persons in whom mental deficiency was linked to "vicious" or "criminal" tendencies. It should be noted at this point that "feeblemindedness" in the British definitional schema was conceptualized as the highest level of mental defectiveness or "amentia" (a term designed to differentiate mental deficiency from "mental disorder" or "dementia").

Meanwhile, in mid-19th century America, the term "feebleminded" was emerging as the superordinal descriptor under which were to be classified "idiots" and other individuals of limited mental ability. In 1848, Samuel G. Howe, a physician, successfully petitioned the Massachusetts legislature for money to open an experimental school for "idiotic" children on the grounds of Perkins Institute for the Blind—of which he was director (Kanner, 1960).

In his 1850 report to the Governor of Massachusetts, Howe proposed a classification system, based on the principle of the capacity for using language, and consisting of three hierarchical categories: "simpletons," "fools," and "idiots" (Sarason & Doris, 1969). The following excerpt indicates that in this report, Howe (possibly as a reaction to Esquirol's conceptualization of idiocy) first proposed the notion of conceptualizing intellectually deviant individuals as "feebleminded":

> This classification assumes that the subjects of it are *not* persons absolutely *devoid of mind,* but merely persons of feeble mind; that the idiot proper is the most feeble, the simpleton the least so. . . . Evil may arise from the misuse of the term *Idiot,* . . . if it causes them to be considered . . . different from other men in being utterly devoid of mind, for it will be considered useless to try to teach those who have no mind at all; but if they are considered as different from others . . . in degree only, . . . as merely having *feeble* minds, then their very feebleness, . . . will commend them to our hearts. (Quoted in Sarason & Doris, 1969, pp. 222-223.)

Howe's classification system apparently never caught on, but the term "feebleminded" began to appear in institutional designations, so that the residential facility which developed out of the Perkins Institute "experimental school" in 1855 was named "Massachusetts School for Idiotic and Feeble-minded Youth" (Kanner, 1960).

It was noted above that the prime contributors to educational programming for intellectually deviant children in the 19th century were physicians. A major exception to the primacy of physicians in early programming was the contribution—in the first decade of the 20th century—of the French psychologist Binet. His donation to the cause was mostly in diagnosis, but he was also much concerned with educational methodology. Consequently, Kirk and Johnson (1951) concluded their discussion of early educational procedures with the observation that: "Educators [during the 19th and early 20th centuries] were willing to delegate the responsibility for the development of methods and techniques in the education of mental defectives to doctors and psychologists" (p. 84). While this observation may not be completely true—witness the establishment of special classes in German public schools as early as 1859 (E. E. Doll, 1962)—it serves to emphasize that the field emerged as an interdisciplinary one at a time when scientific interest in deviant children was establishing a foothold, with a consequent need to formulate scientific criteria for identifying children to whom needed services could be extended. The recognition of this need by the community was manifested in a tentative fashion in Germany, with the work of Ebbinghaus (see Chapter 1); and it crystallized in France when Binet was asked to help devise an objective method for identifying children who were not profiting from "ordinary" education, so that they could be placed into special classes in the school system of Paris.

Binet believed that the then-current classifications by clinical type— which relied primarily on etiological and symptomatic referents—were pedagogically useless, since they did not allow for estimating degree of educational handicap, but that the objective psychological measurement of intelligence was needed to evaluate the extent to which children could profit from educational experiences. The contribution of Binet's metric scales of intelligence (developed in collaboration with the French psychiatrist Simon) to the field of mental retardation was truly revolutionary. More importantly, for purposes of our present discussion, Binet's work emphasized the fact that it was subnormal intellectual functioning which distinguished mental retardation from other disorders of human efficiency, and it led to the emergence of precise, measurable criteria for defining the condition in unequivocal terms which cut across disciplinary and professional lines.

The natural leader in the American movement to define the condition precisely was the organization which had begun in 1876 as the "Association of Medical Officers of American Institutions for Idiotic and Feeble-Minded Persons" (Milligan, 1961). From the beginning, the Association (now AAMD) implicitly included intellectual criteria (first in the form of mental age levels, and subsequently as IQ levels) into its definitional and classification systems. This organizational movement was actually spurred by the work of Goddard, who introduced Binet's measuring device to American Psychology (see Chapter 1).

In 1906, with a change in the name of the Association to the "American Association for the Study of the Feeble-Minded," (AASF), the latter term began to be accepted as generic to the field, and "feeblemindedness" came to be defined as:

> ... a state of mental defect existing from birth or from an early age and due to incomplete or abnormal development in consequence of which, the person is incapable of performing his duties as a member of society in the position of life to which he is born. (Goddard, 1914, p. 4.)

In 1910 the Association adopted Goddard's classification system, based on mental age levels as determined by the Binet-Simon scale, and including three levels of intellectual subnormality under the rubric of "feeblemindedness." The older terms "idiot" and "imbecile" were used to designate the lower levels of functioning, and Goddard coined the term "moron" for the highest level of inadequacy. Since the schema was based directly on Binet's philosophy of measuring social adequacy in terms of intellectual level, the system implicitly defined "feeblemindness" as subnormal mental development which would show up as below-average scores on intelligence tests. The term "moron," which carried the same connotation in American terminology as did "feeblemindedness" in British usage, was defined by Goddard as pertaining to "one who is capable of earning his living under favorable circumstances, but is incapable . . . (a) of competing . . . with his normal fellows, or (b) managing himself and his affairs with ordinaty prudence (1914, p. 4).

In its first manual on terminology and classification, published in 1921, the AASF formally set forth "feebleminded" as the generic term (Gelof, 1963), and in keeping with Terman's (1916) offering of the intelligence quotient as the unit of measured intelligence, the prime definitional criterion for the three levels of feeblemindedness was the IQ (*moron* = 50 to 75, *imbecile* = 25 to 49, *idiot* < 25).

Following the second change in the Association's name, in 1933, to the "American Association on Mental Deficiency" (AAMD), the term "mental deficiency" gradually came to replace "feeblemindedness" in American terminology, although the latter expression clung tenaciously well into the 1950s (Silverstein, 1962).

The term "mental retardation" appeared with the others in professional usage early in the 20th century, and it became increasingly more frequent until it was dominant in the late 1950s (Silverstein, 1962). However, no significant formal definitional change appeared until 1959, when the AAMD promulgated the first official system on terminology and classification (subsequently revised in 1961) in which "mental retardation" was proposed as the universal generic term (Heber, 1959, 1961).

Following the promulgation of the 1959/1961 AAMD system, the general descriptor phrase "mental retardation" was also adopted by the American Psychiatric Association as well as by the World Health Organization (Wilson & Spitzer, 1969). Description and discussion of the 1959/1961 AAMD definition, and of the more current one (Grossman, 1973), will follow an overview of other recent approaches to defining the construct.

Recent Definitions

In delineating the rationale for the development of the 1959/1961 AAMD system, Heber (1962) reiterated:

Historically, mental retardation has been a social, administrative,

> and legal concept, rather than a scientific one. . . . Many . . . pro-
> fessional persons, in recent years, have attempted to formulate a
> more scientific definition and classification of mental retardation;
> usually one which reflected their particular . . . training, interests,
> and theoretical orientation. . . . (pp. 69-70.)

The lack of consistency in the concepts (and consequent classifications) used
by different workers in the field had served to create a good deal of confusion
over the years. Although the intent of the AAMD system was to obviate such
confusion, various approaches to terminology and classification have continued to appear in the literature. Following is a brief overview of different
definitional approaches which have found varying degrees of acceptance
among concerned individuals, in the United States and in other countries.

Emphasis on social competency. The traditional British attitude toward
mental retardation has been to assess it by medical and social criteria, under
the general term "mental deficiency." Here, medical criteria pertained to
etiology, while functional levels were based on criteria of social adequacy.
The categorical descriptions under the previously discussed English Mental
Deficiency Act of 1927 exemplify this biosocial approach in legal definitions.
The British psychiatrist Tredgold (1937), who was influential in furthering
the notion among clinicians that mental deficiency was a behavioral manifestation of organic pathology, proposed a biosocial schema in which a medical
(etiological) classification system was based on a social competency definition:

> Mental deficiency is a state of incomplete mental development
> of such a kind and degree that the individual is incapable of
> adapting himself to the normal environment of his fellows in such
> a way as to maintain existence independently of supervision,
> control, or external support. (Tredgold, 1937, p. 4)

In a paper first published in 1954, the American physician Jervis (1960)
proposed a medical definition very similar to the sociolegal statement of the
English Mental Deficiency Act of 1927. Jervis' definition also incorporated
biosocial criteria:

> Mental deficiency may be defined as a condition of arrested or
> incomplete mental development existing before adolescence,
> caused by disease or genetic constitution and resulting in social
> incompetence. (Jervis, 1960, p. 46)

After a review of the many criteria which previous workers had implicitly or explicitly considered essential to defining the concept, E. A. Doll (1941) offered the following definition, which emphasized social adequacy while incorporating the multiple criteria:

> Mental deficiency is a state of social incompetence obtaining at maturity, or likely to obtain at maturity, resulting from developmental arrest of constitutional (heredity or acquired) origin; the condition is essentially incurable through treatment and unremediable through training. (p. 215)

Emphasis on intellectual level. With the growth of the mental testing movement following Binet's work—which provided a tool for quantifying intellectual ability—and that of Terman (1916), which allowed for encapsulating intellectual level within the concept of IQ, psychometric definitions began to assume a prominent place, particularly among psychologists in the United States. As Robinson and Robinson (1965) put it: "An IQ score of 70 . . . achieved considerable popularity as a cutoff score in defining mental retardation" (p. 32). The most influential IQ-based definitions have been those of Terman and Merrill (1937, 1960) and of Wechsler (1955). Based on the standardization data of their 1937 revision of the Stanford-Binet, Terman and Merrill (1960) applied the classificatory term "mental deficiency" to IQ scores of 69 and below. For Wechsler (1955), "mental deficiency" was likewise statistically defined as an IQ score—on his various intelligence tests—of 69 and below.

It should be noted that despite the clinical application of their cutoff points, neither Terman and Merrill nor Wechsler intended for IQ to be the sole criterion in diagnosing mental retardation. Thus, Terman and Merrill (1960) emphasized that, as far back as 1938, they had cautioned that the classificatory terms delineating various levels were purely statistical and carried no implications of diagnostic significance for IQ categories:

> So, . . . IQs . . . [which] indicate "mental deficiency" with respect to average mentality . . . carry no necessary diagnostic implications such as are usually attached to the term "feeble-mindedness. . . . Many other behaviors contribute to diagnostic categories. (pp. 17, 19)

By the same token, Wechsler (1944) clearly implied that the concept of "mental deficiency" was not a simple entity, whose diagnosis could rest solely on IQ:

Clinical experience shows that there are ... individuals who regularly test as ... mental defectives on psychometric tests but, who nevertheless, are able to adapt and adjust ... [socially]. It is clear that these people are not mentally defective as defined by law or common sense. (p. 53)

The mental retardation-mental deficiency dichotomy. Some 20 years ago, a committee of the World Health Organization (1954) attempted to standardize the international terminology in the field by proposing the use of the general descriptor "mental subnormality," which was defined as "an incomplete or insufficient general development of the mental capacities [p. 6]," and which was to subtend two subgeneric terms: (a) "mental retardation," referring to diminished educational and social performance due to environmental causes, and (b) "mental deficiency," which was to designate "conditions in which the mental capacities ... are diminished as a result of pathological causes, ... " (p. 7). Decrying the use of intelligence test scores as the sole criterion of mental subnormality, the committee observed that intelligence tests had a useful function in the diagnosis of mental subnormality, but that this function was limited because the IQ described only one aspect of the condition, and a given individual's IQ score could differ from time to time.

Foremost advocates in the United States of the mental retardation-mental deficiency dichotomy under the general term "mental subnormality" are Sarason and his colleagues (Sarason & Doris, 1969; Sarason & Gladwin, 1958).

Sarason and Gladwin (1958) expanded the meanings of the terms suggested by the World Health Organization (1954) so as to relate etiology and prognosis of the condition to degree of subnormal functioning. Within that framework, *mental retardation* refers to potentially reversible subaverage intellectual and educational function (IQ roughly 50 to 75), due to social, economic, and cultural factors, in an individual who shows no evidence of central nervous system (CNS) impairment. On the other hand, *mental deficiency* denotes irreversible social and intellectual inadequacy (IQ roughly below 50) as a result of demonstrable CNS pathology. Interestingly enough, Sarason and his associates persisted in their claim that the proposed dichotomy has utility while frankly stating: "In all candor the writers must confess that in our professional activities we have not always been able to be consistent in our position, if only because of the communication problem it may present to others" (Sarason & Doris, 1969, p. 39).

In recognition of various problems of interpretation inherent in British statutes up to that time, the British Mental Health Act of 1959 repealed the Mental Deficiency Acts of 1913 to 1938 and provided two new sociolegal definitions (with medical overtones):

> *Severe subnormality* means a state of arrested or incomplete development of mind, which includes subnormality of intelligence, and is of such a nature or degree that the patient is incapable of living an independent life or of guarding himself against serious exploitation, or will be so incapable when of an age to do so. *Subnormality* means a state of arrested or incomplete development of mind (not amounting to severe subnormality), which includes subnormality of intelligence and is of a nature or degree which requires or is susceptible to medical treatment or other special care or training of the patient. (Hilliard, 1965, p. 28)

While not so specifically stated in these official definitions, the term "severe subnormality" includes the concepts of irreversibility of the social incompetence, CNS pathology, and IQ below 50, while "subnormality" is by implication ameliorable, cultural in origin, and associated with IQ 50 to 75 (Pilkington, 1964). The similarity of these constructs to the dichotomous "mental retardation-mental deficiency" definitions of the 1954 World Health Organization committee and of Sarason and his associates is obvious. However, it is of note that in contrast to the most common British view, which stressed social adequacy almost to the total exclusion of intellectual criteria, the Mental Health Act of 1959 reflected the increasing importance attached to psychometric data, and gave social and intellectual criteria equal consideration.

Educational definitions. Following \Binet's original tenets and as mental testing practices expanded, school progress became the criterion against which IQ scores were validated. Consequently, predicated on the accumulated evidence that IQ scores were good predictors of academic achievement, intelligence test scores were given prominence in educational definitions. However, while IQ soon came to be almost the sole criterion for special class placement, the definitions themselves also placed heavy emphasis on prognosis of social and vocational effectiveness.

The fountainhead for this multiple-criterion educational approach in the United States seems to have been the work of a committee of the 1930 White House Conference on Child Health and Protection (Gearhart, 1972), which established a two-group educational definition—differentiating those below-average children who should not be considered for public schooling of any kind from those who presumably could profit from public (albeit "special") education. In an apparent (and bewildering) confusion of terms, the former group was designated as "feebleminded" (defined as below 50 in IQ, and incapable—by unspecified criteria—of achieving social and vocational adequacy), and the latter was dubbed "mentally retarded" (IQ 50 to 75, and judged capable of eventual social and vocational competence).

Some 20 years later, Kirk and Johnson (1951) suggested a similar two-level definition, also containing a confusion in terminology. They held that the "feebleminded" or "mentally deficient" child (stating that either of these terms—to which no IQ range was attached—was appropriate in the case of a child whose condition was judged to be based on CNS pathology and thus presumed to be irremediable) required custodial care (at home or in an institution) and "would be excluded from both regular and special classes . . . [because he] . . . cannot be educated to be socially competent and occupationally adequate. . . . " (pp. 9, 13). At the higher level, the "mentally handicapped" child was defined as one who earned an IQ score of 50, 60, or 70, and who required—and could profit from—a special curriculum designed to foster social and occupational growth.

Over the years, expansion of the American special class movement to include public school programs for children formerly believed to be "ineducable" gave rise to three-tiered IQ-based educational definitions, reflecting different levels of "potential" for profiting from formal instruction and for achieving social and vocational independence. Kirk's (1972) terminology, which is representative, defines the *educable* mentally retarded child as one whose IQ is within the range of 50-55 to 75-79 and is considered to have (a) educability in academic subjects "at a minimum level" (p. 164), (b) the "capacity" for eventual social independence, and (c) "minimal occupational adequacies" (p. 164). The *trainable* child (IQ 30-35 to 50-55) is one who is not considered educable in the sense of the above criteria, but who has the "potential" for learning (a) self-help skills, (b) social skills in a restricted family or neighborhood context, and (c) "economic usefulness [under close supervision and shelter] . . . " (p. 164). The *totally dependent* or *custodial* child (IQ below 25-30) is defined as being "untrainable" and as needing continued lifelong help with his personal needs.

In another recent educational definition, Dunn (1963) held that special educators up to that point had only assumed responsibility for children with IQs in the approximate range of 30 to 75 and provided "formal" definitions only for *educable* and *trainable* students, adding the criterion of literacy to those delineated in Kirk's schema and suggesting somewhat different IQ criteria. According to Dunn (1963), *educable* mentally retarded pupils (IQ 50-60 to 75-80) "generally possess the capacity to become literate" (p. 9); and *trainable* children (IQ 30-40 to 50-60) "can be expected to develop rudimentary skills in self-care, socialization, and oral communication, but not to become literate" (p. 9).

In a later and carefully reconsidered approach to the definitional problem in special education, Dunn (1973) objected to labeling children as "mentally retarded" for educational purposes, proposing instead the use of the term "general learning disabilities." This concept, while not geared to IQ, still relies operationally on comparative psychometric data, in the form of percentiles:

> Pupils with general learning disabilities are those who require special education because they score no higher than the second percentile for their ethnic or racial subgroup on . . . individual intelligence test batteries administered in their most facile language. (p. 68)

Theory-based definitions. Several attempts to formulate scientific definitions of mental retardation based on specific theoretical formulations have been couched in the language of the neuropsychologist (Benoit, 1959), the behaviorist (Bijou, 1966), and the sociologist (Mercer, 1973).

Benoit's (1959) proposed definition stems from Hebb's (1949) neuropsychological explanation of human behavior, which posits that nerve cells grow and function only in the presence of stimulation. Within that framework, Benoit held:

> Mental retardation may be viewed as a deficit of intellectual function resulting from varied . . . determinants, but having as a common proximate cause a diminished efficiency of the nervous system . . ., [beginning with impaired response to stimulation] thus entailing a lessened general capacity for . . . perceptual and conceptual integration and . . . environmental adjustment. (1959, p. 561)

Bijou (1966), from the standpoint of behavior theory, prefers the term "developmental retardation" and suggested that the condition:

> be treated as observable, objectively defined stimulus-response relationships without recourse to hypothetical mental concepts . . . and hypothetical biological abnormalities. . . . *From this point of view a retarded individual is one who has a limited repertory of behavior shaped by events that constitute his history.* (p. 2)

Mercer (1973), took what she called the "social system perspective" in her definition: "Mental retardation is an achieved status in a social system and the role played by persons holding that status" (p. 36).

Underpinnings of AAMD system. The conglomerate of polyglot definitional approaches covered in the preceding overview makes it apparent that, over the years, the major problems in the promulgation of a precise definition of the condition identified as mental retardation relate to (a) formulation of definitions for purposes of, and/or translating in the languages of, various professions—each stressing particular aspects of the condition, and specifying different and often ambiguous criteria; and (b) use of the construct under different terms, to refer to various groups whose disabilities are not alike in etiology and magnitude. In addition, those definitions which stress adequacy of either social or intellectual behavior as *sole* criteria (of mental retardation, or mental deficiency, or what-have-you) present serious shortcomings. While historically, a social context—or the ability of an individual to adapt to cultural norms—has always provided the framework for judging a given person's level of functioning as "idiotic" or "defective" or "retarded," social difficulties in and of themselves are obviously not confined to such persons. Problems in social adaptation may also be found in those who are severely emotionally disturbed, intellectually gifted, or severely impaired in various sensory-motor functions.

On the other hand, in addition to the fact that proposed IQ-based definitions have established varying intelligence levels as cutoff points for designating an individual as intellectually subnormal, those advocating the sole use of IQ as a criterion must face such problems as a lack of perfect relationship between measured intelligence and competent social behavior, along with fluctuations in a given person's intelligence test scores from one testing period or test instrument to another. It may also be readily appreciated that the criteria by which "mental retardation" is defined not only can have a distinct bearing on the consideration of one's eligibility for services offered to "mentally retarded" individuals in a given setting, but can also be crucial to the communicability, replicability, and interpretation of research findings. Epidemiological research may be particularly vulnerable in the latter regard, since, as Silverstein (1973) so cogently observed, "it is obvious that the prevalence of mental retardation depends on one's definition . . . and the way it is operationalized" (p. 380).

All of the above concerns, together with those discussed in the opening pages of this chapter, make it clear that the major definitional issues with respect to mental retardation as a reliable and valid diagnostic construct may be delineated as follows: The definition must (a) be clear and communicable without regard to the professional affiliation of the user (i.e., it must be an interdisciplinary definition); (b) distinguish mental retardation from other diagnostic constructs; (c) provide unambiguous, consistent, and operational (measurable) criteria for identifying individuals who warrant the given diagnosis; and (d) be useful for treatment and program planning, as well as for research. These considerations underlie the approach used in the terminology and classification systems of the American Association on Mental Deficiency (Grossman, 1973; Heber, 1959, 1961).

AAMD Definitions

The 1959/1961 schema. With the publication of the 1959 AAMD diagnostic manual (Heber, 1959) and its second edition (Heber, 1961), the term "mental retardation" was proposed as the general descriptor for the field, with the stipulation that it incorporated all the meanings that had ever been applied to such constructs as "amentia, feeblemindedness, mental deficiency, mental subnormality, idiocy, imbecility, and moronity, etc." (1961, p. 3). This effort represented an attempt to achieve uniformity in terminology so as to facilitate communication and to help establish valid scientific and clinical criteria as to the meaning of the term "mental retardation"—as well as to provide a rational and consistent basis for grouping persons designated as meeting those criteria.

Consequently, the fifth AAMD *Manual on Terminology and Classification* (Heber, 1961) proffered the following definition, which was designed to cut across interdisciplinary lines: *"Mental retardation refers to subaverage general intellectual functioning which originates during the developmental period and is associated with impairment in adaptive behavior"* (p. 3; italics added). The three major components of this definition were further defined operationally. Thus, *subaverage general intellectual functioning* refers to a score (generally in the form of an IQ) on an objective standardized test of general intelligence which is more than one standard deviation below the mean of the sample upon which the test was standardized; *originating during the developmental period* refers to the requirement that the etiological agent (whatever its nature) was effective before the age of 16—and in emphasizing the necessity for conceptualizing mental retardation in developmental terms, "serves to distinguish . . . it from other disorders of human behavior" (Heber, 1961, p. 3); and *impairment in adaptive behavior* refers to the individual's inability to meet the standards of personal independence and social responsibility which society expects of his peers or age-mates.

The latter criterion is further defined in accordance with the three aspects of adaptation which are deemed most germane to different age groups: (a) rate of *maturation,* which is measured by the rate of development of physical, self-help, and social skills during infancy and early childhood; (b) *learning* ability, which is a prime qualifying condition during the school years; and (c) *social adjustment,* which is particularly relevant to the period of adulthood—where it is gauged by the extent to which the individual is able to function independently in social and vocational pursuits—but which is also important in earlier years when its prime manifestations are adequacy of interpersonal relationships involving parents, other adults, and age-mates.

The prime philosophical position of this AAMD definition—which makes no reference to specific etiology, to physiological "capacity" or "potential," or to "curability"—was that diagnostic and descriptive emphasis must be on current intellectual and adaptive levels and that, consequently, a given individual may meet the definitional criteria of mental retardation at one stage in his development but not at a later one. In the latter event, he would no longer warrant the designation "mentally retarded." (A by-product of this philosophical approach has been to help eliminate the necessity for the construct "psudoretardation." This will be discussed in more detail in the last section of this chapter.)

To facilitate identification of individuals meeting the above criteria, the 1961 schema provided for a behavioral classification—subdivided into the dimensions of *measured intelligence* and *adaptive behavior,* and for a medical classification based on eight etiological groupings. In addition, individuals were to be given an appropriate classification in each of several supplementary categories.

The behavioral classification system was designed to provide the operational base upon which to expand the definition, which specified that before an individual could be designated as "mentally retarded," it was necessary that he satisfy the dual behavioral criteria of subaverage intellectual functioning *and* impaired social-personal adaptation. Therefore, the system provided for the categorization of individuals as to current degree of deviation from the norm in measured intelligence (i.e., "Borderline," "Mild," "Moderate," "Severe," or "Profound" retardation) and in adaptive behavior (i.e., " Mild," "Moderate," "Severe," or "Profound" deviation).

The measured intelligence dimension allowed for classification of current intellectual level based on scores derived through individual administration of standardized objective tests of general intelligence. The choice of appropriate measuring instruments was seen as the responsibility of the clinician, with the expectation that if results from a single test were deemed not representative of an adequate objective assessment, the psychologist would utilize data from a number of scales in order to arrive at a valid diagnostic statement.

In recent years, there has been a proliferation of measuring devices utilized by psychologists for assessment of intelligence level. The reader is referred to Robinson and Robinson (1965, pp. 369-452) and to Fishler (1971) for rather full coverage of psychodiagnosis in mental retardation. However, in current practice (Silverstein, 1970) the most widely used instruments seem to be the Revised Stanford-Binet Intelligence Scale and its derivatives (e.g., Cattell Infant Intelligence Scale, Kuhlmann-Binet), along with the various scales devised by Wechsler (Wechsler Intelligence Scale for Children, Wechsler Adult Intelligence Scale, and Wechsler Preschool and Primary Scale of Intelligence).

In keeping with the statistical assumption that measured intelligence adheres to a Gaussian or "normal" distribution in the general population, and following from the profferred definition, degree of retardation in measured intelligence was scaled into five levels, representing progressive downward deviation from the mean in terms of standard deviation (SD) units. The various levels, with their corresponding descriptive terms, SD values, and representative IQ ranges for Wechsler (SD = 15) and Binet-type (SD = 16) scales are given in Table 3.1.

Table 3.1

**Levels of Retardation in Measured Intelligence According to
Nomenclature, SD Values, and IQ (1961 Manual)**

Retardation in M.I., Descriptive Term	Ranges, SD Values	IQ Ranges	
		SD = 15	SD = 16
None	0.00 to -1.00	85-100	84-100
Borderline	-1.01 to -2.00	70-84	68-83
Mild	-2.01 to -3.00	55-69	52-67
Moderate	-3.01 to -4.00	40-54	36-51
Severe	-4.01 to -5.00	25-39	20-35
Profound	> -5.00	<25	<20

Note: Adapted from Heber (1961).

Provision for the classification of levels of adaptive behavior was much less exact. Heber (1961) noted:

> Precise, objective measures of *Adaptive Behavior* . . . are for the most part presently unavailable. This is due to the fact that few efforts have been directed at developing measures of total adaptation as well as to the imprecision of the norms and standards to which *Adaptive Behavior* refers. (p. 61)

This issue of norms and standards is particularly complicated, since, as has already been pointed out, the behavioral criteria used to evaluate effectiveness of adaptation differ for various age levels. Heber (1961) cautioned that while the Vineland Social Maturity Scale (VSMS) was probably the best single measure then available,[2] it needed to be supplemented by other data which tap the criterion dimensions for different age groups. He suggested that at the preschool level—where maturational criteria are primary—the VSMS be supplemented by selected items from such scales as the Gesell Developmental Schedules (see Chapter 10, herein, by Winsberg); at the school level, standardized tests of academic achievement provide excellent corollary data; and in adulthood, objective and subjective judgments of occupational and social effectiveness, and of family and community adjustment, must be procured.

In order to provide a statistical structure analogous to that utilized in the measured intelligence dimension, the 1961 AAMD manual categorized retardation in adaptive behavior in terms of four levels, represented again by ranges of standard deviation units. The schema is outlined in Table 3.2. It will be noted that, in contrast to those in Table 3.1, the SD ranges in Table 3.2 encompass 1.25 SD units. Although Heber (1961) conceptualized this table as delineating "the limits of the four levels of *Adaptive Behavior* as reflected in Standard Deviation units on the Vineland Social Maturity Scale" (p. 61), he also emphasized that the SD ranges for the levels outlined in Table 3.2 need not be restricted to a particular instrument, such as the VSMS. However, regardless of the measuring devices employed, the various levels represent progressive degrees of negative deviation from the norms and standards of adaptive behavior which may be relevant to the given individual's criterion age-group.

While the preceding definition emphasizes the importance of considering the developmental period (operationally defined as ranging from conception to age 16) with regard to etiology and for conceptualizing mental retardation in developmental terms—a conceptual approach which is seen as differentiating this condition from other behavior disorders—the critical factor in the AAMD concept of mental retardation as a diagnostic construct is the emphasis on the dual criteria of reduced intellectual *and* social adequacy. In addition, the definition implicitly specifies that the subaverage intellectual behavior must be significant enough to make itself known through impairment in any of the several aspects of environmental adaptation (Heber,

---

[2] In 1965, a 5-year Adaptive Behavior Project, directed by Henry Leland, was developed at Parsons State Hospital (Kansas) under the combined auspices of AAMD, the National Institute of Mental Health, and the State of Kansas to develop a measurement device for providing precise, objective criteria—other than those sampled in intelligence tests—by which to describe and classify levels of impairment in adaptive behavior. This led to the eventual publication by AAMD of scales standardized on institutionalized children and adults (Nihira, Foster, Shellhaas, & Leland, 1969, 1974) and on public school children (Lambert, Windmiller, Cole & Figueroa, 1975a, 1975b). The applicability of these instruments to the diagnosis of mental retardation will be discussed in a later section.

Table 3.2

Levels of Retardation in Adaptive Behavior According to Nomenclature and SD Values (1961 Manual)

Retardation in A.B., Descriptive Term	Ranges, SD Values
Mild	−1.01 to −2.25
Moderate	−2.26 to −3.50
Severe	−3.51 to −4.75
Profound	> −4.75

Note: Modified from a similar table in Heber (1961).

1961). Therefore, as Heber (1962) pointed out, within this framework:

> The intellectual and social criteria, . . . are placed in proper perspective: It is the impairment in social adaptation which calls attention to the individual and determines the need for social and legal action on his behalf as a mentally retarded person; *it is the below-average intellectual functioning which distinguishes mental retardation from other disorders of human efficiency.* (p. 71; italics added)

Here we have the crux of the distinction between mental retardation and other diagnostic constructs, regardless of the age range within which the various constructs are applicable.

Following its publication, the fifth AAMD manual saw widespread acceptance and use for more than a decade. Over that period of time, the system was adopted and put into effect by numerous residential facilities and community agencies as well as by other organizations (national and international) whose concerns included that of mental retardation.

As a prime example of the international impact of the 1961 AAMD definition, the World Health Organization (1967), in compiling the eighth revision of the *International Classification of Diseases* (ICD-8), which became effective in 1968, followed the lead of the American Association on Mental Deficiency in designating "mental retardation" as the general term in the international system. Neither ICD-8 nor its adaptation (ICDA)—prepared by the U.S. Public Health Service for use in the United States (U.S. Dept. of Health, Education, and Welfare, 1969)—present formal definitions of the term. However, both versions define the construct operationally in descriptive terms and IQ ranges (as measured by the Stanford-Binet Intelligence Scale), which are identical with those delineated in Table 3.1 for the Borderline, Mild, Moderate, Severe, and Profound levels of measured intelligence. The United Kingdom subsequently incorporated the World Health Organization (1967) teminology and IQ limits for operationally defining "subnormality of intelligence" within the framework of the Mental Health Act of 1959 (Subcommittee on the Classification of Mental Disorders, 1968).

An extremely significant interorganizational consequence, on the national level, was the change in terminology and classification adopted by the American Psychiatric Association (1968). The first edition of its *Diagnostic and Statistical Manual* (American Psychiatric Association, 1952) had employed the term "mental deficiency" with specific reference to those cases of primary (i.e., "ideopathic" or "familial") etiology, or as a supplementary term in cases where mental defect (i.e., low IQ) was associated with a "chronic brain syndrome." The three levels of mental deficiency (defined in terms of IQ) were designated as *mild* (IQ 70-85), *moderate* (50-69), and severe (0-49). With the second edition of the manual (DSM-II), which is based on ICD-8, the American Psychiatric Association (1968) has adopted the superordinal construct "mental retardation," together with the same five relevant descriptive levels (Borderline to Profound mental retardation) and their respective IQ ranges based on SD units. The Association also holds forth the latter as forming an operational base for the measured intelligence dimension of a formal definition that closely parallels the 1961 AAMD formulation—from which it was adapted:

> Mental retardation refers to subnormal general intellectual functioning which originates during the developmental period and is associated with impairment of either learning and social adjustment or maturation, or both. (American Psychiatric Association, 1968, p. 14)

Philosophical concurrence with the AAMD position regarding the dual criteria for diagnosing the condition is implicit in the above definition. However, the DSM-II manual makes it very clear that "the intelligence quotient should not be the only criterion used in making a diagnosis of mental retardation or in evaluating its severity" (American Psychiatric Association, 1968, p. 14). It goes on to caution clinicians that a clinical judgment of the "patient's" behavioral level must be based also on an assessment of developmental history, academic and vocational competence, motor skills, and level of maturity in social and emotional behavior.

Essential recognition by the American Psychiatric Association that it is useful to conceptualize mental retardation as an independent diagnostic construct, regardless of etiology, is provided by the admonition in DSM-II that *"Mental retardation* . . .is to be diagnosed whenever present [i.e., whenever the definitional criteria are satisfied] even if due to some other disorder" (1968, p. 1).

While the 1959/1961 AAMD system had a remarkable impact on terminology and classification in the field, it also raised some professional hackles with regard to the specificity of the definition and the implications of the definitional criteria (e.g., Clausen, 1967, 1972; Garfield & Wittson, 1960a, 1960b; Kidd, 1964; Leland, 1964).

Garfield and Wittson (1960b) raised the early objection that defining subaverage general intelligence as beginning at just more than one standard deviation below the mean allowed too wide a latitude for diagnosing the condition (actually, 16% of the general population would be diagnosed as "mentally retarded" by the sole use of this IQ criterion), and that even with the added criterion of impaired adaptive behavior, there was too great a possibility of diagnostic error. They therefore suggested that "the borderline level should be a separate nonretarded level which is excluded from the more specific categories of mental retardation . . . [and] if an individual's level of functioning is . . . seen as borderline, he should not necessarily be given a diagnosis of mental retardation" (1960b, p. 953). Garfield and Wittson (1960a) then suggested that taking two standard deviations below the mean as a cutoff point (which would result in a theoretical prevalence of little more than 2%) would bring the definition more in line with established points of view and with findings of epidemiological surveys.

Clausen (1967) also disagreed with the use of minus-1 SD as the cutoff point, while arguing strongly for a strictly psychometric definition. Holding that "the essential concern is a social incompetence *caused by* intellectual deficit" (1967, p. 741; italics added), Clausen maintained that social competency is a concept which eludes explicit definition and measurement, since the criteria vary with time of assessment, cultural context, and social level, and since instruments for obtaining precise measures of social adequacy are lacking. Consequently, he objected to the inclusion of the adaptive behavior criterion in the AAMD definition, and he suggested that IQ scores might be the best predictors of the likely occurrence of social incompetence based on intellectual deficit. From this followed his conclusion that:

> When a person with an IQ of 85 (about 1 SD below the mean, corresponding to the AAMD Manual definition) shows impairment of adaptive behavior, the maladaption [sic] is caused by factors other than intellectual, and the person should therefore not be classified as mentally deficient. . . . [Further-

> more] . . . the . . . cutoff point of 70 or 75—corresponding to
> about 2 SD below the mean—is more adequate on the grounds
> that it is primarily below this level that individuals show impair-
> ment of adaptive behavior, caused by low level of general
> intellectual functioning. (Clausen, 1967, p. 743)

Kidd (1964) took issue with several aspects of the definition and put forth a number of proposed modifications. He suggested that (a) for statistical rigor, the modifier "significantly" be inserted before "subaverage" with reference to intellectual functioning; (b) in keeping with the philosophy that origin of the condition is not germane to the purpose of the definition, and in order to avoid semantic hassles over the issue of "true origin," the phrase "manifests itself during" be substituted for "originates during" with regard to the developmental period; and (c) since the term "impairment," in connection with the adaptive behavior aspect of the definition, was too ambiguous with regard to degree of differentiation from the norm, another phrase, such as "significant inadequacy," be employed.

Leland (1964) objected, saying that since the 1961 system explicitly specified that impairment in adaptive behavior was a *reflection* of subaverage intellectual functioning (see Heber, 1961), the concept of adaptive behavior was closely tied to that of measured intelligence rather than to rehabilitation goals. He noted that since individuals could be found to be functioning at different levels in these two aspects of behavior, there was a definite need to consider them as separate and distinct dimensions. Leland further emphasized that from the standpoint of defining precise rehabilitation objectives (which is relevant to the utility of the definition), "those aspects of mental retardation which are measured by the dimension of adaptive behavior can be considered as the more reversible aspects [as opposed to intelligence level or IQ] of the problem" (1964, p. 174).

In a well thought-out paper, which headed a published symposium, Clausen (1972) directly challenged the viewpoint held by Leland and his coworkers (which had by then been reiterated in numerous publications), following up his own earlier arguments against incorporation of the adaptive behavior dimension in the AAMD definition and for maintaining subaverage intellectual functioning as the focus of diagnostic assessment, with minus-2 SD (i.e., IQ about 70) as the cutoff point. The six respondents in the symposium addressed their papers primarily to the issues concerning adaptive behavior, with two (Nagler, 1972; Penrose, 1972) more or less supporting Clausen's stand (although Nagler expressed serious reservations). The other four articles (Blackman, 1972; Leland, 1972; MacMillan & Jones, 1972; Wilson, 1972) reflect very strong disagreement with that position.

Blackman (1972) pointed out that there has been a "widely expressed need to give the definition of mental retardation a reality base that extends beyond the ... intelligence test" (p. 68). Objecting to a strictly IQ-based definition, and in support of the concept of adaptive behavior, he went on to note that "the purpose of the active diagnostician [as opposed to the passive one, whose purpose may be census taking or identifying research subjects] is to categorize mentally retarded individuals in such a way as to point to appropriate remediation" (p. 69). Blackman then concluded:

> For the *active* diagnostic purpose of categorization of retardation leading to treatment or prevention, the definition must include, in addition to psychometric retardation, those behavioral ... components to which the treatment discipline is sensitive. (1972, p. 69)

Leland (1972), presenting an admirable restatement of his position, summed it up in this way:

> There are myriad ways that ... retarded behaviors can be modified. What is needed is the type of definition that the AAMD has proposed, which will help us group children demonstrating these ... behaviors, [and] will make the children available to the services designed for their help. ... The need is not to narrow the definition of mental retardation. ... The need is to narrow and more clearly define specific conditions subsumed under this heading, so that a shift in national priorities ... can be developed. This shift demands an understanding of the elements that will lend themselves to prevention and to reversibility; again, this is the real meaning of the adaptive behavior concept in mental retardation. (p. 79)

MacMillan and Jones (1972) presented a multifaceted contrary response. They objected to the notion of a strictly psychometric definition of mental retardation primarily on the grounds that this would identify a disproportionate number of low-SES and minority children as retarded, since for many reasons this population is at a particular disadvantage with regard to performance on intelligence tests. They also took issue with Clausen's position with regard to adaptive behavior:

> One point that Clausen argues for—namely that scales for assessing adaptive behavior should have preceded its inclusion in the definition ... seems academic. If adaptive behavior is an important parameter of the condition ... , then it should be included in

the definition, regardless of the existence of instruments to assess it. . . . The diagnosis must include the assessment of all parameters of the concept; hence its definition . . . [and] both the diagnosis and definition of mental retardation should include evidence of substandard intellectual functioning *and* impairment in adaptive behavior. If and when objective measures exist, they should be used, but in . . . [their absence] . . ., all available evidence should be considered prior to identification and placement. . . . Obviously it is our contention that the AAMD definition of mental retardation is the best available working definition of the concept. (p. 82)

From his reference point as an educator, Wilson (1972) likewise held forth that the lack of adequate instrumentation for measuring the adaptive behavior variable was not a sound reason for barring its inclusion in the AAMD definition, since in principle it is measurable. He insisted that the concept is educationally relevant, and that it should be part of the official definition of mental retardation.

The 1973 revision. Progress in the field over a 10-year period and the need for a new system which would reflect both the increases in knowledge and changes in philosophy that had occurred since 1961, led to the recent promulgation of a revised AMMD *Manual on Terminology and Classification in Mental Retardation* (Grossman, 1973). The 1973 revision retains important aspects of the preceding system. It provides an operational definition, which emphasizes the dual behavioral criteria,[3] places continued emphasis on current functioning—without regard to etiology, "capacity," or prognosis—and conceptualizes mental retardation as a developmental disability. It also provides a dual behavioral-biomedical classification system. However, there are several significant changes in both the definitional statement and the classification schema.

As Warren (1973) implied, the following current definition seems to have been strongly influenced by the above-noted semantic and philosophical objections to the 1961 statement:

---

[3] Warren (1973), who served on the Editorial Board for the new manual, noted especially that, with regard to the behavioral criteria, "The decision to retain the dual intellectual-adaptive behavior criteria was made after reading the numerous reports on the issue, careful consideration, and much debate. . . . The points of critics were weighed. Recognizing that the final analysis of adaptive behavior is made on the basis of clinical, and sometimes subjective, assessment did not outweigh the necessity of making decisions on 'more than IQ alone' " (p. 2).

> Mental retardation refers to *significantly* subaverage general intellectual functioning *existing concurrently* with *deficits* in adaptive behavior and *manifested during* the developmental period. (Grossman, 1973, p. 11; italics added)

As with the earlier edition, the major definitional components are further defined operationally. Here, *significantly subaverage general intellectual functioning* refers to a score (usually derived in the form of an IQ) on one or more individually administered standardized tests of general intelligence, which is *more than* two standard deviations below the mean of the standardization sample. This modification provides for "deletion of the behavioral category of borderline retardation . . . [and] reflects changing concepts regarding the social capabilities of persons with low intelligence" (Grossman, 1973, p. 5). Thus, on the two most frequently employed measures, the Wechsler scales (SD = 15) and the Stanford-Binet Intelligence Scale (SD = 16), the ceiling levels for classifying retardation in measured intelligence are IQs of 69 and 67, respectively (Table 3.1). Grossman (1973) suggests that the term "Borderline Intelligence" should now be employed for describing the intellectual status of individuals who score between one and two standard deviations below the mean of a particular test. The reader will note that removal of the borderline retardation category meets the objection of Garfield and Wittson (1960a, 1960b) and, by reducing the theoretical prevalence of mental retardation to approximately 2.3%, brings the definition more in line with commonly accepted epidemiological estimates (Tarjan, Wright, Eyman, & Keeran, 1973).

The definitional phrase *manifested during the developmental period,* while still pointing up the need to conceptualize the condition in developmental terms, shifts the emphasis from a concern with the time during which the etiological agent was effective to that during which the individual has met the dual behavioral criteria in the definition. This conceptual shift may have far-reaching ramifications with regard to classification in the field. For example, the syndrome Huntington's Chorea, which is genetically based, *originates* in the developmental period, but typically does not become *manifest* until the individual is well into adulthood. While childhood and juvenile forms of the disease are known, they are exceedingly rare and their clinical features are sufficiently different from that of the classic adult type to warrant consideration as distinct clinical entities (Myrianthopoulos, 1973).

Thus, by the new definition, the adult form of Huntington's Chorea should probably not be classified as a mental retardation syndrome. Operationally, the developmental period is now considered as continuing to *18 years* of age. The manual itself (Grossman, 1973) does not offer any rationale for this extension beyond age 16. However, the change in classification was undoubtedly influenced by mounting evidence that the curve of mental growth does not level off at age 16 (Terman & Merrill, 1937), but that it continues beyond that age (Terman & Merrill, 1960), reaching asymptote between adolescence and adulthood. Thus, based on accumulated research data, Terman and Merrill (1960) set the average adult mental age at 18. A more concrete rationale for extending the period from 16 to 18 years is offered by Polloway and Payne (1975): "Setting the upper limit . . . at 18 corresponds with the approximate age at completion of high school, and as such, provides a common cut-off . . . between adolescence and adulthood" (p. 12).

The expression *deficits in adaptive behavior* refers to the person's relative inability or ineffectiveness in attaining the levels of personal autonomy and social dependability which society expects of his cultural peers or age-mates. This parallels the definition in the Heber (1961) manual. Since efficiency level is always assessed in relation to behavioral standards and expectations for one's chronological age group, deficits in adaptive behavior are again further defined according to different criteria at different developmental levels (i.e., *infancy and early childhood, childhood and early adolescence,* and *late adolescence and adulthood*). Although significantly subaverage intellectual functioning is the *sine qua non* of a diagnosis of mental retardation, it is again stressed that, "it is these deficiences in adaptive behavior which usually determine the need of the individual for programs or services and/or legal action as a mentally retarded person" (Grossman, 1973, p. 13). This consideration—together with the logical notion that, with regard to habilitative efforts, it is the adaptive behavior dimension which is most amenable to change in retarded individuals (Leland, 1964)—calls for some indication of the potential utility of the different criteria for treatment and program planning at the various developmental levels. The 1973 *Manual* provides some such indication while defining the criteria in considerably more detail than in the earlier manual.

During *infancy and early childhood,* maturational delays in the acquisition of skills relating to the following aspects of behavior represent pathognomic criteria for mental retardation: (a) sensory-motor development; (b) communication (including development of speech and language); (c) self-help; and (d) socialization (i.e., social interaction). (See Chapter 10, herein, for an extended discussion of how maturational delays relate to behavioral retardation.) At this level, such developmental deficits "point to the needs for medical services, for early childhood education, or for family guidance" (Grossman, 1973, p. 13).

During *childhood and early adolescence* (i.e., the school years), deficient adaptive behavior is manifested by (a) difficulties in the learning process (acquisition and use of basic academic skills in the classroom and in daily extra-school activities), and (b) relatively inefficient cognitive and social skills for coping with the environment (e.g., utilizing concepts of time and money, employing appropriate self-direction, responding appropriately in group and interpersonal activities). During this period, such "deficits in learning and coping skills indicate needs for specialized educational, pre-vocational, and recreational programs" (Grossman, 1973, p. 13).

At *late adolescence and adulthood,* the qualifying conditions for a continuing diagnosis of mental retardation involve primarily (a) vocational performance (the extent to which the individual is able to maintain himself in gainful employment), and (b) social responsibility (the extent to which the person is able to sustain himself independently in the community and to conform to community standards). Deficits in these areas "determine the needs for vocational training, placement, and a variety of supportive services" (Grossman, 1973, p. 13).

Obviously, the concept of adaptive behavior is highly similar in both the Heber (1961) and Grossman (1973) systems. However, in addition to defining in more detail the criteria for judging deficits in adaptive behavior, the present schema differs from the earlier one in an extremely important aspect. The earlier stipulation that impaired adaptive behavior be considered a *reflection* of subaverage intelligence (Heber, 1961, pp. 3, 4) undoubtedly served to place the adaptive behavior criterion conceptually in a subordinate position relative to that of intellectual functioning. That stipulation was partially involved in Clausen's (1967, 1972) insistence that the definition of mental retardation should be a purely psychometric one; and it may have encouraged general nonconsideration of the adaptive behavior requirement in deriving a diagnosis. In the latter regard, more than 10 years after the promulgation of that requirement, Adams (1973) found that psychologists and physicians were relying almost solely on IQ (to the exclusion of available social competence data) for rendering a diagnostic decision.

While still acknowledging the association between the two behavioral variables, the 1973 revision urges that they be treated as separate and distinct dimensions for both diagnostic and treatment purposes. Thus, the present definition emphasizes their *concurrent existence* rather than their association; and the manual goes on to note that the two dimensions have separate programmatic implications.

> Since the behaviors sampled by current intelligence tests contribute to total adaptation, level of function on measured intelligence will correlate with level of adaptive behavior. There will be, however, frequent individual discrepancies in levels of performance on the two dimensions. . . . Such discrepancies may provide useful information in planning for an individual; level of

measured intelligence and level of adaptive behavior should both be reported. (Grossman, 1973, p. 19)

As noted, the 1973 schema also reflects a dual approach to classification, consisting of a *Behavioral System*—divided into the categories of *measured intelligence* and *adaptive behavior;* a Biomedical System—designed to separate groups according to etiology (or presumed etiology); and a number of supplemental medical and behavioral categories. Unlike the previous arrangement, the current manual lists and defines 10 primary categories or clinical groupings in the Biomedical System. These will be described later in this chapter under AAMD Classification Systems.

In furnishing the operational base upon which to expand the current definition, the Behavioral System again provides for the categorization of individuals with regard to downward deviation from the norm in SD units. With the cutoff taken as more than 2 SDs below the mean, the resulting four levels are designated as "Mild," "Moderate," "Severe," and "Profound" retardation in measured intelligence and in adaptive behavior. Psychological procedures for establishing levels of measured intelligence parallel those of the earlier system; and the various levels—with their corresponding descriptive terms, SD values, and IQ ranges—are delineated in Table 3.3.

Table 3.3

Levels of Retardation in Measured Intelligence According to Nomenclature, SD Values, and IQ (1973 Manual)

Retardation in M.I., Descriptive Term	Ranges, SD Values	IQ Ranges	
		SD = 15	SD = 16
Mild	−2.01 to −3.00	55-69	52-67
Moderate	−3.01 to −4.00	40-54	36-51
Severe	−4.01 to −5.00	25-39	20-35
Profound	> -5.00	< 25	< 20

However, for the adaptive behavior dimension, it was recognized that the minus-2 SD cutoff could be set only "if more precise instruments were available for . . . measurement . . ., and general norms could be precisely stipulated" (Grossman, 1973, p. 19). With the availability of explicit norms of assessing individual levels of adaptive behavior relevant to given criterion age-groups,[4] the application of the suggested cutoff would lead to the classification schema outlined in Table 3.4

Table 3.4

Suggested Levels of Retardation in Adaptive Behavior According to Nomenclature and SD Values (1973 Manual)

Retardation in A.B., Descriptive Term	Ranges, SD Values
Mild	−2.01 to −3.00
Moderate	−3.01 to −4.00
Severe	−4.01 to −5.00
Profound	> −5.00

Adaptive Behavior Norms

Vineland Social Maturity Scale. The problem of explicit norms of adaptive behavior has been a continuing one despite the efforts of Wolfensberger (1962) and Silverstein (1971) to develop needed guidelines. It has been noted that the 1959/1961 AAMD system pointed to the Vineland Social Maturity Scale (VSMS) as the best single measure of adaptive behavior then available, and provided a prototypical schema for describing levels of deviation from the norm in terms of VSMS standard deviation units (Table 3.2). A major obstacle to using the VSMS in this manner for operationalizing the definitional criterion of impaired adaptive behavior is that the means and SDs of the Social Quotient (SQ) scores yielded by the Vineland are not uniform for the various age groups constituting the standardization sample. The SQ means range from 8 to 112, and their SDs range from 6 to 50, over 31 chronological age levels—varying from 0.5 to 30.5 years (E. A. Doll, 1953). This could have two practical consequences: (a) an SQ at one age level may be equivalent (with regard to extent of deviation from the mean at that level) to a much higher or lower SQ at a different age level; and (b), depending on the person's age, a *given* SQ may lead to classifying an individual at any of the four levels of retardation in adaptive behavior delineated in Table 3.2.

---

[4]Stern (1975) listed and described 20 scales used in the assessment of adaptive behavior. However, with the exception of the Vineland Social Maturity Scale, all these instruments are suitable only with either very young and/or severely-to-profoundly retarded, or with institutionalized populations; and all provide either imprecise or tentative norms.

Wolfensberger (1962) first attempted to put some order into this chaotic situation. By way of offering "a practical guideline for clinicians who wish to use the Vineland for coding *Adaptive Behavior*" (p. 453) in accordance with the AAMD schema, he constructed a table giving the Vineland SQ ranges corresponding to the four levels of retardation in adaptive behavior at various chronological ages.

Since Wolfensberger's table allows for the precise categorization of an individual's impairment in adaptive behavior, it should have some clinical utility within the framework for which it was devised; and, of course, a similar table could be constructed to accommodate the current system outlined in Table 3.4. However, as Wolfensberger (1962) pointed out, since SQ scores for the various levels of impairment varied by as much as 61 points between age groups, such an approach is extremely cumbersome for longitudinal assessment or cross-study comparison, indicating the need for converting the ratio SQs ordinarily derived from the VSMS into standard scores.

Silverstein (1971), addressing himself to the latter task, devised a system for converting conventional ratio SQs into deviation social quotients (DSQs), with a mean of 100 and SD = 9. The table which Silverstein provided (1971, p. 351) enables the determination of any (retarded or nonretarded) person's DSQ, given his chronological age and ratio SQ. As such, it can be very useful for operationalizing the definitional criterion of deficient adaptive behavior, thereby enhancing the reliability of the whole definition of mental retardation. With Silverstein's guidelines, the range of DSQs corresponding to the degrees of adaptive behavior deficit delineated in Table 3.4 would be Mild, 73-81; Moderate, 64-72; Severe, 55-63; Profound < 55.

Nevertheless, the current AAMD manual espouses the view that a single score, such as the Vineland Social Quotient, has limited utility beyond administrative and research purposes. It is noted that while scores which provide a general index of adaptive behavior level are useful for classification, overall programming and planning, and facilitating communication among workers in the field, "as with I.Q. scores, individuals who are classified at the same overall level of adaptive behavior may not be 'clinically equivalent' in that they may vary significantly in the various domains of behavior that comprise the overall rating" (Grossman, 1973, p. 20).

Thus, the manual emphasizes that for identifying deficits and training needs preparatory to planning programs of direct service to specific individuals, a single score is less useful than data on the person's functioning level in specific aspects of social competence. While this may be a valid observation, it must be noted that these contingencies are not mutually exclusive. It is, of course, possible within the same conceptual framework to make use of a global score along with subscale, subtest, or "domain" scores with reference to a given individual. We know, for instance, that the widespread use of IQ as a single measure of intellectual ability has not inhibited the development and use of techniques for the clinical assessment of intellectual strengths and weaknesses—or specific aspects of intellectual or educational competence (e.g., Glasser & Zimmerman, 1967; Smith, 1968). Similarly, the use of the Vineland DSQ—or any other global indicator of adaptive behavior level—need not prevent the concomitant application of other devices for assessing relative levels of competence in adaptive behavior domains. With the advent of the AAMD Adaptive Behavior Scale (ABS) (Nihira et al., 1969, 1974), community norms based on the 1974 revision of the ABS (Dervin, 1975; Leland, 1975), and the public school version of the scale (ABS-PS) (Lambert et al., 1975a, 1975b), provisions are at hand for deriving extremely useful information with regard to such assessment.

AAMD Adaptive Behavior Scale. The ABS, developed originally for institutional use, was standardized on approximately 4,000 retarded residents (of both sexes and all levels of retardation in measured intelligence) in 68 facilities in the United States. Subjects ranged in age from 3 to 69 years (11 age categories). The scale consists of two parts, together covering skills associated with independent functioning and with personal and social responsibility and adjustment. All items are grouped under coherent sets of related activities ("behavior domains"). Part One—organized in accordance with developmental expectations—is designed for evaluating various behaviors which are considered important to developing personal independence in day-to-day activities. The 10 domains in this part include: Independent Functioning, Physical Development, Economic Activity, Language Development, Numbers and Time, Domestic Activity, Vocational Activity, Self-Direction, Responsibility, and Socialization. The 14 domains in Part Two are intended to assess maladaptive conduct and personality disturbances—which do not fit easily into any developmental sequence.

Notwithstanding the note in the current AAMD classification manual to the effect that "a forthcoming edition of the [ABS] . . . Manual offers the procedure by which some of the scores can be combined to derive an individual's overall level of adaptive behavior" (Grossman, 1973, p. 19), neither edition of the AAMD Adaptive Behavior Scale provides for obtaining a single, overall ABS score. The 1969 manual (Nihira et al., 1969) delineates means and SDs of domain scores for the normative group. However, in a stated attempt to allow for more meaningful interpretation and utilization of ABS scores, the norms in the 1974 edition (Nihira et al., 1974) are in the form of percentile ranks for domain scores at each of the 11 age categories. When transmitted to a Profile Summary Sheet, these ranks allow for the comparison of individual or group ABS scores with those of a reference group of institutionalized mentally retarded persons of similar age.

ABS community norms. The Adaptive Behavior Project of the Ohio State University has developed preliminary community norms based on the 1974 revision of the ABS (Dervin, 1975; Leland, 1975). As a correlate to the institutional norms, the community data (Dervin, 1975) allow for the comparison of individual or group ABS scores with those of a reference group of community-based retarded individuals of similar age enrolled in given programs.

Public school ABS. The public school version (ABS-PS) is essentially identical in philosophy and format to that of the 1974 revision of the ABS. The scale was standardized on 2,600 California school children of both sexes, ranging in age from 7-3 to 13-2 (spanning grades 2 to 6). The normative sample included children from "Black," "Spanish," "Asian," and "White" ethnic backgrounds and from five educational classifications. The latter were designated as "Regular," "Educable Mentally Retarded (EMR)," "Trainable Mentally Retarded (TMR)," "Educationally Handicapped-Special Class (EH$_1$)," and "Educationally Handicapped-Learning Disability (EH$_2$)."

As with the parent scale, the ABS-PS does not allow for the derivation of a global score. The manual (Lambert et al., 1975a) presents domain norms in the form of means and SDs, and as percentile ranks for each of the five educational classifications at each of six age levels (e.g., 7-3 to 8-2). For Part One, a single set of norms covers both sexes and all ethnic groups. For Part Two, there are separate norms by sex and by ethnic status. The authors suggest that while means and SDs might be used for comparison purposes, it would be more appropriate—for 'educational planning and programming—to employ the Profile Summary Sheet, based on percentile ranks (as with the ABS), to compare the scores of a given child with those of children of the same age in several educational categories. In addition, as a frame of reference for evaluating the adaptive behavior of a given child, the ABS-PS manual contains tables comparing special education and regular class students of each age group on each domain.

Diagnosis and programming. Let us now return to the issue of concomitant application of a global adaptive behavior score and profile, or domain scores for both diagnostic and program-planning purposes. It would, of course, be preferable from the standpoint of stringent measurement technique to employ the same instruments for both purposes—in much the same way the WISC is used with regard to intellectual-cognitive assessment (e.g., Glasser & Zimmerman, 1967). However, it does not seem inappropriate—for satisfying the definitional criteria of impaired adaptive behavior, and for providing guidelines for educational and rehabilitative programming—to supplement the Vineland DSQ, or any other valid and reliable single index, with data from such scales as the ABS and the ABS-PS. That such an approach can be useful in yielding complementary information for decision making, at least among institutionalized severely and profoundly retarded children, is indicated in the work of Gardner and Giampa (1971).

The overall philosophy essentially is summed up in the current manual:

> A valid diagnosis of mental retardation must satisfy the require-
> ments of the definition. . . . Results of intelligence tests can be
> used in relation to the first requirement. . . . The available adap-
> tive behavior scales . . . are not fully satisfactory vis-à-vis the
> second requirement. Therefore, the ultimate determination
> of . . . mental retardation still rests on [standardized scales, sup-
> plemented by] clinical judgment [whenever possible]. Once the
> diagnosis is made, the adaptive behavior scales are useful in
> further specifications. (Grossman, 1973, p. 21)

Nevertheless, there are indications that the AAMD adaptive behavior scales may eventually play a significant role in the diagnosis of mental retardation as well as in facilitating program specificity.

It was noted earlier that, in keeping with the 1959/1961 definition, the original intent of the AAMD Adaptive Behavior Project was to develop a clinical evaluative device for providing precise criteria by which to both describe and classify levels of impairment in adaptive behavior. For various reasons, chief among which was the working philosophy that it was most important first to develop the major behavioral areas on which assessment could be based, attention to what Leland is fond of calling the "bookkeep-ing" aspects of adaptive behavior was postponed. Consequently, as described above, the current ABS procedures do not lend themselves to clinical diagnosis within the intent of the dual definitional criteria.

However, in recognition that some sort of "bookkeeping estimation" of adaptive functioning is required in the overall conceptual scheme of diagnosis and program planning in mental retardation, the Adaptive Behavior Project has developed guidelines for the clinical use of the ABS (Leland & Shoaee, 1975) which might "be serviceable for the purposes of establishing bookkeep-ing levels and other kinds of classification requirements that go with an effective assessment tool" (p. 2).

In what has been designed as a very comprehensive companion to the 1974 ABS Manual (Nihira et al., 1974), Leland and Shoaee developed the notion that the ABS can be used as a preliminary diagnostic tool in individual assessments as well as in planning and evaluating programs for the retarded client; and with regard to the ABS norms, they make the very germane point that:

> Comparison with a reference group will . . . help to determine whether . . . the individual should have the label "mentally retarded." In cases where major domains reflecting personal independence and cognitive function are above the 80th percentile . . ., there is a high probability that the individual does not have a deficit in adaptive behavior and· . . . should not be considered mentally retarded in terms of the definition. (1975, p. 53)

Resolution of Definitional Dilemmas

Reference has already been made to earlier criticisms of the 1959/1961 AAMD definition and the classification system it subtended. As noted, a major source of contention has been the notion that despite the dual definitional criteria, IQ would be (if not *should* be) the sole basis for diagnosing mental retardation, since the adaptive behavior dimension is difficult to operationalize and to assess.

With the advent of the 1973 revision, which even more strongly posits the principle that a diagnosis not be made on the basis of IQ alone, and despite the noted strides in the evaluation of adaptive behavior, fears and contentions concerning the primacy of IQ in the diagnostic process have not died. On the contrary, they have been voiced with renewed vigor. Thus, pointing to the previously mentioned findings by Adams (1973), Filler, Robinson, Smith, Vincent-Smith, Bricker, and Bricker (1975) have cautioned:

> In spite of admonitions . . . [in the 1973 manual] concerning the importance of augmenting results from IQ tests with "clinical judgement," IQ scores will probably continue to be used as the foremost criteria for differential classification. Even those diagnosticians who fully recognize the limitations imposed upon intelligence tests by a number of error factors . . . would place more weight on these test results than those obtained from interviews or rating scales of generally lower reliability. (p. 201)

Fear regarding the central role of the IQ in defining mental retardation is also expressed in an excellent and incisive critique of the current AAMD definition by Baumeister and Muma (1975). Making the point that "psychologists, far more often than any other professionals, have the final responsibility for placing the stamp of 'mental retardation' on individuals" (p. 293), those authors went on to observe that one of the primary functions of a definition is to delimit the nature and scope of a concept. However, they argued, the delimitation process advocated in both the previous schema (Heber, 1961) and the current manual (Grossman, 1973) is predicated on the implicit adoption of a general ability theory of intelligence—which ties together the concepts of retardation and individual intelligence so firmly as to constitute a unitary conception of metal retardation. They further objected that:

> By delineating the concept of MR primarily in terms of IQ, we make it difficult to incorporate MR within other theoretical schemes [factorial, developmental, or learning] .... It is clearly presumptive to evaluate a person's intelligence or adaptive capacities on the basis of a single IQ score. . . . It tells us nothing about internal states of the individual or the processes that mediate socially adaptive behavior. (Baumeister & Muma, 1975, pp. 296-297)

These authors, argued that the dual criterion is meaningless, singing a familiar refrain further on: "adaptive behavior turns out to be a rather vague and ill-defined concept, despite recent efforts to develop measurement scales" (p. 302). Consequently, they hold, the new definition continues to rely prin-cipally on the psychometric conception of mental retardation, and "this ensures the uninterrupted prominence of the IQ score in the labeling process" (p. 302). Nevertheless, Baumeister and Muma acknowledge that in the AAMD scheme there "is clearly an admonition to corroborate obtained [intelli-gence] test results with firsthand evidence concerning adaptive behavior" (1975, p. 303) However, this acknowledgment is tempered by the same fear as that of Filler et al. (1975), to the effect that "the corroborative features of the definition may be dismissed in favor of expediency" (Baumeister & Muma, 1975, p. 303).

As an alternative to what they saw as the IQ criterion for defining mental retardation, and in a stand similar to that of Bijou (1966), Baumeister and Muma (1975) advocated defining human adjustment by a "theory-guided approach . . . that focuses upon the developing organism and its interactions with a dynamic environment" (p. 305), and they suggested an assessment system that seems to defy both operationalization and programmatic imple-mentation at this point in our professional sophistication:

> We should choose our variables from our best understanding of the processes of learning, development, and socialization. In such a system there would not be "MR" but rather a complex and continually changing profile of an individual's adjustments to the continually changing exigencies of his environment. (p. 305)

From their standpoints as psychologists and behavioral scientists, Baumeister and Muma—and those who share their views—present valid arguments that delineate ideal situations with respect to emphasizing individual behavior in given situations, without regard to defining specific diagnostic categories. However, given (a) our present state of knowledge and scientific acumen with regard to human behavior; (b) the multidimensional character of professional involvement with children who, because of inadequate cognitive and social skills, find it hard to adjust facilely to the "continually changing exigencies" of their environment; and (c) the immediate need for an operational approach to identifying and programming for such children, the current AAMD schema offers a more realistic basis for intervention.

Does the AAMD definition of mental retardation force us to continued reliance on intelligence tests and their scores? The answer, of course, must be yes. The theory of intellectual adaptation upon which the definition is based allows for the precise delineation and qualification of intellectual level. The aspect of measured intelligence is a prime differentiating characteristic of the diagnostic construct, and it is one of the important characteristics around which programming must be planned.

Does the AAMD definition really rely on dual criteria? Again, we must say yes, since the definitional system is unequivocal in specifying the requirement. That individual diagnosticians ignore the corroborative features of the definition is not the fault of the definition. The fault lies with the clinician, with his resort to expediency, and with the defeatist philosophy that adaptive behavior defies assessment. The preceding discussion has pointed to important developments in the adaptive behavior arena which dispute that philosophy, and only appropriate training and attitudinal changes can influence clinical practice.

Obviously, there is a great deal of equivocation among the experts as to the definition being primarily psychometric in nature. Indeed, the previously noted responses to Clausen's (1972) symposium presentation indicate strong disagreement with the notion that the definition represents a primarily psychometric conception of mental retardation. I particularly find myself in complete agreement with the contention of the respondents MacMillan and Jones (1972) to the effect that the AAMD approach has yielded the best available working definition of the concept, mental retardation, and with Robinson and Robinson's (1976) conclusions that (a) the practical utility of the AAMD definition far outweighs the problems it doesn't solve, and (b) its emphasis on mental retardation as a symptom that may change over time is especially laudable.

CLASSIFICATION AND LABELING ISSUES

The most definitive, comprehensive discussion of issues related to classification and labeling in mental retardation to appear in recent years has been the report of a federally funded Project on Classification of Exceptional Children (Hobbs 1975a, 1975b). In the sections below, these sources have been drawn upon liberally.

Cromwell et al. (1975) made the point that in addition to clear definitions, diagnostic systems should have coherent and logical structure. Obviously, that structure should be provided by the classification schema which supports the definition. Hobbs (1975a) provided definitions of the terms relevant to the discussion that follows:

> By *classification system* we mean any one of a number of more or less formal and systematic conceptual schemes for describing children and their problems. Some systems classify conditions, some classify children, and some do both. By *classifying* we mean the act of assigning a child or a condition to a general category or to a particular position in a classification system. (p. 43)

The issues surrounding the classification (and consequent labeling) of exceptional children (i.e., those who differ significantly from most other children in some crucial characteristic—such as intellectual, emotional, physical, or socio-economic status) revolve around the notion that such procedures have predominantly negative social implications. These implications may be summed up as follows (Hobbs, 1975a): (a) classification often results in giving the child a label that may seriously affect his opportunities for schooling, housing, and working; (b) professionals often see diagnosis and classification as ends in themselves and make no effort to put appropriate data to use in treatment and programming; (c) classification procedures can be used to perpetuate cultural biases by discriminating against (i.e., "mislabeling") poor and/or minority group children; (d) following classification, some children may be subjected to the harmful effects of institutionalization, or to being otherwise removed from the main currents of childhood experiences—in and out of school; (e) classification and attendant labeling may lead to people's being seen as "different" or "undesirable"; (f) a classificatory label can have negative effects on teacher expectancy regarding pupil achievement, on the attitude of others toward the labeled child, and on the child's self-concept; and (g) finally, the preceding implications emphasize that classification and labeling are potential (if not extant) mechanisms for social control.

However, there are clearly other facets to be considered. Thus, Hobbs (1975a) declared:

> *Classification of exceptional children is essential to get services for them, to plan and organize helping programs, and to determine the outcome of interventive efforts.* . . . Classification and labeling are essential to human communication and problem solving; without categories and concept designators, all complex communicating and thinking stop. We shall address abuses in classification and labeling, but we do not wish to encourage the belief that abuses can be remedied by not classifying. (p. 5)

Also to be considered is the diversity of purposes for which classification schema are designed, since in the final analysis such schema can be appraised only from the standpoint of their stated aims and purposes. Some germane authoritative viewpoints are presented below, followed by a discussion of the AAMD system in particular, proposed alternative classification models, and specific issues with regard to labeling.

Purposes of Classification

Cromwell et al. (1975) stressed interprofessional communication:

> The basic purpose of a classification is to form a dictionary . . . [various professionals] can use as a common basis for communication among themselves. In order to form the basis of communication, the . . . system must be reliable (the terms must be used in the same way by different persons), and the system must have coverage (it must describe the relevant domain of interest). (p. 18)

The manual for the American adaptation of the 8th Revision *International Classification of Diseases* (U.S. Dept. of Health, Education, and Welfare, 1969) emphasizes statistical and scientific usage:

> Classification is fundamental to the quantitative study of any phenomenon. It is recognized as the basis of all scientific generalization and is therefore an essential element in statistical methodology. Uniform definitions and uniform systems of classification are prerequisites in the advancement of scientific knowledge. (p. xii)

Hobbs (1975a) put the accent on practical purposes:

Diagnostic categories provide a rationale for ordering knowledge, making decisions about individual children, organizing school systems and government bureaus, planning budgets, and assessing the outcomes of educational and treatment programs [p. 42]. [Further,] while the system should emphasize the classification of children in ways that will facilitate the delivery of services . . ., it should also yield information illuminating the etiology of handicapping conditions. Understanding of etiology is essential to prevention and may eliminate or reduce the incidence of a . . . condition [p. 235].

In an excellent critique on current classification approaches in mental retardation, Filler et al. (1975), while expressing strong disagreement with the AAMD system, pointed to both practical and scientific applications:

Classification systems in mental retardation provide an objectively specifiable way of delineating populations of individuals who for various reasons are likely to encounter difficulty in acquiring the skills necessary for successful community living. The provision of ways to identify and categorize people is, perhaps, absolutely necessary from the perspective of those responsible for distributing funds for special programs. In addition, scientific efforts to provide explanations of human development assume, as a prerequisite, adequate systems of description. (p. 202)

Finally, in delineating the purposes for developing the AAMD system, the current manual covers all the elements alluded to above:

A classification system is designed primarily to furnish statistical data about groups of cases. The principal use of such a system [in the field of mental retardation] will be to furnish classificatory data on incidence, prevalence, characteristics and concomitant information. Providing a classification system makes possible increased precision in communication, in research work, and in administrative and program planning. (Grossman, 1973, p. 7)

AAMD Classification Systems

It has already been noted that the AAMD schema consists of a dual approach to classification, covering behavioral and biomedical aspects. The

Behavioral System, with which the psychologist is primarily concerned, is employed for classifying individuals according to severity of symptoms (i.e., levels of measured intelligence and adaptive behavior). This system has already been described in detail above.

In both the 1961 and 1973 manuals, the system of biomedical classification was based on the assumption that, for medical purposes, mental retardation could be regarded as a manifestation of an underlying medical condition. However, the present manual emphasizes that "this in no way negates the importance of the social concept of mental retardation since it must be recognized that constructs and classifications are arbitrary language systems which vary according to their intended purpose" (Grossman, 1973, p. 8). Indeed, both editions incorporate the social concept as specific categories within the Biomedical System—which classifies conditions according to the etiology, or presumed etiology, of various clinical syndromes.

The 1961 arrangement provided for the classification of causative conditions within eight major etiological categories. Categories I through VII were intended to identify those cases which were associated with physiological and/or anatomical abnormalities—and where both the developmental retardation and the given "structural" aberration could, with some degree of confidence, be traced back to central nervous system dysfunction.

Category VIII, which emphasized social-behavioral criteria, subtended "Mental Retardation Due to Uncertain (or Presumed Psychologic) Cause with the Functional Reaction Alone Manifest." This category was provided for classifying cases where a comprehensive medical examination had ruled out impairment of the central nervous system as a reasonable basis for the person's deviant intellectual and/or adaptive behavior.

Several coded subunits further specified the types of cases which could be grouped within Category VIII—with the clear implication that in such cases the retardation was to be diagnosed primarily on the basis of behavioral criteria. These subunits included (a) *cultural-familial mental retardation* (a major criterion here was to be subnormal intellectual functioning in at least one parent and in any sibs, and it was assumed that parental inadequacy resulted in cultural deprivation); (b) *mental retardation associated with environmental deprivation* (resulting from either severe sensory deficit or extreme environmental restriction); (c) *psychogenic mental retardation associated with emotional disturbance or with psychotic (or major personality) disorders.*

The influence of the 1961 AAMD definition on the definitional and classification schema of mental retardation subsequently promulgated in the 8th revision of the *International Classification of Diseases* (ICD-8) (World Health Organization, 1967) and its adaptation for use in the United States (ICDA: U.S. Dept. of Health, Education, and Welfare, 1969) and in the ICD-8 based second edition of the American Psychiatric Association (1968) *Diagnostic and Statistical Manual of Mental Disorders* (DSM-II) has already been described. This reciprocal relationship largely influenced the changes made in the 1973 AAMD Biomedical System, whose major etiological divisions, in general, follow those presented in the ICD-8 and DSM-II classifications. The alterations not only represent an attempt to keep the AAMD system consistent and compatible with the other medical classifications, it also reflects an updating of scientific and theoretical concepts together with increased clinical sophistication (Polloway & Payne, 1975).

As mentioned earlier, the current manual lists 10 major etiological groupings. Categories 0 through VI emphasize diseases and conditions of biological defect, which presumably underlie cerebral pathology. Categories VII, VIII, and IX again clearly stress the employment of behavioral criteria in determining etiology. They are therefore more relevant to the work of the psychologist than are the other groupings.

Category VII: *Following Psychiatric Disorder* is for classifying retardation in which cerebral pathology is not in evidence and which is *consequent to* psychotic or other psychiatric conditions rather than *concomitant with* such disorders.

Category VIII: *Environmental Influences* is for cases where cerebral disease or pathology can be ruled out and in which adverse environmental conditions appear to be causative. This category subtends two major classes of unfavorable environmental factors as follows:

1. Psychosocial disadvantage. While this grouping is obviously intended to replace the "cultural-familial" subunit of Category VIII in the earlier system (and which is designated as an "obsolete term" in the current manual), criteria for inclusion herein are very similar to those of the "obsolete" category with regard to the "familial" aspect. However, the present criteria emphasize the "cultural" components of impoverished environments, which include poor housing, inadequate diets, and deficient medical care.

2. Sensory deprivation. This subcategory covers deprivation of sensory experiences occurring as a function of harsh environmental restrictions which are directly related to parent-child interactions. These restrictions include severe maternal deprivation and prolonged isolation and neglect in childhood.

Category IX: *Other Conditions* is provided for classifying cases which involve (a) defects in special senses (e.g., where blindness and/or deafness can be identified as the only causative factors, (b) a multiplicity of biological and social variables, or (c) ill-defined or unknown conditions. It is also for cases which cannot be classified under any of the other categories.

The biomedical classification scheme was developed with a view toward making it useful to personnel in all areas of medicine concerned with retarded individuals. It was designed primarily for facilities (i.e., residential institutions, community clinics) whose primary or sole commitment is to mentally retarded patients or clients. As such, the AAMD Biomedical System "is intended to serve primarily as a statistical classification system of mental retardation" (Grossman, 1973, p. 8).

Proposed New Classification Models

Hobbs (1975a) summed up the conclusions of Filler et al. (1975) and other contributors to the two-volume compendium of current research and opinion regarding the classification of exceptional children (Hobbs, 1975b). In his summary, he seriously questioned the utility of all presently constituted systems, largely on the grounds that the traditional categories of exceptionality do not yield enough information for planning a course of action on behalf of the given child. With specific regard to the diagnosis and classification of mental retardation by any of the three systems currently in use (ICD-8, DSM-II, AAMD), the following are some of the objections which Hobbs set forth: (a) diagnosis is arrived at essentially on the basis of an IQ score—which represents primarily a prediction of academic achievement rather than of general success in living; (b) the ultimate goal of assessment should provide information which can lead to successful social adjustment and community participation on the part of the child; and (c) most importantly, "behavioral classifications (measured intelligence and adaptive behavior), as presently determined, do not lend themselves to the specification of educational goals and of time limits for achieving the goals. . . . Assessment and categorization are not ordinarily linked to specific intervention plans" (Hobbs, 1975a, p. 54).

Obviously, these objections are not completely justified. For example, decisions regarding educational placement of given children must often take into account probable level of achievement at the time of placement. Also, the described attempts at operationalizing the adaptive behavior dimension of the AAMD Behavioral System are designed to provide data which can lead to specific interventive activities in both social and educational spheres.

Warren (1973), in anticipating and discussing some of the stated objections to the AAMD schema, made the extremely cogent point that "users of the system will realize that no system of classification is going to provide a precise blueprint for treatment or programming for individuals needing service" (p. 2). Nevertheless, Filler et al. (1975) and Hobbs (1975a) described what they consider to be ideal systems for providing such precise blueprints without resulting in harmful categorization and labeling.

Filler et al. (1975) advocated a diagnostic and educational system based on Piaget's developmental model, which they term *constructive interaction adaptation system,* in which (they posit) beharior, not children, can be classified. This system (which is also basic to the program described by Bricker and Bricker in Chapter 13 of the present volume) "begins with the reflexive behavior of an infant, moves progressively to complex adult performance, and can form the basis of the functional analysis of behavior" (Filler et al., 1975, p. 217), linking assessment directly to intervention via a developmental approach to mental retardation.

Hobbs (1975a) delineated a strategy vaguely similar to that advocated by Baumeister and Muma (1975), calling it *an ecological approach* to assessing a child's problems and to planning programs for the alleviation of given difficulties:

> With this approach, the child is no longer the sole focus of assessment and intervention. Rather, the problem is seen as residing in the ecological system of which the child is an integral part. . . . Physical and psychological as well as social factors are involved. Thus, assessments and interventions focus on the exchanges between the child, the settings in which he participates, and the significant individuals who interact with him. The objective is . . . to make the total system work. . . . Changes may be brought about through interventions affecting physical, psychological, or social functioning of one or more components of the system. (pp. 113-114)

In addition, Hobbs (1975a) recommended that the federal government make a substantial investment in developing a comprehensive system for diagnosing and classifying exceptional children. It is suggested that such an arrangement should: emphasize services required, not children; deemphasize the familiar categories and emphasize treatment goals; yield information on etiology; and incorporate ecologically oriented profiling systems as outlined in the above approach.

With due recognition and acknowledgment that the views expressed by Hobbs (1975a) and by the contributors to the larger work (Hobbs, 1975b) reflect desirable, albeit ideal, goals with regard to classification and categorization in the field of mental retardation, I can only reiterate that—in view of the exigencies of the field at present, the widespread recognition and employment of the AAMD system, and its manifest usefulness to the majority of personnel who deal with retarded individuals—the current schema represents the best working model of classification now available from the standpoint of the criteria for diagnostic constructs with which this chapter opened.

There is no doubt much room for improvement. However, as Zigler and Phillips (1961) once observed, "systems of classification must be treated as tools for further discovery, not as bases for polemic disputation" (p. 616). The current AAMD system has certainly been the object of much polemic disputation. Nevertheless, there is also much obvious concern and effort, among both adherents and opponents of that schema, toward treating it as a tool for further discovery.

Labeling Issues

It was noted above that a prime objection to classifying children into given categories of exceptionality is that such classification leads to giving the child a categorical label which may have detrimental social and personal consequences. It has also been noted (Hobbs, 1975a) that the use of classificatory labels is often essential to procuring services for exceptional children. Indeed, Guskin, Bartel, and MacMillan (1975) emphasized that, to date, research on the effect of labeling a child as mentally retarded has yielded equivocal results. They therefore urge caution in assuming that labeling automatically and invariably has detrimental effects on the child, and they make the point that a deemphasis on labeling could lead to less services becoming available for children in need of help.

In a most searching analysis of theoretical issues and of the literature pertaining to the effect of the "mentally retarded" label, MacMillan, Jones, and Aloia (1974) noted that the evidence they uncovered failed to support the notion that labeling has long-lasting and debilitating effects on the labeled child, although such effects may very well exist. A great deal of the problem in isolating such effects, they feel, lies with faulty research design and with a confusion on the part of some investigators as to the pertinent issues involved. Noting that concern with issues relating to educational isolation (i.e., special class placement), cultural bias of intelligence tests, and mislabeling of minority children diverts the focus of research from the effect of labeling per se *on the child,* MacMillan et al. (1974) indicated that as far as they are concerned, the following are the critical issues and subissues:

(a) Once the child is labeled, what is the effect of that label on various outcomes (e.g., change in self-concept or level of aspiration; operation of self-fulfilling prophecy of poor performance engendered by expectations of others)?

(b) What is the consequence of mislabeling when the label is inappropriate for the child (assuming labels only damage when they identify a child as less able than he is)?

(c) What is the impact of the label on the performance of any child, regardless of its appropriateness?

(d) How do those who are labeled feel about it?

Pointing to many methodological problems (including questionable instrumentation and often imprecise dependent measures) in the research on labeling, MacMillan et al. (1974) set forth the following conclusions:

(a) Studies on the efficacy of special classes for mentally retarded children do not support the deleterious effects of labeling.

(b) There is no evidence of a direct relationship between labeling and self-concept.

(c) Results of studies on the effect of labeling and/or class placement on peer acceptance are inconclusive and subject to conflicting interpretations.

(d) There is a paucity of evidence to support the strong belief that labeling a child as mentally retarded affects the behavior of others toward him, which in turn influences the performance of the child (self-fulfilling prophecy).

(e) With regard to post-school adjustment of mildly retarded individuals, the label was not found to be a major factor in vocational failure.

(f) None of the research reviewed could trace unsatisfactory outcomes with regard to job status, income, or marital success to any given independent variable such as being labeled mentally retarded.

(g) The reports of educable retarded students and of their parents clearly show that the students are very unhappy at being labeled and at being in special classes. However, it is difficult to separate the effects of either specific variable (labeling and placement).

Having concluded that the available evidence does not support the notion of a deleterious labeling effect in general, MacMillan et al. (1974) stressed that this does not mean that no such effects may exist and that it still needs to be demonstrated that, on the one hand, labels are beneficial and, on the other hand, any possible advantages outweigh possible disadvantages. They went on to discuss the variables that need to be accounted for or controlled in order to do definitive research on how children are affected by the "mentally retarded" label. These variables include:

(a) Multiple labeling (e.g., "mentally retarded" and "culturally disadvantaged").

(b) Formal versus informal labeling (e.g., by agency versus peers).

(c) Person's acceptance or denial of label's validity.

(d) Prelabeling experiences.

(e) Age at being labeled.

(f) Locus of control (extent to which one conceptualizes his ability to determine event outcomes).

(g) Child variables, such as sex, mental age, race, and socioeconomic status.

(h) Situational variables such as institutionalization, and different labels being applied to similar conditions in different settings.

(i) Extent to which labels generalize from one specific context (e.g., school) to another (e.g., home or neighborhood).

(j) With specific regard to research on teacher expectancy, studies must control for the interactions of child and teacher characteristics and of ability levels with levels of expectancy.

In responding to the MacMillan et al. paper, Guskin (1974) posited that:

> The labeling controversy is actually a political argument between those who support the current system of special education and psychological diagnosis as a constructive and altruistic arrangement and those who wish to break up that system because they see it as aggressive and destructive. (p. 263)

Guskin held that the research strategies suggested by MacMillan et al. (1974) are not only unlikely to resolve the political debate, but are extremely difficult and costly to operationalize, and he suggested the more direct approach of developing techniques for modifying the effects of the label. A suggested technique is to train teachers to recognize that the term "retarded" covers a wide range of children's abilities—including some children who are "mislabeled" for various reasons—and to understand that most "retarded" children are accepted as competent by nonretarded peers outside of school and will lead "normal" adult lives.

Payne and Mercer (1975) noted that any word can come to have negative connotations (depending on the associations which accrue to it), and as an example described a situation in which the acronym DISTAR (a commercial program for teaching arithmetic and reading) was used by school children as an epithet against retarded children enrolled in such a program—which was characterized by "concerned" citizens as being for "dumb kids." The authors made the point that generally acceptable terms and definitions may be impossible to attain without education directed at all citizens with regard to understanding retarded persons.

I believe that this section can be brought to an appropriate conclusion with a statement made by MacMillan et al. (1974):

It should be noted, however, that those marginal [retarded] children over whom the debate rages do not appear to benefit maximally from their educational experiences whether they are labeled or not. The task confronting special educators would seem to be to optimize the eductional experience for such children. . . . [rather than] to identify forces on which to place blame (e.g., . . . labels) . . . lest they lose sight of the primary task of teaching . . . the skills and attitudes . . . necessary for . . . success in society. (pp. 257-258)

"PSEUDO RETARDATION" AS A DIAGNOSTIC CONSTRUCT

A major intent of the 1961 AAMD classification system, and of Category VIII in particular, was to render unnecessary the diagnostic construct "pseudo retardation." The 1973 schema implements this intent in much the same way and from the same philosophical standpoint. Let us examine the issues more closely.

In earlier publications (Bialer 1970a, 1970b; in press), I advocated (as have a number of other writers) the universal abandonment of the concept of pseudo retardation because, while it is useless for understanding or enhancing the etiological, diagnostic, or therapeutic aspects of mental retardation, it has persisted in the world literature under a variety of referents. Indeed, it is largely the multiplicity of meanings attached to the term which render it useless as a scientific construct.

The historical underpinnings of the concept have been discussed in detail elsewhere (Bialer, in press). As noted, the major referents of "pseudo retardation" have been related to diagnosis, prognosis, and etiology. Thus, the concept has been used to denote an incorrect original diagnosis based on inadequate or inappropriate assessment, leading to false clinical inferences (Benton, 1962). Obviously, a diagnosis derived from invalid or unreliable data should not be treated as a meaningful entity.

From the prognostic aspect, largely as a function of the criteria delineated by E. A. Doll (1941) for "true" mental deficiency, the diagnosis of mental retardation has been tied to the concepts of genetic "capacity" or "potential" and to the related criterion of "incurability." Thus, any individual who demonstrated competent behavior following an initial diagnosis of mental retardation was judged, post-hoc, to have been not "really" retarded in the first place (i.e., to have been "pseudo" retarded when the diagnosis was made). Surely, post-hoc reasoning of this nature is not conducive to either clinical or scientific progress. Unfortunately, the notion of pseudo retardation as a post-hoc diagnosis continues to be promulgated in professional sources (e.g., Goldenson, 1975).

The etiological referents of the construct are based on the implication that "real" or "basic" mental retardation can be rooted only in irreversible neuropathology. A recent volume edited by Poser (1969) attests to the still-current status of this view among many medical professionals in the field. Nevertheless, Benton (1962) indicated that for those clinicians who adhere to the notion that "true" mental retardation stems only from irreversible CNS impairment, pseudo retardation may denote a "true" defect state in the form of "mental deficiency of atypical etiology" (p. 86), stemming from sensory or cultural deprivation, motor deficit, and/or emotional problems. Benton (1970) traced this meaning of "pseudo" to medical nosology, indicating that while it may be useful in some medical contexts, its employment in the field of mental retardation represents a source of potential confusion. Certainly, if given behavioral manifestations are valid representations of an individual's functional abilities at the time they are observed, it seems illogical to consider them as reflecting a pseudo state. It seems more appropriate to fit them into a broad classification scheme as cases of mental retardation with specific etiological elements.

This broad scheme was the philosophical approach of the AAMD classification system. That approach has rendered the term "pseudo retardation" completely meaningless as a diagnostic construct in three ways: First, the AAMD definition ignores both etiology and prognosis. Second, there is no reference to "capacity," "potential," or "curability," the emphasis being on *current* level of behavioral functioning. From this standpoint, the Behavioral System allows for the contingency that the definitional criteria of mental retardation (although once appropriate) may cease to be applicable at a given point in a person's life (at which point, he or she would no longer be so identified). Third, a broad biomedical framework is provided that is applicable to those cases which, from some of the other reference points outlined above, would not be considered "truly" mentally retarded. On that basis, the concept of pseudo retardation is obviously obsolete and should be discarded completely.

SUMMARY

The concept of mental retardation as a diagnostic construct has been discussed with regard to issues pertaining to the definition of the term and its use in classifying and labeling children. It is posited that the definition of "mental retardation" promulgated by the American Association on Mental Deficiency (AAMD)—together with the classification schema which operationalizes and supports the definition—provides a basis for establishing the term as a reliable and valid diagnostic construct.

Following a historical overview of various definitional approaches here in other countries, as they have related to the care and treatment of the children we would call "mentally retarded," the current AAMD system is discussed at length. It is viewed as an effort to achieve uniformity in terminology, facilitate communication in the field, help establish diagnostic criteria that are reliable and valid for research and clinical purposes, and provide a rational and consistent schema for classifying individuals meeting those criteria. Some proposed new classification models are also described, but it is concluded that the AAMD approach represents the best presently available working model.

Issues regarding classification and labeling of exceptional children are considered from the standpoint of their putative negative social implications. It is noted that assignment of such children to categories is often essential for practical and scientific purposes, that available research evidence does not support the notion of a general debilitating effect of labeling a child "mentally retarded," and that some of the negative consequences (where they do exist) may be offset by the accrual of important benefits. Suggested strategies for more definitive research on labeling are outlined.

Finally, this chapter emphasizes the role of the AAMD system of terminology and classification in performing the much-needed service of rendering obsolete the concept of "pseudo retardation" as a diagnostic construct.

REFERENCES

Adams, J. Adaptive behavior and measured intelligence in the classification of mental retardation. *American Journal of Mental Deficiency,* 1973, *78,* 77-81.

American Psychiatric Association. *Diagnostic and statistical manual, mental disorders.* Washington, D.C.: APA, 1952.

American Psychiatric Association. *Diagnostic and statistical manual of mental disorders* (2nd ed.). Washington, D.C.: APA, 1968.

Baumeister, A. A. The American residential institution: Its history and character. In A. A. Baumeister and E. C. Butterfield (Eds.), *Residential facilities for the mentally retarded.* Chicago; Aldine, 1970, pp. 1-28.

Baumeister, A. A., & Muma, J. R. On defining mental retardation. *Journal of Special Education,* 1975, *9,* 293-306.

Benoit, E. P. Toward a new definition of mental retardation. *American Journal of Mental Deficiency,* 1959, *63,* 559-565.

Benton, A. L. The concept of pseudofeeblemindedness. In E. P. Trapp and P. Himmelstein (Eds.), *Readings on the exceptional child: Research and theory*. New York: Appleton-Century-Crofts, 1962, pp. 82-95.

Benton, A. L. Interactive determinants of mental deficiency. In H. C. Haywood (Ed.), *Social-cultural aspects of mental retardation*. New York: Appleton-Century-Crofts, 1970, pp. 661-671.

Bialer, I. Emotional disturbance and mental retardation: Etiologic and conceptual relationships. In F. J. Menolascino (Ed.), *Psychiatric approaches to mental retardation*. New York: Basic Books, 1970, pp. 68-90. (a)

Bialer, I. Relationship of mental retardation to emotional disturbance and physical disability. In H. C. Haywood (Ed.), *Social-cultural aspects of mental retardation*. New York: Appleton-Century-Crofts, 1970, pp. 607-660. (b)

Bialer, I. Pseudoretardation as a diagnostic construct. *Israel Quarterly of Developmental Paediatrics and Psychology*. In press (1976).

Bijou, S. W. A functional analysis of retarded development. In N. R. Ellis (Ed.), *International review of research in mental retardation* (Vol. 1). New York: Academic Press, 1966, pp. 1-19.

Blackman, L. S. An active-passive dimension in the definition of mental retardation. *Journal of Special Education,* 1972, *6,* 67-70.

Clarke, A. M., & Clarke, A. D. B. Criteria and classification of subnormality. In A. M. Clarke and A. D. B. Clarke (Eds.), *Mental deficiency: The changing outlook* (3rd ed.). New York: The Free Press, 1975, pp. 13-29.

Clausen, J. Mental deficiency—Development of a concept. *American Journal of Mental Deficiency,* 1967, *5,* 727-745.

Clausen, J. Quo vadis, AAMD? *Journal of Special Education,* 1972, *6,* 51-60.

Cromwell, R. L., Blashfield, R. K., & Strauss, J. S. Criteria for classification systems. In N. Hobbs (Ed.), *Issues in the classification of children: A sourcebook on categories, labels, and their consequences* (Vol. 1). San Francisco: Jossey-Bass, 1975, pp.4-25.

Dervin, D. *Community information on the Adaptive Behavior Scale*. Columbus, Ohio: The Ohio State University Adaptive Behavior Project, 1975. (Mimeo)

Doll, E. A. The essentials of an inclusive concept of mental deficiency. *American Journal of Mental Deficiency,* 1941, *46,* 214-219.

Doll, E. A. *The measurement of social competence: A manual for the Vineland Social Maturity Scale*. Minneapolis: Educational Test Bureau, 1953.

Doll, E. E. A historical survey of research and management of mental retardation in the United States. In E. P. Trapp and P. Himmelstein (Eds.), *Readings on the exceptional child: Research and theory*. New York: Appleton-Century-Crofts, 1962, pp. 21-68.

Dunn, L. M. An overview. In L. M. Dunn (Ed.), *Exceptional children in the schools.* New York: Holt, Rinehart and Winston, 1963, pp. 1-51.

Dunn, L. M. Children with moderate and severe general learning disabilities. In L. M. Dunn (Ed.), *Exceptional children in the schools* (2nd ed.). New York: Holt, Rinehart and Winston, 1973, pp. 63-123.

Filler, J. W., Jr., Robinson, C. C., Smith, R. A., Vincent-Smith, L. J., Bricker, D. D., & Bricker, W. A. Mental retardation. In N. Hobbs (Ed.), *Issues in the classification of children: A sourcebook on categories, labels, and their consequences* (Vol. 1). San Francisco: Jossey-Bass, 1975, pp. 194-238.

Fishler, K. Psychological assessment services. In R. Koch and J. C. Dobson (Eds.), *The mentally retarded child and his family: A multidisciplinary handbook.* New York: Brunner/Mazel, 1971, pp. 156-196.

Gardner, J. M., & Giampa, F. L. Utility of three behavioral indices for studying severely and profoundly retarded children. *American Journal of Mental Deficiency,* 1971, *76,* 352-356.

Garfield, S. L., & Wittson, C. Comments on Dr. Cantor's remarks. *American Journal of Mental Deficiency,* 1960, *64,* 957-959. (a)

Garfield, S. L., & Wittson, C. Some reactions to the revised "Manual on Terminology and Classification in Mental Retardation." *American Journal of Mental Deficiency,* 1960, *64,* 951-953. (b)

Gearheart, B. R. The trainable mentally retarded. In B. R. Gearheart (Ed.), *Education of the exceptional child: History, present practices, and trends.* Scranton: Intext, 1972, pp. 15-39.

Gelof, M. Comparisons of systems of classification relating degree of retardation to measured intelligence. *American Journal of Mental Deficiency,* 1963, *68,* 297-317.

Glasser, A. J., & Zimmerman, I. L. *Clinical interpretation of the Wechsler Intelligence Scale for Children (WISC).* New York: Grune & Stratton, 1967.

Goddard, H. H. *Feeble-mindedness: Its causes and consequences.* New York: Macmillan, 1914.

Goldenson, R. M. (Ed.).*The encyclopedia of human behavior: Psychology, psychiatry, and mental health* (rev. ed.). New York: Dell, 1975.

Grossman, H. J. (Ed.). *Manual on terminology and classification in mental retardation* (1973 rev.). Washington, D. C.: American Association on Mental Deficiency, 1973.

Guskin, S. L. Research on labeling retarded persons: Where do we go from here? (A reaction to MacMillan, Jones, and Aloia). *American Journal of Mental Deficiency,* 1974, *79,* 262-264.

Guskin, S. L., Bartel, N. R., & MacMillan, D. L. Perspective on the labeled child. In N. Hobbs (Ed.), *Issues in the classification of children: A sourcebook on categories, labels, and their consequences* (Vol. 2). San Francisco: Jossey-Bass, 1975, pp. 189-212.

Hebb, D. O. *The organization of behavior.* New York: Wiley, 1949.

Heber, R. (Ed.). A manual on terminology and classification in mental retardation. *American Journal of Mental Deficiency,* Monogr. Suppl., 1959, No. 2.

Heber, R. (Ed.). A manual on terminology and classification in mental retardation (2nd ed.). *American Journal of Mental Deficiency,* Monogr. Suppl., 1961.

Heber, R. Mental retardation: Concept and classification. In E. P. Trapp and P. Himmelstein (Eds.), *Readings on the exceptional child: Research and theory.* New York: Appleton-Century-Crofts, 1962, pp. 69-81.

Hilliard, L. T. Historical and legal. In L. T. Hilliard and B. H. Kirman (Eds.), *Mental deficiency.* Boston: Little, Brown, 1965, pp. 1-36.

Hobbs, N. *The futures of children: Categories, labels, and their consequences—Report of the project on classification of exceptional children.* San Francisco: Jossey-Bass, 1975. (a)

Hobbs, N. (Ed.). *Issues in the classification of children: A sourcebook on categories, labels, and their consequences* (2 vols.). San Francisco: Jossey-Bass, 1975. (b)

Itard, J. M. G. *The wild boy of Aveyron* (G. Humphrey & M. Humphrey, Eds. and trans.). New York: Appleton-Century-Crofts, 1962. (Originally published 1894.)

Jervis, G. A. Factors in mental retardation. In J. F. Magary and J. R. Eichorn (Eds.), *The exceptional child: A book of readings.* New York: Holt, Rinehart and Winston, 1960, pp. 45-53.

Kanner, L. Itard, Seguin, Howe—Three pioneers in the education of retarded children. *American Journal of Mental Deficiency,* 1960, *65,* 2-10.

Kanner, L. *A history of the care and study of the mentally retarded.* Springfield, Ill.: Charles C. Thomas, 1964.

Kidd, J. W. Toward a more precise definition of mental retardation. *Mental Retardation,* 1964, *2*(4), 209-212.

Kirk, S. A., *Educating exceptional children* (2nd ed.). Boston: Houghton Mifflin, 1972.

Kirk, S. A., & Johnson, G. O. *Educating the retarded child.* Cambridge, Mass.: Houghton Mifflin, 1951.

Lambert, N. M., Windmiller, M., Cole, L., & Figueroa, R. A. *AAMD Adaptive Behavior Scale: Public school version, 1974 revision: Manual.* Washington, D.C.: American Association on Mental Deficiency, 1975. (a)

Lambert, N. M., Windmiller, M., Cole, L., & Figueroa, R. A. Standardization of a public school version of the AAMD Adaptive Behavior Scale. *Mental Retardation,* 1975, *13*(2), 3-7. (b)

Leland, H. Some thoughts on the current status of adaptive behavior. *Mental Retardation,* 1964, *2*(3), 171-176.

Leland, H. Mental retardation and adaptive behavior. *Journal of Special Education,* 1972, *6,* 71-80.

Leland, H. *Annual report, fiscal year 1974-1975: Adaptive behavior project.* Columbus, Ohio: The Ohio State University Adaptive Behavior Project, 1975. (Mimeo)

Leland, H., & Shoaee, M. *Guidelines for the clinical use of the AAMD Adaptive Behavior Scales.* Columbus, Ohio: The Ohio State University Adaptive Behavior Project, 1975. (Mimeo)

MacMillan, D. L., & Jones, R. L. Lions in search of more Christians. *Journal of Special Education,* 1972, *6,* 81-91.

MacMillan, D. L., Jones, R. L., & Aloia, G. F. The mentally retarded label: A theoretical analysis and review of research. *American Journal of Mental Deficiency,* 1974, *79,* 241-261.

Mercer, J. R. *Labeling the mentally retarded.* Richmond, Calif.: University of California Press, 1973.

Milligan, G. E. History of the American Association on Mental Deficiency. *American Journal of Mental Deficiency,* 1961, *66,* 357-369.

Myrianthopoulos, N. C. Huntington's chorea: The genetic problem five years later. In A. Barbeau, T. N. Chase, and G. W. Paulson (Eds.), *Huntington's chorea: 1872-1972.* New York: Raven Press, 1973, pp. 149-159.

Nagler, B. A change in terms or in concepts? A small step forward or a giant step backward? *Journal of Special Education,* 1972, *6,* 61-64.

Nihira, K., Foster, R., Shellhaas, M., & Leland, H. *Adaptive Behavior Scales: Manual.* Washington, D. C.: American Association on Mental Deficiency, 1969.

Nihira, K., Foster, R., Shellhaas, M., & Leland, H. *AAMD Adaptive Behavior Scale: Manual* (rev. ed.). Washington, D. C.: American Association on Mental Deficiency, 1974.

Payne, J. S., & Mercer, C. D. Definition and prevalence. In J. M. Kauffman and J. S. Payne (Eds.), *Mental retardation: Introduction and personal perspectives.* Columbus, Ohio: Merrill, 1975, pp. 2-48.

Penrose, L. S. Mental deficiency. *Journal of Special Education,* 1972, *6,* 65-66.

Pilkington, T. Mental subnormality in Great Britain. *Journal of Mental Subnormality,* 1964, *10*(19), 113-117.

Polloway, E. A., & Payne, J. S. Comparison of the AAMD Heber and Grossman manuals on terminology and classification in mental retardation. *Mental Retardation,* 1975, *13*(3), 12-14.

Poser, C. M. (Ed.). *Mental retardation: Diagnosis and treatment.* New York: Harper & Row, 1969.

Robinson, H. B., & Robinson, N. M. *The mentally retarded child: A psychological approach.* New York: McGraw-Hill, 1965.

Robinson, N. M., & Robinson, H. B. *The mentally retarded child: A psychological approach* (2nd ed.). New York: McGraw-Hill, 1976.

Sarason, S. B., & Doris, J. *Psychological problems in mental deficiency* (4th ed.). New York: Harper & Row, 1969.

Sarason, S. B., & Gladwin, T. Psychological and cultural problems in mental subnormality. In R. L. Masland, S. B. Sarason, and T. Gladwin, *Mental subnormality.* New York: Basic Books, 1958, pp. 145-400.

Seguin, E. *Idiocy and its treatment by the physiological method.* New York: William Wood, 1866. (Republished. New York: Augustus M. Kelley, 1971.)

Silverstein, A. B. Note on terminology. *American Journal of Mental Deficiency,* 1962, *67,* 303-305.

Silverstein, A. B. The measurement of intelligence. In N. R. Ellis (Ed.), *International review of research in mental retardation* (Vol. 4). New York: Academic Press, 1970, pp. 193-227.

Silverstein, A. B. Deviation social quotients for the Vineland Social Maturity Scale. *American Journal of Mental Deficiency,* 1971, *76,* 348-351.

Silverstein, A. B. Note on prevalence. *American Journal of Mental Deficiency,* 1973, *77,* 380-382.

Smith, R. M. *Clinical teaching: Methods of instruction for the retarded.* New York: McGraw-Hill, 1968.

Stern, A. Appendix A: Tests used in assessment of intellectual ability, adaptive behavior, perceptual-motor skills, and speech and language skills. In B. R. Gearheart and F. W. Litton, *The trainable retarded: A foundations approach.* St. Louis: Mosby, 1975, pp. 232-246.

Subcommittee on Classification of Mental Disorders. *A glossary of mental disorders.* London: Her Majesty's Stationery Office, 1968.

Tarjan, G., Wright, S. W., Eyman, R. K., & Keeran, C. V. Natural history of mental retardation: Some aspects of epidemiology. *American Journal of Mental Deficiency,* 1973, *77,* 369-379.

Terman, L. M. *The measurement of intelligence.* Boston: Houghton Mifflin, 1916.

Terman, L. M., & Merrill, M. A. *Measuring intelligence.* Boston: Houghton Mifflin, 1937.

Terman, L. M., & Merrill, M. A. *Stanford-Binet Intelligence Scale: Manual for the third revision, Form L-M.* Boston: Houghton Mifflin, 1960.

Tredgold, A. F. *A textbook of mental deficiency* (6th ed.). Baltimore: Wood, 1937.

U.S. Dept. of Health, Education, and Welfare. *Eighth revision international classification of diseases: Adapted for use in the United States* (Vol. 1). Washington, D.C.: U.S. Government Printing Office, 1969.

Warren, S. A. Editorial: Classification systems and AAMD. *Mental Retardation,* 1973, *11*(1), 2.

Wechsler, D. *The measurement of adult intelligence* (3rd ed.). Baltimore: Williams & Wilkins, 1944.

Wechsler, D. *Wechsler Adult Intelligence Scale: Manual.* New York: Psychological Corp., 1955.

Wilson, J. B. Is the term "adaptive behavior" educationally relevant? *Journal of Special Education,* 1972, *6,* 93-95.

Wilson, P. T., & Spitzer, R. L. A comparison of three current classification systems for mental retardation. *American Journal of Mental Deficiency,* 1969, *74,* 428-435.

Wolfensberger, W. Age variations in Vineland SQ scores for the four levels of adaptive behavior of the 1959 AAMD behavioral classification. *American Journal of Mental Deficiency,* 1962, *67,* 452-454.

World Health Organization. *Manual of the international statistical classification of diseases, injuries, and causes of death* (8th rev.) (Vol. 1). Geneva: WHO, 1967.

World Health Organization. *The mentally subnormal child.* (World Health Organization technical report series No. 75.) Geneva: WHO, 1954.

Zigler, E., & Phillips, L. Psychiatric diagnosis: A critique. *Journal of Abnormal and Social Psychology,* 1961, *63,* 607-618.

Harvey N. Switzky, a graduate of Brooklyn College of the City University of New York, received his Master's degree in physiological psychology from Brown University in 1965 and his Ph.D. degree in experimental child psychology in 1970. He was a post-doctoral clinical research Fellow in the Institute on Mental Retardation and Intellectual Development (IMRID), John F. Kennedy Center for Research on Education and Human Development at George Peabody College, from 1970 to 1971. He held the position of Research Assistant Professor of Psychology in IMRID from 1971 to 1974. Dr. Switzky was Director of Psychological Services, Chief Psychologist at Northern Wisconsin Colony from 1974 to 1975, and he directed and implemented that institution's efforts to "normalize" the education and habilibation treatment programs for the residents.

At present, Dr. Switzky is an Associate Professor of Special Education at Northern Illinois University, where he is training teachers to instruct severely and profoundly retarded multihandicapped children. He has been a Consulting Editor for the American Journal of Mental Deficiency *from 1973 to 1975 and is presently an Associate Editor for* Exceptional Children. *He has published numerous studies on the learning abilities of retarded and nonretarded children and adults.*

Dr. Switzky's present interests include the analysis of exploratory and play behavior sequences in retarded and nonretarded children, and also the development of assessment models for severely and profoundly retarded children.

Robert J. Gaylord-Ross is an educational psychologist who received his Ph.D. degree from Mississippi State University in 1973. He taught at the University of Wisconsin–Eau Claire (1973-1974), and he was acting chief psychologist at the Northern Wisconsin Colony (institution for retarded persons) from 1974 to 1975. Since 1975 he has been an Assistant Professor of Special Education at the Ferkauf Graduate School of Humanities and Social Sciences, Yeshiva University.

Dr. Gaylord-Ross has published and presented papers on the topics of cognitive development, behavior modification, mental retardation, and self-injurious behavior. He is currently studying the application of behavior modification techniques by parents and teachers for the suppression of self-injurious behavior. The research is being supported by a 2-year grant from the Federal Bureau of Education for the Handicapped.

Behavioral genetics and mental retardation

Harvey N. Switzky and Robert J. Gaylord-Ross

THE GENETIC MODELS

The purpose of this chapter is to examine the principles of Mendelian, Population, and Developmental Genetics in terms of their implications for the prevention, control, and treatment of mental retardation and for the behavioral-genetic analysis of mental retardation. The importance of cytological and biochemical genetic principles for the understanding of certain forms of mental retardation, such as Down's Syndrome—or Trisomy G21 Syndrome (Lejeune, Turpin, & Gautier, 1959) and phenylketonuria (Jervis, 1953; Knox, 1972; Loo, 1967)—necessitates that mental retardation professionals have a thorough understanding of the interrelationships between behavior and genetics. Behavioral genetics (McClearns, 1962) may be informally defined as that science concerned with elucidating the degree or nature of hereditary determination of similarities and differences in the behavior of individuals. One of the oldest beliefs of humankind is that just as physical traits may be inherited and become characteristics of a family or animal species, so may behavioral traits be inherited as well.

The behavioral-genetic analysis of the polygenic theory of inheritance

This chapter was partially written while H. N. Switzky was at the Institute on Mental Retardation and Intellectual Development, The John F. Kennedy Center for Research on Education and Human Development, George Peabody College for Teachers at Nashville, Tennessee, and while both authors were at Northern Wisconsin Colony and Training School, Chippewa Falls, Wisconsin. We are most grateful to Marcelyn Strand, Eunice Pabst, and Joann Mutchler for typing the manuscript, and to Diana Stenner for drawing the figures and proofreading. We would like to thank Irving Mauer, who read an earlier draft of this manuscript and assisted by reacting critically to the material.

of intelligence—as discussed by many scientists (Bronfenbrenner, 1972; Cattell, 1971a, 1971b; Denniston, 1975; Dobzhansky, 1972, 1973; Eckland, 1971, 1972; Eysenck, 1971; Herrnstein, 1971, 1973; Hirsch, 1971, 1972; Jensen, 1969, 1973a, 1973b; Kamin, 1974; Layzer, 1974; Lewontin, 1970a, 1970b, 1974; Morton, 1972, 1974; Rao, Morton, & Yee, 1974; Scarr-Salapatak, 1971a, 1971b; Shockley, 1971; Zigler, 1970)—seemingly has profound implications for the prevention, treatment, and control of mental retardation.

However, Morton (1972, 1974) argued rather convincingly that the study of single gene and chromosomal effects are the most unambiguous and fruitful areas of research for the science of human behavioral genetics. The study of single gene and chromosomal determinants makes it possible to trace the physiological effects of the genetic disturbances to phenotypic expressions of behavior, with minimum interference from the bewildering array of genotype-environmental correlations which exist for polygenetic traits such as measured intelligence.

In accord with this point of view, we have mostly concentrated in this chapter on implications for the prevention, treatment, and control of those mental retardation syndromes which are primarily due to single gene mutations or simple chromosomal aberrations whose mechanisms are more clearly understood. Those who wish to investigate the murky depths of behavioral-genetic analysis of polygenetic inheritance of intelligence can investigate the work of the many scientists enumerated above.

Mendelian Genetics

The origin of the modern field of genetics is traced to the enunciation by the Augustinian monk Gregor Mendel, in 1865, of certain principles that seemed to characterize the mode of action of hereditary factors and the manner in which they are transmitted from one generation to the next. Mendel concentrated his attention on the inheritance in pea plants *(Pisum sativum)* of simple *dichotomous* characteristics such as flower color and size. His greatest innovation was the insistence on counting all the progeny of his plant-crossings and not being content with mere verbal summaries of the typical results. Several morphological characters of pea plants were investigated. Pea plants may differ in the color of their flowers (white-colored), the texture of their seeds (smooth-wrinkled), their size (tall-dwarf), or the color of the rudimentary seed leaves (yellow-green). Mendel found that each plant type bred pure when cross-pollinated with the same variety of plant type.

Mendel started his experiments by cross-pollinating two plant varieties.

In the first-generation hybrid offsping (later named the F_1, or first filial generation) of plants differing with respect to any one of the simple dichotomous characteristics, all plants were uniform and like one of the parents of the pair. The one trait of a pair that produced a visible effect in the F_1 generation was called *dominant* by Mendel. The parental characteristic which was not expressed was called *recessive*. When the F_1 plants were allowed to self-pollinate, plants showing the dominant trait and plants showing the recessive trait were found among the progeny (the F_2, or second filial generation) in a definite 3:1 ratio, but no plants were found which showed intermediate characteristics. It was noted that the recessive plants, when further self-pollinated, always produced offsping (the F_3, or third filial generation) which showed the recessive characteristics. One-third of the dominant plants when self-pollinated (to produce the F_3 generation) showed the dominant characteristics, but two-thirds showed both types of offspring.

To account for these results, Mendel explained them as an indication that each pair of traits depended on a single pair of hereditary factors. Mendel postulated that each parent possessed two elements which determined the particular trait, and each would transmit one of its elements to its offspring. When the parents differed with respect to a characteristic, an element contributed by the one parent might be dominant over that contributed by the other parent, and the progeny would resemble the former. However, the recessive element would not be contaminated in any way by its association with the dominant element. When the individual offspring in turn had descendants, it would pass on the element which it had received from each of its own parents to one-half of its progeny, and the nature of the recessive element passed on would not differ in any way from its nature when transmitted from the original parent. Now, when such a hybrid offspring (F_1) is self-pollinated, the male and female germ cells *(gametes)* will unite at random, and each will contribute one of the elements only. Later, Johannsen (1911) called these Mendelian hereditary factors "genes," which can exist in two (or more) alternative states, called "alleles."

Two types of conditions can be described for any given individual with respect to a particular gene pair. Given the allelic state of the gene from one parent, that from the other parent may be either the same or different. If the two allelic states are the same, the individual is described as *homozygous;* if the two allelic states are different, the individual is described as *heterozygous.* If we characterize one possible allelic state of a gene as A and the other as a (A is dominant over a), there are two homozygous states: AA and aa (e.g., the parents), and one heterozygous state, Aa (e.g., the hybrid offsping). When two hybrids are crossed, yielding an F_2 generation, each gamete produced by the hybrid will be either A or a. Thus, the following combinations can occur during fertilization: AA, Aa, and aa, and these will occur in a 1:2:1 ratio (i.e.,

AA, Aa, Aa, aa). Because of dominance, the *AA* will not be outwardly distinguishable from the *Aa,* except by examination of their offspring, so that the *observable* character will be displayed in a 3:1 ratio.

This was Mendel's *law of segregation:* Genes occur in pairs in the cells of individuals; when gametes are produced, the members of a pair separate so that each gamete receives only one member of the pair. Johannsen (1911) made the fundamental distinction between the *genotype,* which is the genetic composition of the individual (*AA, Aa,* or *aa*) and the *phenotype,* which is the observable trait that is measured (e.g., tall-dwarf, smooth-wrinkled).

Another of Mendel's laws was the *law of independent assortment.* This principle was discovered when pea plants differing in two or more characteristics were crossed. Mendel found that if a pea plant having yellow, round seeds is crossed with one having green, wrinkled seeds (let *AABB* represent the genotype of the yellow round-seeded parent, and *aabb* represent the genotype of the green wrinkled-seeded parent) the F_1 generation will contain hybrids having a phenotype uniformly showing yellow, round seeds, since these elements are dominant. The genotype of these F_1 plants may be represented as *AaBb.* In the F_2 generation resulting from the self-pollination of these plants, the genotype characteristics are combined at random. The genes for green and wrinkled are not bound together simply because these were associated in that combination in the grandparental generation. Thus, the rule of independent assortment refers to the fact that in gamete production, the selection of a particular member of one gene pair does not influence the random selection from another gene pair for inclusion in the same gamete. A double heterozygote pea plant in the F_1 generation, *AaBb,* would produce gametes *AB, Ab, aB,* and *ab* in equal quantities. The crossing of these pea plants *AaBb* X *AaBb* will yield pea plants of four phenotypes: yellow-round seeds, yellow-wrinkled seeds, green-round seeds and green-wrinkled seeds, in the ratio of 9:3:3:1.

Phenotypes are usually the result of genes working together. What does it mean when one speaks of a gene for yellow seeds? It means that if this gene is not present, the yellow pigment will not appear. The phenotype, however, is not solely determined by the genotype. Not all factors display dominance. Mendel noted that the color of the seeds having the genotype for yellow, usually a dominant characteristic, continually varied over quite a range of colors from orange to pale and bright yellow. Blending of a characteristic had occurred. Consequently, two additional factors had to be considered: (a) other genes, which interacted with the gene for yellow (i.e., modifying genes), and (b) environmental factors. The gene for yellow-pigment seeds determined the presence or absence of the yellow pigment; the modifying gene determined the quantity of yellow pigment present. Environmental factors are obviously important as well. Pea plants of the same genotype may differ substantially in phenotype because of differences in environmental determinants such as weather conditions, physical conditions of the soil, and amounts of nutrients in the soil.

Success and Failure of the Early Mendelian Laws

Mendel's work, overlooked for 34 years, was rediscovered and replicated independently in the pea and other plants by Correns (1900), DeVries (1901), and Von Tschermak (1900). Bateson and Saunders (1902), at about the same time, established that Mendel's laws applied to the inheritance of physical traits in the domestic fowl, *Gallus domesticus*. Within a few years of the rediscovery of Mendel's laws, many examples of Mendelian inheritance had been established in animals, plants, and human beings.

The chief procedure for studying genetics in man is the observation of pedigree patterns, i.e., the patterns of distribution of genetic traits (phenotypes) in related people (kindreds). The first pedigree to be interpreted in terms of Mendelian dominant inheritance was studied by Farabee (1905) and concerned the trait of brachydactyly (short fingers).

Farabee found that brachydactyly was expressed in the heterozygote as well as in the homozygote. As illustrated in Figure 4.1 (the hypothetical pedigree for Mendelian dominant inheritance): (a) marriages between heterozygotes and normal individuals produced affected (heterozygote) and nonaffected children in the approximate ratio of 1:1; (b) transmission was vertical in that the trait appeared in and passed from generation to generation; (c) the frequency of the trait was equal in both sexes; and (d) nonaffected parents did not transmit the trait to their children.

Sutton (1903) was the first to posit the theory that the physical vehicles of the hereditary material were the chromosomes which existed in the nucleus of every cell ("the chromosomal theory of heredity"). His main point was that a clear correlation could be established between Mendel's laws and the behavior of the chromosome in meiosis (the process of gamete formation). Sutton noted that: (a) chromosomes are found in pairs; and (b) the members of each pair segregate during meiosis. He thought that to understand the transmission of most inherited traits, one need understand nothing more than the transmission of whole chromosomes through meiosis and fertilization.

An early exception to the law of independent assortment was noted by Bateson and his students (Bateson, Saunders, & Punnett, 1905, 1906). When crosses were made between F_1 dihybrid (*AaBb*) individuals, the phenotypic ratio among the F_2 progeny showed a higher proportion of parental types than the expected 9:3:3:1 distribution. Also, matings between dihybrid

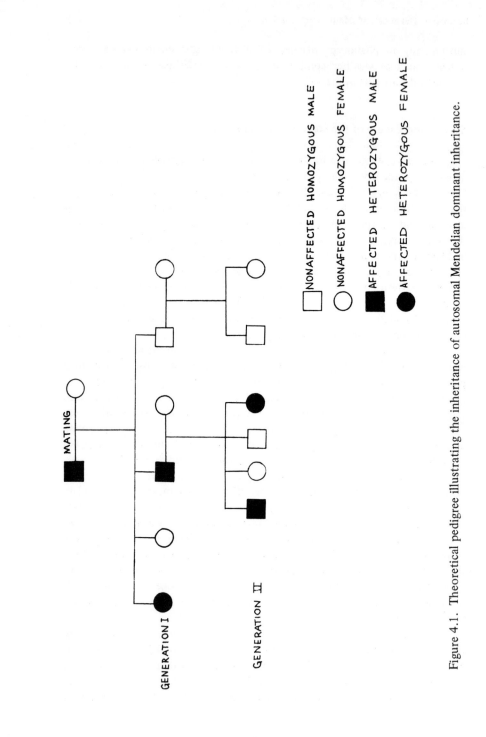

Figure 4.1. Theoretical pedigree illustrating the inheritance of autosomal Mendelian dominant inheritance.

(AaBb) and double recessive *(aabb)* individuals yielded phenotypic ratios among the progeny of approximately 7:1:1:7 rather than the expected 1:1:1:1. This phenomenon, a consequence of *linkage,* was explained by Thomas Hunt Morgan (1919), who proposed that those genes which exhibit nonrandom assortment are arranged, in a linear series, within the same chromosome. Linkage then involves the nonindependent assortment of genes which are not alleles, but which are located on the same chromosome. The law of independent assortment as explicated by Mendel applies only to genes which exist on different chromosomes.

For close to 20 years (approximately 1895-1915) a controversy raged, especially in England, between the biometricians—such as Francis Galton and Karl Pearson—and the exponents of Mendelism, such as Bateson, over the nature of inheritance in man. The traits to which the simple and basic Mendelian rules could be applied most directly were dichotomous discrete traits, whereby the individual may be unambiguously assigned to one or another group. However, the biometricians studied continuously varying characteristics such as intelligence and stature. Thus, rather than finding mutual support in each other's work, the Mendelians and the Galtonians came into acute conflict. It was difficult for the Mendelians to reconcile continuous variation with the type of qualitative, discrete difference mediated by particulate genes with which they had worked. Biometricians such as Pearson, on the other hand, supported the "blending" hypothesis, which held that many traits appeared to blend and distribute themselves in a characteristic "normal" distribution. As far as the Galtonians were concerned, there was little evidence for the discrete nomothetic categorization of traits such as studied by the Mendelians. It appeared to the former group that Mendelian genetics was an unimportant exception to the general rule of the blending of traits, and that the notions of the Mendelians applied only to rare cases of insignificant biological importance.

Mendel himself had laid the ground for the resolution of this conflict by suggesting that a particular characteristic may be due to two or three elements adding together. The work of Nilsson-Ehle (1908), and that of Emerson and East (1913) subsequently showed that if one assumed the operation of (a) a number of monogene pairs, rather than just one pair, each exerting a small and cumulative effect upon the same characteristic; (b) gene transmission in a Mendelian fashion; and (c) the random effects of environment, then the phenotypes obtained would appear to be a continuous normal distribution of characteristics typically studied by the Galtonians, rather than the dichotomous categories studied by the Mendelians. This theory of multiple factor, or quantitative, genetic inheritance was elaborately developed by Fisher (1918) and by Wright (1921). Their work presented convincing demonstrations that the biometric data collected by the Galton School could be derived from multiple factor extensions of Mendel's theory.

Another apparent exception to Mendel's laws had to do with the stability of the distributions of traits inherited in a Mendelian fashion in human populations. In the case of Mendelian dominants like brachydactyly, why does not everyone have brachydactyly? Why shouldn't a dominant trait increase in frequency and replace the recessive trait? Hardy (1908) and Weinberg (1908) deduced from Mendel's law of segregation that the relative proportions of genotypes will remain constant in a population as long as mating is random and no disturbing forces are operating. Populations should be in Hardy-Weinberg equilibrium as long as (a) mating is random, (b) no differential reproductive advantage exists for any genotype, (c) no significant migration exists into or out of the population, (d) the alleles of the locus act additively, (e) no environmental effect exists on the trait in question, and (f) mutation (an abrupt change from one allele to another) is absent.

Population Genetics (Quantitative Genetics)

While Fisher (1918), Haldane (1932), and Wright (1921) extended Mendel's theory to quantitatively varying traits in populations, Hardy (1908), a mathematician at Cambridge University, and Weinberg (1908), a physician at Stuttgart, earlier had independently laid the foundation of population genetics. "Mendelian" genetics has been most useful in understanding the nature of mental retardation syndromes resulting in *qualitative* differences between affected and nonaffected individuals, and which involve only a few genes or only a single gene. "Quantitative" genetics has been useful in understanding the nature of mental retardation syndromes resulting in *quantitative* differences in members of a population (e.g., individuals of low intellectual ability versus individuals of average intellectual ability versus individuals of high intellectual ability). Such dissimilarities are thought to involve the cumulative effects of gene dissimilarities at many loci, although the effects of such dissimilarities are not individually distinguishable.

The theories of quantitative genetics consist of the deduction of the consequences of Mendelian inheritance when extended to the properties of populations and to the simultaneous segregation of genes at many loci. The premise from which the deductions are made is that the inheritance of quantitative differences is by means of genes, and these genes are subject to the Mendelian laws of transmission and may have any of the properties known from Mendelian genetics. One major premise has to do with the notion that the expression of the genotype (as the phenotype) is modifiable by both genetic and nongenetic causes. In order to understand the whole controversy over the recent work of Arthur Jensen (1969, 1973a, 1973b) and his colleagues regarding the genetic basis of intelligence (which as earlier indicated, is not the major focus of this chapter), it is most essential that one has at least a rudimentary grasp of the principles of quantitative genetics.

Developmental Genetics

Developmental processes are subject to continuous genetic and environmental influences, making it particularly difficult to understand the long-term unfolding of a characteristic if only a single developmental period is studied in isolation. However, different genes may be maximally effective at different periods in ontogenetic development of the organism. Thus, the genes responsible for the determination of blood groupings apparently have their effect early in the development of the fetus and result in phenotypes which are highly stable throughout the life span of the individual. On the other hand, hemoglobin type apparently changes very dramatically just before the infant is born because different genes are operating before and after birth. The development of secondary sexual characteristics is another example of how genes may be maximally effective at a particular point in the life span. Again, in Huntington's chorea—Mendelian dominant (characterized by involuntary movements of the head, face, trunk, and/or one or more limbs, progressive central nervous system degeneration, psychosis, and finally death)—fewer than 5% of the cases are manifested before age 25 years, and 33% appear before age 40. In some cases, expression of Huntington's chorea does not develop until after age 70 years. A fundamental question in the area of developmental genetics has to do with the timing of gene action. What determines when a gene is to be active or inactive? Later on in this chapter we shall discuss the Jacob-Monod (1961a, 1961b) operon theory of the regulation of gene action.

The processes of growth are self-stabilizing. All developing organisms, no less than rockets, have their trajectories directed to specific end goals, or targets; and these trajectories are governed by the control systems of their genetic constitution and are powered by energy absorbed from the natural environment. When the organism is deflected from its growth trajectory by acute malnutrition or illness, a restoring force apparently develops as soon as the missing nutrients are supplied or the illness terminated, and the organism seems to "catch up" its original curve. This spurt in growth rate decreases as the organism reaches it original target, and the growth rate slows down to adjust its path onto the old trajectory once again. Tanner (1963) provided considerable empirical evidence on this "catch up" phenomenon in the growth curves of children whose physical maturation had been disturbed by malnutrition or illness. Waddington (1957) referred to this property of returning to the original growth curve, after being pushed off trajectory, as an example of "canalization" or "homeorrhesis" (the maintenance of a flowing or developing situation).

The basic elements for the development of phenotypic characteristics (Waddington, 1962) are stabilized or buffered pathways of change ("creodes"). A system with a multiplicity of genetic deteminants can be described as a point in n-dimensional space; geometrically, the creode may be viewed as a trajectory of this point through the n-dimensional space, directed toward some specified end point. Some phenotypic characteristics are well buffered (deeply canalized) from environmental or genetic changes during the course of development in their creodes, such that when deviations from the trajectory occur as the result of some disturbance, there is a tendency for the system not simply to adopt a new pathway to the old end point, but to return to the original pathway leading toward that point. Other phenotypic characteristics are in creodes which are poorly buffered (shallowly canalized), and are extremely vulnerable to genetic and environmental changes.

In plants, particularly in the development of stem and leaves, environmental influences such as temperature, moisture, and light are known to affect growth and development profoundly. The development of animals is not so strongly influenced by environmental variation within certain limits.

Closely related to the concept of "canalization" is the notion of "reaction range" (Dobzhansky, 1955; Gottesman, 1963, 1968; Gottesman & Heston, 1972). Genotypes are seen as determining a reaction range, which is construed as an indefinite but circumscribed assortment of phenotypes, each of which corresponds to one of the possible environments to which the genotypes may be exposed (see Figure 4.2). However, the ontogeny of a group's or individual's phenotypic norm, or range of reaction, is not predictable in advance.

Evidence on actual norms of reaction in man are very difficult to obtain because equivalent genotypes, as might be represented by sets of identical twins, have not in any systematic way been tested in a variety of environments. Even in animals, where equivalent genotypes can be obtained in greater numbers by inbreeding, and where better experimental control is possible, little work has been done to characterize these norms for the genotypes that occur in natural populations.

In the hypothetical example illustrated in Figure 4.2 (Gottesman, 1963; Gottesman & Heston, 1972), samples of the population with Genotype A have a relatively narrow reaction range (RR*A), which means that even in most favorable environments, the expression of the phenotype is relatively restricted. This function may be compared with individuals of Genotype D, who have relatively wide reaction range (RR*D). The phenotypic expression of a characteristic in this group is extremely sensitive to changes in environment. It follows from the reaction range concept that (a) different

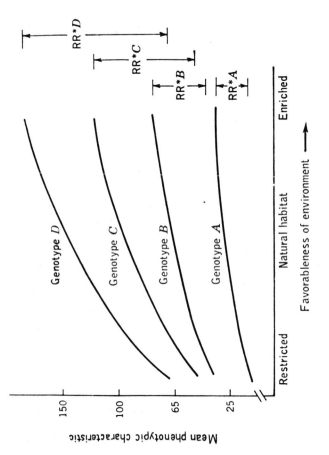

Figure 4.2. Scheme of the reaction range concept for four hypothesized genotypes. (Note: Marked deviation from the natural habitat has a low probability of occurrence. RR signifies reaction range in phenotypic characteristic.) (From "Genetic Aspects of Intelligent Behavior" by I. I. Gottesman, in *Handbook of Mental Deficiency: Psychological Theory and Research* edited by N. R. Ellis Copyright 1963 by McGraw-Hill, Inc. Used with permission of McGraw-Hill Book Co.)

genotypes may produce the same phenotypes (genocopies), (b) different phenotypes may have the same genotypes (phenocopies); and (c) each genotype has its own more or less natural habitat.

To exemplify the use of the reaction-range concept, Gottesman and Heston (1972) applied the model represented in Figure 4.2 to human height variations:

> Each curve in the figure can be construed as representing the phenotypic response of samples of individuals, homogeneous for four different levels of genetic potential for height, who have been reared in various trait-relevant environments (or niches) crudely characterized as restricted, natural habitat, and enriched. Curve Type A could represent a deviant genotype, for example, the one associated with the dominant gene for chondrodystrophic dwarfism. . . . The different environments to which such dwarfs have so far been exposed do not have much effect on their height; the mean height for 15-year-old cases (sexes combined) is only 120 cm. Curve Type B could represent samples of 13-year-old Japanese girls. In contemporary Japan they average 146.1 cm. (= "natural" habitat); 13-year-old girls measured in postwar Japan (1950) only averaged 139.9 cm (= restricted environment nutritionally); 13-year-old Japanese girls born in the United States to Japanese parents averaged 150.5 cm. (= enriched environment). The Reaction Range ($RR*B$) for the genotype represented by 13-year-old Japanese girls under the range of environments sampled would be the largest value minus the lowest, or 10.6 cm. Curve Type C would represent the response of the genotypes of 15-year-old Japanese boys measured at the same times as the girls in B; we are dealing here with sexual dimorphism and a different genotype . . . for height. Postwar boys averaged 151.1 cm; contemporary boys in Japan, 158.2 cm; and contemporary Japanese boys born in the United States, 164.5 cm. for a reaction range of 13.4 cm. all attributable to environmental variations. Curve Type D would represent 15-year-old white American boys who average 168.7 cm. (13-year-old white girls average 155.4 cm.). Examples of the same phenotype with different genotypes are provided by some data on children of Japanese-American white matings (father always white); the 15-year-old boys averaged 164.7 cm. while the 13-year-old girls averaged 151.5 cm. It appears that the hybrids matched the American-born Japanese and were about halfway between contemporary Japanese and white children (under natural habitat conditions). . . The thrust of the reaction

range concept is that both heredity and environment are important in determining trait variation but in different ways, combinations, and degrees, some of which are amenable to dissection for
some traits. (pp. 113-114)

The study of the ontogeny of a phenotypic characteristic is made even more
ambiguous because of the concept of the norm of reaction of a particular
genotype.

BEHAVIORAL-GENETIC ANALYSIS

Just as various morphological characteristics (phenotypes) of plants and
animals can be analyzed using the methods of modern genetic analysis, so the
behavior of animals and humans (which can also be viewed as phenotypes)
may be analyzed by the procedures of behavior genetics. According to
Thiessen (1972), the questions that the behavior geneticist hopes to answer
when analyzing the expression of a behavioral trait are the following:

1. Is the observed behavior influenced by variations in genotype?
2. What proportions of the measured variability of a trait are the
    result of genetic and environmental factors?
3. Given a clear-cut genetic effect, how many genes are operating?
4. What is the frequency with which the gene appears within a
    population or a species group?
5. How is the gene modified by changes in the course of develop-
    ment or by environmental contingencies?
6. What structures and physiological processes intervene between
    the genetic constitution of an organism and the ultimate expres-
    sion of behavior?
7. Does the trait have adaptive significance (i.e., reproductive
    fitness), and is it subject to natural and artificial selection
    pressures?
8. What are the phylogenetic relationships of the behavior with
    related species?

These questions tap all aspects of the interactions among the methods
and techniques of genetics (be they Mendelian, Population, or Developmental
Genetics) and the methods and techniques of psychology. Simply put, the
number of phenotypes possible for a particular measurable behavioral trait is
a function of (a) the number of genotypes available, (b) the number of
environments specified, and (c) the number of interactions between the
possible genotypes and environments.

Scott and Fuller (1963) distinguished between two methodologies in behavioral-genetic analysis, namely, the genotypic orientation and the phenotypic orientation. In genotypic orientation, the investigator is interested in tracing the relationship between the possession of a known genotypic difference in a species and the effects of this genotype on the expression of a behavior through a physiological mechanism. The investigation using the phenotypic orientation starts with the behavior patterns, which are defined as phenotypes, and works backward to find out how they are inherited. The distinctions between these two approaches are not absolute, but a matter of degree only. Consequently, we will not distinguish between the two in our following discussion of genetic behavioral relationships.

Single-Gene (Major Gene) Influences on Behavioral Phenotypes

The Japanese "waltzing" mice syndrome. Japanese "waltzing" or "dancing" mice (Gruneberg, 1952) are characterized by a peculiar syndrome of whirling in circles, head shaking, deafness, lack of rotational dizziness, and inability to balance on an edge or slanting surface. Histological examination shows that these "waltzers" suffer from defects in the vestibular and cochlear apparatus. Breeding experiments and subsequent pedigree analysis conducted by G. von Guaita (1898; see Gruneberg, 1952) and others led to the conclusion that the "waltzing" phenotype is inherited as a Mendelian recessive, as shown in Figure 4.3.

Because of the random assortment of chromosomes into gametes and their subsequent random recombination, aa X aa matings can produce only aa offspring in the F_1 generation (as shown in Figure 4.3, part 1), which can only breed true when inbred in the F_2 generation. On the other hand, aa X AA matings (as in Figure 4.3, part 2) can produce only hybrid Aa offspring in the F_1 generation. Inbreeding the Aa offsprings of the F_1 will produce the classical Mendelian genotypic ratios ($1:4aa,$ $1:2Aa,$ and $1:4AA$) in the F_2 generation. The pedigree pattern of (autosomal) recessive inheritance of the "waltzing" mouse phenotype can be characterized as follows: (a) The expected ratio of nonaffected and affected offspring is approximately 3:1 in matings between heterozygous individuals; (b) transmission is horizontal (i.e., the trait appears and then may "skip" one or more generations before it is seen again); (c) affected offspring have parents that are nonaffected; and (d) male and female offspring are equally affected.

Phenylketonuria. Garrod (1909)—strongly influenced by Bateson—interpreted the pattern of inheritance of certain human biochemical metabolic disorders (cystinuria, albinism, alkaptonuria, and pentosuria) in Mendelian recessive

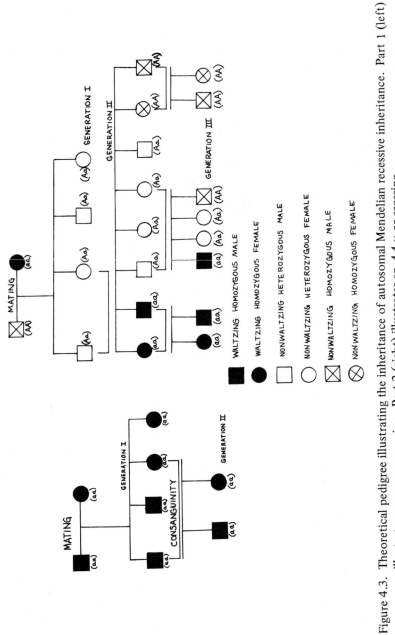

Figure 4.3. Theoretical pedigree illustrating the inheritance of autosomal Mendelian recessive inheritance. Part 1 (left) illustrates an *aa* × *aa* crossing. Part 2 (right) illustrates an *AA* × *aa* crossing.

139

terms. Garrod was the first to focus attention on the relationship between genes and human metabolic reactions, and to posit the notion of "inborn errors of metabolism." Essentially all inborn errors of metabolism are inherited as recessives, with the clinical disorder manifested only in the homozygote. Though the heterozygote usually cannot be identified, some individuals can be identified as heterozygous carriers. Perhaps the best understood of these "inborn errors of metabolism" is phenylketonuria (PKU). Phenylketonuria is typically characterized by a complex syndrome, often including mental retardation, the presence of phenylpyruvic acid in the urine, excessive phenylalanine in the blood, blue eyes, blond hair, fair skin, abnormal electroencephalogram patterns, muscular hypertonicity, micro-cephaly, hyperactive reflexes, and severe temper tantrums (Knox, 1972).

Phenylketonuria is caused by a deficiency of the liver enzyme pheny-lalanine hydroxylase, which normally converts the amino acid phenylalanine to tyrosine (Hsia, 1967; Menkes, 1967). The excessive phenylalanine is converted to phenylpyruvic acid and other metabolites of phenylpyruvic acid, which are excreted in the urine. The excessive phenylalanine also inhibits the production of 5-hydroxytryptamine (serotonin)—an important brain meta-bolite. It is believed that the observed mental retardation is the end result of a critical shortage of brain 5-hydroxytryptamine during early infancy, caused in part by the physiological lack of this metabolite at birth and in part by excessive levels of phenylalanine (Hsia, 1967). The excessive phenylalanine also restrains conversion of tyrosine to melanin, thus accounting for the low levels of pigment in the skin and hair of affected individuals (Dancis & Balis, 1955).

The absence of a critical gene may have more than one phenotypic effect. This is known as *pleiotropism* or *pleiomorphism*. There are no genes for behavior per se. As we shall see in more detail later, genes determine the presence or absence of specific enzymes or proteins, which in turn affect hormone levels, tissue sensitivities, membrane permeabilities, and other biochemical and physiological processes within the body. Behavioral varia-tions and other phenotypic manifestations of gene action are the end products of a long chain of complex biochemical events. The influences of genetic processes on behavior are always indirect.

A phenotypic trait may be highly variable within a population of affected individuals. "Expressivity" refers to the variability in phenotypic expression of a gene among individuals of a particular genotype. Theoretic-ally, the phenotypic effect of a dominant gene A should be seen in all individuals with at least one A allele, as in genotypes AA and Aa. A phenotypic trait determined by a recessive gene a should be manifested in all persons having the genotype aa. If this is true, such genotypes are said to show "complete penetrance," i.e., individuals with a particular genotype can be detected from a control group 100% of the time. This is not always true—due to the interaction of a given gene with other genetic and environmental factors, and also to the nature of given phenotypic characteristics—in which case a gene is said to have "partial or reduced penetrance."

With regard to PKU, if hair color and head size were the only phenotypic traits measured, there would be considerable overlap between phenylketonuric individuals and unaffected individuals, and the genotype would be thought to be nonpenetrating in a great number of persons. If Binet IQ scores were the phenotypic trait being assessed, the overlap between affected and nonaffected people would be less, and the genotype would be said to be nonpenetrant in a smaller number of cases. When blood plasma level of phenylalanine is the phenotype, the separation between affected and nonaffected persons is more complete, with the phenylketonuric group showing higher levels of phenylalanine. In this case, the genotype is more fully penetrant. Penetrance and nonpenetrance are sometimes functions of the preciseness of the methods of analysis.

Galactosemia. Galactosemia is due to the presence of a defective gene which prevents the individual from synthesizing the enzyme alpha-*d*-galactose-1-phosphate uridyl transferase (GPU), necessary for the metabolism of galactose, found in lactose (milk sugar).

A few days after birth, infants with galactosemia vomit, lose weight, and become jaundiced. Eventually, such children may develop cataracts and show mental retardation. The sugar galactose accumulates in the blood and is excreted in the urine. A metabolite of galactose, galactose-1-phosphate, also accumulates in the tissues. The observed phenotypic effects are apparently due to the excessive galactose-1-phosphate rather than to the galactose itself (Sidbury, 1961).

Galactosemia and phenylketonuria are but two inborn errors of metabolism associated with mental retardation. Hsia (1967) lists at least 28 more syndromes.

X-linked traits. Within the nucleus of every human cell are found 22 pairs of homologous autosomal chromosomes and a pair of sex chromosomes which are alike in the female (XX) and morphologically distinct (XY) in the male. In the Denver System of classification, the 22 pairs of autosomal chromosomes are identified by number (1 to 22) in terms of descending order of length and other morphological characteristics, and they are organized into seven groups (A to G). The systematic arrangement and general characteristics of the chromosomes of a given individual are known as a "karyotype." The X chromosome contains many genes. However, it appears that very little genetic information exists on the Y chromosome, except that its presence is essential for the expression of the male phenotype.

Some traits, such as red-green color blindness, are inherited as an X-linked recessive. That is, if a recessive allele for the trait exists on the X chromosome in a male, it cannot have its effects masked by nonexistent dominant alleles on the Y chromosome. Females can produce only X-bearing ova, whereas males can produce X- or Y-bearing sperm. Males will therefore obtain their X chromosome from their mothers, and fathers cannot transmit it to their sons. The trait (i.e., color blindness) will affect only women who are homozygous for the recessive alleles on their (XX) sex chromosomes and only men who possess the recessive allele on their single X chromosome. Women who are either heterozygous for this allele or homozygous dominant, and men who possess the dominant allele on their single X chromosome, will manifest normal color vision. Heterozygous women are carriers of the recessive allele; and if they mate with normal-visioned men, one-half of their sons will show the color-blind trait. The characteristics of X-linked recessive inheritance are illustrated in Figure 4.4.

Such mental retardation syndromes as the Lesch-Nyhan Syndrome (characterized by hyperuricemia [overproduction of uric acid], extreme self-mutilation, spasticity, and choreathetosis—due to complete deficiency of an enzyme of purine metabolism, namely, hypoxanthine-guanine phosphoribosyl transferase) and Hunter's Syndrome (characterized by dwarfism, grotesque facial appearance, joint stiffness, which is due to a defect in mucopolysaccharide metabolism) are both transmitted in an X-linked recessive fashion.

In summary, in X-linked recessive inheritance, (a) transmission does not occur from affected father to son directly, though female offspring of affected males are all carriers; (b) unaffected males do not transmit the trait to any offspring; (c) male offspring of unaffected carrier women have a 50% chance of being affected; and therefore (d) the trait is more often seen in males than in females.

Only a few traits are known to be inherited as X-linked dominants. Examples are Vitamin D-resistant rickets and a rare mental retardation syndrome, Albright's Hereditary Osteodystrophy.

The pedigree patterns of an X-linked dominant trait (see Figure 4.5) resemble autosomal dominant inheritance, except that the trait is transmitted from an affected male to all his daughters but to none of his sons.

Characteristics of X-linked dominant inheritance can be summarized as follows: (a) An affected male transmits the trait to all his daughters and to none of his sons; (b) females tend to be affected about twice as often as males; (c) an affected female transmits the disorder to half her sons and half her daughters; and (d) the heterozygous female tends to be less severely affected than the homozygous male.

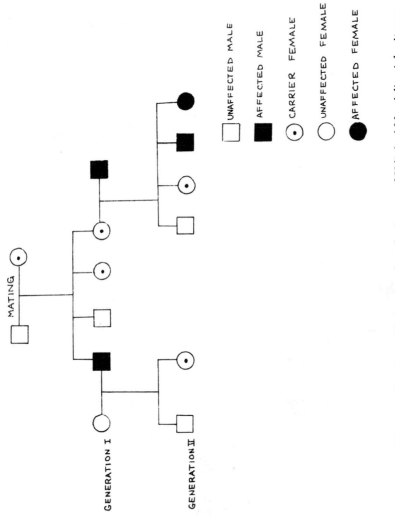

Figure 4.4. Theoretical pedigree illustrating the inheritance of X-linked Mendelian inheritance.

143

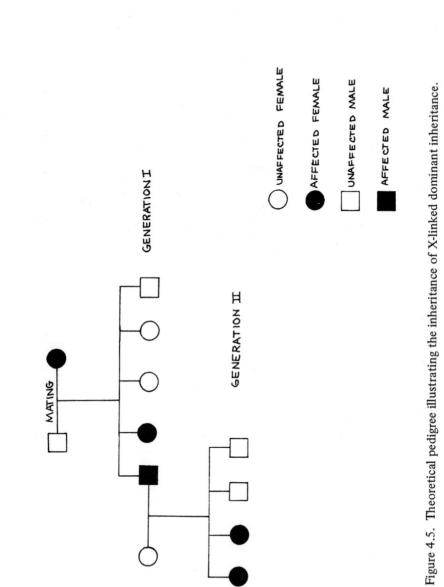

Figure 4.5. Theoretical pedigree illustrating the inheritance of X-linked dominant inheritance.

Chromosomal Abnormalities and Behavioral Phenotypes

Down's syndrome (trisomy G21 syndrome). Down's Syndrome is character-ized by mental retardation, short stature, congenital abnormalities of the heart, simian crease on the palm, and a furrowed and protuding tongue. To the general public, Down's Syndrome is probably the most well-known mental retardation syndrome.

Individuals manifesting Down's Syndrome, instead of possessing the normal complement of 22 pairs of autosomes and a pair of sex chromo-somes—for a total of 46—show an extra autosome G21, for a total of 47 chromosomes (Lejeune, Turpin, & Gautier, 1959). Individuals whose cells show one more than the basic number of a given chromosome are designated as *trisomic.* The most frequent mechanism for this condition is nondisjunc-tion or nonsegregation, i.e., a failure of the G21 chromosomes to separate during meiosis (and sometimes in mitosis). The principal factor in the Trisomy G21 Syndrome is nondisjunction during oogenesis (meiosis). When this occurs, both chromosomes of the G21 pair go to the same daughter cell, with the result that one of the gametes will have the normal complement of chromosomes plus one extra, whereas the other gametes will have one less than the normal complement. A zygote with 47 chromosomes resulting in trisomy of G21 develops when an abnormal ovum (24 chromosomes in-cluding an extra G21) is fertilized by a normal sperm (23 chromosomes).

The nondisjunction of the G21 chromosome may sometimes occur during the early mitosis of a fertilized normal zygote. Down's Syndrome may then also result, with the affected individual showing two or more cell lines with different karyotypes, one normal and the other trisomic for chromo-some G21. This condition is known as *mosaicism.*

Certain individuals with Down's Syndrome display a normal number of chromosomes but altered karyotypes. A close examination of that karyotype reveals two normal chromosomes G21, one normal chromosome D15, and an unpaired large chromosome that is interpreted as resulting from a fusion of at least part of a chromosome 21 with a full chromosome 15 due to a *translocation* (an exchange of parts between two nonhomologous chromo-somes). In cases of Down's Syndrome due to such 15/21 translocation, just as in those due to nondisjunction, the genetic material of chromosome 21 is present in triple dosage. With the translocation type of Down's Syndrome, one parent (the carrier), though phenotypically normal, usually shows a karyotype of only 45 chromosomes, including one chromosome G21, one chromosome D15, and a large translocation 15/21 chromosome. Thus, the offspring zygote resulting from the union of a normal gamete from the noncarrier parent and an abnormal gamete from the carrier parent (who contributed both a G21 chromosome and a 15/21 translocation chromosome) has only 46 chromosomes. However, since there is a triple dosage of genetic material from the G21 chromosome, Down's Syndrome results.

Most males afflicted by Down's Syndrome are infertile; but females may have offspring that are phenotypically normal. Females affected with ordinary Trisomy 21 (Down's) Syndrome will apparently produce two types of ova in equal frequency, those that have one chromosome 21 and those that have two chromosomes 21. In that case, after fertilization with a normal sperm, the former ovum will develop into a normal offspring while the latter ovum will develop into an offspring afflicted with Down's Syndrome. That this mechanism is essentially correct has been supported by Penrose and Smith (1966), who showed that both normal offspring and those with Down's Syndrome have been observed from mothers with Down's Syndrome in about equal frequency. Hanhart, Delhanty, and Penrose (1961) also presented data supporting this mechanism. They studied the karyotypes of an affected mother and her affected daughter, and both showed regular Trisomy G21.

There are many other examples of autosomal chromosomal aberrations which are associated with mental retardation. They include Trisomy E18 Syndrome or Edward's Syndrome (Edwards, Harnden, Cameron, Crosse, & Wolff, 1960) and Trisomy D12 Syndrome or Patau's Syndrome (Patau, Smith, Therman, Inhorn, & Wagner, 1960). Following are some examples of sex chromosome abnormalities which are sometimes accompanied by mental retardation.

Klinefelter's syndrome. Klinefelter, Reifenstein, and Albright (1942) described men who had small testes, sparse body hair, were usually long-legged, were infertile, and showed elevated urinary gonadotrophins and female-like breast development (gynecomastia). Barr and Bertram (1949) found that there was a correlation between the sex of the organism and the presence or absence of sex chromatin (the Barr body) in the interphase nuclei of somatic cells. The presence of this body (chromatin positive) was usually associated with the female phenotype, and its absence (chromatin negative) was usually associated with the male phenotype. It soon became apparent that the presence or absence of a Barr body was not determined by whether the individual appeared to be phenotypically female or male, but rather by the number of X chromosomes present. The maximum number of Barr bodies in a given interphase nucleus is one less than the number of X chromosomes. Bradbury, Burge, and Boccabella (1956), as well as Plunkett and Barr (1956), showed that individuals manifesting Klinefelter's Syndrome were chromatin positive, thus indicating the presence of two X chromosomes. Jacobs and Strong (1959), studying the karyotypes of individuals with Klinefelter's Syndrome, showed the presence of two X chromosomes in addition to a single Y chromosome (47/XXY). Three-quarters of the cases of Klinefelter's Syndrome are of the 47/XXY variety (Court-Brown, Harnden, Jacobs, Maclean, & Mantle, 1964). However, cases are known where even more than two X chromosomes occur in the presence of a Y chromosome. Thus, it is possible to find 48/XXXY (Barr, Shaver, Carr, & Plunkett, 1959), and 49/XXXXY (Fraccaro & Lindsten, 1960) varieties.

Those afflicted with Klinefelter's Syndrome are not necessarily mentally retarded, and may have normal and even superior levels of measured intelligence. Individuals so affected are reported by Stanley Walzer, a psychiatrist at Harvard Medical School, to suffer from speech and language difficulties, and they may become handicapped by a significant reading deficit (Culliton, 1974). It appears that the greater the number of X chromosomes present, the more probable and the more severe the mental retardation. This will be touched upon again below.

The principal mechanism by which Klinfelter's Syndrome is believed to occur is the meiotic nondisjunction of the sex chromosomes. A 47/XXY condition could be produced by the union of an abnormal sperm (XY) with a normal egg (X), but more often is the result of union of an abnormal egg (XX) with a normal sperm (Y). Nondisjunction in early mitosis may also account for the syndrome.

Turner's syndrome (gonadal dysgenesis). Turner (1938) described a syndrome in women characterized by short stature, webbed neck, sterility, infantile development of the external genitalia and accessory sex structures, infantile ovaries, coarctation of the aorta, widely spaced nipples, and sometimes mental retardation. Such individuals were chromatin negative and revealed a karyotype of 45 chromosomes and a single X chromosome (X0) (Barr, 1966). One mechanism of the X0 Syndrome is probably meiotic nondisjunction of the sex chromosomes in either the male or female parent (Crispens, 1971; McKusick, 1964). But the most probable mechanism of Turner's Syndrome is postzygotic mitotic nondisjunction. The likelihood of this mechanism is supported by the high frequency of observed XX/X0 mosaicism (Lindsten, 1963). Monosomy for the X chromosome is in most cases not associated with any impairment of intelligence, though low borderline levels of intelligence may occur in 10% of the cases. This is true for cases of XX/X0 mosaicism as well.

Jacobs' syndrome. Jacobs, Brunton, Melville, Brittain, and McClemont (1965) conducted a survey of 197 mentally retarded males who had violent, dangerous, or criminal propensities and were in a maximum security prison hospital in Scotland. They found 7 of the 197 subjects (3.5%) to have an XYY karyotype and to be unusually tall (mean height of 73.1 inches versus mean heights of men with normal XY karyotype of 67.0 inches). Their findings suggested that the presence of the extra Y chromosome may relate to the degree of mental retardation and to the aggressive characteristics of these residents.

The prevalence of the extra Y chromosome in the population at large is unknown; however, in a heterogeneous sample of 9,327 normal adult males, nine (0.1%) showed the 47/XYY karyotype (Price & Jacobs, 1970). The incidence of this karyotype might be slightly higher (0.1 to 0.2%) among newborn males (Hook, 1973; Shah, 1970).

Many studies have been undertaken to determine if there is an association between the presence of an extra Y chromosome and violent aggressive behavior in males. Usually, the karyotypes of unusually tall males (73.2 inches) with violent behavior residing in penal institutions or institutions for retarded or severely disturbed persons were sampled. In all these studies, the possibility of sampling bias is high, and all data have to be interpreted cautiously. As summarized by Shah (1970), 103 (1.9%) of 5,342 violent males sampled possessed an extra Y chromosome, which is 10 to 20 times the incidence found among newborn infants or in a heterogeneous sample of normal male adults.

It does not absolutely follow that if a male is born with a 47/XYY karyotype he will become a menace to society; however, it seems possible that in the right kind of environment, antisocial behavior may develop with that karyotype. It remains to be scientifically determined as to exactly what kind of environment may elicit antisocial behavior in these cases. Individuals with Jacobs' Syndrome are usually borderline normal in intelligence and show a high frequency of abnormal eletroencephalographic recordings, along with a high incidence of epileptiform conditions.

Sex chromosome abnormalities and intelligence. Vandenberg (1971) put together evidence suggesting that psychometric intelligence decreases as the number of X chromosomes in the karyotype increases. This relationship is outlined in Table 4.1.

Money (1964, 1968) showed that individuals with Turner's Syndrome manifest serious deficiencies in spatial as well as arithmetic abilities. He also reported that the measured intelligence of individuals with Turner's and Klinefelter's syndromes is distributed normally. Since 1968, Stanley Walzer, a psychiatrist, and Park Gerald, a geneticist, both at Harvard Medical School, have been screening all male infants born in the Harvard-affiliated Boston

Table 4.1

Mean Intelligence Scores of Individuals Varying in Sex Chromosome Karyotypes

Number of Y Chromosomes	Number of X Chromosomes					
	0	X	XX	XXX	XXXX	XXXXX
0	Nonviable	100	100	51	40	Untestable
Y	Nonviable	100	84	52	35	Unavailable
YY	Nonviable	76	58	48	Unavailable	Unavailable
YYY	Nonviable	80	├———————— Unavailable ————————┤			

Hospital for Women. This study was undertaken to gather information about the frequency of Jacobs' and Klinefelter's syndromes in the general population and to see whether there was any association between these chromosomal abnormalities and antisocial behavior. Beckwith, a Harvard microbiologist, and his colleagues, together with their group ("Science for People") consider these studies unethical. They recently took formal action to close down Walzer and Gerald's investigations (B.J.C., 1974). The ethical issues raised by Beckwith with regard to this and other studies in human genetics will be discussed in greater detail later.

CURRENT TRENDS AND FUTURE DIRECTIONS FOR THE AMELIORATION OF GENETIC DYSFUNCTIONS

Models of Control of Gene Activity

Many years of work led to the conclusion that the basic mechanism of gene action operated through the production or the control of enzymes or proteins. Proteins or enzymes provide for the development and organization of all tissues and organ systems, and for all metabolic and biochemical activity in the body. The pioneering work of Beadle and Tatum (Beadle, 1945; Beadle & Tatum, 1941) led to the formulation of the one-gene/one-enzyme principle. In recent years, this principle has been redefined to the one-cistron/one-polypeptide concept (Benzer, 1962). Genes not only control protein synthesis, they control the function of other genes.

Avery, MacLeod, and McCarthy (1944) were the first to provide direct evidence for the genetic role of deoxyribonucleic acid (DNA) in the cell nucleus. Many years of research confirmed that, chemically, the gene is DNA (Watson & Crick, 1953a, 1953b). According to the Watson-Crick model, a DNA molecule consists structurally of two long polynucleotides. These comprise a linear sequence of nucleotides, each composed of a pentose sugar (deoxyribose), a simple phosphorus compound (phosphoric acid), and a nitrogenous base (pyrimidines-cytosine [C] or thymine [T] and purines-adenine [A] or guanine [G]). Two polynucleotide chains are coiled around a common axis to form the double helix of DNA, the backbone of each consisting of a regular alternation of the phosphate and sugar groups. Attached to the sugar group, and projecting inward, is one of the nitrogenous bases. Chemical bonds between the bases of each chain hold the double helix together—with a pyrimidine base of one chain always paired with a purine base of the other, such that adenine always pairs with thymine, and guanine with cytosine.

A gene, or a cistron, is the smallest segment of the sequences of nucleotides of DNA, which is capable of coding for a polypeptide and may have a significant effect on the phenotype. The precise sequence of base pairs in a particular gene carries (in this coded form) a specific piece of genetic information. Replication of the DNA occurs by the unwinding and separation of the nucleotide chains, with each chain acting as a template for the synthesis of a new strand. Nucleotide precursors (deoxyribonucleotide triphosphates) fall into position according to base-pairing rules, as mentioned above, so that two precise replicas are produced from one molecule, each of the two with exactly the same sequence of base pairs as the original.

A gene mutation can be viewed as the result of an event which alters the base-pair sequences somewhere along either polynucleotide chain.

Many years of work led to the conclusion that ribonucleic acid (RNA) was involved in the synthesis of proteins in human cells. RNA is a single polynucleotide strand similar to a strand of DNA except that in RNA the sugar is ribose and the pyrimidine bases are uracil and cytosine. Proteins are complex polymers built from polypeptide chains constructed from sequences of amino acids. Protein synthesis occurs primarily in the cytoplasm of the cell (on the ribosome), which consists of protein and ribosomal RNA. Most RNA is synthesized in the nucleus, from where it migrates to the cytoplasm. How is the information in the DNA molecule in the nucleus transmitted to the cytoplasm? The answer is *by way of RNA*. A structural gene is one whose sequence of bases specifies the sequence of amino acids in a protein or polypeptide. Information is transcribed from the sequences of the bases in the DNA molecule as a sequence of bases in an RNA molecule, as described by Nirenberg (1963) and others.

The first step in RNA synthesis involves the separation of the two polynucleotide chains of the DNA so that one of them may serve as a template for the synthesis from available ribonucleotides of a complementary RNA chain. In this process, the same base-pairing rules apply as in DNA except that uracil pairs with adenine for RNA. Thus is formed a strand of RNA carrying the same genetic information as the DNA strand, but the former is coded in a complementary base sequence. This RNA strand (known as "messenger" RNA, or mRNA) then separates from the DNA and passes out of the cell nucleus to the ribosomes. The strands of mRNA attach to the ribosomes and form templates for the formation of polypeptide chains. The transfer of information from RNA to the polypeptide is known as "translation." Transfer RNA (tRNA) transports the amino acids to the mRNA template. It has been demonstrated that triplet sequences of bases in the RNA, which are complementary to sequences in DNA strands, specify an amino acid. Each tRNA strand is specific for a particular amino acid which can be attached to one end of the tRNA molecule, and each contains within its polynucleotide sequence a characteristic base triplet complementary to a base triplet in mRNA which carries codes for that amino acid. The attached amino acid can thus be placed in the correct position for the synthesis of the polypeptide chain defined by the coded sequence of the mRNA which has been transcribed from a particular chain in DNA (i.e., "gene").

A key feature of the processes leading to polypeptide synthesis is that each amino acid in the sequence is designated by a trinucleotide or base triplet in DNA, mRNA, and tRNA. The triplet in mRNA is complementary to that in DNA and also to that in tRNA so that, although the actual bases differ, the same amino acid is specified. For example, three adenines in a row on the DNA molecule (AAA) will be transcribed in mRNA as three uracils (UUU) and translated in tRNA as (AAA). When on the ribosome, this mRNA triplet will attract tRNA with the triplet sequence (AAA). The inherited information coded in the genes can be regarded as a blueprint which determines the structure and regulates the production of all the enzymes and proteins which each human being produces.

How the genes are regulated is far from clear in multicellular organisms. Some hints on these complex processes, at least in microorganisms, have been proposed by Jacob and Monod (1961a, 1961b) in their Operon Model. They proposed that genes could be divided into three types: (a) *structural genes,* which determine the primary amino acid sequence of proteins; (b) *operator genes,* which control the active state of the structural genes; and (c) *repressor genes,* which control the active state of the operator genes.

Operator genes are viewed as being physically very close to one or more structural genes, and together they form an operon. The operon unit in the process of transcription functions to produce mRNA. The basic hypothesis is that the state of the operator, and hence the activity of the associated structural genes, is controlled by a repressor substance (most often a protein) which is the product of a regulator gene. Regulator genes are controlled by cytoplasmic elements, and so are open to environmental control. The repressor protein may bind with the operator and repress structural gene activity. The repressor protein, however, may bind with small molecules (inducers), which do not allow the repressor protein to bind with the operator, thus allowing transcription to occur. If the inducers are absent, the structural genes will be repressed. If the inducers are present, the structural genes will not be repressed. In summary, presence of an inducer turns an operon on, indirectly, and its absence turns an operon off. It is clear that the changes in gene function over the course of development of an organism are probably due to an operon type of system, but the mechanisms are not yet clearly defined in mammalian systems.

Mutation of a structural gene will usually cause a change in the chemical structure of a specific protein, and often in its conformation. Mutation of a regulator gene would probably affect the rates of synthesis of all the proteins determined by the structural genes in the operons it controls, but would not alter their structures. Mutations of the operator genes may result in continuous repression or activation of the structured genes, irrespective of the state of the repressor protein.

Prospects for Genetic Intervention in Man

The spectacular advances in man's understanding of the molecular biology of the gene has not been hidden away from the public in scientific journals. It has been given much publicity in the lay press (e.g., Ausubel, Beckwith, & Janssen, 1974; *Newsday* (Long Island), 1973; *New York Times,* 1968; *Newsweek,* 1974), and it has given rise to much soul searching by some scientists (e.g., Cohen, 1975; B. D. Davis, 1970; Fox & Littlefield, 1971; Friedmann & Roblin, 1972; Lederberg, 1967; Neufeld & Sweeley, 1972; Nirenberg, 1967) as to possible abuses and dangers of interfering directly with man's genetic makeup.

During the past few years, techniques have been worked out for introducing functional genes into mammalian cells by means of animal viruses (Munyon, Kraiselbrud, Davis, & Mann, 1971; Quasba & Aposhian, 1971), bacterial viruses (Merril, Geier, & Petricciani, 1971), and cell fusion techniques (Schwartz, Cook, & Harris, 1971).

Munyon and his group infected mouse cells that lacked a particular enzyme (thymidine kinase) with the animal virus herpes simplex, which apparently introduced the gene for the missing enzyme into the mouse cells. These cells then produced the enzyme specified by this gene, and the new gene seemed to be replicated as the cells divided (i.e., the change was inherited).

Aposhian has proposed that pseudovirions (made up of a normal virus' protein coat) which have enclosed manufactured DNA could be used to deliver new genes into another cell, and that these genes could function and be replicated in the cell. Quasba and Aposhian (1971) constructed a pseudo virion out of the protein coat of the animal virus polyoma containing labeled mouse DNA, and they found that their pseudo virion could infect and deliver the labeled mouse DNA into human cells in vitro.

Bacterial viruses (bacteriophages) consist of a protein shell made up of a polyhedral head, a tail, and a DNA core. Bacteriophages attach themselves tail first to a sensitive bacterium and release only their DNA core into the cell (in contrast to animal viruses, which penetrate cells intact). The DNA of temperate lambda phages becomes incorporated into the bacterial chromosomes, where it persists as a prophage. After a while, the prophages are released into the bacteria, the viral nucleic acids and protein coats are replicated, and new bacteriophages are released into the environment, with the bacterial cells destroyed in the process. Sometimes a portion of the bacterial chromosome may accidently be incorporated into the DNA core of the phage. Zinder and Lederberg (1952) discovered the phenomenon of transduction, a process by which genetic material from one bacterial cell could be carried by a phage (a transducing phage) into another bacterial cell. Following infection, the new host may show characteristics of the old infected bacteria.

Merril, Geier, and Petricciani (1971) used a bacterial virus, lambda phage, which contained the galactose operon obtained from the bacterium *Escherischia coli.* The galactose operon is the set of genes that code for the enzymes which convert galactose to glucose. Merrill et al. (1971) attempted to transfer this operon into fibroblast cells cultured from the skin of a person with galactosemia. The operon was successfully transferred into these cells, and the cells made the GPU transferase enzyme. Thus, lambda bacteriophage DNA can enter human cells and, once there, some of its genes can be replicated, transcribed, and translated.

Cell fusion techniques are yet another way to transfer genes into mammalian cells. When cells are fused or when another nucleus is transplanted into a cell, the dividing time of the multinucleate cell is determined by the nucleus closest to division. This results in the condensation and pulveration of the slower nucleus and a possible incorporation of some of its genes in the foster nucleus. Schwartz, Cook, and Harris (1971) fused chick red-blood cells, which carried the gene for the enzyme inosinic acid pyrophosphorylase, with mouse cells deficient in this enzyme. The chick nuclei were pulverized, with the result that the daughter cells having the mouse nuclei gained the ability to synthesize the missing enzyme. Thus, the chick gene for inosinic acid pyrophosphorylase was replicated and remained functional in the mouse cells. Promising also are techniques which involve chromosomal transfers from bacteria to other bacteria and transfer of chromosomes from toads into bacteria *(Newsweek,* 1974).

Gene therapy. Some researchers think that it is only a matter of time before many of the recessive monogenetic defects of inborn errors of metabolism will be corrected by the addition of the missing operons, using some of the techniques discussed above (B.D. Davis, 1970; Fox & Littlefield, 1971; Friedmann & Roblin, 1972; Nirenberg, 1967). Nevertheless, a number of problems still remain. For example, many human genes are active only in a small number of the cells of the body. Thus, in PKU, it is thought that the cells of the liver lack the enzyme phenylalanine hydroxylase. How is one to deliver the exogeneous operon to the appropriate target organ? How can we ensure that the correct amount of enzymes will be made from the foreign genes? Concentrations of cellular enzymes are so well regulated that neither too much nor too little is made. Will the introduction of exogeneous DNA throw the whole cellular system out of balance, causing greater harm to the recipient?

Most scientists (e.g., Fox & Littlefield, 1971; Friedmann & Roblin, 1972) agree that years of work are still necessary to evaluate the potential side effects or vaunted benefits of such gene therapeutic techniques as replacing defective DNA before these techniques would be used on human patients. However, the desperate nature of the human situation may force some scientists to use therapeutic procedures that others may consider as potentially dangerous. For example, West German scientists *(New York Times,* 1970) injected children suffering from hyperargininemia (a high concentration of the amino acid arginine in the blood and usually associated with mental retardation due to a hereditary deficiency of the enzyme arginase) with Shope Papilloma Virus, a potential cancer-inducing virus. It was hoped that this virus could pass its operon for arginase to the suffering children. Are the risks associated with gene therapy—which may be associated with irreversible and heritable changes in an individual's biological function-ing—equal or superior to the benefits which may be gained by the individual, especially in an area of research as full of unknowns as is manipulation of intracellular DNA? Hyperargininemia is a progressively deteriorating disease that is not known to respond to any therapy. Are high-risk treatments justified in such life-threatening situations? Realistically, each case must be handled individually, with the best interests of the patient always considered primary.

How can gene therapy in humans be controlled so as to avoid potential abuses? For one thing, independent peer review of a potentially high-risk procedure may be attempted. Friedmann and Roblin (1972) feel that all attempts at gene therapy in human patients should be stopped now because of our present lack of understanding; but most scientists are agreed that research in this area still should continue. Such manipulations of the somatic cells of single individuals (or what Lederberg [1967] has called "euphenics," the influencing of specific genes after development has begun in somatic cells) are far less frightening to many than is the systematic alteration of the DNA of the germ cells themselves through eugenics (a type of programmed evolution of populations of human beings). In any case, extensions of the technology that now exist are unlikely to deal with traits such as "intelligence," "motivation," or "personality"—which are probably the result of many genes working together (polygenes). It is unlikely as well that genetically dominant disorders, or disorders resulting from chromosomal aberrations such as Trisomy G21, can be effectively handled unless scientists can surgically remove extra chromosomes or replace dominant cistrons with recessive ones.

Cloning. Extremely frightening to many individuals are the suggestions that identical copies of humans can be produced through asexual reproduction by a process known as "cloning," in much the same way that plant and animal cells are cultivated. All differentiated somatic cells of an animal contain in their nuclei the complete set of genes which could be used for copying the whole organism. In different cells, different subsets of genes are active, and if it should become possible to reverse the regulatory mechanism responsible for this differentiation, any cell could be used to start an embryo. The individual could then be developed in the uterus of a foster mother or in a test tube, and it would be an exact genetic copy of the single parent. Asexual reproduction could thus be used to produce individuals of strictly predictable genetic endowment, practically on an assembly-line basis, without any theoretical limit to the number of clones produced.

Cloning of cells of known genetic structure opens the door to the preservation of genetic makeups of traits which are highly desirable at given times in given environments. At present, this type of cloning has not been achieved with mammals. However, some form of cloning has been carried out with animals. For example, it is now possible to transfer, by microsurgery or by cell fusion, a nucleus into the cytoplasm of a different kind of cell in the same species. In one study, the nucleus of a frog egg was replaced by a nucleus from an intestinal cell of another frog, and subsequent development of the hybrid cell resulted in a genetic replica of a donor frog (Briggs & King, 1959). Also, Mintz (1964) developed a technique of separating the relatively undifferentiated cells of an early mouse embryo. Each of these cells can be used to start a new embryo, with the result that a large set of clones of undetermined genetic structure can be produced.

Cloning of championship livestock of known genetic structure has tremendous incentive value for ranchers. Preservation of the genetic structures of individuals who are especially gifted in the arts and sciences may yield tremendous benefits for society. Yet, who is to decide what traits are desirable and worthy of perpetuation and what traits should be discarded? Will a totalitarian society like the one described by Aldous Huxley (1969) in his novel, *Brave New World,* use cloning techniques to create classes of "alphas, betas, and deltas" so as to enslave its population genetically for the sake of social stability?

A necessary step toward the cloning of humans would be the perfection of techniques of extrauterine fertilization and the development of a technology of reimplanting the developing embryo into a natural or artificial uterus. Apparently, some such technology is available since three test-tube infants *(Minneapolis Tribune,* 1974a) have reportedly been born in Europe within the recent past. In the latter report, a Dr. Douglas Bevis is said to have told the British Medical Association that eggs were removed from the mothers' ovaries and fertilized in a test tube with sperm obtained from the fathers. The fertilized eggs were then put back in the given mother's womb—after growing in the lab for a week—in an attempt to allow these mothers (whose fallopian tubes were blocked) to bear children. However, Bevis *(Minneapolis Tribune,* 1974b) was unable to substantiate any of his claims, and he announced soon after *(Milwaukee Journal,* 1974b) that he was sickened by the publicity given his announcement and that he was giving up research in the field.

Did he fear that admitting such techniques were possible would lead to curtailment in the funding of further research, due to ensuing societal panic over the possible abuses of such a technology? Other events make it appear that this indeed may have been the case. A report written by a panel of scientists of the National Academy of Sciences in September 1972 *(Milwaukee Journal,* 1974c), on the medical, social, and ethical implications of fertilizing human eggs in test tubes, was deemed by a reviewing panel of scientists from the Academy as being too controversial to be published. Publishing the report, according to this latter panel, would make it appear to many as if the National Academy of Sciences approved of research of this nature. Britain's Medical Research Council *(Milwaukee Journal,* 1974d) in response, one assumes, to the controversy over Bevis' claims, decided that no more grants will be given for test-tube baby research until there is solid evidence that there is no risk of abnormal births from such techniques. Nevertheless, some scientists agree (Lederberg, 1967; Watson, 1971) that human clonal propagation and chromosomal manipulations will be possible within the next 20 to 50 years, long before eugenic manipulation of the germ plasma may be possible.

Will society be prepared for the awesome power that scientists will give it for controlling the biological destiny of the individual and the species? Information accumulates far faster than humanity can learn how to use the knowledge wisely. Human beings may be able to program their own cells long before they will be able to assess adequately the long-term consequences of such alterations, long before they will be able to formulate goals, and long before they can resolve the ethical and moral problems which will be raised. The greatest concern of all scientists is that knowledge should be freely available so that decisions can be made adequately—knowledge not for the collective decisions of a handful of professional policymakers, but knowledge that can maximize the role of the individual decision-making power of ordinary men.

Treatment of Developmental Retardation in Man: Inborn Errors of Metabolism

Inborn errors of metabolism are usually due to some recessively inherited defects which result in deficiencies of certain specific gene products (typically an enzyme or hormone) with consequent blockage of the enzymatic conversion of a given metabolite (A). Normally, the conversion process goes through a series of intermediate products (B, C, D, E . . .) until the end product *(N)* is synthesized (A, B, C, D, E, . . . *N)*. Each conversion of a metabolite is under the control of a specific enzyme, which itself is under gene control. If, for example, the biochemical step involved in converting C to D is blocked because of the lack of the enzyme controlling this reaction, compounds D, E, and *N* will not be produced; and any biochemical reactions involving these compounds will also be blocked and will not occur. Thus, compound *C* and its metabolites may accumulate in toxic quantities unless alternative pathways are utilized.

The direct manipulation of the gene (if this is ever attained) is far in the future. However, certain techniques are presently available (Stanbury, Wyngarden, & Fredrickson, 1972) for ameliorating or preventing untoward effects of blocked enzymatic conversion. For example, the end product *N* may be supplied, as in the treatment of metabolic cretinism by supplying exogeneous thyroxine early enough. Another approach is that of limiting, by means of diet therapies—as with PKU—the intake of a precursor which may undergo toxic accumulation. Still other techniques include the use of metabolic inhibitors, or the use of drugs which will deplete the body of a storage substance having toxic properties.

Limiting the dietary intake of the precursors phenylalanine and lactose in the cases of phenylketonuria and galactosemia, respectively, is apparently effective in preventing and treating these genetic diseases. Using the metabolic inhibitor allopurinol to block the action of the enzyme xanthine oxidase has reduced the accumulation of uric acid associated with the Lesch-Nyhan Syndrome. However, the mental retardation associated with this syndrome has not been reversed by this treatment. The massive toxic accumulation of copper associated with Wilson's disease can be depleted by the use of British antilewisite or penicillamine.

Both the induction of metabolizing enzymes and the direct supplying of the blocked enzyme have been successful in certain cases. Further into the future will be actual transplants of organs which will manufacture the critically blocked enzymes. Such an approach has already been used with some reported success in Wilson's disease, as reported by Begab (1974).

Prevention of Developmental Retardation in Man: Limiting the Frequency of Undesirable Genes

Genetic counseling. As regards genetic disorders involving inborn errors of metabolism or chromosomal abnormalities, care should be taken to limit any consanguinous marriages in families afflictéd with these conditions. Another preventive approach is the use of genetic counseling with those who desire offspring in such families. Genetic counseling consists of advising parents or prospective parents of the statistical risks of giving birth to defective children and of alternative ways for satisfying parenthood needs (Begab, 1974). How is genetic counseling to be performed? How are decisions to be made? What should be the counselor's style? These questions are subjective and full of raw and heartfelt emotion (Ausubel, Beckwith, & Janssen, 1974; Beckwith, Elseviers, Gorini, Mandansky, & Csonka, 1975; Carter, 1970; Shaw, 1974; Williams, 1974). The legal-ethical aspects of genetic counseling will be discussed in another section.

Prenatal diagnosis. How does one identify pregnancies that may be at risk? The new techniques of prenatal diagnosis of genetic disease—such a fetoscopy, fetalbiopsy, and particularly amniocentesis—are especially useful (Begab, 1974; Engel, 1972; Friedmann, 1971; Hill & Puck, 1973). The developing fetus within the amniotic cavity is bathed in the amniotic fluid. Suspended in the fluid are viable cells shed from the fetal skin and respiratory tract. Amniocentesis is the surgical process of inserting a sterile needle into the amniotic cavity and withdrawing a small amount of the fluid. By examining the fluid and the cells, one can (in some cases) determine if the growing fetus will develop certain genetic diseases. For example, examining the fetal cells after culturing them will reveal the presence of any chromosomal aberrations such as Trisomy G21.

One of the clearest indications for amniocentesis is the age of the mother. The incidence of gross chromosomal aberration in children born to women over 35 years old is 1 to 2% (Lubs & Ruddle, 1970). Though women over the age of 35 years account for no more than 13% of all pregnancies, they produce 50% of infants afflicted with Down's Syndrome. If selective therapeutic abortion were performed in these cases, the rate of occurrence of this disease would be reduced by as much as 50%. Down's Syndrome represents the largest single category of organic syndromes in mental retardation. The prevention of this disorder could result in much economic benefit to society, as well as in the avoidance of human tragedy (Begab, 1974). It has been estimated that 4,000 infants with Trisomy G21 are born every year in the United States, with the lifetime cost of care of these individuals amounting to at least $1 billion in 1971 (Friedmann, 1971).

Examination of fetal cells (fetal biopsy) for evidence of specific enzyme activity can be done to determine whether or not the fetus has a defective gene. As a case in point, the Lesch-Nyhan Syndrome, a sex-linked disorder—characterized by severe mental retardation in males, involuntary writhing movements (choreoathetosis), and compulsive self-mutilation of the lips and fingertips—is caused by a deficiency in the enzyme hypoxanthine-guanine phosphoribosyl transferase (HGPRT). In examining for this syndrome, fetal cells are cultured and exposed to radioactive hypoxanthine. Normal cells will readily incorporate these metabolites, but HGPRT-deficient cells cannot. When these cells are exposed to X-ray films, the normal cells will show traces of radioactivity, the HGPRT-deficient cells will not. Again, selective therapeutic abortion may be performed if desired by the parents.

A particularly devastating and so far untreatable autosomal recessive genetic disorder is Tay-Sachs disease, which causes blindness, severe retardation, and early death—usually before 3 or 4 years of age. Tay-Sachs disease is due to a deficiency of the enzyme acetylhexosaminidase-A (Okada & O'Brien, 1969), which normally metabolizes a lipid-polysaccharide complex called "GM_2" ganglioside. Absence of the enzyme leads to massive cerebral ganglioside storage. O'Brien, Okada, Fillerup, Veath, Adornato, Brenner, and Lenz (1971) determined many methods of measuring hexosaminidase-A activity in the amniotic fluid and in cultured amniotic cells of affected infants.

More than 40 genetic disorders (Friedmann, 1971; McClearn & DeFries, 1973) can be detected *in utero,* using various biochemical and cytological techniques. Many authorities have suggested that prenatal genetic screening through amniocentesis become a routine part of prenatal care in an attempt to reduce or eliminate the occurrence of genetic diseases that impose a devastating emotional burden on parents and often cause suffering and death in children.

In addition to the mother's age as a variable, a common indicator for the use of amniocentesis is the previous birth of a child with a genetic disease, so-called "retrospective detection." In individuals who have had an afflicted offspring, the probability of having another such child is approximately 1:4 in Mendelian recessive disorders. In such high-risk cases, the technique of amniocentesis will allow parents to lessen the chance of having yet another damaged child at relatively little risk to the mother or developing fetus.

If heterozygous carriers of Mendelian recessive disorders could be identified, and such knowledge was used together with amniocentesis and therapeutic selective abortions when necessary, profound reductions might be realized in the incidence of some genetic diseases.

Heterozygous carriers of Mendelian recessive disorders *(Aa)* in many cases apparently produce less enzymes than do homozygotes for the normal allele *(AA)*. This difference in enzyme activity between heterozygotes and homozygotes can be used to distinguish between them biochemically. Hsia, Discoll, Troll, and Knox (1956) developed a phenylalanine tolerance test which could detect heterozygous carriers for phenylketonuria. In their procedure, phenylalanine was ingested by both normal controls and heterozygous carriers, and plasma phenylalanine levels were measured. Carriers had plasma phenylalanine levels almost twice as high as the controls—indicating a deficiency of the liver enzyme phenylalanine hydroxylase in the carriers. However, it has been noticed that considerable overlap exists in the distribution of plasma phenylalanine in controls (homozygotes) and heterozygous carriers (Knox & Messinger, 1958). The large overlap between indicators of defective gene functioning in carriers and noncarriers makes genetic counseling even more difficult. At present, heterozygote carriers can be detected in over 70 genetic disorders, with various degrees of confidence (Levitan & Montagu, 1971).

Ethical Issues in Genetic Counseling

One of the most difficult and perplexing issues in human genetics is the problem of ethical decision making. Although our technical knowledge of genetic phenomena has increased exponentially during recent years, it is doubtful that there has been a concomitant enlightenment in the domain of the moral implications of genetic applications. The concern with ethics and genetic controls has become especially problematic, due to the pressing ecological demands of poverty and overpopulation. Such problems are both intricate and difficult to analyze because of the intertwining matrix of political and scientific developments. It will be the purpose of this section, then, to disentangle some of the more significant religious, legal, and social factors in order to present a more meaningful overview of issues in genetic counseling.

Historically, the major approach to genetic counseling appeared in the backdrop of Judeo-Christian ethics. When examining this position a bit closer, though, it is evident that Jewish (Talmudic) law was quite different from Roman Catholic precepts (Narot, 1973). On one hand, rabbinical scholars considered the fetus a parasite until brith. This position entailed sacrifice of the fetus in favor of the mother's life when such conflicts arose. Conversely, the Roman Catholic encyclical asserts that at time of conception, the organism is categorically a human being. From this tenet, the Catholic hierarchy has traditionally advocated sacrificing the mother and saving the child—if such a choice must be made. While these choices have not necessarily involved genetic disorders, they have set the tone for dealing with eugenic issues. Currently, the "right to life" advocates assert that the fetus as well as the child must be given full legal and medical protection. The foregoing issues have been germane to the new field of genetic counseling—where the interests of parent, child (or fetus), and physician (or other trained professional) intersect. As will be seen, genetic counseling and possible eugenic control may have a profound influence on the fate of future persons who would be classified as mentally retarded.

Eugenics. Webster's dictionary (1969) defines eugenics as "a science that deals with the improvement (as by control of human mating) of hereditary qualities of a race or breed." Genetic counseling may have the limited scope of dealing solely with the individuals involved in the parent-child-counselor triad. The genetic counselor may discuss the broader social effects of bringing a particular child into the world, but he is more likely to focus on the personal problems that might ensue, given the risks of certain diseases. In eugenics the priorities are reversed. The eugenicist is primarily concerned with the overall ecological effects and their probabilities of occurrence when certain individuals procreate. Population planning through systematic and selective breeding for particular hereditary characteristics is the keynote of eugenics. Obviously, intentional selective breeding has been used with lower organisms, but we are faced with the moral question of whether it is proper to use similar methods with humans.

Before exploring these ethical matters in more detail, a distinction should be made between what are called "positive" and "negative" eugenics. Negative eugenics deals with the avoidance of a particular known disease by intentionally not breeding the carriers of the presumed genetic disorder. For example, through prophylaxis, sterilization, or abortion, those with Klinefelter's Syndrome (XXY) or those who are carriers of Tay-Sach's disease would not be allowed to have children. Negative eugenics operates on tangible disorders, and over a number of generations it is highly probable that the incidence of such genetic diseases would be reduced. When genetic abnormalities can be so accurately isolated, it is likely that popular, as well as moral, support could be gathered for the negative eugenics approach. Still, a pure "right to life" stand would argue that cases with the above disorders or with Down's Syndrome have a fundamental right to be born and live to their fullest, without the intrusion of selective breeding methods (Lejeune, 1973).

In the case of positive eugenics, the issues and questions are much more ambiguous. First, positive eugenics involves the selective breeding of organisms in order to uplift or improve the phenotypical characteristics of a population. Positive eugenics entails mating for more general, polygenetic constructs (e.g., intelligence). Rather than trying to eliminate identifiable gene disorders, as in negative eugenics, positive eugenics tries to encourage assortative mating for certain global nonspecifically gene-linked characteristics. The eugenics movement originated and grew during the late 19th and early 20th century, and then it lost form as a result of the distortions of Nazi Germany. However, there has been a recent rebirth of eugenic interest. Shockley (1972) and Jensen (1969) pointed to the "dysgenic" trends in the United States population, and they believe that positive eugenic steps should be taken to prevent further decline of the average intelligence of the general population. Shockley proposed that the federal government pay parents for not having children, at the rate of $1,000 for every point below 100 in parental IQ. The Shockley proposal is clearly an example of positive eugenics because it does not focus on a specific gene disorder, but rather encourages selective breeding based along a gross measure like intelligence. Thus, it can be seen that positive eugenics is solely concerned with broader, ecological variables; negative eugenics, while it shares that concern, also has implications for individual genetic counseling.

The distinction between societal interests and individual rights has, in fact, been the classical ethical issue for eugenic control. Civic libertarians claim that it is the inalienable right of the person to reproduce without governmental restraints. Such appeals are based on the dictum of natural law, where it is claimed that the right to procreate is self-evident. Recent court rulings affirming the right of the retarded person to reproduce, as well as antisterilization decisions, would seem to support this position. Furthermore, Grad (1967) stated that positive eugenic controls would violate the 5th, 9th, and 14th amendments of the U.S. Constitution. It thus appears questionable whether major eugenic inroads can be made, given the present legal system in the United States.

The opposing view that has argued for the implementation of eugenic programs has not limited its arguments to social-ecological grounds. From a legal standpoint, Morison (1973) questioned whether the right to procreate is self-evident, and Kass (1973) suggested that the rights of man are not immutable and perhaps should be revised. Basically, the eugenic stand appeals to the utilitarian ethic of the greatest good for the greatest number of people. If it can be substantiated that society will greatly benefit with (and suffer without) genetic controls, then the individual must take a subordinate position. In support of utilitarian eugenics is the point that society has always placed limits on the behavior of its citizens, and in times of crises the government has been quite stringent in circumscribing individual freedoms. The eugenicists would state that we are indeed approaching a population crisis (in both quantity and quality) and that certain emergency measures must be taken. Also, it is felt that, in spite of the eugenic programs which should be undertaken, the fundamental value structure of society will not be undermined or changed drastically. Finally, Morison (1973) projected that there would be few direct confrontations between individual and society with eugenic programs.

Genetic counseling—sociolegal implications. It is within this context of individual and societal self-interests that the genetic counselor must function. The genetic counselor must provide information to parents so that *they* can make more educated decisions. The nature of this information revolves largely around the degree of risk of occurrence or recurrence of a particular disorder, given both parents' genetic constitution. Besides transmitting information related to the risks involved, the genetic counselor can be more or less directive in advising parents on the action that should be taken. In the purely nondirective (and legally safest) approach, the counselor would merely provide factual data about the genetic tests and discuss the likelihood of occurrence of the diseases in question. The decision to have children would be left completely up to the parents. Unfortunately, life does not often proceed in such a nondirective vacuum, and counselors are likely to be asked what they would do if they were in the parents' position. The former may, of course, choose not to be directive by sticking to the data presented, and by reiterating that the decision must be left completely in the parents' hands. Carter (1970), though, has taken an intermediate course between directive and nondirective approaches. He defined a low-risk case as having a less than 1:10 probability (usually 1:20) of occurrence, and a high-risk probability as greater than 1:10 (usually 1:4). For low-risk cases, Carter more directly advised that "he" would have the child, if he were in their position. However, when there is a high-risk case, Carter did not try to influence the parents' decision. (For a variety of other opinions, see Restak, 1975).

Although Carter's decision-making model has a definite appeal, and although amniocentesis should make possible a more precise specification of risk, certain legal developments have occurred that further obfuscate the issues at hand. The individual-versus-society dilemma discussed above is perhaps an oversimplification of the situation, since it assumes that the parents will always desire to have the child. However, this may not always be true. In cases in New York and Illinois, recently, a bastard child unsuccessfully sued his parents for damages due to his illegitimate birth (Kilbrandon, 1973). Conceivably, the courts could have ruled in favor of the child, and the parents would have been guilty for failing to abort or to take prophylactic steps. Therefore, in the future, parents must consider their legal responsibilities in deciding to have a child.

The now famous *Gleitman* case (Kilbrandon, 1973) indicated the legal implications for the physician in advising parents. Although the situation involved rubella rather than a genetic disorder, it should nevertheless be instructive and applicable to possible genetic cases. In the *Gleitman* case, the physician did not tell Mrs. Gleitman the possible risks of her having rubella during her pregnancy. Although this was obviously a case of professional negligence, the court ruled against the plaintiff parents. The decision was based on the logical grounds that the alternative would have been to abort, in which case the child would not have been a healthy child, but a nonexistent one. It should be apparent, then, that matters relating to the rights and responsibilities of parent and physician are less than clear, and that these must be redefined in future court decisions. The ramifications of this problem can no longer be couched in the simple terms of free will of parent versus eugenic controls of government. How physicians and others counsel parents, and whether parents decide to have or not to have children in the face of given information, will have pervasive moral as well as legal effects.

Positive eugenics—validity and ethics. Returning to the policy of positive eugenics, it should be restated that positive eugenics is more global in its focus by not trying to eliminate a specific gene disorder. Further, it has been questioned whether positive eugenic programs would work with humans, due to regression effects and the absence of tangible empirical support. Also, Ludmerer (1973) has mentioned the fact that almost all phenotypical traits that follow Mendelian patterns of inheritance are diseases, raising the question of whether positive eugenic breeding is feasible.

Besides doubting the validity of positive eugenics, a more important ethical criticism has been made against the possible implementation of such programs. Williams (1974) expressed the fear that certain ethnic groups (namely, Black Americans) are being singled out for eugenic extinction, based on the evidence that they score lower on standard IQ tests. Williams perceived the sterilization of welfare recipients, as well as the writings of Jensen and Shockley, as part of a genocidal plot to control and eliminate unwanted minority groups. White prejudice, which used to be more blatantly expressed in Jim Crow laws, Williams feels, is now being rationalized for the more educated public through the "scientific racism" of eugenics. Actually, there are historical parallels that support Williams' position. Much of the underlying motivation of the eugenics movement of the early 20th century has been attributed to the desire of the WASP establishment to prevent further migrations of southern and eastern Europeans to the United States (Bremme, 1974). Rather than scientific findings leading to genetic proposals, this interpretation implies that social and political conditions are the prime movers in supporting the science (or pseudoscience) of eugenics, a position argued as well by Kamin (1974). After the extinction of the eugenics movement, due to the excesses of Nazi racism, it could be argued that the 1970s are producing a eugenic renaissance, stemming from the similar sociopolitical needs of the majority to control threatening minority groups.

A similar concern over the abuse of genetic technology has been voiced by a group of contributors to the biochemical study of genetics (Ausubel, Beckwith, & Janssen, 1974). These authors and their group ("Science for People") see incipient evidence of governmental agencies gaining the power to make far-reaching eugenic decisions. Ausubel et al. (1974) are familiar with the recent breakthroughs in genetic technology and fear the application of such a powerful technology to attain sinister ends. The source of their apprehension is not the possibility that a tyrannical dictator will forcefully use eugenic methods, but rather that the power to make eugenic decisions will be subtly transferred to local bureaucrats. The general faith our society has in technology, as well as our recent concern with overpopulation, might justify and set precedents for the taking of eugenic steps. Initially, the actions may be well intentioned and serve good purposes, but eventually there may be no checks and balances on how eugenics measures may go. Already, as Ausubel et al. (1974) cited, legislation in Illinois and New York vaguely defines the standards of who can be sterilized. These authors feel that such vague standards, coupled with the absence of public debate, could lead to genetic screening laws that give:

> state health officials the power to classify additional genetic abnormalities or inherent behavioral traits as defective without legislative approval or public discussion. While screening laws can help anticipate and prevent serious diseases, they can also have the effect of allowing social and political decisions to be made in the antiseptic guise of medicine and genetics [p. 38].

If events developed in this manner, we would, of course, be in the throes of a fascist-type government. What could prevent some local health official from projecting his racist fantasies onto his policy plans?

Ausubel, Beckwith, and Janssen should be pleased to learn that events are not proceeding exactly in the way they feared. The Committee for the

Study of Inborn Errors of Metabolism of the National Academy of Sciences (NAS), after a 2½-year analysis of the state of the art and the politics of genetic screening, concluded that it is not time to recommend community mass-screening programs (Culliton, 1975b). The committee chairman, Barton Childs of the Johns Hopkins University School of Medicine, stressed the fact that genetic screening of asymptomatic individuals should still be considered an experimental procedure in need of considerable evaluation of its potential benefits versus its inherent risks. However, the Committee strongly endorsed the continuation and expansion of genetic screening in the proper setting. The Committee is strongly opposed to mass-screening programs in which groups of citizens are "virtually recruited off the streets to have their genes checked," and it has set forth detailed guidelines on how to go about setting up and evaluating new programs in genetic screening.

The NAS Committee is firmly dedicated to strong citizen participation in setting up genetic screening programs. It has recommended that commissions or "screening authorities" be composed of researchers and lay members who would review all proposed new programs to determine in advance the answers to a number of questions, such as the following:

1. Is the public interested in and prepared to accept screening for the disease in question?
2. Will public facilities such as laboratories be needed? If so, what will the cost be?
3. Will the public need to be educated about the nature and consequences of a particular program? If so, how?
4. Is the proposed screening scientifically accurate? What treatment can be offered to persons identified as having the screened-for condition? Are the treatments effective?

The Committee has emphatically opposed any laws or regulations that make genetic screening mandatory, and it would like to see that procedure, as it matures, become part of general medical practice and not carried out by unprofessionally trained people. Screening should be carried out only when high standards for scientific accuracy and patient follow-up are met (Culliton, 1975b).

The Childs-NAS Committee is aware of the pitfalls that exist, even if individuals are given careful counseling and oral and written information before and after genetic screening. People can become quite confused about the information they have received about their genes (Culliton, 1975b; Horn, 1975; Restak, 1975). They may feel stigmatized and frightened by the knowledge given to them and believe they carry a "bad gene." Some individuals can suffer embarrassment and guilt feelings, and they may conceal their carrier status from future mates. Thus, many may pay high personal costs for the knowledge derived from genetic screening. Therefore, people and the society they live in have to be educated about the knowledge that such a procedure can provide.

The "Science for People" group, especially, as well as the Harvard microbiologist Jonathan Beckwith and Jonathan King of the Massachussetts Institute of Technology, have recently attacked as unethical the 7-year-old chromosomal screening studies of Stanley Walzer and Park Gerald of the Harvard Medical School (Culliton, 1974, 1975a).

Since 1968, Walzer and Gerald have been screening all newborn boys at the Harvard-affiliated Boston Hospital for Women. As noted earlier, the study had two purposes: (a) to gather data about the frequency of 47/XXY (Klinefelter's Syndrome) and 47/XYY (Jacobs' Syndrome) karyotypes in the general population; and (b) to follow up any 47/XXY or 47/XYY children to see whether there was any association between the chromosomal abnormalities and antisocial behavior. Apparently, there is some tenuous evidence that boys with Jacobs' Syndrome are at risk for developing some rather ill-defined behavioral problems and even criminal or antisocial behavior. Gerald believes that while 47/XYY individuals seem to have difficulty controlling themselves, they are certainly not criminals. Walzer reported that some 47/XYY children are hard to handle and that others are perfectly tractable. Both Walzer and Gerald are of the opinion that Jacobs' Syndrome is a disease and that children who have it are entitled to medical treatment just as they would be for any other disease (Culliton, 1974). The frequency of Jacobs' Syndrome is not all that rare. With an incidence of one in a thousand births, it is as common as Down's Syndrome.

It has already been noted that boys with Klinefelter's Syndrome may suffer speech and language difficulties, and may also be handicapped by a significant reading deficit, according to Walzer (Culliton, 1974). Klinefelter's Syndrome, too, is not rare (one in a thousand births). Both Walzer and Gerald believe that in cases of Klinefelter's and Jacobs' syndromes, it is possible to offer useful help in the form of psychological counseling.

The chief antagonist to these studies, Jonathan Beckwith (Culliton, 1974), has objected on several grounds. Beckwith apparently concluded from his review of the literature that (a) Jacobs' Syndrome was a "dangerous myth" which has no meaningful medical or psychological treatment; (b) the stigma of labeling a boy as having either Jacobs' or Klinefelter's Syndrome was so great that behavioral problems may arise as a result of the negative expectations of the parents, a kind of self-fulfilling prophecy; and (c) the overall study was carried out in a grossly unethical manner, since the parents had not been fully informed of the consequences of agreeing to have their babies screened.

It was in the area of informed consent that much of the controversy arose. Beckwith contended that parents should be told not only that they are participating in a search for aberrant chromosomes, but also that, if their child turns out to be afflicted, they will then be asked to consent to further experimental studies of his development. It was argued that parents should be given information about the statistical risks of finding an aberration and the possible courses of action then to be taken. In essence, it was held, the parents should be given a course in genetics. Since this is not possible, Beckwith felt the proper thing to do was to stop the study at once.

Jay Katz, a psychiatrist on the Yale Law School faculty, after reviewing Walzer's Parental Consent Forms, wrote:

> Walzer's initial approach to the parents is neither straightforward enough nor does it comply with what I consider the requirements of informed consent to imply. Elements of "fraud, deceit," and even "duress and overreaching," proscribed by the Nuremberg Code, are clearly present [Culliton, 1974, p. 716].

The blatant attacks on the ethical standards of Walzer have left him feeling persecuted, deeply offended, and emotionally drained. He feels he has conducted his study within the bounds of requirements set up by the hospital, the medical school, and the National Institute of Health, which has just reviewed and funded the study for another 3 years. Apparently, however, there was a grain of truth in Katz's criticism of Walzer's consent forms. Walzer acknowledged that what was considered proper in 1968 might not be considered so in 1975, and so he has continually revised his consent form—which now reflects Beckwith's suggestions. In its present form, parents are asked to give consent after the baby's birth. Before, women were asked for consent while in labor, not the best time to make a well-reasoned decision. Information is now provided about the risk that an aberration will be detected. Parents are told that some aberrations are thought to be related to developmental problems, and they are informed that they may be asked to participate in a further study if any chromosomal variations are present. They are also explicitly told that they do not have to agree to participate in the screening, and that they will not receive less than good medical care if they decide they do not want anyone looking at the baby's chromosomes.

The Human Studies Committee of Harvard Medical School, which must certify that research supported by the Department of Health, Education and Welfare (HEW) meets HEW guidelines for human experimentation, reviewed Walzer's work and agreed that the study complied with requirements that: (a) informed consent be properly obtained, (b) the patients' rights be protected, and (c) the benefits of participating in the study outweigh the risks (Culliton, 1975a).

The scientific and ethical issues raised by the work of Walzer and Gerald were reviewed by Harvard Medical School's standing committee on medical research, chaired by Dana Farnsworth. The Committee decided that the study should continue, and Farnsworth presented the group's opinion to the full medical school, which accepted it. Farnsworth declared (B.J.C., 1974) that research on the genetic basis of behavior is important and worthy of pursuit, that the investigators had behaved ethically and sensitively, and that there was no evidence that the study had harmed any of its participants. Farnsworth, speaking for the Committee (B. J. C., 1974), then cast veiled aspersions on the manner in which Beckwith and his colleagues conducted their opposition. Beckwith's tactic of going to the press was not looked upon with enthusiasm. It was intimated that the attacks on the Walzer study could be construed as an infringement on academic freedom. Beckwith retorted (B. J. C., 1974) that he considered the whole Farnsworth report a "whitewash" and that he intended to keep on trying to block the Walzer-Gerald study.

Beckwith apparently won the battle, since Walzer decided to stop his screening research because of the terrible strain brought on himself and his family by this controversy (Culliton, 1975a). Indeed, even after he won with the faculty, it was clear that the opposition would go on. In fact, new groups (lawyers for the Washington-based Children's Defense Fund) were becoming involved. (For a variety of responses to this controversy, see Beckwith, Elseviers, Gorini, Mandansky, & Csonka, 1975; W.H. Davis, 1975; Mage, 1975).

The question arises, though, whether this concern with the trend of exploratory eugenics is realistic on the one hand, or paranoid or even rational on the other. Perhaps a more insightful way of viewing this matter is to examine our evolving values toward technology. Pirsig (1974) described two types of reactions to our growing technology. The "classicist" appreciates the underlying forms represented by technology, while the "romanticist" views industrial and technological growth as an infringement upon the natural order. Attitudes toward eugenic controls are possibly bifurcating in a similar manner—with eugenicists seeing the necessity of applying technology to the growing population problems, and antieugenic forces holding that certain fundamental values and rights would be compromised by the implementation of genetic technology.

Other Related Issues

Passive euthanasia. In an issue closely related to the ones previously discussed, the Reverend Richard McCormick (*Milwaukee Journal*, 1974a), a Catholic theologian and a Rose Kennedy Professor at the Joseph and Rose Kennedy

Institute for Study of Human Reproduction and Bioethics (Georgetown University), came out in favor of passive euthanasia for deformed infants who have no "potential" for human relations. Father McCormick offered two sets of circumstances where life need not be preserved: (a) where the potential for human relationships is nonexistent, considering the child's mental and physical characteristics; and (b) where the potential, even if it exists, would be utterly submerged and undeveloped in the mere struggle to survive.

The heart of McCormick's argument is that the Judeo-Christian tradition views life as a basic and precious good—but as a relative rather than an absolute good. According to this view, the duty to preserve life must be limited by consideration of other values, and therefore an attitude that preserves it at any cost is one of "idolatry of life."

In an attempt to explore relevant concerns, Barclay (1974) sent out a questionnaire (the "Delphi 2 Questionnaire") to all members of the Division on Mental Retardation of the American Psychological Association, to assess the attitudes of these professionals on various ethical-legal issues. On the matter of the future legal provisions for passive euthanasia in the form of withdrawal of life-prolonging activities, 76% of those responding considered this proposition to be desirable, and 79% of the respondents agreed that this form of passive euthanasia should be legally permissible in the future. However, on the possibilities of passive euthanasia in the form of denying a cure (e.g., failure to perform necessary medications), 70% of those responding considered this proposition to be undesirable, and 73% felt that this form of passive euthanasia should not be made legally permissible in the future.

The McCormick statement will surely break new ground in the complex and hazy land of morality, theology, law, and medico-bio legal ethics. We wonder, however, how McCormick's guidelines could ever be made operational. How does one measure the potential for human relationships? Consider the following incident:

A close friend, his wife, and his three children, one of whom was profoundly retarded, came to visit one of the present authors (Switzky). The profoundly retarded 5-year-old child was placed in his bean-bag chair squarely in the middle of the living room while the other two children went off to play with the host's children. The profoundly retarded child, who was severely brain-injured at birth, remained motorically flaccid and unresponsive to his environment until his mother came over to feed him through a tube, which had been surgically implanted into his stomach (by his father's cousin because no other surgeon would bother). The tube was implanted because the weakness of the boy's swallowing reflex had been causing the child to suffer from aspiration pneumonitis. At the moment the mother started to feed him, the boy started smiling and laughing and making little noises.

Did the "potential" for human relationship exist in this case, or was it so submerged and undeveloped in this child's struggle to survive that the massive amounts of anticonvulsants, muscle relaxants, and antibiotics, along with the surgical procedure given to this child had led to an "idolatry of life"? I (Switzky) do not know. If this boy were mine and he became seriously ill, would I just let him die by denying him a cure? Of, if he remained as healthy as he was, would I let him die by withdrawing from him the life-prolonging drugs? The question is as academic and unrealistic as were the medieval theological discussions concerning the true nature of God. The boy is not my son, and I will not have to make any of these decisions. If he were my son, I would not know what to do until I was forced to make the decision, by myself, or with the help of a counselor.

The point we wish to make is that it is easy to sit down into one's armchair and argue one way or another about the ethics or morality of a particular social-legal action when one is not really that personally involved. It is quite a different story when the one involved is yourself, and the actions which will be undertaken will directly affect you.

Rights of society. Barclay's (1974) Delphi 2 Questionnaire is additionally informative because it taps some of the attitudes of various professional persons who will be called upon to help others (e.g., the federal and state governments, parents, students) make complex decisions on questions of society's legal right to limit by involuntary or compulsory means the number of defective children born into it. Respondents were asked how they felt about the following: (a) sterilization of high-risk individuals who may have better than a 50:50 chance of conceiving a child with a major genetic defect, (b) restricting the number of children a mentally retarded couple could have, (c) abortion of high-risk fetuses, and (d) restricting the female child-bearing period to a maximum of 35 years of age to reduce the probability of defective embryos. On the average, 79% of those responding were against these measures. However, 99% of the responders agreed that society has the right to limit the number of defective children born into it, by encouraging voluntary means such as education, counseling, and improved clinics; and 73% agreed that, just as blood tests for venereal disease are required of couples desiring a marriage license, so genetic counseling, which would include tests to detect genetic defects, should be legally mandatory.

Rights of the individual. The proposed official policy statement of the American Association on Mental Deficiency (1974) on the sterilization of persons who are mentally retarded, emphasized the individual rights of mentally retarded citizens (who have the same rights as other citizens) rather than the rights of society. Since sterilization is a method of contraception available to most adults in North America, this option should be open to most retarded citizens as well. However, no one should be involuntarily sterilized.

The statement suggests that, for legal purposes, individual citizens may be classified into three groups: (a) legally competent persons, (b) legally incompetent persons, and (c) persons of impaired capacity. Legally competent persons should have the right to exercise free and informed choices—without coercion or restraint—in the selection of contraceptive methods so as to assure the maximum possible participation of the individual in decisions regarding his or her reproductive capacity. Legally incompetent persons should not be denied access to sterilization; however, legal, social-ethical, and professional safeguards as outlined below should be applied rigorously to assure that the best interest of the retarded person remains paramount in the decision-making process as reviewed and approved by a court of law.

In reaching its decision concerning sterilization, the court should review and affirm that *all* of the following conditions have been met: (a) The individual is presumed to be physiologically capable of procreation; (b) the individual is, or is likely to be, sexually active in the immediate future; (c) pregnancy would not usually be intended by a competent person facing analogous choices; (d) less drastic alternative contraceptive methods have been proven unworkable or are inapplicable; (e) the guardian of the person agrees that sterilization is a desirable course of action for his or her ward; (f) the court has received advice based on comprehensive medical, psychological, and social evaluations of the individual; (g) the person is represented by legal counsel with a demonstrated competence in dealing with the medical, legal, social, and ethical issues involved in sterilization; and (h) the person, regardless of his or her level of competence, has been granted a full opportunity to express his or her views regarding sterilization, and these views have been taken into account in determining whether to sterilize the individual.

Persons of impaired capacity, or individuals not judged to be legally incompetent in a court of law, are of two types: (a) those who, on the basis of professional assessment, are found to lack the mental capacity to make a reasoned and informed judgment on serious issues such as sterilization; and (b) those who do possess the mental capacity to make an informed judgment on their own behalf, but are under the control of or dependent upon an institution, agency, or individual for their support or survival, and are thus restricted in the freedom to make informed judgments. Persons of impaired capacity can be sterilized only with the approval of a court of law under those conditions specified for legally incompetent persons. It is the intent of the American Association on Mental Deficiency's (1974) proposal to make sure that all retarded citizens are provided with adequate safeguards against unwanted or unnecessary sterilizations.

SUMMARY

From the perspective of modern behavioral-genetics, this chapter has been largely concerned with the implications for the prevention, treatment, and control of mental retardation syndromes that are primarily due to single-gene or simple-chromosomal aberrations.

The history of Mendelian genetics is presented, and Mendel's laws are illustrated by the study of human pedigrees. Multiple factor extensions of Mendel's laws are shown to account for quantitatively varying traits in populations; and it is noted that these extensions, together with data on the stability of genotypes in a population, laid the foundation for modern population genetics.

The discussion of present-day developmental genetics points up that some phenotypic characteristics are not easily changed, even when environmental or genetic forces vary considerably, while other phenotypic characteristics are extremely sensitive to genetic and/or environmental modifications. However, this "range of reaction" is not predictable in advance for a particular phenotype (especially in human beings) because the same genotypes have not in any systematic way been tested in a variety of environments. The basic conclusion is that hereditary and environmental factors are very important in determining phenotypic trait variation, but are operative in a highly ambiguous and unpredictable way.

A number of examples are given of single-gene influences on behavioral phenotypes (including mental retardation syndromes) and their mode of action, along with examples of chromosomal abnormalities, their phenotypic manifestations, and their relationship to psychometric intelligence. The molecular basis of gene activity is considered in terms of the one-gene-one-polypeptide concept, the role of DNA and RNA in heredity, and the increasing realization that genes control not only protein synthesis, but also the function of other genes.

Prospects for genetic intervention in humans (through genetic counseling and other means) for the prevention of mental retardation (and for other purposes as well) are discussed in some detail; and a strong thread weaving through the chapter is the great concern for the extremely complex set of issues revolving around the morel-ethical-religious-legal-social aspects of decisions involving humans' manipulation of their own genotype. It is hoped that critical and analytical thought and discussion generated hereby will in some way help resolve the confusion in this area and replace pure emotionalism with facts so as to promote future scientific inquiry.

REFERENCES

American Association on Mental Deficiency. Sterilization of persons who are mentally retarded. *Mental Retardation,* 1974, *12*(2), 59-61.

Ausubel, F., Beckwith, J., & Janssen, K. The politics of genetic engineering: Who decides who's defective? *Psychology Today,* 1974, *8*(1), 30-43.

Avery, O. T., MacLeod, C. M., & McCarthy, M. Studies on the chemical nature of the substance inducing transformation of pneumococcal types. *Journal of Experimental Medicine,* 1944, *79,* 137-158.

Barclay, A. G. Delphi Questionnaire, Round 2. Personal Communication, 1974.

Barr, M. L. The sex chromosomes in evolution and in medicine. *Canadian Medical Association Journal,* 1966, *95,* 1137-1148.

Barr, M. L., & Bertram, E. G. A morphological distinction between neurones of the male and female, and the behavior of the nucleolar satellite during accelerated nucleoprotein synthesis. *Nature,* 1949, *163,* 676-677.

Barr, M. L., Shaver, E. L., Carr, D. H., & Plunkett, E. R. An unusual sex chromatin pattern in three mentally deficient subjects. *Journal of Mental Deficiency Research,* 1959, *3,* 78-87.

Bateson, W., & Saunders, E. R. Experimental studies in the physiology of heredity. *Reports to Evolution Committee of the Royal Society,* 1902, *1,* 1-160.

Bateson, E., Saunders, E. R., & Punnett, R. C. Experimental studies in the physiology of heredity. *Reports to Evolution Committee of the Royal Society,* 1905, *2,* 1-131.

Bateson, W., Saunders, E. R., & Punnett, R. C. Experimental studies in the physiology of heredity. *Reports to Evolution Committee of the Royal Society,* 1906, *3,* 1-53.

Beadle, G. W. Biochemical genetics. *Chemical Review,* 1945, *37,* 15-96.

Beadle, G. W., & Tatum, E. L. Experimental control of developmental reaction. *American Naturalist,* 1941, *75,* 107-116.

Beckwith, J., Elseviers, D., Gorini, L., Mandansky, L., & Csonka, L. Harvard XYY Study. *Science,* 1975, *187,* 298.

Begab, J. M. The major dilemma of mental retardation: Shall we prevent it? (Some social implications of research in mental retardation). *American Journal of Mental Deficiency,* 1974, *78,* 519-529.

Benzer, S. The fine structure of the gene. *Scientific American,* 1962, *206,* 70-84.

B.J.C. Harvard faculty says XYY study should continue. *Science,* 1974, *186,* 1189.

Bradbury, J. T., Burge, R. G., & Boccabella, R. A. Chromatin test in

Klinefelter's syndrome. *Journal of Clinical Endocrinological Metabolism,* 1956, *16,* 689.

Bremme, D. Development and adoption of intelligence tests in America. Unpublished manuscript, Harvard University, 1974.

Briggs, R., & King T. J. Nucleocytoplasmic interactions in eggs and embryos. In J. Brachet and A. E. Mirsky (Eds.), *The Cell* (Vol. 1). New York: Academic Press, 1959, pp. 537-617.

Bronfenbrenner, U. Is 80% of intelligence genetically determined? In U. Bronfenbrenner (Ed.), *Influences on human development.* Hinsdale, Ill.: Dryden Press, 1972, pp. 118-127.

Carter, C. O. Prospects in genetic counseling. In A. H. Emery (Ed.), *Modern trends in human genetics.* New York: Appleton-Century-Crofts, 1970, pp. 339-349.

Cattell, R. B. *Abilities, their structure, growth and action.* Boston: Houghton Mifflin, 1971. (a)

Cattell, R. B. The structure of intelligence in relation to the nature-nuture controversy. In R. Cancro (Ed.), *Intelligence: Genetic and environmental influences.* New York: Grune & Stratton, 1971, pp. 3-30. (b)

Cohen, S. N. The manipulation of genes. *Scientific American,* 1975, *233,* 24-33.

Correns, C. G. Mendel's Regel uber das verhalten der machkommenschaft der rassen bartarde. *Ber, dt. bot. Ges.,* 1900, *18,* 158-168.

Court-Brown, W. M., Harnden, D. G., Jacobs, P. A., Maclean, N., & Mantle, D. J. *Abnormalities of the sex chromosome complement in man.* (M.R.C. Special Report Series, No. 305.) London: Her Majesty's Stationary Office, 1964.

Crispens, C. G., Jr. *Essentials of medical genetics.* New York: Harper & Row, 1971.

Culliton, B. J. Patients' rights: Harvard is site of battle over X and Y chromosomes. *Science,* 1974, *186,* 715-717.

Culliton, B. J. XYY Harvard research under fire stops newborn screening. *Science,* 1975, *188,* 1284-1285. (a)

Culliton, B. J. Genetic Screening: NAS recommends proceeding with caution. *Science,* 1975, *189,* 119-120. (b)

Dancis, J., & Balis, M. E. A possible mechanism for disturbance in tyrosine metabolism in phenylpyruvic oligophrenia. *Pediatrics,* 1955, *15,* 63-66.

Davis, B. D. Prospects for genetic intervention in man. *Science,* 1970, *170,* 1279-1283.

Davis, W. H. Harvard XYY study. *Science,* 1975, *187,* 298-299.

Denniston, C. Accounting for differences in mean IQ. *Science,* 1975, *187,* 161-162.

DeVries, H. The law of separation of characters in crosses. *Journal of Royal Horticultural Society,* 1901, *25,* 243-248.

Dobzhansky, T. *Evolution, genetics and man.* New York: Wiley, 1955.

Dobzhansky, T. Genetics and the diversity of behavior. *American Psychologist,* 1972, *27,* 523-530.

Dobzhansky, T. Differences are not deficits. *Psychology Today,* 1973, 7(7), 97-101.

Eckland, B. K. Social class and the genetic basis of intelligence. In R. Cancro (Ed.), *Intelligence: Genetic and environmental influences.* New York: Grune & Stratton, 1971, pp. 65-76.

Eckland, B. K. Comments on school effects, gene-environment covariance, and the heritability of intelligence. In L. Ehrman, G. S. Omenn, and E. Caspari (Eds.), *Genetics, environment, and behavior: Implications for educational policy.* New York: Academic Press, 1972, pp. 297-306.

Edwards, J. H., Harnden, D. G., Cameron, A. H., Crosse, V. M., & Wolff, O. H. A new trisomic syndrome. *Lancet,* 1960, *1,* 787-790.

Emerson, R. A., & East, E. M. The inheritance of quantitative characteristics in maize. *University of Nebraska Research Bulletin,* 1913, *2,* 5-120.

Engel, E. The chromosome basis of human heredity. In J. B. Stanbury, J. B. Wyngarden, and D. S. Fredrickson (Eds.), *The metabolic basis of inherited disease.* New York: McGraw-Hill, 1972, pp. 52-79.

Eysenck, H. J. *The IQ Argument.* Freeport, N.Y.: Liberty Press, 1971.

Farabee, W. C. Inheritance of digital malformations in man. *Papers of Peabody Museum of Harvard University,* 1905, *3,* 69-77.

Fisher, R. A. The correlation between relatives on the supposition of Mendelian inheritance. *Transactions Royal Society of Edinburg,* 1918, *52,* 399-433.

Fox, M. S., & Littlefield, J. W. Reservations concerning gene therapy. *Science,* 1971, *173,* 195.

Fraccaro, M., & Lindsten, J. A child with 49 chromosomes. *Lancet,* 1960, *2,* 1303.

Friedmann, T. Prenatal diagnosis of genetic disease. *Scientific American,* 1971, *225,* 34-42.

Friedmann, T., & Roblin, R. Gene therapy for human genetic diseases? *Science,* 1972, *175,* 949-955.

Garrod, A. E. *Inborn errors of metabolism,* London: Oxford University Press, 1909.

Gottesman, I. I. Genetic aspects of intelligence. In N. R. Ellis (Ed.), *The handbook of mental deficiency: Psychological theory and research.* New York: McGraw-Hill, 1963, pp. 253-296.

Gottesman, I. I. Biogenetics of race and class. In M. Deutsch, I. Katz, and A. R. Jensen (Eds.), *Social class, race, and psychological development.* New York: Holt, Rinehart and Winston, 1968, pp. 11-51.

Gottesman, I. I., and Heston, L. L. Human behavioral adaptations: Speculations on their genesis. In L. Ehrman, G. Omenn, and E. Caspari (Eds.), *Genetics, environment, and behavior: Implication for educational policy.* New York: Academic Press, 1972, pp. 105-122.

Grad, F. P. Legislative responses to the new biology. *UCLA Law Review,* 1967, *15,* 480.

Gruneberg, H. *The genetics of the mouse* (2nd ed.). The Hague: Martinus Nijhoff, 1952.

Haldane, J. B. S. A method for investigating recessive characteristics in man. *Journal of Genetics,* 1932, *25,* 251-255.

Hanhart, E., Delhanty, J. D. A., & Penrose, L. S. Trisomy in mother and child. *Lancet,* 1961, *1,* 403.

Hardy, G. H. Mendelian proportions in a mixed population. *Science,* 1908, *28,* 49-50.

Herrnstein, R. J. I.Q. *Atlantic Monthly,* 1971, *228,* 43-64.

Herrnstein, R. J. *I.Q. and the meritocracy.* Boston: Little, Brown, 1973.

Hill, H. Z., & Puck, T. T. Detection of inborn errors of metabolism: Galactosemia. *Science,* 1973, 179, 1136-1139.

Hirsch, J. Behavior-genetic analysis and its biosocial consequences. In R. Cancro (Ed.), *Intelligence: Genetic and environmental influences.* New York: Grune & Stratton, 1971, pp. 88-106.

Hirsch, J. Genetics and competence: Do heritability indices predict educability? In J. McV. Hunt (Ed.), *Human intelligence.* New Brunswick, N.J.: E. P. Dutton, 1972, pp. 7-29.

Hook, E. B. Behavioral implications of the human XYY genotype. *Science,* 1973, *179,* 139-150.

Horn, P. When genetic counseling backfires. *Psychology Today,* 1975, *9*(4); 20,80.

Hsia, D. Y. The hereditary metabolic diseases. In J. Hirsch (Ed.), *Behavior-genetic analysis.* New York: McGraw-Hill, 1967, pp. 176-193.

Hsia, D. Y., Discoll, K. W., Troll, W., & Knox, W. E. Detection by phenylalanine tolerance tests of heterozygous carriers of phenylketonuria. *Nature,* 1956, *178,* 1239-1240.

Huxley, A. L. *Brave New World.* New York: Harper & Row, 1969.

Jacob, F., & Monod, J. Genetic regulatory mechanisms in the synthesis of proteins. *Journal of Molecular Biology,* 1961, *3,* 318-356. (a)

Jacob, F., & Monod, J. On the regulation of the gene activity. *Cold Spring Harbor Symposium on Quantitative Biology,* 1961, *26,* 193-209. (b)

Jacobs, P. A., Brunton, M., Melville, M. M., Brittain, R. P., & McClemont, W. F. Aggressive behavior, mental subnormality and the XYY male. *Nature,* 1965, *208,* 1351-1352.

Jacobs, P. A., & Strong, A. A case of human intersexuality having a possible XXY sex-determining mechanism. *Nature,* 1959, *183,* 302-303.

Jensen, A. R. How much can we boost IQ and scholastic achievement?

Harvard Educational Review, 1969, *39,* 1-123.

Jensen, A. R. *Educability and group differences.* New York: Harper & Row, 1973. (a)

Jensen, A. R. *Genetics and education.* New York: Harper & Row, 1973. (b)

Jervis, G. A. Phenylpyruvic oligophrenia: Deficiency of phenylalanine oxidizing system. *Proceedings of the Society of Experimental Biology and Medicine,* 1953, *82,* 514.

Johannsen, W. The genotype conception of heredity. *American Naturalist,* 1911, *45,* 129.

Kamin, L. J. *The science and politics of IQ.* New York: Wiley, 1974.

Kass, L. R. Implications of prenatal diagnosis for the human right to life. In B. Hilton, D. Callahan, M. Harris, P. Condliffe, and B. Berkley (Eds.), *Ethical issues in human genetics.* New York: Plenum Press, 1973, pp. 185-199.

Kilbrandon, L. The comparative law of genetic counseling. In B. Hilton, D. Callahan, M. Harris, P. Condliffe, and B. Berkley (Eds.), *Ethical issues in human genetics.* New York: Plenum Press, 1973, pp. 245-259.

Klinefelter, H. F., Jr., Reifenstein, E. C., Jr., & Albright, F. Syndrome characterized by gynecomastia, aspermatogenesis without *a*-Leydigism, and increased excretion of follicle-stimulating hormone. *Journal of Clinical Endocrinology,* 1942, *2,* 615-627.

Knox, W. E. Phenylketonuria. In J. B. Stanbury, J. B. Wyngarden, & D. S. Fredrickson (Eds.), *The metabolic basis of inherited disease* (3rd ed.). New York: McGraw-Hill, 1972, pp. 266-295.

Knox, W. E., & Messinger, E. D. The detection in the heterozygote of the metabolic effect of the recessive gene for phenylketonuria. *American Journal of Human Genetics,* 1958, *10,* 53-60.

Layzer, D. Heritability analyses of IQ scores: Science or numerology? *Science,* 1974, *183,* 1259-1266.

Lederberg, J. Dangers of reprogramming cells. *Science,* 1967, *158,* 312.

Lejeune, J. Discussant. In B. Hilton, D. Callahan, M. Harris, P. Condliffe, and B. Berkley (Eds.), *Ethical issues in human genetics.* New York: Plenum Press, 1973, pp. 113-116.

Lejeune, J., Turpin, R., & Gautier, M. Le mongolisme, premier example d'aberration autosomique humaine. *Annals Genetique,* 1959, *2,* 41-49.

Levitan, M., & Montagu, A. *Text book on human genetics.* New York: Oxford University Press, 1971.

Lewontin, R. C. Race and intelligence. *Bulletin of the Atomic Scientist,* 1970, *26,* 2-8. (a)

Lewontin, R. C. Further remarks on race and the genetics of intelligence. *Bulletin of the Atomic Scientist,* 1970, *26,* 23-25. (b)

Lewontin, R. C. Annotation: The analysis of variance and the analysis of causes. *American Journal of Human Genetics,* 1974, *26,* 400-411.

Lindsten, J. *The nature and origin of X chromosome aberrations in Turner's syndrome.* Stockholm: Almquist and Wiksell, 1963.

Newsday (Long Island), January 25, 1973.

Loo, Y. H. Characterization of a new phenylalanine metabolite in phenylketonuria. *Journal of Neurochemistry,* 1967, *14,* 813-821.

Lubs, H. A., & Ruddle, F. H. Chromosomal abnormalities in the human population: Estimates of rates based on New Haven newborn study. *Science,* 1970, *169,* 495.

Ludmerer, K. Discussant. In B. Hilton, D. Callahan, M. Harris, P. Condliffe, and B. Berkley (Eds.), *Ethical issues in human genetics.* New York: Plenum Press, 1973, pp. 402-407.

Mage, M. Harvard XYY study. *Science,* 1975, *187,* 299.

McClearn, G. E. The inheritance of behavior. In L. Postman (Ed.), *Psychology in the making.* New York: Knopf, 1962, pp. 144-252.

McClearn, G. E., & DeFries, J. C. *Introduction to behavioral genetics.* San Francisco: W. H. Freeman, 1973.

McKusick, V. A. *Human genetics.* Englewood Cliffs, N.J.: Prentice-Hall, 1964.

Menkes, J. H. The pathogenesis of mental retardation in phenylketonuria and other inborn errors of amino acid metabolism. *Pediatrics,* 1967, *39,* 297-308.

Merril, C. R., Geier, M. R., & Petricciani, J. C. Bacterial virus gene expression in human cells. *Nature,* 1971, *233,* 398-400.

Milwaukee Journal, July 8, 1974. (a)

Milwaukee Journal, July 19, 1974. (b)

Milwaukee Journal, July 25, 1974. (c)

Milwaukee Journal, July 26, 1974. (d)

Minneapolis Tribune, July 16, 1974. (a)

Minneapolis Tribune, July 17, 1974. (b)

Mintz, B. Synthetic processes and early development in the mammalian egg. *The Journal of Experimental Zoology,* 1964, *157,* 85-100.

Money, J. Two cytogenetic syndromes: Psychological comparisons. I. Intelligence and specific-factor quotients. *Journal of Psychiatric Research,* 1964, *2,* 223-231.

Money, J. Cognitive deficits in Turner's syndrome. In S. G. Vandenberg (Ed.), *Progress in human behavior genetics.* Baltimore: Johns Hopkins Press, 1968, pp. 27-30.

Morgan, T. H. *The physical basis of heredity.* Philadelphia: J. B. Lippincott, 1919.

Morison, R. S. Implications of prenatal diagnosis for the quality of, and right to, human life: Society as a standard. In B. Hilton, D. Callahan, M.

Harris, P. Condliffe, and B. Berkley (Eds.), *Ethical issues in human genetics.* New York: Plenum Press, 1973, pp. 201-211.

Morton, N. E. Human behavioral genetics. In L. Ehrman, G. E. Omenn, and E. Caspari (Eds.), *Genetics, environment, and behavior: Implications for educational policy.* New York: Academic Press, 1972, pp. 247-265.

Morton, N. E. Analysis of family resemblance. *American Journal of Human genetics,* 1974, *26,* 318-330.

Munyon, W., Kraiselbrud, E., Davis, D., & Mann, J. Transfer of thymidine kinase to thymidine kinaseless L. Cells by infection with ultra-violet-irradiated herpes simplex virus. *Journal of Virology,* 1971, *7,* 813-820.

Narot, J. R. The moral and ethical implications of human sexuality as they relate to the retarded. In F. F. de la Cruz, and G. D. LaVeck (Eds.), *Human sexuality and the mentally retarded.* New York: Brunner/Mazel, 1973, pp. 195-205.

Neufeld, E. F. and Sweeley, C. C. Gene therapy for human genetic disease? *Science,* 1972, *178,* 648.

Newsweek, June 17, 1974.

New York Times, September 8, 1968.

New York Times, September 20, 1970.

Nilsson-Ehle, H. Einige ergebnisse von Kreuzungen bei Hafer und Weisen. *Bot Notiser,* 1908, *9,* 257-294.

Nirenberg, M. W. The genetic code: II. *Scientific American,* 1963, *208,* 80-94.

Nirenberg, M. W. Will society be prepared? *Science,* 1967, *157,* 633.

O'Brien, S. J., Okada, S., Fillerup, D. L., Veath, M. L., Adornato, B., Brenner, P. H., & Lenz, J. G. Tay-Sachs disease: Prenatal diagnosis. *Science,* 1971, *172,* 61-64.

Okada, S., & O'Brien, S. J. Tay-Sachs disease: generalized absence of a beta-*d-n*-acetylhexose aminidose component. *Science,* 1969, *165,* 698-700.

Patau, K., Smith, D. W., Therman, E., Inhorn, S. L., & Wagner, H. P. Multiple congenital anomaly caused by an extra autosome. *Lancet,* 1960, *1,* 790-793.

Penrose, L. S., & Smith, G. F. *Down's anomaly.* Boston: Little, Brown, 1966.

Pirsig, R. M. *Zen and the art of motorcycle maintenance.* New York: William Morrow, 1974.

Plunkett, E. R., & Barr, M. L. Testicular dysgenesis affecting semiinferous tubules, principally with chromatin positive nuclei. *Lancet,* 1956, *2,* 853-856.

Price, W. H., & Jacobs, P. A. The 47, XXY male with special reference to behavior. *Seminars in Psychiatry,* 1970, *2,* 30-39.

Quasba, P. K., & Aposhian, H. V. DNA and gene therapy: Transfer of mouse

DNA to human and mouse embryonic cells by polyoma pseudovirions. *Proceedings of the National Academy of Sciences (USA)*, 1971, *68*, 2345-2349.

Rao, D. O., Morton, N. E. & Yee, S. Analysis of family resemblance: II. A linear model for familial correlation. *American Journal of Human Genetics*, 1974, *26*, 331-359.

Restak, R. Genetic Counseling for defective parents—the danger of knowing too much. *Psychology Today*, 1975, *9*(4); 21-23, 88, 92-93.

Scarr-Salapatak, S. Unknowns in the IQ equation. *Science*, 1971, *174*, 1223-128. (a)

Scarr-Salapatak, S. Race, social class, and IQ. *Science*, 1971, *174*, 1285-1295. (b)

Schwartz, A. G., Cook, P. R., & Harris, H. Correction of a genetic defect in a mammalian cell. *Nature New Biology*, 1971, *230*, 5-8.

Scott, J. P., & Fuller, J. L. Behavioral differences. In W. J. Burdette (Ed.), *Methodology in mammalian genetics.* San Francisco: Holden-Day, 1963, pp. 283-296.

Shah, S. A. *Report on the XYY chromosome abnormality.* (USPHS Publication No. 2103.) Washington, D.C.: U.S. Government Printing Office, 1970.

Shaw, M. W. Genetic counseling. *Science*, 1974, *184*, 751.

Shockley, W. Models, mathematics, and the moral obligation to diagnose the origin of Negro IQ deficits. *Review of Education Research*, 1971, *41*, 369-377.

Shockley, W. Dysgenics, geneticity, raceology: A challenge to the intellectual responsibility of educators. *Phi Delta Kappan*, 1972, *53*, 295-307.

Sidbury, J. B., Jr. The role of galactose-1-phosphate in the pathogenesis of galactosemia. In L. I. Gardner (Ed.), *Molecular genetics and human disease.* Springfield, Ill.: Charles C. Thomas, 1961, pp. 61-82.

Stanbury, J. B., Wyngarden, J. B., & Fredrickson, D. S. Inherited variation and metabolic abnormality. In J. B. Stanbury, J. B. Wyngarden, and D. S. Fredrickson (Eds.), *The metabolic basis of inherited disease.* New York: McGraw-Hill, 1972, pp. 3-28.

Sutton, W. S. The chromosomes in heredity. *Biology Bulletin*, 1903, *4*, 231-251.

Tanner, J. M. Regulation of growth in size in mammals. *Nature*, 1963, *199*, 845-850.

Thiessen, D. D. *Gene organization and behavior.* New York: Random House, 1972.

Turner, H. H. A syndrome of infantilism, congential webbed neck, and cubitus valgus. *Endocrinology*, 1938, *123*, 566-574.

Vandenberg, S. G. What do we know today about the inheritance of intelligence and how do we know it? In R. Cancro (Ed.), *Intelligence: Genetic and environmental influences.* New York: Grune & Stratton, 1971, pp. 182-218.

Von Tschermak, E. Uber Kunst Liche kreuzung bei *Pisum Sativum, Ber. dt. bot. Ges.,* 1900, *18,* 232-239.

Waddington, C. H. *The strategy of the genes.* New York: Macmillan, 1957.

Waddington, C. H. *New patterns in genetics and development.* New York: Columbia University Press, 1962.

Watson, J. D. Moving toward the clonal man. *The Atlantic Monthly,* 1971, *227,* 50-53.

Watson, J. D., & Crick, F. H. C. Genetical implications of the structure of deoxyribonucleic acid. *Nature,* 1953, *171,* 964-967. (a)

Watson, J. D. & Crick, F. H. C. Molecular structure of nucleic acids: A structure for deoxyribose nucleic acids. *Nature,* 1953, *171,* 737-738. (b)

Webster's seventh new collegiate dictionary. Springfield; Mass: Merriam, 1969.

Weinberg, W. Uber den nachweis der Vererbung beim Menschen. *Jahresheft Verin Vater Landische Naturk,* Wurttemberg, 1908, *64,* 369-382.

Williams, R. L. The silent mugging of the black community. *Psychology Today,* 1974, *7*(12); 32-41, 101.

Wright, S. Systems of mating. *Genetics,* 1921, *6,* 111-178.

Zigler, E. The nature-nurture issue reconsidered. In H. C. Haywood (Ed.), *Social-cultural aspects of mental retardation.* New York: Appleton-Century-Crofts, 1970, pp. 81-106.

Zinder, N. D., & Lederberg, J. Genetic exchange in Salmonella. *Journal of Bacteriology,* 1952, *64,* 679.

John J. Winters, Jr., received degrees in psychology from Fairleigh Dickinson University (B.A.), the New School for Social Research (M.A.), and New York University (Ph.D.). He has been the recipient of several scholarships and scholastic awards. Since entering the field of Experimental Psychology in 1963 he has been a member of the Research Department at the E. R. Johnstone Training and Research Center, except for a 1-year hiatus during which he was a Research Assistant at Swarthmore College. His research interests are in the development of visual perception, verbal learning, and cognitiion in mentally retarded and nonretarded children, and in adolescents. He is also interested in the methodological problems inherent in conducting behavioral research among those populations.

Dr. Winters is member of the American Psychological Association, Eastern Psychological Association, American Association on Mental Deficiency, American Academy on Mental Retardation, American Association for the Advancement of Science, and the Psychonomic Society. He has served on the Reserach Committee of the American Association on Mental Deficiency, as a consulting editor and book reviewer for the American Journal of Mental Deficiency, as a guest reviewer for other journals, and as an officer in the American Academy on Mental Retardation. As the author of over 40 professional publications, his research reports have been cited by national and international biographical societies.

5

Methodological issues in psychological research with retarded persons

John J. Winters, Jr.

A thorough review of all methodological issues in psychological research with the mentally retarded individual would require a tome with contributions from many authors of diverse interests. Those authors undoubtedly would agree that the problems inherent in the methodology of psychological research with retarded subjects are knotty. The literature is replete with articles discussing methodological problems with persons of average intelligence. When you compound these concerns with those germane to investigating the retarded person, they often take the form of the Gordian knot. Since the field of behavioral research with the retarded person is relatively new, we have not as yet become as verbose as our colleagues in other areas of research. Though this chapter will add to the increasing number of publications which discuss methodological issues in this area, it will not attempt to cover thoroughly, or even to consider, all those that might be of concern, but it will delve into a number of issues to varying degrees.

In the course of arriving at the essence of an issue, a truncated review of the history of the problem is offered. The salient purpose of the review is to emphasize the reason for concern and to grapple with solutions. Along the way the reader may not agree with the proposed solutions. He may dispute some conclusions, and he may feel that insufficient or undue weight has been given to some topics or that some could have been eliminated and others included. However, the author takes refuge in his contention that most researchers in this field, as in others, have some disagreement with the

The author is indebted to Herman H. Spitz and Donald H. Thor for their incisive readings of the manuscript and provocative discussions, to Ms. Barbara Kerstetter and Ms. Patricia Dennison for typing the several drafts of the manuscript, and to Ms. Emilia Ann Winters for her assistance in tabulating data, preparing figures, and general support.

conclusions of others and that it is constructive dissension that perpetuates innovation and progress.

The first major attempt at dealing with a variety of methodological problems in mental retardation was undertaken at the Woods School (Pennsylvania) Symposium in 1959, the proceedings of which have been reported in the *American Journal of Mental Deficiency* (1959, *64,* 227-430). When one reads the papers presented 16 years ago and compares the concerns of that time with those of today, two conclusions become evident: (a) If what was considered a problem then is no longer considered a problem, it is not because it was solved, but because we have gone onto new ones; and (b) if the problem still exists, we have succeeded in becoming a little more sophisticated about how to probe for the solution, but the problem itself often has been little affected. Thus, a perusal of the symposium proceedings will acquaint the reader with the wide variety of past concerns which will still seem very familiar. The reader is also referred to more recent considerations of methodological issues in mental retardation research (e.g., Baumeister & Kellas, 1971; Belmont, 1966, 1971; Denny, 1964; Gardner, 1969; Gerjuoy & Winters, 1969a; Gold, 1973; Lipman, 1963). Some of the issues considered below were also discussed in the latter reviews.

POPULATION COMPARISONS

Equal-MA–Equal-CA Designs

In many psychological experiments the performance of retarded persons is compared with that of intellectually normal persons. Goulet (1968) has trichotomized (as Types I, II, and III) the experimental designs that usually are employed when two such groups are compared. In Type I designs, retarded individuals are compared with those of average intelligence of equal mental age (MA). When the level of mental development is of primary concern, this design is recurrent.

When the two groups are compared in such equal-MA designs, the underlying premise is that any differences that occur may be due to intelligence level, motivation, or chronological age (CA). It is also assumed that though the retarded group is older than the normal group, and their respective past experiences may differ, these differences should have a negligible effect. However, studies which find retarded persons superior to normal individuals of equal MA (e.g., Winters, 1969) indicate that differential experience may affect performance in some tasks. Studies which reveal no differences assume that the MA match was appropriate, and that IQ and experiential differences were not influential. Studies which find persons of average intellect superior conclude that though the MA match was made, IQ or motivational factors were critical.

Zigler (1969), in a position paper, championed the use of the Type I design. His position is that the retarded person progresses through the same sequence of cognitive states as the person of normal intellect, but at a slower rate. The retarded individual also presumably has a more limited upper stage of cognition. This relative growth of cognitive states and upper limit also holds true for individuals of average and superior cognitive development. Essentially, Zigler feels that the MA match equates the developmental level of two sample groups differing in intellectual level, and the cognitive development is sequential with individual limitations on the upper bounds. Though intelligence is a hypothetical construct, at present the best indicator of intellectual development is the intelligence test; therefore, MA is used to equate groups in an experiment. Since, by definition, rate of cognitive development differs for persons of differing IQs, testing two groups of the same MA presupposes the same developmental level.

However, there is at least one main problem with the MA match. It is that, assuming that the intelligence test veridically measures cognitive development, there is no assurance that the experimental task is also an indicator of cognitive development or even a tangential facet of the latter. Any experiments in which retarded and normal persons of equal MA differ, regardless of which is superior in performance, would imply either that MA, or cognitive development, was not equal for both groups or that the experimental task was not related to cognitive development. Further discussion of Type I comparisons can be found in papers by Ellis (1969) and Milgram (1969).

A Type II design is one in which retarded persons are compared with individuals of average intelligence and equal CA. Here, differential performance could result from either the MA or IQ differences of the sample groups. When the level of performance is of primary concern, this design is used. The rationale for a Type II design is that, if normal and retarded individuals differ in intelligence, this difference is related to their CA, since IQ is determined by performance on a task which is related to CA. For example, Ellis' (1969) position is that the differences in adaptive behavior of persons of similar CA determine whether or not one is considered retarded. Thus, when an equal-CA match is performed, the parameter of age is controlled, and the definition of retardation has been met. Ellis, who defends the use of the Type II design, asserts that it is the differences in adaptive behavior that should interest the researcher in mental retardation. To match groups differing in adaptive behavior on MA and assume developmental equivalency is fallacious.

In the Type II design, matches can be made by controlling other independent variables (e.g., socioeconomic background, institutionalization) with the population samples, consequently differing only in level of adaptive behavior. Therefore, this design investigates differences in behavior without assuming accuracy of the IQ test. The investigator is not faced with the dilemma raised by the Type I design, namely, having to explain why subjects who are matched on MA differ on the experimental task. This quandary was also posed by Zigler (1968).

However, the Type II design poses another problem, as pointed out by Ellis (1969). When normal and retarded subjects of equal CA are compared, there is a greater likelihood of floor-and-ceiling effects (which will be discussed later) and of statistical interactions resulting from these artifacts. Baumeister (1967a) discussed these pseudointeractions in greater detail. Also, when performance differs between the normal and retarded groups in this design, we do not know whether the difference is related to IQ or to MA.

Generally, the attitude seems to be that if we can determine how and why retarded and normal presons differ, we can then facilitate the performance of individuals in the lower intelligence group so that they can behave optimally. In the Type I design, if the performance of the two groups is equivalent, as predicted, then the null hypothesis is supported; in the Type II design, emphasis is placed on why they differ. Unfortunately, neither design stresses the reasons for two groups being similar in performance. Possibly, a re-evaluation of the purpose of comparisons is needed, since it might be just as fruitful to emphasize the similarities and then strengthen the relevant behaviors as to emphasize differences and try to improve performance. Emphasizing similarities might be heuristic, since it has been found that the performance of retarded persons can be facilitated on some tasks (Bilsky & Evans, 1970; Gerjuoy & Spitz, 1966; Gerjuoy & Winters, 1970; Gerjuoy, Winters, Pullen, & Spitz, 1969), but transfer of facilitation to related tasks is rare (Bilsky & Evans, 1970; Bilsky, Evans, & Gilbert, 1972).

In reference to the transfer (or lack of it) of newly learned strategies by retarded individuals, Butterfield, Wambold, and Belmont (1973) concluded that training retarded persons on specific tasks was uneconomical in time and effort because generality to similar tasks was restricted. Extensive programmatic research would be required for each of many diversified tasks in order to achieve improvement in overall performance. They suggested that training executive functions (i.e., the process that coordinates these skills) would be more economical and would probably result in a more general theory. This author is in complete agreement with their strategy, although empirically determining which executive functions encompass what skills may not be easy. (See Chapter 7 by Butterfield and Belmont in this volume.)

In the Type III design, equal-MA normal subjects and equal-CA normal subjects (2 groups) are matched with a retarded group. Though this design is the most costly with respect to the number of subjects and experimental time, it yields more information to the investigator who is concerned with identifying the nature of the deficit in retarded individuals. It also yields more information concerning the performance of retarded persons in reference to normal groups. This author cannot agree with the opinion of one opponent of this design that it represents a "cafeteria approach." The addition of another contrast group adds vastly to the information concerning the relative performance of a group of retarded individuals.

As an example of the utilization of the Type III design, Winters (1969) used it in a study employing two different visual tasks. It was found that on one task, both the retarded and normal subjects of equal CA differed from the normals of equal MA, while on the other task, both the retarded and normal subjects of equal MA differed from the normals of equal CA. If only equal-MA or equal-CA groups had been used in either or both tasks, the relative areas of deficiency or efficiency would not have been demonstrated. In another instance, Gerjuoy and Spitz (1966) utilized in a verbal learning task (clustering) the Type III design and added a fourth group, college students. They found that their retarded and normal children, matched on MA, did not differ on the task, but both groups were inferior to the two older normal groups. By manipulation of the word list, the performance of the retarded group was facilitated to the level of the college group. If the older normal groups had not been tested, relative performance could not have been assessed, and information concerning the method of facilitating performance would have been lacking. If the youngest normal children had not been tested, information concerning performance on MA level would have been lacking, since clustering does improve with MA.

This design, however, faces the problems inherent in the other two designs, namely, the assumptions that MA is equal to cognitive development and that if the retarded and equal-CA normal groups are so diverse on MA initially, merely another difference has been found. The advantages are that: (a) The experimenter can gain more information concerning normal behavior in order to evaluate retarded behavior; and (b) by determining how a normal group accomplishes the task, he may be able to apply these strategies to facilitate learning in the mentally retarded person (Butterfield, Wambold, & Belmont, 1973).

But there are some questions as to why we should study normal behavior at all if we are concerned with the behavior of the retarded individual. For example, Baumeister (1967a) contended that, "To understand the behavior of retardates one must study the behavior of retardates. The study of normal behavior is quite irrelevant to this purpose" (pp. 874-875).

His reasoning is that, logically, if laws of behavior of retarded people are the primary concern of investigators in this field, why digress and study the behavior of persons of average intelligence? His argument would be sound—if the information obtained concerning performance by normal groups was not used to change or understand performance of retarded persons. To find that normal and retarded groups do or do not differ, and then just make inferences about the behavior of retarded people, is not a significant contribution to understanding the behavior of retarded persons.

However, the use, misuse, or nonuse of normal groups also depends largely upon whether the experimenter views himself as an investigator of retardation or as a developmental psychologist concerned with laws of human development. The former type of researcher must seriously consider Baumeister's argument, and either restrict his investigations to retarded individuals or utilize information derived from normal behavior to change the behavior of retarded persons. The developmental psychologist need not be too concerned with Baumeister's argument, but this does not free him from the responsibility of studying the development of both normal and retarded persons. Few experimenters test several normal and retarded groups because the approach is uneconomical. As a result, little is learned about the relative development of the two populations. An increased use of the Type III design by researchers would also increase the ratio between the number of normal and retarded persons tested. Consequently, as we include more normal groups in our design, relatively less information is gathered about retarded behavior as compared with normal behavior. Thus, Baumeister's concern becomes even more critical.

An alternative to the above research designs, and one that might alleviate the concern for diminishing amounts of knowledge regarding retarded behavior, is the developmental study. A developmental study may be viewed as one in which *several* levels of an age or IQ parameter are compared by manipulating the number of retarded and normal groups. It may also be considered as an extension of the Type III design, with equal-MA and equal-CA normals matched with additional retarded groups. Such a study might include either several retarded groups varying in MA, CA, or IQ while the normal groups are held constant, or three or more groups of retarded persons who are matched with groups of normals on MA and CA so that the continua of both parameters are investigated. In that way, knowledge of the development of either population could be obtained and comparative analyses performed.

Harter (1967), in her investigation of learning sets in normal and retarded children, extended the Type III design into a developmental study and tested eight groups of subjects, each on two motivational conditions. Four groups were of below-average intelligence, two groups were of average intelligence, and two groups were of above-average intelligence. The three IQ groups were intermatched on MA and CA. With this design it was possible for Harter to investigate the relationships among CA, MA, and IQ as predictors of discrimination learning set performance. Though these data have been reinterpreted recently (Kappauf, 1973), the use of this rare design is a significant contribution to this area of research. Other noteworthy studies using this design have contributed to the understanding not only of retarded and normal behavior, but also of gifted children (Harper, 1965; Paraskevopoulas, 1968a, 1968b). Obviously, this is not a popular design, since the number of subjects tested and the amount of time invested are considerably more than in the previously mentioned typical designs, though it is the most fruitful in gleaning information about normal-retarded behavior.

In order to determine more objectively the number of developmental studies conducted with retarded subjects, three journals were surveyed by the present author. McCandless (1970), the editor of *Developmental Psychology,* reported that 17% of the articles submitted to that journal since its inception in January 1969 have dealt with broad age-range samples, but only 4% of all articles dealt with retarded persons.

In *Child Development,* a journal which specializes in developmental studies, it was found that, over a 10-year period, approximately 4% of the studies used retarded individuals as subjects and about 1% were developmental studies with this population. In the *American Journal of Mental Deficiency,* where all studies reported investigate retardation, 0.1% of papers published in a 10-year period reported developmental studies. Though some outstanding research has been reported in which the development of the retarded individual was the main concern (e.g., Clausen, 1966), it is obvious that there is a dearth of literature in this area. Aside from the previously mentioned difficulties with such research, McCandless (1970) reported that only 31% of developmental studies submitted were accepted. This was due to the employment of small or specialized population samples—from which the authors tried to generalize—and to techniques that were too narrow to be of general use. From these valid criticisms it can be concluded that either (a) those investigators conducting developmental research must sharpen their experimental acumen (Dunn, 1967; Solomon & Lessac, 1968; Wohlwill, 1970), or (b) the criteria for accepting this type of study for publication must differ from those applied to the Type I, II, or III designs. This is not to recommend a lowering of publication standards, but rather to suggest that more consideration be given to the value of developmental studies in this barren area. Naturally, conclusion (a) above is the preferred course.

The last, and least reported, study format is that of longitudinal research. In the longitudinal design, the same subjects are retested over a relatively long period of time. The need for this approach has been reported elsewhere (e.g., Milgram, 1972), and a review of the three previously mentioned journals shows that the number of such published studies is almost nil.

If growth, rate of grow'h, and development are the experimenter's main concern, then the longitudinal study is necessary. It has the advantages of all the previously mentioned designs plus the use of a subject as his own control over an extended period. It should also be apparent that those who are interested in the possible deleterious effects of the environment on growth and retardation, and the possible interaction of the environment and heredity on growth, should initiate their longitudinal research with infants rather than with older subjects. In this way, an experimenter can manipulate or control his independent variables before they have been contaminated, and IQ can then become a dependent variable.

An excellent example of the longitudinal approach is a study being conducted by Heber and his associates (Heber, Dever, & Conry, 1968; Heber, Garber, Harrington, Hoffman, & Falender, 1972). In a high-risk area in Milwaukee, which has a high incidence of mental retardation, Heber and his colleagues screened Black mothers who had IQs above and below 75. Of those below IQ 75, half of the selected subjects were assigned to the experimental group and the other half to the control group. An intervention program for the infants and mothers of the experimental group was initiated shortly after the birth of the infants (CA-3 months) and continued over an extended period (to CA-6 years) to determine whether mental retardation could be prevented or deterred. If, at school age, the experimental children exhibited normal intelligence, then Heber and his associates would have demonstrated that the incidence of mental retardation in high-risk areas can be decreased. If the experimental group exhibited the same retarded behavior as the control group, then it would have demonstrated that this kind of intensive stimulation was not sufficient to overcome factors inherent at birth.

As of December 1972, the mean IQ of the experimental group was approximately 30 points higher than the mean IQ of the control group. However, the control group's mean IQ was never below 90. The investigators have also reported that the experimental and control groups are now in school, and follow-up studies are being performed. This longitudinal project promises to be one of the most critical for determining the effects of early intervention on mental retardation.

Unfortunately, the more demanding the research design, the more infrequent its use becomes. Tulving and Madigan (1970), in a critical review of the research in memory and verbal learning, concluded that less than 10% of the research published could be classified as "worthwhile" and that the other 90% or more "makes one wish that at least some of the writers, faced with the decision of whether to publish or perish, should have seriously considered the latter alternative" (p. 442). This criticism probably could be directed toward researchers in other areas. Though I find it difficult to agree that perishing is preferable to publishing, Tulving and Madigan have made their point. Insistence on more complete designs, along with developmental and longitudinal studies, would reduce the number of publications, but would probably add significantly to "worthwhile" research.

To seek a middle-of-the-road design which would satisfy all possible criticisms and still be economical in time, effort, and money would be both fruitless and naive. Designs are usually dictated by the problem under investigation, whether rate, level of development, or growth is of primary concern. A potpourri of samples (different IQ, MA, and CA levels of normal and retarded groups that are not matched on population parameters) investigated over differing periods of time also is not the solution. A question then arises as to whether the designs generally in use, with all their flaws, are nevertheless the best methods available for investigating the problems. If the design permits an adequate test of the hypotheses, the answer is yes; if the design does not, the answer is no. What should be of primary concern is the trade-off (namely, the scientific value of the information received), in view of the possible flaws of the design, as compared with the information that could have been found if a more extensive design had been used.

Statistical Matching

In experiments comparing normal and retarded groups, the retarded group is usually selected first and the experimenter then strives to acquire as close a match as possible, restricting normal samples to those population parameters predetermined by the retarded sample. In order to ascertain the effect of an independent variable on the dependent measure, the investigator places stringent requirements on the sample matches. Unfortunately, in doing this, we may be doing ourselves a strong disservice. Prehm (1966a) and Stanley (1967) have raised serious objections concerning the use of matched MA and CA groups. Their argument is that when groups are matched individual to individual, or with respect to means and standard deviations, one limits the populations to which one can generalize the findings. Consequently, the results may be biased in favor of the group, or groups, initially superior on the antecedent variable.

It is contended that normal subjects randomly drawn from a population, and randomly assigned to the treatment conditions, would permit greater generalizability of results. Statistical matching, rather than experimental matching, could then be accomplished by the use of analysis of convariance (ANCOVA). Matching on a covariate is held to be superior to matching experimentally (Stanley & Beeman, 1958). This approach apparently would alleviate at least some of the problems facing the experimenter who cannot find adequate normal-retarded or retarded-retarded matches, and it would permit greater extension of the findings. It would also permit the use of multiple groups. However, some problems inherent in using an ANCOVA design could make statistical matching less desirable than experimental matching. For example, there are the underlying assumptions that (a) the regression of the dependent variable on the covariable should be linear, and (b) the correlation coefficient between X and Y should be equal to zero.

As an example, if two groups, retarded and normal, were randomly selected and randomly assigned to a control and experimental condition, the IQ scores could covary, and an ANCOVA would equate groups if the scores of the dependent variable on the covariate are linear (McNemar, 1962) and if the regression lines' slopes do not differ significantly for the two groups (Snedecor, 1956). This method would undoubtedly be superior to experimental matching, but if the assumptions were not met in a given design, the data could be misinterpreted.

Heal (1970) proposed two methods of statistically controlling population variables. In the first method, CA and other control variables would be partialled out of the correlation between IQ and the criterion variable. In this way, the relationship between CA and the control variables would be statistically independent. For the second method Heal proposed, as did Prehm and Stanley, the use of an ANCOVA design.

Another restriction in statistical matching, which was pointed out by Lindquist (1953), is that the covariables in an ANCOVA study should be the *only* relevant factors on which the groups initially differ. Therefore, when normal subjects are compared with institutionalized retarded subjects, or "familial" retarded samples are compared with brain-damaged retarded samples, or when socioeconomic, racial, or other relevant backgrounds differ, an ANCOVA approach may not be suitable. In addition, Lord (1960) mentioned that the covariables must be wholly reliable (i.e., free of errors in measurement), since unreliable covariables do not equate fully. Also, unless the covariables are controlled before the introduction of the treatment variable, the ANCOVA procedure will covary out part of the independent variable. Thus, if the treatment involves different levels of motivation or reward, and the groups vary in amount of reward needed to sustain performance (motivation not being the covariate), the experimenter might eliminate some of the effects of the levels of motivation if an ANCOVA is used.

More recently, Evans and Anastasio (1968), Harris, Bisbee, and Evans (1971), and Sprott (1970) have been concerned with the degree to which one underlying assumption has been met, namely, whether the covariance between the treatment effect and the covariate can be assumed to be zero or whether the expected value must be zero. This issue has not yet been resolved. Harris et al. (1971) indicated that some researchers interpret ANCOVA as removing that variance which is caused by the covariate. This misinterpretation may be due to the similarity between the summary tables used in reporting results of the analysis of variance and ANCOVA procedures. However, the ANCOVA, which eliminates only variance correlated with the covariate, should be considered as any other regression analysis. Rather than use an ANCOVA when there is a high probability that the assumptions are violated, it is possible to employ a multiple-regression analysis. But the underlying assumptions of this analysis must also be met (Darlington, 1968). Cohen (1968) presented an interesting comparison between multiple regression techniques and ANCOVA, with special consideration to curvilinearity and covariates for uncorrelated or correlated independent variables.

In sum, there would appear to be three methodological approaches in comparing normal versus retarded groups. First, the experimenter may use the equal MA and/or equal CA normal matches, thereby possibly restricting the generalizability of the results. Second, the investigator may randomly select subjects from given populations and randomly assign them to experimental treatments. Tests for linearity and regression could then be conducted, and if the underlying assumptions are not violated, ANCOVA or multiple-regression techniques can be used. A third possibility would be to increase the range of the population parameters, but to continue to equate for MA and/or CA. In this way, if the assumptions are not violated, correlational techniques can be used without restricted generalizability. Let us now look at some other issues encountered in formulating effective experimental designs.

VERBAL STIMULI

Familiarity and Meaningfulness

The most common type of psychological experiment in mental retardation, exclusive of that involving applied behavior modification, is in the area of verbal learning (Gardner & Selinger, 1971). Here, the investigator usually presents verbal stimuli visually (words or pictures) and/or auditorily. The stimuli are often controlled for meaningfulness (and sometimes for familiarity), since the stimulus materials for one group of subjects may not have the same meaningfulness and/or familiarity as for another group differing in CA, MA, or IQ. *Familiarity* refers to the experience a subject has had with given stimuli, while *meaningfulness* refers either to the number of associative responses (*m*) a particular subject may have for an item, or to the proportion of subjects who have a particular association for a given item.

Familiarity is usually controlled by using the Thorndike-Lorge (1944) word count of highly familiar stimuli. The experimenter can also familiarize the subject with the stimuli during the experiment so that groups will be equated on this variable. However, this latter procedure is not always successful and does not control for pre-experimental experience. Berry and Baumeister (1971), in an investigation of associative learning, found that 26% of their retarded sample (CA range 12-45 years; IQ range 43-80) had to be excluded from the experiment because of their inability to recognize letters, digits, and words, even though the digits criterion was the most meaningful for nonretarded adults (Battig & Spera, 1962).

Word Association Norms

Control of meaningfulness is usually achieved by applying to the retarded and normal samples the word association norms which have been derived from normal children and adults. The problem of applying the norms of nonretarded groups to retarded groups will be discussed in detail later. However, a question still remains as to the relationship between familiarity and meaningfulness. This relationship remains uncertain (Cramer, 1968), and the criticisms of inaccurate measurement of either apply to both when used with a retarded population.

Much normative data on stimulus meaningfulness have been gathered from adult college students. The more commonly used norms for nonsense syllables are the data collected by Archer (1960), Glaze (1928), Noble (1961), and Underwood and Schultz (1960). The latter authors also derived norms on consonant syllables, dissyllables, bigram and trigram frequencies, and pronouncing capability and response frequencies to single- and two-letter stimuli. Battig and Spera (1962) obtained association values of the numbers 0 to 100; Paivio, Yuille, and Madigan (1968) gathered norms on the concreteness, imagery, and meaningfulness (*m*) of nouns. Interestingly, Paivio et al. (1968) found a reliable but unimpressive relationship between concreteness and meaningfulness (*r* = .56). This finding suggests that what is highly concrete is not necessarily highly meaningful, an assumption which some have made in the past. Also, the relationships between the Thorndike-Lorge (T-L) word count and imagery, concreteness, and meaningfulness were significant but low (*r* = .23, .12, and .33, respectively), indicating that the T-L word count is minimally related to those variables.

The low correlations with the T-L count also could have been due to (a) independence between the number of times words appear in print and their imagery, concreteness, and meaningfulness; or (b) the outdated word count, now over 30 years old. A more recent corpus (Carroll, Davies, & Richman, 1971) is suggested as an alternative to the T-L word count.

Fewer word association norms have been collected for normal children. Entwisle (1966) and Palermo and Jenkins (1963, 1964a, 1964b, 1966) have conducted the bulk of the research in this area. A thorough review and discussion of most word association studies is presented by Cramer (1968).

Prior to 1969, a number of word association norms for retarded persons were published (Eastman & Rosanoff, 1912; Gerjuoy & Gerjuoy, 1965; Horan, 1955, 1956; Otis, 1915; Semmel, Barritt, Bennett, & Perfetti, 1968; Silverstein & McLain, 1961, 1964). The Kent-Rosanoff (1910) word list was used in all but one study (Semmel et al., 1968). Investigators in mental retardation who wanted to compare normal with retarded groups and to vary meaningfulness usually chose the associative norms derived from normal samples, since no comparative norms were available. In at least one instance there was a direct comparison of normal and retarded children on the free-association strength (FAS)—i.e., the strength of associations between words as estimated from normative data of free association tests—of stimulus and response terms when the Palermo-Jenkins (P-J) list was used, in order to determine the applicability of those norms to both populations (Flamer, 1969).

Flamer compared normal children (Mean CA $\cong$ 10 years) with an older retarded group of the same MA and with a retarded group of equal CA on a paired-associates (P-A) task in which three lists with different FAS levels were to be learned. He found that the normals performed better than the retarded group of equal MA, who in turn were superior to the retarded group of equal CA. Also, the FAS levels for the normal and retarded groups of equal MA had the same hierarchy of learning the lists (high FAS > intermediate FAS = low FAS), but differed from the learning hierarchy of the retarded group of equal CA (high FAS > intermediate FAS, high FAS = low FAS, low FAS = intermediate FAS). Flamer concluded that his results suggested the retarded children with the same MA as normal children had similar associative hierarchies and that the word association norms for normal children should be used with retarded children. Because of the nonexistence of word association norms comparing normal and retarded persons, Flamer tried to resolve the problem with best available stimuli, but the different hierarchies of the two higher MA groups, as compared with the lowest MA group on the intermediate and low FAS levels, does suggest that the P-J word list is too inaccurate and inappropriate for use with retarded subjects. The main problem is that when normal and retarded groups are experimentally or statistically matched on MA, the assumption is made that equal-MA groups will have equivalent FAS levels. This assumption is challenged by the study of Griffith, Spitz, and Lipman (1959), who found that their retarded group was approximately 3 years behind the normal sample of equal MA in mediation and concept formation.

Rate and level of learning. Several other significant attempts have been made to control meaningfulness in order to determine the relative rates of learning in normal and retarded subjects. Prehm (1966b) compared normal and retarded groups in a P-A learning task using either nonsense stick figures or pictures from the Peabody Picture Vocabulary Test as stimulus terms, and high- or low-rated consonant-vowel-consonant (CVC) trigrams as response terms. A pilot study indicated that the four possible lists of pairs (figures-low CVC, figures-high CVC, pictures-low CVC, pictures-high CVC) had to differ in list length (3, 6, 6, and 14 pairs, respectively) in order to equate levels of learning. He found that normal persons were superior to retarded persons in acquisition and that level of meaningfulness was significant for normal but not for retarded individuals. Prehm concluded that "meaningfulness" is not an important variable for learning in the retarded child, but this conclusion must be held in abeyance, since levels of "meaningfulness" and list length were confounded.

Drew, Prehm, and Logan (1968), in order to control association value as an experimental variable, compared retarded and normal groups of equal CA on a P-A learning task with two levels of FAS (high and low) on the P-J word list. Their results revealed that the normal group performed better than the retarded group, and both groups were superior in performance on the high FAS lists. Thus, it was found that meaningfulness was important for learning in retarded individuals when list length and meaningfulness were not confounded.

Later, Drew (1969) equated word frequency (T-L word count) on two levels of FAS (high and low) on the P-J work list, and compared retarded and normal groups of equal CA on a P-A learning task. Analyses indicated that although acquisition of the high FAS list was better than the low FAS list for both groups, rate of learning did not differ between the two groups. Therefore, in this last study, level of meaningfulness was as important for the retarded as for the normal subjects, in agreement with Drew et al. (1968) but not with Prehm (1966b). These inconsistent results may be due to the definition of "meaningfulness." In one instance (Prehm, 1966b) the levels of meaningfulness were determined perceptually, which is not uncommon. In the other two studies they were determined by the use of the P-J norms. The studies reviewed to this point indicate the problems inherent in controlling meaningfulness as an experimental variable crucial to learning. Obviously, consistent result are elusive, since the criteria of meaningfulness and familiarity are flexible and sometimes inexact.

Short-term memory. The variable of meaningfulness is also a problem in a related field of investigation, that of short-term memory. Ellis, McCarver and Ashurst (1970) investigated the short-term memory of three retarded groups differing in mean IQ, using a probe technique. In this study the stimuli were exposed sequentially in a horizontal linear array, followed by the test stimulus (probe), which was situated above and in the center of the previously exposed stimuli. The subject's task was to indicate where the test stimulus had appeared in the sequence by pressing the appropriate manipulandum. Each IQ group was tested on high meaningful (pictures) and low-meaningful (nonsense shapes) stimuli. It was hypothesized that high-meaningful stimuli would facilitate performance and that subjects in the higher IQ group would perform better in the primacy portion of the performance curve. It was found that IQ level did facilitate performance in the primacy portion of the curve, which was attributed to a more efficient rehearsal strategy by the more intelligent subjects; but neither the main effect of meaningfulness nor the interaction of IQ with meaningfulness was significant. These results are especially surprising because levels of familiarity also differed. The authors hypothesized that the subjects of high IQ may have implicitly labeled the low-meaningful stimuli, thereby minimizing differences between levels of meaningfulness. Because of a lack of appropriate norms of meaningfulness for these stimuli, researchers in this area of interest have been deprived of materials that could produce more definitive studies.

Norms for retarded children. Gerjuoy and Gerjuoy (1956), pointing out the need for word association norms derived from samples of retarded children, conducted a preliminary study to explore the feasibility of obtaining word association norms from institutionalized, adolescent, mentally retarded subjects. One hundred individually tested subjects from this population were successfully administered the 100 words of the Kent-Rosanoff list, and the frequencies of the most common responses were reported. J. W. Gallagher (1969a, 1969b) then used these "norms" in several studies. In the first study, he compared retarded children with normal children of equal MA and with college students on a P-A learning task with lists of high, low, and nonassociated FAS pairs (J. W. Gallagher, 1969a). The normal subjects' word pairs and FAS values were from the P-J norms; the retarded group's word pairs and FAS values were from the Gerjuoy-Gerjuoy (G-G) norms. He found that the performance of the college students was superior to the equal-MA normal subjects, who were superior to the retarded group. The normal groups made fewer errors on the high and low FAS pairs than on the nonassociated pairs, while the high and low levels did not differ. The retarded group made fewer errors on high FAS pairs than on the low or nonassociated FAS pairs, while these two levels did not differ. Gallagher (1969a) concluded that retarded persons may not be as responsive to low FAS values as are normal individuals.

In order to avoid the problem of the availability of a mediator in learning pairs of words, J. W. Gallagher (1969b) examined P-A chaining in retarded and normal children of equal MA on a single list (A-C) using the multiplicative value of FAS values (A-B X B-C) to determine the strength of A-C pairs. He derived three levels of FAS (high, low, and nonassociated). The word pairs and FAS values for the normal and retarded groups were obtained from the P-J and G-G norms, respectively. It was found that although the normal group was superior to the retarded group, both groups learned the high FAS pairs faster than the low FAS pairs, which were also learned faster than the nonassociated pairs.

Thus, by using multiplicative values of FAS derived from the norms of appropriate population samples, Gallagher avoided the problem of availability of the mediator, and concluded that retarded persons do use associations (i.e., mediate) to facilitate learning. However, he attributed the differential learning rates of his two groups to either (a) the inaccessibility of mediators to his retarded subjects without pretraining, or (b) the presentation method (oral-aural), in which normal and retarded persons may respond differentially. Gallagher (1969b) concluded that future research should utilize normative associative information when examining learning and mediational processes in retarded samples.

On another P-A learning task, Gallagher and Reid (1970) examined the influence of five FAS percentage levels (28, 16, 8, 1, and 0) on the learning of retarded and normal children of equal MA, and of normal subjects with MAs two years lower than those of the retarded group. Of primary concern was why the retarded children had not learned low and nonassociated FAS pairs differentially (Flamer, 1969; J. W. Gallagher, 1969a). As before, the appropriate stimuli were selected from the P-J and G-G lists for each group. The most significant finding was that when the FAS values were high, the performance of the retarded and normal groups of equal MA were similar, though not equivalent. As FAS values decreased, the retarded group's performance became relatively poorer until it was more similar to that of the younger normal sample. These results confirmed the previous findings that low and nonassociated FAS pairs are not learned differentially. The only difference between FAS levels was between the highest (28%) and the next to the lowest (1%) values. The authors concluded that large differences in FAS values are needed to obtain statistically significant differences. The results also indicate, as does the plotting of Gallagher and Reid's (1970) data, that the slopes of the performance curves of the retarded and younger normal groups are more similar to each other than is the slope of either curve to that of the equal-MA normal group. Thus, though an MA match may be more appropriate when FAS values are high, the MA match is seemingly inappropriate at lower FAS levels.

Another possible reason for the deficiency of the retarded person's verbal ability relative to expected ability based on MA has been investigated by this author, in collaboration with Mary Anne Brzoska. Our concern was for the development of the lexicon (i.e., the available dictionary) of a group of retarded children, and of several groups of children and adolescents of average intelligence. We reasoned that if the lexicons of retarded individuals were not comparable to the lexicons of normal individuals of the same MA, then the requisite of an MA match was not met when two groups differing in IQ but equivalent in MA were compared. Our approach to investigating the development of and comparisons of the lexicons of these several groups was to present to the subjects 480 chromatic pictures of common objects and to determine whether the subjects could label each one correctly.

Briefly, 24 noninstitutionalized children classified as retarded (mean CA = 11.89 years, mean MA = 8.46 years, mean IQ = 71.61), 26 kindergarten children (mean CA = 5.67 years), 26 fourth-graders (mean CA = 9.56 years, mean MA = 7.70 years, mean IQ = 101.79), and 21 ninth-graders (mean CA = 14.79 years, mean MA = 15.56 years, mean IQ = 104.77) were tested. Intelligence test scores were not available for the kindergarten children. One of the subject's tasks was to name each picture as it appeared (16-second rate). An adult experimenter recorded the subject's response.

The results most relevant to the several groups' abilities to correctly label the stimuli were: (a) labeling ability was more highly related to MA than to CA, whereas IQ had a minimal effect on performance; (b) the age at which words were estimated to be acquired (AA) or learned, as determined by Carroll and White (1973), was a better indicator of performance for all groups than the commonly used T-L word count; (c) the earlier a word should have been acquired, the greater the retarded group's lag in performance—i.e., there was a differential effect on the retarded group's performance depending upon the estimated AA; and (d) overall, the retarded group's performance was approximately 2 years behind what would be expected on the basis of their MA.

In other words, the T-L word count may not be the most appropriate measure to use when matching normal and retarded groups on verbal learning tasks. The words that are listed as the most frequent by Thorndike and Lorge (1944) produced the greatest decrement in the retarded group's performance relative to their MA. Even more confounding is the finding that although the retarded group performed approximately 2 years behind their expected MA level, this estimate is based on performance on the total corpus of 480 stimuli. As pictures vary in ease of labeling, so does the relative performance of the retarded group. Given these results, in conjunction with those cited above, the question arises as to which parameter to use when comparing normal and retarded groups. At present the only tentative answer is that it depends upon the task (i.e., whether the task requires naming pictures, forming associations, and so forth). What is obvious is that matching solely on MA may not be the most efficient method and that more efficient techniques must be sought. It would be discouraging to think that experimental hypotheses are being unduly influenced by inequities in the stimuli, but the foregoing results do suggest this possibility.

For some time now, researchers in the area of verbal learning have been aware of the need for association frequencies of specific items for various subject groups. Deese (1959) stated that "at the very least, . . . experiments in which different groups of Ss are compared for their ability to remember specific items should either present data on association frequencies for the groups concerned or make certain that such association frequencies are well controlled" (p. 22). Until 1969, no investigator of verbal learning in mental retardation could comply with the latter suggestion since norms comparing normal and retarded groups were not available, although J. W. Gallagher's previously cited studies, in which he used different norms with different populations, came the closest.

In a seminal study, Gerjuoy and Winters (1969b) tested 997 institutionalized adjescent mentally retarded persons on a word association task. There were approximately 100 males and 100 females at each of five age levels (11, 13, 15, 17, and 19 years). The 200 P-J words were orally administered to individual subjects who were instructed to respond with the first word they thought of, and the experimenter recorded the responses verbatim.

Comparisons (Rho) were made between the five most frequent responses given by the nonretarded subjects of the P-J sample and by the retarded subjects in this study for each stimulus word within each grade-, CA-, and IQ-sex category. The data were combined over sex, since no difference for this variable was found. Figure 5.1 depicts the correlations of the five most frequent responses between each $\overline{CA}$ retarded group and the eight normal groups. Figure 5.2 represents the correlations of the five most frequent responses between each $\overline{IQ}$-retarded group and the eight normal groups.

Aside from individual group comparisons, which have been reported elsewhere (Gerjuoy & Winters, 1969b), the main findings were as follows:

1. The slopes of the two sets of curves are similar and constantly decline, indicating that as the normal group's MA increases, there are fewer word associations that are also given by the retarded groups.

2. The $\overline{\text{IQ}}$ comparisons (Fig. 5.2) produce generally higher correlations than $\overline{\text{CA}}$ comparisons (Fig. 5.1).

3. When comparable MA groups are represented, the correlations of the five most frequent responses are higher than when comparisons are made with retarded persons whose MAs are lower than those of the normal sample.

4. In order to obtain a higher correlation between the two populations, it is necessary to match the retarded subjects with lower-MA normal subjects. This is consistent with previous findings (Gallagher & Reid, 1970; Griffith, Spitz & Lipman, 1959) that the performance of retarded persons is more akin to a lower-MA normal group than to an equal-MA normal group.

5. As MA decreases, the relationship between the word association responses of the retarded and normal groups of equal MA also decrease. Thus, the MA level of both the retarded and normal groups matched on MA can significantly effect relative performance.

It should also be noted that the highest correlation between the two groups was .60 and that the relationship occurred when the retarded group's $\overline{\text{MA}}$ was 135.15 months and the normal sample's $\overline{\text{MA}}$ was 108 months (see Fig. 5.2). Though this correlation is significant, group comparisons are not the most efficient. In order to seek relationships that would not solely reflect group comparisons, but would also indicate the values of the stimulus words, the data were reported in a different format by Winters and Kahn (1970, 1971). They reported comparisons between the five most frequent word associations of the normal groups and the five most frequent word associations of the institutionalized retarded groups for each of the 200 stimulus words. The 1970 study presented tables which compared each of five $\overline{\text{MA}}$ levels of the retarded sample (92, 102, 108, 116, and 135 months) with the $\overline{\text{MA}}$ of the normal subjects (167 months). The 1971 study presented tables which compared each of the four $\overline{\text{MA}}$ levels of the retarded sample with each of the eight $\overline{\text{MA}}$ levels of the normal sample (see Fig. 5.1 for the population parameters). It is intended that these tables be used when an experimenter wants to control for FAS or meaningfulness on a verbal learning task, and for comparing normal and retarded samples who comply with the population parameters described therein.

It should be pointed out that there are two general restrictions on these

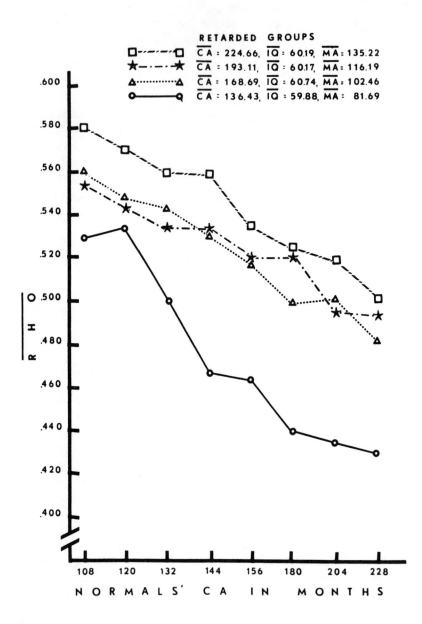

Figure 5.1. Correlations of the retarded groups' five most frequent responses with the normal groups' (Palermo & Jenkins) five most frequent responses as a function of increasing CA in the normal and retarded groups.

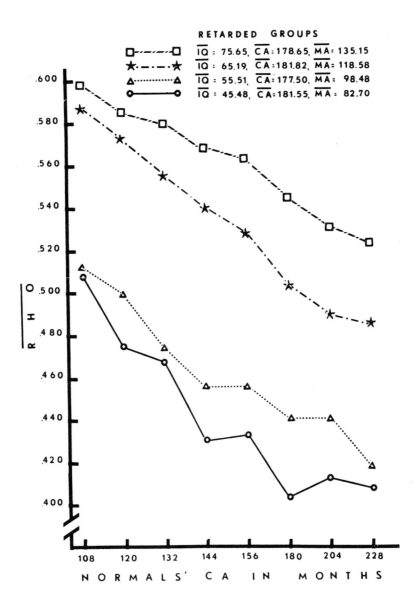

Figure 5.2. Correlations of the retarded groups' five most frequent responses with the normal groups' (Palermo & Jenkins) five most frequent responses as a function of increasing IQ in the retarded groups and increasing CA in the normal groups.

data. The first is that Palermo and Jenkins' (1964a) youngest normal $\overline{MA}$ group was 108 months, while Gerjuoy and Winters (1969b) had two younger $\overline{MA}$ retarded groups (82 and 102 months). As a result, equal $\overline{MA}$ comparisons could not be made below $\overline{MA}$ 108 months. Second, the retarded sample in the latter study consisted of institutionalized individuals.

In order to extend the relationship between the associations of normal and retarded persons downward below $\overline{MA}$ 108, Harris Kahn of the University of Connecticut[1] is comparing the word associations of the Gerjuoy and Winters (1969b) retarded sample with the word associations of normal children in grades 1 through 4 (Palermo & Jenkins, 1966). When Kahn's analysis is completed, comparisons of word associations will have been made between normal subjects, whose $\overline{MA}$s range from 72 to 228 months, and retarded subjects, whose $\overline{MA}$s range between 82 and 135 months.

Institutionalization and word associations. As for institutionalization as a variable in word association norms, J. W. Gallagher and Baumeister have collected free association data on 100 words from the P-J norms (Baumeister & Kellas, 1971). Their study included 400 institutionalized retarded persons from four institutions, 100 noninstitutionalized retarded persons, and 100 normal children (grades 3, 4, and 5). They found considerable equivalence of norms. However, some significant differences were found, including differences between institutions. Thus, the derived normative associative data were not completely interchangeable among these various groups. It may also be true that normative associative data are not completely interchangeable between *any* groups with differing backgrounds and population parameters.

The finding of considerable equivalence of norms among retarded persons, though the norms are not completely interchangeable, is encouraging because it suggests some commonality of word associations among the groups that Baumeister and his colleagues investigated. However, in those studies which investigated the word associations of retarded individuals, 1,400 retarded subjects were institutionalized while only 100 retarded subjects were noninstitutionalized. Undoubtedly, more basic information is needed concerning that 96% of the retarded population which is noninstitutionalized; as Baumeister and Kellas (1971) pointed out, normative data on other language characteristics of the retarded population are needed as well.

It is becoming more apparent that hypotheses concerning cognition, verbal learning, and concept formation are susceptible to the stimulus materials being used and that the MA match is becoming antiquated. Thus, it is imperative that more efficient control of the stimuli be achieved and that matches between normal and retarded groups be based on task-relevant

---

[1] Personal communication, June 15, 1971.

parameters rather than on classical techniques. This can be accomplished only by conducting the required basic research on the stimuli to be used with the population under investigation.

Consideration of the preceding selected experiments leads to several tentative conclusions concerning research in verbal learning. One conclusion is that retarded persons have a lower language development than their normal MA counterparts (Griffith, Spitz, & Lipman, 1959; Gallagher & Reid, 1970). Thus, an MA match between normals and retarded groups is not always the most appropriate comparison. Another inference is that the relationship between MA and meaningfulness is more curvilinear in the retarded person than in the normal person (Gallagher & Reid, 1970). A third observation is that when inappropriate norms are used to control levels of meaningfulness, the hierarchy of performance of retarded and normal groups of equal MA is inconsistent (Flamer, 1969). Fourth, it may be concluded that the use of multiplicative FAS values from appropriate normative data is a valid indicator of FAS and alleviates experimentally induced mediational techniques when investigating verbal mediation (J. W. Gallagher, 1969b). Fifth, one is left with the impression that when levels of meaningfulness are not derived from appropriate normative data, the results are confounded and interpretations of the data can be inconclusive (Ellis, McCarver, & Ashurst, 1970; Prehm, 1966b). Last, preliminary evidence indicates that the lexicons of normal and retarded persons of equal MA are not equivalent which, if supported by future research, stipulates that the retarded group should perform at a lower level than their equal MA counterparts in verbal learning tasks.

FLOOR AND CEILING EFFECTS[2]

Floor and ceiling effects are among the chronic problems that influence the results of experiments which compare the performance of normal and retarded persons. Haywood (1970) referred to them as "the perennial problem . . . with which we are painfully acquainted" (p. 9). These effects imply that the difficulty or ease of a task affects performance. The following definitions are offered in order to describe these effects more accurately.

When an independent variable is expected to produce a substantial improvement in group performance, but cannot do so because the group is already performing close to maximum on the task, then we say that a *ceiling effect* exists. When an independent variable is expected to produce a substantial decrease in group performance, but cannot do so because the

---

[2] The author is grateful to John M. Belmont for his erudite comments on a previous draft of this section.

group is already performing close to minimum on the task, then we say that a *floor effect* exists. Figure 5.3 shows examples of these two effects. Lines A and A′ depict the floor effect, and lines B and B′ depict the ceiling effect.

These artifacts are usually unpredictable (except in extreme cases), and few attempts have been made to evaluate them. When either effect is in evidence, the investigator may treat them as a flaw in the experiment, or he may choose to ignore them and to interpret his results as if the effects did not exist. However, the concern for the presence of either effect is real, since they can cause findings to be misinterpreted.

Along with other problems in research methods with normal and retarded persons, Baumeister (1967a) discussed the contamination of experimental interactions by floor and ceiling effects. Of particular concern is the possible occurrence of a Group X Condition pseudo interaction if any group performs at ceiling (or floor) while the other group varies between conditions. Examples of this can be seen in Figure 5.4. Group A performs at "ceiling," Group B at "floor," and Group C varies between conditions. Groups X Conditions interactions would be found for both Groups A and C, and Groups B and C.

One fallacious interpretation of such interactions would be that as the condition varied, there was a differential effect on each group. Obviously, if the performance of one group cannot vary between conditions because of the nature of the task, the interaction is spurious. However, Baumeister (1967a), in a didactic vein, attempted to cope with this problem by suggesting that investigators look at the distribution of scores about a point on a curve. He contended that if the distribution is skewed, this would indicate the presence of an artifact, and results should be interpreted accordingly.

Berkson and Cantor (1962), who were also concerned with possible artifacts introduced by floor and ceiling effects, have suggested that the means and standard deviations (SDs) of group responses be examined throughout the entire experiment. Initially, the means and SDs of the correct responses should be small, but both measures should increase as performance improves. If limits are placed on performance, group means will converge and SDs will decrease. Aside from initial and final performance, the SDs should remain constant. Hence, Berkson and Cantor maintained that comparisons based on these measures can detect the possible operation of floor and/or ceiling effects.

An empirical method of avoiding such artifacts would be to conduct pilot studies on a specific task, with specific samples, to determine whether the task is affected by the given effect. By varying the task, possible floor and ceiling effects might be eliminated. A number of investigators have resorted to this empirical method for avoiding contaminating effects. For example, Anders (1971), in a study comparing college-level and retarded subjects on a

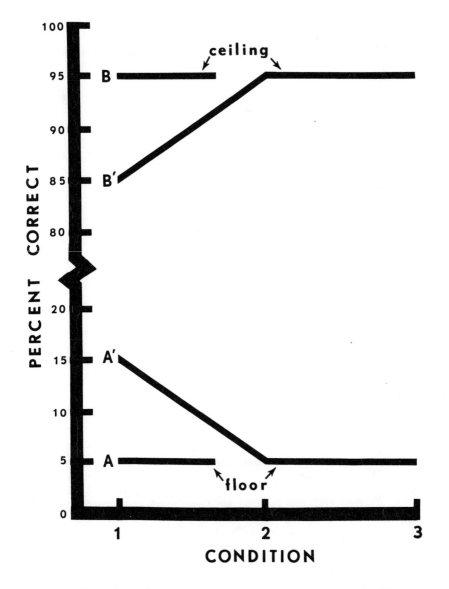

Figure 5.3. Hypothetical percentage of correct responses as a result of three conditions to demonstrate possible floor and ceiling effects on three performance curves.

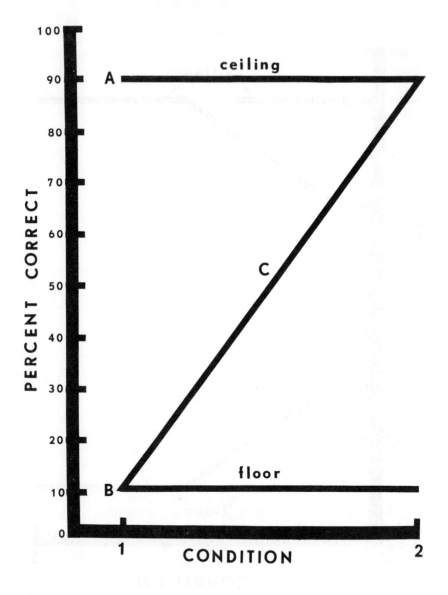

Figure 5.4. Hypothetical percentage of correct responses as a result of two conditions to demonstrate possible floor and ceiling effects and pseudo-interactions of the performance curves.

short-term memory task, tested 10 additional retarded subjects in a pilot study to determine the appropriate number of stimuli to be used with each group, and to equate the difficulty of the interpolated task that was given during a retention interval. The college subjects received a 12-item list and counted backward by 3s during the retention interval, while the retarded subjects viewed an 8-item list and counted backward by 1s during the retention interval. Anders succeeded in avoiding the floor and ceiling effects during the main experiment, and suggested that this method of matching subjects to the task be adopted by those who wish to compare groups of different intelligence levels.

Prehm (1966b) also used a pilot study to determine appropriate lengths of tests and levels of meaningfulness in a verbal learning task with normal and retarded persons. In the main experiment, he varied list length and levels of meaningfulness for each group, and based his interpretation on the finding that level of meaningfulness was not a significant variable for the retarded subjects but was significant for normal subjects. Nevertheless, in the studies by both Anders and Prehm, treatment conditions were confounded between groups, and the results must be interpreted with this in mind. Unfortunately, little information is available about the relative performance of retarded and normal subjects as a result of artifacts introduced by floor and ceiling effects. Because of the variations in the type of task, stimulus materials, population parameters, comparative groups, and so forth, it would be extremely difficult to determine beforehand whether a specific task with specific groups would exhibit these effects. An investigator must rely on previous experience, his intuition, or a pilot study (the last being the most reasonable). Though it would be a monumental task, it would be extremely valuable to researchers in mental retardation if one were to compile the knowledge gained thus far concerning the specific conditions under which the floor and ceiling effects are elicited. It would not only help investigators to avoid the problem, but it would also supply valuable information concerning the behavior of retarded and normal groups on a wide variety of tasks.

Though the experimenter has, after much effort, eliminated these unwanted artifacts, he also has further restricted his experimental findings to those conditions which may be unique in many ways (e.g., type of stimuli, rate of presentation, intervening tasks). As a result, information concerning the conditions under which these artifacts would exist also have been eliminated. When we discard information in an attempt to avoid floor and ceiling effects, we consequently eliminate knowledge concerning limits or capacity of performance. An alternative approach would be to analyze for the two separate effects and to interpret the data that are not affected by this phenomenon, without sacrificing evidence regarding information capacity or efficiency. It is clear that there is a need to consider more seriously the massive power of these artifacts and to attempt to measure them. Consequently, the following section is devoted to a proposed method for detecting the given effects.

Identification of Floor and Ceiling Effects

Two criteria that should be met in order to recognize these effects appropriately are (a) any resultant effects should be task-relevant, and (b) performance of one group should not be compared with performance of another group to determine whether either effect is present. The first criterion is posited because the nature of the task should dictate whether it is too easy or too difficult. The second criterion is important because it is the performance of specific groups, not relative performance, that is of interest in determining the existence of these effects.

As mentioned previously, Baumeister (1967a) stressed the importance of a skewed distribution of scores as an indication of the operation of floor and ceiling effects. This is true, to a point, since if a floor effect is present, the distribution of scores about a point on a curve should be skewed upward; but if a ceiling effect is present, the distribution of scores about a point should be skewed downward. This skewness will exist if there is an appreciable distribution of scores, but if the subjects are all performing at a high or low level, the distribution may be minimally skewed, or not skewed at all. As an example, if a task requires correct recognition of tachistocopically exposed words presented sequentially at several exposure times (e.g., 0.01, 0.10, and 1.0 second), correct responses may be nil at the fastest rate and perfect at the longest rate. Thus, there is no distribution of scores to indicate skewness at those two extreme exposure times.

It has also been noted that Berkson and Cantor (1962) proposed comparing means and SDs of the various groups over conditions and trials to determine whether the magnitude of the means and SDs changed within and between groups. Theoretically, the restrictions of the task would determine the group means and SDs; and comparisons could be made between converging the diverging curves. When curves are not parallel and the SDs decrease, an artifact may be present. The use of changes in variability in scores as a criterion is apparently a more efficient method, since no assumptions must be made about the shape of the distribution of points in a curve. But Berkson and Cantor did not suggest a method for determining the degree to which the means and SDs must covary in order to be considered pathognomonic of artifacts. If within-group comparisons are made among several levels of conditions, and a group is found to perform consistently close to floor or ceiling (as illustrated by Groups A and B in Fig. 5.4), comparisons of their means and SDs would be misleading.

Belmont and Butterfield (1969) define ceiling and floor effects as those points which are at or near asymptote, or chance level. The presence of either effect can then be determined by making statistical comparisons between the distribution of scores that are suspect of being at ceiling or floor and a distribution of scores that are not suspect (i.e., a reference distribution). By eliminating the mean differences between the two sets of scores so that each score in the two distributions is algebraically corrected, and then comparing the two distributions with the Kolmogorov-Smirnov or Chi-square tests, the presence of these effects can be determined. The premise is that the distribution of scores that is suspect will be skewed relative to the distribution that is not near asymptote or chance.

This empirical definition is commendable, since it is the first which states explicit how to determine these nebulous effects. However, there may be some problems inherent in such an analysis. First, the suspect distribution is being compared with a reference distribution, which in turn has its own skewness about each point. Thus, direction of skewness of the reference distribution will affect the comparison. Second, when two curves are present, one being near-asymptote and the other near-chance, either or both may or may not have skewed distributions. If their respective distributions do differ, either or both could reflect an effect. Also, it is not unexpected that the distribution of scores about a point, which reflects chance performance, would be normally distributed, especially since the Gaussian distribution depicts a chance distribution. Third, if both curves suggest the same effect (either floor or ceiling), the distribution of scores about a point would be skewed in the same direction and no differences would occur. In this case it would become arbitrary as to which distribution is the suspect distribution and which is the reference distribution.

As mentioned previously, it would be more desirable to be able to determine whether performance of a group reflects either effect, independent of performance by other groups. In this way, all distributions could be tested regardless of relative performance. Skewness as an indicator of an abnormal distribution is not necessarily the best criterion, since skewed distributions can occur when neither effect is evident, and they may not occur when performance is maximal or minimal. Thus, it might be more meaningful to compare the variance of a real distribution of scores with the variance of a hypothetical distribution. The resultant effects are then task-relevant—i.e., the level of performance is determined by the ease or difficulty of the task rather than by comparable performance of other groups, or of the same group at other levels.

Proposed methods of analyses for floor and ceiling effects. Two methods of analyzing for floor and ceiling effects are proposed here. These analyses are intended for data that are binary when the dependent measure is dichotomous. This does not mean that continuous data are not affected by floor and ceiling effects. It means that any attempt to apply these analyses to continuous data would be inappropriate. The first method is appropriate when scores are distributed about a point on a performance curve. The second method is appropriate when there is no distribution of scores about a point on a curve, but the relative performance of a group of subjects on a dichotomous task (e.g., Yes-No, Pass-Fail) determines the percentage of those who said "Yes," or who passed. The first approach will be discussed in some detail; the second will be mentioned briefly.

For the first method of analysis, it is suggested that if a level of performance is suspect, the variance of the distribution of scores about the suspect point should be compared with the variance of the task. The variance of the task can be determined by using the binomial distribution, npq, when n is the number of correct responses required for 100% performance *(not cases)*, p is .50 and q is .50. As n increases, the array of scores approaches the normal distribution. The reason for assigning .50 to p and q is that (since the probabilities of achieving any discrete score on any task is not known) equal probability is given to achieving scores above and below the hypothetical mean score of the task with the scores normally distributed about the mean. Then an F ratio can be found between the variances, with the variance of the binomial distribution as the numerator and the variance of the real distribution as the denominator. The degrees of freedom (df) for both the numerator and denominator would be the number of scores minus 1. Since there is a restriction on which variance is in the numerator and which is in the denominator, the ratio will be a one-tailed test in most F tables. Where the F ratio is significant, this would indicate that the floor or ceiling effect is present.

As an example, if a task has a maximum of 10 correct responses, n = 10, p = .50, and q = .50. The mean of the task is np (5) and the variance is 2.5 with SD = 1.58. Thus, on all tasks the mean will always be one-half the possible total correct, and the variance one-half the mean; and those which have the same total possible correct (n) will have the same means and variances.

Belmont and Butterfield (1969) cited Holden's (1966) experiment as an instance where the ceiling effect was demonstrated. They stated that, by inspection, it was apparent that the curve of Holden's 16-year-olds was at ceiling, since the slopes of the curve could not vary upward. Holden's data were analyzed by the present author to determine empirically which groups in which conditions performed at ceiling or floor.

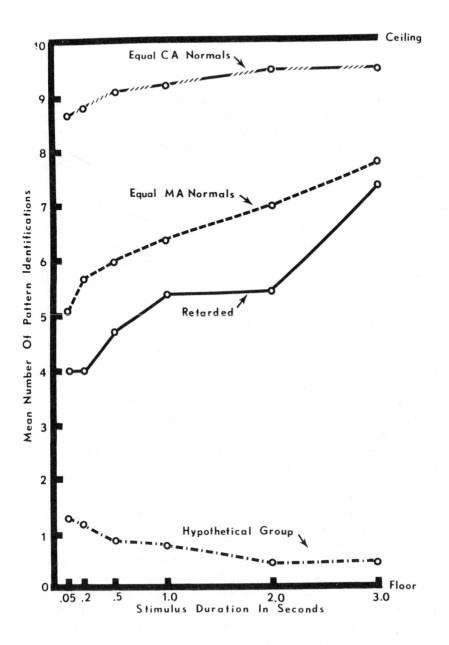

Figure 5.5. Mean number of correct pattern identifications per stimulus duration for each group (after Holden, 1966). The hypothetical curve represents the inverse performance of the equal-CA normal subjects.

Figure 5.5 shows the performance curves of Holden's experiment.[3] Included in this figure is a hypothetical curve which shows the inverse performance of Holden's oldest normal subjects in order to illustrate the floor effect and permit analyses with real numbers.

Analyses were performed on the scores of the three groups and the hypothetical group (Fig. 5.5) at each stimulus duration, using both the Kolmogorov-Smirnov test with adjusted means (Siegel, 1956) and the F-test comparison. The main results were as follows: The Kolmogorov-Smirnov test revealed that: (a) the distribution of the scores of the oldest normal subjects differed at every point from the score distributions of the hypothetical group, though both curves are suspect; (b) the differences between the score distributions of both the older and younger normal subjects decreased as stimulus duration increased until 3.0-second exposure time; (c) at no exposure time were the differences between the distribution of scores significant, suggesting that neither group was at ceiling; (d) the score distributions of the younger normal sample differed from those of the hypothetical group at every exposure time, but they differed from the distribution of scores from the retarded sample only at the .05-, 1.0-, and 3.0-second exposure times; (e) the retarded group also differed from the hypothetical group at every exposure time with lesser differences as exposure time decreased; and (f) differences were less between the hypothetical group and the retarded group at the shorter exposures, whereas the difference values (K_D) increased as the two curves diverged.

When the proposed analysis (F ratio) was performed on Holden's (1966) groups and the hypothetical group, it was found that (a) neither the older normal subjects nor the hypothetical groups demonstrated either effect at the shorter exposures (.05 and .2 second), but the former group exhibited the ceiling effect and the latter group the floor effect at all other exposure rates; and (b) neither the retarded group nor the equal-MA normal group demonstrated either effect. The F values of the retarded group were consistently lower than the comparable values of the younger normal group, but this reflects the larger variability of the retarded group's data (Baumeister, 1968a).

When Holden's data were again analyzed, eliminating scores that were at ceiling, it was found that one main effect and the interaction were no longer present. As a result, a portion of Holden's data has been reinterpreted. However, while this experiment is only one of many that have produced such artifacts, it is one of the few that have undergone such scrutiny. Nevertheless, this is one example of the possible use of this type of analysis for determining floor and ceiling effects.

---

[3]The author thanks Edward A. Holden, Jr., for supplying the data for reanalysis.

The second analysis, which was presented in detail in an earlier publication (Winters, 1972), should be used when each subject contributes one dichotomous score to each level of the experimental condition. An arcsin distribution can then be used, based on the percentage of subjects who responded in a determined manner. To facilitate this analysis, Winters (1972) presented a table which indicates maximum and minimum performance. To reiterate, these analyses are not intended for data that are continuous. Possibly, the method suggested by Berkson and Cantor (1962) should be followed with continuous data, since their approach examines measures of variability and permits within-group comparisons.

Belmont and Butterfield (1969) aptly pointed out that the "difficulty with ceiling and floor effects occurs frequently, but its significance is not widely appreciated. These effects are very difficult to avoid, and they may easily invalidate conclusions of differential forgetting as a function of age or intelligence" (p. 35-36). As critical and widespread as these artifacts are in research in mental retardation, only a few authors have attempted to solve the problem. The suggestions made here are yet another attempt, hopefully more refined, at coping with these phenomena.

INSTITUTIONALIZATION

Two related issues regarding behavioral research with retarded subjects will be considered in this section: (a) comparative effects of institutionalization versus noninstitutionalization, and (b) the effect of length of institutionalization.

Institutionalization versus Noninstitutionalization

Of the approximately 6 million retarded persons in the United States (below IQ 70), 4% are institutionalized (Robinson & Robinson, 1976). When studies are conducted using retarded subjects, we must consider how that 4% compares with the 96% who are not institutionalized. The concern is real, since a large portion of the research in mental retardation is conducted with institutionalized retarded persons. As a result, when hypotheses are tested, using this selective retarded group, the question arises as to whether the results can be generalized to the remainder of the retarded population.

There are several cogent reasons why institutionalized retarded individuals are such popular subjects. First, since they are a captive population, there is no need to migrate from one setting to another for large samples. Second, there is greater assurance that you have a retarded sample.

In some public school systems many students are in special classes for the retarded learner, not because they score low on an intelligence test and demonstrate maladaptive behavior, but because they present discipline problems. Hence, the classification of "retarded" becomes even more ambiguous. Third, the test scores, or information required concerning any given matching variable, are not always available when noninstitutionalized retarded individuals are used, since many of the students are not given the relevant tests or the tests used may vary among students in a class, depending upon the choice of the incumbent school psychologists. In some instances, students are placed in special education classes on the basis of group tests. If the experimenter wishes to use the retarded students in the public school, it is frequently necessary, and indeed is advisable, for him to administer a common test to all potential subjects. Nevertheless, while using institutionalized populations presents a number of advantages, if these subjects differ in important respects from their noninstitutionalized counterparts, generalization from experimental findings will be severely restricted.

Adequate reviews of studies which have compared institutionalized and noninstitutionalized retarded groups on a number of variables have been reported elsewhere (Baumeister & Butterfield, 1970; Butterfield, 1967; Klaber, 1970). (On these and other related points that follow, see also the chapter on institutionalization by Sternlicht and Bialer in this volume.)

Generally, when institutionalized and noninstitutionalized groups are compared, the former sample does not fare too well. Of the studies that have compared these two groups, Centerwall and Centerwall (1960), Kugel and Regue (1961), and Stedman, Eichorn, Griffin, and Gooch (1962) have found that the general development of the community groups was superior to the general development of the institutionalized groups. This has also been found to hold for personality development (Goldfarb, 1943, 1955).

With particular relevance to research methodology, Lyle (1959, 1960) found that institutionalized and noninstitutionalized retarded children did not differ on the nonverbal scores of an intelligence test, but the former group was significantly lower on verbal scores. These two studies, at least, should give us some insight as to the parameters on which to match normal and retarded subjects. Lyle found that the verbal scores of the institutionalized retarded persons were depressed, thus decreasing the full scale score. This signifies that when comparing institutionalized and noninstitutionalized retarded groups matched on the full scale score, the institutionalized subjects should do worse in a verbal learning task. If two retarded groups (institutionalized and noninstitutionalized) are compared with normal individuals of equal MA, the hierarchy of performance on a verbal learning task should be: normal sample, noninstitutionalized retarded group, institutionalized retarded subjects—in descending order of verbal competency. This is the hierarchy that is often found in such research (e.g., Baumeister, 1968b; Winters & Harvey, 1970). Therefore, another pertinent variable on which to match subjects would appear to be the verbal scores of an intelligence test.

Goulet (1968) reported that, of seven investigations in which retarded persons and normal controls of equal MA were compared on P-A learning tasks, three studies showed that the normal groups were superior in learning over the retarded groups (Iscoe & Semler, 1964; Jensen, 1965; Rieber, 1964), whereas four studies report no differences in learning (Cantor & Ryan, 1962; Girardeau & Ellis, 1964; Heckman, 1966; Ring & Palermo, 1961). Two of the studies, in which normal samples were superior, used institutionalized retarded groups; and three studies, in which the two groups did not differ, used noninstitutionalized retarded groups. In spite of the wide ranges of CA, MA, and IQ in these seven studies, the noninstitutionalized retarded groups performed better than institutionalized retarded groups on the various verbal tasks. This would tend to confirm Lyle's (1959, 1960) findings.

On performance tasks, Baumeister (1967b) concluded that the mentally retarded subjects were less retarded in motor learning than in other areas, suggesting that motor skills represent a process that is less related to intellectual deficiency. Also, most intelligence tests measure verbal skills more intensively than nonverbal skills. Malpass (1963) found that retarded individuals demonstrate less motor competence than equal-CA normal persons, but he noted that as intelligence level increases among retarded samples, and as precise movements, complex skills, and motor coordination become less stringent requirements in task performance, the differences diminish. It has also been found (Baumeister, Hawkins, & Holland, 1966) that when retarded persons and equal-CA normal subjects were compared on a rotary pursuit task, the latter were initially superior; but differences disappeared when the retarded individuals were given practice. It is evident that retarded persons are not so deficient in motor skills as they are in verbal skills when compared with normal controls. This points to the need to use the appropriate intelligence test measure (verbal or performance score) as a matching standard, whether or not the retarded sample is institutionalized. Gordon and Haywood (1969) pre-experimentally matched "familial" and "brain damaged" retarded persons on intelligence test verbal scores in order to investigate verbal learning ability, but to this author's knowledge no studies have been conducted comparing institutionalized and noninstitutionalized retarded persons with normal individuals, with the three groups pre-experimentally matched on verbal and performance scores.

Length of Institutionalization

It sometimes has been hypothesized that the length of time spent in an institution might have a deleterious effect on learning in retarded individuals. For example, Baumeister (1968b) found a positive correlation between length of institutionalization and trials to criterion on a verbal learning task. However, Butterfield (1967) aptly pointed out that because institutionalized retarded persons have been found to be not as intelligent as noninstitutionalized retarded persons does not mean that the institutional environment caused the intellectual difference. The institutionalized group may have been committed because they were less intelligent to begin with. A great deal of research has addressed itself to determining the differential effects of institutional and community backgrounds on intellectual and academic development in retarded children. The results, however, have been equivocal.

Crissey (1937) and Kephart and Strauss (1940) found that the earlier a retarded person is institutionalized, the greater the IQ loss, when compared with retarded individuals who were institutionalized at a later age. Butterfield (1967) also reported that institutionalization has been found to have a deleterious effect on personality and verbal skills. However, it has also been found that length of institutionalization is unrelated to IQ change in young adult and adult residents (Clarke & Clarke, 1954; Clarke, Clarke, & Reiman, 1958).

Skeels and Dye (1939) compared the development of two groups of children in institutional settings. One group of children, which was placed in an institution for retarded persons, was cared for by the attendants and older retarded residents. They received individual attention and affection. The other group of children was in an orphanage. After 2 years, most of the children in the institution were placed in adoptive homes and, prior to placement, showed gains in intelligence. The orphanage group showed no such gains. A follow-up study of the two groups (Skeels, 1966) revealed that those who were reared in the adoptive homes became productive citizens, while most of those who were reared in the orphanage were adult residents in institutions for retarded people. These studies indicate that the early experiences of a child are extremely influential on his development and that institutions for the retarded child need not necessarily be detrimental. The latter indication is in agreement with findings reported by Butterfield (1967) and Butterfield and Zigler (1965). From Butterfield's (1967) review of the effects of length of institutionalization, at least two points are noteworthy: (a) The results of many earlier studies, which typically did not use control groups, were misinterpreted as to the effects of institutionalization; and (b) more sophisticated recent studies (circa 1962) have revealed that length of institutionalization is unrelated to IQ change for older retarded residents.

More recently, Balla, Styfco, and Zigler (1971) found that there was no correlation between any of their dependent measures and the ratio between length of institutionalization and CA when their subjects' MAs were 6, 7, 8, and 10 years. In another study, Balla, McCarthy, & Zigler (1971) found with retarded residents at three MA levels (7, 9, and 11.6 years) that those subjects who were institutionalized at a younger age were less wary of nonretarded adults than those institutionalized at an older age.

ETIOLOGICAL DIFFERENCES IN BEHAVIORAL RESEARCH

The problems inherent in determining etiological differences and in conducting research with different etiological groups have been discussed by others (e.g., Gladwin, 1959; Masland, 1959; Pasamanick, 1959). This section is concerned only with the utilization of brain-injured (BI) and nonbrain-injured (NBI) retarded subjects in behavioral research.

Since the studies conducted by Werner and Strauss (circa, 1940) with BI retarded persons, there has been considerable research comparing BI and NBI retarded groups, with continuing controversy as to the wisdom of such comparisons. There are two major schools of thought in that controversy. One maintains that the groups differ sufficently to warrant the consideration of etiology in an experiment. The other maintains that the existing evidence does not indicate that BI and NBI retarded individuals, when matched on IQ, differ in enough characteristics to warrant the use of eiology as an important independent variable. Let us first consider the argument that etiology should not be employed as an independent variable.

Clausen (1966) tested 276 institutionalized mentally retarded persons, all with no gross central nervous system pathology, who were designated as "familials," "organics," "unexplained," "mixed," "mongoloids," and "not classifiable." They were compared with 112 normal subjects on 33 measures which included tests of motor ability, verbal ability, and intelligence. The subjects were tested over a period of approximately 2½ years. Clausen found that for the wide variety of measures used, deficiency of skills was unrelated to moderate neurological impairment. Those measures which reflected such impairment were fine finger and gross body coordination, muscular strength, and eye dominance. As noted, retarded persons with profound neurological impairment were not included in the study. Thus, Clausen's results suggest that, unless the organic impairment is severe or there is concern for those differences Clausen found in his moderately impaired group, it would be more expeditious not to be concerned with BI-NBI differences.

J. J. Gallagher (1957) compared 24 pairs of BI and NBI

institutionalized retarded individuals on 22 measures of perception, language, learning, personality, and behavior. He found no differences in quantitative measures of learning, aptitude, or perception. The main differences were in the area of personality. Gallagher concluded that general mental development was more important than any unique and specific intellectual factors. Thus, again it was found that behavioral measures did not clearly distinguish the two etiological groups.

Arguments for deemphasizing etiological differences have also been made by such workers as Bijou, Ellis, Leland, and Spitz. Considering them in alphabetical order, Bijou (1966) stated that medical categories such as "familial," "intracranial birth lesions," "cretin," and "mongoloid" refer to anatomical and physiological characteristics of the individual, and that no assumption need be made that these categories can account for reduced psychological development. Bijou feels, as do some others of his convictions, that the medical diagnosis does not reflect or coincide with level of performance on behavioral tasks.

Ellis (1969) pointed out that if behavioral deficits (regardless of etiology) can be determined, this generality has more merit than seeking specific behaviors for each etiology. He based the reason for seeking more general behavior on his observation that different etiological groups are rarely characterized by behavioral differences.

Leland (1969) refuted the use of etiological classification as indicators of behavioral determinants for slightly different reasons. He feels that when a retarded person is classified, either by etiology or IQ level, this may restrict or prevent that person's participation in some training program. According to Leland, it is the individual's ability that should determine treatment and not the classification system, with which we are often too preoccupied.

Spitz (1963) took the position that all retarded persons have a deficit in the structure or functioning of the central nervous system, and that consequently all are "brain damaged" to some degree. Thus, except where there is severe or profound CNS impairment, the dichotomy becomes tenuous. Spitz also stated that both the more carefully controlled research by J. J. Gallagher and the failure to replicate the findings of Werner and Strauss refute previously found differences between BI and NBI retarded persons. Spitz further stated that "we have not yet reached a point where a brain-damaged child can automatically be categorized without first knowing how he performs on certain tests, especially when the overlap of scores with endogenous Ss is considered" (p. 16).

Briefly, the research of Clausen and J. J. Gallagher has caused much doubt as to whether BI and NBI retarded individuals differ on enough behavioral measures to warrant using etiology as an independent variable. Aside from the insufficient evidence that BI and NBI retarded persons differ behaviorally (Ellis) and the conclusion that the determination of BI and NBI is vague (Spitz), this dichotomy serves no useful purpose (Leland) and is not related to behavior (Bijou).

Among the chief proponents of the stand that etiology should be considered, Zigler and his associates contended that seeking behavioral differences in BI and NBI retarded samples is important. Zigler (1969) championed the consideration of etiology as a variable in all research in mental retardation on the basis that such BI and NBI subjects differ with respect to both cognitive development and the nature of cognitive functioning, and that there is sufficient evidence to dictate that we should attend to etiology when we perform research with retarded individuals. He further argued that if you consider etiology as a variable and find no differences, you have lost nothing. On the other hand, if you do not attend to etiology, you are using subjects who are more heterogeneous than need be, and you are also ignoring any differences that might exist.

The generative research by Zigler and his associates prohibits a thorough review here of their studies. The reader is referred to Balla, Styfco, and Zigler (1971) and to Yando and Zigler (1971) for an appraisal of research in which etiology is a variable. Nevertheless, the etiological dichotomy is crucial to Zigler, since the developmental mode of cognitive growth, with which he is associated, applies to the NBI retarded group only. Thus, in order to test the parameters of this model, Zigler would have to either exclude or, at least, take into account the BI group. A question then arises as to whether those researchers who do not concur with the developmental model are committed to control for etiology when, in their opinion, it is not an important consideration. (For an in-depth discussion of Zigler's theoretical orientation, see the chapter by Schonebaum & Zinober in this volume.)

As yet, there is no theory of mental retardation. Whether one will ever be found, or if it would differ from any other theory of human behavior, is dubious. In any case, we have not evolved laws of general behavior of the retarded person. If found, these laws may not differ significantly from those already known. The efforts expended in investigating comparisons between dichotomized segments of the mentally retarded population may not produce the most efficient yield of information toward general laws. This is not to imply that there are *no* differences between institutionalized and noninstitutionalized retarded populations, that length of institutionalization has *no* effect on behavior, or that there are *no* etiological differences. If the research had not been conducted, we would not know the differences or similarities that do exist. Belmont (1971), as an example, offered an excellent review of the literature in which the behavior of mongoloid persons is compared with the behavior of nonmongoloid individuals. If the previous research had not been conducted and Belmont had not reviewed it, he could not have proposed seven hypotheses about the behavior of mongoloid individuals. It is a question of value. Are we to occupy limited research time and energy in investigating the ever-increasing differences that might be found within the retarded population, or should our efforts be directed toward a more molar approach to mental retardation with intrapopulation differences secondary? Any science has as its basic tenet the quest for general or universal laws. This also should be our first principle.

QUANTITATIVE VERSUS QUALITATIVE DIFFERENCES

Periodically, authors commit themselves to a view of whether the major differences between normal and retarded persons are quantitative or qualitative. This can be a crucial issue, since it underlies the logic of many population comparisons. The general attitude is that the differences are quantitative and thay any apparent qualitative differences are superficial. We will examine more closely here the possibility that profound qualitative differences do exist.

Warren (1934) defined quality as "an aspect, attribute, characteristic, or fundamental dimension of experience, which involves variation in kind and not in degree" (p. 221). This is distinguished from quantity, which is "a characteristic whose variations admit of numerical expression" (p. 221). To extend these definitions into more relevant terms, the former involves differences of type; the latter involves differences of magnitude. Thus, a quantitative difference can be described on a continuum of measurement, whereas a qualitative difference suggests no such continuum.

Baumeister and Kellas (1971) stated that the group differences in intelligence level which they observed are quantitative, not qualitative. For those investigators, processes that control learning are considered quantitative, and they vary only in degree among intelligence levels. Those authors also hold that the problems in mental retardation are developmental rather than pathological and that, as a result, it is the process of growth (quantitative) not deviancy (qualitative) which concerns those of us in the area. An underlying assumption might be that growth proceeds along a single continuum, whereas deviancy does not. However, the possibility also exists that the generic term "growth" applies to more than one type of measurement and that there are different types of "growth."

Estes (1970) stated: "It does seem clear that none of the learning or retention processes that have been analyzed in normal human learners in the laboratory differ qualitatively in the mentally defective, except at the most profound retarded level (below IQ of 30). Quantitative differences in rate of acquisition of knowledge or skill are generally demonstrable as a function of

IQ, with relationships generally slight for simpler laboratory tests and larger for more complex ones, but tending to disappear when MA is equated" (p. 69-70). Thus, Estes observed that though qualitative differences between normal and retarded persons might exist when a person's IQ is below 30, learning differences above this level are quantitative. He based this opinion on the observation that, although we lack detailed experimental analysis, the combination of the cognitive developmental processes that have been identified as characteristic of normal growth only appear to be qualitatively different from forms of learning observed in the young normal child, in the mentally retarded child, and in animals.

It would be difficult for anyone to evaluate qualitative differences between nonretarded persons (e.g., IQ = 100) and retarded individuals with IQs of 70, 60, 50, 40, and 30. Undoubtedly, as IQ increases and MA approaches CA, quantitative differences do tend to disappear. However, the conclusion that no observable qualitative differences occur within this range of 70 IQ points (30 to 100) may be based on inconclusive evidence. There is almost unanimous agreement that a normal 8-year-old child (MA = 8 years, IQ = 100) is not the same as a 12-year-old retarded child with the same (8-year) MA (IQ = 66), since their experiences differ so greatly. Yet, when we discuss cognitive development and learning, there is a tendency to view these differences as quantitative.

There is a general tendency among researchers in this area to agree that normal-retarded group differences are quantitative, since the data do suggest this conclusion. However, evidence is available that at least some differences in cognitive processing and development are qualitative. One example is a study by Stedman (1963). He compared retarded (IQ = 64) and normal persons of equal CA (over 15 years old) on a free recall task in which pairs belonging to the same semantic category were presented. There were five pairs in each of six different categories. Stedman concluded that analyses of percentage of clustering by category for each subject level suggested a qualitatively different recall process in retarded subjects.

Further support for the importance of qualitative differences in learning has been found in the research concerning rehearsal strategies in learning. Ellis (1970) hypothesized that the reason for normal-retarded group differences in list learning is due to the relative deficiency in rehearsal by the lower intellectual group. Since this group does not covertly rehearse items to the same degree as do normal subjects, they do not recall as much, especially in the primacy portion of the list. Subsequent research has supported this hypothesis. While this may be viewed as a quantitative difference in amount of rehearsal, it also suggests that the strategy of learning differs with each group, thereby affecting the amount of learning. Butterfield, Wambold, and Belmont (1973) reported that the strategies of groups with normal and subnormal intelligence do, in fact, differ—which would suggest qualitative differences.

For over 10 years, Spitz (1963, 1973) supported the tenet that normal-retarded group differences in learning and cognition are due to the differences in organizational strategies, which implies qualitative differences. While channel capacity cannot account for the gross inferior performance of the educable retarded child (Spitz, 1973), differing organizational strategies can do so. More recently it has been found that groups with average and below-average intelligence differ on both the order in which they recall items in a list and in the consistency of their order of recall (Winters & Attlee, 1974).

Brown (in press) contended that, in the development of memory, there are qualitative changes, and that the nature and extent of differences in knowledge during development are determined by the extent to which a task or situation is dependent upon one or several different memorial processes. As the child matures, we should expect qualitative differences in his ability to perceive and remember relationships and events. In a related article, Brown (1974) suggested that in normal-retarded sample comparisons, the retarded population should be deficient on a task if performance depends upon the *use* of these processes, since they are not always available to the immature subject. Thus, it is not necessarily the amount of processing, but the nature and availability of the processing that are critical in the development of learning and normal-retarded group differences.

As to whether differences in performance among groups that are above, at, or below average intelligence are quantitative or qualitative depends as much upon the way the question is posed as it does on the experimental design. One cannot pose an "either/or" question; the question should be directed at the aspect of behavior under investigation and the type(s) of differences or similarities being sought. We have made relatively few excursions into this domain although the question of quantitative-qualitative differences is becoming more recurrent.

EXTERNAL AND INTERNAL CRITICISMS OF MR RESEARCH

The main purpose of this chapter is to discuss issues of concern or controversy regarding research in the field of mental retardation from the standpoint of the author's experience and theoretical framework. Consequently, the views expressed herein may be biased. Sporadic attempts to be as critical of ourselves as we are of others frequently fail because of vested interests. What we need occasionally is for an authority who is not in the same area of research (retardation) to be critical of our endeavors.

Fortunately, this has been done by Estes (1970), who is an authority in learning theory and is not primarily concerned with mental retardation per se. Thus, his critical and incisive view of research in that field could offer some useful insights. Paramount here are the concerns for the methods and purposes of research in mental retardation. This concern warrants special consideration, since as Estes discusses methodological issues in mental retardation at the same time he questions the direction in which we are going. If our direction needs a reevaluation, so does our methodology.

Following are some of the main suggestions proffered by Estes (1970):

1. We should modify our mode of assessment of the retarded individual so that, instead of intelligence tests, we use general performance on various tasks under standard situations and evaluate the rate of gain in performance. Thus, the spectrum of measured performance would be much larger, and the performance profile of a subject would be more descriptive of his level and relative rate of learning.

2. Multiple normal control groups should be compared with retarded groups so as to match groups on opportunities to learn. This approach, coupled with Baumeister's suggestions, would solve several problems in types of design used and would permit more refined questions.

3. Concerning the use of MA and CA matches, Estes opposes this type of control, since higher IQ subjects, who have greater rates of development, are not matches for retarded subjects. He also contends that since opportunities to learn are not the same for normal and retarded persons, and since the subject brings to the experimental setting his previous knowledge and experience, the assumption that subjects are matched is fallacious.

4. With regard to the emphasis in research findings, that of *differences* between normal and retarded groups, Estes believes the emphasis should not be on disability but on the resources which an individual might utilize to compensate for the particular pathology. This has been stated here, and elsewhere by others, but it merits restating.

5. Long-term studies should be conducted to provide evidence concerning the reversibility of the retarded individual's deficiency in cognitive abilities. Estes is probably concerned here with the feasibility of reversing cognitive regression, and of increasing or stabilizing the IQ rate. With the exception of the research by Heber et al. (1968, 1972), little has been done by way of

longitudinal studies in which behavior is manipulated in an attempt to influence MA development.

In sum, Estes essentially suggested a total reevaluation of designs, methods, purposes, and emphasis. His criticisms of this area of research have merit, but the problems involved in facilitating the proposed changes are monumental.

Ellis' (1971) attitude toward these views was one of general acceptance with qualifications. He agreed in part with what Estes said but feels that (a) behavioral research in mental retardation is still rather young, and we are still investigating what we can and cannot do; and (b) since Estes based his suggestions on studies in which only substantial results were found, his review was "rather diminutive in comparison to what it might have been" (Ellis, 1971, p. 418); and (c), the omission of findings generated by the research of Luria and of O'Connor was notable. Nevertheless, Ellis felt that Estes' opinions were veridical, objective, fair, and critical without being pejorative.

Spitz (1971) took a somewhat different view of Estes' approach. After paying tribute to the monumental task which Estes undertook, Spitz suggested a series of other books in which the reader could find more comprehensive and thorough reviews of the relevant topics. He also felt that Estes was not aware of the full extent of the revolution taking place in Psychology. Spitz noted that the effect of ethology (i.e., knowledge of species-specific behavior) was not mentioned by Estes, that Piaget was mentioned only once, and that the section on mental development in Estes' book was the least comprehensive.

As a final point, Spitz criticized Estes for giving the impression "that retardates without brain damage suffer from the effect of inadequate learning histories. [and that] They have not had the same learning opportunities as normals and therefore comparisons with normals are of little value for any theoretical purpose. The implications of this view are devastating, and I leave it to the reader to follow them to their devious end" (1971, p. 418).

Since most of the criticisms of Estes' book have been adequately dealt with by Ellis and Spitz, I would like to expound on one point only. Essential to Estes' position, and a recurrent theme throughout his critique, is his opinion that differences in learning ability can be inferred from performance at a given time only if previous opportunities to learn have been equated for individuals being compared. Consequently, normal and retarded subjects must be matched on learning opportunities. It is for this reason that Estes feels that there is little theoretical value to learning research with the mentally retarded person. It is also for this reason that he suggested that multiple normal groups who vary in opportunities to learn be compared with retarded groups.

Estes recognizes that deficiencies in memory input and in

opportunities for vaired learning experiences in early life may produce irreversible changes in adult performance in learning situations, as well as emotional and motivational disturbances. However, he feels that controls should be found for opportunities to learn. In order to avoid the dilemma of unequal learning opportunities, Estes suggested that investigators of mental retardation use tasks that are least influenced by previous learning histories (e.g., classical conditioning) and that investigation of learning capacities of retarded subjects, when compared to normal individuals, be held in abeyance until much more is known about how to equate for opportunities to learn over varying time spans.

This places us at an impasse, since (a) retarded persons cannot possibly have opportunities to learn equal to that of nonretarded persons; (b) we have no measure of learning opportunities; (c) even if we could measure it, subjects of higher IQ can take better advantage of opportunities to learn, thereby creating additional inequality; (d) we cannot experimentally control what we cannot measure; and (e) we must therefore wait for an operational definition of, and a means of measuring, "opportunity to learn" before proceeding with any experiment in which learning experiences may influence the results. Estes prescribed a very difficult task, since—regardless of the influence of genetic or sociocultural factors on intellectual development—we cannot at present control either factor.

The present author cannot agree that there is, for any theoretical purpose, little value to the research conducted thus far. Admittedly, loose methodology needs tightening, but there is no point in discarding theories or hypotheses, especially when they are testable, because of flaws in the mechanics. If this were the case, we would have little or no theory in any field. A possible solution would be, as Estes suggested in his reference to the use of a broad section of performance tasks, to equate subjects on the stimuli (e.g., meaningfulness, familiarity, language development) and then investigate learning. In this way, at least, we can equate the groups' abilities in the initial phase of an experiment, which is one of Estes' main concerns. It is impossible to predict whether given hypotheses would be more viable if these requisites were met, but there probably would be more confidence in our results and interpretations.

SUMMARY AND CONCLUSIONS

As stated in the beginning of this chapter, the topics selected for discussion do not necessarily represent those that all investigators might consider as the most critical. There have been forays into some of these topics and more extended excursions into others. An attempt has been made here to be as encompassing as possible, while at the same time being selective so as to extract the essence of each issue. If there have been any expectations that any problem or issue would be resolved here, then this work has not met those expectations; if the reader has sought information concerning the nature of some issues and techniques or approaches to dealing with them, then this chapter is more in keeping with those expectations.

Ellis (1971) pointed out that this is a relatively new area of research and that we are still exploring what we can do. His reference to the length of time we have concerned ourselves with behavioral research with the mentally retarded individual is evident in that some of the "pioneers" in this field are very much alive and productive. (It was only some 16 years ago, at the Woods School Symposium, that a concerted effort was made to delve into the problems and deficiencies of research with mentally retarded groups.) That we are still exploring what we can do is evident in the contents of this chapter. If one views this vehicle as yet another exploration into the morass of issues concerning research methodology with the mentally retarded person, then it is viewed in its proper perspective.

One of the emphases here, and a common thread throughout, has been the concern for normal-retarded group and retarded-retarded group comparisons and the parameters on which the groups have been matched. When matched on age parameters (equal MA and/or equal CA), we should be wary as to the interpretations of some of our findings, especially those that may be influenced by matching techniques or by floor and ceiling effects. When retarded groups are compared (e.g., institutionalized and noninstitutionalized), other considerations should be given to the matching variables and the nature of the task. The assumption that equal-MA means equal-lives is erroneous. That subjects matched on an extra-experimental task parameter are also matched on stimulus meaningfulness, associations, or availability is also an error in reasoning.

As yet, there is no theory of mental retardation, and there is no hard-and-fast rule to test any such theory, if indeed one will ever exist. Nevertheless, the techniques and strategies of investigating the behavior of retarded persons must be guided by methodological acumen if we are ever to derive new laws of human behavior, or attempt to explain the old ones.

REFERENCES

Anders, T. R. Short-term memory for serially presented supraspan information in nonretarded and mentally retarded individuals. *American Journal of Mental Deficiency,* 1971, *75,* 571-578.

Archer, E. J. A re-evaluation of the meaningfulness of all possible CVC trigrams. *Psychological Monographs,* 1960, *74*(10, Whole No. 497).

Balla, D., McCarthy, E., & Zigler, E. Some correlates of negative reaction tendencies in institutionalized retarded children. *Journal of Psychology*, 1971, *79*, 77-84.

Balla, D., Styfco, S. J., & Zigler, E. Use of the opposition concept and outer directedness in intellectually-average, familial retarded, and organically retarded children. *American Journal of Mental Deficiency*, 1971, *75*, 663-680.

Battig, W. F., & Spera, A. J. Rated association values of numbers 0-100. *Journal of Verbal Behavior*, 1962, *1*, 200-202.

Baumeister, A. A. Problems in comparative studies of mental retardates and normals. *American Journal of Mental Deficiency*, 1967, *71*, 869-875. (a)

Baumeister, A. A. Learning abilities of the mentally retarded. In A. A. Baumeister (Ed.), *Mental retardation: Appraisal, education, and rehabilitation.* Chicago: Aldine, 1967, pp. 180-211. (b)

Baumeister, A. A. Behavioral inadequacy and variability of performance. *American Journal of Mental Deficiency*, 1968, *73*, 477-483. (a)

Baumeister, A. A. Paired-associate learning by institutionalized and noninstitutionalized retardates and normal children. *American Journal of Mental Deficiency*, 1968, *73*, 102-104. (b)

Baumeister, A. A., & Butterfield, E. (Eds.). *Residential facilities for the mentally retarded.* Chicago: Aldine, 1970.

Baumeister, A. A., Hawkins, W. F., & Holland, J. Motor learning and knowledge of results. *American Journal of Mental Deficiency*, 1966, *70*, 590-594.

Baumeister, A. A., & Kellas, G. Process variables in the paired-associate learning of retardates. In N. R. Ellis (Ed.), *International review of research in mental retardation* (Vol. 5). New York: Academic Press, 1971, pp. 221-270.

Belmont, J. M. Long-term memory in mental retardates. In N. R. Ellis (Ed.), *International review of research in mental retardation* (Vol. 1). New York: Academic Press, 1966, pp. 219-255.

Belmont, J. M. Medical-behavioral research in retardation. In N. R. Ellis (Ed.), *International review of research in mental retardation* (Vol. 5). New York: Academic Press, 1971, pp. 1-81.

Belmont, J. M. & Butterfield, E. C. The relations of short-term memory to development and intelligence. In L. P. Lipsitt and H. W. Reese (Eds.), *Advances in child development and behavior* (Vol. 4). New York: Academic Press, 1969, pp. 29-82.

Berkson, G., & Cantor, G. N. A note on method in comparisons of learning in normals and the mentally retarded. *American Journal of Mental Deficiency*, 1962, *67*, 475-477.

Berry, F. M., & Baumeister, A. A. Cue selection and meaningfulness in the paired-associates learning of retardates. *American Journal of Mental Deficiency,* 1971, *75,* 456-462.

Bijou, S. W. A functional analysis of retarded development in normal and retarded children. In N. R. Ellis (Ed.), *International review of research in mental retardation* (Vol. 1). New York: Academic Press, 1966, pp. 1-19.

Bilsky, L., & Evans, R. A. N. Use of associative clustering technique in the study of reading disability: Effects of list organization. *American Journal of Mental Deficiency,* 1970, *74,* 771-776.

Bilsky, L., Evans, R. A., Gilbert, L. Generalization of associative clustering tendencies in mentally retarded adolescents: Effects of novel stimuli. *American Journal of Mental Deficiency,* 1972, *77,* 77-84.

Brown, A. L. The role of strategic behavior in retardate memory. In N. R. Ellis (Ed.), *International review of research in mental retardation* (Vol. 7). New York: Academic Press, 1974, pp. 55-111.

Brown, A. L. The development of memory: Knowing, knowing about knowing, and knowing how to know. In H. W. Reese (Ed.), *Advances in child development and behavior* (Vol. 10). New York: Academic Press (in press).

Butterfield, E. C. The role of environmental factors in the treatment of institutionalized mental retardates. In A. A. Baumeister (Ed.), *Mental retardation: Appraisal, education, and rehabilitation.* Chicago: Aldine, 1967, pp. 120-137.

Butterfield, E. C., Wambold, C., & Belmont, J. M. On the theory and practice of improving short-term memory. *American Journal of Mental Deficiency,* 1973, *77,* 654-669.

Butterfield, E. C. & Zigler, E. The influence of differing institutional social climates on the effectiveness of social reinforcement in the mentally retarded. *American Journal of Mental Deficiency,* 1965, *78,* 48-56.

Cantor, G. N., & Ryan, T. J. Retention of verbal paired-associates in normals and retardates. *American Journal of Mental Deficiency,* 1962, *66,* 861-865.

Carroll, J. B., Davies, P., & Richman, B. *The American heritage word frequency book.* New York: Houghton Mifflin, 1971.

Carroll, J. B., & White, M. N. Age-of-acquisition norms for 220 picturable nouns. *Journal of Verbal Learning and Verbal Behavior,* 1973, *12,* 563-576.

Centerwall, S. A., & Centerwall, W. R. A study of children with mongolism reared in the home compared to those reared away from home. *Pediatrics,* 1960, *25,* 678-685.

Clarke, A. D. B., & Clarke, A. M. Cognitive changes in the feebleminded.

British Journal of Psychology, 1954, *45*, 173-179.

Clarke, A. D. B., Clarke, A. M., & Reiman, S. Cognitive and social changes in the feebleminded—three further studies. *British Journal of Psychology*, 1958, *49*, 144-157.

Clausen, J. *Ability structure and subgroups in mental retardation.* Washington, D. C.: Spartan Books, 1966.

Cohen, J. Multiple regression as a general data-analytic system. *Psychological Bulletin*, 1968, *70*, 426-443.

Cramer, P. *Word association.* New York: Academic Press, 1968.

Crissey, O. L. The mental development of children of the same IQ in differing institutional environments. *Child Development*, 1937, *8*, 217-220.

Darlington, R. B. Multiple regression in psychological research and practice. *Psychological Bulletin*, 1968, *69*, 161-182.

Deese, J. On the predictions of occurrence of particular verbal intrusions in immediate recall. *Journal of Experimental Psychology*, 1959, *58*, 17-22.

Denny, M. R. Research in learning and performance. In H. A. Stevens and R. Heber (Eds.), *Mental retardation: A review of research.* Chicago: University of Chicago Press, 1964, pp. 100-142.

Drew, C. J. Associative learning as a function of material associative strength and MA. *American Journal of Mental Deficiency*, 1969, *74*, 369-372.

Drew, C. J., Prehm, H. J., & Logan, D. R. Paired associate learning performance as a function of association value of materials. *American Journal of Mental Deficiency*, 1968, *73*, 294-297.

Dunn, B. E. Some problems with the experimental method. *Psychological Reports*, 1967, *21*, 15-18.

Eastman, F. C., & Rosanoff, A. J. Association in feeble-minded and delinquent children. *American Journal of Insanity*, 1912, *69*, 125-141.

Ellis, N. R. A behavioral research strategy in mental retardation: Defense and critique. *American Journal of Mental Deficiency*, 1969, *73*, 557-566.

Ellis, N. R. Memory processes in retardates and normals. In N. R. Ellis (Ed.), *International review of research in mental retardation* (Vol. 4). New York: Academic Press, 1970. pp. 1-32.

Ellis, N. R. Learning theory. *Contemporary Psychology: A Journal of Reviews*, 1971, *16*, 417-418.

Ellis, N. R., McCarver, R. B., & Ashurst, H. M., Jr. Short-term memory in the retarded: Ability level and stimulus meaningfulness. *American Journal of Mental Deficiency*, 1970, *75*, 72-80.

Entwisle, D. R. *Word associations of young children.* Baltimore: The Johns Hopkins Press, 1966.

Estes, W. K. *Learning theory and mental development.* New York: Academic Press, 1970.

Evans, S. H., & Anastasio, E. J. Misuse of analysis of covariance when treatment effect and covariate are confounded. *Psychological Bulletin,* 1968, *69,* 225-234.

Flamer, G. B. Paired-associate learning of retarded children as a function of the normative associations of normal children. *Developmental Psychology,* 1969, *1,* 436-439.

Gallagher, J. J. A comparison of brain-injured and non-brain-injured mentally retarded children on several psychological variables *Monographs of the Society for Research in Child Development,* 1957, *22* (2, Whole No. 65).

Gallagher, J. W. The effect of association value and stimulus-response relationship on paired-associate learning. *American Journal of Mental Deficiency,* 1969, *73,* 768-773. (a)

Gallagher, J. W. Mediation as a function of associative chains in normal and retarded children. *American Journal of Mental Deficiency,* 1969, *73,* 886-889. (b)

Gallagher, J. W., & Reid, D. R. Effect of five free association strength values on paired-associate learning. *American Journal of Mental Deficiency,* 1970, *75,* 33-38.

Gardner, J. M. Behavior modification in mental retardation: Search for an adequate paradigm. *American Journal of Mental Deficiency,* 1969, *73,* 844-851.

Gardner, J. M., & Selinger, S. Trends in learning research with the mentally retarded. *American Journal of Mental Deficiency,* 1971, *75,* 733-738.

Gerjuoy, I. R., & Gerjuoy, H. Preliminary word-association norms for institutionalized adolescent retardates. *Psychonomic Science,* 1965, *2,* 91-92.

Gerjuoy, I. R., & Spitz, H. H. Associative clustering in free recall: Intellectual and developmental variables. *American Journal of Mental Deficiency,* 1966, *70,* 918-927.

Gerjuoy, I. R., & Winters, J. J., Jr. Psychological research in mental retardation. *Mental Retardation,* 1969, *7*(4), 4-10. (a)

Gerjuoy, I. R., & Winters, J. J., Jr. *Word association norms: Adolescent retardates.* Project report, E. R. Johnstone Training and Research Center. Grant no. HD 01706. Washington D. C.: National Institute of Child Health and Human Development, 1969. (b)

Gerjuoy, I. R., & Winters, J. J., Jr. Subjective organization by EMR adolescents in free recall: Bimodal presentation. *American Journal of Mental Deficiency,* 1970, *74,* 509-516.

Gerjuoy, I. R., Winters, J. J., Jr., Pullen, M. M., & Spitz, H. H. Subjective organization by retardates and normals during free recall of visual stimuli. *American Journal of Mental Deficiency,* 1969, *73,* 791-797.

Girardeau, F. L., & Ellis, N. R. Rote verbal learning by normal and mentally retarded children. *American Journal of Mental Deficiency*, 1964, *68*, 525-532.

Gladwin, T. Methodologies applicable to the study of learning deficits. *American Journal of Mental Deficiency*, 1959, *64*, 311-315.

Glaze, J. J. The association value of non-sense syllables. *Journal of Genetic Psychology*, 1928, *35*, 255-269.

Gold, M. W. Research on the vocational habilitation of the retarded: The present, the future. In N. R. Ellis (Ed.), *International review of research in mental retardation* (Vol. 6). New York: Academic Press, 1973, pp. 97-147.

Goldfarb, W. The effects of early institutional care on adolescent personality. *Journal of Experimental Education*, 1943, *12*, 106-129.

Goldfarb, W. Emotional and intellectual consequences on psychologic deprivation in infancy: A reevaluation. In P. H. Hoch and J. Zubin (Eds.), *Psychopathology of childhood*. New York: Grune & Stratton, 1955, pp. 105-119.

Gordon, J. E., & Haywood, H. C. Input deficit in cultural-familial retardates: Effects of stimulus enrichment. *American Journal of Mental Deficiency*, 1969, *73*, 604-610.

Goulet, L. R. Verbal learning and memory research with retardates: An attempt to assess developmental trends. In N. R. Ellis (Ed.), *International review of research in mental retardation* (Vol. 3). New York: Academic Press, 1968, pp. 97-134.

Griffith, B. C., Spitz, H. H., & Lipman, R. S. Verbal mediation and concept formation in retarded and normal subjects. *Journal of Experimental Psychology*, 1959, *58*, 247-251.

Harris, D. R., Bisbee, C. T., & Evans, S. H. Further comments—Misuse of analysis of covariance. *Psychological Bulletin*, 1971, *75*, 220-222.

Harter, S. Discrimination learning set in children as a function of IQ and MA. *Journal of Experimental Child Psychology*, 1965, *2*, 31-43.

Harter, S. Mental age, IQ, and motivational factors in the discrimination learning set performance of normal and retarded children. *Journal of Experimental Child Psychology*, 1967, *5*, 123-141.

Haywood, H. C. Mental retardation as an extension of the developmental laboratory. *American Journal of Mental Deficiency*, 1970, *75*, 5-9.

Heal, L. W. Research strategies and research goals in the scientific study of the mentally subnormal. *American Journal of Mental Deficiency*, 1970, *75*, 10-15.

Heber, R., Dever, R., & Conry, J. The influence of environment and genetic variables on intellectual development. In H. J. Prehm, L. A. Hamerlynch, and J. E. Crosson (Eds.), *Behavioral research in mental retardation* (Monograph No. 1). Eugene, Oregon: University of Oregon, 1968, pp. 1-22.

Heber, R., Garber, H., Harrington, S., Hoffman, C., & Falender, C. *Rehabilitation of families at risk for mental retardation: Progress report.* Madison, Wisconsin: Rehabilitation Research and Training Center in Mental Retardation, University of Wisconsin, 1972.

Heckman, B. Varied exposure durations in paired-associate learning in normal and retarded children. *American Journal of Mental Deficiency,* 1966, *70,* 709-713.

Holden, E. A. Jr., Stimulus duration and subnormality in visual pattern recognition. *Journal of Comparative and Physiological Psychology,* 1966, *62,* 167-170.

Horan, E. M. Word association frequency tables of mentally retarded children. New York: Columbia University, 1965. (Unpublished doctoral dissertation)

Horan, E. M. Word association frequency tables of mentally retarded children. *Journal of Consulting Psychology,* 1956, *20,* 22.

Iscoe, I., & Semler, I. J. Paired-associate learning in normal and mentally retarded children as a function of four experimental conditions. *Journal of Comparative and Physiological Psychology,* 1964, *57,* 387-392.

Jensen, A. R. Rote learning in retarded adults and normal children. *American Journal of Mental Deficiency,* 1965, *69,* 828-834.

Kappauf, W. E. Studying the relationship of task performance to the variables of chronological age, mental age, and IQ. In N. R. Ellis (Ed.), *International review of research in mental retardation* (Vol. 6). New York: Academic Press, 1973, pp. 257-317.

Kent, G. H., & Rosanoff, A. J. A study of association in insanity. *American Journey of Insanity,* 1910, *67,* 37-96, 317-390.

Kephart, N. C., & Strauss, A. A. A clinical factor influencing variations in IQ. *American Journal of Orthopsychiatry,* 1940, *10,* 343-350.

Klaber, M. Institutional programming and research: A vital partnership in action. In A. A. Baumeister and E. Butterfield (Eds.), *Residential facilities for the mentally retarded.* Chicago: Aldine, 1970, pp. 163-200.

Kugel, R. B., & Regue, D. A comparison of mongoloid children. *Journal of the American Medical Association,* 1961, *175,* 959-961.

Leland, J. The relationship between "intelligence" and mental retardation. *American Journal of Mental Deficiency,* 1969, *73,* 533-535.

Lindquist, E. F. *Design and analysis of experiments in psychology and education.* Boston: Houghton Mifflin, 1953.

Lipman, R. S. Learning: Verbal, perceptual-motor, and classical conditioning. In N. R. Ellis (Ed.), *Handbook of mental deficiency: Psychological theory and research.* New York: McGraw-Hill, 1963, pp. 391-423.

Lord, F. M. Large-sample covariance analysis when the control variable is fallible. *Journal of the American Statistical Association,* 1960, *55,* 307-321.

Lyle, J. G. The effect of an institution environment upon the verbal development of imbecile children: I. Verbal intelligence. *Journal of Mental Deficiency Research,* 1959, *3* 122-128.

Lyle, J. G. The effect of an institution environment upon the verbal development of imbecile children: II. Speech and language. *Journal of Mental Deficiency Research,* 1960, *4,* 1-13.

Malpass, L. F. Motor skills in mental deficiency. In N. R. Ellis (Ed.), *Handbook of mental deficiency: Psychological theory and research.* New York: McGraw-Hill, 1963, pp. 602-631.

Masland, R. L. Methodological approaches to research in etiology. *American Journal of Mental Deficiency,* 1959, *64,* 305-310.

McCandless, B. Editorial. *Developmental Psychology,* 1970, *2,* 1-7.

McNemar, Q. *Psychological statistics* (3rd ed.). New York: Wiley, 1962.

Milgram, N. A. The rationale and irrational in Zigler's motivational approach to mental retardation. *American Journal of Mental Deficiency,* 1969, *73,* 527-535.

Milgram, N. A. MR and mental illness—A proposal for conceptual unity. *Mental Retardation,* 1972, *10*(6), 29-31.

Noble, C. E. Measurements and association value (a), rated associations (a′) and scaled meaningfulness (m) for the 2100 CVC combinations of the English alphabet. *Psychological Reports,* 1961, *8,* 487-521.

Otis, M. A. A study of association in defectives. *Journal of Educational Psychology,* 1915, *6,* 271-288.

Paivio, A., Yuille, J. C., & Madigan, S. Concreteness, imagery and meaningfulness values for 925 nouns. *Journal of Experimental Psychology Monograph,* 1968, *76* (1, Pt. 2).

Palermo, D. S., & Jenkins, J. J. Free association responses to the primary responses of the Palermo-Jenkins word association norms for grade school children. *Research Bulletin No. 37.* Pennsylvania State University, 1963.

Palermo, D. S., & Jenkins, J. J. *Word association norms: Grade school through college.* Minneapolis: University of Minnesota Press, 1964. (a)

Palermo, D. S., & Jenkins, J. J. Changes in the word associations of fourth and fifth grade children from 1916 to 1961. *Research Bulletin No. 41.* Pennsylvania State University, 1964. (b)

Palermo, D. S., & Jenkins, J. J. Oral word association norms for children in grades one through four. *Research Bulletin No. 60.* University Park, Pa.: Pennsylvania State University, 1966.

Paraskevopoulos, I. Developmental stages for decoding symmetry in retarded and gifted children. *American Journal of Mental Deficiency,* 1968, *73,* 447-454. (a)

Paraskevopoulos, I. Symmetry, recall, and preference in relation to chronological age. *Journal of Experimental Child Psychology,* 1968, *6,* 254-264. (b)

Pasamanick, B. Research on the influence of sociocultural variables upon organic factors in mental retardation. *American Journal of Mental Deficiency,* 1959, *64,* 316-320.

Prehm, H. J. Verbal learning research in mental retardation. *American Journal of Mental Deficiency,* 1966, *71,* 42-47. (a)

Prehm, H. J. Associative learning in retarded and normal children as a function of task difficulty and meaningfulness. *American Journal of Mental Deficiency,* 1966, *70,* 860-865. (b)

Rieber, M. Verbal mediation in normal and retarded children. *American Journal of Mental Deficiency,* 1964, *68,* 634-641.

Ring, E. M., & Palermo, D. S. Paired-associate learning of normal and retarded children. *American Journal of Mental Deficiency,* 1961, *66,* 100-107.

Robinson, N. M., & Robinson, H. B. *The mentally retarded child: A psychological approach.* (2nd ed.) New York: McGraw-Hill, 1976.

Semmel, M. I., Barritt, L. S., Bennett, S. W., & Perfetti, C. A. A grammatical analysis of word associations of educable mentally retarded and normal children. *American Journal of Mental Deficiency,* 1968, *72,* 567-576.

Siegel, S. *Nonparametric statistics for the behavioral sciences.* New York: McGraw-Hill, 1956.

Silverstein, A. B., & McLain, R. E. Associative processes of the mentally retarded: I. An exploratory study. *American Journal of Mental Deficiency,* 1961, *65,* 761-765.

Silverstein, A. B., & McLain, R. E. Associative processes of the mentally retarded: II. Effects of selected background variables. *American Journal of Mental Deficiency,* 1964, *69,* 440-445.

Skeels, H. M. Adult status of children with contrasting early life experiences. *Monographs of the Society for Research in Child Development,* 1966, *31*(3, Whole No. 105).

Skeels, H. M., & Dye, H. B. A study of the effects of differential stimulations on mentally retarded children. *Proceedings and Addresses of the American Association on Mental Deficiency,* 1939, *44,* 114-136.

Snedecor, G. W. *Statistical methods applied to experiments in agriculture and biology* (5th ed.). Ames, Iowa: Iowa State College Press, 1956.

Solomon, R. L., & Lessac, M. S. A control group design for experimental studies of developmental processes. *Psychological Bulletin,* 1968, *70,* 145-150.

Spitz, H. H. Field theory in mental deficiency. In N. R. Ellis (Ed.), *Handbook of mental deficiency: Psychological theory and research.* New York: McGraw-Hill, 1963, pp. 11-40.

Spitz, H. H. Book reviews. *Behavior Therapy,* 1971, *2,* 417-418.

Spitz, H. H. The channel capacity of educable mental retardates. In D. K. Routh (Ed.), *The experimental psychology of mental retardation.* Chicago: Aldine, 1973, pp. 133-156.

Sprott, D. A. Note on Evans and Anastasio on the analysis of covariance. *Psychological Bulletin,* 1970, *73,* 303-306.

Stanley, J. C. Problems in equating groups in mental retardation research. *Journal of Special Education,* 1967, *1,* 241-256.

Stanley, J. C., & Beeman, E. Y. Restricted generalization, bias and power that may result from matching groups, *Psychological Newsletter* (New York University), 1958, *9,* 88-102.

Stedman, D. J. Associative clustering of semantic categories in normal and retarded subjects. *American Journal of Mental Deficiency,* 1963, *67,* 700-704.

Stedman, D. J., Eichorn, D. H., Griffin, J., & Gooch, B. A. A comparative study of the growth and developmental trend of institutionalized and non-institutionalized retarded children. In R. L. Cromwell (Ed.), *Abstracts of Peabody Studies in Mental Retardation,* 1962, *2,* 81. (Abstract)

Thorndike, E. L., Lorge, I. *Teacher's word book of 30,000 words.* New York: Teachers College, Columbia University, 1944.

Tulving, E., & Madigan, S. A. Memory and verbal learning. *Annual Review of Psychology,* 1970, *21,* 437-484.

Underwood, B. J., & Schultz, R. W. *Meaningfulness and verbal learning.* Philadelphia: Lippincott, 1960.

Warren, H. C. *Dictionary of psychology.* Cambridge, Mass: Houghton Mifflin, 1934.

Winters, J. J., Jr. A comparison of normals and retardates on physiological and experiential visual illusions. *American Journal of Mental Deficiency,* 1969, *73,* 956-962.

Winters, J. J., Jr. Proposed analyses of floor and ceiling effects. *American Journal of Mental Deficiency,* 1972, *77,* 296-300.

Winters, J. J., Jr., & Attlee, L. C. The von Restorff effect and measures of organization in normals and retardates. *Memory and Cognition,* 1974, *2,* 301-305.

Winters, J. J., Jr., & Harvey, F. A. Effects of two presentation methods on the paired-associate learning of normals and retardates. Paper presented at the meeting of the American Association on Mental Deficiency, Washington, D.C., May 1970.

Winters, J. J., Jr., & Kahn, H. Word-association norms of adolescent mental retardates. *Psychonomic Monograph Supplements,* 1970, *3* (8, Whole No. 40).

Winters, J. J., Jr., & Kahn, H. Word-associations norms: A comparison of adolescent mental retardates and normals. *Psychonomic Monograph Supplements,* 1971, *4* (8, Whole No. 56).

Wohlwill, J. F. The age variable in psychological research. *Psychological Review,* 1970, *77,* 49-64.

Yando, R., & Zigler, E. Outerdirectedness in the problem-solving of institutionalized and noninstitutionalized normal and retarded children. *Developmental Psychology,* 1971, *4,* 277-288.

Zigler, E. Mental retardation. *International encyclopedia of the social sciences.* New York: Macmillan & Free Press, 1968, pp. 226-247.

Zigler, E. Developmental versus difference theories of mental retardation and the problem of motivation. *American Journal of Mental Deficiency,* 1969, *73,* 536-556.

Reuben M. Schonebaum is Chief Psychologist of the Developmental Evaluation Center at the Shield Institute for Mental Retardation in Queens County of New York City. He attended New York City public schools and Queens College of the City University of New York. He first developed an interest in mental retardation when serving as a teaching aide at the Westchester Assocation for Retarded Children. Subsequently, he attended the graduate programs in clinical psychology and experimental child psychology at the University of Connecticut, where he received his Master's degree in 1968 and his Ph.D. degree in 1971.

While a graduate student, Dr. Schonebaum was a USPH Fellow in mental health and an NIMH trainee in mental retardation, and completed a research intership at Kennedy Child Study Center, New York. He taught courses in clinical and developmental psychology in the Graduate School of Arts and Sciences at Fordham University, New York, from 1970 to 1976. He is a member of Division 33 of the American Psychological Association and of the Division 33 Task Force on Learning Disabilities.

Dr. Schonebaum has published research studies on the development of human information processing, and has contributed book reviews to the American Journal of Mental Deficiency *and to* Child Development Abstracts and Bibliography. *He has been a consulting reviewer for the* Journal of Experimental Child Psychology. *His principal interests are in mental retardation, learning disabilities, and behavior genetics.*

Joan Wagner Zinober received her B.A. degree in psychology in 1967 from Michigan State University. Subsequently, she attended the University of Connecticut, where she received an M.A. in child and developmental psychology in 1967 and a Ph.D. in child and developmental psychology in 1970. From 1969 to 1971, Dr. Zinober was Assistant Professor of Educational Psychology at New York University. Following that, she spent one year as a research coordinator for the U.S. Office of Education in Washington, D.C.

Since 1972, Dr. Zinober has been Director of Research and Evaluation at the Hillsborough Community Mental Health Center in Tampa, Florida. She is also Clinical Assistant Professor of Psychiatry at the University of South Florida School of Medicine. Dr. Zinober's main field of interest at the present time is program evaluation of community mental health activities.

She is a member of the Council on Research and Evaluation of the National Council of Community Mental Health Centers. She is also a field instructor for Florida State University and is Agency Supervisor at the Hillsborough Community Mental Health Center for Florida State University graduate students in program evaluation.

Dr. Zinober has published a number of papers and book chapters, both in the field of developmental psychology and in the field of program evaluation in community mental health. She has presented papers on program evaluation at various state and national meetings.

6

Learning and memory in mental retardation:
The defect-developmental distinction re-evaluated

Reuben M. Schonebaum and Joan W. Zinober

THE ISSUE

Almost two decades ago, Anastasi (1958) examined the distinction between hereditary and environmental factors in the development of behavioral differences. She noted then that the controversy had focused on the issue of whether heredity or environment contributed more to individual differences in a trait—particularly, intelligence—and she argued that the appropriate question was not "how much," but "how" these factors contributed to the development of behavior. In a similar fashion, the distinction between "defect" and "developmental" interpretations of differences between retarded and normal people on learning and memory tasks has become controversial in recent years (Ellis, 1969; Milgram, 1969, 1973; Zigler, 1969, 1973) and seems to have diverted attention away from a more central issue. It has raised the question of whether performance differences indicate that retarded individuals are cognitively less efficient than normal persons, but it has obscured the question of how they are less efficient.

Since the developmental position assumes that retarded and normal individuals equated for developmental level should perform equally well, a great deal of investigative effort has been devoted to explaining why

The authors wish to express their thanks and appreciation to Dr. Sheldon Kastner for his help in the initial draft of this manuscript. We also wish to extend our gratitude to Margie Schonebaum for providing a critical reading of the paper; to Linda Landi for preparing the final manuscript; and to Linda Dunkerley for preparing the figures.

differences in performance between retarded and normal subjects matched on mental age have been found repeatedly. Edward Zigler (1966a, 1966b, 1967, 1969, 1973), for example, suggested that retarded-normal performance differences are a function of the unique experiential history of the retarded individual. He has concluded that the degree of social deprivation and amount of failure experienced by retarded people foster motivational tendencies which impede performance on traditional measures of learning and memory, but that, when these factors are taken into account, there should be no cognitive differences related to intelligence.

The experimental literature provides ample evidence that normal subjects outperform retarded subjects on a variety of learning and memory tasks (Belmont & Butterfield, 1969; Ellis, 1970; Spitz, 1973; Zeaman & House, 1966). Therefore, the issue is not whether retarded individuals are less efficient in learning and memory, but how the steps taken by an individual who learns readily and remembers well differ from the responses which comprise the behavioral pattern of the less efficient person. The plan of this chapter is to review the distinctions between defect and developmental interpretations of retarded-normal performance differences advocated by Zigler and to analyze the assumptions underlying the developmental view. It will be suggested that a more fruitful approach to the understanding of retarded behavior is to be found in an evaluation of the component processes mobilized by a person in the performance of a task. Several lines of research employing this strategy have yielded knowledge about the operations that contribute to typical levels of performance and offer the possibility of a more retarded behavior is to be found in an evaluation of the component processes mobilized by a person in the performance of a task. Several lines of research programs, one dealing with discrimination learning and the other with short-term memory, will be outlined to illustrate the approach.

The Defect-Developmental Distinction

"Organic" versus "familial" retardation.[1] Zigler, as the leading spokesman of the developmental position, presented the major principles of organic versus

---

[1]The authors are aware that terms such as "cultural-familial," "organic," and "familial" are no longer in general use as descriptive or categorical terms for mentally retarded individuals. However, in order to maintain consistency with the terminology used by Zigler in his work, and by others in related discussions of etiology, the terms will be used in the text of this paper and will be placed in quotation marks whenever they appear.

familial retardation in a number of publications (Zigler, 1966a, 1966b, 1967, 1969, 1973). In his writings, he drew attention to the variety of clinical phenomena which are encompassed by the term "mentally retarded," and he argued that this occurs because a subnormal intelligence-test score has been used as the chief criterion for assigning individuals to this category. To Zigler, it is the heterogeneity of this group which has led to a great deal of confusion about the importance of cognitive "defects" and how they contribute to the limited abilities of mentally retarded individuals. Therefore, Zigler sought to clarify the distinctions among the different groups of people who share the characteristic of subnormal intelligence and proposed to treat separately only the performance of individuals whose impairments exceed those due to normal intellectual variation.

Zigler based his distinction between types of retardation on etiological considerations. He noted that some retarded persons are affected by obvious neurological abnormalities due to injury, infection, or hereditary metabolic disorders. Examples of this "organic" type of retardation include Strauss' exogenous syndrome, secondary microcephaly, and phenylketonuria. Although known physical defects account for a sizable proportion of the retarded population, particularly those with moderate to profound retardation, they do not account for the majority. The largest number of retarded individuals fall into the "mildly retarded" intelligence classification and typically have IQs above 50. They do not have clearly discernible medical defects. Instead, they are identified primarily by limited intellectual functioning. Other family members (particularly parents and siblings) of mildly retarded persons also often show intellectual retardation of the same degree, and therefore these individuals are commonly labeled "cultural-familial." Zigler views retarded people in this category as representing the downward extension of the normal distribution of intelligence.

The distribution of phenotypic intelligence. Several models based on the assumption of polygenic inheritance have been proposed to account for the continuous nature of the intelligence distribution. Simply stated, polygenic models involve the hypothesis that intellectual capacity is under the control of several genes rather than one or two major genes. Each polygene, if present in an individual genotype, adds an equal amount of phenotypic intelligence. Therefore, the more "positive" genes a person has, the more intelligent he can be, and the fewer "positive" genes he has, the less intelligent he is likely to be. A simple model, incorporating only five pairs of additive genes, can yield a distribution of phenotypic intelligence which corresponds fairly accurately to distributions of scores from intelligence tests.

Several of Zigler's conclusions about the two types of mental retardation fit well with a polygenic interpretation of intellectual differences. For one thing, "cultural-familial" retardation can be understood in terms of an overall distribution of a complex trait called "intelligence," with the lower end of the distribution classified as the retarded range. Zigler (1967) stated: "With this approach, the familial retardate may be viewekd as normal, where normal is defined as meaning an integral part of the distribution of intelligence that we would expect from the normal manifestations of the genetic pool in our population" (p. 293).

The same processes that account for normal cognitive functioning also account for the performance of individuals with "familial" retardation. Furthermore, "organic" retardation can be seen to fall outside the normal distribution because of exceptional prenatal, paranatal, or postnatal events unrelated to the usual genetic variation in a population. The individual with "organic" retardation is abnormal in the sense that his limited intellectual functioning is the result of an abnormal physiological process. Logically, at least from an etiological perspective, the performance of "organically impaired" individuals should be treated differently from the performance of individuals with "cultural-familial" retardation. The latter can be distinguished from others in the population only because they do more poorly on intelligence tests and academic tasks, while the former can be distinguished both intellectually and physiologically.

Zigler believes that there has been a tendency to overgeneralize the knowledge that certain forms of retardation have a neurological basis, and that this has resulted in the assumption that all retarded persons have a physiological taint, although one which is not always clinically detectable. He referred to this view as the "defect" or "difference" orientation (Zigler, 1966b). Among the theories that Zigler classified as defect positions are those which attribute the performance of retarded individuals to the rigidity of boundaries between regions in the cognitive structure (Kounin, 1941a, 1941b), to inadequate neural satiation (Spitz, 1963), to an impaired stimulus trace (Ellis, 1963), to a dissociation between verbal and motor systems (Luria, 1963), and to a deficient attention mechanism (Zeaman & House, 1963). There is an obvious variety in these theories, but Zigler asserted that their kinship lies in a common effort to relate retarded-normal performance differences to differences in cognitive structure.

Importantly, for Zigler, a hypothesis of cognitive dysfunction carries with it the implication that all retarded individuals have physiological defects, although he does acknowledge that "[the] theoretical language of some defect theoreticians is explicitly physiological, that of others is non-physiological, while that of others remains vague" (Zigler, 1967, p. 294).

Rate and level of cognitive development. The interpretation of retarded-normal performance differences advocated by Zigler follows from the etiological distinction he made between "organic" and "familial" retardation. As noted, Zigler contended that the "defect" interpretation is appropriate for behavioral differences between "organically impaired" and normal individuals, since the former do have obvious physiological defects. However, this is not the case for individuals with "cultural-familial" retardation, and their performance should be understood in terms of the variability in characteristics ostensibly related to normal genetic combinations. These are the rate of cognitive development and the cognitive level attained when development approaches its asymptote at maturity.

The developmental orientation assumes that the individual with "familial" retardation progresses through the same early cognitive stages as the normal child, but at a slower rate. Consequently, the child with "familial" retardation will have failed to reach more advanced cognitive stages when further development is attenuated by age. Both normal and retarded children show evidence of a regular progression through cognitive stages until middle or late adolescence (Woodward, 1963). The chief difference is that retarded children reach a particular cognitive stage at a later time than normal children, and they do not reach the more advanced stages at all. By the same token, the developmental orientation implies that when the cognitive levels of individuals have been assessed accurately, retarded and normal children who are at the same point in cognitive development should perform comparably on learning and memory tasks.

In contrast to the application of a physiological interpretation to the deficits in cognitive functioning shown by "organically retarded" individuals, Zigler did not accept the notion that individuals with "familial" retardation are organically impaired and that therefore this group should not perform less well when compared with normal children at a similar stage of cognitive development.

The most commonly used measure of cognitive growth is the mental age (MA) score, derived from performance on global tests of intelligence, such as the Stanford-Binet. Zigler acknowledged that these traditional methods of estimating MA are not perfect measures of cognitive development. Intelligence tests tend to be samples of universally taught information and skills, and include tasks which can be administered to individuals over a relatively wide age range, rather than be procedures for evaluating whether or not an individual uses the type of solution appropriate to a particular stage of cognitive development. Nevertheless, Zigler believes that, at present, standard intelligence tests are the best available methods for tapping the complex of cognitive processes which are reflected in behaviors characteristic of different cognitive stages. Zigler assumes that, in a general way, the MA score can be viewed as the product of the same cognitive processes in different people, regardless of their ages or IQ scores. Thus, classifying individuals according to their MA scores arranges them into groups having relatively homogeneous cognitive attainment. From the developmental perspective, children receiving similar MA scores should be at virtually the same cognitive stage, even though they may differ in age and rate of development.

Reinforcement and motivation. As noted, the defect and developmental positions on performance differences between normal and retarded individuals are divided on the question of whether there is always some form of organic impairment associated wtih mental retardation. They are also divided on the question of whether the IQ score or the MA score is correlated with an individual's level of performance. In practical terms, the question is whether the performance of retarded persons should be evaluated by comparing them with normal individuals of the same chronological age (i.e., time since birth) or of the same mental age (i.e., approximately equal with respect to general cognitive attainment).[2]

It has been pointed out that the developmental position assumes that retarded subjects, with the exclusion of "organically impaired" individuals, function exactly like normal persons of the same mental age. From this standpoint, MA-matched retarded and normal individuals may differ in both chronological age and IQ score, but these differences are irrelevant as far as performance on learning and memory tasks is concerned. However, performance differences between MA-matched normal and retarded subjects have been reported often, and the ready conclusion from such findings is that they are attributable to IQ-score differences. Zigler argued vigorously that this conclusion is fostered by the failure to consider some of the more subtle distinctions between normal and retarded persons than their IQ scores. A major difference between retarded and normal individuals—and the one that has been the focus of Zigler's work—is that retarded subjects often live in special institutions, while most intellectually normal persons and many mildly retarded people live at home with their families. Therefore, Zigler maintained that the factor of institutionalization, as well as that of low IQ scores should be considered as a correlate of mental retardation and as a cause of performance differences between MA-matched normal and retarded subjects.

Although Zigler assumed the cognitive similarity of normal and "familial-retarded" individuals who have been matched for MA, he referred to differences in the motivational histories of the two groups as a means of explaining why their performance is sometimes found to differ. He noted that

---

[2] See the chapter by Winters in this volume.

the experience of someone who is retarded is unique and that, apart from any direct effects of the specific handicap, this experience has an influence on the individual's problem-solving strategies. The environment of the retarded person holds out a different set of responses, expectancies, and reinforcements from that of the normal child. In his world, the retarded child is more prone to experiencing failure as a result of his efforts. He is less likely to obtain social approval from adults for his behavior, and, particularly if he is institutionalized, he is less likely to have had satisfactory interactions with adults.

The work of Zigler and his associates led them to conclude, on the one hand, that the unique experiential history of retarded children may foster a heightened motivation to interact with adults and to seek out approval from them (Green & Zigler, 1962; Zigler, 1961, 1963). On the other hand, it has also been concluded that the larger proportion of failure experienced by retarded individuals (as compared to normal children) tends to produce in the retarded child a sense of mistrust or wariness toward adults (Shallenberg & Zigler, 1961; Zigler, 1958) and a generally lower expectancy for achieving success in the performance of a task (Stevenson & Zigler, 1958). Institutionalization seems also to have an important effect on the value of different reinforcers for retarded residents. They apparently perform better when they are working for tangible rewards, such as small toys, than when they are rewarded by knowledge of the correctness of their responses (Stevenson & Zigler, 1957; Zigler & deLabry, 1962). Retarded individuals also have been found to be "outerdirected" (Green & Zigler, 1962; Turnure & Zigler, 1964; Zigler, Hodgden, & Stevenson, 1958). That is, retarded subjects tend to focus on extraneous cues in a problem situation, looking to irrelevant aspects of the task or to reactions of the experimenter for information to direct their responses, rather than searching their own frames of reference for solutions.

Thus, consistent motivational characteristics seem to be acquired by retarded individuals as a consequence of their relative deprivation of positive social experiences. These various tendencies are seen as contributing jointly to the less flexible and less efficient performance of retarded subjects on the tasks used to assess cognitive functioning (e.g., intelligence tests). Zigler implies that these motivational differences, rather than some single deficiency inherent in retardation, are reflected in the discrepancies observed when comparing the performance levels of normal and retarded individuals of the same general cognitive level.

Evaluation of the Developmental Position

Validity of etiological distinctions. The "two-group" approach to mental retardation advanced by Zigler implies that retardation is more likely to have an organic cause in individuals who are physiologically defective than in individuals who are distinguished by a level of intellectual functioning for which there is no apparent relation to neurological impairment. Therefore, seeking out the abnormal physiological structures underlying mental retardation in the former group is an appropriate task, with the hope that fuller knowledge of the causes will result in adequate diagnosis and effective procedures for remediation of the intellectual disability.

At the same time, although the etiology of "familial" retardation "constitutes the greatest mystery" (Zigler, 1967, p. 298), Zigler feels it is wrong to attempt to solve it, arguing instead that there is no pathology or defect in individuals who lack physical symptoms. It should be clear that Zigler draws a parallel between discernible medical abnormalties and neurological impairment, and between the absence of gross physical impairments and normal cognitive functioning. In fact, there is no more justification for these inferences than for the assumption of damage to the central nervous system on the basis of poor intellectual performance.

To date, there is little evidence to indicate the nature of the relationship between neurological functions and the processes of learning and memory. Although we know that central nervous system damage has consequences for general intellectual abilities, we do not know which of the various cognitive functions are affected by injuries to specific areas of the brain. Furthermore, in spite of the fact that we know that certain genetic, metabolic, and infectious diseases are associated with a higher incidence of severe and profound retardation, our knowledge of how these diverse etiologies influence intellectual functioning is still limited. At the same time, we cannot be certain that the absence of gross physiological symptoms in retarded individuals indicates that the neurological structures which affect intelligence are intact. There is general agreement that leraning and memory are correlated with physiological changes and, to the extent that they are, retarded performance is likely to involve deficiencies at the neural level. Nevertheless, the current state of our knowledge is not sufficient to permit a judgment as to the validity of etiological distinctions or causal hypotheses about mental retardation.

The developmental interpretation of mental retardation is essentially homological. It assumes that since normal individuals and those with "familial" retardation are physically similar, in the sense that neither group shows the outward signs of an abnormal physiological process, they are functionally identical. Zigler asserts that, regardless of IQ score, individuals of the same general developmental level share the same cognitive processes. He emphasized the continuity between normal and retarded cognitive functioning when he noted that these groups differ only in their positions on the distribution of intelligence due to normal polygenic variation. In short, from the developmental perspective, the differences between normal and retarded people are differences in the degree of intellect rather than differences in the kind of cognitive processes they employ.

It is good scientific practice to assume the null hypothesis—in this case that there are no differences in cognitive functioning between normally intelligent and "familial-retarded" individuals. However, the effect of the homological assumption may be to divert effort away from investigations of how subjects at different points along the distribution of intelligence deal with learning and memory tasks. Zigler depreciated the work of some of those who offer hypotheses about other variables that might be related to intelligence by referring to them as "defect" theorists and by suggesting that they assume that all retarded persons suffer from physiological abnormalities. It seems, rather, that these workers are providing a stimulus for tests of the null hypothesis of no functional differences between normal and retarded individuals, and that such investigations will yield data relevant to the homological assumption.

The alternative question. As Zigler (1967, 1969, 1973) noted, normal individuals and those with "familial" retardation do differ in two important respects: (a) the rate of development, and (b) the final level of cognitive ability attained. Zigler claimed that these are the only significant differences, and therefore he concluded that when groups of retarded and normal subjects are matched on mental age, they should perform equally well. This prediction is dependent in part upon the aspects of cognitive functioning which are measured or evaluated. Zigler tends to be concerned more with the terminal behaviors (or end products of performance) than with how an individual arrives at a response. But it may well be that less intelligent individuals and those with normal and higher intelligence, when they work at the same kinds of tasks, do so in different ways.

By the same token, it seems reasonable to contend that the growth of cognitive abilities is influenced by the way in which an individual deals with the environmental tasks that face him throughout his development. Thus, an individual's performance on intelligence tests, and, in turn, his rate of development and level of cognitive attainment as estimated by his IQ and MA scores, respectively, may reflect his particular way of processing the information at his disposal. Such a view implies not that retarded individuals are physiologically defective, but rather that they go about arriving at terminal behaviors in a fashion which is different from that used by people of normal intelligence.

To the extent that our concern is for the rehabilitation of behavior, and not merely for the demarcation of distinctions, our attention should be focused on the processes that produce the behavior. The end result of an inidividual's performance—his IQ or MA score, the number of errors he makes in solving a problem, the amount of information he retains after a brief interval—are not nearly so informative about the source of his difficulties as what we learn about how the person went about achieving that end result. The study of terminal behaviors and comparisons between high and low scorers on some index leads us only to the conclusion that people who perform well on one measure, such as an intelligence test, tend also to perform well on other (related) measures such as problem-solving tasks; and, conversely, that those who perform poorly on the first also perform poorly on the others. These results have lead to statements which say, in effect, "mentally retarded individuals are retarded because they perform in a retarded way." We are still left with a nagging sense of not having answered the material and relevant question: "What is it about mentally retarded individuals that makes them perform in a retarded way?" The answer certainly is not "low intelligence," nor is it a "negative reinforcement history." Both concepts are descriptive rather than explanatory.

Zigler (1966a, 1966b, 1973) stated that performance differences between groups of normal and "familial-retarded" individuals equated for cognitive development are attributable to the influence of nonintellective factors, particularly to the degree of social deprivation and amount of failure experience. He maintains that when these factors are controlled in comparisons of normal and retarded subjects matched on mental age, there will be no residual differences between them. Although motivational variables of the sort studied by Zigler and his colleagues may control certain aspects of performance, it is not likely that these same motivational variables are responsible for producing slower rates of development and less mature levels of cognitive attainment. Modifying the environments of retarded children may make them less prone to develop the personality characteristics which impair their performance, but retarded children will still be substantially different from normal children of the same mental age. It is important to note that while the performance of normal children tends to improve with age, a retarded child's performance improves less rapidly with age. The implication is that retarded and normal individuals differ in their abilities to utilize information and to develop increasingly more efficient problem-solving procedures.

The goal from an educational and psychological perspective is to understand and improve the problem-solving abilities of retarded individuals. One way of achieving this end is to increase our knowledge about the component processes and responses that comprise the total behavior patterns of retarded subjects. We know that "retarded" behavior is less efficient than "normal" behavior, but it remains to be seen just *how* it is inefficient. Insight into the "how" of retarded behavior can be gained by studying what the retarded person does when he has to learn or remember something. It will also be necessary to establish the sequence of events which leads to the most efficient completion of a task. This requires the development of innovative techniques for separating and observing each of the spontaneous, instantaneous steps in a learning and memory process. Then comparisons can be made between what the normally intelligent individual and the retarded person does. This, in turn, can yield a better understanding of how the retarded individual is inefficient in the selection, modification, and application of procedures for particular task requirements.

The next section presents a brief overview of two research programs which approach retarded-normal performance differences by seeking to evaluate the component processes used by an individual to arrive at the solution of two kinds of problems, discrimination learning and short-term memory. The methods and the results of these investigations themselves provide the best evidence of the utility of a process-oriented approach to answering the question of how retarded and normal individuals differ.

STUDIES OF COMPONENT PROCESSES IN LEARNING AND MEMORY

Attention

One of the processes which affects the efficiency of learning is the ability of individuals to initially attend to the most informative aspects of a problem situation. The amount and kind of information taken in by a person influence the rate at which he solves a problem and, ultimately, whether he arrives at a solution at all. An individual who monitors only a small portion of the information available to him, or who does not readily discriminate between relevant and irrelevant aspects of a task, will perform in an inefficient fashion. He will learn slowly because he does not have enough information to solve the problem, and he will remember little because he cannot retrieve from his memory what is not there.

The concept of attention in learning refers to the process by which an individual focuses selectively on certain aspects of a stimulus situation to which he is exposed. His response presumably is based on these stimuli attributes, while it is unaffected by attributes to which he does not attend. This view of attention derives from an interest in the discrimination task as a typical learning situation and the attempt to develop theoretical accounts of the phenomena of discrimination learning (Bower & Trabasso, 1964; House & Zeaman, 1963; Lovejoy, 1965, 1966; Restle, 1955, 1962; Sutherland, 1959; Trabasso, 1963; Trabasso & Bower, 1968; Zeaman & House, 1963). In the discrimination task, the person must choose between two (or more) objects, pictures, or patterns, and in this manner demonstrate that he has learned which one of the two is consistently correct (or rewarded). Although this appears to be a simple task, the principles involved are fairly complex, and they presumably evoke those skills and processes involved in everyday problem situations.

As with so many other learning tasks, there is a tendency for the results of research in simple discriminative learning to indicate that the overall performance of retarded subjects is inferior to that of normal subjects, even when mental age is controlled (Ellis, Hawkins, Pryer, & Jones, 1963; House & Zeaman, 1958; Rieber, 1964; Ross, Hetherington, & Wray, 1965; Rudel, 1959). The general finding has been that *performance* in discrimination-learning tasks is related to intelligence (House & Zeaman, 1958; Zeaman & House, 1966), and all too often this result has been interpreted as meaning that *learning rate* is a function of intelligence. Certainly, traditional learning curves portray a linear increase in the slopes of learning functions with increasing intelligence, and this could mean that retarded individuals learn more slowly than normal subjects (see Figure 6.1).

Backward learning curves. One of the difficulties in interpreting performance differences observed in traditional learning functions is that they tend to obscure the rather varied performance of the individuals who contribute to the group curve. Any two points along the learning function may actually represent different samples of subjects, since individuals achieve criterion on different trials. Two things can be done to improve the way the group function represents the characteristics of individual performance: First, subjects can be grouped in terms of the trial block on which criterion is achieved, and, second, the criterion trial block for each group can be equated and performance can be plotted *backward* from the criterion block (Hayes, 1953). The resulting "backward learning curve" tends to sharpen the features of the group function in the vicinity of the criterion trial block (see Figure 6.2). When this is done with discrimination-task data from groups of normal and retarded subjects, two things not apparent in forward learning curves become evident: (a) The final slopes of the approach to criterion, or learning rates, for all groups are highly similar; and (b) the difference among groups

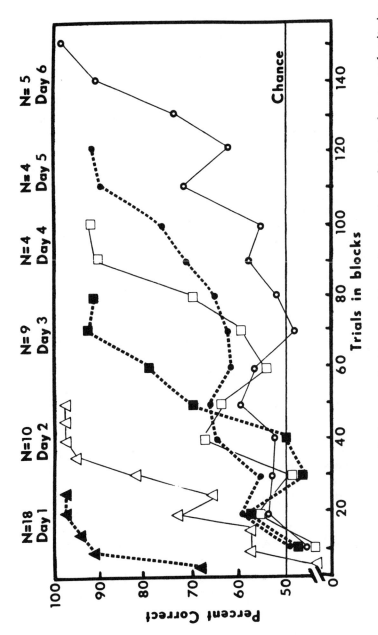

Figure 6.1. Forward learning curves of subgroups of subjects requiring various numbers of training days to reach criterion. The number of subjects in each group appears at the top. (From "The Role of Attention in Retardate Discrimination Learning" by D. Zeaman and B.J. House, in *Handbook of Mental Deficiency* edited by N. R. Ellis. Copyright 1963 by McGraw-Hill, Inc. Used with permission of McGraw-Hill Book Co.)

255

lies in the lengths of the portions of the curves which precede the rise in performance to criterion (Zeaman & House, 1963).

Thus, backward learning curves suggest the startling conclusion that retarded and normal individuals do not differ in learning rate, and that learning rate is not related to IQ (Zeaman & House, 1966). At the same time, retarded and normal subjects do appear to differ with regard to the time spent at the chance level of performance (i.e., the time it takes for the performance level to start to change from chance). This difference needs to be analyzed to determine whether it represents a fundamental difference in the way learning proceeds in normal and retarded individuals, or whether it is due to some other developmental difference that is unrelated to the underlying learning process.

Zeaman and House (1963) suggested a model of learning which accounts for the differences between normal and retarded subjects in overall performance on discrimination tasks and for the specific difference between them in terms of the lengths of the chance portions of their backward learning curves. This model proposes that in order to solve a discrimination problem, a person must learn to do two things: (a) pay attention to a relevant dimension (such as shape, color, or size) on which the stimuli differ, and (b) choose the correct value (such as triangle versus circle, red versus green, large versus small) on that dimension. Thus, from the perspective of Zeaman and House's "Attention Theory," problem solution is represented as involving the learning of two distinct classes of responses, namely, observing or attention responses, and instrumental or approach responses.

An instrumental response consists of making a choice among the several stimulus objects available on a trial of a problem. The observing response mediates between the perception of the stimulus and the person's choice, and it exposes to the subject the specific values of the stimulus dimension observed. Dimensions were defined by Zeaman and House (1963) as "broad classes of cues having a common discriminative property (p. 168)." Objects typically differ along several dimensions. For example, the stimuli in a problem might differ in Color and Shape (see Figure 6.3).

If a person attends to a particular dimension (e.g., Color) and picks a particular value on that dimension (e.g., red), *and* his choice is rewarded (e.g., he receives an "M & M" or is told "correct"), then he will be more likely to attend to that dimension and to choose the same value on that dimension the next time. Similarly, if his choice is not reinforced, he will be less likely to attend to the same dimension again. Therefore, the probability of attending to a particular dimension increases or decreases from trial to trial as a result of reinforcement.

Ultimately, the relevant dimension becomes the one which the person is most likely to choose, because only his choice of the correct value on the

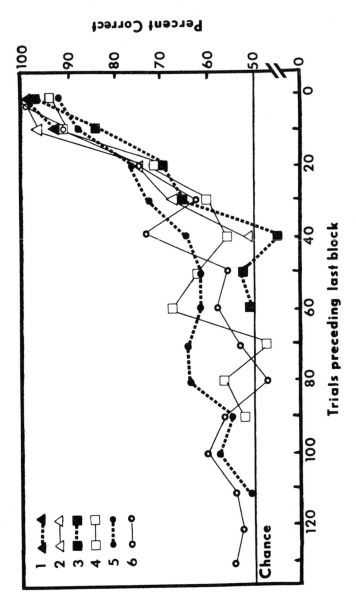

Figure 6.2. The functions of Figure 6.1 have been regrouped prior to averaging for a backward learning curve. The contrast in form of backward and forward learning curves is marked. (From "The Role of Attention in Retardate Discrimination Learning" by D. Zeaman and B. J. House, in *Handbook of Mental Deficiency* edited by N. R. Ellis. Copyright 1963 by McGraw-Hill Book Co.)

TRAINING PROBLEM

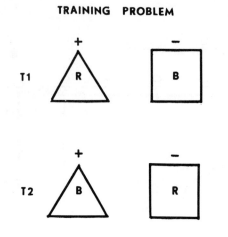

TRANSFER PROBLEMS

ID Sʜɪꜰᴛ   **ED** Sʜɪꜰᴛ

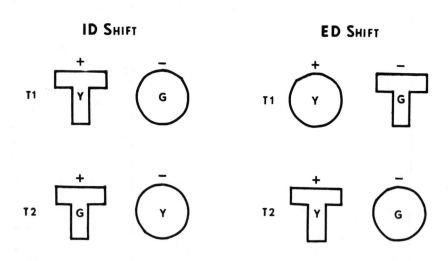

Figure 6.3. Examples of intradimensional and extradimensional shifts used to
assess the transfer of attention responses in discrimination learning.

relevant dimension is consistently rewarded. Once the subject has learned to attend to the relevant dimension with a greater probability than any other dimension, his performance will begin to improve. In terms of a two-choice discrimination task, this is the point at which the subject's responses begin to be correct more than half of the time. Furthermore, this is reflected in the backward learning curve by a relatively rapid change from responding at chance level to responding correctly all the time. The length of the portion of the curve which precedes the rise in performance is thus a function of how long it takes an individual to learn to attend to the relevant dimension more frequently than to any other dimension.

Transfer of attention. The validity of Zeaman and House's analysis of the steps leading to the solution of discrimination-learning problems has been supported by demonstrations of the effects of the transfer of attention responses (Campione, Hyman, & Zeaman, 1965; Dickerson, 1966; Furth & Youniss, 1964; House & Zeaman, 1962; Isaacs & Duncan, 1962; Shepp & Turrisi, 1966). Transfer of training is indicated when performance on a problem is influenced by the solution of a previous problem. If it is assumed that attention, like other learned responses, can be transferred from one situation to another, then the expectation would be that it should be easier to learn the second of two discrimination problems in which the same dimension is relevant than when the relevant dimension is changed between problems.

The case where the subject is trained on two problems having the same relevant dimension is referred to as an "intradimensional" (ID) shift. The other situation, where the relevant dimensions of the two problems differ, is called an "extradimensional" (ED) shift. If the values of each of the dimensions are changed between problems, so as to preclude the transfer of instrumental learning, then any differences in performance between ID-shift and ED-shift problems can be attributed to the transfer of attention responses. In general, an ID shift should be learned faster than an ED shift because, in the first kind of transfer problem, the person is already attending to the appropriate aspects of the stimuli as a result of the prior training. However, an ED shift requires that the subject first extinguish an inappropriate attention response before learning to attend to the newly relevant dimension of the transfer problem.

Normal children and college students consistently learn ID shifts faster than ED shifts (Dickerson, 1966; Eimas, 1966; Furth & Youniss, 1964; Isaacs & Duncan, 1962). Zeaman and his colleagues found that retarded subjects also show this characteristic ID-ED shift difference (Campione, Hyman, & Zeaman, 1965, House & Zeaman, 1962; Shepp & Turrisi, 1966). Thus, the evidence suggests that both retarded and normal subjects solve discrimination-learning problems in the same fashion, that is by learning to attend to the relevant stimulus dimension as well as to make the correct choice on that dimension.

Although the implication of these findings is that retarded and normal individuals learn the same chain of component responses, the question remains as to why the discrimination-learning performance of retarded subjects is generally less adequate than that of nonretarded subjects. One possibility is that the difference lies in the selection and application of attention responses to meet the requirements of a specific problem. For example, individuals may differ with respect to their initial tendencies to attend to the particular dimensions of the stimuli in a problem. In fact, some subjects show a marked preference for certain dimensions over others (Heal, Bransky, & Mankinen, 1966; Wolff, 1966). Furthermore, people do not always attend to all available stimulus dimensions, and a proportion of subjects—particularly those at a lower developmental level—tend to limit their attention to only a few dimensions at a time (House & Zeaman, 1963; Ingalls & Dickerson, 1969; Schonebaum, 1973). As a result, a person's success in a discrimination task depends largely on whether or not the relevant dimension of a problem is one of those to which he attends at the outset.

The probability of making an attention response to a relevant dimension at the beginning of a problem naturally influences the length of the presolution period, since performance improves rapidly only when an individual is more likely to attend to the relevant dimension than to any other. If the relevant dimension is one to which the person is likely to attend initially, then his performance can improve above chance level in a few trials. On the other hand, if he attends to an irrelevant dimension at the outset, then solution will take longer. Zeaman and House (1963) suggested that the poor performance of retarded subjects on discrimination problems is largely due to the fact that they have low initial probabilities of attending to the stimulus dimensions (usually, Form or Color) most often relevant in discrimination learning experiments. Consequently, they spend more time at a chance level of performance than do nonretarded subjects, who are more likely to attend to Form and Color. Retarded individuals, however, frequently choose to attend to dimensions, such as Left-Right Position, which are not selected first as often by normal subjects. Thus, when one of the dimensions favored by retarded individuals is made relevant, they can solve the problem quickly. Under these circumstances, the performance of retarded subjects may be superior to that of normally intelligent subjects (e.g., Weir & Stevenson, 1959).

Several conclusions about learning by retarded individuals can be drawn from the study of the component responses which contribute to performance in discrimination problems and transfer tasks. First, the difference between normal and retarded subjects in overall discrimination performance is not necessarily attributable to differences in simple learning rate. Analyses of original learning of discrimination problems by groups of subjects separated according to intelligence, especially when depicted in terms of backward learning functions, indicate comparable learning rates. Second, comparisons of ID-ED shift differences for normal and retarded subjects show that problem solution involves essentially the same process in both groups, and that retarded as well as normal persons are capable of learning to attend to the relevant dimensions of a discrimination problem.

Apparently, performance differences between retarded and normal subjects are not due to a "defective" attention mechanism. Rather, the chief difference between retarded and normal individuals seems to be in their ability to select the appropriate attention response at the outset of a problem.

Rehearsal and Retrieval

Like attention, *rehearsal* is a process that influences the acquisition of information by the individual. This is the mechanism by which items held in a temporary store (primary memory) are kept active. These items are either lost (by simple decay) or are transferred to the permanent store of secondary memory (Waugh & Norman, 1965). Persons who are deficient in their ability to rehearse will have lower recall scores and take longer to solve a problem, particularly when task demands are high, because they must rely on the most recently acquired information.

Retrieval, on the other hand, refers to the search through memory for items placed in storage. Memory-scanning strategies typically follow characteristic patterns, as reflected in the response latency functions, depending upon such factors as the type of material being retrieved, the number of items in store, and the response requirements of the recall or recognition task (Sternberg, 1969). These different retrieval patterns may be an indication of the plan of search used by a person in his effort to accomplish efficient and accurate performance on a particular task. Individuals who lack appropriate retrieval strategies will show less accurate recall and slower problem-solving behavior, even if they are capable of rehearsing and retaining the material, since they do not have ready access to the information in memory.

In traditional memory tasks—involving a train-test procedure—the focus has been on accuracy of recall (i.e., the proportion of list items retained after exposure and a brief retention interval). Performance on such a task is influenced by the manner in which items are learned and maintained in memory, the rate of loss from memory (or forgetting), and the manner in which items that have been learned and retained are located and retrieved from memory. Accurate short-term recall reflects the combined efficiency of all these processes. When performance is less than perfect, it is not possible to evaluate on the basis of recall scores alone whether one or the other, or some combination of the component processes, is operating at a less than efficient level. The typically poor short-term recall performance of retarded persons thus is difficult to interpret. The quantitative inferiority of the "memory" of retarded individuals may be an indication of an inefficient acquisition process, storage system, or retrieval strategy, or a combination of these.

One of the alternatives, a "leaky" storage or relatively high rate of forgetting, may be readily ruled out as a cause of poor recall by retarded subjects. Recent reviews of the short-term memory literature comparing the performance of retarded subjects with that of nonretarded subjects have concluded that rate of forgetting is unrelated to intelligence (Belmont, 1972; Belmont & Butterfield, 1969). When differences in amount of information initially encoded are considered, and subjects are equated on the level of immediate recall, they show equal forgetting. Thus, the retarded person's inferior recall performance cannot be attributed to an inadequate retention mechanism. This leaves, as possible explanations of retarded-normal recall differences, discrepancies in one or both of the following processes: (a) acquisition or learning of material, and (b) search and retrieval strategy. It also leaves the technical problem of isolating the acquisition and retrieval processes and obtaining direct measures of each, independent of the amount of information recalled by an individual.

Evaluating component processes. A unique solution to this problem has been provided by Belmont and Butterfield (1971a, 1971b), Butterfield and Belmont (1971), Butterfield, Wambold, and Belmont (1973), and by Butterfield and Belmont in this volume. Their "inductive naturalistic method" involves the application of a serial-learning device developed by Ellis (1970) and allows the investigator to observe components of the process which precede the correct recall of an item, as well as to count the number of items recalled correctly. The apparatus, shown in Figure 6.4, consists of a row of nine plexiglas buttons, with a tenth button centered above. A stimulus item, usually a single consonant, is rear-projected on one of the transparent buttons momentarily when it is pressed by the subject.

The subject can proceed at his own pace in successively exposing the stimulus items. After exposing each of the items, the subject then presses the upper button, which exposes a probe item. The subject's task usually is to recall the position of the probe in the training "list" and to press the appropriate button below. He is allowed only one opportunity per trial to find the correct consonant. Therefore, the procedure is essentially a one-trial serial learning task, with the subject pacing acquisition and administering the probe himself. Furthermore, the experimenter can observe and record the time taken by the subject both to "press-to-see" the next item after the offset of each previous item and to probe his memory after the last item.

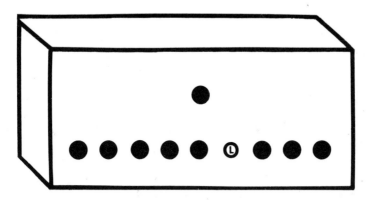

Figure 6.4. Subject console used in Belmont and Butterfield's studies of acquisition and retrieval processes. The probe button appears at the top. (From "The Relations of Short-Term Memory to Development and Intelligence" by J. M. Belmont and E. C. Butterfield, in *Advances in Child Development and Behavior,* Vol. 4, edited by L. P. Lipsitt and H. W. Reese. Copyright 1969, by Academic Press, Inc. Used with permission.)

Normal adult subjects tend to show consistent patterns of pauses between stimuli from trial to trial. Some subjects pause after every item; some move quickly from button to button, pausing only after every two or three items; and others pause not at all before pressing for the probe item. Although different subjects manifest a variety of pause patterns, individuals tend to pause at the same points in a list (see Figure 6.5). Belmont and Butterfield (1969, 1971a, 1971b) assume that these characteristic pause patterns reflect the subject's attempt to employ an efficient strategy for learning the position of each item in a list. Each pause corresponds to some activity on the part of the subject, namely, his *rehearsal* of an item or group of items in order to facilitate his recall when the probe appears. Belmont and Butterfield's (1971a, 1971b; Butterfield and Belmont, 1971) data indicate that nonretarded adults generally engage in spontaneous active rehearsal on eight-or nine-item consonant lists, usually pausing at the early (after the third item) and middle (after the sixth item) portions of a list, when they rehearse all items already exposed.

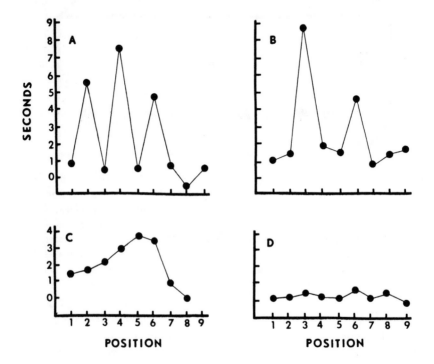

Figure 6.5. Mean hesitation patterns for the last 10 trials of four subjects who employed different acquisition strategies. (From "The Relations of Short-Term Memory to Development and Intelligence" by J. M. Belmont and E. C. Butterfield, in *Advances in Child Development and Behavior,* Vol. 4, edited by L. P. Lipsitt and H. W. Reese. Copyright 1969, by Academic Press, Inc. Used with permission.)

Furthermore, normal adults typically do *not* pause when they do not have to; i.e., they do not rehearse the final items on a list. This passive nonrehearsal phase of the adult acquisition strategy fits well with the notion of an ephemeral "echo box" memory (Waugh & Norman, 1965) and is adequate to serve efficient recall when the subject can test his memory immediately after exposure. Finally, normal adult subjects make use of both echo-memory and active rehearsal to construct a complex acquisition strategy. They do not rehearse the first few items on a list, but instead rely on passive nonrehearsal to collect several items in an "echo box" for subsequent rehearsal (usually after exposure of the third item). Then this procedure is repeated for the next few items. The remaining items are added to memory without active rehearsal, as noted previously. The modal adult strategy is, then: expose items 1-3; rehearse items 1-3; expose items 4-6; rehearse items 4-6 (1-6); expose items 7-9; probe! The net result of this combination of passive nonrehearsal and active rehearsal is highly efficient recall at each position in the serial list.

To this point, the retrieval process has not been mentioned because Belmont and Butterfield's "press-to-see" method allows for the evaluation of acquisition in a recall task unconfounded by the effects of retention and retrieval. However, information about the manner in which items are retrieved from memory is recoverable from their procedure by an analysis of correct response latencies following the exposure of the probe item. The analysis of response latency is similar to that used by Sternberg (1969) and allows the investigator to distinguish among several strategies available to the subject when searching his memory for a match to the probe item.

Belmont and Butterfield's (1971b) response latency data lead to two conclusions: (a) A subject's retrieval strategy is responsive to the way in which he places items in memory, and (b) passively and actively learned materials are retrieved from memory in different ways. Passive-nonrehearsed items (those from the end of a list) yield flat serial-position functions; i.e., it takes about the same amount of time for an individual to respond to a probe item from any one of the positions at the end of a list. On the other hand, actively rehearsed items show marked serial-position effects; the farther down the list an item is, the longer it takes for the subject to respond after exposing the probe item. This seems to be because the subject retrieves an item from memory by first searching for the first item rehearsed, then the second, and so on. When he finds the item that matches the probe, he ends the search. Therefore, retrieval from the active memory is best characterized as a slow, serial, and self-terminating process (Butterfield & Belmont, 1971).

An important aspect of the recall behavior of nonretarded individuals is the adaptability of their mnemonic strategies. They show the ability to tailor combinations of passive nonrehearsal and active rehearsal—as well as to alter search and retrieval—to suit the needs of a particular task (Belmont & Butterfield, 1969, 1971a, 1971b; Butterfield & Belmont, 1971). When lists are short, echo memory may be used exclusively. When lists are long, rehearsable chunks of items are formed in echo memory and then rehearsed actively. Significantly, items from the end of a list are also searched first because they are retained in the evanescent echo memory and will be lost if not retrieved immediately.

Another demonstration of the flexibility of acquisition strategies in normal adults involves the use of repeated lists. Here the subject can relax his organization of items into rehearsable chunks as each item becomes learned through repeated presentations, and his pattern of pauses should become increasingly flatter over trials (Belmont & Butterfield, 1969). Other studies show a similar modification of acquisition strategies to match changes in the retrieval requirement or retention interval (Butterfield, Belmont, & Peltzman, 1971; Kellas & Butterfield, 1971).

Recall strategies in retarded individuals. To what extent can the poor-recall accuracy of retarded individuals be explained by differences in their acquisition (rehearsal) and retrieval (search) strategies when compared with those of nonretarded adults? First, the finding that retarded subjects and normal adults recall items from final serial positions on a list equally well suggests that retarded individuals can and do use passive nonrehearsal efficiently (Belmont & Butterfield, 1969, 1971a, 1971b; Butterfield, Wambold, & Belmont, 1973; Ellis, 1970). At the same time, several studies provide evidence suggesting that retarded subjects are less able to make use of rehearsal in an active memory because their recall for items from the initial positions of a list is poorer than that of normal individuals (Belmont & Butterfield, 1969, 1971a; Butterfield, Wambold, & Belmont, 1973; Ellis, 1970; O'Connor & Hermelin, 1965).

Direct evidence of the difference in acquisition processes between retarded and nonretarded individuals is provided by an examination of pause patterns across serial positions in the "press-to-see" task (Belmont & Butterfield, 1969, 1971a). Twenty-one institutionalized, mildly retarded adults were compared with 14 college students on a 7-item list. The retarded subjects showed relatively short and equal pauses across each of the positions (except for the initial position). The difference between the retarded adults and the undergraduates was most marked in the middle of the list, and the interaction between serial position and intellectual level was statistically significant ($p < .005$). This is strong evidence that the poor-recall accuracy of retarded individuals is at least partly due to their failure to engage in spontaneous active rehearsal.

It does not necessarily follow, however, that retarded individuals are *unable* to rehearse; there may be several reasons why they do not rehearse. The absence of spontaneous rehearsal in developmentally young individuals might be an indirect result of inefficient storage or retrieval mechanisms. If learned material is lost from memory at a rapid rate, or if it is not readily recoverable from memory, then there would likely be only a small gain in recall accuracy from active rehearsal. It has already been noted that retarded subjects are not especially disadvantaged with respect to rate of forgetting when compared with normal individuals. But, there is some indication that their retrieval processes are not comparable. For one thing, when retarded adults were instructed to rehearse the initial items on a six-letter list, normal adults still recalled many more of the rehearsed items than did the retarded subjects, although the recall accuracy of the retarded adults was greatly improved by requiring them to use an identical rehearsal strategy (Belmont & Butterfield, 1971b).

Furthermore, a comparison of the correct response latencies for the normal adults and a selected group of the trained retarded subjects whose recall accuracy was as high as that of the nonretarded subjects revealed that the retarded adults took longer to respond correctly at each of the rehearsed positions, although the two groups had comparable serial-position functions for correct response latency (Belmont & Butterfield, 1971a). The form of the latency function for this subsample of retarded subjects who recalled at a high level after rehearsal instruction seems to imply that retarded individuals search through their active memory in the same serial, self-terminating fashion as do normal adults. The difference apparently lies in the fact that retarded subjects gain access to their active memory less readily and therefore are slower to retrieve information.

It seems also that retarded individuals are less skilled at tailoring passive and active acquisition strategies according to the recall requirements of a task (Belmont & Butterfield, 1971b; Butterfield, Wambold, & Belmont, 1973). Although normal adults combine passive nonrehearsal with active rehearsal when a task requires that they be able to recall any item and its position in a relatively long list, retarded subjects tend to persist in using a passive procedure, regardless of the recall task requirements. Also, when retarded subjects were induced to employ an active-passive learning strategy—by giving them practice in exposing a few letters in rapid succession, then rehearsing them aloud, and then exposing the remaining letters and immediately pressing to see the probe—their recall accuracy after training did not show much improvement over a pretraining test, although a larger proportion of subjects showed evidence of active rehearsal after training than before training (Butterfield, Wambold, & Belmont, 1973).

This discrepancy between the effects of rehearsal training on pause time as against recall accuracy might be attributable to the failure of the retarded subjects to use a retrieval strategy which was appropriate for their newly learned acquisition strategy. Recall accuracy should be most efficient if the passive memory is searched prior to the active memory because the former is more rapidly evanescent. Retarded individuals, who seem to use a passive acquisition strategy almost exclusively, are not likely to have developed retrieval strategies which could be coordinated to a combined active-passive acquisition procedure. In fact, instruction in the use of active rehearsal seemed to foster a tendency for the retarded subjects to search for actively learned items before passively learned ones, with an attendant improvement of recall for items from the beginning of the list at the expense of recall for later items (Butterfield, Wambold, & Belmont, 1973).

The relative deficiency in recall accuracy by retarded subjects seems to be the result of the interplay of several differences in the way that they go about learning and searching for information in memory as compared with the procedures employed by normal adults. In particular, these differences are (a) a tendency to use passive nonrehearsal exclusively in learning items, and a failure to use an active rehearsal strategy, regardless of the recall task requirements; (b) a less accessible active memory (when active rehearsal is induced by training procedures); and (c) the absence of habitual retrieval strategies which can be coordinated to combined active-passive acquisition strategies.

On the positive side, it should be noted that retarded individuals have demonstrated the ability to use each of the component processes necessary for accurate recall, particularly when trained appropriately. They do have an adequate capacity for passive nonrehearsal, they can actively rehearse items after relevant training, and they can accurately recall the rehearsed items. Finally, they can combine passive and active mnemonic strategies, and they can search through passive memory before attempting to retrieve items from the active store if they are first trained to use a retrieval strategy which is suited for the induced learning strategy. Emphasizing the assets of retarded subjects disclosed by their investigations of short-term recall, Butterfield, Wambold, and Belmont (1973) noted that their subjects "did not lack the memory processes for accurate performance in this task. What they did lack was spontaneous access to the processes and coordination among them" (p. 668). (In their chapter in the present book, Butterfield and Belmont elaborate upon their most recent work in the areas outlined above.)

SUMMARY AND CONCLUSIONS

The distinction between "defect" and "developmental" interpretations of retarded-normal performance differences has given importance to the question of whether retarded individuals are cognitively less efficient than normal individuals. Zigler, who supports the developmental view, has suggested that retarded subjects have been assessed as cognitively different from normal subjects primarily because investigators have included both "organically impaired" and "familial-retarded" subjects in their studies of learning and memory. According to this position, children with "familial" retardation differ from normally intelligent individuals only in their rate of cognitive development and in the final level of ability achieved.

It follows, then, that "familial-retarded" and normal subjects equated for developmental level are expected to perform equally well. The research efforts of scientists committed to this view have tended to focus on the question of why retarded subjects frequently perform more poorly than do normals matched on mental age. The explanation favored by Zigler and his collaborators is that the performance of children with "familial" retardation on learning and memory tasks is impeded by unique motivational tendencies which they develop because they are subject to an unusual degree of social deprivation and failure experience.

The "two group" approach assumes that mental retardation in individuals who show evidence of an abnormal physiological process is more likely to have an organic cause than have individuals who differ from normal children only in their cognitive development. However, the present state of knowledge about the relationships between brain physiology and cognitive functioning is not sufficient to decide this matter conclusively. Another aspect of the etiological distinction is that "familial-retarded" and normal individuals of the same developmental level are assumed not to differ in their cognitive processes by reason of the fact that they are physically similar. This assumption is essentially homological because it relates similarity of function to the absence of apparent physiological differences between normally intelligent and "familial-retarded" individuals.

Substantial evidence that nonintellective, motivational factors influence the efficency of the performance of "familial-retarded" subjects was reported by Zigler and his colleagues. Nevertheless, it is not likely that these variables produce the slower rates of development and less mature levels of cognitive attainment characteristic of mental retardation. Rather, rate of cognitive growth and developmental level reflect the effectiveness with which an individual selects, modifies, and applies the component processes that contribute to his performance. Therefore, the issues in the interpretation of findings from studies of learning and memory is not whether performance differences indicate that retarded individuals are less congnitively efficient than normal subjects, but *how* they are less efficient.

Two groups of investigators who examined the latter question are House and Zeaman (in the area of discrimination learning) and Belmont and

Butterfield (in the area of short-term recall). Although the research of these two groups differs with regard to the task studied and the experimental procedures used, some general conclusions follow from their findings. Their results provide evidence that retarded persons are capable of using the component processes of attention in discrimination learning, and of rehearsal and retrieval in short-term recall. In this respect, retarded individuals are not "defective." On the other hand, they seem less likely than normal individuals to select and modify these processes according to the specific requirements of a task. Retarded subjects fail to use some of the response strategies available to them. For example, they initially attend only to certain dimensions in a discrimination problem, and they use passive nonrehearsal exclusively in a recall task. Therefore, the relatively poor performance of retarded subjects on learning and memory tasks seems to be related to the inefficient manner in which they coordinate the steps leading to the completion of a task, rather than to their lack of certain cognitive processes.

The utility of separating and evaluating the component processes which underlie performance is that it permits comparisons to be made between normal and retarded people in terms of the sequence of events in which they engage when they are asked to learn or remember something. Knowing how an individual goes about a task will ultimately provide a fuller understanding of how the behavior of the retarded person is inefficient.

REFERENCES

Anastasi, A. Heredity, environment, and the question "how?" *Psychological Review,* 1958, *65,* 197-208.

Belmont, J. M. Relations of age and intelligence to short-term color memory. *Child Development,* 1972, *43,* 19-29.

Belmont, J. M., & Butterfield, E. C. The relations of short-term memory to development and intelligence. In L. C. Lipsitt and H. W. Reese (Eds.), *Advances in child development and behavior* (Vol. 4). New York: Academic Press, 1969, pp. 29-82..

Belmont, J. M., & Butterfield, E. C. Learning strategies as determinants of memory deficiencies. *Cognitive Psychology,* 1971, *2,* 411-420. (a)

Belmont, J. M., & Butterfield, E. C. What the development of short-term memory is. *Human Development,* 1971, *14,* 236-248. (b)

Bower, G. H., & Trabasso, T. Concept identification. In R. C. Atkinson (Ed.), *Studies in mathematical psychology.* Stanford: Stanford University Press, 1964, pp. 32-94.

Butterfield, E. C., & Belmont, J. M. Relations of storage and retrieval strategies as short-term memory processes. *Journal of Experimental*

Psychology, 1971, *89,* 319-328.

Butterfield, E. C., Belmont, J. M., & Peltzman, D. J. Effects of recall requirement of acquisition strategy. *Journal of Experimental Psychology,* 1971, *90,* 347-348.

Butterfield, E. C., Wambold, C., & Belmont, J. M. On the theory and practice of improving short-term memory. *American Journal of Mental Deficiency,* 1973, *77,* 654-669.

Campione, J., Hyman, L., & Zeaman, D. Dimensional shifts and reversals in retardate discrimination learning. *Journal of Experimental Child Psychology,* 1965, *2,* 255-263.

Dickerson, D. J. Performance of preschool children on three discrimination shifts. *Psychonomic Science,* 1966, *4,* 417-418.

Eimas, P. D. Effects of overtraining and age on intradimensional and extradimensional shifts. *Journal of Experimental Child Psychology,* 1966, *3,* 348-355.

Ellis, N. R. The stimulus trace and behavioral inadequacy. In N. R. Ellis (Ed.), *Handbook of mental deficiency.* New York: McGraw-Hill, 1963, pp. 134-158.

Ellis, N.R. A behavioral research strategy in mental retardation: Defense and critique. *American Journal of Mental Deficiency,* 1969, *73,* 557-566.

Ellis, N. R. Memory processes in retardates and normals. In N. R. Ellis (Ed.), *International review of research in mental retardation* (Vol. 4). New York: Academic Press, 1970, pp. 1-32.

Ellis, N. R., Hawkins, W. F., Pryer, M. W., & Jones, R. W. Distraction effects in oddity learning by normal and mentally defective humans. *American Journal of Mental Deficiency,* 1963, *67,* 576-583.

Furth, H. C., & Youniss, J. Effect of overtraining on three discrimination shifts in children. *Journal of Comparative and Physiological Psychology,* 1964, *57,* 290-293.

Green, C., & Zigler, E. Social deprivation and the performance of retarded and normal children on a satiation type task. *Child Development,* 1962, *33,* 499-508.

Hayes, K. J. The backward curve: A method for the study of learning. *Psychological Review,* 1953, *60,* 269-275.

Heal, L. W., Bransky, M. L., & Mankinen, R. L. The role of dimensional preference in reversal and nonreversal shifts of retardates. *Psychonomic Science,* 1966, *6,* 505-510.

House, B. J., & Zeaman, D. A comparison of discrimination learning in normal and mentally defective children. *Child Development,* 1958, *29,* 411-416.

House, B. J. & Zeaman, D. Reversal and nonreversal shifts in discrimination learning in retardates. *Journal of Experimental Psychology.* 1962, *63,* 444-451.

House, B. J. & Zeaman, D. Miniature experiments in the discrimination learning of retardates. In L. P. Lipsitt and C. C. Spiker (Eds.), *Advances in child development and behavior* (Vol. 1). New York: Academic Press, 1963, pp. 313-374.

Ingalls, R. P., & Dickerson, D. J. Development of hypothesis behavior in human concept identification. *Developmental Psychology*, 1969, *1*, 707-716.

Isaacs, I. D., & Duncan, C. P. Reversal and nonreversal shifts within and between dimensions in concept formation. *Journal of Experimental Psychology*, 1962, *64*, 580-585.

Kellas, G., & Butterfield, E. C. Effect of response requirement and type of material on acquisition and retention performance in short-term memory. *Journal of Experimental Psychology*, 1971, *88*, 50-56.

Kounin, J. S. Experimental studies of rigidity: I. The measurement of rigidity in normal and feeble-minded persons. *Character and Personality*, 1941, *9*, 251-272. (a)

Kounin, J. S. Experimental studies of rigidity: II. The explanatory power of the concept of rigidity as applied to feeble-mindedness. *Character and Personality*, 1941, *9*, 273-282. (b)

Lovejoy, E. P. An attention theory of discrimination learning. *Journal of Mathematical Psychology*, 1965, *2*, 342-362.

Lovejoy, E. P. Analysis of the overlearning reversal effect. *Psychological Review*, 1966, *73*, 87-103.

Luria, A. R. Psychological studies of mental deficiency in the Soviet Union. In N. R. Ellis (Ed.), *Handbook of mental deficiency*. New York: McGraw-Hill, 1963, pp. 342-362.

Milgram, N. A. The rational and irrational in Zigler's motivational approach to mental retardation. *American Journal of Mental Deficiency*, 1969, *73*, 527-532.

Milgram, N. A. Cognition and language in mental retardation: Distinctions and implications. In D.K. Routh (Ed.), *The experimental psychology of mental retardation*. Chicago: Aldine, 1973, pp. 157-230.

O'Connor, N., & Hermelin, B. Input restriction and immediate memory decay in normal and subnormal children. *Quarterly Journal of Experimental Psychology*, 1965, *17*, 323-328.

Reiber, M. Verbal mediation in normal and retarded children. *American Journal of Mental Deficiency*, 1964, *68*, 634-641.

Restle, F. A theory of discrimination learning. *Psychological Review*, 1955, *62*, 11-20.

Restle, F. The selection of strategies in cue learning. *Psychological Review*, 1962, *69*, 329-343.

Ross, L. E., Hetherington, M., & Wray, N. P. Delay of reward and the learning of a size problem by normal and retarded children. *Child Development,* 1965, *36,* 509-517.

Rudel, R. G. The absolute response in tests of generalization in normal and retarded children. *American Journal of Psychology,* 1959, *72,* 401-408.

Schonebaum, R. M. A developmental study of differences in initial coding and recoding of hypothesis information. *Journal of Experimental Child Psychology,* 1973, *16,* 413-423.

Shallenberger, P., & Zigler, E. Rigidity, negative reaction tendencies, and cosatiation effects in normal and feeble-minded children. *Journal of Abnormal and Social Psychology,* 1961, *63,* 20-26.

Shepp, B. E., & Turrisi, F. D. Learning and transfer of mediating responses in discriminative learning. In N. R. Ellis (Ed.), *International review of research in mental retardation* (Vol. 2). New York: Academic Press, 1966, pp. 85-121.

Spitz, H. H. Field theory in mental deficiency. In N. R. Ellis (Ed.), *Handbook of mental deficiency.* New York: McGraw-Hill, 1963, pp. 11-40.

Spitz, H. H. The channel capacity of educable mental retardates. In D. K. Routh (Ed.), *The experimental psychology of mental retardation.* Chicago: Aldine, 1973, pp. 133-156.

Sternberg, S. Memory-scanning: Mental processes revealed by reaction-time experiments. *American Scientist,* 1969, *57,* 421-457.

Stevenson, H. W., & Zigler, E. Discrimination learning and rigidity in normal and feebleminded individuals. *Journal of Personality,* 1957, *25,* 699-711.

Stevenson, H. W., & Zigler, E. Probability learning in children. *Journal of Experimental Psychology,* 1958, *56,* 185-192.

Sutherland, N.S. Stimulus analyzing mechanisms. In *Proceedings of the symposium of the mechanization of thought processes* (Vol. 2). London: Her Majesty's Stationery Office, 1959, pp. 575-609.

Trabasso, T. Stimulus emphasis and all-or-none learning of concept identification. *Journal of Experimental Psychology,* 1963, *65,* 395-406.

Trabasso, T., & Bower, G. H. *Attention in learning.* New York: Wiley, 1968.

Turnure, J., & Zigler, E. Outer-directedness in the problem solving of normal and retarded children. *Journal of Abnormal and Social Psychology,* 1964, *69,* 427-436.

Waugh, N. C., & Norman, D. A. Primary memory. *Psychological Review,* 1965, *72,* 89-104.

Weir, M. W., & Stevenson, H. W. The effect of verbalization in children's learning as a function of chronological age. *Child Development,* 1959, *30,* 143-149.

Wolff, J. L. The role of dimensional preference in discrimination learning.

Psychonomic Science, 1966, *5,* 455-456.

Woodward, M. The application of Piaget's theory to research in mental deficiency. In N. R. Ellis (Ed.), *Handbook of mental deficiency.* New York: McGraw-Hill, 1963, pp. 297-324.

Zeaman, D., & House, B. J. The role of attention in retardate discrimination learning. In N. R. Ellis (Ed.), *Handbook of mental deficiency.* New York: McGraw-Hill, 1963, pp. 159-223.

Zeaman, D., & House, B. J. The relation of IQ and learning. In R. M. Gagne (Ed.), *Learning and individual differences.* Columbus, Ohio: Chas E. Merrill, 1966, pp. 192-217.

Zigler, E. The effect of pre-institutional social deprivation on the performance of feebleminded children. Austin: University of Texas, 1958. (Unpublished doctoral dissertation)

Zigler, E. Social deprivation and rigidity in the performance of feebleminded children. *Journal of Abnormal and Social Psychology,* 1961, *62,* 413-421.

Zigler, E. Rigidity and social reinforcement effects in the performance of institutionalized and non-institutionalized normal and retarded children. *Journal of Personality,* 1963, *31,* 258-269.

Zigler, E. Mental retardation: Current issues and approaches. In M. L. Hoffman and W. F. Hoffman (Eds.), *Review of child development* (Vol. 2). New York: Russell Sage Foundation, 1966, pp. 107-168. (a)

Zigler, E. Research on personality structure in the retardate In N. R. Ellis (Ed.), *International review of research in mental retardation* (Vol. 1). New York: Academic Press, 1966, pp. 77-108. (b)

Zigler, E. Familial mental retardation: A continuing dilemma. *Science,* 1967, *155,* 292-298.

Zigler, E. Developmental versus difference theories of mental retardation and the problem of motivation. *American Journal of Mental Deficiency,* 1969, *73,* 536-556.

Ziegler, E. The retarded child as a whole person. In D. K. Routh (Ed.), *The experimental psychology of mental retardation.* Chicago: Aldine, 1973, pp. 231-232.

Zigler, E., & deLabry, J. Concept-switching in middle-class, lower-class, and retarded children. *Journal of Abnormal and Social Psychology,* 1962, *65,* 267-273.

Zigler, E., Hodgden, L., & Stevenson, H. W. The effect of support and nonsupport of the performance of normal and feebleminded children. *Journal of Personality,* 1958, *26,* 106-122.

Earl C. Butterfield received his Ph.D. in psychology from George Peabody College in 1963. He pursued his research career in mental retardation from 1963 to 1967 at Yale University, and since then at the University of Kansas. He is currently Professor of Psychology and Pediatrics, Co-Director of the Ralph L. Smith Mental Retardation Research Center, and President-Elect of the American Psychological Association's Division on Mental Retardation. He has worked collaboratively with Dr. John Belmont since 1966 on the study of cognitive development as it pertains to mental retardation.

John M. Belmont received his Ph.D. in experimental psychology in the mental retardation program at the University of Alabama in 1966. Since then he has actively collaborated with Dr. Earl Butterfield in the area of cognitive development, holding a research appointment at Yale University from 1966-1972 and an associate professorship at the University of Kansas Medical Center (Pediatrics) from 1972 to the present. Dr. Belmont is a Center Investigator at the Ralph L. Smith Mental Retardation Research Center, where he is also Research Training Coordinator.

7

Assessing and improving the executive cognitive functions of mentally retarded people

Earl C. Butterfield and John M. Belmont

The issues we discuss here arise from our research with mentally retarded and normal children, and from our reading of current findings and theories of how normal adults process information. We introduce the issues with brief overviews of our work and that of others. Having thus raised some critical questions about how to assess and improve cognition, we propose a strategy for answering the questions and describe some recently collected data which illustrate how successful that strategy could be.

THE ISSUES

In 1967 we began a program of research aimed at understanding the development of the information-processing aspects of intelligence. At that time we made a major simplifying assumption, which was that the laboratory study of children's memory functions would clearly reflect their information-processing strategies. We chose memory as this vehicle because the science of mnemonics seemed to offer a suitably wide range of background data about normal adults, and of methods which could be elaborated to expose the developmental character of information processing.

The preparation of this report and the data described in it were supported by Public Health Service grants HD-00870, HD-00183, and HD-02528. We are deeply indebted to the following members of the Shawnee Mission (Kansas) Public School District for making it possible to collect the data reported here: Dr. Ralph Chalender, Assistant Superintendent; Ernest Kumpf, Principal of the Roesland School; Wayne Morris, Principal of the Prairie School; Charles Rocklage, Principal of the Indian Hills Junior High School; and Richard Trast, Associate Principal of the Shawnee Mission East High School.

We investigated three memory functions: information acquisition, information retention, and information retrieval. A review of the developmental research on *long-term* retention showed that this function does not vary with age or IQ (Belmont, 1966). Finding, too, that *short-term* retention has no developmental properties (Belmont, 1967, 1972; Belmont & Butterfield, 1969), we decided to concentrate on information acquisition (input) and retrieval (output), and we described a set of procedures by which these two functions would be objectively separated and independently measured (Belmont & Butterfield, 1969; Butterfield & Belmont, 1971). A series of basic developmental studies with these procedures demonstrated a substantial growth in the child's use of active information-processing strategies. Young nonretarded and retarded children showed little of the highly organized spontaneous input or output behavior clearly shown by older normal children and adults (Belmont & Butterfield, 1971a, 1971b; Butterfield & Belmont, 1972).

At that point it seemed appropriate to try to improve children's memory performance by teaching them to use active cognitive strategies. Our first working hypothesis was that children would improve their information processing if they were trained to use mature input strategies. To test this notion, we trained young normal and retarded children to use input strategies which we knew to be suitable for the memory task we had been studying. The training improved the children's performance, but did not raise it to adult levels. Continuing along the same lines, then, our revised hypothesis was that adequate training would require attention to output as well as to input processes. We proceeded to teach these children to use an output strategy which we knew to be consistent with the input strategy we had already taught them. Although the combined instruction resulted in further gains, the youngsters still did not perform at adult levels. The reason for this failure was suggested by their protocols: Every retarded child adequately performed the input and output components of the combined strategy, but few managed to coordinate these to promote a harmonious flow of information. Our final effort therefore involved training them to coordinate input and output, and this led to virtually perfect memory. Retarded adolescents' recall rose to 114% of the level of untrained normal adults (Butterfield, Wambold, & Belmont, 1973).

Brown, Campione, Bray, and Wilcox (1973) also showed that retarded children who do very poorly on a pretest will perform with virtually perfect accuracy when they are trained to use appropriate task-specific, information-processing stategies. The training methods in this study differed from those of Butterfield et. al. (1973) because target behaviors and task difficulty differed between the studies. Nevertheless, these first two absolute successes at removing particular cognitive deficiencies in retarded children may be ascribed to a shared reliance upon recent advances in basic experimental and developmental theories of cognition (Atkinson & Shiffrin, 1968; Belmont & Butterfield, 1971a, 1971b; Brown, 1972; Butterfield & Belmont, 1971; Ellis, 1970; Flavell, Friedrics, & Hoyt, 1970).

Brown et al. (1973) and Butterfield et al. (1973) shared the current theoretical view that competent cognition requires an active, deliberate, planful search for solutions to the information-processing problem at hand, and that retarded people do not so search. Their training experiments were based on the premise that when a plan is given to the child—i.e., if the experimenter decides which cognitive tactics the child will use in what order—the child will perform as if he had invented the strategy himself. Given that the instructed strategies did in fact work perfectly, the question becomes: What do these findings say about how to analyze and improve the cognition of developmentally delayed children?

Despite the similarity of their empirical studies, Brown (1974) and Butterfield et al. (1973) answered this question entirely differently. The crux of the disagreement is whether it would be more profitable to train strategies for the solution of specific tasks, or to train the process of planning solutions regardless of the particular task. Brown favored the former because she suspected "that the lack of a general intention to use strategies (and the capacity to invent them) is a structural limitation of the immature memorizer" (1974, p. 103). She therefore leaned heavily toward the solution of training a variety of well-studied strategies in hopes that these would spontaneously transfer to novel situations. She quite correctly viewed strategy transfer and generalization as the central measures of success for her orientation. Moreover, she correctly specified that before she could train strategies, she would need to analyze the strategic and capacity requirements of a large number of specific tasks.

We rejected this approach. For one thing, it appears to be economically unsound because devising such a remedial program "to induce general cognitive competence in retarded persons . . . would require systematic analyses of one cognitive domain after another, over a tremendous diversity of domains, with applied experiments along the way to show how to improve each component skill. . . . The conglomerate enterprise would . . . be enormous, and its intermediate payoff unsure" (Butterfield et al., 1973, p. 668). In favor of the alternative approach, we noted that normal and retarded children

> can perform all of the component processes required for excellent performance on one particular memory task. . . . What they did lack was spontaneous access to the processes and coordination among them. If this failure of executive control is transsituational . . . then the appropriate level of analysis for

future research is the level of selecting, sequencing, and coordinating processes that are in the cognitive repertoire. Trying to train *executive function* instead of the particular skills for whose success it must ultimately be responsible may save much effort and yield more general theory in the bargain. (Butterfield et al., 1973, p. 668)

This view assumes at the outset that there is no irremediable limitation on the retarded child's willingness or capacity to make an active, planful approach to information-processing problems. All we need do is understand the several creative processes which together we call the "executive function." Then we can arrange special educational procedures that will improve the child's executive functioning, thereby avoiding the overwhelming undertaking of outfitting him with many cognitive strategies, which he would then have to generalize for himself. This aim is the exact converse of Brown's hope that "once a strategic repertoire is acquired, the problem of the general factor disappears" (1974, p. 102). The difference between these orientations is that Brown focused on the *control processes* responsible for regulating the flow of information, while we have focused on the *executive functions* responsible for organizing the control processes into strategies.

Control Processes and Executive Functions

Contemporary theorists (Atkinson & Shiffrin, 1968; Greeno & Bjork, 1973; Reitman, 1970) distinguish the executive function from the control processes which it regulates. In common sense, the distinction works itself out nicely. For example, let the goal be to decide how much our groceries will cost. At the executive level, we choose to estimate their several probable costs by slightly increasing the last prices paid, and then adding up the estimates. To actually solve the problem, the executive must then invoke the relevant control processes for item location, inflation, and addition. During the whole procedure, moreover, the executive might maintain vigilance by invoking supplementary control processes to check the emerging results against subjective criteria for plausibility, until the last answer is obtained.

In the theoretical literature, the executive function is far more diversified than the foregoing introspection might suggest. Reitman (1970) nicely documented this complexity with his descriptions of adults' reports about how they invent solutions to memory problems. Anderson and Bower (1973) also acknowledged the wide range of the executive's planning and organizing functions. They assigned these to an interfacer whose responsibility it was to interpret and parse incoming information and to coordinate its flow through the various short- and long-term memory features of their model of human memory. Along similar lines, Greeno and Bjork (1973) expended the traditional-box flow diagram of the information processor to include the executive function, which oversees the human analyzer's decisions regarding selective attention, rehearsal, long-term memory searches, readiness to recall, and so forth.

In all these theoretical statements, the control processes are seen to be the operations by which we work upon the information available, or retrieve it from memory, in order to perform a cognitive task. By contrast, the executive function is the means by which we select, sequence, evaluate, revise, or abandon these operations. Thus, control processes (or sequences of them) are the goal-directed tactics of cognition; their deployment is the objective outcome of executive planning and revision. In view of this distinction, a primary issue is: *Can an educationally useful theory of cognition concern itself with cognitive control processes to the exclusion of the executive functions of cognition?*

If executive functions could be ignored, as Brown maintains, it would be substantially easier to generate findings from which to build an educationally useful theory of cognitive development. The reason is simply that the measurement of executive functions has yet to be refined. In contrast, not only are control processes currently measurable, but also the direct instruction of control processing has already met with notable success. Indeed, if we consider studies which have directly instructed young normal and retarded children to use task-specific control processes, and compare them to studies which have not given direct instruction (but have arranged the task situation to increase the likelihood of successful information processing), it is clear that the former are about twice as effective as the latter.[1]

Against these arguments for focusing primarily upon control processing, we would note that despite their large immediate effects, the studies which have trained control process strategies have not resulted in either long-term retention of the instructed strategies or generalization of the strategies from the original task to novel tasks (Borkowski, 1974). We view these failures as crucial evidence for the necessity to engage the executive functions in any cognitive training program. Both long-term retention and (especially)

---

[1]On the average, Brown et al. (1973), Butterfield et al. (1973), Gerjuoy and Spitz (1966), Jensen (1965), Jensen and Rohwer (1963), Keeney et al. (1967), Kellas et al. (1973), Kingsley and Hagen (1969), Moely et al. (1969), and Turnure and Thurlow (1973) effected a 60% gain in information processing, while Baumeister et al. (1966), Cole et al. (1971), Gerjuoy and Spitz (1966), Heckman (1966), Jacobs and Foshee (1971), Lance (1965), and Ring (1965) effected an average increase of only 34%.

generalization imply that the child sees and correctly evaluates the information-processing requirements of a task relative to his knowledge of appropriate control processes. This evaluation is an executive function, and since each cognitively demanding situation has its own information-processing requirements, the child will need to be taught to use his executive function to tailor his control processing to meet those demands. In our view, these executive functions are close to what is meant by intelligence. Therefore, instruction on executive functioning rather than on control processes should be the better preparation for behaving intelligently in the world at large. Within this position, a key methodological question is: *How are we to assess executive functions so as to plan and evaluate our efforts to train them?*

Measuring Executive Functions

The role of control processes. In spite of the recent emergence of the executive function as a general theoretical construct, there has been very little effort to study it. Indeed, because of its very complexity, Reitman (1970) advocated a method of minimizing the executive by systematically instructing subjects to use highly specific sequences of control processes. This procedure assigns the executive function to the experimenter, rather than to the subject, in an effort to reduce unexplained variability in dependent measures resulting from spontaneous executive decisions by the subjects. This procedure of Reitman's and that of introspective reporting are the only methods so far described for either controlling or measuring the executive function. The discrepancy between its theoretical acknowledgment and the near absence of experimental studies has resulted, we suppose, from the relative novelty of empirical investigations of the subordinate control processes. Since the control processes are the subjects of the executive function, they would seem to be the most promising indices of its operation. A firm basis of measurment for the control processes would therefore precede measurements of their overseer.

When Atkinson and Shiffrin (1968, p. 116) argued that control mechanisms are central to information processing, they mentioned only two methods for studying them: introspective report and highly inferential mathematical modeling. They might also have cited direct induction of rehearsal (e.g., Wickelgren, 1965) or its prevention (e.g., Glanzer & Meinzer, 1967), and the inferential method of observing the effects of situational variables on the subject's kind or amount of control processing (Glanzer & Cunitz, 1966). Although none of these methods permits the measurement of spontaneous control processing, in recent years its active, spontaneous character has come alive with the following important advances in measurement:

1. Ellis and Dugas (1968) showed that the amount of time a normal adult devotes to list learning in a subject-paced situation is a measure of his rehearsal processes. Belmont and Butterfield (1969) and Flavell et al. (1970) confirmed this general finding with children, and Wilkes and Kennedy (1969) and Butterfield and Belmont (1971) showed that the pauses in the subject-paced situation are finely related to temporal properties of recall, which in turn reflect information retrieval processes.

2. Rundus and Atkinson (1970) reported an overt rehearsal method by which tape recordings were scored for number of rehearsals and size of rehearsal set. Kellas, McCauley, and McFarland (1975) related these overt rehearsal measures to the temporal measures of rehearsal noted above.

3. Flavell et al. (1970) showed that children's input control processes can be measured by observing spontaneous overt verbalizations.

4. Montague et al. (1970) had the subject push a button whenever he found himself rehearsing. This permits an overt response to indicate covert rehearsal even during some competing overt activity (Kroll & Kellicut, 1972).

5. Pollio, Richards, and Lucas (1969) successfully timed tape-recorded recall protocols to measure output processes previously indexed by measures of the order in which items are recalled. Ashcraft and Kellas (1974) related this output time measure to the temporal measure of rehearsal for retarded and normal children.

6. Anders (1973) showed that trial-by-trial structured introspection about retrieval searches is a reliable and useful indicator of retrieval processing in situations where there is no experimenter-defined structure in the lists.

These objective techniques clearly will not allow us to measure all of the rich variety of control processes available to the mature information processor. They nevertheless provide the basis for beginning to study the executive function, with the first step being to clearly define the construct.

Executive Functions Defined

We propose the follwing definition of executive functioning, although it would be quite unworkable without objective measures of control processes:

> *Executive function is exhibited when the subject spontaneously changes a control process or sequence of control processes as a reasonable response to an objective change in an information processing task.*

The definition requires that the child's change of control processes be spontaneous, and that it be a reasonable response to the task change precipitating it. What is meant by reasonable response? Atkinson and Shiffrin (1968) observed that the appropriate control processes for some tasks can be deduced rationally, while for other tasks they must be determined by experimental analysis. The situation is identical for task changes. For example, if a person has been actively rehearsing every new list in a changing-list memory experiment, and a particular list is then repeated several times, the person's only reasonable response is to rehearse less as he more thoroughly learns that list. Other task changes do not yield so easily to rational analysis. Rather, one must examine the behavior of some reference group of effective information processors to discover the reasonable executive changes. For studies of normal and retarded children, normal adults comprise the reference group, so a research program aimed at diagnosing and treating executive function deficits of mentally retarded people will necessarily begin by examining normal adult performance.

QUESTIONS OF RESEARCH STRATEGY

Studying Normal Adults

Before training effective cognition, one must know what it is. This knowledge has two parts. First, there are the strategies involved in mature approaches to specific information-processing requirements. Then there is the level of accuracy achieved when effective thinkers use mature strategies. The strategies themselves will stand as models to be taught. The concomitant accuracy will stand as the ultimate standard by which to judge the efficacy of the training.

Identifying effective strategies. A question of real importance is why one does not draw on the accumulated knowledge of general experimental psychology to discover effective strategies. Why not simply choose tasks which have already been widely used with college students? The answer is that general experimental psychologists have inferred strategies from measurements of recall accuracy. The problem with this method is that we must judge the efficacy of a strategy, for efficacy judgments depend on accuracy measures. We are left with no independent measure of the strategy itself. This is completely unsatisfactory when one is searching for specific relationships between strategies and levels of accuracy. So, we must abandon inferential devices and adopt independent measures of strategy. We cannot, however, do this within the experimentalists' nomothetic approach, which dictates that conclusions be based on group averages. A strategy suggested by a group average necessarily ignores the wide variability among the individual strategies contibuting to the average (Belmont & Butterfield, 1969). The picture of an average strategy leading to an average level of accuracy destroys all strategy/accuracy relationships, preserving not even the worst among them as a potential model for cognitive training and efficacy evaluation. Thus, we are obliged to adopt independent measures of strategy and an idiographic approach in which individual differences become the *sine qua non* of understanding, where once thay were error variance.

Our studies of normal adults, which led to successful memory training of retarded children, amply illustrate and (we think) practically justify this research approach: We gave normal adults control over the presentation of to-be-remembered items, and then analyzed the temporal patterns of the resulting learning and recall activity. From these patterns we isolated input and output strategies (Belmont & Butterfield, 1969; Butterfield & Belmont, 1971; Butterfield, Belmont, & Peltzman, 1971). As it happened, the ultimate training regimen required judicious combinations of input and output strategies (Butterfield et al., 1973), and this requirement simply never would have been met without independent measures of individual adults' strategies and the accuracies they yield.

Since, as enumerated above, there are now many direct measures of cognitive strategies in a variety of situations, there is no evident reason why aspiring instructors of cognition should not undertake preliminary normal-adult studies, according to this approach, even when preparing to train executive functions rather than control processes. It is a matter of extending the approach to include identification and hence refined measurement of executive functions, which in turn can be developed into workable training procedures.

Setting standards. The study of normal adults contributes importantly to defining standards for those who would improve retarded children's thinking. The rule of thumb which we have found useful and attainable (Butterfield et al., 1973) is that our training routines are sufficiently refined when they lead mentally retarded children to perform as well as or better than uninstructed normal adults. While this may turn out to be an impossible standard for other cognitive functions, a clear specification of adult levels of accuracy is an important benchmark against which to judge the performance of specially instructed retarded children. It keeps the instructor humble.

Studying Normal Children

We have argued that it is necessary to study normal children of several ages, after studying normal adults, and before trying to train mentally retarded people (Butterfield et al., 1973). This must seem an inefficient strategy to those who aspire to improve the lot of the mentally retarded individual. After all, why not proceed directly from the normal adult data to applications with deficient children? For one thing, the economics of experimentation dictate that whenever possible, pilot work should be done with normal children. They are always more plentiful, usually more accessible, and sometimes easier to work with. The prime limitation on this rule is that retarded children may not respond to training procedures as normal children do. In at least a general way, the researcher will therefore need to show that mental age (MA) is the best predictor of the results of training efforts.

Another reason for studying normal children is to determine that the cognitive skill in question, be it control process or executive function, does in fact develop with age. This requires relatively large numbers of children over wide MA ranges, but confident knowledge of such development, including its timing and character, can give valuable insight into possible types and probable outcomes of training efforts. Moreover, it will establish the age below which the skill is normally entirely lacking. The latter point is important because special procedures are needed to study (and hence, we assume, to increase the efficacy of) processes which are not seen in the child's spontaneous cognitive repertoire.

STUDIES OF EXECUTIVE FUNCTIONING

The experiments reported below were designed to meet the foregoing methodological requirements. Together, they illustrate the means of providing empirical bases needed for developing cognitive training procedures for retarded children. The first experiment takes the simple but essential step of showing that training procedures found to be sucessful with normal children will probably work equally well with our ultimate target population. The second and third experiments, designed to establish the normal development of certain control processes, incidently suggested that executive functioning also develops. Experiments 4 and 5 were hence designed to directly demonstrate the operation of several executive functions in normal adults and their development in normal children. The youngest children in these studies used so little spontaneous control processing, however, that we could not confidently describe their executive functions. Therefore, in Experiments 6 and 7, we trained adults and children in the use of task-specific strategies in order to establish a baseline of measurable control processing which the subjects could then change as evidence of active executive functioning.

Experiment 1: Effect of Strategy Instruction on Three IQ Groups at MA 9 years, 6 months

In this experiment Clark Wambold[2] shows that children at one mental age respond identically to cognitive instruction regardless of their IQ.

Method. Wambold selected 16 children from each of three IQ groups: Retarded ($\overline{IQ}$ = 77), Normal ($\overline{IQ}$ =100), and Gifted ($\overline{IQ}$ = 124). The average MA for each group was 9-6.

The experiment involved a 2-day procedure. On the first day, all children were treated identically. They exposed the letters of each of 29 6-letter lists, at their own rate, by pressing a button each time they wished to see a new letter. Each letter appeared behind a different window on the apparatus. Each list was followed by a recall period. The children's interletter-input pause times were automatically recorded. Their vocal recall of each list was tape recorded.

On the first five lists, the children were free to recall the six letters in any order (Free Recall). On the remaining 24 lists, they were instructed to recall the last three letters in the sequence of presentation and then the first three in the sequence. This 4-5-6-1-2-3 order was termed "Circular Recall."

On the second day, eight of the 16 children in each IQ group were given 24 more Circular Recall trials, exactly as on Day 1. This was the Day 2 Uninstructed Condition. The other eight subjects were taught to use a specific input strategy to match the Circular Recall requirement. This was the Instructed Condition. Here, the children were told to expose the first three letters, saying each aloud one as it appeared. They were then to pause and rehearse the first three letters aloud as a group three times. They then

---

[2] Clark Wambold conducted this experiment while working as a Postdoctoral Research Trainee with Earl Butterfield.

exposed the last three letters, saying each aloud once, and began their circular recall immediately following their pronunciation of the last letter.

Results. Figure 7.1 shows the recall accuracy from each of the three IQ levels. It can be seen that there are no appreciable IQ effects, regardless of whether the children were engaging in Free or Circular Recall on Day 1, or were Instructed or Uninstructed on Day 2.

Figure 7.2 shows the pause times for Day 2's Instructed and Uninstructed groups. Within each group, children paused similarly, regardless of their IQ, though there was, of course, a large instructional effect. Analysis and classification of each child's pausing pattern yielded the same results. Thus, the similar average patterns did not mask interesting individual differences among the retarded, average, and gifted children.

Figure 7.3 summarizes recall accuracy results collapsed over IQ. It shows the character of the changes in accuracy that occurred in all groups. In the Day 1 Free Recall and Uninstructed Circular Recall functions, it can be seen that under the Circular Recall requirement, all groups performed less accurately in the first three serial positions, but more accurately in the last three. This complex alteration in the serial position curve as a function of recall requirement strongly suggests a similarity of cognitive processing among children of different IQs but like MAs. Comparing Day 1 Uninstructed with Day 2 Uninstructed shows a practice effect, but only for the last three serial positions. This complex alteration, which was present for all three IQ groups, again illustrates a common cognitive process. Finally, comparing the Day 2 Uninstructed and Instructed shows that the input strategy markedly improved recall accuracy, but only at the first serial positions. This is yet a third alteration indicative of basically similar cognition among the IQ groups.

Discussion. This single experiment cannot guarantee that all children of like MA, regardless of IQ will respond similarly to cognitive training under all conditions. For the domain of tasks that we report on here, however, it seems fair to conclude that we can learn much about mentally retarded children by studying normal ones. This gives us the economic advantages of being able to focus on normal children while making only occasional confirmatory studies of retarded children. Moreover, this essentially developmental strategy automatically establishes a broader generality than can be achieved by studying children at only one psychometric intelligence level.

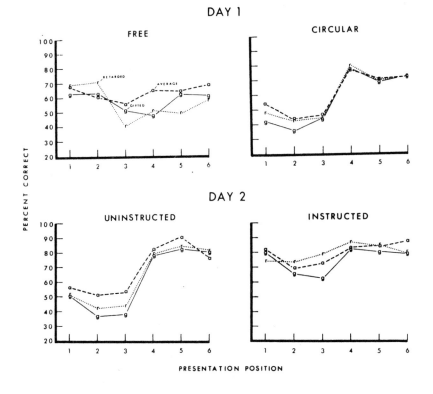

Figure 7.1. Recall accuracy as a function of input position for Day 1 Free and Circular Recall, and for Day 2 Circular Recall with and without input-strategy instructions. The three groups were retarded (r), average (a), and gifted (g) children of MA 9-6 (Exp. 1).

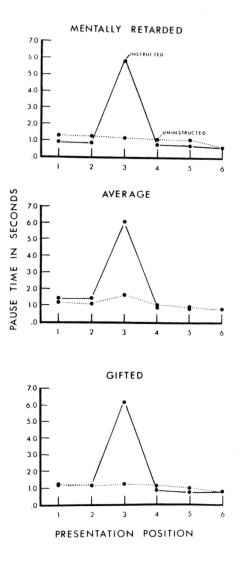

Figure 7.2. Input interletter pause times as a function of input position for retarded, average, and gifted children on Day 2, with and without input-strategy instruction (Exp. 1).

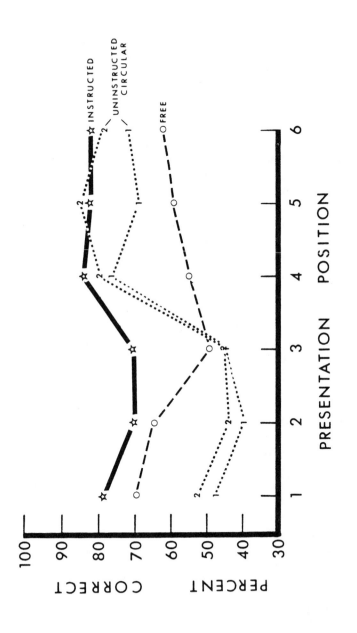

Figure 7.3. Recall accuracy data from Figure 7.1 collapsed across IQ for direct comparison of Day 1 Free (o–o) and Circular (1–1) uninstructed children with Day 2 uninstructed (2–2) and instructed (☆——☆) children (Exp.1).

Experiment 2:   Effects of Between-Subjects Variation of Recall Response Requirement on Spontaneous Input Strategy as a Function of Age

The second reason for studying normal children is to determine that the cognitive functions under study develop with age. This experiment, conducted by Peter Shackleton,[3] shows that input control processing does develop. Moreover, it suggests that the executive function responsible for invoking particular input processing also develops.

Method. Shackleton studied 40 intellectually average children at each of four age levels: 8, 10, 12, and 14 years. The stimulus presentation and data-recording techniques were identical to those used by Wambold in Experiment 1. As before, the children were free to input six-letter lists at their own rate. Twenty children at each age were given Free Recall. The other 20 were given Position Recall, in which a randomly selected letter from the list was exposed in a window at the end of the list, and the child then pushed the window where he recalled its having appeared previously. All children received 15 lists in a single sitting.

Results. Figure 7.4 shows average input pause time (top) and recall accuracy (bottom) as a function of serial position at each age level under each response requirement. The pause-time functions show a curvilinear developmental trend for both requirements. That is, the youngest children show relatively little pausing, older ones show much greater activity, and the oldest are intermediate. Of notable interest is the finding that this trend has different developmental timing for the two response requirements. For Free Recall, the large increase in input processing occurs between ages 8 and 10 years, with 12- and 14-year-olds dropping to an intermediate level. For Position Recall, the maximal increase is found between ages 10 and 12, with 14-year-olds thereafter showing a modest decrease in activity. The development of active pausing strategies for Position Recall thus lags about 2 years behind that for Free Recall.

Figure 7.4 (bottom) shows that recall accuracy increases with age, commensurate with the development of active input processing, though the details of this development are largely obscured by the ceiling on measurement. Nevertheless, the decrease in older children's pausing is not accompanied by reduced recall accuracy, suggesting that the pause-time decrease is not a regression, but rather a strategy refinement leading to increased information-processing efficiency.

---

[3] Peter Shackleton conducted this experiment under Earl Butterfield's supervision in lieu of a Master's thesis for the University of Kansas Department of Psychology.

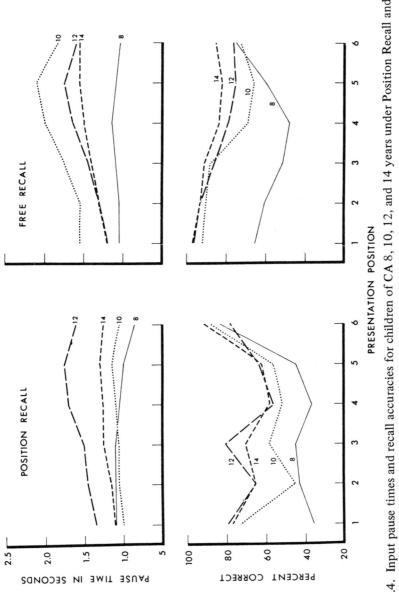

Figure 7.4. Input pause times and recall accuracies for children of CA 8, 10, 12, and 14 years under Position Recall and Free Recall (Exp. 2).

293

Discussion. This study shows that rehearsal control processes do develop, and it suggests that executive functions which control rehearsal also develop. The second point is not completely sure because, for one thing, between-subjects comparisons cannot show children changing their strategies in reaction to changes in the response requirement. We do know, however, that the 12- and 14-year-olds rehearse under both requirements, and their recall is higher than the younger children's. Rehearsal is thus seen to be the mature strategy for both requirements. It may then be noted that the 10-year-olds recognize the utility of rehearsing under Free Recall, but not under Position Recall. The 10-year-old's executive is evidently misled by the Position Recall task, in spite of the child's clear command over the rehearsal control processes. Older children are not likewise misled by the objective dissimilarities between the two tasks, finding that a similar strategy works well for both.

Experiment 3:   Effects of Within-Subjects Variation of Recall Response Requirement on Spontaneous Input Strategy at Age 10

Immediately following the Shackleton study, Lui Leichtman and Wendy Turnbull[4] attempted to remove all doubt about Shackleton's findings for 10-year-olds. They eliminated the possibility of a sampling error having caused the 10-year-old's difference in input processing by having new samples of 10-year-old's difference in input processing by having new samples of 10-year-old children perform both Free Recall and Position Recall.

Method. Ten children, age 10 years, received 15 trials of Free Recall, followed by 15 trials of Position Recall. Ten others received these recall requirements in the reverse order. Otherwise, the experiment was similar to Shackleton's, except that Leichtman and Turnbull's lists contained seven not six items.

Results and Discussion. Figure 7.5 displays Shackleton's pause time results for the between-subjects response requirement comparison versus Leichtman and Turnbull's times for the two orders of within-subjects comparison. In their principal interactions, the three sets of pause times are quite comparable, so we may confidently conclude that 10-year-olds recognize the importance of rehearsing in preparation for Free Recall, but not for Position Recall. In conjunction with Shackleton's findings for younger and older children, these data stand as indirect evidence that executive functions do develop, at least between the ages of 8 and 12 years.

Within this group of introductory experiments, that by Leichtman and Turnbull was the only within-subjects demonstration of spontaneous changes

---

[4]Lui Leichtman and Wendy Turnbull conducted this experiment as a research practicum under the supervision of John Belmont and Earl Butterfield in the University of Kansas Department of Psychology.

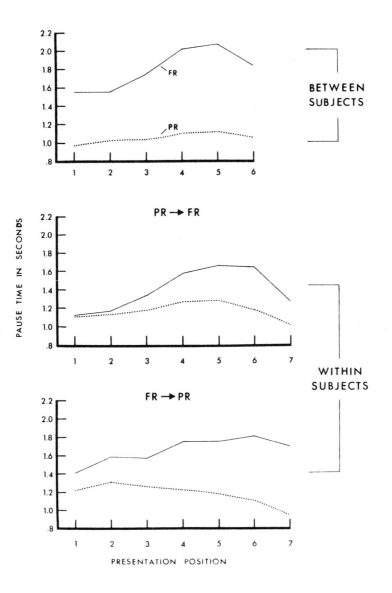

Figure 7.5. Experiment 2 between-subjects comparison of 10-year-olds' pause times for Position Recall and Free Recall versus Experiment 3 within-subjects comparisons of these conditions. PR→FR refers to the order in which subjects received Position Recall and Free Recall.

in control processes resulting from variation in task demands. These changes were noted at only one age level, and it turned out that the changes were unreasonable, judging from what we know about mature information processing on the two tasks. In view of our earlier definition of executive function, it thus appears that these experiments have done little to elaborate the development of adaptive executive functioning, though they have very well served their original purpose of demonstrating active systematic development in the control processes responsible for mature performance in this kind of laboratory task.

To permit the study of executive functioning to move ahead, we decided on a series of task variations which mature thinkers would respond to with easily measurable, large changes in control processing. The basis for task selection was a study described briefly by Belmont and Butterfield (1969). Inasmuch as this was the first fine-grain study of normal adult executive functions, we report it here in detail as Experiment 4. It is concerned with three general functions: *strategy selection, revision,* and *reinstatement.* To these we added *strategy monitoring* in our 1974 developmental study, reported below as Experiment 5.

Experiment 4:   Executive Functions of Strategy Selection, Revision, and Reinstatement by Normal Adults

Method and results. This experiment uses the Position Recall task on 36 lists, presented in groups of nine lists, with each list containing nine letters. Ten college students pace themselves through these lists in one sitting. As before, each item in the list appears in a separate location. At the end of each list, the person is required to indicate where a randomly selected letter had appeared in that list.

The study begins with a series of nine different lists, each of which is presented once. This changing-lists condition makes a very high demand on information-processing skills, and there are strategy changes as a function of practice as the adult subject comes to grips with the task's largely hidden complexities. Figure 7.6 shows that, on the average, adults take eight or nine trials to *select* a relatively stable strategy. During those initial trials with changing lists (top panel, dotted line), the strategy changes represent the executive search for an adequate solution to the mnemonic problem. The task change required by our definition of executive functioning is simply the addition of new lists. Adults begin by using an active, cumulative rehearsal strategy to input all items in a list. This is evidenced by the sharply rising pause-time function, most clearly evident in the first two trials. By Trial 5, we see a much more efficient strategy involving active cumulative rehearsal of the

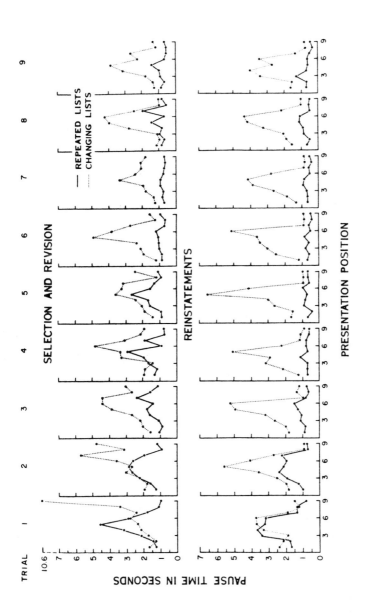

Figure 7.6. Normal adults' input pause times for 9-trial blocks of changing (c) and repeated (r) lists administered in the order c-r-c-r to illustrate the executive functions of strategy selection, revision, and reinstatement (Exp. 4; adapted from Belmont & Butterfield, 1969, Fig. 9).

first several items in the list, and relatively passive processing for the terminal items. These trial-by-trial strategy changes illustrate what we mean by strategy selection: It constitutes the changes in control processes which occur before a person settles on a stable strategy to meet the information-processing demands of the first task he receives in our laboratory.

After the nine strategy-selection lists, the experiment makes a major (unannounced) task change. Instead of presenting a different list on each trial, a particular list is presented repeatedly for nine trials, with a different position being probed randomly on each trial. The change in control processing to conform to this very easy mnemonic problem is seen in the solid lines of the top panel of Figure 7.6. Here, the leftmost line is for a novel list; all the others are for repetitions of that list. The change is dramatic: All subjects *revise* the active/passive strategy they have maintained under the changing-list condition. Having learned the repeated list, it is no longer necessary to actively memorize it on each trial, and so the pausing patterns become flat and low, reflecting relatively passive processing of all in the list. This progressive change from the active/passive strategy to the totally passive one, which in this case took about five or six trials, illustrates what we mean by *strategy revision:* It constitutes the changes in control processes by which a person adopts a new stable strategy following a variation in the information processing demands of a task for which he has previously stabilized a different strategy.

The experiment continues with another unannounced major task change, which is simply to reinstitute the trial-by-trial changing-list condition with which it began. The subjects' concomitant strategy changes are immediate and profound: The active/passive strategy is reinstated on the very first trial, as seen in the leftmost dotted line of the bottom panel of Figure 7.6.

This change illustrates what we mean by *strategy reinstatement:* It comprises\the change in control processes by which the person stabilizes an old strategy following the reintroduction of a task for which he had previously stabilized the strategy. Since reinstatement implies that the executive decisions are based upon recognition of a problem for which a strategy was once selected, reinstatement requires that strategy stabilization be accomplished in fewer trials than the original strategy selection. The most efficient reinstatement would be stable reversion to the old strategy on the first reexposure to the old problem. Judging from the relatively stable form of the pause patterns over the second set of changing lists, it seems that the normal adults in this study exhibited highly efficient reinstatement.

The study provided another occasion to observe strategy reinstatement by changing for a second time to the repeated-list condition. As seen in the solid line of the bottom panel of Figure 7.6, subjects reinstated the unremarkable low, flat, pausing pattern after two or three list repetitions, which is probably close to being the most efficient possible reinstatement for the repeated-list condition.

Discussion. This study firmly established the practicality of measuring adult executive function according to the changed-task/changed-strategy criterion. We might simply have repeated this study at several ages to constitute the developmental stage of our proposed research strategy. We decided, however, to do the developmental work with a task that would lead adult subjects to adopt highly similar but complex spontaneous input strategies. By reducing individual strategy differences while maintaining strategy sophistication, we supposed we could detect relatively small age-related differences in executive functioning.

We wished also to include a fourth executive function, *strategy monitoring*, so we used alternating series of changing and repeated lists; but late in the last series of repeated lists, we introduced small changes in the repeated list to probe for the monitoring function. By *monitoring* we mean the person's continuous evaluation of his strategy to determine its success with a particular task. Such monitoring is essential to strategy selection, revision, and reinstatement. Moreover, it is required for maintaining a stabilized strategy because such maintenance is appropriate only as long as the task demands remain unchanged. The point at which a subject discovers a task change (or, in effect, realizes that his current strategy is no longer serviceable) must depend upon the current focus of monitoring activity. If, for example, he is chiefly concerned with the correctness of his information output, then an indication that his output is unsuccessful may signal the need for a strategy change. If, on the other hand, his strategy maintenance depends upon monitoring some relatively stable character of the task itself, then a change in the task would provide the effective signal. We challenged the monitoring function by making changes in the task which must be detected *during list presentation* by a task-focused monitor.

Experiment 5:   Development of Strategy Selection, Revision, Reinstatement, and Monitoring from Age 10 to Adulthood

Method. This study involves 60 intellectually average school children, 20 each at ages 10, 12, and 17 years (nominal adults). It is patterned after Experiment 4 in that there are again alternating series of changing and repeated lists. Here, however, the subject views lists containing eight words (singular common nouns in the third-grade reading vocabulary), and he outputs every list under a Circular Recall (6-7-8-1-2-3-4-5) requirement in which he must recall the

Table 7.1

Sequence of Lists by Trial in Experiment 5

Trial	1	2	3	4	5	6	7	8	9
List	1	2	3	4	5	6	7	8	9

Trial	10	11	12	13	14	15	16	17	18
List	10	10	10	10	10	10	10	10	10

Trial	19	20	21	22	23	24	25
List	11	12	13	14	15	16	17

Trial	26	27	28	29	20	31[a]	32	33	34[a]	35	36	37[a]
List	18	18	18	18	18	18	18	18	18	18	18	18

[a]On these trials List 18 is modified by replacing two adjacent words with previously unseen words. List 18 is otherwise unchanged during the last 12 trials.

300

last three words and then the first five.

Table 7.1 shows the sequence of list by trial. Each list number in the table signifies a group of eight words, none of which appears in any other list. Thus, each list is unique through Trial 10, and List 10 is thereafter repeated through Trial 18. Unique lists are then seen from Trial 19 through Trial 26 (Lists 11 to 18), and List 18 is finally repeated to the end of the experiment. Note that on Trials 31, 34, and 37, List 18 is modified by replacing two old words with two new, one-time-only words. the new pairs appear in serial positions 4 and 5, 6 and 7, and 1 and 2 on Trials 31, 34, and 37, respectively.

Results. Figure 7.7 (top) presents the adults' average pause times over the first 18 trials, broken down into the first nine (changing) lists, and the following nine (repeated) lists. Trials 19-25 (second group of changing lists) and Trials 26-30 (second group of repeated lists prior to modifications) are shown in Figure 7.7 (bottom).

Considering the first 18 trials, in view of Figure 7.6 (top), it is clear that this experiment generally duplicates Experiment 4's highly systematic results for strategy selection and revision. In the present data, however, the adults initially stabilized their basic strategy on Trial 4. This is decidedly sooner than in the Position Recall study. The strategy is also more stable from trial to trial, and its dissolution under list-repetition (strategy revision) is more rapid, complete and more reliable than previously.

Figure 7.7 (insert) compares the strategy on Trial 10 to that on Trial 19. Inasmuch as this comparison is between the last novel list prior to list repetition and the first novel list following repetition, we conclude that reinstatement of the original is immediate, and the reinstated strategy is the same as the original strategy in nearly every measurable detail.

Reinstatement of the low, flat, revised strategy for repeated lists (Trials 26 and beyond) is virtually complete on Trial 28. This two-trial reinstatement is about two trials faster than the first revision (Trial 10 and beyond), which was complete on Trial 14, having taken four trials. The saving is thus about 50%. This result duplicates the quicker reinstatement than original revision seen in Experiment 4 (three trials versus six: a saving of 50%). Moreover, the first revision is faster in Experiment 5 than in Experiment 4 (four trials versus six), as is reinstatement of the revised strategy (two trials versus three). This second reinstatement is also more reliable than in Experiment 4.

In summary, the adult subjects in Experiment 5 exhibited strategy selection, revision, and reinstatement functions like those found under the Position Recall requirement of Experiment 4; but in all respects the Circular Recall requirement results in faster solutions to the original and subsequently varied information-processing requirements, and the solutions are more reliable. Finally, both experiments showed faster reinstatements than original

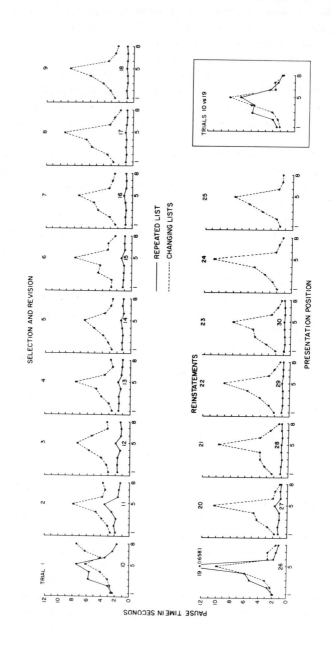

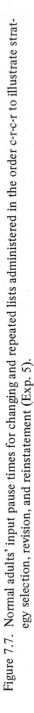

Figure 7.7. Normal adults' input pause times for changing and repeated lists administered in the order c-r-c-r to illustrate strategy selection, revision, and reinstatement (Exp. 5).

302

inventions (could "reinstatement" otherwise be given the name?"), the savings being about equal in the two experiments.

Figure 7.8 shows the age comparisons for Experiment 5. Adult data are a rearrangement of Figure 7.7. We note that some development of executive functioning may be seen following nearly every critical task change in this experiment. The 10-year-olds take about eight trials to stabilize their initial strategy selection, while 12-year-olds and adults require only four trials. In spite of formal similarities among the initial strategies (see, e.g., Trial 8), there is a steady age progression in the amount of time devoted to item input, and this trend is restricted primarily to rehearsal activity leading up to and including the fifth item. This relationship of age to input activity is mirrored in the recall accuracy: Over the first five serial positions on Trials 8, 9, and 10 combined, recall was at 79%, 65%, and 45% for adults, 12-year-olds, and 10-year-olds, respectively. Since these trials are the 10-year-olds' first three stabilized trials, we also compared them with the older groups' first three stabilized trials (4, 5, and 6). This analysis still showed the older groups to be well above the 10 year-olds (74% and 60% versus 45%), so we conclude that increasing age is accompanied by more rapid strategy selection and by more effective selection.

Starting with Trial 11, the first repetition of List 10, there is a progressive strategy revision in all groups. The resulting decrease in input activity is both absolutely and relatively greater in the adults, and the final outcome is that all groups show low, flat, pausing patterns, with the adults now devoting less rather than more input time than the others (see, e.g., Trial 14). The group difference after revision is small, however, and it may represent nothing more interesting than greater reading speed in the older subjects. (With auditory presentation, the three groups might well perform identically on the repeated lists.) In any case, by Trial 12, all groups are recalling the repeated list perfectly.

Strategy reinstatement begins on Trial 19. Looking at the gross formal similarities between Trial 19 and Trial 10, as already reported for the adults, it appears that reinstatement by 12-year-olds and 10-year-olds is not as precise as adult reinstatement. In both younger groups, there appears to be a dynamic reinstatement process, which continues up to about Trial 21 for the 12-year-olds and up to about Trial 23 for the 10-year-olds. In addition to formal dissimilarities between the original stable strategy and the first reinstatements in the younger groups, there are differences in the levels of input processing, suggesting that at the beginning of reinstatement, the children are underestimating the amount as well as the form of rehearsal necessary for the postrepetiton task. From these analyses, it appears that the development of reinstatement involves both the form of the strategy and the overall amount of input activity. Adults show immediate, stable

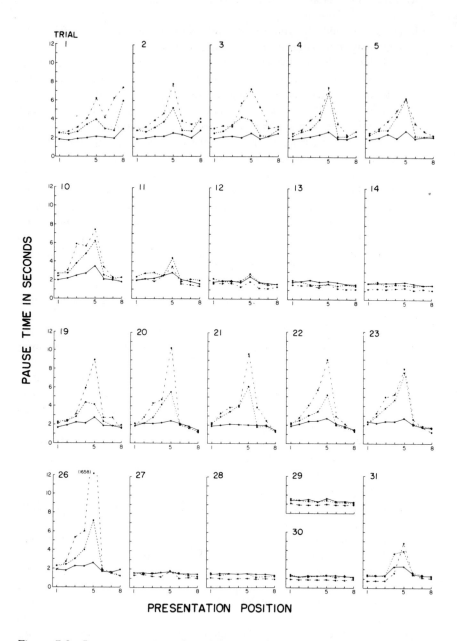

Figure 7.8. Input pause times for adults, and for 12- and 10-year-olds, illustrating the development of strategy selections, revision, reinstatement, and monitoring (Exp. 5).

304

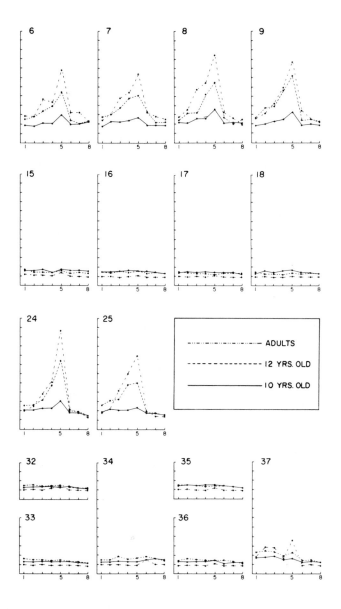

Figure 7.8. (Cont.)

reinstatement of form and level. Twelve-year-olds show immediate reinstatement of form, but they lag in reinstating their original level. Ten-year-olds lag on both dimensions.

It will be recalled that List 18 is presented for the first time on Trial 26 and is repeated unmodified through Trial 30. This provides the occasion to observe reinstatement of the low, flat patterns for repeated lists first seen as a stable strategy revision on about Trial 14. The reinstatement seen in trials 26 through 30 looks formally identical to the original revision, but it is completed by all groups within two trials. This is the same saving as was reported above for the adults. As on the first set of repeated lists, the adults are again seen to be spending the least, rather than the most, input time once revision has been completely reinstated. This second revision thus shows no major developmental differences, but it is the only exception (in the first 30 trials of this experiment) to the general finding of large, systematic developmental changes in the executive functions of strategy selection, revision, and reinstatement.

Trial 31 provides the first opportunity in this experiment to observe the development of the executive monitoring function. On this trial, a small change was made in the list which had been presented on the five preceding trials; namely, new words were substituted for the previous ones at positions 4 and 5 only. The data showed developmental differences in both the form and level of the strategy modifications made as a result of the subjects' monitoring of this change in a familiar list. When the adults encountered the new word at Position 4, they paused only slightly more at that position than they had on the previous trial. Following the second new word, at Position 5, they markedly increased their study time. Thus, adults responded to the new words at positions 4 and 5 by pausing appreciably only following the fifth position. Twelve-year-olds paused about as much overall at positions 4 and 5 as did the adults, but they distributed their pause time more equally over the two positions. Thus, they showed a much greater pause at Position 4 than the adults did, and than they themselves had done on the previous trial. While they paused more at Position 5 than they had on the previous trial, they did not pause here as much as the adults. This pattern suggests that they did not appreciate, as adults did, that they could delay rehearsing the new fourth item until after seeing the fifth. The 10-year-olds responded to the modifications at positions 4 and 5 much like the 12-year-olds, but their overall level of pausing was lower. Thus, there were both form and level differences in response to the changed task between all three age groups. This is substantial evidence that the monitoring function develops and that it relates to a person's understanding of how his control processes can serve him.

On trials 32 and 33, the list which had been presented on trials 26 through 30 was presented again. The pattern of flat low pauses seen on Trial 30 is also seen on both trials 32 and 33. On Trial 34, new words were inserted into the list at positions 6 and 7. None of the groups responded much to this modification, although there is some suggestion that this particular change should evoke only a modest response, since it occurred in the portion of this list for which rehearsal is not necessary. We are disinclined to make anything of the very small age-related differences on Trial 34.

On trials 35 and 36, the list presented on trials 26 through 30 was presented again, and again all age groups produced the low, flat, pause pattern characteristic of a thoroughly familiar list. The list was repeated on the last list, Trial 37, but this time new words were substituted at the first two positions. All groups paused at these two positions as if they were seeing another new list, but all showed a lowered pause time after the fourth word, by which time they should have determined that the list was only partly new. Finally, all groups paused more following the fifth word than they had on the two preceding trials. Presumably they were integrating the two new words into a chunk with the familiar three at positions 3 through 5. The adults took more time to do this than the two younger groups, again showing development of the executive function of monitoring.

Discussion. The question that must now be faced is whether the apparent differences in executive functioning revealed by this experiment are somehow an artifact of differences in the amount of control processing used by the three age groups. We doubt that this is true, but we acknowledge that the 10-year-olds used very little active rehearsal, and that might have led to an underestimation of their executive capability with the present procedure. The next experiment explores the feasibility of observing executive changes using instructed control-processing strategies. Here, we instructed adults where to rehearse, and we then repeated lists to see whether they would appropriately revise the instructed strategy. We reasoned that if they did, we might use instructed strategies to examine executive functions of young children, who normally show very little spontaneous control processing.

Experiment 6: Adult's Revison of an Instructed Input Strategy

In this experiment, which was reported by Butterfield and Belmont (1972), adults were instructed to use a three-part input strategy to learn lists of nine letters for a position recall task.

Method. Subjects were asked to quickly expose the first five letters, then pause to rehearse those five until they judged they knew them well enough to rapidly expose the next two letters, and then rehearse them until they knew them well enough to rehearse the first seven together as group. When they knew all seven well enough, they then went rapidly through the last two items and immediately exposed the probe. The subjects were not told that some of the lists would be repeated. In fact, the first three lists in each group of four were repeated from group to group over 12 groups, yielding three different repeated lists and 12 different changing lists in 36 trials (thus, R_1, R_2, R_3, C_1, R_1, R_2, R_3, C_2; ... ; R_1, R_2, R_3, C_{12}).

Results. Figure 7.9 shows the rehearsal pauses for repeated and changing lists for the first, second, and third blocks of 12 trials. These adults decreased their pausing (at positions 5 and 7) across trial blocks for the repeated lists, but not for the changing lists. Comparison of these findings with those in Figure 7.6 show that these instructed adults did not revise their strategy as rapidly as the uninstructed ones in Experiment 3, but this is not surprising because here they were told to use a particular input strategy. Thus, to revise their strategy, they had to behave in a sense contrary to instructions.

Discussion. These findings, like those of Belmont and Butterfield (1969), show that adults readily distinguish previously rehearsed lists from new lists and that they adjust their rehearsal, continuously taking into account what they have already learned. More important, the findings show the feasibility of using instructed strategies to study executive function.

Experiment 7:   Ten-Year-Olds' Revision and Reinstatement of an Instructed Strategy and Their Monitoring of Task Changes

Method. This experiment with 10 intellectually average 10-year-old children combines the procedures of the two proceding experiments. As in Experiment 5, a new list is presented on each of the first 10 trials. Trials 11 through 18 are repetitions of the list used on Trial 10. Trials 19 through 26 are again changing lists, and the list presented on Trial 26 is repeated on trials 27 through 30. On Trial 31, the fourth and fifth words of this list are replaced with ones not previously used in the experiment. The previously repeated list is then given again on trials 32 and 33, and on Trial 34 its fifth and sixth words are replaced with new ones. Following two more repetitions of the previously repeated list, the experiment concludes on Trial 37, in which the first two words are replaced with new ones. As in Experiment 5, each list is recalled in the circular, 6-7-8-1-2-3-4-5 order. However, following the first three trials (on which they are allowed to pause as they please), subjects are

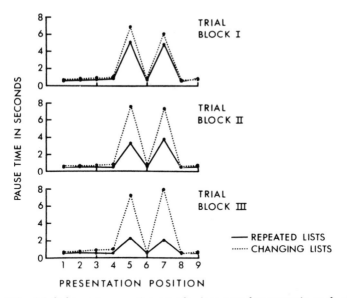

Figure 7.9. Adults' input pause times under instructed strategy in each of 3 blocks of 12 trials, each block containing repeated and changing lists (Exp. 6; adapted from Butterfield & Belmont, 1972, Fig.4).

instructed to use cumulative rehearsal of the first five words and passive attention for the last three. Subjects are not forewarned at the time of list changes, repetitions, or modifications.

Results and discussion. Figure 7.10, which is organized like Figure 7.8 for Experiment 5, shows the trial-by-trial pause times of the 10-year-olds who participated in Experiment 7. The first three trials show that these children were somewhat more active than the 10-year-olds in Experiment 5, but the instruction following the third trial nevertheless markedly increased their rehearsal processing of the first five words. Their use of the instructed strategy is highly reliable across trials 4 through 10. Because of the instruction, we cannot conclude anything about their initial input-strategy selection, for we ourselves selected the strategy in order to observe how they would revise, reinstate, and monitor it.

Beginning at Trial 11, it is apparent that these 10-year-olds did appropriately revise their strategy as a consequence of list repetition. Like the adults in Experiment 6, they took more trials than their age mates in Experiment 5 to accomplish this revision. They never did show a completely flat, low, pause pattern, in that there was still a modest peak at Position 5 on Trial 18. Nevertheless, the revision across trials 10 through 18 is dramatic and reasonable.

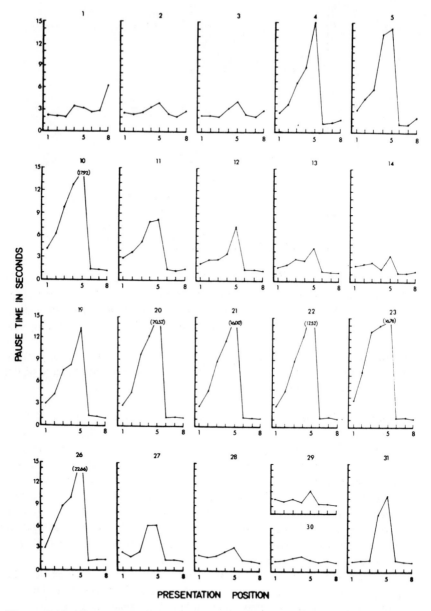

Figure 7.10. Experiment 7 input pause times for 10-year-old normal children, illustrating the feasibility of using input strategy instruction to study strategy revision, reinstatement, and monitoring. The list sequence is identical to Exp. 5.

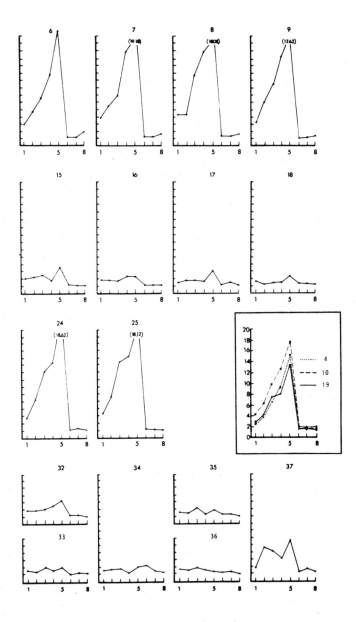

Figure 7.10. (Cont.)

311

Reinstatement of the original instructed strategy occurred on the first new list (Trial 19). The precision of this reinstatement is shown in Figure 7.10 (insert), which compares the pauses of the subjects on trials 4, 10, and 19, which were, respectively: (a) the first trial on which the subjects used the instructed strategy; (b) the last trial prior to the list repetition which precipitated the first revision; and (c) the first trial on which they could have reinstated the instructed strategy. The insert shows a great similarity in all details of the pause patterns for these trials.

An exaimination of trials 19 through 26 shows that this instantly reinstated strategy was used highly reliably throughout the second block of changing lists. Thus, under the instructed-strategy condition, the 10-year-olds reinstated their active strategy more rapidly than did the uninstructed 10-year-olds of Experiment 5. In fact, they reinstated as rapidly as the adults in Experiment 5. Precisely why strategy instruction should result in more mature reinstatement is not clear, but it may reflect the fact that the instruction defined a clear-cut strategy for the subjects. Under the uninstructed conditions of Experiment 5, they may have immediately recognized the need to reinstate their strategy, but may not have had as explicit an understanding of what they had previously done to solve the task's information-processing requirements. The more rapid reinstatement in Experiment 7 would then result from the reduced need to redefine an effective version of their previous strategy.

These subjects' second revision, beginning on Trial 27 and proceeding through Trial 30, was achieved more rapidly than their first one (trials 11 through 18). This is exactly consistent with the findings of Experiment 5, but we cannot here calculate a savings in revision trials because the subjects did not reach a stable flat strategy for either of the two revisions. Nevertheless, the more rapid decrease in pauses across trials 27 through 30 than across trials 11 through 14 justifies the conclusion that the second revision was proceeding more rapidly and would have been accomplished sooner.

The strategy modification of these instructed 10-year-olds on Trial 31 reveals similarities to that of both the 12-year-olds and the adults of Experiment 5. It is considerably more dramatic than the corresponding revision of the uninstructed 10-year-olds (see Figure 7.8). Its form is more similar to that of the 12-year-olds than of the adults in Experiment 5. Thus, there are marked pauses following both the fourth and fifth (new) words (like 12-year-olds) rather than only following the fifth word (like adults). However, this greater similarity to the uninstructed 12-year-olds may be unremarkable, since the instructed strategy itself led to relatively much longer pauses at Position 4 than those made spontaneously by the adults in Experiment 5. Perhaps the mature response to a modification at positions 4 and 5 is to perform at those positions as one does in a completely novel list.

To evaluate this possibility, we will need to instruct adults as well as children to use a particular input strategy. It is nevertheless clear from the data of Trial 31 that executive decisions to modify a strategy are revealed much more clearly for young children who have been instructed than for those who have not (see Figures 7.8 and 7.10, Trial 31).

As in Experiment 5, the modification on Trial 32 is unremarkable. Changing words in the passively acquired terminal portion of the list results in only modest observable changes. In contrast, the changes in strategy on Trial 37 are accentuated for these children compared to those in Experiment 5. The form of this modified strategy is precisely like that of the adults and seventh graders in Experiment 5, but, as on Trial 31, it is greatly (and most helpfully) exaggerated.

This experiment shows that executive functions can be studied even in children who normally exhibit practically no spontaneous control processing. It surely leaves unanswered many questions about the early development of executive functions, but in combination with Experiment 6 it shows that answers can be obtained and that the way to achieve this is to instruct people of different ages to use common strategies, and then modify the task.

CONCLUSIONS

We find great encouragement in these first experimental data about executive functions. They show that there is no methodological obstacle to the developmental investigation of strategy selection, revision, reinstatement, and monitoring, They strongly suggest that we will be able to compare the executive functions of mentally retarded and nonretarded people. In short, they establish the feasibility of a program of research which is focused on the executive component of cognition. By doing that, they provide an operational alternative to focusing simply upon control processes in a fixed-task paradigm, which up to now seemed the most promising way to seek an educationally useful, theoretical view of cognitive development. While these data do not provide an answer to the question of whether more effective cognitive instruction for the mentally retarded person will come (a) from studying control processes themselves, or (b) from using control processes to study executive functions, the data do set the stage for resolving this issue. In view of the current lack of effective cognitive training curricula, we conclude that the very existence of these two alternative approaches to developing theoretically based instructional routines is a major advance.

SUMMARY

Two groups of investigators, including the present authors, have recently shown that the cognitive performance of mentally retarded children can be raised at least to the level of untrained average adults by instructing the children to use mature cognitive control processes. Both demonstrations depend upon recent advances in basic and developmental theories of cognition, and both raise the question of how to extend these theoretical views to yield maximal educational utility for mentally retarded children. The issue is whether to expand the theory of control processing or the theory of executive functions. One group favors the former. We argue for the latter. In this chapter, we have concerned ourselves with establishing the feasibility of studying executive functions and their development, in order to provide an operational alternative to the study of control processing.

We defined executive functions in terms of control processes as follows: *Executive function is exhibited when the subject changes a control process or sequence of control processes as a reasonable response to an objective change in an information-processing task.* We then elaborated a research approach to the study of executive functions, and we described seven experiments which establish the practicality and promise of that approach. Its first step is to secure a basic understanding of the executive functions of intellectually average adults. We presented data from several experiments that provide this understanding with respect to the executive functions of strategy selection, revision, reinstatement, and monitoring.

Having identified executive functions by studying adults, the second phase of the proposed research approach is to determine whether their use develops with age. This is done by studying average children of different ages. We presented data from several such experiments to show that strategy selection, revision, reinstatement, and monitoring do develop. These experiments also establish a technique for studying the executive functions of children who do not spontaneously exhibit control processing. The technique is to train them to use specific control-processing strategies, and then change the task for which they were trained in such a way that a mature executive would modify the instructed strategy. This technique was shown to work with young children and with adults.

The third step of the proposed research approach is to compare the performance of mentally retarded and intellectually average children. We argued that average and subnormal children of the same mental age should respond similarly to cognitive training, and we presented data which establish that they do so for the experimental procedures we employ. The final step of our approach, yet to be implemented, will be to design instructional techniques to instill normal adult executive functions in mentally retarded children.

REFERENCES

Anders, T. R. A high-speed self-terminating search of short-term memory. *Journal of Experimental Psychology,* 1973, *97,* 34-40.

Anderson, J. R. & Bower, G. H. *Human associative memory.* New York: Wiley, 1973.

Ashcraft, M. H., & Kellas, G. Organization in normal and retarded children: Temporal aspects of storage and retrieval. *Journal of Experimental Psychology,* 1974, *103,* 502-508.

Atkinson, R. C., & Shiffrin, R. M. Human memory: A proposed system and its control processes. In K. W. Spence and J. T. Spence (Eds.), *The psychology of learning and motivation.* New York: Academic Press, 1968, pp. 89-195.

Baumeister, A., Hawkins, W., & Davis, P. Stimulus-response durations in paired-associates learning of normals and retardates. *American Journal of Mental Deficiency,* 1966, *70,* 580-584.

Belmont, J. M. Long-term memory in mental retardation. In N. R. Ellis (Ed.), *International review of research in mental retardation* (Vol. 1). New York: Academic Press, 1966, pp. 219-255.

Belmont, J. M. Perceptual short-term memory in children, retardates and adults. *Journal of Experimental Child Psychology,* 1967, *5,* 114-122.

Belmont, J. M. Relations of age and intelligence to short-term color memory. *Child Development,* 1972, *43,* 19-29.

Belmont, J. M. & Butterfield, E. C. The relations of short-term memory to development and intelligence. In L. C. Lipsitt and H. W. Reese (Eds.), *Advances in child development and behavior.* New York: Academic Press, 1969, pp. 29-82.

Belmont, J. M., & Butterfield, E. C. Learning strategies as determinants of memory deficiencies. *Cognitive Psychology,* 1971, *2,* 411-420. (a)

Belmont, J. M., & Butterfield, E. C. What the development of short-term memory is. *Human Development,* 1971, *14,* 236-248. (b)

Borkowski, J., & Wanshcura, P. Mediational processes in the retarded. In N. R. Ellis (Ed.), *International review of research in mental retardation* (Vol. 7). New York: Academic Press, 1974, pp. 1-54.

Brown, A. L. Context and recency cues in the recognition memory of retarded children and adolescents. *American Journal of Mental Deficiency,* 1972, *77,* 54-58.

Brown, A. L. The role of strategic behavior in retardate memory. In N. R. Ellis (Ed.), *International review of research in mental retardation* (Vol. 7). New York: Academic Press, 1974, pp. 55-111.

Brown, A. L., Campione, J. C. Bray, N. W., & Wilcox, B. L. Keeping track of changing variables: Effects of rehearsal training and rehearsal prevention in normal and retarded adolescents. *Journal of Experimental Psychology*, 1973, *101*, 123-131.

Butterfield, E. C. & Belmont, J. M. Relations of storage and retrieval strategies as short-term memory processes. *Journal of Experimental Psychology*, 1971, *89*, 319-328.

Butterfield, E. C., & Belmont, J. M. The role of verbal processes in short-term memory. IN R. L. Schiefelbusch (Ed.), *Language research with the mentally retarded.* Baltimore: University Park Press, 1972, pp. 231-248.

Butterfield, E. C., Belmont, J. M. & Peltzman, D. J. Effects of recall requirement on acquisition strategy. *Journal of Experimental Psychology*, 1971, *90*, 347-348.

Butterfield, E. C., Wambold, C., & Belmont, J. M. On the theory and practice of improving short-term memory. *American Journal of Mental Deficiency*, 1973, *77*, 654-669.

Cole, M., Frankel, F., & Sharp, D. Development of free recall learning in children. *Developmental Psychology*, 1971, *4*, 109-123.

Ellis, N. R. Memory processes in retardates and normals. In N. R. Ellis (Ed.), *International review of research in mental retardation* (Vol. 4). New York: Academic Press, 1970, pp. 1-32.

Ellis, N. R., & Dugas, J. The serial position effect in short-term memory under E- and S-paced conditions. *Psychonomic Science*, 1968, *12*, 55-56.

Flavell, J. H. First discussant's comments: What is memory development the development of? *Human Development*, 1971, *14*, 272-278.

Flavell, J. H., Friedrichs, A. G., & Hoyt, J. D. Developmental changes in memorization processes. *Cognitive Psychology*, 1970, *1*, 324-340.

Gerjuoy, I., & Spitz, H. Associative clustering in free recall: Intellectual and developmental variables. *American Journal of Mental Deficiency*, 1966, *70*, 918-927.

Glanzer, M., & Cunitz, A. Two storage mechanisms in free recall. *Journal of Verbal Learning and Verbal Behavior*, 1966, *5*, 351-360.

Glanzer, M., & Meinzer, A. The effects of intralist activity on free recall. *Journal of Verbal Learning and Verbal Behavior*, 1967, *6*, 928-935.

Greeno, J. G., & Bjork, R. A. Mathematical learning theory and the new "mental forestry." *Annual Review of Psychology*, 1973, *24*, 81-116.

Heckman, B. Varied exposure durations in paired-associate learning in normal and retarded children. *American Journal of Mental Deficiency*, 1966, *70*, 709-713.

Jacobs, J. W., & Foshee, D. P. Use of the von Restorff effect to condition rehearsal in retarded children. *American Journal of Mental Deficiency*, 1971, *76*, 313-318.

Jensen, A. Rote learning in retarded adults and normal children. *American*

Journal of Mental Deficiency, 1965, *69,* 828-834.

Jensen, A., & Rohwer, W. The effect of verbal mediation on the learning and retardation of paired-associates by retarded adults. *American Journal of Mental Deficiency,* 1963, *68,* 80-84.

Keeney, T. J., Cannizzo, S. R., & Flavell, J. H. Spontaneous and induced verbal rehearsal in a recall task. *Child Development,* 1967, *38,* 953-966.

Kellas, G., Ashcraft, M. H., & Johnson, N. S. Rehearsal processes in the short-term memory performance of mildly retarded adolescents. *American Journal of Mental Deficiency,* 1973, 77, 670-679.

Kellas, G., McCauley, C., & McFarland, K. Reexamination of externalized rehearsal. *Journal of Experimental Psychology: Human Learning and Memory,* 1975, *104,* 84-90.

Kingsley, P. R., & Hagen, J. W. Induced versus spontaneous rehearsal in short-term memory in nursery school children. *Developmental Psychology,* 1969, *1,* 40-46.

Kroll, N., & Kellicut, M. H. Short-term recall as a function of covert rehearsal and intervening task. *Journal of Verbal Learning and Verbal Behavior,* 1972, *11,* 196-204.

Lance, W. Effects of meaningfulness and overlearning on retention in normal and retarded adolescents. *American Journal of Mental Deficiency,* 1965, *70,* 270-275.

Moely, B. E., Olson, F. A., Halwes, T. G., & Flavell, J. H. Production deficiency in young children's clustered recall. *Developmental Psychology,* 1969, *1,* 26-34.

Montague, W. E., Kiess, H. O., Hillix, W. A., & Harris, R. Variation in reports of covert rehearsal and in short-term memory produced by differential payoff. *Journal of Experimental Psychology,* 1970, *83,* 249-254.

Pollio, H. R., Richards, S., & Lucas, R. Temporal properties of category recall. *Journal of Verbal Learning and Verbal Behavior,* 1969, *8,* 529-536.

Reitman, W. What does it take to remember? In D. Norman (Ed.), *Models of human memory.* New York: Academic press, 1970, pp. 469-509.

Ring, E. The effect of anticipation interval on paired-associate learning in retarded and normal children. *American Journal of Mental Deficiency,* 1965, *70,* 466-470.

Rundus, D., & Atkinson, R. C. Rehearsal processes in free recall: A procedure for direct observation. *Journal of Verbal Learning and Verbal Behavior,* 1970, *9,* 99-105.

Turnure, J. E., & Thurlow, M. L. Verbal elaboration and the promotion of transfer of training in educable mentally retarded children. *Journal of Experimental Child Psychology,* 1973, *15,* 137-148.

Wickelgren, W. A. Acoustic similarity and intrusion errors in short-term memory. *Journal of Experimental Psychology,* 1965, *70,* 102-108.

Wilkes, A. L., & Kennedy, R. A. Relationship between pausing and retrieval latency in sentences of varying grammatical form. *Journal of Experimental Psychology,* 1969, *79,* 241-245.

Paul Heintz, a graduate of Newark State College, received his M.A. and Ed.D. degrees from Teachers College, Columbia University, with specializations in mental retardation, administration, and educational psychology. At Columbia, he was a Federal Fellow in Mental Retardation from 1963 to 1965 and served as a research assistant to Leonard Blackman from 1965 to 1966.

Dr. Heintz taught in special classes and developed programs for "mainstreaming" educable mentally retarded pupils in the Plainfield, New Jersey, public schools between 1957 and 1963. He was affiliated with the adjunct faculties of Kean College and Rutgers University, and served as Assistant Professor of Education at Seton Hall University (1966-1968).

Dr. Heintz joined the faculty of New York University in 1968 and is currently Associate Professor of Educational Psychology and Director of Graduate Programs in Special Education in the School of Education, Health, Nursing, and Arts Professions. He holds membership in the American Association on Mental Deficiency and the American Psychological Association, and served as a consulting editor to the American Journal of Mental Deficiency between 1973 and 1975. He has also served as a member of the Superintendent's Advisory Committee on the Handicapped, and as a consultant to the Board of Examiners and the Office of Educational Evaluation for the Board of Education of the city of New York.

His current writing and research interests include educational intelligence, learning, curriculum, and teacher expectancy. He is presently writing a book on the theory and application of educational intelligence to curriculum development.

Leonard S. Blackman did his undergraduate work at the City College of New York and Syracuse University, receiving his B.A. degree from the latter institution in 1950 while majoring in psychology. He also received his M.S. (Education) degree, majoring in developmental psychology, from Syracuse University in 1951. After specializing in developmental and educational psychology, he was awarded the Ph.D. degree by the University of Illinois in 1954.

Dr. Blackman's concern with the special education of the mentally retarded child and the research issues and procedures most likely to illuminate that concern began with a post-doctoral Ford Foundation Fellowship in mental retardation, awarded to him by the Institute for Research on Exceptional Children at the University of Illinois under the supervision of Dr. Samuel A. Kirk. This Fellowship enabled Dr. Blackman to supplement a predominantly theoretical and research-oriented program in psychology with a program concentrating on the special characteristics of mentally retarded people and the educational and vocational programs developed for their training.

This expanded application and orientation was applied to his first professional position as Director of Research at the Edward R. Johnstone Training and Research Center in Bordentown, New Jersey, where he served from 1956 to 1962 and was one of the early investigators in the use of automated self-instructional devices in the education of mentally retarded children.

Since 1962, Dr. Blackman has been a member of the Special Education faculty at Teachers College, Columbia University. During this period, he has made a significant contribution to the planning and ultimate construction of the Research and Demonstration Center for the Eduation of the Handicapped at Teachers College, and has devoted considerable time to the research advisement of doctoral students. Dr. Blackman's recent research efforts, currently being supported by the National Institute of Child Health and Human Development, have been in the area of designing and evaluating procedures for upgrading the cognitive functioning of educable mentally retarded children and adolescents.

8

Psychoeducational considerations with the mentally retarded child

Paul Heintz and Leonard S. Blackman

BACKGROUND AND DELINEATION OF ISSUES

Relationship of General and Special Education

Historically, special education has functioned as a derivative of general education. With the advent of compulsory education, the schools were faced with the new responsibility of providing an education for children who did not possess the usual academic propensities for traditional school learning. Perhaps of greater concern to educators during the early 1900s were the anticipated adverse effects on nonretarded children of including pupils with subaverage intellectual functioning in the regular grades. Both the teachers and the nonretarded students whom they instructed were unable or unwilling to tolerate the presence of the retarded child, either because he was a "dragging anchor" academically or because of his disruptive behavior. The original motives for initiating special, segregated programs for the mentally retarded pupil clearly stemmed from a "relief" philosophy for the benefit of general educators and their pupils (Kirk & Johnson, 1951).

After World War II, the number of public school special classes for mentally retarded students accelerated at a rapid pace. During this growth period, special educators developed their own cadre of dedicated, knowledgeable professionals, who envisioned their mission in a far more positive light. They believed that special classes existed for the purpose of providing the most propitious educational arrangements for children who would have been denied this privilege had they remained in the regular class. Thus, the justification for special education shifted from that of being primarily a dumping ground for problem children to one that focused on fulfilling those needs of the mentally retarded pupil which ostensibly could not be met in the heterogeneous regular class.

Although special education for the mentally retarded child became recognized as a specialized subarea within the field of education, it has continued to be influenced by the same forces, issues, and crises that have, over the years, shaped the major events within general education. With few exceptions, the major curriculum guides developed for the retarded group have simply mirrored the concerns and emphases of general educators at various points in time. This can be seen in Descoeudres' (1928) emphasis on Dewey's concept of "learning by doing" and Inskeep's (1926) watered-down version of the regular curriculum during the 1920s. Also, there has been wide agreement in recent years that the goals set forth by the National Education Association (1946), which included self-realization, human relationships, economic efficiency, and civic responsibility, are appropriate departure points for modifying the special class curriculum (Goldstein & Seigle, 1958). It has been suggested that these goals are as applicable to and appropriate for the so-called educable retarded child as for the nonretarded student (Kirk, 1962; Smith, 1968). An examination of the more widely used curriculum guides for the retarded classes indicates that the guides do not differ to any great extent from those offered normal groups. Even the influence of "Sputnik" may have affected special educators in much the same way that it affected general educators. Following that historic event during the late 1950s and during the 1960s, this was reflected in the emphasis on skill acquisition among retarded pupils (Blackman, 1967).

More recently, the issues of integration of minority groups, equality of educational opportunity, as well as increased sensitivity toward social problems in general have filtered down to special educators, convulsing them in the same way as it has general educators. Although inquiries into and criticisms of the efficacy of special classes in fostering academic and social growth among retarded pupils are not recent phenomena (Bennett, 1932; Pertsch, 1936), educational practices with that group are currently being attacked on moral grounds by practitioners within the field of special education (Dunn, 1968) and on constitutional issues by individuals who are both in and outside the educational establishment (Lippman & Goldberg, 1973).

Issues in general education. At the same time that social forces continue to make greater demands on both special and general educators in terms of appropriate pupil placement and administrative arrangements, there is a concurrent movement to develop a more scientific basis for instruction and curriculum development. This is being accomplished as a result of the growing body of knowledge concerning psychological processes in learners, together with increasingly sophisticated efforts to understand curricula and instruction. In contrast to fields like medicine, psychology, biochemistry and genetics, where phrases like "scientific inquiry," "scientific methods," and "applications of science" have become the verbal badges of the professional insider, the educator is still somewhat wary and ambivalent (Blackman, 1967) in adopting such distinctions. Most of our schools of education have almost institutionalized a balanced division between those who prefer the controlled experiment as a way of producing data and results which can be applied to reshaping the mission and methods of the schools, and those who see education essentially as an art form which loses its vitality and comprehensibility in the face of efforts to fractionate the gestalt called teacher-pupil interaction and classroom environment. Highet (1955), for example, emphatically stated that "scientific teaching, even of scientific subjects, will be inadequate as long as both teachers and pupils are human beings" (pp. vii-viii).

There are other barriers to the educators' full-fledged commitment to the application of scientific principles and methodology to the instruction of children. Those who have been the most influential in pushing for greater rigor and systematization in the structuring of children's learning environments are often perceived as aliens because they frequently represent disciplines other than education. Even professional educators are resistant to "aliens," particularly in view of the rather vociferous criticism directed toward them from that source. Cronbach (1967), for example, characterized as generally inefficient most teachers' informal attempts at making modifications for pupil differences, based on teacher intuition. Educators feel further threatened by claims that while it is their responsibility to make curriculum decisions or to determine what should be taught, it is the exclusive role of the psychologist to make decisions regarding appropriate instructional methods for pupils exhibiting educationally significant deviations from the norm (Carroll, 1967).

In many quarters, science in education has been narrowly construed as being totally synonymous with the several educational derivatives of operant conditioning principles (Skinner, 1968). These have been variously labeled as self- or automated instruction, behavior modification, reinforcement therapy, and token economy programs, among others. Many educators have been suspicious of these programs because, since the time of Dewey, they have considered themselves humanists first and pedagogues second. They have been at once fascinated and repelled by the psychologists' preoccupation with behavior as the only and ultimate reality in education. They have observed, with apprehensive interest, the psychologists' heavy-handed but often productive forays into the area of academic skill development. Finally, where psychologists have ventured into programs or emotional and social redevelopment, the educators have cringed at what they have perceived as sometimes callous and arrogant, and always mechanistic, intervention programs.

Much that has been carried out under the heading of educational research has contributed little to improve the status of scientific inquiry among educators as a respectable means of extending knowledge about teaching. Although a lack of familiarity with the scientific approach on the part of many educators may contribute to this situation, educational research in the past has been, unfortunately, largely sterile. Smith (1970), for example, characterized the bulk of educational research as being of "the lamp-post variety") i.e., research directions that are guided by the availability of funding for "high priority" areas).

It is not surprising, therefore, that general educators have not trampled each other in their rush to board the "science in education" bandwagon. After all, the great majority of normal children manage to learn rather successfully from the time-honored techniques. At least some of the remaining children are helped to some degree by remedial and tutorial procedures. Hence, in the education of normal children, there is little motivation to change a reasonably comfortable set of objectives and procedures for the more scientific approach to education being fostered by a set of research-oriented "hostiles."

Issues in special education. When the special education of the mentally retarded student is considered, however, words like "comfortable" and "successful" must be replaced with words like "uncomfortable" and "disappointing." The promise of the special class for the mentally retarded child was that the specially trained teacher, the small number of children in the room, the special curriculum and unique methods and materials, and the noncompetitive environment would all combine to produce an educational opportunity for these children that could not be equaled by the regular class.

A number of research studies conducted since the early 1930s have explored the efficacy, in terms of academic achievement and social adjustment, of placing mentally retarded children in special classes, as compared to keeping them in regular classes. Reviews of the findings of these studies revealed that, almost without exception, the special classes were not fulfilling their promise (Blackman & Heintz, 1966; Kirk, 1964). Despite some methodological flaws, the data consistently showed that as far as academic achievement was concerned, educable mentally retarded pupils in regular classes were doing at least as well as, and often significantly better than, those in special classes.

The results of other studies have indicated that the special class environment may be superior to the regular class in promoting positive personal and social development among educable retarded children (Baldwin, 1958; Blatt, 1958; Johnson, 1950; Lapp, 1957). These studies, however, have been criticized for their reliance on subjective teacher ratings and on sociometric data, as well as for not being able to control for the selection of pupils in special or regular classes. Mayer (1966), taking a somewhat different tack, failed to find support for the hypothesis that retarded children placed in a special class early in their school lives would have developed more positive self-concepts than those who were placed at a later time. Meyerowitz (1962) also reported that after one year in a special class, young educable retarded children were more derogatory toward themselves than were their peers, who had been allowed to remain in a regular first grade. Research findings on the value of special programs for trainable retarded students have been equally disappointing (Kirk, 1964). This type of frustration and disappointment with current programs for the mentally retarded pupil is hardly conducive to maintaining the status quo.

Dunn (1968), in expressing a concern over the possible negative effects of the special-class teacher's expectancy level, urged that alternative educational placements be considered for the vast majority of socioculturally deprived children who are labeled as "educable mentally retarded" and routinely assigned to special classes. According to Dunn, the usual practice of having the school psychologist determine eligibility for special-class placement has in large measure led to ". . . digging the educational graves of many racially and/or economically disadvantaged children by using a WISC or Binet IQ score to justify the label 'mentally retarded.' This term then becomes a destructive, self-fulfilling prophecy" (p. 9).

Kirk (1972) also warned about the possible drawbacks of placing in special classes those children who come from lower sociocultural backgrounds because special-class teachers' expectations may not be sufficiently high. While stating that the evidence on the effects of labeling a low-functioning child (who may not be low in general intelligence) "retarded" is far from conclusive, Kirk suggested that those children who lack the advantages of the majority population should not be placed in a special class.

Placement in special classes for the mildly retarded students, with its prior requirement of diagnosing and therefore labeling a child mentally retarded, has also been severely criticized because of its devastating effects on the individual's sense of personal worth. The similarity of treatment received by handicapped people and by ethnic and racial groups because of their minority status position in society has received empirical support over the years (Wright, 1960). Most of the literature concerning the negative effects on the self-concept of the retarded individual who is singled out as having deviant characteristics has focused on the school years, but Edgerton (1967) reported that mildly retarded adults were possessed with an overriding need to reject the notion that the label "mentally retarded" was applicable and/or appropriate for them.

Often the arguments against special-class placement and labeling of the mildly retarded person have not gone beyond the discussion stage in the literature. The merits of various administrative provisions for the retarded pupil have been debated (Dunn 1963, 1973; Guskin & Spicker, 1968), but little has been done to effect wide change in the most commonly found administrative arrangement in the United States—namely, the special-class unit integrated into the regular school building. Yet, Goldberg and Blackman (1965) raised the question ". . . as to whether the administrative and physical aspects of this integration have succeeded in engendering appropriate social and psychological ramifications . . . " (p. 30). They hold the position that integration is an administrative and pedagogical "state of mind" rather than merely a physical arrangement. Thus, a special class ostensibly integrated into a regular school may be effectively isolated if either the administrator or the teacher, or both, fail to implement those activities and develop those attitudes that will make integration psychologically and socially meaningful.

In comparing different types of special-class administrative arrangements, we find little conclusive evidence at the present time to support the superiority of any one of the sociopsychological environments generated by truly integrated, unintegrated, and segregated special classes. Goldberg and Blackman's question is concerned with the ramifications of the integrated special class in what is essentially a segregated special-class framework. In view of the more recent proposals for abolishing the special-class system, thereby integrating into regular classes, the individual pupils formerly labeled as mentally retarded, the same issues pertain regarding the psychological meaningfulness of this integration for the individual.

Whatever pupil placement patterns are utilized for the mentally retarded child, the major problems faced by special educators in their attempts to develop educational strategies which will prove to be superior to past efforts include finding suitable answers to the following questions: (a) What are the behaviors that will define academic, social, and vocational competence in the mentally retarded person? (b) Based on these desired behaviors, what new content is to be included in the special curriculum, and how is it to be organized? (c) How is the selected content to be transmitted to the retarded student in ways that are more effective than past efforts have been? (d) What are the important components of learning style, task requirements, and delivery system characteristics that must be considered in transmitting the content selected? Answers to the first two questions are central to curriculum development decisions, while the last two questions form the nucleus for the development of effective instructional strategies.

ATTEMPTS AT RESOLUTION AND CURRENT STATUS OF ISSUES

Sources of Data for Curriculum Content and Instructional Strategies

The field of curriculum is currently undergoing rapid growth and change in the makeup of personnel as well as in the body of knowledge being developed. Curriculum, as a field of study, is steadily attracting the involvement of greater numbers of psychologists, social scientists, and measurement and evaluation specialists (McNeil, 1969) as well as educators with specializations in the preceding areas. The involvement of these specialists in curriculum development has resulted in an increased concern for formulating more systematic approaches to curriculum building. In recent years there have been greater efforts to determine how the concepts of measurement and evaluation, as employed in the behavioral sciences, can be utilized in understanding the effects on the learner of including specific content in the curriculum. Specialists are attempting to integrate the growing body of knowledge in psychology and education in their efforts to develop new curriculum models and to specify curriculum objectives in more precise behavioral terms. Although the field of curriculum has witnessed a significant growth of ideas over the past few years, attempts at implementing these newer notions are still in the infancy stage.

While directions taken in both special and general education have been influenced by similar forces and events over the years, a number of factors unique to the education of the mentally retarded child have resulted in differences that are worthy of mention. Special educators have devoted their major efforts and resources to administrative and organizational aspects, and have given only minimal attention to curriculum and instructional provisions for which the administrative arrangements were originally intended (Meyen, 1968). Until recently, few college or university centers offered training programs specifically in the area of curriculum building for the mentally retarded pupil. This is unfortunate because the need for a systematic approach to structuring a sequential program is perhaps greater for those pupils than for the "normal student" (Meyen, 1968).

The basic procedural elements involved in curriculum building are essentially the same in special and general education, and are relatively independent of the population for whom the course of study is intended. Despite this fact, the curriculum-building skills of general educators rarely have been utilized by special educators. Yet, it is interesting to note that the generally fragmented curriculum efforts in special education tend to parallel the more highly developed curriculum models in general education. Simches and Bohn (1963) examined the major curriculum guides that had been developed for the educable mentally retarded student, and concluded that the programs existing at that time did not differ appreciably from those offered nonretarded groups.

McNeil (1969), in analyzing the forces that influence curriculum making in general education, described three major data sources for formulating objectives. These were: subject matter, society, and the learner. It is not surprising, therefore, that the forces currently impacting curriculum development for the mentally retarded child can be divided into three similar broad areas. First, the movement in general education toward the acceleration of academic skill development has its counterpart in the special education of the mentally retarded person. Second, there are recently updated versions of curricula designed to provide mentally retarded children with the traditional virtues of social and vocational competence. Third, the "learning disability" movement has placed the deviant learner at the hub of the curriculum.

Mastery of subject matter. While the importance of academic achievement in the education of the mentally retarded pupil has been traditionally ranked behind such areas as personal, social, and occupational development, special educators have nonetheless considered academic skills to be an important component of the curriculum for the retarded learner. The curricula developed during the early 1930s placed major emphasis on such areas as sense training, the unit of experience, and occupational education (Rothstein, 1971). But all had some provisions for including the minimal "tool" subjects of reading and arithmetic. Kirk and Johnson (1951), while stressing a "mental health" approach to the development of curriculum for the retarded student, felt that it was necessary to remind special educators of the importance for all retarded children to learn to read to the "best of their ability" (p. 183). In what probably was, and perhaps still is, the single most widely used and imitated curriculum guide for the retarded scholar in the United States, Goldstein and Siegle (1958) included specific knowledges in such areas as arithmetic, language arts, and science. However, these curriculum specialists emphasized, as did most of the specialists preceding them, that academic competence was primarily important in that it led to skills needed for success in those major life functions that persist throughout the lifetime of every individual.

In examining the area of academic skills in the curriculum for the retarded child, two features stand out. First, only two major (if rather simplistic) principles for modifying the organization and content to be included in the curriculum were available to special educators from the beginning of special classes for retarded groups in the early 1930s to as late as the 1960s. Briefly, these principles were that content should be presented at a *gradual rate* and on a *concrete level* (Kirk & Johnson, 1951). Other suggestions for modifications were simply variations of these two principles. For example, the widespread use of drill and repetition in special classes resulted in a slower rate of presentation, whereas the unit or project method emphasized the presentation of content in real or concrete situations. Interestingly, Scott (1966) pointed out that variable and irrelevant stimuli are frequently introduced to the retarded learner as a result of attempts to provide concrete examples during instruction. Thus, one of the most commonly applied principles of curriculum selection may have contributed inadvertently to the large measure of failure experienced by retarded children during initial learning.

Since the introduction of variable and irrelevant stimuli significantly reduces the chances of success during initial learning, a secondary consequence of introducing a variety of concrete materials may be the introduction of failure sets in the retarded learner. The learner, after being repeatedly exposed to failure experiences, simply stops attending to the task parameters and is often unable to solve subsequent simpler problems due to this failure set (Scott, 1966). Cromwell's (1963) work on failure avoidance in the mentally retarded individual provides a theoretical basis for this phenomenon.

Related to the limitations imposed by an emphasis on concretistic instruction, there has been, and continues to be, general disagreement among authorities concerning the appropriate levels of academic skills to be included in the special curriculum. That there has been disagreement in this area is hardly surprising in view of the ambiguity that has characterized the literature dealing with learning ability among the mentally retarded population. For example, Bijou (1952) maintained that, from a learning-teaching point of view, the retarded child is different from the normal child of comparable mental age in that the retarded child appears unable to progress academically commensurate with the level expected on the basis of his mental age. House and Zeaman (1959), after finding differences between retarded and normal children in discrimination learning, suggested that the results confirmed the long-standing suspicions of teachers of mentally retarded students that mental-age scores obtained from intelligence tests were overestimating the learning ability of their pupils. Osborne (1960), reflecting a similar point of view, stated that "it has long been obvious to workers in the field of mental retardation that a fourteen-year-old boy with a mental age of seven functions quite differently from a normal seven-year-old boy, intellectually as well as emotionally and socially" (p. 351).

Dunn (1963), in defining the educable mentally retarded child, pointed out that a youngster with an IQ of 75 will have reached the capacity to perform at the beginning of the seventh-grade level at age 16. During the same discussion, however, Dunn indicated that "a rough rule of thumb is to say that most 'educable' pupils will, in late adolescence, have the capacity, on the average, to achieve somewhere around the grade four to five level" (pp. 71-72). Although lacking specificity, the statement implies that teachers could expect most educable pupils to achieve approximately two years below mental age expectancy when the pupils reach the age of leaving school. As for the retarded pupils with IQs in the 50 to 59 range, Dunn maintained that most authorities recognize that few pupils in this intellectual range will have the ability to read.

The results of numerous investigations on the actual level of academic achievement attained by mentally retarded pupils are far from consistent. A number of studies (Bennett, 1929; Bensberg, 1953; Blatt, 1958; Daly & Lee, 1960; Jacobs, 1957; Merrill, 1924) have indicated that the majority of retarded pupils are able to attain success in academic skills when this success is defined as achieving at a level commensurate with mental age (MA) expectancy or at a level comparable to that of normal children of similar mental age. Other studies, investigating the same areas of academic achievement and using similar criteria, have found that mentally retarded children do not perform at their MA expectancy levels (Cassidy & Stanton, 1959; Dunn, 1954; Moran, 1960). Finally, other investigators, using the same comparison criteria, have found that retarded children attain successful achievement in some academic areas, but fail in others (Bennett, 1932; Bliesmere, 1962; Boyle, 1959; Brown & Lind, 1931, Cruickshank, 1948a, 1948b; Dunn, 1954; Groelle, 1961; Hoyt, Meranski, & Snell, 1924; Pertsch, 1936; Renshaw, 1919).

Attempts to determine the factors that result in varying levels of achievement among the mentally retarded groups in the studies cited above are unfortunately obfuscated by the variety of curricula used, as well as by the variability among the teachers and administrative arrangements under which the learning occurred. Conspicuously absent from the research literature is evidence that the organization of academic content differed from the traditional grade-sequencing of academic skills followed in the regular grades—a sequence that has some philosophical and logical justification, but as yet has little empirical validity. There is evidence to indicate that both the curriculum organization provided for the majority of normal pupils in the academic areas and the instruction that has derived from that organization have shared many of the inadequacies previously described in special education. Research by Bellack, Kliebard, Hyman, and Smith (1965) revealed that teachers—despite differences in the ability levels, size, and background of their classes—spent two-thirds to three-quarters of their instructional time asking and reacting to questions based on isolated bits of factual information.

Further concern over the state of the regular school curriculum was expressed by scientists shortly after Sputnik I, during the late 1950s and early 1960s (Bruner, 1960). The feeling among these scientists was that advances in knowledge within their disciplines were not being reflected in appropriate curricula, with the consequence that the schools were not training persons who were academically prepared to make sound decisions. An additional area of concern among the scientists was the perceived gap between what was being taught in the elementary and secondary schools and that which was offered within institutions of higher education. All these concerns led to the now famous "Woods Hole Conference" where some 35 scientists, scholars, psychologists, and educators met to discuss how education in mathematics and science might be upgraded in the schools. The proceedings of this conference were published (Bruner, 1960) in what was perhaps the most influential educational work of the early 1960s.

While the interests shared by the participants at Woods Hole were primarily directed toward curriculum reform for intellectually normal and gifted children, two recurring themes of the conference emphasized the benefits that would accrue to the less able learner from curricula that were organized around the structure of knowledge. As stated by Bruner (1960), these themes were ". . . any subject matter can be taught effectively in some intellectually honest form to any child at any stage of development" (p. 33), and "good teaching that emphasizes the structure of a subject is probably even more valuable for the less able student than for the gifted one, for it is the former rather than the latter who is most easily thrown off the track by poor teaching" (p. 9).

More specifically, Bruner (1960) posited that building curricula that reflect the fundamental structure of fields of knowledge (such as language, mathematics, and history) would be superior to the traditional curricula, in that the former would make academic subjects more comprehensible. The increased comprehensibility would be a direct outcome of the emphasis on understanding fundamentals rather than simply the mastery of facts and techniques. Stated in other terms, this structured approach would emphasize the teaching and learning of content and processes that exemplify the key concepts underlying and unifying specific subject matter (Phenix, 1964), which in turn would facilitate the learning of the specific academic facts and skills.

For example, if the learner is able to grasp one of the key notions within mathematics, that of absolute consistency within the same system (Phenix, 1964, p. 74), then it is suggested that particular instances of quantities in arithmetic problems must always be the same. Piaget's (1952) work has demonstrated that understanding of computations involved in simple addition and substraction is not possible unless the learner has grasped the concept of conservation of quantity. Past research findings have indicated that mentally retarded learners, in contrast to intellectually normal pupils, are not naturally set to learn (Denny, 1964). Retarded students, when compared with their nonretarded peers, have demonstrated inferiority in a variety of concept utilization skills.

The evidence provided by the studies cited above strongly suggests that the mentally retarded child, as opposed to the nonretarded child, will require greater assistance in recognizing the key concepts that underlie the basic academic subject matter in the special educational setting. Intellectually normal children probably have been able to grasp some of the key concepts that constitute the structure of various types of subject matter even when they are not taught directly. Retarded pupils, however, because of their difficulty in abstraction and concept utilization, have found the same academic material more difficult to learn.

On the other hand, the performance of educable mentally retarded children improves, often dramatically, when material is organized for them and when strategies are supplied to them (Cobb & Barnard, 1971; Holden, 1971; Ryan, Chivers, & Redding, 1969; Spitz, 1966; Spitz, Goettler, & Webreck, 1972). Some studies indicate that retarded students do not permanently incorporate these induced strategies (Bilsky & Evans, 1970; Gerjuoy & Alvarez, 1969; Jensen & Rohwer, 1963; Milgram, 1967), while other studies report more permanent effects (Martin, 1967; McIvor, 1972; Ross, 1971. In view of these findings, it would appear that mentally retarded students should be given assistance in organization at every level of subject matter in order to maximize their opportunities for more efficient acquisition of academic skills.

Another reason offered for designing curricula according to the structure of subject matter is that memory of details is enhanced. Gestalt psychologists have long emphasized the central roles of "meaning" and "structure" or "wholeness" in facilitating learning. As Brown (1958) stressed, "meaningful learning is learning that fits into a structure. Meaningful material is material in which there are systematic relations among the elements" (p. 71). Spitz (1966) also pointed out that, according to the Gestaltists, bits of information are not so important in learning and memory as are the "organizational agents." On the basis of these views, while grouping bits of information is superior for facilitating learning, in comparison to presenting isolated bits, emphasizing the principle or system on which the elements are organized is likely to be superior to both. Similarly, Ausubel (1966) developed the concept of "advance organizers" to emphasize the importance of priming the learner with broader conceptual structures as a way of anchoring subsequently presented information.

The issue as to the most effective way in which to organize material becomes critical when viewed within Spitz's theoretical conception of mental retardation, in which an organizational deficit is postulated as a major cause of the retarded child's inability to learn at a level comparable with that of normal children. This position holds that retarded individuals are characterized by a deficiency in "input" or "filing." "Put in simple terms, normals frequently act on the incoming information in ways which aid their learning and memory: retardates frequently do not act on the incoming material, or act on it in ways that hinder learning and memory" (Spitz, 1966, p. 53). The major implication of the latter position is that material presented to retarded learners should be in a highly organized state in order to compensate for the existing organizational deficit.

Further support for the efficaciousness of structuring curricular content is available from data that indicate facilitation of rehearsal behavior when material is organized on a meaningful basis (Ellis, 1970). An increase in rehearsal of incoming stimuli leads in turn to greater efficiency in both storage and ultimate retrieval.

Improvement of transfer of training is postulated as a third specific consequence of stressing fundamental principles underlying the structure of subject matter. Bruner (1960) described the process in the following way: "To understand something as a specific instance of a more general case—which is what understanding a more fundamental principle or structure means—is to have learned not only a specific thing but also a model for understanding other things like it that one may encounter" (p. 25).

Katz (1964) and Kaufman and Prehm (1966), after reviewing a large number of studies on transfer, concluded that most retarded individuals have the ability to transfer learning strategies. Studies by McIvor (1972) and Bean (1968), providing cognitive strategy training programs in classrooms, further supported this finding. McIntyre and Dingman (1963), however, reported that the ability to transfer was related to IQ level. Thus, while mentally retarded individuals, in the main, have demonstrated some transfer ability, organizing curriculum content on the basis of fundamental ideas is likely to facilitate still greater transfer.

Additional support for the efficacy of designing curriculum content on the basis of the inherent structure of given fields of knowledge is given by the work of Gagne (1970). A central, recurring theme proposed by Gagne is that there are eight varieties of learning that currently can be distinguished, and which can be ordered within an hierarchical framework (see Gagne, 1970; pp. 65, 66). The varieties of learning proposed by Gagne (presented in descending hierarchical order) are problem solving (Type 8), rules (Type 7), concepts (Type 6), discriminations (Type 5), verbal associations (Type 4), chains (Type 3), stimulus- response connections (Type 2), and signal learning (Type 1). In this hierarchy, each lower type serves as a prerequisite for those on the higher levels (e.g., the learning of two or more rules is a prerequisite for problem solving). Further, it is proposed that an analysis of subject matter skills is most effectively carried out within the eight varieties of learning proposed by Gagne. According to him, the essence of the basic tool subjects that have comprised the traditional curricula of the schools is not clearly conveyed by the commonly used labels of "reading," "writing," and "arithmetic." Much more basic than subject matter areas are the capabilities found in discriminations, chains, and concepts that constitute those activities, such as observing, counting, drawing, and classifying, which are involved in learning subject matter. The organization of curricula based on the preceding analysis would, according to Gagne, facilitate the learning of the more advanced principles found in academic areas.

In contrast to the epistemological approach toward discovering the structure of subject matter proposed by Bruner (1960) and Phenix (1964), Gagne's learning hierarchies would be derived from empirical data obtained from an analysis of academic tasks. Gagne described the process as follows:

> When a task to be learned is analyzed into simpler capabilities that need to be learned as prerequisites, and when such an analysis is continued progressively to the point of delineating an entire set of capabilities having an ordered relation to each other (in the sense that in each case prerequisite capabilities are represented as subordinate in position, indicating that they need to be previously learned), one has a learning hierarchy. (1970, p. 238)

Interestingly, Gagne suggested that learning hierarchies exist within topics rather than within broad subject-matter fields. Some empirical support has been obtained for the existence of learning hierarchies within various topics in the field of mathematics (Gagne, 1962; Gagne & Bassler, 1963; Gagne & Paradise, 1961; Gagne & staff, 1965). Although these findings may not be surprising to most educators, the significance of Gagne's work lies in the fact that it has provided a viable method of mapping the order in which the subject matter can be organized in order to maximize success at various stages of learning. Of immediate, practical value are the data that describe subskills within topics already analyzed and reported by Gagne and his associates.

The interest and research activities of both psychologists and curriculum specialists in concepts and concept learning over the past two decades have served as the impetus for recent efforts to formulate a model of conceptual learning and development which presumably has direct relevance to the teaching of concepts drawn from subject-matter areas, curriculum materials, and related assessment procedures (Klausmeier & Hooper, 1974). The model provides a framework for analyzing only one type of learning, concept learning, since it is posited that an individual begins to learn a concept at a simple level in early childhood and continues to learn the same concept at successively more complex levels into adulthood. All concepts are considered to be acquired as a result of learning experiences, and thus directed learning is emphasized while maturational and readiness principles, as traditionally used in psychology, are deemphasized.

Research generated within the model is currently examining among pupils at different levels of conceptual development the effects on concept learning of varying the quantity of concept attributes (relevant and irrelevant) during instruction, as well as the number of examples and nonexamples that lead to effective instructional sequences. Analyses of some 120 concepts drawn from the areas of mathematics, language arts, science, and social science have been conducted, thus providing preliminary data for the establishment of an empirically validated instructional system for teaching key concepts within the academic areas.

Additional recent efforts at empirically establishing the order in which subject matter skills are efficiently learned have been carried out in the area of reading. Coleman (1970), in examining the learning of four types of reading-related skills among preschoolers, provided information on the relative difficulty of learning (a) 50 words commonly used in teaching beginning reading, (b) grapheme-morpheme associations, (c) phonic blends, and (d) printing the letters of the alphabet.

A major goal of Coleman in pursuing his line of inquiry was to demonstrate a technique for collecting a data base for a reading technology. He argued that, unlike the engineer who is able to transform knowledge from the physical sciences into useful tables by using straightforward mathematical operations, the educator does not have at his disposal mathematical formulas for transforming knowledge generated from the research in learning. To eliminate this void in education, and specifically in reading, Coleman proposed that research be directed at calibrating language units according to ease of learning them within particular language subskills. In order to permit the direct application of the results to the classroom, Coleman's strategy involves the examination of language units actually used in reading instruction, as well as using children who have not yet learned the language unit skills. Thus, in contrast to the common practice in psychology of examining the effects of variables suspected of influencing the acquisition of artificial language habits (e.g., meaningfulness as related to learning nonsense syllables) among mature learner populations, Coleman (1970) used preschool children as "calipers to calibrate language units" (p. 4) contained in real reading materials.

One of the more obvious values of the data tables provided by Coleman is that they identify in a straightforward manner the degree of difficulty in learning letters, words, and sounds. The information provided in the tables can be used immediately by the teacher in organizing a reading program for children who are struggling with beginning reading. In a similar vein, Dunn-Rankin (1968) empirically verified the order of difficulty in making visual discriminations between letters.

In addition, the data collected by Coleman also suggest general characteristics of easy and difficult skills (e.g., nouns that denote animate objects, such as "kitten" and "cow," are easier to learn than those that do not; consonant-vowel syllables are more difficult to learn to blend than are vowel-consonant syllables). When provided with the preceding information, the teacher is able to transform reading materials that are part of the larger reading program into tentative "learnability sequences," even though they have not been directly examined with naive subjects. In view of the retarded child's demonstrated propensity for developing failure-avoidance behavior (Cromwell, 1963), data on easy-to-difficult sequencing are probably more critical to the special-class teacher than to the teacher of intellectually normal children.

The identification of parameters that differentiate the relative difficulty of arithmetic problems included in the elementary school curriculum was the major focus of an investigation by Suppes, Jerman, and Brian (1968). Building on the findings of studies that have rank-ordered the difficulty levels in learning addition, subtraction, and multiplication combinations used in beginning arithmetic problems, Suppes and his colleagues examined the effects on ease of learning arithmetic of such factors as memory requirements, sequential changes, and magnitudes of largest and smallest quantities contained in problems. Using errors as well as success latencies[1] as criterion variables in stepwise regression analyses, the investigators found the memory requirement (number of digits that must be held in memory) to be the most important predictor of both criterion variables. Thus, in planning the sequencing of arithmetic skills at the elementary school level for normal children, the variable of memory deficit in mentally retarded children (Ellis, 1970), however, the special-class teacher must be even more finely attuned to the memory requirements of the specific arithmetic tasks presented.

Curriculum in the social context. The daily needs and activities of individuals living in contemporary society have provided a second major source of curriculum content in both general and special education. Since the early 1900s, major figures in education have developed curriculum objectives on the basis of an analysis of the demands made on the individual within the community in such areas as health, family, and civic and vocational life (McNeil, 1969). Most of the earlier efforts of curriculum specialists in general

---

[1]Interestingly, Gagne (1970) suggested that a hesitation on the part of the learner results in some degree of extinction of a correct response, as do errors and omissions.

and special education, which were directed at analyzing the competencies needed for successful citizenship, must be characterized as being of the armchair variety. These specialists carried out their "analyses" of cummunity-based needs and activities for the average citizen, and they developed their subsequent recommendations for curriculum content on factors that seemingly distinguished between the successful and the unsuccessful citizen. However, rather than basing their analyses on empirical evidence, the requisite knowledge and skills for successful community adjustment were determined on the basis of what seemed most reasonable to the curriculum specialists at any given time.

Recent efforts in curriculum building for the mentally retarded child, as exemplified by the "Social Learning Curriculum" (SLC)—suggested by Goldstein (1969) and by Goldstein, Mischio, Heiss, Melnick, Frafkin, & Clerico (1970)—also have socio-occupational competence as their major goal, with academic content included in instances where such content is judged necessary for the achievement of competence in social and occupational areas. While the major purposes of most recent efforts do not differ from those of the past, the procedures utilized in generating curriculum objectives for the SLC represent a unique approach. Underlying the development of the SLC is the basic premise that, since the major emphasis of the curriculum is on the preparation of the retarded student for later community adjustment, the logical source of curriculum objectives would be based on the behavior of retarded adults already in the community. Toward that end, such data were collected from a representative cross section of rehabilitation and social agencies serving mentally retarded individuals across the country. Using the critical incident technique, special attention was directed toward identifying commonly observed *undesirable* behaviors among such individuals. The survey revealed a considerable degree of homogeneity of behavior traits, both across the agencies and across situations. For example, overdependence, which was reported as a major negative trait by each agency, appeared within the context of situations in the areas of occupational adjustment, family life, leisure-time activities, and interpersonal interactions.

Goldstein and his colleagues (1969, 1970), having collected examples of hundreds of negative or self-defeating behaviors exhibited by older mentally retarded individuals, formulated the curriculum objectives of the SLC by translating the obtained negative behaviors into lessons for their positive counterparts. The statements supplied by the agency personnel were further categorized into the areas of concepts, facts, and behavioral skills. The given positive behaviors, along with the requisite concepts, facts, and skills, constitute the basic content of the SLC. Thus, this curriculum represents a departure from most traditional curriculum-building efforts in that its content is based on empirically derived needs and problems as encountered by mentally retarded people in their attempts to adjust in an increasingly complex society.

In view of the major emphasis placed on social and occupational adequacy in curricular offerings for the retarded student, it is not surprising that community adjustment among mentally retarded individuals has been a major area of research interest over the years. Baller (1936), in a classic follow-up study of adults who earlier had been judged mentally retarded, found that 39% were successfully self-supporting. Charles (1953), in a follow-up of Baller's study, reported that 83% of the original group of retarded individuals who had been located were self-supporting, and 75% of these subjects were living in single dwellings. Finally, Kennedy (1948) reported that the differences in vocational and social adjustment between a group of 256 mentally retarded adults and a nonretarded control group were not substantial. Dunn (1963) summarized the results of these and other community-based studies by stating that "as adults, most former educable pupils marry, raise families, and find competitive employment" (p. 117). Kirk (1962) concluded that under favorable social and economic conditions, educable mentally retarded individuals are able to adjust to society and lead a normal community existence. Although lacking specificity, these statements can be interpreted as being quite positive and optimistic in describing the retarded adult's prospects for successful community adjustment.

Heber and Dever (1970) reviewed the research completed prior to 1960 on community adjustment of mentally retarded persons, and they suggested that many of the reported studies were overly optimistic in their interpretations of the success that had been achieved by retarded subjects. Among their chief criticisms were (a) Findings that mentally retarded adults do as well as "normals" on the same kinds of jobs were reported without a consideration of the type of level of work involved; and (b) comparisons of mentally retarded and normal subjects on social adjustment indices were made without a critical assessment of whether the social behaviors of the nonretarded subjects were worth emulating. Heber and Dever (1970) suggested that most of the normal workers with whom the retarded employees had been compared for the purpose of determining vocational adjustment were probably themselves marginally employable and thus held hard-to-fill jobs. In addition, socially "acceptable" norms were often provided by individuals who, for a variety of reasons, came from "slum" neighborhoods with a high incidence of social problems. In short, the studies apparently found the mentally retarded subjects to be as successful in vocational and social adjustment as the least successful normal individuals.

Other recent follow-up studies that have closely scrutinized the lives of mentally retarded persons also provide findings that are in sharp contrast to those reported earlier. For example, Windle (1962) found that approximately

40 to 50% of a group of 296 retarded individuals who had been released from an institution were reinstitutionalized within a 5-year period. The major reasons for the retarded subjects' failure to adjust in the community included (a) antisocial behavior (crimes, sexual misbehavior); (b) inadequate work performance (inability to take orders, anxiety, poor self-evaluation); and (c) inadequate interpersonal relations.

Perhaps the clearest and most comprehensive picture of the struggles that occur when the formerly institutionalized retarded adult tries to function independently in the community is provided by Edgerton (1967). That author's major purpose was to determine the degree of community success experienced by mildly retarded adults who had been judged by the institution staff as being prepared to face life "on the outside." The results of the study are unique in that they provide some of the most detailed descriptions of the daily lives of mentally retarded adults.

Edgerton and his staff carried out extensive interviews with the individuals involved, and they frequently accompanied them to their jobs, on shopping trips, and during leisure time activities. The profiles that emerged for most of the retarded adults who had been able to avoid reinstitutionalization cannot be judged to reflect successful adjustment by any reasonable criteria. Since community employment was a necessary condition for the release from the institution, all former residents had employment when they were discharged. However, at the time of follow-up, most of them were only marginal from an economic standpoint—as demonstrated by their indebtedness, their lack of job security, and, most of all, their lack of marketable job skills. In the area of leisure time activities, the former institutional residents did not appear to differ from their normal counterparts of low socioeconomic status. This, however, can hardly be interpreted as a positive finding because the retarded adults spent most of their time watching television. Few had hobbies, and one of their more unusual recreational activities was simply riding buses back and forth for sightseeing purposes. Quality of housing and conditions of cleanliness and hygiene were, more frequently than not, noticeably substandard.

Perhaps the portion of Edgerton's study that provided the greatest insight into the unhappiness and general anxiety of the retarded adult is that which details the feelings and attitudes of these exresidents. Two major concerns of these individuals influenced their day-to-day activities at least as much as did their struggles to survive economically. These were (a) the need to deny to themselves that they were or ever had been "mentally retarded," and (b) the need for "passing" for normal by hiding their incompetence from others. Thus, many of their daily activities were motivated not by a sense of personal fulfillment, but by a desire to appear like their normal counterparts. For most of the former institutional residents, the task of passing was extremely difficult. They were conscious of the constant danger of "being discovered" because of their inability to complete an employment application, obtain a driver's license, use "proper" words during necessary interactions with others, accumulate possessions or even have children—since most were sterilized.

In contrast to the figures provided by earlier studies, Edgerton (1967) estimated that only 3 of 48 persons in his sample could be considered fully independent, while a total of 38 were classified as either "heavily" or "completely" dependent. In short, special education and rehabilitation programs, which had been provided these retarded individuals within what may be judged to be a progressive institution, were not sufficient to prepare them adequately to face the daily requirements of and activities in a community setting.

Since the earlier discussed Social Learning Curriculum was organized around the reported activities of mentally retarded individuals who were similar to those in Edgerton's study, it is not surprising that the SLC's goal ". . . is to produce mature individuals who can think critically and act independently to such an extent that they are socially and occupationally competent" (Goldstein, 1969; p. 3). To achieve this goal, the selection and organization of curriculum content were at all times guided by considerations of socio-occupational competence. Skills in other areas (e.g., academic, motor) were included only if they could be judged to be requisite to socio-occupational adequacy.

With respect to the organization of specific content within individual SLC instructional sequences and lessons, Goldstein (1969) advocated the use of the inductive teaching method (ITM) whenever possible (Minskoff, 1967). Group discussion is the primary vehicle implementing the ITM, and instruction is organized so that the learner is systematically guided through a problem-solving sequence involving a series of increasingly complex teacher-initiated questions. These require responses involving labels, details, inferences, predictions, and generalizations. The teacher-initiated questions are structured in such a way as to force the pupil to focus on cues needed to solve specific problems largely independently of the teacher. The learner is also supplied with immediate feedback (both positive and negative) about his performance, and he is asked to reevaluate his response and respond again, if necessary.

A unique feature of the ITM, as modified for use in the SLC, is that the teacher does not provide the pupils with the correct response. This hopefully facilitates reduction of the dependency behavior commonly found among retarded children and, perhaps, even encouraged by some special class practices. Guskin (1963), for example, argued that the dependency behavior exhibited by the retarded person may be due in part to the education and training procedures used by individuals whose definition of mental retardation emphasizes a dependency component. Since it is proposed that the problem-solving ITM be used consistently, for most of the school day within a SLC framework and for an average school career lasting 12 years, it would appear reasonable to expect some degree of carryover to the daily problem-solving behavior of the post-school retarded adult. However, the determination of the empirical efficacy of these procedures awaits follow-up studies.

The retarded learner as a data source. A third major data source for obtaining curriculum content and for designing instructional methods in both general and special education is the learner himself. Within the history of general education there have been efforts, in varying degrees, to stimulate the learner to initiate curriculum activities based on his stated interests, concerns, and needs. In these situations, the learner, in effect, has been encouraged to share with the teacher the responsibility of determining what was to be included in the curriculum. The most recent version of a "child-centered" curriculum is the open classroom plan, which has become increasingly popular in general education. While some attention has been given to developing curricula based on the ostensible interests of the mentally retarded student, over the years the approach has played only a relatively minor role in the shaping of curricula for the retarded child.

Since the early 1960s, however, the deviant characteristics of the mentally retarded learner have served as a major source for generating curriculum objectives and instructional strategies for the special-class program. Up to that time, educators in general had expressed the need for recognizing the universality of individual differences in interests and aptitudes among *all* learners in planning curriculum, although specific techniques for acting on this recognition were not generally available to the educator. For special education, Kirk (1962) suggested that differences within the learner himself were as crucial to educational planning as were interindividual differences. He pointed out that a common characteristic of the exceptional child was the within-child growth discrepancy in such areas as motor, language, speech, academic, and social development. The relatively greater intraindividual variability in mentally retarded children (as compared to nonretarded subjects) in more basic psychological processes has also been confirmed in laboratory research (Baumeister & Kellas, 1968).

Early in the 1960s, the interests of a growing number of special educators were directed toward a group of children who, it was felt, did not fall within any of the traditional categories of exceptionality but who were nevertheless primarily characterized by a pattern of intraindividual discrepancies in development which frequently resulted in a learning disability and subsequent school failure. Bateman (1964), in one of the earlier definitions of "learning disabilities," succinctly stated the still prevalent general conceptualization of most special educators:

> Regardless of the lack of agreement about etiology, definition, incidence, and treatment of special learning disabilities . . ., the child with learning disabilities is perhaps best described as one who manifests an educationally significant discrepancy between his apparent capacity for language behavior and his actual level of language functioning. (p. 167)

Most current definitions of the concept "learning disability" continue to stress impairment in language behavior or behaviors related to language, including such areas as visual-motor functioning and reading ability, as well as communication skills. While numerous positions regarding the etiology of learning disabilities have been proposed (McCarthy & McCarthy, 1969), most definitions exclude mental retardation and/or cultural deprivation as a contributing or parallel process in this syndrome (Johnson & Myklebust, 1967).

The more recent conceptualization of learning disabilities by Kirk and McCarthy (1971), however, emphasized the need to focus on discrepant abilities without specifying other criteria which must be met by the learner in order to profit from a learning disability classroom program. They suggested that the presence of abilities and relative disabilities (i.e., discrepant abilities) can exist in children traditionally classified as mentally retarded, as well as in other handicapped children, and in learners who are otherwise considered to be normal. According to Kirk and McCarthy (1971), it is even conceivable that:

> Some children classified as mentally retarded may in fact not be retarded but have been so categorized because their specific disabilities in certain functions have caused them to test low on general intelligence tests. These children might do better if placed in a program designed to ameliorate their special disabilities rather than in a program for the mentally retarded. (p. 442)

While psychologists and educators have used standardized tests over the years to determine the intellectual, educational, and personality development of individual pupils relative to particular reference groups, a learning disability curriculum approach (LDCA) rests on the use of instruments specifically designed to assess the relative strengths and weaknesses in developmental factors within an individual pupil. These two uses of tests differ both with respect to purpose as well as, in most cases, to specificity of factors assessed.

The major purpose for using tests such as the Stanford-Binet or the Metropolitan Achievement Test has been to classify or label pupils with respect to level of general intellectual or educational functioning. While the above tests are included within the *modus operandi* of the LDCA to determine the degree of discrepancy between an individual's general intellectual functioning and his academic achievement, the major purpose of testing in a learning disability program is to arrive at a diagnostic profile that focuses on narrowly defined factors for each pupil. The diagnostic profile, in turn, provides data for the specification of an educational or remedial program for the pupil. Unless the results of a testing program for a particular student lead to specific treatment or remediation, it cannot be considered a diagnosis (Kirk & McCarthy, 1961).

The use of diagnostic tests which fall within the areas of academic achievement (particularly reading) to assess a learner's particular strengths and weaknesses in subskills has been fairly common in most school systems for some time. The learning disability movement in special education, with its central requirement for basing the selection of all curriculum content and instructional strategies on the results of a diagnostic profile, has resulted in the proliferation of "new" diagnostic "tests." This, in turn, has been sustained by a continuing search for more relevant diagnostic factors. These factors, for the most part, have been defined in terms of those perceptual, motor, cognitive, and language processes held to be prerequisite to the development of general academic skills. The developmental factors that have been emphasized most frequently in the learning disability literature include such areas as perceptual-motor functioning (Kephart, 1971; Sloan, 1955), visual and auditory perception (Frostig, Lefever, & Whittlesey, 1964; Koppitz, 1962), linguistic functioning (Kirk, McCarthy, & Kirk, 1968), and intersensory integration (Birch & Belmont, 1964).

The information obtained from a learning disability evaluation is primarily intended to serve as a guide for making decisions about teaching techniques that would exploit a learner's strengths. A corollary to this approach has placed the major emphasis on upgrading the deficiencies of the deviant learner through training and remediation. Thus, with increasing frequency, instructional objectives in academic and social areas for the retarded student have taken a secondary position of importance to the training of motor and perceptual skills. Bateman (1967), in discussing a learning disabilities approach to teaching educable mentally retarded children, stated that this approach:

> ... redirects our attention to question-asking as the foundation of teaching and curriculum planning, to specific factors affecting and determining learning processes, to individual appraisal of

patterns of cognitive abilities, to a re-examination of a philosophy of teaching through strengths or to weaknesses, and to the need for direct teaching of the processes of thinking rather than the products of someone else's thinking. (p. 25)

There have been some attempts to assess and remediate the disabled learner's weaknesses within the framework of cognitive models or theories of intellectual structure. Efforts to develop a theoretical framework for the specific purpose of influencing the selection of curriculum content within a cognitive orientation are not new in general education. An early effort in that direction was the "Taxonomy of Educational Objectives" (Bloom, Engelhardt, Furst, Hill, & Krathwohl, 1956) whose major purpose was to provide educators with a wide range of possible objectives in the cognitive area, along with a yardstick for evaluating the extent to which cognitive skills were included within any given instructional unit. An additional objective of the taxonomy was to assist teachers in specifying objectives more clearly, with the expectation that this would simplify the planning and evaluation of the effects of instruction.

The taxonomy promulgated by Bloom and his colleagues (1956) contains six major classes within the cognitive domain: knowledge, comprehension, application, analysis, synthesis, and evaluation. The classes were conceived as being roughly hierarchical in nature, with ". . . the objectives in one class . . . likely to make use of and be built on the behaviors found in the preceding classes in this list" (p. 18). The area of knowledge was listed as a separate independent class, while the other five were grouped under the broad category of intellectual abilities and skills.

Implicit in this taxonomic formulation of a cognitive domain for guiding the development of educational objectives is a conviction that intellectual abilities and skills are educable. Stated in other words, the exposure of a learner to an educational program in which curriculum objectives are systematically selected on the basis of their being representative of particular cognitive abilities should lead to an increment in intellectual abilities within the learner. As stated by Bloom et al. (1956), an increase in intellectual abilities and skills in the learner would be demonstrated by an increase in the ability to ". . . find appropriate information and techniques in his previous experience to bring to bear on new problems and situations" (p. 38).

In contrast to the indirect advocacy given to educating intellectual and learning abilities by the foregoing workers, Meeker (1969) proposed that "cognitive therapy" be provided for pupils experiencing learning difficulties in school. Meeker, in criticizing the continuing use of traditionally accepted curricula with exceptional children, singled out the mentally retarded group as perhaps being most adversely affected by this practice. While recognizing the current attempts at modifying teaching methodologies for exceptional children, she indicated the unfortunate tendency for the goals to remain the same with regard to the subject matter in the curriculum.

In an effort to influence educators and psychologists to bring about changes in structuring curricula within special education, Meeker developed a system whereby curriculum content may be selected to reflect the abilities contained in Guilford's (1967) structure-of-intellect (SOI) model. Meeker's purposes in undertaking the development of this system were to "... interpret a complex psychological model of intelligence for use within the existing framework of curriculum ... and ... to show that cognitive therapy can properly be accomplished within the domain of the school ... " (1969, p. ix). Meeker, in anticipating some objection to a proposal for offering cognitive therapy to pupils on the grounds that abilities within an individual are fairly stable, removed any doubts about her position regarding the educability of intellectual abilities by stating that it is possible to deal directly with a learner who is low in memory (one of Guilford's intellectual operations) by remediating his memory skills.

While standardized intelligence tests traditionally have been used to place children in various clinical and/or psychometric categories of intellectual funtioning, Meeker suggested that there are occasions when the results of intelligence tests can and should be used diagnostically. Specifically, she stated that "... the child should be so taught as to eradicate a specific disability or deficit found in his intellectual responses" (1969, p. 111). To accomplish this, Meeker devised a mapping procedure for assigning test items from the Stanford-Binet and Wechsler scales to the appropriate cell in Guilford's SOI. As Meeker recognized, one of the problems encountered in categorizing Stanford-Binet and Wechsler test items in the SOI cells is that the results of factor analytic studies have indicated that the traditional test items in most cases are not "pure" measures of intellectual abilities. Thus, in the instances where there were questions about the most appropriate cell assignments for test items, the items were either assigned to a SOI cell that appeared to be the best fit, or they were assigned to a SOI cell that appeared to be the best fit, or they were assigned to two or more cells. Meeker indicated that initial data collected to determine whether children who scored high on Stanford-Binet items also scored high on Guilford tests provided "essential substantiation" that this was the case.

As a result of the mapping procedure devised by Meeker (1969), it is now possible to examine the performance of children on individual test items, to determine whether there are patterns of strengths and weaknesses in any of the five operations or products, and to decide on the type of content (figural, symbolic, or semantic) with which the child is best able to deal. After charting these results, individual deficits can be remediated either through the use of curriculum and methodological suggestions provided by Meeker or by those informally designed according to SOI cell definitions. Thus, if a learner scored below expectancy levels on those Stanford-Binet items that consistently correspond to Guilford's memory cells, Meeker would suggest that the pupil be exposed to curricula and methods designed to improve directly the intellectual operation of memory.

A cautionary note should be sounded regarding Meeker's proposals to upgrade the functioning of mentally retarded individuals on cognitive factors extracted from mature normal populations. Conceivably, the Guilford model may not be applicable in all respects to the mentally retarded learner. The works of Clausen (1966, 1967), Meyers, Orpet, Sitkei, & Watts (1962), and Blackman and Burger (1972) may be instructive in this regard.

The notion that intellectual abilities are amenable to, or perhaps developed as a result of, specific training or educational experiences has been strongly set forth by Staats (1963, 1968, 1971) for a number of years. While recognizing that his views are in direct contrast to those currently held by most members of the scientific community, Staats posited that, with the exception of children who exhibit observable physical defects, all children are equal at birth in their ability to acquire intellectual skills. Using the argument that it is now not possible to detect systematic differences between the brains of a "genius" and an "idiot" with regard to tissue, electric wave activity, or chemical composition, Staats proposed that ". . . *we all*, as members of the species, inherit a brain capable of handling all the learning tasks our world presents" (1971, p. 267). He further suggested that if there are any interindividual differences in inherited learning mechanisms or neural structures, they are differences that are not requisite to any of the intellectual tasks presently required of man. Within the same realm of thought, Staats stated that while there had not been a biological evolution in man's brain since the time of the caveman—and there will be none in the future—man has and will continue to become more intelligent.

The question of whether it is possible to modify the level of intellectual functioning of the young mentally retarded child through formal educational interventions has been the subject of a number of investigations. Such studies, in most cases, have been conducted at the preschool and primary grade levels, since it is commonly held that if intellectual abilities can be increased, the chances for success are greatest during the early years. Kirk (1958), in an effort to determine the feasibility of influencing changes in the mental development of young educable retarded children, provided his experimental subjects with a daily 6-hour nursery school program in both community and institutional settings. The results of his study indicated that the retarded subjects in both settings, who were exposed to the experimental program made significantly greater gains on IQ measures than control groups who had not received the enriched program. The community control subjects also tended to show gains in IQ scores after entering school, while the experimental children showed no further gains in IQ. The greatest gains within all groups were made by those subjects coming from the most deprived environment who did not exhibit organic involvements.

Goldstein, Moss, and Jordan (1965), in their study of special class efficacy, tested the hypothesis that mentally retarded children placed in special classes would show greater development in intellectual functioning than would comparable children placed in the regular grades. After screening 1,938 children at the beginning of the first grade in three counties in Illinois, where primary-level special classes were not in existence, the experimenters identified 129 children who scored at or below an IQ of 85. The children were then randomly placed in special classes or in regular first-grade classes. The results of the study indicated that both special and regular class groups made significant gains in IQ over the first year, with no differences between groups. The gains made by subjects in both groups were dramatic, with a gain of 12 or 13 points not uncommon. Analyses carried out at the end of the 4-year study again revealed no differences between special and regular class groups. As was the case in the Kirk preschool study, subjects made their greatest gains during the first year of exposure to formal schooling, with a general leveling off during the next 3 years.

Hodges, McCandless, and Spicker (1971) examined the effects of exposing 5-year-old psychosocially deprived children, whose initial IQs were between 50 and 85, to various diagnostically based experimental curricula. Included within their research objectives was the development of curriculum strategies that would be effective in improving cognitive, affective, and motoric deficits among their subjects, and the prevention of future mental and educational retardation. Interestingly, the experimenters' approach to developing their instructional strategies included the use of the Stanford-Binet Intelligence Scale (1960 revision) and the Columbia Mental Maturity Scale to develop curriculum content, as well as to provide pre- and posttest measures of intellectual functioning. The experimental group and an at-home control group exhibited gains of approximately one standard deviation or more in Stanford-Binet IQs (21 and 15 points, respectively) over the 3-year experimental period. Children who had been assigned to a traditional kindergarten program gained an average of 11 IQ points over the same period.

None of the above studies provided clear-cut results for supporting the superiority of "special" curricula over "regular" or traditional curricula in raising the intellectual functioning of young retarded subjects. In some cases, control subjects not receiving early special attention later caught up to and therefore erased the initial superiority in IQ gain exhibited by the experimental subjects. In other cases, there were no differences between groups, and in still others significant differences were reported with the use of one IQ measure but not with another.

The major contribution of the above studies to a learning disability curriculum model for the mentally retarded child is the common finding that initial intellectual functioning among educable retarded children can be raised by exposing them to cognitively oriented curricula during their early years. The IQ gains exhibited by children who tested within the 50 to 85 range tended to be substantial, psychometrically, with gains as much as one standard deviation in magnitude not uncommon. Since IQ gains tended to level off after a year of formal schooling, the effects of exposing low-functioning children to cognitively oriented curricula over their entire school careers need to be examined.

The most dramatic exploration of the effects of early and largely direct training and/or stimulation of intellectual skills among preschoolers was that of Heber, Garber, Harrington, Hoffman, and Falender (1972). Their subjects were drawn from an inner-city area that comprised approximately 2½% of the city's population, yet yielded one-third of the educable mentally retarded students known to the schools. The risk of obtaining from this area an IQ below 80 at age 14 for a child whose mother's IQ was below 80 was determined to be approximately 80%.

Heber et al. (1972) selected 40 mothers with IQs less than 80 and assigned them to experimental and control groups using a modified random selection system based on an alternative monthly assignment of newly born infants to a particular group. One-half of the infants of these mothers received an intensive stimulation program, beginning shortly after birth (CA 3 months) and lasting through the preschool years (CA 6 years). During the child's early months in the program, an "infant teacher" spent the entire day in the home while the mother was provided vocational training elsewhere. As soon as permission was secured from the mother, each experimental infant was taken to a center for the entire day, where one-to-one training continued in such areas as perceptual-motor, cognitive-language, reading, and mathematical problem solving. As subjects progressed in years, their special training was provided in small groups of six to eight children. At the end of approximately 5½ years, the experimental group obtained an average IQ score of 124, while the mean scores of the control group and of a contrast group (control siblings) were 94 and 83, respectively. Thus, the experimental group surpassed the control group by more than two standard deviations and the contrast group by almost three standard deviation units.

The preceding study was criticized by Page (1972) on a number of grounds. Because the stimulation program utilized by Heber et al. (1972) contained materials which approximated materials used in infant intelligence tests, Page suggested that the study merely demonstrated that it is possible to train subjects on test items used in these intelligence tests. However, scrutiny of the toys, books, and games selected for the preschool child in most middle-class homes, as well as the language models available, suggests that these materials and models could also be described as being similar, in some respects, to intelligence test items. Thus, the Heber group's "training for the test" might be construed as presenting programs and materials that differ more in degree than in kind from the materials, activities, and skills frequently selected for middle-class children because they have high "educational value." The efficacy of the approach used by Heber and his associates, however, cannot be evaluated until the experimental subjects enter school and are able to demonstrate the acquisition of those complex academic and social skills commensurate with their reported intelligence levels.

While the learning disability curriculum model is currently the single most popular special educational approach, it has come under attack on a number of grounds. Mann (1971a, 1971b), for example, has raised questions about the validity of a number of central principles and procedures underlying a learning disability approach. He questioned whether the current measurement practices and instruments used in a typical learning disability program could result in the differentiating of (a) various handicapped groups, (b) handicapped and nonhandicapped groups, or (c) specific abilities and subabilities. In addition to challenging the sophistication of the testing procedures currently in use, Mann suggested that while the theoretical positions held by the learning disability proponents are particularly appealing to individuals working with handicapped children, they are either overly simplistic (contrary to much of the data on ability testing) or have been long rejected as being untenable in psychology. He concluded that claims concerning the measurement of (a) underlying basic abilities or functions and their strengths and weaknesses, (b) special constructs identified in the learning disability movement, (c) abilities most crucial to normal functioning and development, and (d) "remediable" abilities are nothing more than theoretical "hubris." In short, Mann suggested that the diagnosis and remediation carried out in a learning disability approach are not more effective than traditional educational programming with its more global emphasis.

An examination of Mann's (1971a, 1971b) analysis of the learning disability movement and related practices reveals that the procedures under attack in this special area are strikingly similar to the daily activities carried out by general educators in their efforts to accurately assess school readiness, reading readiness, reading disabilities, general intellectual ability, and interests. Normal pupils who are found to be "not ready" are given more time and perhaps added stimulation to become ready. Thus, older "ready" pupils are placed in slow, average, or fast first grades, and unmotivated pupils in the more progressive school systems are provided with counseling and therapy. In both general education and special education, as efforts to utilize the available constructs and data generated by testing programs increase (often combined with unwarranted enthusiasm as to their applicability to classroom programming on the part of the tests' consumers), the possibility of introducing error, and therefore invalid procedures, may also increase. Special educators have perhaps been guilty of committing more errors or of using invalid procedures more frequently than have general educators, but these sins have been committed in response to being faced with the task of educating learners who had already demonstrated in most cases that they were unresponsive to the learning environments provided by general education.

The revelation that general and special educators are, on occasion, unwittingly guilty of invalid practices should come as a surprise only to those who (a) are not familiar with the proper use and interpretation of such concepts and constructs as intelligence, perception, learning, motivation, and self-concept; and (b) who are unaware of the limitations of current educational and psychological tests and measurements, vis-à-vis valid educational programming. It would seem that a call for an increase in knowledge in the preceding areas would be of greater benefit to educators and children than would an overall indictment of general educational practice.

FUTURE DIRECTIONS

The three sources of data described in the preceding section as exerting a heavy influence on both curriculum development and the design of instructional methods in special education are (a) the knowledge structure of subject matter, (b) descriptions of social competence in mentally retarded learners, and (c) analysis of their learning disabilities. The second data source, which concerns the descriptions of social competence, is almost exclusively concerned with issues of curriculum development. Indeed, the Social Learning Curriculum (Goldstein, 1969), currently under field evaluation, is a direct expression of that focus.

The first and third data sources, having to do with the structure of subject matter and with an analysis of the learning disabilities of the mentally retarded child, provide the conceptual framework for a program of educational research with mentally retarded students, suggested earlier by Blackman (1967).

Taxonomic Models for Educational Technology

Blackman (1967) maintained that the effective modification of the classroom behavior of mentally retarded children depends first on the development of a "school-relevant taxonomy of their psychoeducational characteristics." By psychoeducational characteristics is meant "an analysis of the retarded child's profile of abilities and deficits in a wide range of psychological processes such as perception, learning, cognition, retention, transfer, attention, discrimination, and language among others" (p. 8).

This, in essence, defines the approach as bearing on the learning-disabilities issue. The proposed taxonomic approach also maintains that knowledge of a retarded learner's disabilities has ". . . little educational utility independent of its relevancy to school; that is, a comparable understanding of the psychoeducational prerequisites for acquiring specific school tasks" (p. 8). The stress on understanding the nature of school tasks as the second anchor point in the taxonomy reflects, only in part, the subject-matter approach. As described earlier in this chapter, the contribution of understanding subject matter to the development of curriculum and methods was to enable the sequencing of school tasks based on the indigenous properties of the knowledge structure within these tasks. That is, school tasks could be ordered in terms of a complexity-based, layered hierarchy of the skills and understandings required in the successful acquisition of these tasks. However, the crucial emphasis on understanding school tasks in Blackman's (1967) taxonomic model bears on the relevance of the learner's psychological assets and disabilities to the subject matter being acquired. Subject matter, therefore, must be understood not only in terms of its own logical structure, but also in terms of the demands that it places on the perceptual, learning, and cognitive abilities of the learner for whom the didactic material is targeted. The former emphasis speaks to how subject matter should be organized for presentation based on its own knowledge structure. The latter speaks to the appropriateness of certain subject-matter structures for mentally retarded learners.

There is a line of research implied in this analysis of the relationship between subject-matter structure and learner disabilities. First, the elements of a didactic sequence must be placed in a logical hierarchical order, while at the same time defining the most effective stimulus environments for presenting each of the elements. The effectiveness of both the order and the particular stimulus environments must be empirically validated with large samples of normal learners. Secondly, there is a need to investigate the effectiveness of particular stimulus components as well as instructional sequences for mentally retarded learners. The patterns of cognitive disabilities in the mentally retarded student in such areas as perceptual organization and short-term memory, already well-documented in this chapter, will provide clues for modifying both the stimulus environments within the elements of an instructional sequence and, conceivably, the ordering of these elements.

A further component of Blackman's taxonomic system deals with instructional systems on those ". . . processes, steps, or strategies by which the learner is moved by the teacher and/or some technological extension of the teacher toward mastery of appropriate educational content" (1967, p. 9). The total teaching system, therefore, includes (a) an analysis of the learner's strengths and disabilities, (b) an analysis of both the logical and "learner-demand" structure of subject matter, and (c) the instructional system designed as a derivation from (a) and (b).

As described in an earlier section of this chapter, the research on educationally relevant learning disabilities has been extensive and continues to expand. Empirical research aiming to determine the knowledge structure hierarchy for any given subject-matter sequence is relatively meager and is undergoing conceptual modification. The research aimed at empirically verifying those psychological processes inherent in the acquisition of subject matter (primarily reading) is, with some exceptions (Blackman & Burger, 1972; Samuels & Anderson, 1973), still developing. It should be no surprise, therefore, to find that research on the efficacy of instructional systems developed after extensive investigations on the complementary characteristics of subject matter and learner is almost nonexistent.

One major research effort in the "taxonomic tradition" by Tannenbaum (1970) must be considered prototypic in the sense that the backup research on learner and subject-matter characteristics does not yet permit the comprehensiveness of coverage on these variables that a complete taxonomy will ultimately require.

Nevertheless, Tannenbaum (1970) developed a rather well-structured taxonomic system for designing instructional strategies that will cater to the needs and predispositions of handicapped learners. This system evolved from the premise that: "The teacher's instructional goal is to achieve a 'goodness of fit' between the pupil's functioning capacity and preferred learning style on the one hand and the organization of content and strategies for instructional transmission on the other" (p. 13).

Tannenbaum's Taxonomy is divided into seven components, three of which are concerned with the "What" (or content) of instruction, while four have to do with the "How" (or strategy) of instruction. Based on the criterion of maximizing the child's engagement in the classroom, and ultimately his achievements, it is the teacher's job to select the most appropriate pedagogical alternatives stipulated in the Taxonomy.

The three components of the Taxonomy representing the content area are an analysis of (a) Basic Skills, (b) Basic Sub-Skills (grouped under the respective basic skills), and (c) Sequence Levels (a categorization of materials according to difficulty). Clearly, the particulars of this portion of the Taxonomy will vary, depending upon the academic skill being taught. Thus, based upon an epistemological analysis of the subject matter under consideration, the basic skills, subskills, and sequence levels will be appropriate to reading, arithmetic, social studies, or whatever other content is being taught.

The four strategy components are divided into (a) Instructional Methods, (b) Instructional Modes, (c) Communication Input, and (d) Communication Output. *Instructional Method* suggests alternatives for organizing pupils for a formal teaching-learning experience. These include, among others, teacher-led total group, teacher-led small group, student-led small group, and student-student tutorial. The *Instructional Modes* strategy stipulates transactional styles between the learner and the teaching stimuli, such as play-chance, test response, exposition, and role playing. *Communication Input* points to the learner's sensory modalities which are available for mediating the instructional stimuli. They include visual, auditory, motoric, visual-motoric, and auditory-motoric modalities. *Communication Output* lists the channels to be used by the pupil to demonstrate the correctness of processing the information received by the input channel. The channels include no response, oral response, motoric response, and oral-motor response.

The Taxonomy, therefore, provides one program of individualized instruction by offering the classroom teacher "specific guidelines for diagnosing learning needs and styles and for analyzing instructional materials and strategies" (Tannenbaum, 1970, p. 24). One of the inescapable characteristics of research evaluating the effectiveness of taxonomic instruction relates to the fact that instructional strategies must be designed so as to be congruent with the particular pattern of learning abilities and disabilities manifested by the individual deviant learner. The practical and economic implications of a total commitment to the individual learner in the development of educational services is, at the moment, difficult to fathom. A total commitment to the progress made by the individual, nonreplicable learner in setting research goals is equally provocative. Before research on the individual learner's response to direct educational intervention can be achieved, prior study using the more traditional forms of large group research is necessary to identify those perceptual, learning, and cognitive processes critical to subject-matter acquisition as well as the most effective forms of stimulus environments and learning sequences.

Blackman (1972) anticipated this issue when he suggested that:

> Concern for the progress of the individual child is a radical notion for the research enterprise and poses certain problems. . . . The factors that affect the child's performance over time become the first stage of the central research question. The second stage is the evaluation of techniques, developed after these factors have been identified, which are designed to bring the child's level of performance and rate of progress to a more satisfactory state. . . . It is a model that subverts those values in research which insist upon the generalizability of findings. Clearly, that set of experiments which identifies those variables which impede learning and which will then develop effective remedial procedures for an N of 1 will say little about the effectiveness of these procedures for a second or third child, or for an entire class. The value system for this type of research holds that the important finding is the unique procedure that will work with a particular child. The generalization of an intervention procedure, when it ultimately occurs, will result from the accretion of a large number of $N = 1$ experiments that have replicated the successful treatment procedure for a specifiable set of children's aptitudes. (p. 187-188)

In summary, the model being proposed for generating research in the special education of the mentally retarded child rests on the premise that programs of educational intervention will be directed at the individual child. His abilities and disabilities will be marked, their relevance to specified sets of subject matter sequences will be established, and instructional systems will be designed that will take both into account. The effectiveness of these procedures will be evaluated objectively as a function of the retarded learner's acquisition of skills over time. The model suggests finally that the central research topic is to be ". . . the research subject himself—the unsuccessful child, his incapacities, and the remediation thereof . . . " (Blackman, 1972, p. 187).

SUMMARY

Historically, the same political, social, and economic forces that have shaped curriculum and methods for the broad range of normal children have had comparable effects on the special education of mentally retarded children. Recently, however, special education programs, particularly for the mildly mentally retarded student, have attracted special scrutiny. As a consequence, they are coming under increasing criticism on the basis of both educational research data and social pressures.

The so-called special-class efficacy studies have been disappointing in that little evidence has been produced to show that special classes accelerate the development of either academic or social skills of retarded children. Community groups decry the continued segregation of the disproportionately large numbers of minority and disadvantaged children typically found in special classes organized for the mentally retarded pupil. These groups are promoting a "mainstreaming" approach.

In response to these pressures, special educators are searching for a more scientific framework from which to derive those curricula and methods that are more likely to prove effective in educating the mentally retarded child. Three major sources of data that have influenced the development of new programs and practices in this field are discussed in the present chapter. They include data on (a) the structure of subject matter, (b) the demands of society, and (c) the abilities and disabilities of the learner.

The total teaching system described rests upon an analysis of the learner's assets and deficits, an understanding of the cognitive demands of particular subject-matter tasks, and the design of an instructional delivery system derived from the interface of learner and task characteristics. Future directions for research are projected that will further define both the structure and the learner demand characteristics of school tasks, and that will verify empirically the effectiveness of the entire teaching system. Since the system is devoted to educational intervention on behalf of the individual deviant learner, the implications and tactics of $N = 1$ research are discussed.

REFERENCES

Ausubel, D. P. The use of advance organizers in the learning and retention of meaningful verbal material. *Journal of Educational Psychology*, 1966, *51*, 267-272.

Baldwin, W. K. The social position of the educable mentally retarded child in the regular grades in the public schools. *Exceptional Children*, 1958, *25*, 106-108.

Baller, W. R. A study of the present social status of a group of adults who, when they were in elementary schools, were classified as mentally deficient. *Genetic Psychology Monographs*, 1936, *18*, 165-244.

Bateman, B. Learning disabilities—yesterday, today, tomorrow. *Exceptional Children*, 1964, *4*, 167-177.

Bateman, B. Implications of a learning disability approach for teaching educable retardates. *Mental Retardation,* 1967, *5*(3), 23-25.

Baumeister, A. A., & Kellas, G. Intra-subject response variability in relation to intelligence. *Journal of Abnormal Psychology,* 1968, *73,* 421-423.

Bean, F. X. The effect of classroom instruction upon the class inclusion behavior of the educable mentally retarded. New York: Teachers College, Columbia University, 1968. (Unpublished doctoral dissertation)

Bellack, A., Kliebard, H. M., Hyman, R. T., & Smith, F. L. *The language of the classroom* (Part 2). Cooperative research project No. 2023. New York: Teachers College, Columbia University, 1965.

Bennett, A. Reading ability in special classes. *Journal of Educational Research,* 1929, *20,* 236-238.

Bennett, A. *A comparative study of subnormal children in the elementary grades.* New York: Bureau of Publications, Teachers College, Columbia University, 1932.

Bensberg, G. S., Jr. The relation of academic achievement of mental defectives to mental age, sex, institutionalization, and etiology. *American Journal of Mental Deficiency,* 1953, *58,* 327-330.

Bijou, S. W. The special problem of motivation in the academic learning of mentally retarded children. *Exceptional Children,* 1952, *19,* 103.

Bilsky, L., & Evans, R. A. Use of associative clustering technique in the study of reading disability: Effects of list organization. *American Journal of Mental Deficiency,* 1970, *74,* 771-776.

Birch, H. G., & Belmont, L. Auditory-visual integration in normal and retarded readers. *American Journal of Orthopsychiatry,* 1964, *34,* 852-861.

Blackman, L. S. The dimensions of a science of special education. *Mental Retardation,* 1967, *5*(4), 7-11.

Blackman, L. S. Research and the classroom: Mahomet and the mountain revisited. *Exceptional Children,* 1972, *39,* 181-191.

Blackman, L. S., & Burger, A. L. Psychological factors related to early reading behavior of EMR and nonretarded children. *American Journal of Mental Deficiency,* 1972, *77,* 212-229.

Blackman, L. S., & Heintz, P. The mentally retarded. *Review of Educational Research,* 1966, *36,* 5-36.

Blatt, B. The physical, personality, and academic status of children who are mentally retarded attending special classes as compared with children who are mentally retarded attending regular classes. *American Journal of Mental Deficiency,* 1958, *62,* 810-818.

Bliesmere, E. P. B. A comparison of bright and dull children of comparable mental ages with respect to various reading abilities. *Dissertation Abstracts,* 1962, *12,* 694.

Bloom, B. S., Engelhardt, M. D., Furst, E. J., Hill, W. H., & Krathwohl, D. *Taxonomy of educational objectives; the classification of educational goals. Handbook I: Cognitive domain.* New York: David McKay, 1956.

Boyle, R. C. *How can reading be taught to educable adolescents who have not learned to read?* Washington, D.C.: U.S. Government Printing Office, 1959.

Brown, A. W., & Lind, C. School achievement in relation to mental age—a comparative study. *Journal of Educational Psychology,* 1931, *22,* 561-576.

Brown, R. *Words and things.* New York: The Free Press of Glencoe, 1958.

Bruner, J. S. *The process of education.* New York: Vintage, 1960.

Carroll, J. B. Discussion of Cronbach's paper: Instructional methods and individual differences. In R. M. Gagne (Ed.), *Learning and individual differences.* Columbus, Ohio: Charles E. Merrill, 1967, pp. 40-44.

Cassidy, V. M., & Stanton, J. E. *An investigation of factors involved in the educational placement of mentally retarded children: A study of differences between children in special and regular classes in Ohio.* Columbus, Ohio: The Ohio State University Press, 1959.

Charles, D. C. Ability and accomplishment of persons earlier judged mentally deficient. *Genetic Psychology Monographs,* 1953, *47,* 3-71.

Clausen, J. *Ability structure and subgroups in mental retardation.* Washington, D.C.: Spartan, 1966.

Clausen, J. Mental deficiency—development of concept. *American Journal of Mental Deficiency, 1967,* 71, 727-745.

Cobb, J. H., & Barnard, J. W. Differential effects of implicit associative values on short-term recall of retarded and nonretarded children. *American Journal of Mental Deficiency,* 1971, *76,* 130-135.

Coleman, E. B. Collecting a data base for a reading technology. *Journal of Educational Psychology,* 1970, *61*(4, Part 2), 1-23.

Cromwell, R. L. A social learning approach to mental retardation. In N. R. Ellis (Ed.), *Handbook of mental deficiency.* New York: McGraw-Hill, 1963, pp. 41-91.

Cronbach, L. J. How can instruction be applied to individual differences? In R. M. Gagne (Ed.), *Learning and individual differences.* Columbus, Ohio: Charles E. Merrill, 1967, pp. 23-29.

Cruickshank, W. M. Arithmetic ability of mentally retarded children: I. Ability to differentiate extraneous materials from needed arithmetic facts. *Journal of Educational Research,* 1948, *42,* 279-288. (a)

Cruickshank, W. M. Arithmetic ability of mentally retarded children: II. Understanding arithmetic processes. *Journal of Educational Research,* 1948, *42,* 279-288. (b)

Daly, W. C., & Lee, R. H. Reading disabilities in a group of M-R children:

Incidence and treatment. *Training School Bulletin,* 1960, *57,* 85-93.

Denny, M. R. Research in learning and performance. In H. A. Stevens and R. Heber (Eds.), *Mental Retardation.* Chicago: University of Chicago Press, 1964, pp. 100-142.

Descoeudres, A. *The education of mentally defective children.* Boston: Heath, 1928.

Dunn, L. M. A comparison of the reading processes of mentally retarded and normal boys of the same mental age. *Monographs of the Society for Research in Child Development,* 1954, *19,* 7-99.

Dunn, L. M. (Ed.) *Exceptional Children in the Schools.* New York: Holt, Rinehart and Winston, 1963.

Dunn, L. M. Special education for the mildly retarded—is much of it justifiable? *Exceptional Children,* 1968, *35,* 5-22.

Dunn, L. M. (Ed.) *Exceptional children in the schools: Special education in transition* (2nd ed.). New York: Holt, Rinehart and Winston, 1973.

Dunn-Rankin, P. The similarity of lower-case letters of the English alphabet. *Journal of Verbal Learning and Verbal Behavior,* 1968, *7,* 990-995.

Edgerton, R. B. *The cloak of competence.* Berkeley: University of California Press, 1967.

Ellis, N. R. Memory processes in retardates and normals. In N. R. Ellis (Ed.), *International review of research in mental retardation* (Vol. 4). New York: Academic Press, 1970, pp. 1-32.

Frostig, M., Lefever, W., and Whittlesey, M. S. *Frostig Developmental Test of Visual Perception.* Palo Alto, Calif.: Consulting Psychologists Press, 1964.

Gagne, R. M. The acquisition of knowledge. *Psychological Review,* 1962, *69,* 355-365.

Gagne, R. M. *The conditions of learning.* New York: Holt, Rinehart and Winston, 1970.

Gagne, R. M., & Bassler, O. C. Study of retention of some topics of elementary non-metric geometry. *Journal of Educational Psychology,* 1963, *54,* 123-131.

Gagne, R. M., & Paradise, N. E. Abilities and learning sets in knowledge acquisition. *Psychological Monographs,* 1961, *75* (14, Whole No. 518).

Gagne, R. M. and staff. University of Maryland math project: Some factors in learning non-metric geometry. *Monographs of the Society for Research in Child Development,* 1965, *30* (1, 42-49).

Gerjuoy, I. R., & Alvarez, J. M. Transfer of learning in associative clustering of retardates and normals. *American Journal of Mental Deficiency,* 1969, *73,* 733-738.

Goldberg, I. I., & Blackman, L. S. The special class: Parasitic, endophytic, or symbiotic cell in the body pedagogic. *Mental Retardation,* 1965, *3*(2), 30-31.

Goldstein, H. Construction of a social learning curriculum. *Focus on exceptional children,* 1969, *1,* 1-10.

Goldstein, H., Mischio, G. S., Heiss, W. F., Melnick, G., Frafkin, M., & Clerico, L. *A proposal for a research and development center in curriculum for the mentally retarded.* New York: Yeshiva University, 1970.

Goldstein, H., Moss, J., & Jordan, L. J. *The efficacy of special class training on the development of mentally retarded children.* Cooperative Research Project No. 619. Washington, D.C.: U.S. Government Printing Office, 1965.

Goldstein, H., & Siegle, D. M. *A curriculum guide for teachers of the educable mentally handicapped.* Danville, Ill.: Interstate Printers and Publishers, 1958.

Groelle, M. C. Reading survey tests given to educable mentally retarded children. *Exceptional Children,* 1961, *27,* 443-448.

Guilford, J. P. *The nature of human intelligence.* New York: McGraw-Hill, 1967.

Guskin, S. L., & Spicker, H. H. Educational research in mental retardation. In N. R. Ellis (Ed.), International review of research in mental retardation (Vol. 3). New York: Academic Press, 1968, pp. 217-278.

Heber, R., & Dever, R. Education and rehabilitation of the mentally retarded. In H. C. Haywood (Ed.), *Social-cultural aspects of mental retardation.*

Heber, R., Garber, H., Harrington, S., Hoffman, C., & Falender, C. *Rehabilitation of families at risk for mental retardation.* Progress report. Madison, Wis.: Rehabilitation Research and Training Center in Mental Retardation, University of Wisconsin, 1972.

Highet, G. *The art of teaching.* New York: Vantage, 1955.

Hodges, W. L., McCandless, B., & Spicker, H. *Diagnostic teaching for preschool children.* Arlington, Va.: Council for Exceptional Children, 1971.

Holden, E. A., Jr. Effects of temporal grouping on unimodal and multimodal sequential information processing in nonretarded and retarded subjects. *American Journal of Mental Deficiency*, 1971, *76*, 181-184.

House, B. J., & Zeaman, D. Visual discrimination learning in normal and mentally defective children. *Child Development*, 1959, *29*, 411-416.

Hoyt, M., Meranski, S., & Snell, J. Mental age and school attainment of 1,007 retarded children in Massachusetts. *Journal of Educational Psychology*, 1924, *15*, 297-301.

Inskeep, A. D. *Teaching dull and retarded children*. New York: Macmillan, 1926.

Jacobs, J. N. A study of performances of slow learners in the Cincinnati Public Schools on mental achievement tests. *American Journal of Mental Deficiency*, 1957, *63*, 238-243.

Jensen, A. R., & Rohwer, W. D., Jr. The effect of verbal mediation on the learning and retention of paired associates by retarded adults. *American Journal of Mental Deficiency*, 1963, *68*, 80-84.

Johnson, G. O. A study of the social position of the mentally handicapped children in the regular grades. *American Journal of Mental Deficiency*, 1950, *55*, 60-89.

Johnson, D. J., & Myklebust, H. R. *Learning disabilities*. New York: Grune & Stratton, 1967.

Katz, P. J. Another look at transfer of learning and mental retardation. *Mental Retardation*, 1964, *2*, 177-183.

Kaufman, M. E., & Prehm, H. J. A review of research on learning set and transfer of training in mental defectives. In N. R. Ellis (Ed.), *International review of research in mental retardation* (Vol. 2). New York: Academic Press, 1966, pp. 123-149.

Kennedy, R. J. R. *The social adjustment of morons in a Connecticut city*. Westport, Conn.: Commission to Survey Resources in Connecticut, 1948.

Kephart, N. C. *The slow learner in the classroom,* (2nd ed.) Columbus, Ohio: Charles E. Merrill, 1971.

Kirk, S. A. *Early education of the mentally retarded: An experimental study*. Urbana, Ill.: University of Illinois Press, 1958.

Kirk, S. A. *Educating exceptional children*. Boston: Houghton Mifflin, 1962.

Kirk, S. A. *Educating exceptional children* (2nd ed.). Boston: Houghton Mifflin, 1972.

Kirk, S. A. Research in education. In H. A. Stevens and R. Heber (Eds.), *Mental retardation*. Chicago: University of Chicago Press, 1964, pp. 57-99.

Kirk, S. A., & Johnson, G. O. *Educating the mentally retarded child.* Boston: Houghton Mifflin, 1951.

Kirk, S. A., & McCarthy, J. J. The Illinois Test of Psycholinguistic Abilities: An approach to differential diagnosis. *American Journal of Mental Deficiency,* 1961, *66,* 399-412.

Kirk, S. A., & McCarthy, J. J. Learning disabilities. *The encyclopedia of education,* 1971, *5,* 441-446.

Kirk, S. A. McCarthy, J. J., & Kirk, W. D. *Illinois Test of Psycholinguistic Abilities.* Urbana, Ill.: University of Illinois Press, 1968.

Klausmeier, H. J., & Hooper, F. H. Conceptual development and instruction. In F. N. Kerlinger (Ed.), *Review of research in education* (Vol. 2). Itasca, Ill.: F. E. Peacock, 1974, pp. 3-54.

Koppitz, E. M. *Bender Visual-motor Gestalt Test for Children.* Beverly Hills, Calif.: Western Psychological Services, 1962.

Lapp, E. R. A study of the social adjustment of slow learning children who were assigned part-time to regular grades. *American Journal of Mental Deficiency,* 1957, *62,* 254-262.

Lippman, L., & Goldberg I. I. *Right to education: Anatomy of the Pennsylvania case and its implications for exceptional children.* New York: Teachers College Press, Columbia University, 1973.

Mann, L. Perceptual training revisited: The training of nothing at all. *Rehabilitation Literature,* 1971, *32,* 322-335. (a)

Mann, L. Psychometric phrenology and the new faculty psychology: The case against ability assessment and training. *The Journal of Special Education,* 1971, *5,* 3-14. (b)

Mayer, L. C. The relationship of early special class placement and the self-concepts of mentally handicapped children. *Exceptional Children,* 1966, *33,* 77-81.

Martin C. J. Associative learning strategies employed by deaf, blind, retarded, and normal children. Project No. 5-069, Grant No. 5-0405-4-11-3, Office of Education, U.S. Department of Health, Education, and Welfare. Washington, D.C.: U.S. Government Printing office, 1967.

McCarthy, J. J., & McCarthy, J. F. *Learning disabilities.* Boston: Allyn & Bacon, 1969.

McIntyre, R. B., & Dingman, H. F. Mental age vs. learning ability: An investigation of transfer of training between hierarchical levels. *American Journal of Mental Deficiency,* 1963, *68,* 396-403.

McIvor, W. B. Evaluation of strategy-oriented training programs on the verbal abstraction performance of EMRs. *American Journal of Mental*

Deficiency, 1972, *76,* 652-657.

McNeil, J. D. Forces influencing curriculum. *Review of Educational Research,* 1969, *39,* 293-318.

Meeker, M. N. *The structure of intellect: Its interpretations and uses.* Columbus, Ohio: Charles E. Merrill, 1969.

Merrill, M. A. On the relation of intelligence to achievement in the case of mentally retarded children. *Comparative Psychological Monographs,* 1924, *11,* 1-100.

Meyen, E. L. The education of the mentally-retarded—A systematic error in curriculum development. *Education and Training of the Mentally Retarded,* 1968, *3,* 164-168.

Meyerowitz, J. H. Self-derogation in young retardates and special class placement. *Child Development,* 1962, *33,* 443-451.

Meyers, C. E., Orpet, R. E., Sitkei, E. G., & Watts, C. A. Primary abilities at mental age six. *Monographs of the Society for Research in Child Development,* 1962, *27* (1, Whole No. 82).

Milgram, N. A. Retention of mediation set in paired associate learning of normal children and retardates. *Journal of Experimental Child Psychology,* 1967, *5,* 341-349.

Minskoff, E. H. *An analysis of the teacher-pupil verbal interaction in special classes for the mentally retarded.* New York: Yeshiva University, 1967.

Moran, R. E. Levels of attainment of educable subnormal adolescents. *British Journal of Educational Psychology,* 1960, *30,* 201-210.

National Education Association. *Policies for education in democracy.* Washington, D.C.: NEA, 1946.

Osborne, W. J. Associative clustering in organic and familiar retardates. *American Journal of Mental Deficiency,* 1960, *65,* 351-357.

Page, E. B. Miracle in Milwaukee: Raising the I.Q. *Educational Researcher,* 1972, *1,* 8-16.

Pertsch, F. C. *A comparative study of the progress of subnormal pupils in the grades and in special classes.* New York: Bureau of Publications, Teachers College, Columbia University, 1936.

Phenix, P. *Realms of meaning.* New York: McGraw-Hill, 1964.

Piaget, J. *The child's conception of number.* New York: Humanities Press, 1952.

Renshaw, S. The abilities of pupils in Detroit prevocational classes. *Journal of Educational Psychology,* 1919, *10,* 83-94.

Ross, D. Retention and transfer of mediation set in paired associate learning of educable retarded children. *Journal of Educational Psychology,*

1971, *62*, 322-327.

Rothstein, J. H. *Mental retardation: Readings and resources* (2nd ed.). New York: Holt, Rinehart and Winston, 1971.

Ryan, J. F., Chivers, J., & Redding, G. Short-term memory and rehearsal in educable subnormals. *American Journal of Mental Deficiency*, 1969, *74*, 218-22.

Samuels, S. J., & Anderson, R. H. Visual recognition memory, paired associate learning, and reading achievement. *Journal of Educational Psychology*, 1973, *65*, 160-167.

Scott, K. G. Engineering attention: Some rules for the classroom. *Education and Training of the Mentally Retarded*, 1966, *1*, 125-129.

Simches, G., & Bohn, R. J. Issues in curriculum research and responsibility. *Mental Retardation*, 1963, *1*, 84-87; 115-117.

Skinner, B. F. *The technology of teaching*. New York: Appleton-Century-Crofts, 1968.

Sloan, W. The Lincoln-Oseretsky motor development scale. *Genetic Psychology Monographs*, 1955, *51*, 183-252.

Smith, M. D. Significant differences: Get away from the lamp-post, researcher, you're sufficiently lit now. *Educational Researcher*, 1970, *21*, 4-6.

Smith, R. *Clinical teaching: Methods of instruction for the retarded*. New York: McGraw-Hill, 1968.

Spitz, H. H. The role of input organization in the learning and memory of mental retardates. In N. R. Ellis (Ed.), *International review of research in mental retardation* (Vol. 2). New York: Academic Press, 1966, pp. 29-56.

Spitz, H. H., Goettler, D. R., & Webreck, C. A. Effects of two types of redundancy on visual digit span performance of retardates and varying aged normals. *Developmental Psychology*, 1972, *6*, 92-103.

Staats, A. W. *Child learning, intelligence, and personality*. New York: Harper & Row, 1971.

Staats, A. W. *Complex human behavior*. New York: Holt, Rinehart and Winston, 1963.

Staats, A, W. *Learning, language, and cognition*. New York: Holt, Rinehart and Winston, 1968.

Suppes, P., Jerman, M., & Brian, D. *Computer assisted instruction*. New York: Academic Press, 1968.

Tannenbaum, A. *The taxonomic instruction project: An introduction to taxonomic instruction*. Research & Demonstration Center for the

Education of Handicapped Children, Teachers College, Columbia
University, New York, N.Y., June 1970. (Unpublished manuscript)
Windle, C. D. Prognosis of mental subnormals. *American Journal of Mental
Deficiency,* 1962, *66* (Monogr. Suppl. 5).
Wright, B. *Physical disability: A psychological approach.* New York: Harper
& Row, 1960.

John E. Gordon did his undergraduate study at George Washington University. He received his M.A. and Ph.D. degrees from George Peabody College, with a major in clinical psychology and a minor in special education (mental retardation).

He was a recipient of an NIMH training fellowship in mental retardation at Peabody, which led to studies relating to intellectual potential of mentally retarded persons. Interests in clinical neuropsychology were developed during the course of research investigations on verbal abstracting behavior of organically impaired and cultural-familial mentally retarded persons. These interests in the learning problems of brain-damaged children were continued and broadened while on his clinical internship in the neuropsychology and child psychiatry departments of Tufts New England Medical Center Hospitals.

Currently, Dr. Gordon is Assistant Professor of Clinical Psychology at Temple University, where his research and training interests include neuropsychology, mental retardation, learning disorders in children and adults, and service delivery systems for persons with developmental disabilities. He has been a consulting editor to the American Journal of Mental Deficiency *and is the editor of a book entitled,* Developmental Disabilities: An Orientation to Cerebral Palsy, Epilepsy, and Mental Retardation.

In addition to previous assignments as Associate Director (and Acting Director) of Temple University Developmental Disabilities Center and as an alternate member of the Pennsylvania State Developmental Disabilities Council, he is currently a neuropsychology consultant to the Community Epilepsy Center at University of Pennsylvania Graduate Hospital and to a variety of state and federal mental health and mental retardation facilities.

9

Neuropsychology and mental retardation

John E. Gordon

DELINEATION OF THE ISSUES

Mental retardation is generally accepted as a generic term to denote a broad range of maladies which occur within the developmental period and have in common the behavioral effects of lowered general intellectual and adaptive abilities (Grossman, 1973; Heber, 1961, 1970). It has long been assumed that specific etiologic conditions exert characterisitc effects on afflicted individuals, such that the behavioral consequences result in distinct and identifiable patterns which are related to and dependent on the specific etiology. When brain damage is considered to be the primary etiologic factor in mental retardation, it is expected that there are characteristic behavioral consequences which are malevolently unique to these retarded persons, as compared to those where the basic etiology consists of inherited or familial and/or sociocultural or environmental influences. The search for differential diagnostic technology and the documentation of specific behavioral consequences of brain damage have produced a prodigious amount of reported research, much of which is confusing if not contradictory.

Neuropsychology can be most generally defined as the study of brain-behavior relationships; and clinical neuropsychologists apply the knowledge and techniques derived from such study to the diagnosis and treatment of "brain-damaged" persons (Haywood & Gordon, 1970). Stemming from the research of Strauss and his associates, it has been suggested that "exogenous" or "brain-damaged" individuals have in common "disturbances in perception, thinking, and emotional behavior, either separately or in combination" (Strauss & Lehtinen, 1947, p. 4) as a result of their brain injuries. Haywood (1968), in combining the foregoing three areas

367

of disturbance, differentiated two primary types of behavioral effects of brain damage: (a) intellectual or ability deficits (which may be both general and specific), and (b) personality· disorders. The intellectual or ability deficits which frequently accompany cerebral dysfunction due to brain damage include impairments in speech and other language functions—both expressive and receptive, perceptual disorders, disturbances of concept formation, sensory deficits and suppressions, and motor deficits—including pareses and plegias. Personality disorders accompanying brain lesions frequently mimic functional (i.e., nonorganic) disturbances and, particularly in children, are manifested by such symptoms as unpredictable personality change, hyperkinesis, depression, distractibility, and erratic aggressivity. Regardless of the number and type of deficit areas studied (an issue to be discussed later), the goals of neuropsychological assessment are to (a) evaluate the current level of behavioral functioning in an individual presumed to be brain damaged, (b) infer the etiologic factors responsible for the dysfunctional behaviors, and (c) recommend rehabilitative treatment or training programs which will have the greatest chance for increasing the individual's overall functional level.

This chapter focuses specifically on issues pertinent to the relationship between neuropsychology and mental retardation. It should be emphasized at the outset that I am convinced that the neuropsychodiagnostic statement "brain damage," as it has been usually applied to mentally retarded persons, has little or no clinical utility. Such a diagnosis is always an inference which rarely can be adequately validated. There is no such thing as either an "organic" or a behavioral syndrome which is unique or pathognomonic to "brain damaged" mentally retarded persons. The diagnostic statement is useless with regard to identifying the medical, educational, psychological, or social intervention necessary for habilitation or rehabilitation. Furthermore, the diagnosis not only fails to provide accurate prognostic information; it also too frequently establishes artificial limitations on opportunities for growth because of the negative social and professional attitudes associated with the term "brain damaged." Neuropsychological study of mental retardation, nevertheless, is not only critical to the understanding of that condition, but is also essential to a truly comprehensive understanding of behavior in general, since all behavior is mediated by the brain. Within that context, this chapter attempts to cover the following issues:What is the meaning of the concept of "brain damage" as it relates to mental retardation? What are the treatment implications of the detection of deficits consequential to actual brain injury in mentally retarded persons? Is there validity in the neuropsychodiagnosis of mentally retarded individuals? Can such diagnoses be accomplished reliably? If so, what are the approaches, and for what purposes?

THE ROLE OF BRAIN-BEHAVIOR RELATIONSHIPS IN UNDERSTAND-ING MENTAL RETARDATION

Etiology and Behavior

Mental retardation can be most aptly considered a clinical syndrome rather than a disease entity. Its definition (Grossman, 1973) depends on behavioral, not organic, symptomatology (i.e., subaverage intelligence and deficits in adaptive behavior) and the time of life during which the behavioral symptoms become manifest (i.e., the developmental period). By some estimates, there are perhaps over 200 specific causes of mental retardation. Some of these (e.g., Tay-Sach's Disease) may have a rather invariable influence on the severity of mental retardation and on life itself. However, most of the etiologic conditions produce mental retardation in varying degrees from profound to mild, *if at all,* depending on a number of factors. These include the extent, locus, and type of brain lession (if any), premorbid ability, at what point the cerebral injury occurs in the developmental sequence (e.g., in utero, at birth, during early or late childhood), and the implementation of early and effective treatment and subsequent training opportunities. Also of great importance are the psychological, familial, and sociocultural environments in which the child develops and is maintained.

It should be abundantly clear that a given etiology does not, in and of itself, determine the ultimate behavioral consequences. But before elaborating further on this point, I would like to discuss some issues related to the causes, classification, and epidemiology of mental retardation.

A Two-Dimensional View of Mental Retardation

Since mental retardation is currently defined in behavioral terms, we may say that the only common feature among all mentally retarded persons is impaired intellectual ability (see Chapter 3). The factors which act to suppress intellectual functioning can be divided into two categories: organic and functional. While the organic factors have their genesis in pathological conditions of the brain, the functional determinants relate to a host of environmental influences, the greatest of which (in terms of frequency) are adverse sociocultural and familial conditions. Further, functional mental retardation traditionally has been considered more optimistically in terms of intellectual potential and learning ability.

Heber (1970) estimated that of the total population of mentally retarded persons, no more than 10 to 20% present *demonstrable* structural pathology of the nervous system. He pointed out that this type of retardation, "in which pathology of the central nervous system is a presenting feature" (p. 4), does not respect socioeconomic, ethnic, or racial boundaries" (i.e., all levels of each are equally represented). Further, from a behavioral standpoint, Heber described this group of mentally retarded persons as generally, *but not always,* having measured IQs below 55 and functioning either as "trainable" or untrainable students in school, or as severely impaired in adaptive behavior in adult life. Clearly, Heber identified this pathological group as the one which constitutes the "excess" of mentally retarded persons to be found at the lower end or the Gaussian (normal curve) distribution of intelligence (Dingman & Tarjan, 1960).

The remaining 80 to 90% of all mentally retarded persons, according to Heber, do not present obvious *gross* cerebral pathology. While the basic cause(s) of this type of retardation is (are) unknown, the primary factors which have been implicated include familial (or inherited) low intelligence (i.e., those cases which fit the normal distribution of intelligence) and/or those adverse conditions which are associated with poverty. Members of this mentally retarded group may not manifest gross brain pathology, but they may nevertheless have central nervous system involvement which cannot be detected with present methods of examination. These persons are described as being in the mild range of retardation and "educable" within their school-age years. As adults, they generally exhibit moderate to mild impairments in adaptive behavior.[1]

It should be noted that this tendency to dichotomize mental retardation into two basic categories has a history of over a hundred years. Further, while the emphases have cycled and recycled with regard to focusing either on what the "organic" retarded group *could not* do, or the "functionally" retarded group *could* do, the "organic" mentally retarded person has historically been perceived as having comparatively limited potential. For example, Seguin (1866/1971) classified mentally retarded individuals into the two categories of *profound* and *superficial* idiocy. Profound idiots were characterized as mentally defective individuals who actually had lesions in the central nervous system (i.e., evident cerebral pathology). Superficial idiots, however, were so classified because in such cases the peripheral nervous system, rather than the brain itself, was considered to be damaged or weakened (i.e., they had defective receptors). This latter group was seen as being prevented from utilizing environmental stimuli to effect the maximum learning and performance of which they might

---

[1] When such persons are not classified as mentally retarded but present perceptual, thinking, and/or emotional problems which relate to academic underachievement, they are considered "learning disabled" or "minimally brain damaged" (see Haywood & Gordon, 1970).

be capable because only weakened or distorted impressions were gained through their impaired senses. Although educational methods for these two types of retarded children were functionally the same, it was principally the latter group for whom Seguin developed his sense training or "physiological" method of education.

The following sampling of diagnostic terms further demonstrates the attempt to view mental retardation as two-dimensional: primary-secondary amentia (Tredgold, 1937); subcultural-pathological (Lewis, 1933); endogenous-exogenous (Strauss & Lehtinen, 1947); nonbrain-injured-brain-injured (Gallagher, 1957); familial-nonfamilial (Doll, 1946); physiologic-pathologic or functional-organic (Tarjan, 1961); mental deficiency-mental retardation (Sarason, 1959); environmentally or culturally deprived, and nonorganic versus organically impaired (Alley, 1969). The two-dimensional view has been fostered primarily because of what we know—or, more accurately, what we do *not* know—about neuropathology of mental retardation.

Neuropathology of Mental Retardation

Neuropathological study of mental retardation (i.e., post-mortem observation) cannot at this time provide clear-cut answers to the question of whether or not all mentally retarded persons so observed had organic brain damage (Malamud, 1964; Warkany & Dignan, 1973), for the following reasons: (a) Even at autopsy, there is no way to determine etiology in many types of observed neuropathology; (b) at autopsy the pathogenesis of the findings is unclear because the end stage of the process is being studied; and (c) the current state of the art, which may change with technological progress, is not sufficiently advanced.

Given these very realistic limitations, the findings from the neuropathology laboratories are astounding. For instance, after performing 282 necropsies of an institutionalized mentally retarded population, Crome (1960) found established syndromes in 32% of the sample and unclassified anomalies in 68% of the cases, some of which had multiple lesions.

In another investigation, which took place over an approximately 14-year period, Malamud (1964) performed consecutive autopsies on 1,410 unselected mentally retarded persons who came from three California hospitals. He found the following prevalence rates for each classification: malformations, 61%; malformations plus destructive processes, 4%; destructive processes, 25.5%; metabolic and degenerative disorders, 5%; neoplastic disorders, 2%; and no definite pathology, 2.5%. While it is to be expected that more severe forms of mental retardation are associated with early death and that individuals with these forms of retardation have a greater tendency to be institutionalized, Malamud's sample included 11% "high-grade defectives." An analysis of the relationship between neuropathological findings and level of intellectual classification revealed that there was a significantly higher ratio of "low- to high-grade defectives" in the group with gross lesions (11.5:1) versus the group with "milder" lesions (6.5:1). Additionally, in the group which had no definite pathology, the ratio of "low- to high-grade defectives" was 2.5:1.

It is clear from Malamud's study that the more severely retarded the population, the more severe and frequent the neuropathological findings. However, it is also quite clear that persons with the milder forms of mental retardation (including individuals in the "borderline" category) are not necessarily without both mild and severe neuropathology. The reverse is equally true for severely retarded persons (i.e., they may or may not demonstrate neuropathology).

In summary, and taking into cognizance the neuropathologist's methodological limitations, it would be frivolous to assume that mental retardation divides itself into two neat, nonoverlapping categories—brain damaged and nonbrain damaged, or "organic" and "functional." The primary point is, as Masland (1958) stated, "brain injury can operate throughout the whole range of [subaverage] intelligence and, in fact, . . . minor degrees of injury are far more common than are the severe and grossly evident ones" (p. 11).

While it appears that the diagnosis of "brain damage" or "nonbrain damage" has depended mostly on psychological data, sociomedical history, and physical neurological examinations, these are at best inferential and perhaps unrelated to the neuropathological evidence. This issue will be returned to and focused on later.

Issues Related to Classification and Epidemiology of Mental Retardation

Like its predecessor (Heber, 1961), the most recent revision of the American Association on Mental Deficiency (AAMD) *Manual on Terminology and Classification in Mental Retardation* (Grossman, 1973) offers two approaches to the classification of mental retardation: biomedical and behavioral (see Chapter 3). One of the major limitations inherent in such a dual approach to classification (and one recognized in both editions of the Manual) is the inability of either approach to predict the other reliably. That is, by knowing the presumed (biomedical) etiology of the disorder, one does not necessarily know how impaired the person is in his intellectual and/or adaptive behavior. Further, as Grossman stated: "Individuals with the same medical diagnosis and the same level of measured intelligence and of adaptive behavior may still differ widely in patterns of ability, in signs and stigmata, and in a variety of characteristics not included in the medical and psychological evaluations used to arrive at classifications" (1973, p. 6).

The issue of individual differences which are likely to be manifest even among persons similarly classified is more properly within the province of *diagnosis*. Leland (1968) warned that classification is not synonymous with diagnosis. Classification is seen as a definitional approach to identifying both the etiological origins of the condition (AAMD Biomedical Classification) and the extent of the impairment (AAMD Behavioral Classification). Further, the purposes of classification are held to include, among other things, "bookkeeping" which will (a) permit understanding of incidence and prevalence of various conditions leading to mental retardation, (b) enable careful research on cause and function (broadly speaking), (c) make possible administrative and program planning, and (d) aid in increasing diagnostic accuracy.

Diagnosis, on the other hand, not only defines the causative factors of the problem, but it also provides information regarding the individual's current level of functioning and (ideally) indicates the treatment or training necessary to modify or improve the person's behavioral level. The purposes of diagnosis, therefore, are more specifically oriented toward the individual mentally retarded person.

The neuropsychologist is keenly interested in classification because the existing classification scheme, in part, predetermines the diagnostic options that are available for comparison with his behavioral data. More importantly, however, the lack of correspondence between the biomedical and behavioral classifications is the primary focus of the discipline of neuropsychology, which is attempting to "elucidate the relations between behavior and the structure and functions of the nervous system" (Benton, 1974, p. 47). For the clinical neuropsychologist, individual diagnosis is important not only for providing a clear understanding of the clinical aspects of the persons under study—including making individual program recommendations—but also for providing the data which will help clarify brain-behavior relationships, thereby facilitating the more general purposes of classification.

Since epidemiology, the study of disease in populations (D. M. Reed, 1972), is to a large extent dependent on classification—(and is, in fact, one of the primary purposes of classification), we should be aware of some of the methodological limitations involved. That the frequency of brain damage in mental retardation is high is supported by the preliminary evidence from the neuropathologist's laboratory. However, specific incidence and prevalence rates of the various neuropathological conditions which can cause mental retardation are at best only *estimates*. There are a number of reasons for this state of affairs.

First, as has been noted, true or accurate etiological diagnoses may depend on more adequate evaluative techniques than are either commonly employed (neuropathological examinations) or than currently exist. For example, Burns (1960) pointed out in his study of behavioral differences between neuropathological types of mentally retarded persons that ". . . a few years ago children with phenylketonuria would have fit into 'familial retardation,' as undoubtedly many undiscovered 'inborn errors of metabolism' now do" (p. 329). Similarly, Tarjan (1961), extolling the advances made in chromosomal research, found Klinefelter's syndrome to be about eight times as great in an institutional sample of mentally retarded individuals as in the general population. He indicated that most of these residents had a prior diagnosis of "idiopathic" mental deficiency.

Second, while the American Association on Mental Deficiency has developed a widely used classification scheme (Grossman, 1973; Heber, 1961), causation is unknown in most cases. Tarjan (1961) estimated that the diagnosis of "undifferentiated" or "familial" is still used with nearly half of the institutionalized retarded population, and that the probability of nonspecific diagnosis is even greater among noninstitutionalized retarded persons. Heber (1970) presented data which support Tarjan's estimates. Of the mentally retarded population which resided in public institutions in 1963, 53.2% were considered clearly nonorganic (35.7% "presumed psychological cause," of which 13.4% were "cultural-familial" and an additional 17.6% were "unclassified"). Additionally, 29.2% were diagnosed as of unknown but organic etiology (23.4% were "unknown prenatal influences," of which 8.3% were labeled "Mongolism," and another 5.9% were classified as "unknown structural reaction"). Heber (1970) made the interesting point that despite a decrease in the percentage of unclassified first admission patients over a 4-year period (1960-1963), and despite the facts that institutional staff constitute a relatively sophisticated diagnostic resource and that mentally retarded persons who are institutionalized tend to be those with more clearly identifiable pathologies, "74.26 percent of the institution population was classified in essentially unknown categories" (p. 31).

Third, the classification schemes used to categorize mentally retarded persons may vary according to the purpose for which such information is gathered (e.g., psychological, medical, sociological, educational). Discussing the epidemiologic approach, D. M. Reed (1972) referred to the enormous difficulties of developing incidence and prevalence rates when classifications vary according to discipline needs.

Another problem related specifically to the classification of mental retardation was noted by Polloway and Payne (1975). They pointed out that etiological classification systems change as a result not only of recent scientific inquiry and thought, but also according to changes in social values and emphases, making obsolete the previous specific etiologic categories. For example, the present AAMD classification no longer includes "cultural-familial" retardation and has eliminated the "borderline retardation" level of measured intelligence. The deletion of the borderline category results in a decrease of 13.6% in the prevalence of mental retardation in the general population, when IQ alone is considered. Thus, it is obvious that the frequency of various pathological conditions related to mental retardation will be influenced by the very definition used to classify the syndrome being studied, as well as by changes in the definitional practices of those reporting the statistical information.

The epidemiologist's job is to accumulate the descriptive data which permit categorization, analysis of consistencies, inferences with regard to causation, and (hopefully) evaluation of the effectiveness of large-scale preventive and therapeutic measures (D. M. Reed, 1972; Sternfeld, 1975). The problems of acquiring accurate and precise incidence and prevalence information—the basic data of epidemiologic study—represent major hurdles for the epidemiologists of mental retardation and render the accuracy of their conclusions suspect.

The neuropsychologist is interested in delineating relationships between brain and behavior. To the extent that given estimates (and we must agree that often these can only be *minimal* estimates) of neuropathology in the mentally retarded population are accurate, adequate support can be offered for continued neuropsychological investigation. Furthermore, the information derived from such study should help to bridge the gap between diagnosis and classification.

Behavioral Correlates of Brain Damage in Mental Retardation

If mental retardation represents a behavioral manifestation of cerebral dysfunction, due to either structural lesions or functional limitations (e.g., consider the neuropathological evidence related to "functional" retardation; also see Haywood & Tapp, 1966; Hebb, 1949), then progress in our understanding of brain-behavior relationships should contribute to a more comprehensive understanding of mental retardation.

Much of what is known today of the behavioral correlates of brain damage is derived from the experimental animal neuropsychology laboratory (also referred to as the field of psychobiology) and from clinical neuropsychological investigations of humans with acquired cerebral lesions (cf., Benton, 1969; Halstead, 1947; Khanna, 1968; Klebanoff, Singer, & Wilensky, 1954; Luria, 1965, 1966a, 1966b, 1973; Meyer & Meyer, 1963; Miller, 1972; Milner & Glickman, 1965; Penfield & Roberts, 1959; Pribram,

1969; Reitan, 1966a, 1968; Reitan & Davison, 1974; Smith & Philippus, 1969). While the goals of these two branches of the discipline of neuropsychology are broadly similar, their methods, limitations, and conclusions vary considerably.

Experimental animal neuropsychology, in seeking to understand the relationships between behavior and the structure and function of the nervous system, has as its techniques the means to induce changes in the nervous systems of its animal subjects by surgical, electrical, or chemical intervention, and to measure objectively the associated behavioral responses. Since precise autopsy and histological information can be made immediately available (by sacrificing the animal), experimental neuropsychologists can also study the effect that environmental manipulation has on the neural structure of the subject's brain. This approach has an additional advantage inasmuch as it can control for pre-experimental experiences of its subjects, and to some extent even for the effects of heredity, through rather sophisticated rearing and breeding procedures.

Clinical neuropsychology, in attempting to define brain-behavior relationships, studies the behavior of humans who are referred because of "accidents of nature." Investigations by clinical neuropsychologists are relegated to indirect, inferential study of the brain (as is the clinical study of neurology for the most part) by measuring specific behaviors of persons with diagnosed brain lesions, comparing them on the same behavioral measures with presumably nonbrain-damaged persons, and relating the differences to what is known of the nature and extent of the brain lesion. This approach is necessarily more inferential than that of the experimental neuropsychologist because complete knowledge of the person's cerebral status is infrequently available and often unobtainable.[2] Typically, the clinical neuropsychologist must depend on other diagnostic techniques (e.g., neurological physical examinations and laboratory studies, neurosurgical evidence, autopsy information) for the probable nature and extent of the cerebral lesion. Furthermore, rarely (if ever) is accurate or reliable information concerning the premorbid status of the brain available to the clinical neuropsychologist.

As Benton (1970b) pointed out, clinical neuropsychology has particular relevance for the study of mental retardation. The experimental neuropsychologists have provided a tremendous amount of information about basic sensory, motor, and perceptual brain processes. However, many important behavioral functions which distinguish mentally retarded from nonmentally retarded persons are distinctly human and simply are not present in animals.

---

[2] Notable progress, however, is being made. For example, Milner's (1965) research on memory, Penfield & Roberts' (1959) work on speech and language functions, and Gazzaniga's (1970) split-brain research.

The most reliable data the clinical neuropsychologist has been able to develop have come from previously "normal" adult patients who have acquired a well-delineated central nervous system disorder. Not until all the specific factors affecting brain-behavior relationships which have thus far been identified (e.g., extent of brain damage, locus, laterality, chronicity, age at acquisition, type of lesion, premorbid ability structure) are controlled experimentally will there be a clear conceptual model of neuropsychology (Birch, 1964; Deutsch & Schumer, 1970; Haywood, 1968; Reitan, 1966a; Ross, 1968; Sarason, 1959; Smith, 1969; Yates, 1954). The existing data are far from definitive, and to apply data from brain-damaged "normal" adults to mentally retarded persons (all of whom manifest their "mental retardation" in childhood as a matter of definition), therefore means that comparisons between the two populations must again be inferential if a generalized model of brain-behavior relationships is to be developed. The more frequent research approaches focusing on "brain damaged" mentally retarded samples involve direct behavioral comparison with "nonorganic" mentally retarded persons of similar age and IQ. Some of the inherent limitations of this procedure will be discussed specifically in the next section. Generally, however, this approach is myopic and falls short of establishing any unified understanding of brain-behavior relationships.

Notable exceptions to the latter generalization are the studies by Benton (1970b) and by Matthews and his colleagues (Matthews, 1974; Matthews & Reitan, 1961, 1962, 1963). Such investigations are advancing our understanding of brain functioning by examining such higher processes as abstraction ability, language functions, and psychomotor and somesthetic skills in mentally retarded subjects, and by attempting to correlate their findings with what is known concerning the structure and functioning of the nervous system. Continued research along these lines by those and other investigators, with additional study of nonretarded samples at various age and IQ levels, should prove fruitful for an increased understanding of the behavioral correlates of brain damage in retarded persons.

PROBLEMS AND ISSUES IN NEUROPSYCHOLOGICAL STUDY OF RETARDED PERSONS

Much of what is known today of the behavioral correlates of brain damage is conflicting. This state of confusion exists in spite of a great deal of research information which has been steadily accumulating since the French physiologist Flourens in 1824 (Halstead, 1947) extirpated given areas of animal brains and observed the corresponding behavioral responses. Since, it is said, "the brain does not function in a chaotic manner" (Yacorzynski,

1965, p. 658) our manner of thinking and our methods may be the responsible forces imposing chaos where order is present.

This would be the most parsimonious explanation in view of the simplistic notions attributed to complex brain functions by both clinicians and researchers, the heated debates over theoretical issues diversely explaining commonly observed events, and the contradictory data evolving from ill-designed experiments using incompatible methodologies on poorly established samples. Perhaps it is time to reevaluate our theories and methods of neuropsychology, with particular emphasis on the issues relating to the study of mentally retarded persons.

Basic Assumptions and the Inferential Process

The study of neuropsychology requires several basic assumptions regarding (a) the nature of the nervous system, (b) the impact that insults to the nervous system have on behavior, and (c) the ability of psychological tests to measure this impact. The first such assumption, which is widely accepted, is that the brain is the principal mediating organ of behavior. The brain receives input stimuli (afferent impulses) from its sensory receptors, prepares itself for activity and sends the stimuli to appropriate areas in the cortex (reticular activating system), interprets the stimuli (perception) and plans its response (association and motor planning), and sends impulses out (efferent impulses) to the musculature of the body for a behavioral (motor) response to the original stimuli. Thus, it is assumed that it is the brain which coordinates the incoming stimuli with the outgoing behavioral response. When behavior is nonadaptive to the environmental stimuli or is relatively ineffectual in response to such stimuli, and we ascertain that the sensory and motor apparatus is operating efficiently, it may be inferred that the brain is dysfunctional. The fact that any of these processes can be affected by experience, attitudes, emotional state (which may itself be a function of complex brain activity; see Pribram, 1969), or structural anomaly complicates the understanding of brain-behavior relations.

In order to study the structure and function of the brain and to relate its integrity to specific behavioral responses in a lawful manner, it must be assumed additionally that all people are similar with regard to the brain's anatomy. While there is some variability among individuals with respect to brain weight and exact anatomical definition, for the most part the structure of the brain is basically the same across the normal human species. Furthermore, it must be assumed that there is functional similarity of the brain among normally behaving people. While this appears to be true, the exact nature of this similarity is unknown, and it is a focus of theoretical debate. Since the brain is the mediating organ of behavior, it can be expected that the behavior of the organism will be affected when it is structurally damaged. At the heart of the theoretical controversy is whether this behavioral alteration is general—and due to the whole brain's response to the insult—or whether it is specifically dependent on which part of the brain has been destroyed.

In either case, neuropsychologists assume that the status of the brain can be determined by evaluating behavior. This is admittedly an inferential process. Nevertheless, to the extent that the manifest behaviors under evaluation adequately represent the diversity of the brain's functioning, the inferences regarding cerebral status may be considered valid.

However, several other factors are involved in evaluating the validity of brain-behavior inferences. In humans, knowledge of the premorbid state of cerebral and/or behavioral function would seem crucial to the determination of brain impairment. Unfortunately, with people, premorbid central nervous system or behavioral references are rarely available because neurological and/or psychological evaluations are typically initiated only for the purpose of identifying the cause of some presenting problem. Even where premorbid status can be inferred from an individual's medical, developmental, educational, and social history, reliability of the information is frequently questionable.

Thus, without direct knowledge of the behavioral or neurological status of the given individual prior to the occurrence of his problem, his behavior can only be compared to that of a nonpathological control or contrast group to determine how deviant it is. This group comparison rests on the aforenoted assumption that behavioral functioning is similar across given groups of people with nonpathological brains—allowing for some individual differences due to the unique interaction between an individual's genetic/biological constitution and the environment in which he develops. Furthermore, since the workings of the brain are influenced by the age of the organism, and perhaps by other factors as well (e.g., sex, socioeconomic status, current residence such as psychiatric institution, hospital, or home), the control-contrast group needs to be selected accordingly.

In sum, therefore, two of the problems which potentially weaken the inferential process are (a) the lack of direct premorbid information regarding the behavioral and neurological status of the person under study, and (b) the adequacy of the comparison group with regard to controlling for important factors which may influence behavior. An additional problem relates to the "nonpathology" of the control group. Since it is a logical impossibility to be able to prove the *nonexistence* of anything, the certainty of the control group's nonpathology is always equivocal. Thus, to facilitate comparing the behavior of a presumed brain-damaged person to that of a nonpathological group, it is imperative that the neuropsychologist establish stringent diagnostic criteria for the selection of his control group.

Other factors relating to the validity of neuropsychological inferences may depend on the type of validity under consideration. For example, *concurrent validity* can be demonstrated if the neuropsychological assessment can independently establish the status of the brain with accuracy consistent with that of other diagnostic methods (e.g., neurological, neuropathological, neurosurgical). However, since this type of validity is intimately associated with the reliability and validity of the other methods, the neuropsychologist will need to be acquainted with them as well. It is possible that, with the understanding of lawful brain-behavior interconnections, neuropsychology could contribute independent diagnostic information to the data gathered from other sources, whose techniques may be less sensitive under certain circumstances. This could result not only in more accurate clinical diagnoses, but also in a better understanding of cerebral structure and function.

To the extent that neuropsychodiagnosis can provide accurate prognoses regarding individual response to treatment or training programs, it also will have *predictive validity*. However, since the empirical determination of predictive validity requires directly measuring the behavioral criteria to be predicted (see Maher, 1963), careful analysis of criterion measures, rather than overdependence on *face validity*, is required to determine just what neuropsychodiagnosis predicts or does not predict.

Finally, the testing instruments used by neuropsychologists must be evaluated carefully. A test can be conceptualized as a method of obtaining a sample of behavior which will enable one to predict its degree of adherence to some criterion in a presumably more efficient manner than that allowed by observation of an individual's entire behavioral repertoire. Therefore, some testing error is expected and can be tolerated for the sake of efficiency. However, too much extraneous error (error variance) can seriously limit the validity of neuropsychological inferences. One major source of such error may be the lack of precision in obtaining the normative data. Standardized tests permit comparisons between the person with presumed brain damage and the control-contrast (or norm) group with regard to possible behavioral differences. They also tend to increase the reliability of any observed differences by objectively defining the operational procedures. However, even with standardized measurements, unreliable test results may be obtained because of the considerable individual variability in test-taking behavior as well as in previous exposure to the test content. Consequently, neuropsychological tests must be differentially sensitive to etiologic conditions beyond that which may relate to specific situational stresses, individual fluxes in motivation, and cultural-experiential backgrounds. It also becomes obvious that such testing instruments must be extensively cross-validated before being considered clinically useful.

Furthermore, the demonstrated concurrent or predictive validity of neuropsychological tests derived from highly controlled empirical research may have to be reexamined with regard to their diagnostic use in a clinical situation. For example, Meehl and Rosen (1955) pointed out that validation studies often establish artificial *base rates* as a result of their sampling procedures. In other words, given two groups of subjects (e.g., braindamaged and nonbrain-damaged) of equal sample size, the probability of correctly classifying a subject from the test results is 50% on the basis of chance alone. The differential sensitivity of the test, therefore, will depend on the distribution of the diagnostic conditions within the population to which the test is being applied. When a test is used clinically, often the base rate is not known. Also, an instrument which distinguishes between two or more groups of subjects at a level of significance acceptable to research standards may not be adequate according to clinical standards.

For example, a test may differentiate a group of persons having a neoplastic brain disease from nonbrain-damaged groups at the .05 level of significance. However, wrongly classifying this type of neurological disorder (false negative) 5% of the time is clearly inadequate clinically and could have dire consequences for the person being evaluated. Therefore, scrutiny of the validating research concerning neuropsychodiagnostic tests and caution in their application to clinical populations are minimal prerequisites for establishing the efficacy of neuropsychological inferences.

Theoretical Approaches and Their Implications

It is axiomatic that to perceive the totality of any given event is humanly impossible. Therefore, a theory-based approach enables the observer to selectively perceive in an orderly and logical fashion. To the extent that science proceeds in successive approximations, if a theory helps in increasing our knowledge, it is maintained. If, to the contrary, our perceptions and ordering of the data do not yield increased clarity and knowledge, then the theory is either refined or discarded (Kuhn, 1970).

Our understanding of brain-behavior relationships has been simultaneously advanced and confused by essentially two competing theoretical orientations: the holistic theory and the localization of function theory. Some 150 years ago, Flourens (1824) concluded from his animal research that, while there were certain parts of the brain which have functions of a rather specific nature, the brain works in a unitary manner, as a single system, with regard to intellectual and all other behavior. This belief that intelligence was an inseparable function of the activity of the entire cerebrum was diametrically opposed to the then-current *Zeitgeist* of Phrenology, which held that specific areas of the brain could be considered centers in which complex forms of mental activity were "localized" (including such faculties as honesty, love for parents, and greed). Since that time, neuropsychological theory has been enmeshed in fervent disagreement. The historical controversy between the "holistic" and "localization of function" schools is well documented elsewhere (cf., Boring, 1950; Halstead, 1947; Head, 1926; Luria, 1973; Stevens, 1971; Yacorzynski, 1965). However, a brief summary may be helpful for appreciating the current implications of the argument with regard to the neuropsychological study of mental retardation.

The scientific search for localized functions in the brain was given impetus by two mid-19th century discoveries. First, Broca in 1861 (Halstead, 1947), upon performing the autopsy of a patient who had aphasia, discovered cortical lesions and softening in the left cerebral hemisphere. Through inference, Broca concluded that the speech center (which consequently bears his name) was located at the base of the third frontal convolution of the left cerebral hemisphere. Then 9 years later, in 1870, Fritsch and Hitzig (Halstead, 1947) electrically explored the dog brain and determined well defined cortical areas of motor functioning. Subsequent to these two discoveries, there ensued a great amount of brain research concerned with localizing sensory, motor, perceptual, language, and other cognitive activities. At the same time, many researchers were generating skepticism regarding the localization of higher mental abilities (e.g., Ferrier, 1886; Goltz, 1881; Loeb, 1902).

Most investigators did not deny the localized nature of sensory and motor functions, but they were not convinced that cognitive behavior could be so finely discerned. Franz (1907, 1915), however, brought into question the localization of even the more basic functions by demonstrating the ability of animals to relearn a lost response following experimental extirpation of areas of their brains. Also, Jackson (see Taylor, 1931-1932), arguing against the complete localization of language, suggested that the occurrence of a behavioral response (e.g., aphasic jargon) following cerebral insult cannot be due to the destroyed tissue. It was argued that since that tissue is no longer functional the behavioral responses which are observed must be attributed to the remaining intact tissue.

Lashley's (1929) principles of "mass action" and "equipotentiality" dealt more serious blows to the localization theory. He was able to demonstrate, by ablating animal brains, that the extent of loss of previously learned habits was a direct result of the amount of tissue (mass) removed, independent of the site of the damage. Furthermore, Lashley held that relearning the lost habit could be achieved because other parts of the brain which were still intact could assume, within limits, the function of the destroyed tissue.[3] Goldstein (1939, 1940) after observing World War I veterans who had sustained head injuries, made another important contribution. Following in the Gestalt tradition, he determined that while the cerebral damage could effect specific losses, depending on the areas involved, "general disturbances" of complex forms of mental activity (e.g., abstract thinking) were common in all the cases studied. Goldstein's conclusion that these general disturbances were likewise a function of brain insult and that they were essentially of no localized significance stimulated an ongoing search for specific qualitative behavioral differences between brain-damaged and nonbrain-damaged persons.

Holistic theorists posit that if the brain is impaired at any cerebral site, for any reason, then the behavioral manifestations should be obvious. Said differently, brain-damaged persons are qualitatively different from nonbrain-damaged persons, and these differences should be behaviorally observable as pathognomonic signs on the basic of *interindividual* comparisons. The tasks of the researcher are to identify the differences, to develop measuring devices which will permit classification of these behavioral differences, and to verify their differential diagnostic usefulness. The clinician is then responsible for selecting those tests which will enable him better to observe his patient in order to determine if the patient's behavior is characteristic or pathognomonic of brain damage—following which, he can recommend appropriate treatment or training programs.

Unsurprisingly, the clinical neuropsychological assessment of persons suspected of having cerebral injury will be guided, in large part, by the theoretical orientation of the clinical—whether or not he is himself aware of it. For example, since an holistic neuropsychologist assumes that the brain operates as a unitary system of complex interconnecting communication pathways, the tests he employs will be largely determined by that assumption. Psychological tests based on the research of Goldstein (e.g., Goldstein-Scheerer impairment test series), Piotrowski (Rorschach organic sign approach), Bender (e.g., Bender Visual-Motor Gestalt Test and Canter Background Interference Procedure Test), and others (see Smith & Philippus, 1969) subscribe to the holistic point of view.

One of the major flaws in the holistic approach—besides its denial of the vast amount of research data supporting the notion of widespread location of cerebral function (see Miller, 1972)—is the nature of the "reversed inference process" which it generates between research and clinical activities. A good example, particularly relevant for neuropsychological assessment of

---

[3] Lashley's work has been criticized (see Birch, 1964; Yacorzynski, 1965), and alternative explanations for mass action and equipotentiality have been offered (Luria, 1969, 1973).

mentally retarded persons, stems from the research of Strauss and his associates (Strauss & Kephart, 1955; Strauss & Lehtinen, 1947). Attempting to extend to children the conceptions derived from Goldstein's work on brain-injured adults, Strauss compared "brain-injured" (exogenous) and "familial" (endogenous) mentally retarded children on a variety of behavioral tasks. He defined the brain-injured child (Strauss & Lehtinen, 1947) as one:

> who before, during, or after birth has received an injury to or suffered from an infection of the brain. As a result of such organic impairment, defects of the neuromotor system may be present or absent; however, such a child may show disturbances in perception, thinking, and emotional behavior, either separately or in combination. (p. 4)

The original definition (which preceded that quoted above) had been operationalized to include three biological criteria for establishing the neurological diagnosis: (a) neurological signs of brain injury, (b) history of the neurological impairment, and (c) no history of mental retardation in the family. "Familial" mentally retarded persons, whose major differential symptomatic characteristic was the absence of demonstrable cerebral insult, were expected to perform on the behavioral tasks in a manner consistent with their mental level and to show relatively intact perceptual, cognitive, and emotional abilities in comparison to "brain-injured" mentally retarded persons.

On the basis of their research, so convinced were Strauss and Lehtinen (1947) of these brain-behavior relationships that they suggested classifying children as "brain injured" even in the absence of the biological criteria if only the behavioral "disturbances" were observed. Thus, what was once an independent variable (brain damage)—used to establish related dependent variables (behavior)—had become, through a reversed inference process, the dependent variable. The obvious result is confusion. As Haywood (1967) pointed out, all of Strauss's behavioral signs "are also prominently associated with severe emotional disturbance, specifically with schizophrenia, acute brain injury, and frequently with primary mental retardation" (p. 4). In other words, because it can be demonstrated that a particular "brain-damaged" group exhibits a behavioral symptom, it does not necessarily hold true that a person who manifests that symptom has a damaged brain. We are beginning to recognize that brain-behavior interconnections are not of a simple isomorphic nature (Benton, 1974).

The strict localization of function approach stipulates that the behavioral effects of brain damage depend mostly on the site of the insult. The fact that all higher mental abilities have not yet been localized is explained by the Russian neuropsychologist Luria (1969), a leading, current proponent of this point of view. Higher mental functions, according to Luria, are a result of developmental learning within a social context and always represent *complex functional systems* based on jointly working zones of the brain cortex: *"Only special analyses of the structure of these functions and those physiological mechanisms by means of which they are realized, permit us to grasp their complex structure and to specify more exactly those factors of which they are composed" (p. 8).*

In other words, since higher mental processes are a complex functional system, more thorough analysis of the units of the system would have to be achieved to localize the brain areas collectively responsible for a given behavior. In response to the "mass action" of Lashley and to Goldstein's "general disturbances" of function, Luria (1969) stated:

> It becomes completely understandable that a higher (mental) function may suffer as a result of the destruction of *any link which is part of the structure of a complex functional system* and, consequently, may be disturbed even when centers differ greatly in location. However, and this is specially important, *when one or another link has been lost, the whole functional system will be disturbed in a particular way,* and symptoms of disturbances of one or another higher [mental] function will have a *completely different structure, depending on the location of the damage.* (pp. 8-9).

One of the major criticisms of this approach is that the degree of localization will depend on how the cerebral site is defined anatomically. Much of the human research relating to localization of higher mental processes has assumed that cerebral geography possesses functional specificity. Studies have compared persons with cerebral lesions in one lobe versus another, right versus left hemispheres, and anterior versus posterior locations. It is known, for example, that each lobe may have its own symptomatology (Smith, 1969). However, lobes of the brain are not functional divisions; rather they are arbitrarily defined gross structures labeled according to the cranial bones they underlie.

Related to this requirement of increased neuroanatomical specificity is the problem of establishing accurate neurological criteria for the site of the injury. In the experimental animal studies, extirpations and ablations, for example, can cause more general cerebral damage than just to the localized areas thought to be under study. This additional injury, which is difficult to assess, can occur because of damage to the circulatory system and because of necrotic processes which may be initiated by surgical intervention. With humans, specific localizing criteria typically are derived from the neurological sciences. The approaches used for establishing neurological criteria will be evaluated shortly, but suffice it to say for now that neurological data supporting specific localization of brain injury are too often inferential and equivocal.

It is primarily because of the criterion problem that the training background of the clinical neuropsychologist should include functional neuroanatomy and neurology in addition to psychometric assessment, psychopathology, and research methodology. He should also become more than superficially knowledgeable about various appropriate treatment and training programs (e.g., special education; rehabilitation approaches which may involve psychiatric care, speech and hearing therapy, physical therapy, and occupational therapy; psychotherapy, and biological therapies). In most cases, the in-depth multidisciplinary experience required for this type of neuropsychological training is not feasible. While participating closely as a member of an interdisciplinary team of specialists is a viable and realistic alternative, it is no substitute for becoming intimately aware of the diagnostic techniques and methodological limitations of colleagues in neurology, allied health fields, and education.

Another limitation of the localization of function approach is the diversity of specialization among its adherents. Most neuropsychologists who ascribe to this school become specialists in the structure of given areas of the brain and/or in their function. In order to construct an integrated conceptual understanding of brain-behavior interaction, the specialists on the lobes of the brain (or more specific neuroanatomical sites) will have to begin relating to the functional specialists who are studying such processes as biological intelligence, language, abstract thinking, memory, perception, vision, audition, somesthesia and the other senses, and motor and psychomotor functioning. Otherwise, proponents of the localization of function point of view will be as myopic and noncontributory to developing a comprehensive neuropsychological theory as are their holistic protagonists.

Furthermore, the localization neuropsychologists will continue to be criticized correctly by the Gestaltists, who opine that the total is more than the sum of its part. This is particularly relevant with regard to the research data that have accrued regarding characteristics (in addition to location) of cerebral insult which affect behavioral functioning. For example, the type of insult (e.g., neoplastic disease, cerebral vascular disease, congenital malformations, head trauma) will relate not only to the neurological sequelae but also to their behavioral consequences (see Reitan & Davison, 1974). Obviously, the more extensive the damage, the greater the behavioral disturbances expected (although exceptions are not unknown; see Hebb, 1939; Matarazzo, 1972). Also laterality, acuteness of onset, age and developmental stage at acquisition of the brain damage, and length of time between onset and psychological examination have been shown to exert certain influences on the behavioral correlates of brain lesions (Birch, 1964; Corah, Anthony, Painter, Stern, & Thurston, 1965; Deutsch & Schumer, 1970; Eisenberg, 1964; Graham, Ernshart, Thurston & Craft, 1962; Haywood, 1968; H.B.C. Reed, 1968; Reitan, 1966a; Sarason & Doris, 1969; Smith, 1969; Teuber & Rudel, 1962).

The clinical neuropsychological assessment approach by those who are theoretically oriented toward the localization-of-function school must provide a comprehensive battery of tests to ensure that all functional areas of the brain are adequately assessed. Additionally, they will perform functional *intraindividual* comparisons to achieve insight regarding the cerebral location of the impairment. For instance, they may compare the functioning of the right side of the body with the left (to determine in which cerebral hemisphere the lesion is located); expressive versus receptive language functions (anterior versus posterior lesion); motor versus tactile, auditory, or visual senses (frontal versus parietal, temporal, or occipital lobes, respectively). Some of the psychological tests and procedures which have evolved from this point of view include The Illinois Test of Psycholinguistic Abilities (see Bateman, 1964), pattern analyses of the Wechsler intelligence scales (see, Klove, 1974; Matarazzo, 1972), Halstead's Neuropsychological Battery (Halstead; 1947) and its modifications by Reitan (1966a) and others (see, Reitan & Davison, 1974, especially the chapter by Matthews regarding neuropsychological testing of mentally retarded persons), and the Laboratory Method developed by L'Abate (1968).

It is clear that the brain is a complex organ which currently is incompletely understood from anatomical, neuropathological, and functional perspectives. The two theoretical approaches discussed above, which have dominated neuropsychological inquiry, have demonstrated a great amount of heuristic value and have produced a tremendous amount of empirical data. It is widely accepted that brain damage can, and often does, produce impairment of general intelligence as well as of other specific higher mental functions which depend on the location of the cerebral injury. However, too much is known regarding the other characteristics of neurological lesions which influence behavior to accept the primacy of one theoretical approach over the other. Both approaches possess inherent limitations which prevent an integrated understanding of behavior as it relates to the nature and function of the nervous system.

With regard to mental retardation, perhaps what is needed is an alternative way of viewing brain-behavior relationships. Since, by definition, mental retardation occurs during the developmental period, it would be logical to apply a developmental model to neuropsychology (Birch & Lefford, 1964; Luria, 1963; Ross, 1968). Here the emphasis would be on the interdependent stages of development of both nervous system and behavior. The interference which specific types of brain damage and their anatomical foci exert on cortical and functional differentiation and integration could become the focus of neuropsychological study. From the behavioral side, it would appear to be particularly fruitful to explore the neuropsychological dimensions of Piaget's approach to cognitive development. Also, since a developmental neuropsychology would include all stages of life, this model may facilitate the incorporation of the current differences existing in the clinical neuropsychological research findings between children and adults, and provide a better framework for understanding the process of aging.

Neuropsychological assessments of retarded individuals based on both the holistic and localization of function approaches are seriously inadequate. The theoretical debates and the ensuing contradictory and confusing research results—as much as lack of understanding regarding the highly specific nature of brain-behavior interdependence—probably are significantly responsible for the rather simplistic notions and tests many psychologists employ in confronting diagnostic questions regarding brain damage in mentally retarded persons. But, regardless of how complex the issues are, the application of misconceptions can hardly contribute clarity. Psychologists must become more aware of the influence exerted by their explicit or implicit theories concerning brain-behavior relationships on (a) the selection of their psychometric instruments, (b) the clinical inferences they make in interpreting their assessment data, and (c) the recommendations they offer to solve the problems they identify.

Given the enormous complexity of the brain, it is apparent that single tests cannot adequately encompass a representative sample of brain functions. Also, because in the case of cerebral insult it is the remaining intact brain tissue that is responsible for the observed responses (adaptive and maladaptive), behavioral profiles of both weaknesses and strengths are required to understand the alterations among behavioral relationships caused by brain damage. Thus, specific tests must be used in conjunction with other more general instruments to permit at least minimally adequate neuropsychological inferences. The Halstead-Reitan Neurological Test Battery currently represents the most sophisticated and comprehensive psychometric approach to the study of brain-behavior relationships in mentally retarded persons (Matthews, 1974; Reitan, 1966a). However, Haywood (1967) suggested that the following procedures need to be employed by the psychologist before rendering a diagnosis:

> Assessment of intellectual ability using *both* verbal and non-verbal tests; assessment of social functioning, using a measure like the Vineland Social Maturity Scale; assessment of

neuropsychological functions, using something like the Halstead-Reitan neuropsychological procedures that have clear standardized norms; further assessment of perceptual functioning, using instruments such as the Kephart tests, the Frostig tests, and consultation with a neurologist and/or specialist in the particular area of functioning which is thought to be deficient; educational assessment using standardized tests of educational achievement, and in particular using such diagnostic reading tests as the Durrell Analysis of Reading Difficulty and the Triggs Reading Survey; sensory examination to test for deficiencies in vision and hearing; personality assessment involving the use of clinical interviews and standardized instruments for personality diagnosis. (pp. 11-12)

The chances of overlooking subtle behavioral effects of brain damage will be diminished significantly with such an exhaustive diagnostic survey. In addition, it makes possible the development of a behavioral profile of strengths and weakness in basic abilities and learning achievement to be used for recommending specific treatment and/or training. Such a profile could also be used to investigate brain-behavior relationships by considering it a baseline reference against which to compare behavioral gains made by one or another treatment or training program.

Validity of Neuropsychological Research in Mental Retardation

Research on the behavioral correlates of cerebral insult in mental retardation generally has been of the post-hoc type (Maher, 1963). Because most "brain-damaged" mentally retarded persons acquire their neurologic status from genetic, intrauterine, or perinatal influences, it is not possible to assess either their cerebral or behavioral status prior to the injury. Thus, neuropsychological studies of such retarded individuals necessarily occur some time after the injury. The experimental paradigm most often used has involved two groups of retarded subjects—selected on the basis of presumed etiology (e.g., "organic" versus "cultural-familial"), administering behavioral tasks to each, statistically measuring the group differences, and drawing conclusions—usually based on the a priori theoretical assumptions of the investigator regarding brain-behavior relationships. Each aspect of this research process is open to criticism and has contributed significantly to our confusion in understanding the neuropsychology of mental retardation. Since the measuring devices used for, and the diagnostic inferences drawn from, the clinical neuropsychological assessment of mentally retarded persons are based on such research, it is important to evaluate the validity of the methods employed.

Etiologic classifications. The classifications of "brain-damaged" and "cultural-familial" are themselves only general terms that include a variety of etiologic conditions. For example, the "brain-damaged" group may include subjects whose injury was caused by birth trauma, unknown congenital encephalopathy, infections, intoxicants, closed head injuries sustained postnatally, neoplasms, prematurity, and various unknown or uncertain circumstances. Also, as previously noted, it is apparent that in addition to the type of the lesion, such important factors as the extent of the injury, its locus, laterality, chronicity, suddenness of onset, velocity of progression, the person's age and developmental stage at acquisition, and his premorbid ability structure all vary unsystematically within this group. Even if the "brain-damaged" group were constituted to be very homogeneous with regard to the AAMD Biomedical Classification, it is obvious that these other factors would greatly affect the variability of the behavioral correlates. For example, it is impossible without much supplemental information, to characterize *behaviorally* a specific child who has sustained a closed head trauma or who has ingested lead-based paint, much less an infant whose condition has been diagnosed as being due to "unknown etiology with structural reactions manifest."

An example of the possible effects of combining heterogeneous groups of adults with cerebral lesions has been offered by Reitan (1955). In a study comparing individuals with left and right cerebral damage as to their scores on the Wechsler-Bellevue Intelligence Scale, he found that of the 11 subtests in this scale, subjects with lesions of the right cerebral hemisphere obtained their *second lowest* mean score on Block Design—a measure considered sensitive to brain injury. However, those with left cerebral lesions achieved their *next-to-highest* mean score on the Block Design subtest. On the basis of these findings, it would be expected that if these two groups were to be combined into a single "brain-damaged" sample, their overall performance on Block Design would appear as an average score in the middle of the subtest distribution, with a relatively large standard deviation. Gallagher (1957) noted this *cancellation effect* and consequently did not rely on gross group averages (the approach most often reported in the research literature) to compare his "brain-injured" and "nonbrain-injured" mentally retarded subjects. Instead, Gallagher analyzed his data by ranking all his subjects on the performance measures in order to get an accurate picture of the score distributions in the groups.

While the "cultural-familial" retarded group is typically more homogeneous, these persons may still vary considerably in several ways: proven mental retardation in the nuclear family, amount of sociocultural and environmental deprivation, and medical problems other than those that are assumed to affect brain structures. Additionally, in a comprehensive review of the literature comparing concept formation-abstract thinking and learning between "brain-damaged" and "cultural-familial" mentally retarded persons, Gordon (1972) found that all the studies were of institutionalized persons. Institutionalization frequently represents an environmentally depriving situation that affects intellectual functioning (Badt, 1958; Sarason & Doris, 1969; Zigler, 1962, 1967). Since preinstitutional environments were not formally evaluated and/or systematically controlled in most of the studies reviewed, it is not only possible but also quite probable that the mental retardation observed in the research subjects was multiply determined.

Furthermore, the earlier-reported results of the neuropathological and epidemiological studies, the effect early experience can have on morphological changes within the nervous system (Haywood & Tapp, 1966), and the multitude of diverse factors which have been associated with the prenatal and early postnatal development of culturally deprived infants (Kennedy, 1968), point to the probability that the "nonbrain-damaged" mentally retarded residents would possess more neurological deficits than expected. Indeed, "cultural-familial" mentally retarded persons are often found to manifest neurological signs which are not dissimilar to those of their "brain-damaged" peers (Benda, 1944; Benton, 1955, 1959, 1964; Feldman, 1953; Reitan, 1966a; Yakovlev & Farrel, 1941). Taking into consideration both the heterogeneity of the "brain damaged" and "cultural-familial" groups and the possible overlap of etiologic factors among them, it is not surprising to find that large intragroup differences obfuscate intergroup comparisons.

Another major limitation in this area of research stems from the individualized and often either vague or nonexistent operational definitions assigned to the terms "brain damage" and "cultural-familial" by the various investigators. It is difficult, and at times impossible, to codify the results from the various projects and to arrive at valid general conclusions concerning brain-behavior associations when the subject classifications are not comparable across the individual studies. It is as if the researchers had a blind and naive faith in the holistic neuropsychological theory and operated under the assumption that, since a "brain-damaged" mentally retarded person has a damaged brain, he should behave in "organic" ways which essentially are inferior to those of his "cultural-familial" peers. Further, he should thus behave regardless of the nature or extent of the damage or the original criteria used to establish the etiologic classification. This overly simplistic notion of brain function has not contributed very much to our conceptual understanding of brain-behavior relationships (actually it has helped confuse the issues), nor has it or is it likely to discover the "critical" factors or criteria it seeks (Reitan, 1974) which will improve the diagnostic value of neuropsychological assessment.

Differential diagnostic criteria. In addition to the idiosyncratic terms and their associated definitions (when present), further confusion is created by the varying methods used to differentiate the two groups of mentally retarded subjects. The diagnoses have been based on a variety of techniques, ranging in quality from complete and thorough multidisciplinary examinations (physical, neurological, biochemical, chromosomal, and physiological laboratory tests—in addition to psychological, social, developmental, anthropometric, and educational evaluation) to diagnostic classifications by a single mental ,health professional who may base his findings on cursory examinations and inadequate medical, developmental, and/or social histories. The lack of importance accorded to classification by some researchers is indicated by their failure to report even the diagnostic method employed in selecting their subjects. When one subject group (i.e., the "cultural-familial") is primarily determined on the basis of *absence* of demonstrable brain damage, then what goes undetected as a result of poor diagnostic criteria may add to the lack of distinction between the groups and, moreover, to fallacious conclusions.

Since neuropsychology has as its goal the understanding of the *relationships* between brain and behavior, it matters little whether the dependent variable under immediate study is the brain or behavior. For a complete understanding of the nature of the relationship at one time or another, each must serve independently to predict the other. More critical is the need for both variables to be explicitly defined and measured. As previously mentioned, experimental neuropsychologists can often control the precise nature and extent of the cerebral lesion against which to correlate the animal subject's altered behavior. Furthermore, by reversing the independent and dependent variables, they may be able to determine the effect of experiential manipulation on their subjects' brains. However, for clinical neuropsychologists working with human beings, such precision usually is not feasible. Much more typical for clinical neuropsychology is the attempt to relate observable and measurable behavior to existing cerebral impairment. Since it is known that the nature and extent of the brain damage (independent variables) will affect the behavioral consequences (dependent variables), how is information regarding the interrelationship of these variables obtained?

The most obvious method of acquiring *direct* information concerning the cerebral status of an individual is through immediate observation. Neurosurgeons often have the opportunity to view directly the cortical structures and to see the lesion first hand. Thus, they frequently may be able to provide specific information with regard to type, extent, and locus of the cerebral impairment. However, neurosurgery is not the treatment of choice for many types of central nervous system disorders. Even when it is, in many cases, the patient cannot provide valid responses for the prior neuropsychological assessment because of such factors as physical discomfort, fear, high anxiety, or varying states of unconsciousness. Sometimes, as in the instance of emergency surgery, there is little time available for testing prior to the operation. When the patient can be given a reliable neuropsychological evaluation, neurosurgical evidence may offer very rewarding criterion data against which to compare the behavioral measures.

However, at least three problems have been well documented regarding neurosurgical findings. First, specific localization of cerebral structures is not always possible because of the individual variability and condition of the brain. Second, neurosurgery infrequently involves the entire cerebrum. (Having found one lesion, the neurosurgeon may not explore for others.) Third, the neurosurgeon's diagnosis is not always supported by other criteria. For example, Reitan (1966a) reported a case where the neurosurgeon removed what he diagnosed as a neoplasm (glioma), but histological examination of the tissue failed to support that diagnosis. Reitan went on to make the point that there have been several similar uncorroborated clinical diagnoses in patients he evaluated. While such patients could not be included in his research as subjects with non-neoplastic diseases, neither could they be included with confidence as members of a group with confirmed neoplasms.

Another method of directly observing a brain lesion is by postmortem examination. But comparing neuropsychological data with pathology reports also can occasionally lead to spurious results. Due to the cooperative and attentional requirements of the testing situation, there is usually a fairly large time lapse between psychological assessment and death. Consequently, the cause of death may be completely unrelated to the neuropsychological test findings or, if there is a relationship, the nature of the lesion may have changed over time (i.e., it may have gotten progressively worse). Thus, the brain-behavior principles inferred from such direct but inexact criterion information would be inaccurate. Furthermore, retrospective neuropsychological analysis based on pathologic examination of death tissue is risky because the pathologist cannot provide information regarding pathogenesis of the disorder if he studies only the end stage of the process. Finally, the amount of postmortem neuropathology found in patients who had in life manifested neither neurological nor behavioral symptoms of such pathology is high. Unless autopsy data from appropriate control groups become available, postmortem criteria of the behavioral correlates of brain damage must remain tentative.

The *indirect* methods of establishing differential diagnostic criteria for use in clinical neuropsychological research rely mostly on the diagnostic methods of neurologists (see Kennedy & Ramirez, 1964). The neurologist attempts to combine the data he gathers from a variety of sources (e.g., history, physical examination, and special laboratory tests and procedures such as electroencephalography and contrast studies) in order to establish a diagnosis. The adequacy of this inferential approach depends on the validity of the clinical methods used, the nature of the patient and his symptomatology, and the clinical experience of the neurologist. Since uncertainties in each aspect of the inferential process can weaken the certainty of the diagnostic conclusions, there are serious implications when such conclusions are used as criteria for neuropsychological study.

In evaluating the efficacy of the neurological diagnostic process, it should be noted that the neurologist usually cannot specify prior to his examination exactly what methods he will use or what their relative value will be. The diagnostic approach is not standardized, and his choice of methods depends on the information he receives from each of the prior methods employed in the course of the examination. Furthermore, his observational approach essentially is oriented toward the "all-or-none" phenomenon (i.e., the response is either normal or abnormal). Whenever measurements are taken, they are subjectively interpreted and reported.

Additional tests which the neurologist may request are also subjectively evaluated, although in cases of demonstrable gross brain abnormality, the interjudge reliability can be high. These additional tests are usually of diagnostic value only for specific types of cerebral damage, and because they may involve certain risks to the patient (except for the electroencephalogram and skull X-ray), they may be requested only after the neurologist has determined that the worth of the additional diagnostic information warrants the risks and discomfort involved for his patient. Thus, not only are neurological examinations not standardized, but those methods which could permit more definitive diagnostic inferences often are potentially too dangerous to the patient to be performed routinely.

For purposes of establishing a neurological diagnosis of brain damage in mentally retarded persons, the medical and developmental history, physical neurological examination, electroencephalogram (EEG), and skull X-rays are the most common techniques employed. With these nonintrusive methods, the neurologist may be able to detect a cortical lesion, particularly if it is acute, progressive, focal, or lateralized to one side of the body, and if it affects the motor or sensory cortex. However, very few mentally retarded persons who are chosen for either neuropsychological research or clinical study possess such disorders of the nervous system. Their brain damage, when it can be documented, tends to be chronic, static, and diffuse, and to interfere with higher mental functions more than with specific sensory or motor functions on either side of the body. Rarely are the more intrusive measures—such as pneumoencephalograms or anigiograms—requested by the neurologist because in most cases the nature of the presenting problem (i.e., mental retardation) does not warrant exposing the patient to such aversive procedures.

Too often, then, the neurologist cannot offer unequivocal support for the diagnosis of brain damage in mentally retarded persons, and he relies heavily on data from the patient's history when the physical examination and laboratory studies are unrevealing. Even when some of his diagnostic findings are suggestive (as opposed to pathognomonic) of brain injury, they may lack high interjudge reliability and differential diagnostic validity. For example, Kennedy and Ramirez (1964) reported that on the basis of EEG tracings, "depending on one's definition of normal, 'abnormalities' have been found in 15 to 40 percent of normal children" (p. 16).

It would, of course, be inaccurate to conclude that neurology has little to offer by way of criterion information for neuropsychological study of mentally retarded persons. What is being suggested, however, is that the diagnostic methods and inferential process of neurology are of variable validity; and it is important to establish under what conditions and with what degree of confidence neurologic evidence may comprise acceptable criteria for establishing brain-behavior relationships.

While the establishment of neurologic evidence of cerebral dysfunction is important to the clinical neuropsychological study of mental retardation, perhaps of equal importance is the problem of neurologically determining that no brain damage exists. If the neurological methods for providing criterion information are nonstandardized, sometimes unreliable, and frequently of questionable validity with the retarded population, then inferential conclusions based on *negative* neurological findings are clearly untenable. Yet, the "cultural-familial" mentally retarded group is established in just this fashion when the results of neurological assessment are used as differential criteria for selecting subject samples.

When neurological criteria are not specifically used, then the most frequent criteria reportedly employed to select "brain-damaged" and "cultural-familial" mentally retarded subjects are hospital diagnoses. The general unreliability of this classification procedure is notorious, and will not be further discussed here. However, one aspect of the data that are frequently utilized to establish hospital diagnoses is particularly important and may help explain why any differences between the two retarded groups have been found.

Since the diagnosis of "mental retardation" relates to impaired intellectual and adaptive functioning, it is safe to assume that the label rather invariably has been applied on the basis of at least a psychological evaluation. Consequently, hospital diagnoses must, in part, rely on the behavioral data obtained by the psychologist. However, one of the requirements of establishing valid relationships between two events is that they both be defined independently (Maher, 1963). Clearly, when the criteria establishing the independent variable (brain damage) are also used to measure the dependent variable (behavior), whatever relationship exists may have nothing whatsoever to do with etiology. Gordon (1972) examined this hypothesis by reclassifying the same group of subjects according to three major classes of criteria: (a) neurological diagnoses (established on the basis of extensive medical and neurological examination); (b) neuropsychological diagnoses (two experienced child clinical neuropsychologists interpreted the Halstead-Reitan Battery for dichotomous classification without knowledge of the medical diagnoses); and (c) dual screening (those subjects who were classified the same by both medical and neuropsychological diagnoses) and comparing the resultant "brain-damaged" and "nonbrain-damaged" groups on behavioral measures of verbal abstracting and verbal learning.

Gordon found that the differential behavioral performances between the two diagnostic groups were predicted best by the neuropsychological classification (e.g., diagnosis of "organicity"), second best by the dual screening approach, and least well by medical diagnoses. He concluded that behavioral classification of cerebral status is a better predictor of overt behavior than are neurological diagnoses, even when the latter are well documented independently of behavioral criteria. This would be particularly true if the subjects in the brain-damaged ("organic") group were heterogeneous with regard to their neurological diagnoses.

Confusion between the *fact* of "brain damage" (i.e., structural impairment of cerebral tissue) and the *concept* of "organicity" (i.e., a behavioral syndrome frequently found to be associated with brain-damaged persons—see Dunn, 1968; Strauss & Lehtinen, 1947) may relate to the lack of consistency in the research literature on brain-behavior relationships. These two terms are *not* synonymous. "Brain damage" needs to be determined on the basis of nonbehavioral neurological evidence. The meaning of the concept for neuropsychological research may be limited unless the multidimensional nature of the structural impairment can be determined. "Organicity," however, may be caused by *some* kinds of brain damage, but not by others according to Birch (1964). But, as Maher (1963) stated: "For accurate inferences to be drawn, it is necessary not only that the relationship between the etiological factor and the response be empirically established, but that it be a relationship not also found between the response and some other etiological factor" (p. 240).

Groups of children with differing etiologic diagnoses have been observed to manifest "organic" behavior (Haywood, 1967). Thus, "organicity" can be observed and described by psychologists, but it does not necessarily involve structural brain damage and certainly not all types of structural impairment. Consequently, the extent to which the behavioral syndrome of "organicity" is used to establish hospital diagnoses may determine the degree of behavioral differences found between "brain-damaged" and "cultural-familial" mentally retarded groups in the reported research.

What is required of neuropsychological research with mentally retarded persons (and, indeed, with all "brain-damaged" populations) is complete and unambiguous specification of the diagnostic criteria used to classify the groups under study. Not until this is accomplished can the results of such investigations be adequately evaluated in order to develop a clear understanding of brain-behavior relationships.

Diversity of behavioral measures. Another factor that contributes to general confusion in this area of research is the variety of tasks used to measure what is presumably the same brain function. As Teuber and Rudel (1962) showed, the *nature* of the task and the *age* of the subject at the time the task is presented will determine the nature of the deficit observed or not observed. This should be kept in mind when researchers make the theoretical jump in their discussions from highly specific operational definitions of dependent variables to indiscriminant or global use of terms referring to the supposed underlying (and static) abilities or traits which are assumed to differentiate "brain-damaged" from "cultural-familial" mentally retarded individuals.

Two other studies support Teuber and Rudel's assertion concerning the dynamic nature of various indices of the neurological and behavioral impairment associated with brain damage. Graham et al. (1962) investigated the effects of perinatal anoxia on subsequent behavior and found that at age 3, the anoxic children scored significantly below their controls on all tests of cognitive function, as well as demonstrating significantly more positive and "suggestive" neurological signs. Further, there were no group differences on impairment in perceptual-motor functions. When these same children were evaluated four years later at age 7 (Corah et al., 1965), the anoxic children were no longer significantly deficient in general intelligence (although they were still poorer in vocabulary performance compared to the control group), and they were no longer demonstrating more signs of neurological impairment. However, the anoxic group then showed relative deficits in perceptual-motor performance and attention.

It is obvious from these studies that a deficit, if observed at all, may be manifested in different ways at different ages. If a lucid understanding of brain-behavior associations is to be achieved, it will be necessary for all investigators to use a uniform battery of standardized behavioral measures which have norms established on the basis of at least chronological age and IQ. This conclusion is directly relevant to research on the behavioral differences between "brain-damaged" and "cultural-familial" retarded persons, where confusing and sometimes conflicting findings of various studies result from failure to consider the different subject and task characteristics.

PURPOSES OF NEUROPSYCHOLOGICAL ASSESSMENT IN MENTAL RETARDATION

No assessment procedure is performed in a vacuum. It is always initiated by and oriented toward answering a set of questions. As earlier outlined, the purposes of clinical neuropsychological assessment, in general, are to evaluate and describe the current behavioral status of an individual presumed to be brain damaged, to infer the etiologic factors responsible for any dysfunctional behaviors, and to recommend appropriate rehabilitative treatment or training programs. The relative values of these goals, specifically with regard to mentally retarded persons, are particularly important to assess in view of the many research problems which have been identified.

Neurological Labeling

A neuropsychological assessment which leads to a neurological label of "brain damage," especially when based on either a single test or pathognomic signs approach, has limited utility as it is typically applied. The holistic neuropsychological concept of the "organic" behavioral syndrome in children (e.g., distractability, hyperkinesis, concrete thinking, and perceptual disorders) has not been supported as representing either a general symptom complex for all "brain-damage" groups or even as being pathognomic for some. Children with different etiologies have been known to manifest similar behavioral patterns. Just as important is the fact that children who do not manifest the "organic" syndrome do not necessarily have unimpaired brains. Many children with cerebral pathology display remarkably different behavior, including hypoactivity and age-appropriate attentional, conceptual, and perceptual skills. Furthermore, the people classified as " brain-damaged mentally retarded" represent a heterogeneous etiologic group; and it must be repeated that their behaviors cannot be generally described or predicted without more specific knowledge about (a) the nature of the lesion (e.g., type, locus, extent, laterality, chronicity, suddenness of onset, and rate of change), and (b) the brain-damaged person (e.g., premorbid ability, age, and developmental stage at acquisition of the lesion and at the time of evaluation). Even when neuropsychological assessment points to a diagnosis of "brain damage," convincing confirmation may be unavailable because of the frequent lack of unequivocal independent neurological criteria for mentally retarded individuals.

With regard to treatment implications, Ross (1968) refers to the "Rumpelstiltskin fixation " in clinical diagnostic practice. The search for *the* cause (i.e., the name of the "ill-tempered dwarf"), in the hope that by finding it the problem can be resolved, is not so relevant for mental retardation as it might be for other types of problems. Mental retardation is a behavioral syndrome, not a disease entity. Certainly, when a retarded person is physically sick, diagnostic procedures should be employed to identify the problem for appropriate medical resolution. However, most retarded individuals do not suffer from an acute and/ or progressively deteriorating neurological disorder which must be diagnosed and treated. They suffer from intellectual deficits and consequent learning problems for which neurology has no curative treatment.

In actuality, the application of neurological labels such as "brain damage " to some mentally retarded people has had a rather *antitherapeutic* effect. The implication of the label is that such a person could never exceed his current level of performance because of permanent structural limitations in the brain. Currently, there is a lack of consistent research support for the notion of a general limitation in learning or intellectual potential among "brain-damaged" mentally retarded persons compared to their "cultural familiar" peers (Gordon, 1972). Thus, the danger in labeling a retarded child as "brain damaged" is that unwarranted pessimistic attitudes are generated, which can lead in a "self-fulfilling" manner to limited educational, vocational, and social development (Gordon, 1975).

Nevertheless, neurological labeling may have considerable clinical and research value under certain conditions. For example, if a mentally retarded child's cognitive or affective abilities should begin to deteriorate, early determination of the cause of the behavioral decline would be critical. In this situation, the question of structural brain damage may have medical- surgical significance, warranting neuropsychological inquiry to help the multidisciplinary team arrive at an etiologic understanding of the person's altered behavior. However, since the behavioral correlates of cerebral injury are so varied, an extensive battery of tests is required to ensure that adequate samples of behaviors are assessed before a diagnostic opinion is rendered (see, Haywood, 1967). Such a battery should be designed to evaluate not only the general intellectual and ability deficits frequently found in mentally retarded individuals with brain lesions, but also the total range of specific behavioral alterations which have been demonstrated empirically to relate to impaired cerebral functioning. Without such comprehensiveness, a false negative diagnosis (i.e.,"no brain damage") may be the result of a lack of appropriate and reliable assessment data, which could lead to a time lag and irreversible impairment before the true cause of the child's problem surfaces.

Furthermore, it is obvious that the greater the degree of specificity that the neuropsychologist can offer about the type and nature of the lesion, the more valuable will be his diagnostic contribution. Consequently, the test battery should permit both *inter*individual and *intra*individual comparisons in order to facilitate the analysis of any differential patterns of behavioral funtion and dysfunction which may be related to the lesion. Occasionally (but rarely), the neuropsychodiagnosis of "brain damage" without further specification may have some value beyond that which is available from other diagnostic sources. It certainly would have value if the psychologist were the initial professional person contacted concerning an acute and/or progressively deteriorating behavioral problem, inasmuch as appropriate referrals and early intervention could then be initiated. To the extent that accurate neurological classification can be independently derived from neuropsychological assessment, our understanding of behavior as it relates to pathological conditions of the brain will have been demonstrated.

Educational Prescriptions

While neurological labeling has some value under the limited conditions described above, there is no empirical evidence demonstrating the differential effectiveness of educational programs specifically designed for "brain-damaged" mentally retarded children when compared to their "nonbrain-damaged" peers (see, Dunn, 1968; Gordon, 1972; Johnson, 1968). In general, the traditional educational philosophy of emphasizing clinical symptomatology for class placement (e.g., mental retardation, brain damage, emotional disturbance, physical or sensory handicap) is waning (Dybwad, 1975; Haywood & Gordon, 1970). Homogeneous grouping of children according to diagnostic classification for teaching purposes simply has not proved to be efficacious. Implicit in this unitary or holistic approach is the notion that all children who share the same general descriptive diagnosis are equivalent in their learning abilities and disabilities. This assumption is untenable in view of the often arbitrary nature of the classification criteria established by public educational systems. As Blanco (1972) queried, "Although many children have been classified (by school psychologists), how many have been heldped?" (p. 3) Furthermore, as has been repeatedly emphasized above, it is just as invalid to expect that all children with a given diagnosis (e.g.,"brain-damage") possess similar intellectual and behavioral characteristics as it is to expect that all children who are not so diagnosed are alike.

Reitan (1964, 1966b) offered some very suggestive evidence that if a child's learning problem is caused by damage in certain cortical areas, differential teaching strategies are required to educate him successfully.

However, most "brain-damaged" mentally retarded children do not possess such highly specific lesions. Responding to the lack of behavioral consistency among retarded children classified as brain damaged, Gallagher (1957) questioned the practical usefulness of etiologic diagnosis and emphasized the need to study the individual child within a behavioral context. He pointed out that in his comprehensive investigation:

> The distribution of cases, even where there were significant differences between groups, showed that many of the brain-injured children did not have the unfavorable characteristics that might be assigned to them as a group. Educational provisions made for brain-injured children on the basis of such overall group differences would not be any more applicable to some brain-injured children than they would be to the familial children. . . . To ask the question another way: Does the educator not gain more information from the fact that the child is perceptually disturbed then from the fact that he is brain-injured? (pp. 68-69)

There is some evidence that special education teachers agree with Gallagher. In a study reported by Mackie, Williams, and Dunn (1960), 150 "superior" teachers of mentally retarded children were asked to rank in order of importance a list of 100 competencies needed by teachers of mentally retarded students. The results showed that the ability to recognize the individual differences of each retarded pupil, the ability to provide a flexible, individual curriculum, and the ability to interpret the behavior of such pupils in terms of physical, psychological, and environmental factors were rated as "very important" (rank orders of 1, 4, and 5, respectively). However, having knowledge of the clinical types of mental retardation and the ability to apply the Strauss technique (Strauss & Lehtinen, 1947) ranked 77th and 94th in importance of competencies needed. Therefore, according to these "superior" special teachers, the mentally retarded student needs to be recognized as a whole and unique person, and educational programming must take into account his individual pattern of behaviors.

Thus, the educational value of neuropsychological assessment of mentally retarded children resides more often in the behavioral patterns disclosed by the assessment process than in the resulting diagnostic classification. The classification of a mentally retarded child as "brain damaged," even if independently verified, provides little specific information regarding the unique patterns of abilities and disabilities which relate to the functional integrity of the brain. Knowing the individual child's strengths and weaknesses appears to be the most valuable approach to planning for his educational needs. Gallagher (1960) demonstrated the effectiveness of such an educational approach. He provided a group of brain-injured retarded children with a three-year tutoring program based on their individual strengths and weaknesses. When compared to a control group, these specially tutored children improved significantly in the areas of attention span and general intellectual performance.

In conclusion, an approach to neuropsychological assessment whose goal is to establish diagnostic classifications would seem to have limited educational value for most mentally retarded children. In contrast, a comprehensive neuropsychological assessment procedure, such as advocated by Haywood (1967) and outlined in an earlier section of this chapter enables the clinician to draw inferences about the status of the child's brain functioning and to construct cognitive, perceptual, and emotional profiles which depict his strong and weak points. These profiles can then be used as the basic data for developing specific prescriptions for individual educational programming (see Blanco, 1972; Sapir & Nitzburg, 1973). They can also serve as a behavioral reference point against which to evaluate change as a function of educational input, thereby providing information on the modifiability of brain-behavior relationships through experiential intervention.

Prognosis of Social and Vocational Adjustment

If the field of neuropsychology is to gain credence among mental retardation specialists, it must demonstrate its value in helping to provide sound planning for the education and habilitation of the mentally retarded person. Some years ago, H. B. C. Reed (1968) pointed out that research in this area was notably lacking. Efforts toward filling the gap are still sorely needed.

One of the major reasons for the lack of this kind of neuropsychological research—despite a great deal of interest and almost univeral agreement as to its importance—is the complexity of the issues involved. The validity of using neuropsychological assessment to predict future events depends specifically on the ability to measure the criterion variables objectively. By that token, social and vocational competence have yet to be successfully predicted for mentally retarded persons by any measure—probably because the important dimensions of such competence have yet to be identified to the satisfaction of all concerned. (See Chapter 3 for the discussion on measurement of social competence.) In any case, the task of the neuropsychologist is to demonstrate that measure of the neurological status of the brain—as ascertained through neuropsychological assessment and measures of social and vocational competence are meaningfully related. Matthews (1974) is currently engaged in such a research project. On a continuing basis, he and his associates are administering a modified version of the Halstead-Reitan Neuropsychological Test Battery—along with a variety of vocational tests, personality measures, and behavioral ratings—to mildly retarded subjects who are enrolled in an intensive vocational assessment, training, and placement program with subsequent placement in various jobs. In this follow-up study, the criteria of vocational and social competence are degree of successful job placement and independent living in the community for six months or longer. This investigation should permit some conclusions regarding the predictive utility of the measure used, as well as provide information concerning the relationship between neuropsychological measures and those of social and vocational adjustment.

From another standpoint, H. B. C. Reed (1968) suggested that intellectual abilities may be the important determinants of how a person solves problems, whether they be educational, vocational, or interpersonal in nature. Benton's (1970a) interactive model for understanding intellectual functionaing of mentally retarded persons may provide a fruitful alternative approach for predicting social-vocational adjustment. The model is based on the notion that intellectual behavior is the product of a number of determining factors of different types. These factors include: cerebral status, sensory status, motor status, emotional status, and cultural status Benton suggested that by subdividing each of these factors (which are construed as continuous variables) into three to five levels, a predictive "formula" could be derived for the given individual, and the "formula" could be tested for its predictive sensitivity with regard to his social and vocational adjustment. While the criteria of successful habilitation still must be meaningfully and operationally defined, Benton's model (with the addition of a motivational status factor) permits the full appreciation of the complexity of human adaptive behavior. A comprehensive neuropsychological assessment could provide a great deal of the information needed to generate the "formula."

Undoubtedly, the ultimate value of the neuropsychological study of mentally retarded persons will be determined not only by helping to establish lawful relationships between the brain and behavior, but also by its ability to successfully apply that understanding to the development of appropriate educational, training, and habilitative programs aimed at maximizing the behavioral potential of each person.

SUMMARY

In focusing specifically on the association between neuropsychology (study of brain-behavior relationships) and mental retardation, it was noted that the goals of neuropsychological assessment, in general, are to evaluate behavior in a person with presumed cerebral pathology, infer the etiological basis of any behavioral dysfunction, and recommend appropriate rehabilitative treatment or training. Consequently, this chapter covers issues concerning the dichotomous concepts of "organic" mental retardation, the role of theory in neuropsychodiagnosis, reliability and validity of neuropsychological assessment of retarded persons, neuropsychological research in mental retardation (with particular emphasis on problems in establishing neurological and behavioral criteria), and the role of neuropsychodiagnosis in achieving social, vocational, and educational goals with retarded individuals.

A neuropsychodiagnostic approach is suggested which allows the clinician to construct cognitive, perceptual, and emotional profiles—depicting the retarded child's strengths and weaknesses—for purposes of individual educational prescriptions and as reference points for evaluating the modifiability of brain-behavior relationships through experience. It has been posited that this assessment procedure requires a cooperative interdisciplinary orientation and will demonstrate its greatest value in understanding human behavior if a developmental model is applied.

REFERENCES

Alley, G. R. Comparative constructional praxis performance of organically impaired and cultural-familial mental retardates. *American Journal of Mental Deficiency,* 1969 *74,* 279-282.

Badt, M. I. Levels of abstraction in vocabulary definitions of mentally retarded school children. *American Journal of Mental Deficiency,* 1958, *63.* 241- 246.

Bateman, B. *The Illinois Test of Psycholinguistic abilities in current research.* Urbana, Ill.: Institute for Research on Exceptional Children, 1964.

Benda, C. E. The familial imbecile or oligo-encephaly as a morbid entity. *American Journal of Mental Deficiency,* 1944, *49,* 32-42.

Benton, A. L. Right-left discrimination and finger localization in defective children. *Archives of Neurology and Psychiatry,* 1955, *74,* 583-589.

Benton, A. L. *Right-left discrimination and finger localization: Development and pathology.* New York: Harper & Row, 1959.

Benton, A. L. Psychological evaluation and differential diagnosis. In H. A. Stevens and R. Heber (Eds.), *Mental retardation: A review of research.* Chicago: University of Chicago Press, 1964, p. 16-56.

Benton, A. L. (Ed.) *Contributions to clinical neuropsychology.* Chicago: Aldine, 1969.

Benton, A. L. Interactive determinants of mental deficiency. In H. C. Haywood (Ed.), *Social-cultural aspects of mental retardation.* New York: Appleton-Century-Crofts, 1970, p. 661-671 (a).

Benton, A. L. Neuropsychological aspects of mental retardation. *Journal of Special Education,* 1970, *4,* 3-11. (b)

Benton, A. L. Clinical neuropsychology of childhood: An overview. In R. M Reitan and L. A. Davison (Eds.), *Clinical neuropsychology: Current status and applications.* New York: Wiley, 1974, p. 47-52.

Birch, H. G., (Ed.) *Brain damage in children: The biological and social aspects.* Baltimore: Williams & Wilkins, 1964.

Birch, H. G., & Lefford, A. Two strategies for studying perception in "brain-damaged" children. In H. G. Birch (Ed.), *Brain damage in children. The biological and social aspects.* Baltimore: Williams & Wilkins, 1964, p. 46-60.

Blanco, R. *Prescriptions for children with learning and adjustment problems.* Springfield, Ill: Charles C Thomas, 1972.

Boring, E. G. *A history of experimental psychology* (2nd ed.). New York: Appleton-Century-Crofts,1950.

Broca, P. Remarques sur le siege de la faculté du langue articule, suivies d'une observation d'aphemie (perte de la parole). *Bull. Soc. Anat., 2nd ser.,* 1861, *36,* 330-357. (Cited in W. C. Halstead, *Brain and intelligence.* Chicago: University of Chicago Press, 1947.)

Burns, R. C. Behavioral differences between brain-injured and brain-deficient children grouped according to neuropathological types. *American Journal of Mental Deficiency,* 1960, *65,* 326-334.

Corah, N. L., Anthony, E. J., Painter, P., Stern, J. A., & Thurston, D. Effects of perinatal anoxia after seven years. *Psychological Monographs,* 1965, *79* (3, Whole No. 596).

Crome, L. The brain and mental retardation. *British Medical Journal,* 1960, *1,* 897-904.

Deutsch, C. P., & Schumer, F. *Brain-damaged Children: A modality oriented exploration of performance.* New York: Brunner/ Mazel 1970.

Dingman, H. F., & Tarjan, G. Mild mental retardation and the normal curve. *American Journal of Mental Deficiency,* 1960, *64,* 991-994.

Doll, E. A. Practical limitations of the endogenous-exogenous classification of mental defectives. *American Journal of Mental Deficiency,* 1946, *50,* 503-511.

Dunn, L. M. Minimal brain dysfunction: A dilemma for educators. In H. C. Haywood (Ed.) *Brain damage in school age children.* Washington, D.C.: The Council for Exceptional Children, 1968, pp. 161-181.

Dybwad, G. Where do we go from here? In J. E. Gordon (Ed.), *Developmental disabilities: An orientation to epilepsy, cerebral palsy, and mental retardation.* Harrisburg, Pa.: Pennsylvania Developmental Disabilities Council, 1975, pp. 299-313.

Eisenberg, L. Behavioral manifestations of cerebral damage in childhood. In H. G. Birch (Ed.), *Brain damage in children: The biological and social aspects.* Baltimore: Williams & Wilkins, 1964, pp. 61-73.

Feldman, I. S. Psychological differences among moron and borderline mental defectives as a function of etiology. *American Journal of Mental Deficiency,* 1953, *57*, 484-494.

Ferrier, D. *The functions of the brain.* London: Smith, Elder, 1886.

Flourens, P. J. M. *Recherches experimentalles sur les propriétés et les functions du systeme nerveux dans les animaux vertèbres.* Paris: 1824. (Cited in W. C. Halstead, *Brain and intelligence.* Chicago: University of Chicago Press, 1947.)

Franz, S. I. On the functions of the cerebrum: The frontal lobes. *Archives of Psychology,* New York, 1907, *1*, No. 2.

Franz, S. I. Variations in distributions of the motor centers. *Psychological Review Monograph,* 1915, *19*, No. 1.

Fritsch, G., & Hitzig, E. *Ueber die electrische erregbarkeit des grosshirn. Arch. f. Anat. u. Physiol.,* 1870, *37*, 300-332. (Cited in W. C. Halstead, *Brain and intelligence.* Chicago: University of Chicago Press, 1947.)

Gallagher, J. J. Comparison of brain-injured and non-brain-injured mentally retarded children on several psychological variables. *Monographs of the Society for Research in Child Development,* 1957, 22 (2, Serial No. 65).

Gallagher, J. J. *The tutoring of brain-injured mentally retarded children.* Springfield, Ill.: Charles C Thomas, 1960.

Gazzaniga, M. S. *The bisected brain.* New York: Appleton-Century-Crofts, 1970.

Goldstein, K. *The Organism.* New York: American Book Co., 1939.

Goldstein, K. *Human Nature.* Cambridge Mass. Harvard University Press, 1940.

Goltz, F. Uber die verrichtungen des grosshirns, *Arch f. d. Physiol.,* 1881, 1-49. (Cited in W. C. Halstead, *Brain and intelligence.* Chicago: University of Chicago Press, 1947.)

Gordon, J. E. *Intellectual potential in mentally retarded persons: Effect of stimulus enrichment on verbal abstraction and verbal learning.* Ann Arbor, Mich.: University Microfilms, 1972, No. 72-25380. (Doctoral dissertation, George Peabody College).

Gordon, J. E. The service needs of cerebral palsied adults. In J. E. Gordon (Ed.), *Developmental disabilities: An orientation to epilepsy, cerebral palsy, and mental retardation.* Harrisburg, Pa.: Pennsylvania Developmental Disabilities Council, 1975, pp. 155-162.

Graham, F. K., Ernhart, C. B., Thurston, D., & Craft, M. Development three years after perinatal anoxia and other potentially damaging newborn experiences. *Psychological Monographs,* 1962, *76* (3, Whole No. 522).

Grossman, H. J. (Ed.) *Manual on terminology and classification in mental retardation : 1973 revision.* Washington, D.C.: American Association on Mental Deficiency, 1973.

Halstead, W. C. *Brain and intelligence.* Chicago: University of Chicago Press, 1947.

Haywood, H. C. Perceptual handicap: Fact or artifact? *Child Study,* 1967, *28,* 2-14.

Haywood, H. C. Introduction to clinical neuropsychology. In H. C. Haywood (Ed.), *Brain damage in school age children.* Washington, D.C.: The Council for Exceptional Children, 1968, pp. 3-19.

Haywood, H. C., & Gordon, J. E. Neuropsychology and learning disorders. *Pediatric Clinics of North America,* 1970, *17,* 337-346.

Haywood, H. C., & Tapp, J. T. Experience and the development of adaptive behavior. In N. R. Ellis (Ed.), *International review of research in mental retardation.* (Vol.1). New York: Academic Press, 1966, pp. 109-151.

Head, H. *Aphasia and kindred disorders of speech.* (2 vols). New York: Macmillan, 1926.

Hebb, D. O. Intelligence in man after large removals of cerebral tissue: Report of four left frontal lobe cases. *Journal of General Psychology,* 1939, *21,* 437-446.

Hebb, D. O. *The organization of behavior.* New York: Wiley, 1949.

Heber, R. (Ed.) A manual on terminology and classification in mental retardation (2nd ed.). *American Journal of Mental Deficiency,* Monogr. Suppl., 1961.

Heber, R. *Epidemiology of mental retardation.* Springfield, Ill.: Charles C Thomas, 1970.

Johnson, J. T. The relevance of "brain damage" for the fields of psychology and special education. *IMRID Papers and Reports,* 1968, *5* (21; entire issue). Available from George Peabody College, Nashville, Tenn.

Kennedy, W. A. Cultural deprivation: Its role in central nervous system functioning. In J. L. Khanna (Ed.), *Brain damage and mental retardation.* Springfield, Ill.: Charles C Thomas, 1968, pp. 110-120.

Kennedy, C., & Ramirez, L. S. Brain damage as a cause of behavior disturbance in children. In H. G. Birch (Ed.), *Brain damage in children: The biological and social aspects.* Baltimore: Williams & Wilkins, 1964, pp. 13-23.

Khanna, J. L. (Ed.) *Brain damage and mental retardation.* Springfield, Ill.: Charles C Thomas, 1968.

Klebanoff, S. G., Singer, J. L., & Wilensky, H. Psychological consequences of brain lesions and ablations. *Psychological Bulletin,* 1954, *51*, 1-42.

Klove, H. Validation studies in adult clinical neuropsychology. In R. M. Reitan and L. A. Davison (Eds.), *Clinical neuropsychology: Current status and applications.* New York: Wiley, 1974, pp. 211-236.

Kuhn, T. S. *The structure of scientific revolutions.* Chicago: The University of Chicago Press, 1970.

L'Abate, L. Screening children with cerebral dysfunctions through the laboratory method. In H. C. Haywood (Ed.), *Brain damage in school age children.* Washington, D.C.: The Council for Exceptional Children, 1968, pp. 128-158.

Lashley, K. S. *Brain mechanisms and intelligence.* Chicago: University of Chicago Press, 1929.

Leland, H. An overview of the problem of the psychological evaluation in mental retardation. In J. L. Khanna (Ed.), *Brain damage and mental retardation.* Springfield, Ill.: Charles C Thomas, 1968, pp. 3-16.

Lewis, E. D. Types of mental deficiency and their social significance. *Journal of Mental Science,* 1933, *79*, 298-304.

Loeb, J. *Comparative physiology of the brain and comparative psychology.* New York: G. P. Putnam's Sons, 1902.

Luria, A. R. (Ed.) *The mentally retarded child.* New York: Macmillan, 1963.

Luria, A. R. Neuropsychological analysis of focal brain lesions. In B. B. Wolman (Ed.), *Handbook of clinical psychology.* New York: McGraw-Hill, 1965, pp. 689-754.

Luria, A. R. *Higher cortical functions in man.* New York: Basic Books, 1966. (a)

Luria, A. R. *Human brain and psychological processes.* New York: Harper & Row, 1966. (b)

Luria, A. R. Neuropsychology in the local diagnosis of brain damage. In W. L. Smith and M. J. Philippus (Eds.), *Neuropsychological testing in organic brain dysfunction.* Springfield, Ill.: Charles C. Thomas, 1969, p. 5-21.

Luria, A. R. *The working brain: An introduction to neuropsychology.* New York Basic Books, 1973.

Mackie, R. P., Williams, H. M., & Dunn, L. M. *Teachers of children who are mentally retarded.* Washington, D. C.: U.S. Government Printing Office, 1960.

Maher, B. A. Intelligence and brain damage. In N. R. Ellis (Ed.), *Handbook of mental deficiency: Psychological theory and research.* New York: McGraw-Hill, 1963, pp. 224-252.

Malamud, N. Neuropathology. In H. A. Stevens and R. Heber (Eds.), *Mental retardation: A review of research.* Chicago: University of Chicago Press, 1964, p. 429-452.

Masland, R. L. The prevention of mental subnormality. In R. L. Masland, S. B. Sarason, and T. Gladwin. *Mental Subnormality.* New York: Basic Books, 1958, pp. 11-141.

Matarazzo, J. D. *Wechsler's measurement and appraisal of adult intelligence,* (5th ed.) . Baltimore: Wilkins & Wilkins, 1972.

Matthews, C. G. Applications of neuropsychological test methods in mentally retarded subjects. In R. M. Reitan and L. A. Davison (Eds.), *Clinical neuropsychology: Current status and applications.* New York: Wiley, 1974, pp. 267-287.

Matthews, C. G., & Reitan, R. M. Comparisons of abstraction ability in retardates and in patients with cerebral lesions. *Perceptual and Motor Skills,* 1961, *13*, 327-333.

Matthews, C. G., & Reitan, R. M. Psychomotor abilities of retardates and patients with cerebral lesions. *American Journal of Mental Deficiency,* 1962, *66*, 607-612.

Matthews, C. G., & Reitan, R. M. Relationship of differential abstraction ability levels to psychological test performances in mentally retarded subjects. *American Journal of Mental Deficiency,* 1963, *68*, 235-244.

Meehl, P. E., & Rosen, A. Antecedent probability and the efficiency of psychometric signs, patterns, or cutting scores. *Psychological Bulletin,* 1955, *52*, 194-216.

Meyer, D. R., & Meyer, P. M. Brain functions. *Annual Review of Psychology,* 1963, *14*, 155-173.

Miller, E. *Clinical neuropsychology.* Baltimore: Penguin Books, 1972.

Milner, B. Memory disturbance after bilateral hippocampal lesions. In P. Milner and S. Glickman (Eds.), *Cognitive processes and the brain.* New York: Van Nostrand, 1965, pp. 97-111.

Milner, P., & Glickman, S. (Eds.) *Cognitive processes and the brain.* New York: Van Nostrand, 1965.

Penfield, W., & Roberts, L. *Speech and brain mechanisms.* Princeton, N.J.: Princeton University Press, 1959.

Polloway, E. A., & Payne, J. S. Comparison of the AAMD Heber and Grossman manuals on terminology and classification in mental retardation. *Mental Retardation,* 1975, *13* (3), 12-14.

Pribram, K. H. (Ed.) *Brain and behavior.* (4 vols.) Baltimore: Penguin Books, 1969.

Reed, D. M. The epidemiologic approach. In M. Alter and W. A. Hauser (Eds.) *The epidemiology of epilepsy: A workshop.* (NINDS Monograph No. 14, U. S. Department of Health, Education, and Welfare, National Institutes of Health Publication No. 74-390). Washington, D.C.: U. S. Government Printing Office, 1972.

Reed, H. B. C., Jr. The use of psychological tests in diagnosing brain damage in school children. In H. C. Haywood (Ed.), *Brain damage in school age children.* Washington, D.C.: The Council for Exceptional Children, 1968, pp. 109-127.

Reitan, R. M. Certain differential effects of left and right cerebral lesions in human adults. *Journal of Comparative and Physiological Psychology,* 1955, *48,* 474-477.

Reitan, R. M. Relationships between neurological and psychological variables and their implications for reading instruction. In H. A. Robinson (Ed.), *Meeting individual differences in reading.* Chicago: University of Chicago Press, 1964, pp. 100-110.

Reitan, R. M. A research program on the psychological effects of brain lesions in human beings. In N. R. Ellis (Ed.), *International review of research in mental retardation.* (Vol. 1). New York: Academic Press, 1966, pp. 153-169. (a)

Reitan, R. M. The needs of teachers for specialized information in the area of neuropsychology. In W. M. Cruickshank (Ed.), *The teachers of brain-injured children.* Syracuse, N.Y.: Syracuse University Press, 1966, pp. 223-243. (b)

Reitan, R. M. Psychological assessment of deficits associated with brain lesions in subjects with normal and abnormal intelligence. In J. L. Khanna (Ed.), *Brain damage and mental retardation.* Springfield, Ill.: Charles C Thomas, 1968, pp. 44-87.

Reitan, R. M. Methodological problems in clinical neuropsychology. In R. M. Reitan and L. A. Davison (Eds.), *Clinical neuropsychology: Current status and application.* New York: Wiley, 1974, pp. 19-46.

Reitan, R. M., & Davison, L. A. (Eds.) *Clinical neuropsychology: Current status and application.* New York: Wiley, 1974.

Ross, A. O. Conceptual issues in the evaluation of brain damage. In J. L. Khanna (Ed.), *Brain damage and mental retardation.* Springfield, Ill.: Charles C Thomas, 1968, pp. 20-43.

Sapir, S. G., & Nitzburg, A. C. (Eds.) *Children with learning problems.* New York: Brunner/Mazel, 1973.

Sarason, S. B. *Psychological problems in mental deficiency* (3rd ed.). New York: Harper & Row, 1959.

Sarason, S. B., & Doris, J. *Psychological problems in mental deficiency* (4th ed.). New York: Harper & Row, 1969.

Seguin, E. *Idiocy: And its treatment by the physiological method.* New York: William Wood, 1866. (Republished New York: Augustus M. Kelley, 1971).

Smith, A. Ambiguities in concepts and studies of "brain damage" and "organicity." In W. L. Smith and M. J. Philippus (Eds.), *Neuropsychological testing in organic brain dysfunction.* Springfield, Ill.: Charles C Thomas, 1969, pp. 22-48.

Smith, W. L., & Philippus, M. J. (Eds.) *Neuropsychological testing in organic brain dysfunction.* Springfield, Ill.: Charles C Thomas, 1969.

Sternfeld, L. Project prevention. In J. E. Gordon (Ed.), *Developmental disabilities: An orientation to epilepsy, cerebral palsy, and mental retardation.* Harrisburg, Pa.: Pennsylvania Developmental Disabilities Council, 1975, pp. 201-206.

Stevens, L. A. *Explorers of the brain.* New York: Alfred A. Knopf, 1971.

Strauss, A., & Kephart, N. *Psychopathology and education of the brain-injured child* (Vol. 2) *Progress in theory and clinic.* New York: Grune & Stratton, 1955.

Strauss, A., & Lehtinen, L. *Psychopathology and education of the brain-injured child.* New York: Grune & Stratton, 1947.

Tarjan, G. Studies of organic etiologic factors. In G. Caplan (Ed.), *Prevention of mental disorders in children.* New York: Basic Books, 1961, pp. 31-51.

Taylor, J. *Selected writings of John Hughlings Jackson* (2 Vols.). London: Hodder, 1931-1932.

Teuber, H. L., & Rudel, R. G. Behaviour after cerebral lesions in children and adults. *Developmental Medicine and Child Neurology,* 1962, *4,* 3-20.

Tredgold, A. F. *A text book on mental deficiency* (6th ed.). Baltimore: Williams & Wilkins, 1937.

Warkany, J., & Dignan, P. St. J. Congenital malformations: Microcephaly. In J. Wortis (Ed.), *Mental retardation and developmental disabilities: An annual review.* (Vol.5). New York: Brunner/Mazel, 1973, pp. 113-135.

Yacorzynski, G. K. Organic mental disorders, In B. Wolman (Ed.), *Handbook of clinical psychology.* New York: McGraw-Hill, 1965, pp. 653-688.

Yakovlev, P., & Farrel, M. J. Influence on locomotion of the plantar reflex in normal and in physically and mentally inferior persons. *Archives of Neurology and Psychiatry,* 1941, *46,* 322-330.

Yates, A. J. The validity of some psychological tests of brain damage. *Psychological Bulletin,* 1954, *51,* 359-379.

Zigler, E. Social deprivation in familial and organic retardates. *Psychological Reports,* 1962, *10,* 370.

Zigler, E. Familial mental retardation: A continuing dilemma. *Science,* 1967, *155,* 292-298.

Bertrand G. Winsberg graduate from Roosevelt University in Chicago and received his M.D. degree from the University of Michigan, where he also received his training in adult and child psychiatry. His graduate work at Michigan led to an M.S. degree in psychiatry. Following this, he studied Developmental Neuropsychiatry with Dr. Hilda Knobloch at Mt. Sinai Hospital Medical School of the City University of New York.

Since 1968, Dr. Winsberg has been the Director of the Child Psychiatric Evaluation Research Unit of the New York State Department of Mental Hygiene. He is also Clinical Associate Professor of Child Psychiatry at Downstate Medical Center of the State University of New York.

Dr. Winsberg's research work has been in the areas of clinical evaluative research, developmental psychopharmacology, and pediatric neuropsychiatry. He is also actively involved in training individuals for service in mental health facilities. Thus, he has taught neuropsychiatry to medical students, social workers, psychologists, pediatricians, psychiatrists, medical associates, and nurses.

Recently, Dr. Winsberg has participated in the formation of a program of developmental neuropsychiatry at the State University of New York at Stony Brook. The material contained in this chapter will provide the basic curriculum content of the training course for mental health care practitioners.

10

Neuropsychiatric issues in developmental subnormality

Bertrand G. Winsberg

BACKGROUND AND DELINEATION OF ISSUES

The first fully systematic infant developmental examination—and still among the most widely used—is the Gesell Developmental and Neurological Examination (Gesell & Amatruda, 1941, 1947). However, much confusion remains with regard to its implications and appropriate use among professionals who work with handicapped populations. The psychologist who uses developmental instruments for diagnostic purposes frequently is handicapped by a lack of familiarity with developmental issues in the medical sciences.

The author is familiar with the terminology of the American Association on Mental Deficiency, which does not accept the distinction between "mental deficiency" and "mental retardation," by which the former term is taken to refer to subnormal intellectual performance of organic derivation and the latter to that of nonorganic etiology. Nevertheless, in this chapter, that distinction between the terms is followed so that the discussions will conform more closely to the terminology used by Knobloch and Pasamanick (1974) in the 3rd edition of *Gesell and Amatruda's Developmental Diagnosis* and thereby keep the conceptual issues clear. From a neuropsychiatric perspective, as I hope this chapter will make clear, these distinctions must be kept so that meaningful treatment and research may proceed.

Much of the research and theoretical material presented in the chapter is taken from the recently completed 3rd edition of *Gesell and Amatruda's Developmental Diagnosis* by Drs. Hilda Knobloch and Benjamin Pasamanick (1974), with whom the author has both worked and studied. In particular, extensive use has been made of the Introduction and of Chapters 5 and 11, and this use is acknowledged here rather than in the text. This body of material is inseparably part of the author's orientation, which has been derived from his many years of personal and professional association with Drs. Knobloch and Pasamanick. Their review of this chapter and their suggestions for modification to enhance its clarity are gratefully acknowledged.

This deficiency often hinders his ability to interpret his data adequately and, consequently, to suggest the best possible treatment alternatives. Also, a common belief among many workers in child development is that the Gesell Developmental and Neurological Examination has no predictive value. This belief has contributed to the trend which minimizes the importance of data on infant behavior—as derived from the Gesell scale—for the prediction of clinical outcome; and it is founded on a lack of understanding of the instrument and on oversimplified attempts in its use. The public health relevance of early and accurate diagnosis of neuropsychiatric conditions in children is of clear and major importance. Only then can adequate treatment and planning commence, etiologic factors causing disease be identified, and the principal goal of medicine (i.e., primary prevention) be realized.

This chapter indicates that, other than for preliminary screening purposes, interpretation of the data obtained from the Gesell examination cannot be rendered by the novice, however well he may be trained in other aspects of psychological diagnosis. An understanding of medical issues which relate to infant performance must be well grasped if infant behavior is to be understood adequately and a meaningful diagnosis derived. The diagnostician (psychological or otherwise) who might wish to employ the Gesell Developmental and Neurological Examination must do so only after adequate preparation and training. Successful use cannot be accomplished solely with the materials accompanying the examination kit. The conduct of the examination and many of these issues are treated at length in the 3rd edition of *Gesell and Amatruda's Developmental Diagnosis* (Knobloch & Pasamanick, 1974).

A principal aim of this chapter is to orient the reader to the appropriate use and interpretation of Gesell's Developmental and Neurological Examination and to present some of the work and thinking which it has stimulated in pediatric neuropsychiatry. In addition, recent epidemiologic research pertaining to this area will be discussed. I will present data indicating that the Gesell examination, when used appropriately, is a reliable, valid tool for general clinical deployment; and I will report on recent work which substantiates previous findings that it is a sensitive indicator of even minor neurological dysfunction in infancy. The implications of Gesellian developmental diagnosis for current areas of research and clinical treatment of children constitute the final section.

Historical Antecedents

The Industrial Revolution in the 19th century gave impetus to a burgeoning science of child development; toward the end of the century this converged in systematic attempts to record the behavioral and intellectual development of children. At the beginning of the current century, Gesell received his early training and subsequent doctorate (in 1906) in educational psychology at Clark University, the major American center of the day in the area of child development, where he was among other students of G. Stanley Hall who were to have an impact on the field. At Clark, Gesell became concerned with the then-current Zeitgeist in psychology and medicine, that of finding the simplest norms of cognitive performance which might indicate impaired neurological integrity. These concerns led him to the study of medicine, first at Wisconsin, and then at Yale—where, after receiving his medical degree in 1915, he remained throughout the greater part of his subsequent productive career.

Studying a large number of normal children, and supplementing these observations by those of an even greater number of infants and children who presented developmental deviations and defects, Gesell began mapping the behavior of the fetus, the infant, and the very young child. He established norms, tested hypotheses, and constructed theories that were explanatory of the stages of behavioral change which led to the final product, the human adult.

Gesell was ever alert to new instrumentation which could be of assistance in his research; and the motion picture became a powerful tool in his armamentarium. Using hundreds of thousands of feet of film over the years, he demonstrated not only that developmental patterns could be identified, but that their occurrence could be predicted reliably. Development ceased to be a vague abstraction; instead, it came to be seen as an organic process which yields to scientific analysis and to diagnostic appraisal. During the half-century of his productive life, he poured forth hundreds of papers, monographs, and books, the sum and substance of which are probably best summarized in one of his later books, *The Embryology of Behavior* (Gesell, 1945). Gesell was active on behalf of children—both the sick and the well—throughout his life, concerning himself with problems of mental subnormality as well as with issues relating to adoption, child guidance, and justice. When he thought the time was ripe to apply his accumulated knowledge toward clinical pediatric neuropsychiatry, Gesell recruited the pediatrician Catherine Amatruda. Together, they established a clinic in New Haven, Connecticut, for diagnosis, guidance, and teaching purposes in the area of child development.

Through Gesell's intensive study of over 10,000 normal and abnormal infants, systematic examination procedures were developed and observations were made. These procedures and observations were reported in two major works, *Developmental Diagnosis* (Gesell & Amatruda, 1941) and *The Embryology of Behavior* (Gesell, 1945). From this groundwork, Gesell

H=History
O=Observation

	36 Weeks	40 Weeks (KEY AGE)	44 Weeks
Adaptive	Cube: grasps 3rd cube (*40w) Cube: hits, pushes cube with cube (*15m) Cup-cube: cube against cup (*44w) Pellet & bottle: approaches bottle first (*40w) Ring string: manipulates string	Cube: matches 2 cubes (*15m) Cup-cube: fingers cube in cup (*44w) Pellet: index finger approach Pellet & bottle: approaches pellet first Pellet & bottle: grasps pellet Pellet in bottle: regards pellet if drops out Bell: grasps by handle Bell: waves or shakes	Cup-cube: removes cube from cup Cup-cube: (demonstration) cube into cup without release (*52w) Pellet in bottle: points at pellet through glass (*18m) Bell: regards & pokes clapper Ring-string: approaches string first
Gross Motor	Sit: 10 minutes plus, steady Sit: leans forward, reerects Stand: holds rail, full weight (*48w)	Sit: indefinitely, steady Sit: goes over to prone Stand: pulls to feet at rail (*15m) Prone: creeps (*15m)	Stand: at rail, lifts & replaces foot (*48w)
Fine Motor	Cube: radial digital grasp Pellet: prehends, scissors grasp (*40w)	Cube: crude release (*15m) Pellet: grasps promptly Pellet: inferior pincer grasp (*48w) Ring-string: plucks string easily	Bell: grasps by top of handle
Language	Vocalization: da-da or equivalent (*40w) Vocalization: imitates sounds Comprehension: responds to name no-no	Vocabulary: dada & mama with meaning Vocabulary: 1 "word" Comprehension: bye, patacake	
Personal Social	Feeding: holds bottle (*15m) Feeding: feeds self cracker	Social: waves bye, patacake (*...)	Social: extends toy to person without release (*52w) Feeding: milk from cup in part (*15m) Mirror: reaches image of ball in mirror (*52w)

Figure 10.1. The 40-week Gesell schedule. (From *Gesell and Amatruda's Developmental Diagnosis*, 3rd edition, edited by H. Knobloch and B. Pasamanick. Copyright 1974 by Harper & Row. Used with permission.)

developed an instrument which was felt to be sensitive to a number of areas relevant to neurological integrity in infants. These behavioral fields or areas include (a) Adaptive,[1] (b) Motor (both fine and gross), (c) Language, and (d) Personal-Social. Additionally, as part of the formal examination, the clinician obtains a description of any abnormalities in neuromotor integration. Figure 10.1 presents a sample of the Gesell schedule, covering the behaviors assessed at the 36- to 44-week age level. Figures 10.2 through 10.5 are samples of the recording form for the examination, with an itemization of some of the abnormal neuromotor signs which are looked for during the assessment.

The basis for evaluating the five behavioral areas is the developmental quotient (DQ), which expresses the rate of development at any given age as the ratio between the child's maturity age—as obtained from the Gesell schedules—and his chronological age, in a manner analogous to the derivation of the ratio IQ, i.e., DQ = (Maturity Age/Chronological Age) X 100. Each of the five behavioral areas generates a DQ which may be used in helping to determine a diagnosis. However, it is the Adaptive DQ which is related to later intellectual performance. Accordingly, it is the adaptive-level score which has been found to offer the highest predictive validity for intelligence tests administered at school age. The items constituting the areas of development chosen by Gesell were selected in accordance with his interest in the evolving nervous system. Apparently, simple infant behaviors (e.g., securing a small object) are derived from a number of discrete behaviors which are termed developmental patterns (e.g., the development of vision and visual pursuit, conceptual development). The emergence of specific patterns are illustrated in Tables 10.1 and 10.2. Table 10.1 describes the behaviors involved in the integration of visual perception (regard for an object) and motor prehension into a coordinated behavior—visual regard and grasp of a toy—from arm activation at 16 weeks of age to the two-hand grasp at 24 weeks. Table 10.2 traces the development of fine motor prehension and grasp, from mutual fingering at 16 weeks to the 36-week radial-digital grasp of a cube.

The integration of various developmental patterns in temporal sequence (as illustrated in Tables 10.1 and 10.2) requires normal neuronal maturation. Consequently, deviations from normal integrative patterns must be interpreted clinically for the diagnosis of neurological disabilities. The normal patterns of integration are delineated in the recording form illustrated in

---

[1]The term "Adaptive" connotes the problem-solving interaction between the infant and his environment. It is the end product of the integration of a number of separate behavioral dimensions (e.g., perceptual, orientational, manual, verbal), and might be considered equivalent to what is thought to be measured by tests of intelligence.

DEVELOPMENTAL AND NEUROLOGIC EVALUATION FORM
Form 5B

IDENTIFYING INFORMATION:

Name:_____ Case Number:_____

Hospital Number:_____

Date of Birth:_____Expected Date of Birth:_____
Examination Date:_____Corrected Birth Date:_____
Race and Sex: 1-WM; 2-WF; 3-BM;4-BF; 5-OM; 6-OF (Circle
one.)
Birth Weight: grams (_____lbs and ozs.)

Amount of Prematurity in Days:

Age in Weeks (Code 000 if months) Age is corrected for
prematurity.
Age in months, to nearest half month (Code 000 if weeks)
Corrected.

FIRST THREE PAGES ARE SUMMARY PAGES; TURN TO PAGE 4 TO BEGIN RECORDING.

DIAGNOSTIC SUMMARY:

INTELLECTUAL:_____

NEUROMOTOR:_____

SEIZURES:_____

SPECIAL SENSORY:_____

QUALITATIVE:_____

SPECIFIC DISEASES OR SYNDROMES:_____

MATURITY LEVELS:

Range	Develop-mental Quotient	Weeks	Months	(Delete inapplicable word.)
___	___	_____..._____	...General Developmental Level
___	___	_____..._____	...Gross Motor Behavior
___	___	_____..._____	...Fine Motor Behavior
___	___	_____..._____	...Adaptive Behavior
___	___	_____..._____	...Language Behavior
___	___	_____..._____	...Personal-Social Behavior
		_____..._____	...Stanford-Binet Mental Age

INTELLECTUAL POTENTIAL: (Circle one number in each column)
0. Felt to be adequately predictive
1. Indicative of present function but modifying factors present
2. Inadequate for precise evaluation   Specify: _____
3. Inadequate for evaluation

Figure 10.2. A page of the Developmental and Neurological Evaluation Form
(5B). (Modified from *Gesell and Amatruda's Developmental Diagnosis,* 3rd edition, edited by H. Knobloch and B. Pasamanick.
Copyright 1974 by Harper & Row. Used with permission.)

CLINICAL EVALUATION OF INTELLECTUAL POTENTIAL

IN NORMAL RANGE
0. Superior
1. High Average
2. Average
3. Low Average
4. Dull Normal
5. Indeterminate, not defective

MENTAL DEFICIENCY PRESENT OR LIKELY
6. Borderline Dull
7. Borderline Defective
8. Defective
9. Undecided

NEUROMOTOR STATUS: (Circle one number in each column)
    Posture locomotion, movement control, muscle tone, coordination
    and manipulation, reflexes, etc.

TYPE OF NEUROMOTOR ABNORMALITY:
0. No abnormality
1. Due to disease outside of the central nervous system (e.g., renal or
    cardiac, marked malnutrition, acute disease, arthrogryposis, etc.)
    Specify:_____

2. Indicative of Chronic Organic Brain Disease
3. Other central nervous system disease (e.g., anterior horn cell,
    degenerative disease, brain tumor, myelomeningocele, etc.)
    Specify:_____

4. Multiple conditions
    Specify:_____

9. Undecided

DEGREE OF NEUROMOTOR ABNORMALITY:
0. No abnormality

0. Motor Behavior normal for chronologic age
1. Gross motor normal for chronologic age,
    minimal fine motor abnormalities
2. Gross motor normal for chronologic age,
    minor fine motor abnormalities
3. Motor retardation without abnormal signs
    for level of function

4. Abnormal neuromotor signs of
    no clinical significance
5. Abnormal neuromotor signs of
    minor degree
6. Abnormal neuromotor signs of
    marked degree

4. Motor retardation with abnormal signs
    of no clinical significance
5. Motor retardation with abnormal signs
    of minor degree
6. Motor retardation with abnormal signs
    of marked degree
7. Abnormal neuromotor signs of severe degree: qualitative change,
    e.g., "Cerebral Palsy," specific syndrome, etc.
    Specify type:_____

9. Undecided

Figure 10.3. A page of the Developmental and Neurological Evaluation Form (5B). (Modified from *Gesell and Amatruda's Developmental Diagnosis,* 3rd edition, edited by H. Knobloch and B. Pasamanick. Copyright 1974 by Harper & Row. Used with permission.)

419

	Increased		Decreased	
0.	Not increased	0.	Not decreased	
1.	Questionably increased	1.	Questionably decreased	
2.	Increased	2.	Decreased	
3.	Unsustained clonus	3.	Absent	
4.	Increased stretch reflexes	9.	No data	
5.	Sustained clonus			
9.	No data			

Clinical
Evaluation
0-4

	Right	Left	Right	Left	Right	Left
Biceps.......	____	.... ____	.... ____	.... ____	____	____
Triceps......	____	.... ____	.... ____	.... ____	____	____
Knee.........	____	.... ____	.... ____	.... ____	____	____
Ankle........	____	.... ____	.... ____	.... ____	____	____

OTHER NEUROMOTOR ABNORMALITIES:

The remainder of the abnormal neuromotor patterns must be considered in terms of the adaptive maturity age level of the child. An older child with a significant motor handicap may have abnormal patterns at some or all of the infant levels as well as in the patterns for children.

AGE LEVEL selected for case: (Circle one number.)
Asterisks below, and in margins, indicate age at which patterns become abnormal.
4. 16 weeks (15-25)]......................***
3. 28 weeks (26-35)]......................**
2. 40 weeks (36+)]......................*
1. Children (when independent locomotion attained; usually 15 months)

(CHECK ONE SPACE FOR EACH NUMBERED ITEM IN LEFT HAND COLUMN, AT APPROPRIATE AGE LEVEL. Cross out all the items above age level selected for the patient.)

INFANT PATTERNS:

Head	0. Normal	1. Question Present	2. Mild Degree	3. Moderate Degree	4. Severe Degree	9. No Data
|¯Retraction............						
* Backward sagging......	____	____	____	____	____	____
* Forward sagging.......	____	____	____	____	____	____
* Sideward sagging.....R	____	____	____	____	____	____
|_ L	____	____	____	____	____	____

Supine						
|¯Persisting tonic- R	____	____	____	____	____	____
↓ neck-reflex.......L	____	____	____	____	____	____
* Extension of leg.....R	____	____	____	____	____	____
* L	____	____	____	____	____	____
| Scissoring............	____	____	____	____	____	____
|_						

Figure 10.4. A page of the Developmental and Neurological Evaluation Form (5B). (Modified from *Gesell and Amatruda's Developmental Diagnosis,* 3rd edition, edited by H. Knobloch and B. Pasamanick. Copyright 1974 by Harper & Row. Used with permission.)

	0. Normal	1. Question Present	2. Mild Degree	3. Moderate Degree	4. Severe Degree	9. No Data

Sitting

* Persisting tonic-neck-reflex..R						
* L						
* Extension of leg..............R						
* L						
Narrow base with leg ....R						
adduction...................L						
* Flexion of knee and hip.......R						
* L						
* Hyperextension of back.........						
* Rounding of back..............						

Standing

Extension of leg..............R						
* L						
Scissoring.....................						
* Plantar flexion of toes.......R						
......................................L						
* Abnormal postures of feet.....R						
......................................L						

Specify abnormality for last category:_____

* Standing on narrow base........						
Standing on wide base..........						
Standing on toes..............R						
......................................L						
Withdrawal of leg.............R						
......................................L						
* Flexion at knee and hip.......R						
......................................L						
Knee hyperextended, hip.......R						
flexed L						
Knee hyperextended and ....R						
hip extended...............L						

Arms and Hands

Adduction of arm..............R						
......................................L						
Flexion of elbow..............R						
* L						
Flexion of wrist..............R						
* L						
Pronation of arm..............R						
* L						
Extension of elbow............R						
......................................L						

Figure 10.5. A page of the Developmental and Neurological Evaluation Form (5B). (Modified from *Gesell and Amatruda's Developmental Diagnosis,* 3rd edition, edited by H. Knobloch and B. Pasamanick. Copyright 1974 by Harper & Row. Used with permission.)

Arms and hands (con't.)	0. Normal	1. Question Present	2. Mild Degree	3. Moderate Degree	4. Severe Degree	9. No Data
* Abnormal posturing...........R	_____	_____	_____	_____	_____	_____
L						

Specify abnormality for last category:

	0. Normal	1. Question Present	2. Mild Degree	3. Moderate Degree	4. Severe Degree	9. No Data
Fisted hand..................R						
* L						
Thumb adducted in palm.......R						
* L						
Withdrawal from grasp........R						
* L						
Excessive strength of grasp..R						
L						
Abduction of arm.............R						
L						
* Failure to use arms independently..............						
* Maldirected reaching.........R						
L						
Requires support to move.....R						
L						
Difficulty retaining.........R						
L						
Extensive extension in or....R						
abruptness of release L						
Incoordinated transfer.......R						
L						
Exaggerated casting..........R						
L						
* Cascading....................R						
L						
Difficulty in release........R						
L						
Poking, tipping..............R						
L						
Whole hand grasp.............R						
L						
Curling fingers into palm....R						
for pellet L						

Figure 10.5. (cont.)

Table 10.1

Development of Visual Perception and Motor Prehension

Age and Activity	Developmental Pattern
16 weeks (Activation on sight and taking toy to mouth)	The first manifestation of approach is seen in the activation of the arms on sight of a toy at 16 weeks. Simultaneously, the beginnings of acquisition are seen when looking from hand to object leads to bringing the toy to the infant's third hand—his mouth. This exploitative behavior has not been observed until now because the infant has not been able, except visually, to pursue actively the objects which impinge upon his supine existence.
20 Weeks (Approach with both hands)	Activation yields to approach, and at 20 weeks the infant brings both hands toward a toy with increasing precision of arm movement.
20 Weeks (Grasp when held near hand)	Although he approaches, he takes toy only if it is held near his hand.
24 Weeks (Two-hand approach and grasp)	At 24 weeks, eye-hand toy relationships are so perfected as to enable the infant to sight, approach, and take a toy with both hands. Approach and grasp have evolved from the integration of visual perception, active grasp, and reaching into a single coordinated movement.

Note. Abstracted from the narrative of the film, "Developmental Evaluation in Infancy," prepared by Dr. H. Knobloch. Available from the Department of Photography and Cinema, the Ohio State University, Columbus, Ohio 43210.

423

Table 10.2

Development of Fine Motor Prehension and Grasp

Age and Activity	Developmental Pattern
16 Weeks (Mutual fingering) (Clutches at clothes)	At 16 weeks, the infant is under the limitation of postural symmetry. He brings his hands together and engages in mutual fingering. This behavior is a reflection of one state in his central nervous system maturation. In addition, he scratches, fingers, and clutches at his clothes or at a blanket.
20 Weeks (Scratches at a tabletop)	At 20 weeks, this exploitative scratching is seen at the tabletop or in prone. This primitive fingering shows fine motor growth. The hands are free from the fisted position while the fingers are becoming emancipated and can now begin to work independently.
20 Weeks (Precarious grasp of cube)	A toy placed in the hand is held precariously, usually at the ulnar side of the palm. Initially digital differentiation occurs with a large object (e.g., a cube).

24 Weeks (Whole hand grasp of cube)

By 24 weeks, progression to the radial side has begun. The infant not only grasps a cube, but also holds it in the center of his palm with all his fingers. This primitive pattern of prehension is a whole-hand palmar grasp.

28 Weeks (Radial-palmar grasp of cube)

Promp prehension of the pellet will eventually result from this specialization of the radial digits. This more advanced asymmetry is foreshadowed at 28 weeks as the infant grasps a toy and holds it at the radial side of the palm. This radial-palmar grasp foretells thumb opposition.

36 Weeks and Thereafter (Radial-digital grasp of cube)

At 36 weeks, the fingertips are beginning to come under voluntary control. Because a cube-sized object is held with the ends of the thumb, index, and third fingers, grasp of it is now called radial-digital. It can become no more precise.

_____

Note. Abstracted from the narrative of the film, "Developmental Evaluation in Infancy," prepared by Dr. H. Knobloch. Available from the Department of Photography and Cinema, the Ohio State University, Columbus, Ohio 43210.

Figures 10.2 through 10.5. It should be noted that, through the use of asterisks, the recording form indicates the age at which the appearance or persistence of various patterns are abnormal.

Reliability and Validity of the DQ

Before theoretical considerations and examination procedures could be expected to receive general clinical acceptance, it was necessary to establish the reliability and validity of the diagnostic interpretation derived from the examination. The reliability of the DQ was established through interexaminer and test-retest procedures (Knobloch & Pasamanick, 1960). Interexaminer reliability of clinical examinations performed on over 100 infants by 18 different examiners was found to be .98. Test-retest reliability for 65 infants, examined within time intervals ranging from a few hours to a few days by two examiners, was found to be .82. These data indicate that Gesell DQs are of respectable reliability for general clinical use.

Extensive work has been done on the predictive and construct validity of the Gesell examination. However, before this work is reviewed, it is necessary to make clear the underlying assumption involved with its use. A basic assumption is that if normal neurointegration—and concomitant normal functioning—are present in infancy, the consequent normal development will manifest itself as such at later follow-up on instruments designed to measure neurointegration—provided that no intervening events (e.g., physical injury, infection) have caused damage to the central nervous system.

The prediction of later (usually school age) intelligence from the Adaptive area of the Gesell examination has caused considerable problems in the developmental literature. In particular, such attempts have proved unsuccessful in the hands of psychologists, many without specialized training in its use (for a recent review on the predictive validity of developmental tests, see Stott & Ball, 1965). This lack of training has led to a misinterpretation of the data obtained on the Adaptive schedule and to the general impression that it is too heavily dependent on motor items (Fishler, 1971).

The appropriate use of scoring procedures and the diagnostic interpretation of derived scores are discussed in great detail by Knobloch and Pasamanick (1974). As delineated by them, the procedure allows for the special treatment of adaptive items which cannot be performed because of motor deficit. As an example, consider the child with athetosis who cannot match two cubes at 40 weeks. The fine motor integration necessary to perform this behavior adequately is also reflected in the fine motor scale (e.g., grasping a pellet or plucking a string). In assessing such a child, these items would be scored as either "abnormal" or "absent," depending on the child's indication of his ability to understand and attempt the task. Should the child attempt to match two cubes, but prove incapable because of his motor handicap, the fine and gross motor schedules would reflect this impairment but he would not be penalized in the scoring of the Adaptive DQ. Further, in determining the quotient which will be utilized for the prediction of later intellectual development, the Language DQ must also be considered. A higher Language quotient than Adaptive quotient should serve as a sign that the latter is too low; and this finding should be weighed along with other clinical data in deriving an overall score. Obviously, the use of the schedules involves much more than a simple check-off of behavioral items.

It must be emphasized and appreciated that in predicting later test performance, adverse sociocultural events (e.g., social disruption, inadequate education) which may depress intellectual performance must be given careful consideration. Nevertheless, the depressant effects of such factors on IQ test scores and on school performance will not be dwelt upon here, since these have received attention elsewhere in this volume and in other reviews (see Jencks, 1972).

Another important consideration in determining the validity of the developmental examination is the extent to which it is clear as to what the test is designed to detect and what predictions may follow from the findings. The primary purpose of the examination is the identification of the infant with such severe organic brain disease that normal development is precluded even under optimal circumstances. Another purpose is the differentiation of neuromotor and sensory defect from intellectual impairment. Concomitantly, by a careful consideration of demographic data, one might hope to discriminate between disease of the nervous system and extraindividual environmental factors, which may act differentially to depress developmental rates. On the basis of test performance alone, it is impossible to detect the normal infant who may later appear as socioculturally retarded, or conversely, to identify the normal child who will later demonstrate superior performance because of the quality and availability of educational opportunity. In these latter instances, as will be discussed later, it is social class—with its accompanying effects on educational and social opportunities—which may be expected to be the best indicators of later performance. It is for these reasons, among others, that predictive validity studies by many investigators have failed to demonstrate meaningful associations.

In validity studies conducted on a variety of groups composed of infants with normal intellectual "potential" (i.e., normal Adaptive scores), the correlation coefficients found between infant and later examinations are all about .50 (Knobloch & Pasamanick, 1974). These diverse groups included a sample of black infants reexamined at age 7, a group of noninstitutionalized infants recommended for adoption placement and seen at age 5, 300 infants reevaluated at age 3, and 200 followed up in the early school period, at about age 7. Further work showed (Knobloch & Pasamanick, 1974) that when a sample is composed only of infants with neuromotor and intellectual defects, or when those with mental deficiency are included in the total sample, the correlations between early and later examinations rise to .70. When the correlations are weighted by using a stepwise regression procedure accounting for parental socioeconomic status and seizures after the infant examination, they rise to .75 for infants with DQs above 80 and to .85 for the total group. With regard to the "normal" sample, 75% of the 300 infants seen at age 3, and 60% of the 200 infants reexamined at school age, had changed less than 15 DQ points between the two examinations (Knobloch & Pasamanick, 1974). Physicians who have conducted studies in the United Kingdom on the predictive validity of the Gesell examination have obtained similar results (Drillien, 1961; Illingsworth, 1961).

Such findings indicate that the contentions of many professionals concerned with infant assessment, to the effect that the infant examination is both unreliable and lacking in predictive validity, must be modified. This is of more than academic interest. The specification of the prevalence of developmental disorders among children, as well as the provision and planning of services for them, is contingent on early identification. It is clear from the work reviewed above that the Gesell examination is an instrument which is both reliable and predictive of performance on intelligence tests beyond infancy. Furthermore, more recent follow-up studies with other developmental instruments, such as the Bayley Mental Scale (Holden, 1972; Ireton, Thwing, & Gravem, 1970), demonstrate that the weak predictive validity obtained among normal infants is considerably strengthened when socioeconomic variables are included in the correlational matrix. Although in the study by Ireton et al., the correlations reported for Stanford-Binet IQ at age 4 and the Bayley score at age 8 months are low (.28 for males and .23 for females) and consequently unacceptable for general clinical use, they are statistically significant and substantially higher than the zero correlation previously obtained by Bayley (1955). The Holden study, on the other hand, found the Bayley scale to predict poorer (although normal) intellectual functioning on the Stanford-Binet and Wechsler Intelligence Scale for Children (WISC) in 8-year-old children who were 1 month retarded at 8 months of age, as contrasted to a normal group. In that study, the discriminatory ability of the Bayley was "impressively" increased when combined with both a child's poorer performance on motor tests and a clinical judgment of abnormality. The large variability in latter IQ scores caused Holden to conclude that mental deficiency could not be predicted in individual cases. However, Holden's selection of children who did not manifest mental deficiency (DQs of 87) requires reservations about his conclusions.

Another recent investigation, using the Cattell Infant Intelligence Scale (Werner, Honzik, & Smith, 1968), found significant correlations (.49) between 20-month DQs and school-age IQ, which was further enhanced (.58) when medical and socioeconomic status were included by multiple correlation procedures. In a later section, I will comment further on statistical procedures which may be employed for validity studies and for the specification of factors leading to neonatal risk.

The above correlational data have been presented because of the emphasis on such numerical concerns in the literature. However, they are not the most important aspects of child development which require examination. In children without organic impairment, school-age tests of intelligence have limited usefulness as indices of the validity of methods assessing infant development. Errors of *clinical application* will be avoided if the clinician remembers that the DQ and IQ refer to the *end products* of development. In and of themselves, these scores do not reflect such important variables as the etiology of given defects and deviations, the medical history of the child, and differences in environmental and experiential factors during the course of maturation. Therefore, the diagnostician must not only have knowledge of central nervous processes and of clinical entities and syndromes, but must also weigh all these qualifying considerations and interpret the various quotients accordingly. Ultimately, the clinician must determine whether a given DQ or IQ is really predictive, or whether modifying factors are present.

Neuropsychiatric Disorders as a Continuum

With particular relevance to the present chapter, it is important to understand the association between mental deficiency and various other neuropsychiatric conditions originating during fetal life, infancy, and childhood. These conditions include cerebral palsy, convulsive disorders, and the "hyperkinetic syndrome."

There is reason to believe that mental deficiency constitutes but one of many related conditions afflicting the central nervous system and which fall within a continuum of neuropsychiatric disorders in children. Validity studies must, of necessity, consider the broad range of defects which might result from noxious insults to the fetus, infant, or mother. Perhaps comprehension of the problem will be enhanced if the issues are presented in historical perspective.

An analysis of data obtained in a study conducted in New Haven, Connecticut, in the early 1940s, indicated that black infants achieved Gesell scores at levels which would have been expected for white infants

(Pasamanick, 1946). Further, the growth curves for weight and height of black infants were comparable to those reported for white babies, a finding which at the time was contrary to those of other studies. A further analysis of the data for both groups suggested that weight and height were directly associated with performance in adaptive behavior on the Gesell examination. A reasonable explanation for these findings was that they were a consequence of the more equitable distribution of food by rationing which had occurred during World War II.

The implication of the latter study, to the effect that nutrition might be a major factor in child development, formed the basis for a number of subsequent prospective and quasi-retrospective epidemiologic investigations on the association between maternal nutrition and infant development. This series of investigations (Knobloch & Pasamanick, 1966; Pasamanick & Knobloch, 1966), was guided by a hypothetical formulation, termed "a continuum of reproductive casualty," which has been supported to a greater or lesser degree by a number of later investigations by other workers—as discussed below.

The continuum of reproductive casualty. At this point, I will review the concept and the earlier work it generated, and will bring the issues up to date by focusing principally on the work done since the time of the last two reviews cited above.

The concept of reproductive casualty has been implicit in the writings of other concerned workers for almost three-quarters of a century (e.g., Ballantyne, 1902, 1904; Gesell 1945). Therefore, an enormous body of literature on the subject has accumulated and continues to proliferate.

The expression "continuum of reproductive casualty" was coined some years ago to denote the sequelae of harmful events occurring during pregnancy and parturition, and resulting in damage to the fetus or newborn—such insult being located mainly in the central nervous system. The various sequelae were seen as forming a continuum from fetal death through varying degrees of disability in the child. The term "reproductive casualty" was used to replace a somewhat older term, "reproductive wastage," which was applied chiefly to fetal and neonatal deaths. It was felt that "wastage" was an invidious word when applied to children at any time and that, in any event, it was incorrect if used for a host of minor disabilities such as motor, perceptual, intellectual, learning, and behavior disorders.

The basic formulation stems from a number of propositions:

> (a) Since prematurity and complications of pregnancy are associated with fetal and neonatal death, usually on the basis of injury to the brain, there must remain a fraction of children so

injured who do not die.

(b) Depending upon the nature, degree, and location of the damage, the survivors may develop a series of disorders, covering a wide range of severity. This range may extend from cerebral palsy, convulsive disorders, and mental deficiency through various types of behavioral and learning disabilities—which result from lesser damage that is nevertheless sufficient to disorganize behavioral development and to lower stress threshold.

(c) These abnormalities of pregnancy are associated with certain (usually socioeconomically determined) life experiences.

(d) Consequent to socioeconomic variables, the latter abnormalities and their resulting neuropsychiatric disorders are found in greater aggregation among the poor.

The extent of potentially noxious factors which may have an adverse effect on the fetus *in utero* ranges from environmental influences affecting the mother to various (as yet poorly understood) medical conditions. In the latter instance, remedial measures are difficult (sometimes impossible) to institute, and some diseases lead to such unavoidable sequelae as those associated with maternal herpes simplex virus (Florman, Gershon, Blackett, & Nahmias, 1973; Nahmias, Josey, Naib, Freeman, Fernandez, & Wheeler, 1971), diabetes (Churchill, Berendes, & Nemore, 1969), cytomegalic inclusion disease (Monif, Egan, Held, & Eitzman, 1972; Reynolds, Stagno, Hosty, Tiller, & Alford, 1973), and proteinuria (Rosenbaum, Churchill, Shakhashiri, & Moody, 1969). In the case of potentially noxious environmental circumstances, public health intervention toward the prevention of disability may be possible. Noxious environmental conditions with adverse sequelae include cigarette smoking (Davie, Butler, & Goldstein, 1972), air pollution (Lave & Seskin, 1970), hard water supply (Crawford, Gardner, & Sedgewick, 1972), radiation effects (Blot & Miller, 1973; Sternglass, 1969), drugs medically administered during pregnancy—such as anticonvulsants (Lowe, 1973) and antibiotics and salicylates (National Academy of Sciences, 1970)—anesthetic gas inhalation among pregnant nurses (Cohen, Belleville, & Brown, 1971), and maternal narcotic addiction (Pierson, Howard, & Kleber, 1972; Zelson, 1973). A most important environmental consideration is the availability and quality of health care. This will be reviewed in more detail subsequently.

Research on Reproductive Casualty

The prospective and quasi-retrospective studies conducted pursuant to the reproductive casualty formulation sought to relate neuropsychiatric conditions in children to various factors attending their conception and delivery. In the retrospective studies, information was gathered from hospital charts on such items as the number of previous pregnancies, abortions, stillbirths, premature and neonatal deaths, complications of pregnancy, labor, and delivery, operative delivery procedures, birth weight, and neonatal course. The prospective studies were concerned in large measure with the problem of the predictive validity of the infant neurological examination; and discussion of them will be deferred to a later section.

Retrospective studies. Table 10.3 summarizes the results of the various quasi-retrospective studies conducted by Pasamanick and Knobloch (1966) in Baltimore, Maryland, and Columbus, Ohio—concerning the association between neuropsychiatric disability in children and complications of pregnancy, prematurity, and neonatal abnormalities.

The data in Table 10.3 indicate that five of the first seven clinical entities studied have been found to be significantly associated both with complications of pregnancy and with prematurity. These are *cerebral palsy, mental deficiency, epilepsy, behavior disorders,* and *reading disabilities.* A sixth condition, *tics,* was found to be significantly associated with complications but not with prematurity, although slight differences in the predicted direction were found for neonatal abnormality.

No differences were found between the study subjects and those in the control groups in the incidence of prolonged and difficult labor and of various operative procedures during delivery—such as use of mid- or high forceps, Caesarean section, breech extraction, or internal version and extraction—which were previously assumed to be responsible for birth injuries. Rather, those differences which were found were associated with the prolonged and probably anoxia-producing complications of pregnancy, such as toxemia and maternal bleeding. When all the disabilities were pooled, breech deliveries were also significantly associated in the non-White population.

As indicated in Table 10.3, five other conditions were studied: *strabismus, hearing defects, school accidents, infantile autism,* and *juvenile delinquency.* Strabismus, largely due to muscle paralysis or imbalance, had previously been found to be common, particularly in infants, as one of the symptoms of a syndrome of minimal brain damage; and it has been described as present in cerebral palsy and other known sequelae of brain damage. It was therefore not too surprising to find quite a strong and significant association of complications of pregnancy and prematurity with this condition in children who had no other apparent evidence of brain damage.

Two other general observations were made. First, in both the

Table 10.3

Maternal and Fetal Factors in Neuropsychiatric Disorders

Disorder	Number of Children in Study Group White	Number of Children in Study Group Non-White	One or More Complications in Pregnancy (%) Study Group W	One or More Complications in Pregnancy (%) Study Group N	One or More Complications in Pregnancy (%) Control Group W	One or More Complications in Pregnancy (%) Control Group N	Prematurity[a] (%) Study Group W	Prematurity[a] (%) Study Group N	Prematurity[a] (%) Control Group W	Prematurity[a] (%) Control Group N	Neonatal Abnormalities[b] (%) Study Group W	Neonatal Abnormalities[b] (%) Study Group N	Neonatal Abnormalities[b] (%) Control Group W	Neonatal Abnormalities[b] (%) Control Group N
Cerebral Palsy	561[c]	—	38.0		21.0		22.0		5.0		—		—	
Epilepsy	274	122	27.7	50.8	18.8	43.4	12.9	15.3	3.8	12.3	17.2	13.6	5.7	3.3
Mental Deficiency	404	235	34.4	60.0	25.2	55.0	16.3	18.4	7.0	11.6	18.0	7.7	7.5	6.1
Behavioral Disorders	625	215	33.0	64.0	25.0	51.0	6.0	17.0	2.0	5.0	5.0	4.0	3.0	2.0
Reading Disorders	205	—	37.6	—	21.5	—	11.5	—	4.6	—	7.8	—	3.9	—
Tics	51	—	33.3		17.6		4.0		6.0		37.3		25.5	
Speech Disorders	272	—	25.0	—	19.0	—	5.0	—	8.0	—	9.0	—	11.0	—
Strabismus	398		22.9		16.1		13.6		7.8		22.4		13.8	
Hearing Disorders	124		24.0		11.5		16.1		7.3		17.1		13.3	
Accidents in School Children	725		17.8		16.3		8.0		5.2		15.0		12.8	
Autism	50		51.0		17.0		21.0		12.0		64.0		28.0	
Juvenile Delinquency	300		8.5		11.1		3.6		3.8		—		—	

Note. From "Retrospective Studies on the Epidemiology of Reproductive Casualty: Old and New," by B. Pasamanick and H. Knobloch. *Merrill-Palmer Quarterly,* 1966, *12,* 1-26. Copyright 1966 by the Merrill-Palmer Institute. Reprinted by Permission.

[a]Birth weights 2,500 gm (5.5 lb) or less.
[b]Convulsions, cyanosis, and asphyxia.
[c]Data appearing in center of columns reflect undifferentiated White and non-White totals.

experimental and control groups, the incidence of abnormalities of pregnancy was much higher in the non-Whites than in the Whites. Second, the differences between study cases and controls tended to be greater in the more severe clinical conditions (e.g., cerebral palsy, epilepsy, autism), and the differences tended to decrease with the severity of the listed disorders.

As is generally found in submitting any hypothesis to validation, various subsequent studies by other investigators have supported the initial findings, while others have failed to yield support. For example, the early Baltimore studies clearly implicated toxemia of pregnancy as one of the factors among the various identifiable gestational and obstetrical complications associated with neuropsychiatric disability in childhood. On the other hand, in the preliminary analysis of the British Perinatal Data (Davie et al., 1972), no association was found betwen toxemia (and various other obstetrical complications) and "recognized handicap" at school age, as reported by the teacher. Another British study (Barker & Edwards, 1967), looking at the educational test scores of some 50,000 11-year-old children in Birmingham, England, found a small but definite link between poor test performance and several obstetrical and gestational variables (e.g., short gestation period, toxemia, occipito-posterior presentation, and birth in an ambulance). The latter findings are all the more notable because these authors excluded from consideration children most likely to be impaired; for example, children in special schools for the handicapped, or those classified as "borderline subnormal." Similarly, investigators in the Ontario Perinatal Study (Buck, 1970) found pre-eclampsia to be associated with slight, but nonetheless significant, impairment in various intellectual, behavioral, and neurological dependent measures among their population. However, in the Ontario group, no association was obtained between other pregnancy problems and the dependent measures used.

Rutter, Tizard, and Whitmore (1970) studied 141 British children in their Isle of Wight project and reported finding no association betwen intellectual and reading retardation in the children and toxemia of pregnancy or other obstetrical problems in the mothers. On the other hand, Birch, Richardson, Baird, Horobin, and Illsley (1970) found a clear overrepresentation of pre-eclamptic toxemia, as well as other obstetrical complications, in a mentally subnormal population in Aberdeen, Scotland. In recent studies on American school children with psychiatric disorders, McNeil and Wiegerink (1971) and McNeil, Wiegerink, and Dozier (1970) also found a high prevalence of pregnancy and birth complications in a heterogeneous group of behaviorally impaired children. However, the populations employed by Rutter and his associates and by McNeil's group are typical of a number of other investigations in being too small to provide an adequate test of the contributions of the factors considered.

Sociocultural issues. The work done with regard to the identification of high-risk variables which might be predictive of eventual neuropsychiatric disability is complicated by the possible interaction of socioenvironmental variables (e.g., social class, sibship, ordinality). A number of investigators have suggested data analysis procedures which might bring to light the basis for some of the reported discrepancies (see Gottfried, 1973, for a general review). For example, in an exploratory study, Smith, Flick, Ferris, and Sellman (1972), using the procedures of multivariate discriminant function analysis to test the concept of a continuum of reproductive casualty, found support for the concept. They described a procedure for the analysis of the relationship between a number of risk factors and intellectual development in 7-year-old children.

Another recently reported and extensive follow-up study using multivariate analysis is that of Neligan, Prudham, and Steiner (1974). They investigated the contributions of breech delivery and clinical asphyxia—as these interact with low birth weight and socioeconomic status—to eventual neuropsychiatric disorders among surviving infants at ages 5 and 10, years. Data from survivors of asphyxia and of breech of delivery—taking into account socioeconomic status and (where it occurred) low birth weight—were compared to those from children of nonstigmatized pregnancies. Dependent measures included intelligence tests at 5 and 10 years of age and behavior ratings from teachers at 10 years. It was found that low birth weight, social class, and number of previous pregnancies had the greatest depressing effect on later IQ. The factors of asphyxia and breech delivery had little effect on IQ scores when considered independently of the birth weight and social class variables. The strongest support for the reproductive casualty hypothesis was found for the survivors of low birth weight.

As with the major syndromes outlined above, universal support for the more minor conditions in the reproductive casualty continuum (e.g., learning and behavior disorders) has not been found. This may be due in part to the protective effect exerted by improved health and nutritional status among some of the populations studied as compared to that of the subjects in the earlier investigations in Baltimore and Columbus. The inconsistencies may also be a consequence of the general lack of attention in many studies to the possible interaction of some of the potentially noxious variables in combination (e.g., toxemia or asphyxia plus low birth weight). It should again be noted that in the research conducted in Baltimore and Columbus, the degree of neuropsychiatric deficit was found to be associated with the number of reported pregnancy and birth complications in each subject.

A clear finding of the retrospective studies by Pasamanick and Knobloch (1966) was the disproportionately higher prevalence of pregnancy and birth complications among non-White mothers as compared to White mothers. These observations were taken to be a consequence of the relative inadequacy of health care provided for non-White populations, even when social class was controlled. It must be noted that in no sense can control of the social class variable in epidemiological investigations be expected to account adequately for the adverse effects of racial discrimination and its sequelae, the inequitable allocation of resources among poor non-White Americans.

These early findings have been corroborated repeatedly by later investigations, most recently in a study conducted by the National Academy of Sciences (Kessner, 1973), which again found the shameful disproportionately high neonatal and maternal mortality rates among American Blacks, as contrasted to Whites. That study indicated that should all women receive adequate health care services before and during pregnancy, the infant mortality rate could be reduced by as much as 33%. Although the findings pertaining to the differential prognosis among groups of differing socioeconomic status in the British and Ontario Perinatal Studies are not so blatantly apparent as those found with American populations, they also show the adverse effects of lowered socioeconomic status on pregnancy outcome.

Prospective studies. Two prospective studies which attempt to delineate the effects of organic brain disease, as identified during infancy, to clinical outcome are reviewed by Knobloch and Pasamanick (1974). As with the retrospective studies reviewed above, these latter investigations were conducted in Baltimore, Maryland, and Columbus, Ohio.

Three hundred infants examined with the Gesell schedule at 40 weeks in a Baltimore Study of Prematures were reexamined at 3 years of age. Differences among these children appeared to emerge only in those aspects of behavior which have a neurological substrate—as determined by the extent of neuromotor abnormality—and not in other areas, such as peer relations or intrafamilial interaction patterns. Bowel and bladder control, both daytime and nighttime, were achieved by a greater percentage of 3-year-olds who had been diagnosed as having normal neuromotor status in infancy than in those who had manifested minor neuromotor abnormalities. Conversely, the lowest rates of success were found in those children who had shown marked neuromotor impairment at 40 weeks. In addition, the quality of assessed behavioral integration of the children at age 3 correlated positively with the intactness of their neuromotor status in infancy. Thus, the proportion of 3-year-olds showing some degree of disorganization increased from 15% to 20% to 60%, concomitantly with changes in ratings of infant neuromotor status from "normal" to "mild impairment," to "markedly severe impairment."

The ability to maintain average intellectual status is probably one of the most important aspects of behavior. The percentage of children who at age 3 had failed to maintain a low-average or better intellectual level increased from 6% in those with normal infant neuromotor status to 14% in those with minor abnormalities, and to 33% in the small number with marked abnormalities in infancy. In another sample followed longitudinally to age 3, rates for failure to maintain normal intellectual status were 5% in normal infants and 25% in those with minor neuromotor impairment. These findings together with further longitudinal data (Knobloch & Pasamanick, 1974) suggest that most of the infants who deteriorate have done so by age 3, and any further decline with increasing age will occur essentially in those children showing evidence of impairment as infants. It is further suggested that part of the lowering of IQ-test scores that occurs in children with antecedent impairment may be due to their inability to respond to the stress presented by the structure of the classroom and the psychological testing situation.

The interrelationships between infant DQ, neuromotor status, and school-age IQ, as well as the influence of socioeconomic status and the frequency of subsequent seizure activity of those children, were studied in the Columbus, Ohio, population. Table 10.4 lists the battery of tests employed at school age to evaluate a number of clinically relevant areas.

As in the Baltimore study, there was a significant, systematic, direct relationship between infant neuromotor status and later performance in the Columbus sample on all of these tests. However, the IQ-test scores correlated highly with almost all other tests administered on follow-up, and IQ appears to be a major factor in all aspects of function. In the case of school-age minimal brain dysfunction (which by definition includes only those children with near-average or better intelligence), further analysis is necessary to determine if the infant neuromotor diagnosis has an influence on later behavior independently of its effect on the IQ-test score. Consequently, the data were submitted to closer inspection for that purpose.

Of the 136 children whose IQ was above 75, 93 were of normal neuromotor status as infants, and 43 had previously shown minor or marked neuromotor impairment. Each of these groups (normal-as-infants versus impaired-as-infants) was further divided into subgroups of children who had IQ scores of 96 or more, on the one hand, and IQs between 76 and 95, on the other. It was found that of the 93 who were normal in infancy, approximately 66% had a school-age IQ of 96 or more, while of the 43 previously impaired infants, only about 50% were in the upper-IQ range. While the total number of children involved was relatively small, the data further indicate that infant neuromotor status had a behavioral influence independently of IQ. Thus, as compared to the upper-IQ-normal-as-infants

Table 10.4

**Test Battery Used in School-Age Follow-up of Children
Examined in Infancy**

1. Audio-Visual Integration Test
2. Bender Visual-Motor Gestalt Test
3. California Achievement Test: Selected Tests of:
   Arithmetic
   Handwriting
   Reading
   Spelling
4. Finger-Tapping Speed
5. Garfield Motor Impersistence Test
6. Illinois Test of Psycholinguistic Abilities: Subtests
   Auditory Decoding
   Auditory Vocal Automatic
   Motor Encoding
   Visual Motor Sequencing
7. Kinsbourne-Warrington Test of Finger Agnosia: Subtests
   In Between
   Same-Different
8. Language Function Tests:
   Auditory Associative Learning
   Ideational Fluency
   Inductive Reasoning
   Speech Discrimination
   Speech Mimicry
   Verbal Fluency
9. Oseretsky Tests of Motor Proficiency (Gollintz Revision)
10. Birch Perceptual-Motor and Perceptual-Motor Sequencing Test
11. Prechtl Choretic Movement Test
12. Stanford-Binet, Form L-M
13. Wechsler Intelligence Scale for Children: Subtests
    Coding
    Mazes

subjects, fewer of the upper-IQ-impaired-as-infants group had average or better performance in the following areas: The Oseretsky Tests of Motor Proficiency, the Reading and Spelling subtests of the California Achievement Test, the Bender Visual-Motor Gestalt Test, the Auditory Vocal Automatic and Auditory Decoding subtests of the Illinois Test of Psycholinguistic Abilities, the Garfield Motor Impersistence Test, the Same-Different subtest of the Kinsbourne-Warrington Test of Finger Agnosia, and the Analysis and Synthesis subtests of the Birch Perceptual-Motor and Perceptual-Motor Sequencing Test. Trends on other tests were in the same direction, but did not reach statistical significance. The behaviors sampled by these tests correspond to the kind of difficulties which are considered components of the minimal brain damage syndrome at school age.

An additional point worthy of note was the greater number of pregnancy and birth complications in the case of infants with marked neuromotor impairment as compared to the nonimpaired sample. Even though the sample sizes were small, results are analogous to those found in the earlier Baltimore studies on reproductive casualty, and they are consistent with at least some of the previously reviewed current studies on the association between pregnancy and birth complications and neuropsychiatric disorders in childhood.

CURRENT IMPLICATIONS OF THE ISSUES

In the preceding sections, it has been argued that the Gesell Developmental and Neurological Examination is both a reliable and valid instrument for the assessment of general neurological and intellectual integrity in infants. Additionally, the evidence has been reviewed which indicates that the diagnosis of neuropsychiatric conditions in infancy is often validated by tests which identify impairment in school-age children.

It has also been noted that psychological studies which find infant tests to be invalid for prediction of latter intellectual status have been conducted by clinicians who either ignored or did not have access to the clinical-medical information which must be used concomitantly with test data in establishing accurate diagnostic assessments of infant neurological and intellectual status. Another possible reason for the given negative findings may be a homogeneously high socioeconomic status among the particular sample or population studied. It is most likely for these reasons, along with often inadequate sampling size, that many longitudinal studies which relate infant tests to later functioning have failed to find meaningful associations.

The material reviewed above has obvious implications for the field of developmental retardation. The orientation which the clinician/investigator must assume in either conducting his work or appraising the work of others was originally expressed by Gesell and Amatruda (1947) in referring to the diagnosis of minimal cerebral dysfunction or impairment. Nevertheless, their comments, which follow, apply to the total problem of organic brain disease (e.g., seizures, mental deficiencies) in the infant:

> The diagnosis of minimal cerebral impairment is not always supported by the paranatal and neonatal history. The diagnosis rests upon the nature and historical development of the neuromotor and sensory deviations and deficits. Here, as elsewhere, one must take the total behavior picture into account and must reconcile the findings of successive examinations. Even when there is a portentous history which would seem to point unmistakably to devastating or selective injury of severe degree, it is well to place the utmost reliance on the behavior. . . . On the other hand, an entirely negative prenatal history and an uneventful neonatal period may nevertheless demand a diagnosis of minimal brain damage because of persisting or gradually diminishing neuromotor signs. In obscure or doubtful cases, the following is a safe rule: Do not assume that there has certainly been a cerebral injury, but assume that every child who is born alive has run the universal risk of such injury. (p. 240)

Sociocultural Considerations

The lack of consideration of developmental diagnosis for establishment or exclusion of organicity among infant populations confounds the findings of many clinical studies and, in some instances, casts doubts on their necessity. Consider, for example, Heber and Garber's well-known study (1972) on so-called familial retardation.

Taking children at age 3 or 4, Heber and Garber sought to determine the extent to which their subjects' presumed "potential" for mental retardation could be prevented. They selected their study children on the basis of maternal IQ ($\leqslant 70$), with "confidence" that many of their children would be identified as retarded with advancing age. A sample of children whose mothers achieved IQ scores of 100 or above served as a comparison or control group.

Initial findings indicated that the experimental subjects—who were involved in an individual academic program—manifested marked acceleration (approximately a 33 IQ-point superiority) relative to the control children. This study was formulated in full awareness of considerations pertaining to the nature-nurture controversy, and it was conducted on children who were the offspring of so-called retarded parents. Nevertheless, we must assume in the absence of data to the contrary that the majority of the study children were not organically impaired. Furthermore, while the prevalence of pregnancy and birth complications in the mothers of the experimental group would be expected to be greater than that found among women of higher socioeconomic status, it would probably be no higher than that found among the mothers of the control group. Within this context, the findings pertaining to the acquisition of behaviors by the experimental group were of a magnitude which Heber and Garber say they found difficult to believe. The Gesellian would find nothing surprising in the derived data. He would conclude that infants without acquisition-limiting organic brain disease would be expected to manifest normal growth and development, provided the opportunities for such development are made available.

In another study, which was not directed specifically to the problem of retardation (Eisenberg, 1967), Head Start data give evidence of improved performance by children receiving educational services, followed by a decline in their performance once such services are terminated—again, nothing surprising. Given an intact organism, academic performance (as is all learning) is obviously contingent on the availability of educational opportunity.

Role of developmental biology. Since the problems associated with retardation and behavioral genetics are not within the purview of this chapter (see Switzky & Gaylord-Ross, this volume), I will not dwell on them here except briefly. The populations studied relative to intellectual retardation of presumed sociocultural or "familial" (i.e., genetic) derivation almost invariably are those constituting ethnic minorities. These populations are most poorly served by our health, education, and welfare systems, and are consequently at highest risk for the development of neuropsychiatric disability. As has been repeatedly argued, the continued investigation of the relationship between genetic and intellectual variables among the poor is a form of scientific racism (Pasamanick, 1971). The biological developmentalist cannot entertain a hypothesis pertaining to cognitive differences among various ethnic or racial minorities under conditions of social inequities which affect the subject's performance on the dependent measures which are used. Further, he considers of only trivial scientific concern whatever "true" racial or ethnic differences may exist.

A line of investigation on which biological developmental considerations may have some bearing is represented in the area of cross-national studies on cultural differences, as exemplified in the work of Kagan and his associates (Kagan & Klein, 1973). These workers have investigated \cognitive development in peasant Guatemalan children, as contrasted with those in an urban, middle-class Boston population, using cross-sectional methods. Any such cross-sectional assessment must suffer, a priori, by a failure to consider both the higher prevalence of fetal death in the rural group and the higher probability of central nervous system pathology in the surviving later-age rural populations. Unfortunately, interpretation of whatever between- or within-group differences are found is extremely hazardous without a full awareness of such considerations. For example, Kagan and Klein found "accelerated" performance among 11-year-old Guatemalan children, as contrasted to the performance of Guatemalan infants, on various cognitive dependent measures, leading to the conclusion that "infant retardation seems to be partially reversible" (1973, p. 957). Actually, this may represent no true acceleration at all, but rather the effects of a "weeding out"—by death or other calamity—of previously poorer-performing, organically impaired children. Alternatively, the poor performance of Guatemalan infants could just as likely be associated with nutritional deficiencies which may be corrected as the infant becomes ambulatory and more capable of elaborating on his diet. An awareness on the part of the investigators of medical and nutritional problems in the Guatemalan sample might have avoided such ambiguity. This is particularly important because inadequate nutrition among infants and school children is known to have an adverse effect on growth and intellectual development (Birch & Gussow, 1970).

Geographically closer to home are those studies addressed to the problem of "individual differences" (Escalona, 1968) and "temperament" (Thomas, Chess, & Birch, 1968). These investigators have sought to relate various patterns of infant behavior to later personality outcome. In the studies by Thomas et al., a number of infants identified as having behavioral patterns putatively predisposing to later abnormal behavior have evidenced such deviance on follow-up investigation. Recent work by English investigators (Graham, Rutter, & George, 1973) have supported these findings. However, in the absence of evidence to the contrary, the behavioral deviance manifested by many of the study children can as likely be attributed to prior undiagnosed organic brain disease, as to biologically innate differences. The failure to include such considerations renders hazardous any conclusion about the predictive validity of infant behavior assessments to later "personality."

Current work on environmental toxins—perhaps best typified by lead-poisoning investigations—may prove to be unproductive for similar reasons. In this work, the association between a history of lead burdening and adverse development has been interpreted as possibly causal (David, Clark, & Voeller, 1972; Pueschel, Kopito, & Schwachman, 1972). However, without the exclusion of possible organicity in the populations studied prior to exposure to lead, no meaningful conclusion about the nature or the extent of the association can be derived.

Implications for Pediatric Medicine

Of much more immediate importance to health care than the research areas discussed above are the implications of developmental assessment to clinical pediatric medicine. The underemployment of such assessment is illustrated by some current developments in health-care legislation. For example, in 1972 the U.S. Congress, in an amendment to the Economic Opportunity Act (P.L. 92-424), specified that 10% of Head Start services be allocated to the care of children with "developmental disabilities." Regrettably, in the New York City area, as in most other areas, no data are available as to the prevalence of pre-school children in the developmental age range who are in need of special services for developmental disability. The preceding discussion points up the irony that this unfortunate ignorance is totally avoidable, since a reliable screening instrument is available to identify high-risk infants and toddlers who are in need of more intensive assessment (Knobloch, Sherard, & Pasamanick, 1966). Health-care planning cannot proceed without difficulty in the absence of prevalence and incidence data.

Further comment about the identification and diagnosis of children at risk is warranted. The diagnostician has incumbent upon him the establishment or exclusion of disease, by which is meant pathological functioning of an organ or a group of organ systems. The failure of medicine to adequately use developmental assessment procedures for the establishment of disease has permitted extravagant speculations about the etiology of various types of behavioral disorders. A number of intervention procedures—proposed and conducted with disregard of the disease concept—have been promulgated, many with little demonstrable effectiveness (e.g., the psychotherapies and milieu therapies). It is my opinion that progress in the development of appropriate medical treatment has suffered, and will continue to suffer, from this lack of consideration.

The dearth of trained manpower for administering and interpreting developmental measures has been commented upon above. Nevertheless, it must be stressed that, in the absence of such manpower, little progress in terms of planning for services can ensue.

Behavioral versus medical models of treatment. Since behavior modification procedures are increasingly being used in hospitals and clinics for the treatment of patients who have received a diagnosis of organic brain disease, some comments are required about the differences (and their implications) between the behavioral and medical models. Of particular relevance is the failure of the behaviorist to consider acquisition-limiting impairment of the central nervous system. For example, the behavioral model, which is discussed at length by Watson in this volume, has been summarized by Bijou (1966) as follows:

> It is suggested that developmental retardation be treated as observable, objectively defined stimulus-response relationships without recourse to hypothetical mental concepts such as "defective intelligence" and hypothetical biological abnormalities such as "clinically inferred brain injury." From this point of view a retarded individual is one who has a limited repertory of behavior shaped by events that constitute his history. Retardation is not conceived of as a symptom. (p. 2)

In contrast, the developmental-medical model states that, in the presence of a diseased organism, intellectual impairment and behavioral deviance are direct consequences of the disease state. The concept of disease assumes an etiological agent (frequently unknown, but presumably knowable) and indicates a prognosis or prediction of events dependent on both the etiology of the condition and the demonstrated effectiveness of treatment. The function of treatment as conducted within this model is that of altering the prognosis in a favorable direction. In the case of behavioral deviance which is not consequent to disease, the physician has no particular treatment competence. His professional function ceases, insofar as his expertise is concerned, when disease is excluded, although his contributions may continue as a function of his involvement as a concerned citizen or administrator.

The behavioral therapist generally avoids speculation about both the etiology and the prognosis of deviant behavior, as these are conceptualized within the disease model. Rather, behavioral impairment is defined, without recourse to a health-illness dimension, as socially unacceptable behavior. Nevertheless, both models concur in the desirability of attenuating symptoms (or the frequency of deviant responses) so that the suffering of the patient is diminished. Consequently, a mutually accepted criterion of treatment effectiveness is the diminution of such behaviors or symptoms. The medical model, however, imposes an additional criterion of effectiveness, that of favorably altering the prognosis—ideally by controlling the etiological factors causing disease.

These differences have considerable practical implications. Questions—such as: "What are the child's prospects for future development?"

"What long-term plans should be made for his care?" "What resources should society allocate for the care of retarded or otherwise handicapped children?"—cannot be answered by the behaviorist working within the context of his model. Since prognosis as defined above is not relevant to the behaviorist, such questions, which are of clear public health relevance, remain unanswered. Additionally, the failure to render a diagnosis or to discuss limitations imposed by central nervous system impairment (since, from a theoretical standpoint, these variables are irrelevant) may serve to raise the expectations of parents—who are ready to clutch at any available straw—to unrealistic heights. The physician must consider the nurturance of such unfounded expectations to be clinically detrimental.

Finally, since within the behavioral model, deviance is socially defined, the concept of illness, with all it implies, is not considered in the clinical practice of many behavior therapists functioning in a pediatric mental health setting. Consequently, danger exists that children with only trivial behavioral deviance, which may or may not be based on disease states, will receive treatment which would be deemed unnecessary from the medical perspective. When appropriately used, the medical model (constrained as it is by the disease concept) does not allow for such ambiguity.

With reference to specific medical treatment, the information derived from developmental diagnosis has implications for pharmacotherapy of children with behavioral disorders. I have indicated that there is often sufficient diagnostic information, both medical and psychological, to obligate the primary diagnosis of chronic organic brain disease for many patients. As pertains to psychiatric disorders of childhood, this diagnosis is in contrast to such generally utilized descriptive terms as childhood psychosis, hyperkinetic reaction, and learning disabilities.

The establishment of a diagnosis has serious implications for psychopharmacological treatment of children. In planning drug therapy of severe behavior disorders in children, for example, it is commonly assumed that the phenothiazines, which are of unquestioned value for the treatment of adult schizophrenia, will likewise be of use for children who receive the clinical diagnosis of schizophrenia. Unfortunately, there is no support for this assumption; furthermore, the use of phenothiazine compounds is not without potential risk. On the other hand, the considerably less toxic psychostimulants have been shown to be of benefit for the attenuation of deviant behaviors among hospitalized children with organically based hyperactive and aggressive behavior disorders (Winsberg, Press, Bialer, & Kupietz, 1974), most of whom at one time had received the diagnosis of schizophrenia. Still, psychostimulants tend to be withheld from children who, at the hands of clinicians who are unfamiliar with the issues, may receive a primary diagnosis of schizophrenia rather than the more appropriate diagnosis of organic brain disease.

Research in pediatric psychopharmacology also tends to be confused by this issue. The appeal for subject-sample homogeneity, by which is usually meant diagnostic homogeneity, frequently leads to obscuring the end result by aggregating on the basis of common intellectual level the research samples with both organic disorders (which one might expect to respond to drug therapy) and nonorganic behavior disorders (for which drug management should play no part). A sample consisting of both behaviorally disordered mentally defective children and behaviorally disordered organic children with normal intelligence is much more homogeneous than is a group of behaviorally impaired normals, some of whom are organic, the others not. The only communality among this latter hypothetical group is the manifestation of behavior disorders. Developmental neuropsychiatric considerations can allow for etiological grouping (where such grouping seems to have relevance for appropriate treatment) not allowed by descriptive categorization.

Every experienced clinician has knowledge of many children who were misdiagnosed in their early years and suffer tragic consequences such as needless institutionalization. On the other hand, the same clinicians can point to cases of obviously impaired children who in infancy were judged to be of "normal potential." The anguish which misinformed parents and their afflicted children frequently suffer as a consequence of diagnosis and prognosis rendered in the absence of adequate evaluation (by usually well-meaning clinicians) is in large measure avoidable by the judicious use of the Gesell Developmental and Neurological Examination.

SUMMARY

The aim of this chapter has been to focus on some of the more current neuropsychiatric issues in developmental retardation. Towards that end, much of its content has been addressed to the status of the developmental assessment of the infant, using the Gesell Developmental and Neurological Examination, and to the implications this procedure has for a number of areas of pressing importance for pediatric neuropsychiatry. The material covered shows that the Gesell examination, when appropriately used, is a reliable and valid instrument for the identification of abnormal functioning among infants in a number of behavioral areas—including adaptive behavior, language, and motor integrity—and that such abnormality is indicative of organic brain disease. It is emphasized that the early identification of such illness is of central importance for clinical care of children with neuropsychiatric conditions and for the planning of relevant health-care delivery systems. The discussion has endeavored to show that the failure to consider infant neurological status in much current research, in such diverse areas as cognition and psychopharmacology, complicates the interpretation of the findings. Thus, the principal goal of this chapter has been to encourage the reader, be he clinician, health-care planner, or researcher, to attend to these issues (many of which remain controversial) in the conduct of his work.

One of the major obstacles to improving health care for children is the lack of incorporation of sound developmental principles in much current clinical activity. The design of health-care delivery systems for children with neuropsychiatric disorders is dependent on the determination of the prevalence and incidence of such conditions among children, and on the specification, whenever possible, of their etiological factors. It is evident that planning for the provision of services in the case of children who manifest developmental subnormality cannot proceed adequately without attention to the issues raised in this chapter.

REFERENCES

Ballantyne, J. W. *Manual on antenatal pathology: The Foetus.* Edinburgh: William Green and Sons, 1902.

Ballantyne, J. W. *Manual on antenatal pathology: The Embryo.* Edinburgh: William Green and Sons, 1904.

Barker, D. J. P., & Edwards, J. H. Obstetric complications and school performance. *British Medical Journal,* 1967, *3,* 695-699.

Bayley, N. On the growth of intelligence. *American Psychologist,* 1955, *10,* 805-818.

Bijou, S. W. A functional analysis of retarded development. In N. R. Ellis (Ed.), *International review of research in mental retardation.* (Vol. 1). New York: Academic Press, 1966, pp. 1-19.

Birch, H. G., & Gussow, J. D. *Disadvantaged children, health, nutrition, and school failure.* New York: Grune & Stratton, 1970.

Birch, H. G., Richardson, S. A., Baird, D., Horobin, G., & Illsley, R. *Mental subnormality in the community.* Baltimore: Williams and Wilkins, 1970.

Blot, W. J., & Miller, R. W. Mental retardation following in utero exposure to the atomic bombs of Hiroshima and Nagasaki. *Radiology,* 1973, *106,* 617-619.

Buck, C. Examples of current studies of reproductive casualty. In H. C. Haywood (Ed.), *Social-cultural aspects of mental retardation.* New York: Appleton-Century-Crofts, 1970, pp. 737-744.

Churchill, J. A., Berendes, H. W., & Nemore, J. Neuropsychological deficits in children of diabetic mothers. *American Journal of Obstetrics and Gynecology,* 1969, *105,* 257-268.

Cohen, E. N., Belleville, J. W., & Brown, B. W. Anesthesia, pregnancy and miscarriage: A study of operating room nurses and anesthetists. *Anesthesiology,* 1971, *35,* 343-347.

Crawford, M. D., Gardner, M. J., & Sedgewick, P. A. Infant mortality and hardness of local water supplies. *The Lancet,* 1972, *1,* 988-992.

David, O., Clark, J., & Voeller, K. Lead and hyperactivity. *The Lancet,* 1972, *2,* 900-903.

Davie, R., Butler, N., & Goldstein, H. *From birth to seven: A report of the national child development study.* London: William Cloves and Sons, 1972.

Drillien, C. M. Longitudinal study of growth and development of prematurely and maturely born children: VII, Mental development 2-5 years. *Archives of Diseases of Children,* 1961, *36,* 233-240.

Eisenberg, L. Clinical considerations in the psychiatric evaluation of intelligence. In J. Zubin and G. A. Jervis (Eds.), *Psychopathology of mental development.* New York: Grune & Stratton, 1967, pp. 502-513.

Escalona, S. K. *The roots of individuality, normal patterns of development in infancy.* Chicago: Aldine, 1968.

Fishler, K. Psychological assessment services. In R. Koch and J. C. Dobson (Eds.), *The mentally retarded child and his family: A multidisciplinary handbook.* New York: Brunner/Mazel, 1971, pp. 156-196.

Florman, A. L., Gershon, A. A., Blackett, P. R., & Nahmias, A. J. Intrauterine infection with herpes simplex virus: Resultant congenital malformations. *Journal of the American Medical Association,* 1973, *225,* 129-132.

Gesell, A. *The embryology of behavior: The beginnings of the human mind.* New York: Harper & Row, 1945.

Gesell, A., & Amatruda, C. S. *Developmental diagnosis.* New York: Paul B. Hoeber, 19741.

Gesell, A., & Amatruda, C. S. *Developmental diagnosis.* (2nd ed.) New York: Harper & Row, 1947.

Gottfried, A. W. Intellectual consequences of perinatal anoxia. *Psychological Bulletin,* 1973, *80,* 231-242.

Graham, P., Rutter, M., & George, S. Temperamental characteristics as predictors of behavior disorders in children. *American Journal of Orthopsychiatry,* 1973, *43,* 328-339.

Heber, R., & Garber, H. An experiment in prevention of cultural-familial mental retardation. In D. A. A. Primrose (Ed.), *Proceedings of the second congress of the International Association for the Scientific Study of Mental Deficiency.* Amsterdam: Swets and Zeitlinger, 1972, pp. 31-35.

Holden, R. H. Prediction of mental retardation in infancy. *Mental Retardation*, 1972, *10* (1), 28-30.

Illingsworth, R. S. The predictive value of developmental tests in the first year with special reference to the diagnosis of mental subnormality. *Journal of Child Psychology and Psychiatry*. 1961, *2*, 210-215.

Ireton, H., Thwing, E., & Gravem, H. Infant mental development and neurological status, family socioeconomic status and intelligence at age four. *Child Development*, 1970, *41*, 937-945.

Jencks, C. *Inequality: A reassessment of the effect of family and schooling in America.* New York: Basic Books, 1972.

Kagan, J., & Klein, R. E. Cross-cultural perspectives on early development. *American Psychologist*, 1973, *28*, 947-961.

Kessner, D. M. *Infant death: An analysis by maternal risk and health care.* Washington, D. C.: National Academy of Sciences, 1973.

Knobloch, H., & Pasamanick, B. An evaluation of the consistency and predictive value of the 40 week Gesell developmental schedule. In *Psychiatric research report 13: Child development and child psychiatry.* Washington, D. C.: American Psychiatric Association, 1960.

Knobloch, H., & Pasamanick, B. Prospective studies on the epidemiology of reproductive casualty. *Merrill-Palmer Quarterly*, 1966, *12*, 27-43.

Knobloch, H., & Pasamanick, B. (Eds.) *Gesell and Amatruda's developmental diagnosis* (3rd ed.). New York: Harper & Row, 1974.

Knobloch, H., Sherard, E., & Pasamanick, B. A developmental screening inventory for infants. *Pediatrics*, 1966, *38*, 1095-1104.

Lave, L. B., & Seskin, E. P. Air pollution and human health. *Science*, 1970, *169*, 723-733.

Lowe, C. R. Congenital malformations among infants born to epileptic women. *The Lancet*, 1973, *1*, 9-10.

McNeil, T. F., & Wiegerink, R. Behavioral patterns and pregnancy and birth complication histories in psychologically disturbed children. *Journal of Nervous and Mental Disease*, 1971, *152*, 315-323.

McNeil, T. F., Wiegerink, R., & Dozier, E. J. Pregnancy and birth complications in the birth of seriously, moderately and mildly behaviorally disturbed children. *Journal of Nervous and Mental Disease*, 1970, *151*, 24-34.

Monif, G. R. G., Egan, E. A., Held, B., & Eitzman, D. V. The correlation of maternal cytomegalovirus infection during various stages in gestation with neonatal involvement. *Journal of Pediatrics*, 1972, *80*, 17-20.

Nahmias, A. J., Josey, W. E., Naib, Z. M., Freeman, M. G., Fernandez, R. J., & Wheeler, J. H. Perinatal risk associated with maternal genital herpes simplex virus infection. *American Journal of Obstetrics and Gynecology*, 1971, *110*, 825-837.

National Academy of Sciences. *Maternal nutrition and the course of pregnancy.* Washington, D.C.: NAS, 1970.

Neligan, G., Prudham, D., & Steiner, H. *The formative years: Birth, family, and development in Newcastle upon Tyne.* London: Oxford University Press, 1974.

Pasamanick, B. A comparative study of the behavioral development of Negro infants. *Journal of Genetic Psychology,* 1946, *69,* 3-44.

Pasamanick, B. A child is being beaten. *American Journal of Orthopsychiatry,* 1971, *4,* 540-556.

Pasamanick, B., & Knobloch, H. Retrospective studies on the epidemiology of reproductive casualty: Old and new. *Merrill-Palmer Quarterly,* 1966, *12,* 1-26.

Pierson, P. S., Howard, P., & Kleber, H. D. Sudden deaths in infants born to methadone-maintained addicts. *Journal of the American Medical Association,* 1972, *220,* 1733-1734.

Peuschel, S. M., Kopito, L., & Schwachman, H. Children with an increased lead burden: A screening follow-up study. *Journal of the American Medical Association,* 1972, *222,* 462-466.

Reynolds, D. W., Stagno, S., Hosty, T. S., Tiller, M., & Alford, C. A. Maternal cytomegalovirus excretion and perinatal infection. *New England Journal of Medicine,* 1973, *289,* 1-6.

Rosenbaum, A. L., Churchill, J. A., Shakhashiri, Z. A., & Moody, R. L. Neuropsychologic outcome of children whose mothers had proteinuria during pregnancy. *Obstetrics & Gynecology,* 1969, *33,* 118-123.

Rutter, M., Tizard, J., & Whitmore, K. *Education, health and behavior.* New York: Wiley, 1970.

Smith, A. C., Flick, G. L., Ferris, G. S., & Sellman, A. H. Prediction of developmental outcome at seven years from prenatal, perinatal and postnatal events. *Child Development,* 1972, *43,* 495-507.

Sternglass, E. J. Infant mortality and nuclear tests. *Bulletin of the Atomic Scientists,* 1969, *15,* 18-21.

Stott, L. H., & Ball, R. S. Infant and preschool mental tests: Review and evaluation. *Monographs of the Society for Research in Child Development,* 1965, *30* (3, Serial No. 101).

Thomas, A., Chess, S., & Birch, H. G. *Temperament and behavior disorders in children.* New York: New York University Press, 1968.

Werner, E., Honzik, M., & Smith, R. Prediction of intelligence and achievement at ten years from twenty months pediatric and psychologic examinations. *Child Development,* 1968, *39,* 1063-1075.

Winsberg, B. G., Press, M., Bialer, I., & Kupietz, S. Dextroamphetamine and methylphenidate in the treatment of hyperactive/aggressive children. *Pediatrics,* 1974, *53,* 236-241.

Zelson, C. Infant of the addicted mother. *New England Journal of Medicine,*
     1973, *288,* 1393-1395.

Manny Sternlicht biographical information: see page 2.

11

Issues in counseling and psychotherapy with mentally retarded individuals

Manny Sternlicht

BACKGROUND AND DELINEATION OF ISSUES

Although much work has been performed in the area of counseling and psychotherapy with mentally retarded populations, no systematic, definitive, and comprehensive body of knowledge has yet evolved. (The interested reader is referred to Sternlicht, 1966, and Bialer, 1967, for extended compendia in the sphere of psychotherapy with retarded people.)

Perhaps this is because psychotherapy is more of an art than a science. Or, more likely, perhaps the crucial variables are so "tacky" that they defy resolution by our currently inadequate scientific procedures. Those significant variables that must be considered by any practitioner in this sphere may be subsumed within four major classes of critical issues: (a) interaction issues, (b) structural issues, (c) method issues, and (d) outcome issues. This chapter attempts to clearly delineate these crucial issues and to offer as definitive a resolution of them as is currently possible.

In order to establish a common frame of reference, my definition of "mental retardation" is the one officially espoused by the American Association on Mental Deficiency, namely, that "Mental Retardation refers to significantly subaverage general intellectual functioning existing concurrently with deficits in adaptive behavior, and manifested during the developmental period (Grossman, 1973, p. 11)." Mental retardation represents essentially a behavioral or social classification; it is a collective term encompassing many heterogeneous conditions, all having in common a lack of intellectual prowess. It is a symptomological syndrome comprising an intellectual deficit and some form of emotional reaction to that deficit.

The definition of "counseling and psychotherapy" poses some difficulties, since almost every psychotherapist has his own idea of what is meant by these terms. I do not believe that "counseling" and "psychotherapy" are mutually exclusive processes, but that counseling may be subsumed under the rubric of psychotherapy as a less intensive psychotherapeutic category. Rather than add another definition of psychotherapy, I am quite comfortable with that offered by Leland & Smith (1962), which is that "psychotherapy [is] . . . any planned attempt based on a close interpersonal relationship to create behavioral change in the patient, regardless of the materials or procedures used" (p. 622). There are three major points of emphasis in this definition that should be highlighted.

First, "any planned attempt" subtly suggests that the actual carrying out of a psychotherapeutic program can be performed by an individual with a minimal amount of training and experience, as long as the program has been adequately designed by a psychotherapist who is well qualified in the area. Second, the need for "a close interpersonal relationship" is an important focus, one which serves to differentiate counseling and psychotherapy from some of the forms of conditioning and behavior therapies that have recently emerged; in addition, a warm, close relationship seems necessary in order to maximize self-revealing behavior on the part of the retarded person. The third and final point to note is that of the creation of "behavioral change" in the individual. With the retarded individual, it is difficult, if not impossible, to assess therapeutic benefit except as it is reflected on an overt behavioral level, especially since the retarded client's developmental difficulties generally reside in the sphere of overt functioning.

Difficulties in Resolution of Issues

Without unduly oversimplifying the current state of affairs, the major factor accounting for the persistence of the various classes of critical issues is the lack of a systematic and comprehensive theory dealing with psychotherapy with the mentally retarded person. Integral in developing and synthesizing such a theory is intimate knowledge in at least three essential areas: a theory of the personality of the retarded individual, an understanding of the relationships of retarded persons in society, and an awareness of the available specialized psychotherapeutic procedures and techniques. At this time, we have, or at least are beginning to have, a fairly reasonable understanding of the latter two necessities, but the first point continues to remain a mystery. That is, we now possess an effective armamentarium of therapeutic procedures for use with a mentally retarded population, and we also have a kind of philosophical system of values which considers the relationships of retarded individuals within and to their societal settings. (This latter system is being constantly updated, especially so as the retarded person interacts and communicates more frequently with us consequent to becoming more and more visible in the community.) What we do not have, however, is an adequate conceptualization of the personality of these individuals (see Sternlicht & Deutsch, 1972). This is a signal lack, since, as Tillich (1952) declared, no therapeutic theory can be developed without an implicit or explicit image of man.

The reasons for this lack are not overly difficult to comprehend. Basically, most of the professional workers in the field come heavily laden with intellectualized and verbal proficiencies, with an intellectually oriented system of values and beliefs. These individuals generally find it nearly impossible to fully understand the phenomenology of mental retardation, to be able to view the world from the eyes of a retarded individual. The psychological world of the latter is alien to the logically ordered adult mind of the therapist. It is relatively easy for us to completely empathize with an individual who is physically handicapped, since nearly all of us have, or have had, physically handicapping conditions of one type or another at some time in our lives (e.g., myopia, fractures, headaches). In addition, we also can readily empathize with a person who is emotionally disturbed, since all of us have had periods of psychotic-like behavior at one time or another, at least in terms of idiosyncratic thinking or behaving such as might occur when one "falls in love" or when one mourns the loss of a loved one. But how can we view the world through the eyes of someone with limited intellectual resources? Our experiential background fails us, and our cognitive processes abhor the notion.

Then, too, almost every retarded individual will encounter some degree of perceptual distortion of objective reality, even if it only assumes the form of not being able to correctly comprehend the nuances of what is transpiring in a social situation. This is especially significant because the particular style and personality of an individual is built not upon objective reality, but rather upon the subjective view that the person takes of the facts of life. Because the retarded child needs a much longer period of time to differentiate himself from the world around him, he encounters great difficulty in establishing stable differences, and his view of himself and the world will be limited in scope and clarity, and will be subject to various distortions depending upon the nature of his intellectual limitations. Menolascino (1968) found that psychiatric disorders in mentally retarded children occurred relatively frequently, but that these differed qualitatively from those observed in nonretarded children. This is not surprising, because the quantity and quality of opportunities for the retarded child to develop socially and biologically are nearly alwasy delayed and distorted. The emotional difficulties of retarded individuals arise directly from a lack of competency to deal effectively and appropriately with their psychological, social, and physical environments. Behavioral disturbance, after the degree of intellectual deficit itself, represents the single most important cause of institutionalization of the mentally retarded resident.

Another factor that helps to account for the well-recognized and lamented paucity of data in the area is the reluctance of professional personnel to work psychotherapeutically with a retarded clientele. Aside from the phenomenological difficulties already referred to, most psychotherapists have invested heavily in intellectually oriented and verbally laden therapeutic skills and processes. These processes, for the most part, have been found to be ineffective with the retarded client; and clinicians have been loathe to work with a population that they are ill equipped to deal with. Another factor which plays a great role in the reluctance of professionals to become therapeutically involved with this population is the viewpoint of limited therapeutic gain. That is, it is reasoned that even if a psychotherapeutic regimen were to be wholly effective from an emotional standpoint, the retarded person would still continue to function on a limited intellectual level, and he would most likely not be able to make any significant, creative contributions to society. On the other hand, so the reasoning goes, if one were to work with, for example, a schizophrenic child, and the therapeutic program were fully effective, then there is always the possibility that the "cured" individual might creatively contribute to the betterment of society.

What is overlooked, however, whether intentionally or otherwise, is that the psychotherapist who works with the retarded client literally puts himself on the "firing line" in a way that is never the case when working psychotherapeutically with almost any other type of population. This is the case because the retarded individual has a "known" upper limit of intellectual and cognitive functioning, and if the therapeutic assistance does not enable the retarded client to behave on the level which that limit would lead us to expect, then the fault lies with the therapist entirely. Many psychotherapists are reluctant to take on such an ego-threatening challenge. In many respects, it may be easier to work with a neurotically or psychotically disturbed group, since psychotherapeutic effectiveness is exceedingly difficult to measure in these cases, and if the therapist is at all successful in affecting any kind of positive behavioral change, then the success is there for all to see.

INTERACTION ISSUES

Client Variables

Before one can attempt an effective program of psychotherapy with the mentally retarded person, one must first consider the purposes and uses for which the therapy is directed. Appropriate and suitable goals must be spelled out as fully as possible; without preset end points, no psychotherapeutic regimen with this population can ever be wholly successful. While there may be many rather specific therapeutic targets, depending upon the particular needs of the given client, psychotherapeutic goals essentially can be subsumed under two broad rubrics: preventive (anticipatory) psychotherapy, and ameliorative psychotherapy. In the preventive, or anticipatory, category, we would consider all forms of counseling and psychotherapy which are designed primarily to prepare the retarded individual for coping with those kinds of behavioral problems that he might be expected to encounter both in the immediate and in the not-too-distant future. Regardless of whether the retarded individual is institutionalized or living in the community, the focus here would be upon adequate functioning within an open community setting.

Under the treatment rubric, we would consider all those psychotherapeutic endeavors devised in an attempt to either ameliorate or to eliminate entirely, if at all possible, any emotional disturbances negatively affecting overall satisfactory behavioral responsiveness. This type of treatment program would thereby aim at improving and enhancing personal effectiveness and self-actualization in all spheres of living. (In an institutional environment, this should be carried out without any regard for possible potential situational change; e.g., community placement.)

There are only two essential requirements to be met by retarded clients in order to participate in a therapeutic program, aside from the patently obvious "need for assistance" factor. I view a motivational criterion as a necessary *sine qua non.* That is to say, some degree of motivation on the part of the individual undergoing a psychotherapeutic situation must be apparent; the client must exhibit some willingness or readiness for change. Then, too, the potential therapeutic candidate will need at least a minimum amount of intellective capabilities in order to be able to profit from some degree of assistance. I am not thinking here in terms of any minimum IQ—although a significant element in determining an individual's capacity for coping with environmental stresses and pressures is the degree of mental retardation—but rather in terms of capabilities for expressive and receptive communication. Parenthetically, Halpern, Mathiew, and Butler (1968) commented on the latter point, even as did Ayer and Butler (1969). If an individual can comprehend the essence of what is occurring during a therapeutic session, and if he can be stimulated to communicate his needs and desires, then he ought to be capable of profiting from psychotherapy, other factors being equal. Theoretically, nearly all mildly and moderately retarded individuals are able to profit from a therapeutic endeavor, while those who are profoundly retarded usually are not; and severely retarded persons must be considered on a wholly individual basis.

In my own experiences, however, I have encountered two types of retarded clients who do not seem to be able to profit from psychotherapeutic work. These are core homosexuals and those individuals who seem to be under some significant speech pressure. The former group consists not of transient or incarcerated homosexuals, who engage in unisexual activities owing to the lack of available and appropriate sexual objects of gratification, but rather of persons who are truly homosexual in terms of their basic personality patterns; while the latter group is composed of individuals who (presumably on account of neurological dysfunctioning) simply are unable to inhibit their motor impulses to a sufficient extent so that they can remain silent for any great length of time. I have employed almost every psychotherapeutic approach and medium to reach these two groups, but without any notable success. Interestingly enough, nearly all these kinds of clients that I have worked with have been either mildly retarded or of borderline subnormal intelligence, thereby further compounding the difficulty in comprehending why these two groups should be so resistant to psychotherapeutic assistance.

Psychotherapist Variables

Ideally, anybody who works psychotherapeutically with a mentally retarded population should have a great deal of understanding of these individuals as well as an eager willingness and enthusiasm to participate with them on whatever level of functioning they may be operating at any given point in time. The therapist must have maximum confidence in what the retarded client can do and can accomplish, and, within limits, he should neither underestimate nor overestimate. He must be cognizant of the dictum that anything which increases the retarded person's life space is to be desired.

Personality factors are of predominant importance; extreme professionalism is not called for, but the qualities of a good mothering individual are. The ability to love is absolutely essential, if love is viewed not so much as emotion as "action undertaken with the aim of fostering happiness and growth in the person loved" (Jourard, 1971, p. 51). The therapist must have the courage and capacity to use himself in the therapeutic experience for the betterment of his charges.

There are several qualifications that a therapist dealing with the mentally retarded client should have, and these of course include the obvious; namely, some knowledge of the phenomenology of such individuals, a knowledge of the field of mental retardation per se, and a working familiarity with the broad principles of psychotherapeutic treatment, especially as specifically related to the retarded individual. The therapist will have to try to empathize with the retarded person and to intimately relate with him on his level, particularly if the client is behaving on a more infantile plane. A good deal of experience in intensive daily contact with a retarded population is particularly valuable in this regard, as is the possession of uncommonly good common sense. Further, the psychotherapist must have faith in what he is doing. He must be willing to view himself as he really is, to become subjectively involved with his clients and not be on an aloof, detached, or semidetached plane; and he also must be able to derive satisfactions from the work that he is doing—client satisfactions alone are inadequate.

I have found that the age or sex of the therapist assumes no real importance. In terms of capability to carry out the content and course of a psychotherapeutic program, the kind of therapist that I would opt for to work with the retarded client is in some senses similar to that spelled out by London (1964), in his notion of the two necessary characteristics of action therapists:

> 1. The therapist assumes a much greater influence over the detailed conduct of the treatment sessions, and possibly over the outside life of the patient, than Insight therapists would. 2. The therapist is much more responsible for the outcome of treatment, that is, for whatever changes take place in the patient, than are Insight therapists. (p. 78)

Thus, the therapist will have to assume an active role in the management of his client. The therapist will need to be in constant touch with the staff and the parents concerning the client's progress, and he will be expected to provide the dynamic formulations necessary to coordinate the total team's efforts in an attempt to initiate and maintain a uniform and consistent therapeutic approach. Finally, the therapist must be sufficiently flexible, innovative, versatile, and insightful to change his direction and approach should it become warranted.

Familial Variables

When working therapeutically with a retarded individual, his human background milieu, especially his familial situations, must be taken into full account. By the time a retarded individual comes for help, he already has been molded by familial interactions and their consequences. Not only must the retarded client's order of birth and the number and ages of siblings and parents be taken into account, but also his meaning to and significance for the family. The attitudes which especially parents assume toward their retarded child, and the manner in which they act toward him, play a highly significant role in the client's formative development.

If the child is institutionalized, then his alter family (i.e., attendant personnel) must be taken into account. One cannot hope to work therapeutically with an individual without also trying to gear his environmental background toward a similarly helpful and positive direction. Contacts with parents and parental surrogates, as well as with other significant relational individuals, must be held regularly on an ongoing basis, especially to instill the value of consistency and firmness in dealing with the retarded child. Therapeutic suggestions may have to be given to the entire family, with the concurrent necessity for ensuring that a cooperative spirit is maintained. On occasion, family therapy may be warranted, especially where the family needs to develop modes of attack against critical upsets; at any rate, very often treatment of the retarded person calls for counseling of the whole family. Then, too, as Farber and Ryckman (1965) stated, "Families with a (severely) mentally retarded child face many problems which may occur in the marital relationship, the interaction between parents and their mentally retarded or normal children, or in the relationship between the retarded child and his normal siblings" (p. 1). The family frequently needs improved strategies for effectively interacting not only with their retarded member, but frequently with each other in an open, accepting, and uncompromising\fashion. Sometimes this can be accomplished within a quasi-educational framework, while at other times more intensive in-depth treatment is necessary.

STRUCTURAL ISSUES

Individual versus Group Variables

When I refer to structural issues, I am really thinking about the type of structuring that is a part and parcel of any group psychotherapy situation.

Because of the lack of adequately trained personnel in the area of psychotherapy with retarded populations, because of the lack of interest of many clinicians in the sphere, and because of the magnitude of the needs involved and of some similarities in these needs, group psychotherapy becomes the preferred mode of treatment and habilitation. Only rarely does a retarded person display the need to be seen solely on an individual basis, and occasionally individual work may be utilized as a desirable supplement to group work. (In individual psychotherapy, there is a need for flexible planning, and the length of each session should be variable—ranging from 20 minutes to 1 hour.) In some cases, group therapy might be the natural follow-up to individual work at that point when the client's ego strengths have reached the degree where he is capable of tolerating interaction of an unpredictable nature with his peers.

One of the most outstanding assets of group therapy with the retarded person is the demonstration of the availability of alternate behavioral models. Behavior which is exhibited by the group members or presented by the therapist, and which is found acceptable by the group, becomes identified and noted by the client as eminently desirable. Then, too, the group approach is especially appropriate for retarded adolescents, as it offers them the opportunity to deal with an adult (the therapist) in the presence of other adolescents. This opportunity affords the adolescent with an invaluable experience, namely, how to relate to adults in an effective manner vis-à-vis his own unique adolescent needs and drives.

I have discovered that, in group counseling and psychotherapy with retarded people, it is eminently desirable for treatment (ameliorative) groups to be organized on a closed-end basis, while preventive groups are best maintained on an open-ended basis. The reason for this view with regard to preventive groups is twofold: First, a member who "graduates" from the program can be invited to return and discuss some of his experiences with the group, thereby serving as a visible indication of the successful possibilities inherent in the psychotherapeutic activity and also as a successful motivational reinforcer. Second, a new addition to the group serves as a reminder to the remaining members of the degree of progress that they have made; the older members, in turn, can function as effective role models for the initiate.

In most group psychotherapy programs, there exists a "magic number" type of approach relevant to the optimal number of participants in a typical group therapy setting. As a result of my experiences, I have found that the ideal group situation with retarded clients is one which accommodates between 12 and 16 clients, with a modal number of 14. I am fully cognizant of the fact that such a relatively large number of clients will require a maximum amount of activity and output on the part of the group therapist, but if the group consists of much less than 12 members, there is a great risk that relatively little therapeutic action will occur. If the group is much larger than 16, the members may become unruly at times and somewhat difficult to control, which may eventuate in a total disruption of the therapeutic effort.

I do not feel the need for any especial diagnostic group composition. Rather, the members of a group should be selected solely upon the criteria of their needs (i.e., preset therapeutic goals), their communicative capabilities, and their motivation for undergoing the experience. Within gross limits, age and sex are not considered to be particularly crucial variables, nor are overt or underlying behavioral and personality dynamics. Diagnoses per se are unimportant; levels of behavioral functioning, or potential functioning, qualify as the *sine qua non*. Needless to say, the goals (preventive or treatment) of the group experience should be clearly defined and understood by all group participants.

No great successes have been encountered with the use of co-therapists, and I would not at all recommend this procedure. This is so because of the great amount of time necessary to effectively coordinate communications, which vitiates any potential advantages of the co-therapist system. Then, too, the basic rationale for the utilization of co-therapists is the emulation of a typical family setting; however, many institutionalized retarded residents do not have a family situation to return to, and there would be no purposes in fostering hopes and wishes which may not be capable of fulfillment. On this latter note, most of the experiences of those doing group therapy with retarded individuals have been within an institutional setting. This is not accidental, since it is exceedingly difficult to get 14 or so retarded persons in the community together on a regular basis (problems with transportation, time, etc.).

For group therapy to be maximally effective, a rather large area of physical space is needed, thus permitting some members of the group the opportunity to get up and walk around the room should the need for such activity arise. Further, the room itself should be relatively free of any kind of potentially distracting stimuli, such as paintings or notices, and, if at all possible, it should be entirely decorated (painted) by the clients themselves. No particular furniture is needed, aside from an adequate number of reasonably comfortable chairs and some end tables. Group sessions ordinarily should last between 1 and 1½ hours, with the exact termination point best left variable and determined in accordance with how the group is proceeding at that point in time. That is, if a particular therapeutic area has been successfully covered and an hour has gone by, then that might be the appropriate time to terminate that session. On the other hand, if the group is still in the midst of working through some sphere of difficulty at the end of the hour, then the session could continue for an additional half-hour.

Meetings should be held on at least a weekly basis, although occasionally it is desirable to schedule twice-weekly sessions with treatment groups. Brief short-term group therapy does not generally appear to be especially effective.

Milieu Variables

While I feel that it may be impossible to really have a total program of milieu therapy in any facility for the mentally retarded individual, certainly there are supportive aspects of the environment that can be created which will maximize the (therapeutic) growth and development of that individual. The environment, human as well as nonhuman (physical), should be modified as much as possible in such a way as to maximize the probable occurrence of successful experiences and to minimize the likelihood of the client's experiencing failure situations. This is especially needed, since all of us are aware that our background of experiences is a key motivational component. In addition, as Vail (1956) stated, "The environment necessary for the treatment of mental defectives is a controlled, supportive one which protects the individual until he is able to develop his resources; one which provides the educational materials to hasten this development; which recognizes the maturation of these potentialities for peaceful, productive, and harmonious participation in society, and willingly grants his release and independence at the proper time" (p. 170). The retarded person must have access to whatever space, time, materials, equipment, people, and activities may be necessary for his therapeutic enhancement.

Just as any topnotch child guidance clinic would need to work therapeutically with the parents as well as with the children-clients, so too I believe that any effective work with the retarded child involves some auxiliary therapeutic contact with those persons upon whom the client is dependent (e.g., parents or care personnel), depending upon where the client resides. When a retarded person lives at home with his family and is being seen in the community, I insist upon seeing one or both parents as well, perhaps on a one-to-four basis; i.e., one session with the parent(s) for every four sessions with the client. At least partially, this is done in order to create the most suitable therapeutic environment at home, by counseling the parents as to how best to handle their retarded son or daughter. In addition, this counseling process offers a source of continuous two-way communications and feedback, as well as serving as a vehicle for the resolution of any other familial difficulties that may exist. The same reasoning also holds true in the institutional setting, where members of the child-care staff function as parent-surrogates, and where they should be directly involved in the overall treatment program.

Then, too, the physical environment has important consequences, since the specific types of forms and colors employed in an architectural design can have a positive or negative effect. Lighting intensity should be adequate for clear form recognitions, and spaces and rooms should be so arranged as to satisfy the retarded clientele's physical and psychological needs. The physical surroundings may communicate support and safety, or may signal expectations of insecurity and uncertainty.

Buildings for retarded children need to provide some degree of privacy for each child, have childlike attributes, and provide a sense of security, intimacy, and familiarity. Sound levels also need to be effectively controlled, and all levels and types of impinging stimulation need to be monitored and controlled. In the final analysis, however, the requirements for an environment which is designed to be therapeutic are not really different from the general requirements for total psychological growth and well-being.

METHOD ISSUES

Process Variables

Role of therapist. Obviously, the role and function of the psychotherapist, per se, is all-important in therapeutic work with the retarded client. Very few of us, if any, would deny that the therapist is the only "instrument" or "technique" in the therapeutic session; that is, therapist variables certainly are more important than therapeutic-media variables. In many respects, the solution to the effectiveness of therapeutic endeavors resides in the therapist's sensitivities, personality, and background—recognizing, of course, the dynamic nature of the therapeutic situation, with its duality of interpersonal interactions. As a simplistic example, sharing of experiences or disclosures by the therapist will often invite a similar reaction on the part of the client. Then, too, the therapist, via his behavior, establishes a behavioral model for the client, in addition to serving as a source of needed information. Further, the therapist working with a group of retarded persons will have to be prepared to lead the group toward its preset goals until several of the group members develop the ability to assume some of these leadership aspects.

In institutional settings, the therapist needs to explore and to evaluate fully the effects that certain current institutional features may have in developing restrictions, inhibitions, and various additional forms of deterrents which may hinder or block the possibility of generating fresh solutions in typical problem areas. It is manifest that such built-in restrictions (whether institutionally imposed or self-imposed) may reduce the freedom and potentiality of a mentally retarded individual. In this light, too, the therapist has to learn how to prevent and/or circumscribe any unnecessary rules and needless restrictions—which may create any narrowing down of developmental potentiality—from being built into our facilities and into our institutionalized residents.

The therapist must be aware that all hostilities and resistances experienced toward the institution, and toward authorities in general, may be projected symbolically onto him. He must develop techniques to bring these out into the open in order to allow for catharsis and irrational transference exposure, and thus to help the group members give up compulsive rebellion against the restrictions and frustrations imposed by authorities and to learn to accept the facts of life, including the unpleasantnesses and the unfairnesses of institutions and authorities. These attitudes seem to wholly permeate the resident's daily behavior, and they serve, in some degree, to delimit psychotherapy from the start. On the other hand, working with an institutionalized population offers the therapist a magnificent opportunity for manipulating and controlling the resident's nearly total environmental milieu, thereby ascertaining that all the needs of the individual are being met.

The current utilization of combined individual and group psychotherapy suggests that therapeutic approaches are presently being employed with a greater awareness and acknowledgment of the unique and dynamic needs of different clients. In these cases, results are generally superior when the same therapist works with the client in both the individual and the group sessions, mainly on account of the lack of any kind of communicative hindrances. In this regard, one must bear in mind that not all members of a group are able to be reached with equal facility. Further, each psychotherapeutic plan must be in some way individualized, to take full account of each client's needs, personality structure, and level of functioning. The planning approaches to a therapeutic regimen for the retarded individual are not especially dissimilar to those utilized with nonretarded persons. Substantial differences may be found, however, in the range and level of applicability of these approaches.

Client-therapist interactions. The dynamic interactions within the therapeutic setting must be so structured as to provide an appropriate setting and psychological climate within which easy rapport and open communication will "naturally" occur. Among the areas that will need to be highlighted, as both complementary and supplementary to the primary spheres of effective and efficient environmental adjustment and adaptation (be this environment either the community or the institution), are those relating to adequate motivations, familial and peer group relationships, relationships with authoritarian figures, control of unacceptable behavior patterns, and self-concept enhancement via opportunities for successful experiences. In this regard, opportunities for some degree of cathartic ventilation are a must, as the client needs to express and to come in contact with his feelings and emotions. The latter is basic to the patently necessary follow-through of learning and assuming modes and techniques for preventing involvement in situations which may lead to tensions and frustrations, as well as for attaining techniques for the amelioration and elimination of those tensions that do occur. Improved impulse control is needed, as are enhanced social sensitivities and awarenesses, together with the resolution of any difficulties or inadequacies in satisfactory sexual identifications. Thus, means of satisfying sexual needs within a societally approved framework also need to be developed. Because help and assistance in these areas may be required from time to time, the retarded client also will need to be taught how and where to go for such appropriate succor.

The therapeutic experience. The focus of the therapeutic experience should be on the "here and now" rather than upon inquiry into past history; and illustrative anecdotal explanations based upon the retarded individual's own recent experiences ought to be fully utilized. Clarification of existing attitudes is important. Because mentally retarded people have fewer resources to draw upon than do their nonhandicapped peers, there is a need to avoid long periods of silence, lest therapeutic action be lost and the periods be misinterpreted as acts of hostile rejection. The client needs to be directly involved with an awareness of his own physical processes and corporeal body, as such emphasis will be helpful in making the retarded client increasingly aware of those communications emanating from within himself.

Transference and resistance. It is quite feasible to establish a transference relationship relatively early in the game because resistances are the exceptions rather than the rule, owing to inadequate and insufficient affectional contacts on the part of the retarded client. This transference situation can be adroitly manipulated so as to reduce anxiety, increase tolerances, and improve behavioral and communicative adequacy. The tempo of therapeutic progress will be determined by permitting the client to proceed at his own individualized rate. Opportunities for cathartic processes will have to be initiated and encouraged, as well as opportunities for significant reality testing. Failure-inducing possibilities have to be avoided like the plague, as indeed must any kind of procedure which might serve to hinder the development of badly needed feelings of mastery and security. Situations may need to be created which would elicit acting-out activity related to the retarded person's basic problems, while situations ought to be shunned which might provoke diffuse hyperkinetic behavior. Outlets also will be needed which would allow the client to enjoy so-called forbidden pleasures in socially acceptable substitute ways that are within the grasp of the individual's attainment.

Group interactions. In group psychotherapy, the attention of the retarded client is redirected away from himself and toward the others in the group and their problems. The group setting helps the individual to develop meaningful relationships with others, thereby becoming more relaxed as a consequence of feeling less unique, via a developing awareness of shared common experiences and difficulties. This also serves to reduce feelings of anger and guilt, thereby promoting greater communicative facilities. As self-consciousness decreases, additional active (rather than merely voluntary) participation can be encouraged and stimulated. In the group situation, the participants can be guided in the exploration of different, alternative means of behaviorally responding and in working through those problems encountered in establishing and maintaining effective interpersonal relationships.

Among the major benefits to be derived from group work are stimulation and socialization. Greater social development can be gleaned, as well as (a) better utilization of personality assets toward efficiently dealing with social relationships, family or institution situations; and (b) more realistic awareness of the nature and meaning of the individual's intellectual limitations.

Stages in therapy. One can differentiate between successive stages in the progression of any ongoing psychotherapeutic program, although the demarcations will necessarily be "fuzzy" and overlapping. In encapsulated form, the initial sessions are normally devoted to a "warming-up" process, where appropriate therapeutic relationships are established and then buttressed, and the limits tested. This is followed by the middle phases, where opportunities are provided and manipulated for cathartic expression of anxious and aggressive feelings in a relatively safe and structured environment and in the presence of a supportive therapist. Problems of a personal, social, and/or pre-vocational and vocational nature are intensively worked through here, and individual resources are developed and enhanced. In the concluding stages, the client is encouraged to behave in those ways consonant with his newly developed self-confidence and reliance.

Technique Variables

For ease of presentation, the various types of therapeutic techniques employed with mentally retarded clients can be dichotomized into those procedures that are essentially traditional in cast and those that are of a more novel nature. If, as expressed by Sinclair Lewis in *Arrowsmith,* technique is the beginning of science, then we have at least a commencement to a science of counseling and psychotherapy with the retarded person. A slew of psychotherapeutic techniques and procedures are now available that have been specifically devised for such individuals, and there are others that have been appropriately modified for use with a retarded population.

Traditional approaches. Among the more traditionally oriented techniques that are suitable for use with the retarded client—and that also have been utilized with other populations—are those derived from the fine arts. Dancing, music, and song are especially beneficial for the retarded individual, who is essentially nonverbal anyway. These procedures tend to be particularly useful in assisting that individual to develop, or to enhance an appropriate self-image, and to assist in producing creative self-expression, as well as to permit him the opportunity for developing needed social and personal prowess. Many references are available in this sphere (e.g., McDermott, 1954; Rosen, 1954; Weigl, 1959), but I have found the use of an instrumental band to be of especial therapeutic help (I am indebted to Joseph Lombardi, the former Bandmaster at Willowbrook Developmental Center, for his invaluable assistance in what follows).

The proper use of instruments and arrangements in band work can create a therapeutic milieu, particularly for two types of retarded youngsters: (a) those exhibiting behavior problems of an hostile, aggressive, acting-out nature, and (b) those who are overly passive and submissive. The trumpet, drums, and cymbal are the instruments of choice for the aggressive group, while the saxophone and the clarinet are more appropriate for the passive group. The first week in the band is the most vital. Individual instruction is provided, and success must be assured every beginner (and usually the production of sound constitutes ample reward). After the student has command of a few notes, he is put into a group playing the same instrument, and then the new players are ready for the beginners band. At this point, each "musician" becomes aware of his role (the musical arrangements are designed so that each player has the same notes). The aggressive client's behavior now becomes socially acceptable, through the loud sound of the trumpet; and, via the clarinet, the passive client now receives a sense of achievement without feeling the need to compete. As the beginners advance to the intermediate band level, the musical arrangements assume increasing importance, as they become the vehicles through which the role and position of each player are molded and reinforced. In the final, advanced stage, the musical arrangements are such that each section is dependent upon the other. This results in strong group identifications, in the diminishment of hostile and aggressive behaviors, and in increased self-confidence, all of which generalize well beyond the bandroom situation.

The use of finger painting and clay modeling as therapeutic media also are quite outstanding and cogent for use with retarded groups. I have also used various types of projective techniques in a therapeutic fashion; for example, by offering a client a blank piece of paper and asking him to draw a picture of a person. When he finished, I then asked him to draw a better picture of a person—repeating this request until the client was able to draw a picture of a quite recognizable person, thereby enhancing his own self-concept, in terms of what he could now do.

Another traditional type of therapeutic variable is the use of catharsis, as exemplified in play therapy, sociodrama, and psychodrama. The types of play activities that I employ are very similar to those that are traditionally used with children, and this is so because, as far as the mental age is concerned, many of our retarded individuals do act as if they were children. While this technique is most suitable for children, it can be used with adolescents and adults, and even with the more severely retarded adults. The type of play therapy that seems to be most effective is either activity group therapy or the use of puppetry in group therapy. I do not use psychodrama as it was originally envisioned by Moreno, but have adapted it to the form of a kind of role-playing situation, which is of especial benefit to the preventive group therapeutic situation. Here, because the retarded person is unable to engage in effective vicarious living, we actually (on a concrete basis) act out a specific type of employment situation, thereby giving the retarded individual some familiarity with what he might encounter in a typical real-life employment situation. Or members of the group will be assigned various specific roles and encouraged to "play out" specific problems that need to be dealt with. There is also educational therapy and tutorial counseling, but these would be useful mostly in a classroom, and especially employed by teachers, so I will not emphasize them at this point.

Novel approaches. A procedure that is relatively new, but one which is based upon older established principles of milieu therapy, is motivation therapy. Basically, the motivation technique is a structured, simple group interaction, designed to promote meaningful resident interchanges with adults, with peers, and with the environment generally. It is especially valuable for attendant staff as a technique whereby the attendant can reach his charges in a meaningful and constructive way over and beyond the custodial care which traditionally constitutes the major role of living-unit personnel.

The potential values of the program for the mentally retarded person are twofold. First, the retarded individual would benefit from being able to relate in a useful and meaningful way to his human and nonhuman environmental surroundings (in terms of adjusting more effectively to institutional living, being eligible for community placement, or being more amenable for intensive psychotherapy or other types of group programs). Second, the attendant's understanding of his charges would increase greatly, with a concomitant significant boost in his general morale. This would result in the attendant's becoming less a "custodian" and more an interacting aide, gaining satisfaction from accomplishing something constructive and worthwhile.

These motivation values are attained primarily through aide-client contacts, within a conceptualization of five carefully organized "steps":

1.   The Climate of Acceptance
2.   A Bridge to Reality
3.   Sharing the World We Live In
4.   An Appreciation of the Work of the World
5.   The Climate of Appreciation

Very briefly, a group of five or six retarded individuals meet 5 days a week if possible, for half-hour sessions. The clients are seated in a circle, with the aide-leader in the center; various "props" are used extensively. Among the directives given to the aide-leader are such as the following: "We want to interest the resident in the objective world, stimulate the resident, give him something to think about and possibly talk about. Make him part of a group. You can use as subject matter any topic . . . such as Nature, Hobbies, Sports, Food, Clothes, and whenever possible incorporate . . . the activities of daily living (ADL)." Stress is placed upon a consistency in the time and frequency of attentional contacts (Sternlicht, Siegel, & Deutsch, 1971).

Another procedure which is relatively new and emerging, but again is one based upon older, established principles (in this case those of learning and conditioning) is that of behavior shaping (or behavior modification). These techniques are not discussed in this chapter, but treated separately in chapter 12, since there is some dispute as to whether or not behavior modification is a psychotherapeutic approach per se.

Moving on now to those therapeutic techniques that are of a more novel nature, especially as applied to retarded clients, one may commence by talking about hypnosis (hypnotherapy). Hypnotic procedures have only rarely been utilized with retarded people, although we know that they are hypnotically susceptible (Sternlicht & Wanderer, 1963). What we do not know, however, is what would occur were a retarded individual to be hypnotically age-regressed. Would he return to an earlier developmental level, an earlier CA, or MA, or IQ, or . . . ? Surely, this represents a procedure that is worthy of further investigation!

Another novel procedure, which is especially advantageous in establishing initial rapport, is that of "Indian Hand-Wrestling" (Sternlicht, 1964). This procedure represents nothing more than the effective manipulation of a "gimmick." I developed this technique as a consequence of seeing in group psychotherapy a group of very hostile and delinquent acting-out retarded adolescents. I had lost two groups because I did not realize the dynamics of what was going on, and the literature was no guide. My analysis of the situation indicated that what these boys respected most was group force. Accordingly, I had to demonstrate to them that the therapist was stronger than anybody in the group. I placed two end tables in a corner of the room, one end table being slightly higher than the other. As the therapist entered the room, he was met by a mass of hostility, and he immediately asked for the strongest person in the room. Three hands went up, whereupon—since only one person could be the strongest—fighting matches were held between two of the three. The peer group formed a circle, which also ensured that there would be no "dirty play" involved, and these two residents fought it out. After one was declared a victor, he then fought with the third person. A final victor emerged, who was presumably the strongest individual in the group. Then the therapist stated that he would show that he was stronger than anybody by having an Indian hand wrestle with the victor. The therapist nonchalantly proceeded to sit by the table that was a bit higher than the other and immediately knocked down the resident's arm. A protest ensued, to the effect that the resident was not prepared, and so on, and this procedure was repeated. This time, the therapist made no immediate attempt to push the arm down, but instead just looked at the rest of the residents, cracked some jokes, and then finally knocked the arm down. The residents were completely in awe of the therapist's prowess, and therapeutic work was able to begin immediately. A similar procedure, labeled the "Silence-Insult" technique, was evolved for a comparable group of female acting-out, delinquent retarded adolescents. Since it was deemed wise not to employ any kind of physical contact, the therapist merely sat quietly observing first one resident and then another resident. After about 20 minutes of all kinds of obscene language on the part of the group, one of its members asked the therapist what he was doing. The therapist mentioned that he was being silent, as his way of insulting the group. This provoked a very lengthy and excellent initial discussion on the meaning of insults.

Other procedures that have been found to have wide applications in group psychotherapy have been the "Trial by Jury" and the "Alternative Guidance" techniques. In the former, one individual voluntarily offers to be on trial, while a defending attorney and prosecuting attorney are selected from the group, with the rest of the group serving as the jury. The therapist then serves as the judge, and the procedure normally takes a full session. The jury itself decides upon an appropriate punishment technique, which is nearly always enforced, since it is a peer-derived one and not an authoritarian one. The latter procedure (Wanderer & Sternlicht, 1964) involves explaining to the residents that there are several types of responses available to any given stimulation or provocation. For example, it is pointed out that if a resident rushes by and hits another on a shoulder, the immediate response need not be to hit back, but rather to consider the possible reasons for the behavior—perhaps it was an accident, perhaps the supervisor should be notified, or perhaps the other resident should be spoken to. It is amazing how impoverished the behavioral repertoire of the retarded resident is, particularly when it comes to responding to any actions which may be regarded as aggressive in nature.

Another procedure that has been found effective, especially for those individuals who are afraid of going to sleep at night, is the procedure known as Shadow Therapy (Robertson, 1964). In this procedure, a projector is used to illuminate a blank white space in the darkened room, and the therapist acts out certain kinds of pantomimes in the white space. The client is then encouraged to do the same and gradually learns that he has some control over his shadows, and that shadows are caused by effects of illumination and not by supernatural causes. Also, noisemakers can be used in an analogous manner as a way of enabling the client to understand that he can have some control over the quantity of noise that is made, as well as the fact that he can learn a degree of perceptual selectivity by tuning down those noises that have no direct relevance to him.

Another excellent nonverbal therapeutic medium is the use of balloons. I have employed balloons in many ways, even as a tranquilizing agent. Used as such, the client is instructed to go into a darkened room, to sit in a comfortable chair and lock the door, and then to just gradually rub an inflated balloon against his cheek for several minutes. This usually results in a nostalgic reflection of some pleasant early childhood experiences, which acts in a very tranquilizing manner. The choice of colors of balloons selected can also be used to illustrate the influences of sexuality in our society, in terms of which color is employed. In addition, the resident can be asked to blow up the balloon and then tie a knot at the end. It may be pointed out, depending on whether the balloon is filled to its utmost or whether there is a large reservoir of safety, that this is similar to the way in which an individual tests his control limits—does he go to the very extreme permissible, or does he leave himself with a margin of caution and safety? In addition, the way in which the client breaks a balloon can also be used as an indication of the way in which he handles aggression. Does he react immediately and directly and seem to enjoy the job of breaking the balloons, or is he very cautious and fearful of breaking the balloons? Most of these kinds of interpretations can be pointed out in an essentially nonverbal manner, by liberal use of pantomime.

In like manner, I also make very great use of mirrors in psychotherapy, especially to point out to the individual the way in which he appears to other people. Very often, institutionalized retarded individuals do not have access to a mirror, and are unaware of their appearance and posture as other people would see them. Using a three-dimensional mirror, the resident can see the way in which other people view him, and can make appropriate modifications in his postural stance, if so warranted. In addition, within a group psychotherapeutic setting, the client's peers can also offer him some comments along these lines, as a kind of consensual validation. Another way of effecting this same kind of dynamic approach is via the use of instant audio-visual feedback or closed-circuit television, where the resident can see himself on tape or video as other people have seen him.

Being psychoanalytically oriented, I have also attempted dream interpretations, but I found that the dreams of retarded persons seem to be essentially rather childish and immature, and are not really easily adaptable to dream interpretation per se. Accordingly, as a way of utilizing this technique, movies shown to clients can be interrupted in the middle, or just a middle segment or ending of a movie can be shown, and the client can be asked to fantasize what the remaining section of the movie would have been. These fantasies can then be interpreted in an almost identical manner to the way in which dreams are generally interpreted.

Photographs are also very helpful in this regard, by way of giving the clients a chance to learn that you cannot always "judge a book by its cover," and that sometimes outward appearances can be deceptive.

The use of magic tricks is also a valuable psychotherapeutic aid, especially as a way of building ego support and confidence. Very simple kinds of magic tricks can be taught to the clients, who then immediately get some degree of confidence and also immediately show off these tricks to their peers.

OUTCOME ISSUES

Efficiency and Effectiveness of Counseling and Psychotherapy

Many questions still remain in the area of counseling and psychotherapy with the mentally retarded client. One series of questions relates to the outcomes of therapy, and this refers not only to effectiveness (i.e., does psychotherapy work?), but also to the efficiency of the operations (i.e., is a maximum amount of return obtained for the amount of investment given?). At this time we have no significant answers as to the efficiency of procedures, and our answers as to effectiveness still are in a relatively rudimentary stage; process research is practically nonexistent (see Bialer, 1967). The reason for the lack of definitiveness in this sphere may well be related to the manifold difficulties in dealing with psychotherapeutic procedures generally.

Experimental results in the physical sciences are relatively easy to replicate, since different scientists, applying exactly identical procedures to equivalent materials under precisely similar conditions with alternately accurate measuring instruments, can be expected to attain comparable findings. Such a degree of precision is rarely ever approximated in psychotherapy research for many reasons. For one, the current measuring devices and instruments that we have available are relatively insensitive and too general; for another, we have not yet been able to effectively isolate all of those variables that may play a pertinent role. This is especially difficult if one considers that the relationship between the therapist and the client, with its inherent uniqueness—a uniqueness which cannot reasonably be duplicated—may be the all-important factor.

In many respects, the broad question of whether or not psychotherapy with the retarded person is effective is a meaningless one because of the many variations in types of retarded clients (each with his own idiosyncratic set of problems and symptoms) and in types of therapeutic activities. Rather, the question must be delineated in terms of fairly specific types of psychotherapeutic endeavors and specific retarded populations, with temporal and environmental variables being spelled out in full detail and in relation to specific effects (i.e., types of outcomes). Situational influences on behavior need to be brought more integratively into the predictive system, and perhaps more emphasis needs to be placed upon the precise specification of the outcome criteria. In essence, then, it is hopeless to make judgments and predictions about outcome issues until such time as we have paid sufficient attention to variables in the retarded client, the therapist, the methods of therapy, the therapist-client interaction, and the surrounding life situation.

As Cowen and Trippe (1963) stated, "We have reached the point where uncontrolled observation and armchair speculation must be augmented by controlled, objective experimentation (p. 577)." Unfortunately, the impact of quantitative research on the practice of psychotherapy has been negligible. Clinical research and quantitative research have tended to remain distant from each other, and the scattered reports which manage to find their way into therapists' hands often have contradictory findings and lack clinical sophistication in their conception, execution, and interpretation. To be able to evaluate and assess outcomes in psychotherapy with the retarded client, one must have a well-formulated treatment plan before the commencement of the actual treatment for a specific retarded clientele, and it must be followed without change during any given therapy session. Only in this way can procedures be fully evaluated. (Of course, once a session has been completed and recorded, needed changes in treatment can be effected.) In addition, we need more holistic measurement devices for the detection of behavioral changes that are consonant and compatible with the complexities of personality, with more sophisticated expectations of change. That is, critical attention needs to be given to the detection of very small gains as indicators of success. This latter need, however, may well have to wait until adequate objective outcome criteria are fully detailed and spelled out.

Another factor that must be taken into account in research in this sphere, but one which is markedly identifiable by its omission, is the requirement for long-range evaluation of therapeutic outcomes. Thus, evidence is needed for the determination of whether or not the benefits derived from any psychotherapeutic procedure are long-lasting and relatively "permanent."

Notwithstanding the paucity of well-controlled and detailed studies in the efficacy and effectiveness of counseling and psychotherapy with mentally retarded populations, there are a sufficient number of "gross" studies available to support the conclusion that psychotherapy is a most useful means of improving the personality and social behavior of most retarded individuals with behavioral difficulties, and that the use of preventive counseling and therapeutic modalities is particularly helpful and cogent.

Efficacy of Specific Orientations

To the question of which methodological techniques and approaches work best with which types of retarded clients and under which particular types of situational influences, perhaps the best way to determine the answer is to take a global view of the available psychotherapeutic literature. This is to be found in Tables 11.1, 11.2, 11.3, and 11.4, which briefly summarize and highlight certain salient features in much of the available research literature. Even a cursory review of the results will highlight the relative efficacy of those approaches that are basically nonverbal and directive, and I can fully support this finding on the basis of my own experiences in the field (Sternlicht, 1966).

Further, from a situational viewpoint, therapeutic success is especially likely if the client is living at home (i.e., noninstitutionalized). Presumably, this is a reflection of the greater supports (especially emotional) that the

Table 11.1

Group Psychotherapy with Institutionalized Retarded Clients

Study	Sex	No.	Age	IQ Range	Primarily Verbal	Primarily Nonverbal	Primarily Directive	Primarily Non-directive	Duration & Special Information	Results
Appel & Martin (1957)	M, F	10 F; 10 M	Children	–	X		X		2 ea. wk. for 1 yr. (continuing). *Aim:* Adaptation to community	S
Bryer & Wagner (1963)	M	16	Young adults	48-90		X	X		12 wk.	S
D'Angelo (1962)	F	52: (divided into 2 groups)	–	–	X			X	1 hr. each wk. for 6 mo. in experimental group	F
Dentler & Mackler (1961)	M	29	6-12	Mean IQ = 56		X (deprivation; seclusion)	X (Authoritarian)		Observations by aides all day for 3 wk.; Sociometric tests during 3 mo. orientation	S if what is desired is "manageable patients," not really a therapy)
de Palma (1956)	M	40: (5 groups, 8 in each)	1 adolescent group; 4 adult groups	"Imbeciles"; "low grade morons"	X		X		20 sessions, 45 min. each	MS

	Sex	No. of Subjects	Age	IQ					Duration / Comments	Outcome
Fine & Dawson (1964)	F	65: (divided into 7 groups of 8 each)	15-30	50+ (mild retardation)	X		X	X	1 hr. each wk. for 2½ yr. (Special co-operation with community)	S
Gorlow, et al. (1963)	F	42: (6 groups of 7 each)	15-23	50-80	X			X	1 hr., 3 times each wk. for 12 wk.	F
Heimlich (1960)	M, F	3: (2 withdrawn; 1 hyperactive)	8-16	—		X (Music)		X	2 yr. (An attempt at communication with treatment-resistant children)	S
Joseph & Heimlich (1959)	M, F	3: (2 withdrawn; 1 hyperactive)	Children	—		X (Music)		X	½ hr. twice each wk. for 2 yr.	S
Kaldeck (1958)	M, F	104: (10-14 in group)	17-40	"Close to 50"	X		X (changed from passive to active)		1 hr. twice each wk. for 30 mo. (25 subjects placed in community)	S

Table 11.1 – Continued

Study	Sex	No.	Age	IQ Range	Primarily Verbal	Primarily Nonverbal	Primarily Directive	Primarily Non-directive	Duration & Special Information	Results
Kaufman (1963)	M	8	18-25	61-67	X		X		Once a wk. for 1 yr. (Supplemented by experiences outside institution)	S (6 of 8 permanently in community)
Leland et al. (1959)	M	8	4-9	50-75; (4 aggressive, 4 withdrawn)		X (Play therapy)		X	1 mo.	MS
McKinney & Keele (1963)	M	48: (24 E group; 24 C group)	8-18	30 or below (severe)		X ("Mothering")		X	At least 4 hr. per day for 4 wk.	S
Miezio (1967)	M, F	17	12-19	50-70		X		X	18 mo.	S
Murphy (1957)	M, F	64	—	"Low and Middle Grade"		X (Music)		X	—	S
Murphy (1958)	M, F	Entire institution (1,100)	Mean age = 24	"Low and Middle Grade": (under 10-47)		X (Music)		X	"Live" music for 4 wk., ½ hr. each wk.	S

Study	Sex	N	CA	IQ					Duration / Frequency	Outcome
Snyder & Sechrest (1959)	M	16	Mean CA = 19	Mean: IQ = 62	X		X (minimal interaction)		13 wk., once a wk.	S
Sternlicht (1965)	F	10-14 (in each of 3 groups)	14-20	37-70	X	X (Activity)	X		90 min. a wk., 2 groups for 1 yr.; 1 group for 15 mo.	S
Stubblebine (1957)	M	6	19-55	55-105 (epileptic)	X			X	1 hr., twice a wk. for 22 wk.	F
Subotnik & Callahan (1959)	M	8	8-12	53-88		X (Play therapy)		X	Short-term treatment: 16 sessions twice each wk. for 8 wk.	F
Tavris (1961)	M	5	19-29	Under 40 (severe)	X		X		Once a wk. for several mo. (A nonverbal communication of attitudes noted by author)	MS
Wanderer & Sternlicht (1964)	M, F	11 groups (9-15 in each)	9-54	40-72	X		X		1 hr. each wk. for 2 yr.	S
Wilcox & Guthrie (1957)	F	97 (divided into 3 groups)	15-43	53-90	X		X		1 hr., 3 times each wk. for 25 sessions (mixed groups essential for success)	S

Table 11.2

Group Psychotherapy with Noninstitutionalized Retarded Clients

Study	Sex	No.	Age	IQ Range	Primarily Verbal	Primarily Nonverbal	Primarily Directive	Primarily Non-directive	Duration & Special Information	Results
Alvin (1959)	M, F,	24	7-16	22-50: (severely retarded)		X (Music)	X		34 concerts	S
Bevan (1960)	—	2	—	—		X (Activity)		X	Unknown duration	S
Chess (1962)	M, F: (M = 27; F = 10)	37 (Report based on 19)	4-16	<30-72	X	X (Play)	X	X	6 or more sessions. (Individualized therapy to child's intellectual level)	S
Long (1959)	M, F	10: (5 M; 5 F)	5-17	Under 50: (severely retarded)		X (Role-playing)	X		15 sessions (feels need of maturity)	MS
McDaniel (1960)	M, F	—	16-32	Mean IQ = 52		X (Sociometric manipulation)	X		2 sessions, and tested at end of 6 wk.	S

480

Study	Sex	N	Age	IQ				Procedure / Comments	Outcome
Pilkey (1961)	M, F	16: (experimental and control groups)	13-16	58-79	X (psychodrama)	X	X	1 hr., twice each wk. for 4 wk; 6 wk. trial. (Aim: increase empathic ability)	S
Ricker et al. (1967)	171: (57	Young "Educable adults	"Educable" (mild retardation)	X	X (Film)	X	X	2 hr. each wk. for 17 wk. (excellent attempt to eliminate bias)	S
Scheidlinger et al. (1962)	M	1	10	74	X (Activity)	X	X	5-yr. case history of one subject in a group.	S (Worked where individual therapy failed)
Tyson (1957)	M, F	85: (divided into small groups)	Young children	—	X	X (Music)	X	In 1 mo., all children had over 150 appointments	S
Weigl (1959)	M, F	5-10	5-15	40-75	X	X (Music)	X	45 min., once each wk. (a continuous program)	S (in facilitating relationships)

Table 11.3

Individual Psychotherapy with Institutionalized Retarded Clients

Study	Sex	No.	Age	IQ (Range)	Primarily Verbal	Primarily Nonverbal	Primarily Directive	Primarily Non-directive	Duration & Special Information	Results
Ayer & Butler (1969)	M, F	27	Adolescents	40-85	X		X		Up to 24 sessions	S
Bryer & Wagner (1963)	M	16	Young adults	48-90		X	X		12 wk.	S
Friedman (1961)	M	1	24	57	X			X	18 mo.	S
Glass (1957)	M	1	12	60-78 (repeated testing)		X	X		¾ hr. twice each wk. for 8 mo.	(S)
Heister (1954)	M, F	14	Children	44-75		X	X		1 yr.	S
Mundy (1957)	M, F	25	Children (5 to 12)	40+		X		X	9 mo. to 1 yr.	S

Table 11.4

Individual Psychotherapy with Noninstitutionalized Retarded Clients

Study	Sex	No.	Age	IQ (Range)	Primarily Verbal	Primarily Nonverbal	Primarily Directive	Primarily Non-directive	Duration & Special Information	Results
Dichter (1962)	M	1	10	72		X		X	6 mo.	S
Knight et al. (1957)	M	1	11	72	X		X		1 yr. (1 morning each per wk.)	S
White (1959)	M	1	4	"In high 60s"		X	X		Once each wk. for a "few mo."	S

families of these clients can and do provide, supports which apparently are not forthcoming when they are in an institutional setting. While admittedly the outcome criteria in these studies often are vague and untenable (from a strictly experimental point of view), and efforts need to be made to develop comprehensive yet statistically operational outcome devices, the effectiveness of counseling and psychotherapy with the mentally retarded client is not left in doubt. However, no controlled studies are available which would shed any light on the efficiency of these particular procedures, and this must await future work.

FUTURE TRENDS

Therapeutic Innovations

We are currently in the midst of an era of crescive search for solutions, for ways of assisting the retarded person in developing his maximal potential for self-growth and development, and in efficiently relating to his environment. Because of the retarded individual's unique problems in the spheres of intellective functioning and verbal facilities, more traditionally oriented psychotherapeutic approaches have usually been pointless. The inherent multifarious difficulties that impede our truly effectively communicating and relating with the retarded person have led clinicians in this field—rather, *have forced*—clinicians to create new conceptualizations of counseling and psychotherapeutic procedures.

As a starter, I am firmly convinced that many common everyday objects can be much more efficiently employed therapeutically than they currently are. For example, what would be the effects on his future behavior if a retarded individual were able to more-or-less completely view himself as others do? A room with sides and ceiling that are completely mirrored might do wonders here. (I would not have the floor mirrored as well because locomotor difficulties might abound.) Arts and crafts can be more constructively employed, and the myriad things that one can create with balloons are endless. Noise plays a major role in our environment—why not use noisemakers as a means of exploring this area? How about aiding the retarded client in comprehending everyday manipulations, as Goldin's (1966) children's book, *Salt,* does?

In terms of mirrors, too, one also can employ a regular full-length mirror as well as several that reflect body distortion (in common use in amusement parks), with these latter mirrors utilized in illustrating how feelings can be distorted, and so forth.

The retarded person needs to have an adequate self-concept and self-image. Perhaps improvements in these areas could be facilitated by the employment of cosmeticians, by the use of a psychogalvanometer (to aid in the understanding of the client's feelings and emotions), and by working with photographs of (retarded and nonretarded) individuals. Empathy might be ideally explored via this latter technique. A personality adjective checklist might be creatively utilized as well. An additional value in the use of a cosmetician is the physical contact between the beautician and the client, since touch can have a supportive impact far beyond the use of words.

The possibility of marathon group therapy is one that has not yet been attempted with retarded groups, but it offers very interesting possibilities. Such a situation could occur when a group meets together for therapeutic purposes for an entire day, with time out only for breakfast, lunch, and supper, which are brought into the room. Presumably, the clients could be allowed freedom of access; and this may very well be a suitable kind of intensive treatment-type group psychotherapy with a retarded population. The possibility of seeing a group of retarded individuals for an entire afternoon and allowing them to walk in and out of the therapeutic situation as they please seems promising. Then, too, the concept of offering retarded clients a recess period during group therapy may serve the same therapeutic functions as do alternate group therapy sessions with nonretarded clients.

As noted above, balloons can be manipulated in many ways, some of which have already been highlighted. An illustration of still another use to which they can be put is in the development of a more effective self-concept, with consequent differentiation of self from others. For example, a therapist can demonstrate Sheldon's three body types by taping three different kinds of balloons (e.g., tall, thin; short, fat; and "just right") on the wall. If further clarification is desired, corresponding photographs can be pasted on the balloons. An issue that comes to mind at this juncture is whether we should stimulate one sensory modality at a time (single-channel inputs) or several senses (multichannel inputs). If deemed therapeutically appropriate, our balloons could be "odorized" to indicate various human odors. I am certain that other such possibilities will readily come to mind; for instance, the association of smell with relevant emotional feeling states.

The innovative therapist can manipulate a tape recording so that his retarded clients will hear sounds (e.g., grunts) normally associated with emotional states, and this can lead into a session on how to interpret effectively other people's feelings and reactions as well as one's own. On a visual plane, this also could be accomplished by having the clients study facial expressions closely (either "live" or from photographs). With other kinds of tape recordings, the clients can try to guess what the speaker is going to do next, and why. This all can be accomplished within a pantomime framework. Or we can show the conclusion of a film and have the clients act out what they imagine was the beginning.

Hand puppets can be utilized by the retarded clients to express their feelings about a tape recording or about a film, or to act- out various kinds of roles. Problem situations can be enacted, with hand puppets or via dramatic play therapy (Bach, 1950), concerning things that bother the retarded person and how these things can be changed. Immediate feedback can be provided by permitting retarded subjects to test their conclusion directly against the consequences of their manipulations.

The possibilities are virtually endless. A kaleidoscope can be used to facilitate an understanding of an environment that is constantly in flux, while the potential therapeutic uses of such objects as felt boards and overhead projectors are relatively transparent. Autoinstructional devices (e.g., teaching machines) with pictures or cartoons, or diagrams only, can readily substitute as a type of nonverbal alternative guidance procedure. Television can be employed as a therapeutic medium, as can costume play therapy (Marcus, 1966).

There is a multiplicity of models of identification that are available for use in the development of effective ego-ideals, including the viewing of successfuly placed retarded persons in real-life (or on-the-job) situations and via film biographies.

Planned covert communications will have to be made in a basically unspoken, silent language. Knowledge will have to be offered concerning the utilization of those cues available in the milieu as a guide toward specific socially acceptable (copying) behavior. The therapeutic session will have to offer the client the unique opportunity to explore and to understand himself. We should increase the richness of stimulus input into the retarded person's repertoire of knowledge and allow him occasions to work with such inputs. (The retarded client also must learn to control his inputs and outputs.)

At best, many of these ideas may serve as but speculative approaches. They are offered as possible procedures designed to focus upon a still most tacky problem area.

Programmatic and Conceptual Innovations

The environment of retarded individuals must be totally oriented toward satisfying their needs; as such, the environment must be a wholly humanizing one. Daily routines will have to be designed so as to facilitate a maximum of independent functioning as well as maximizing social and emotional development; and sensory-perceptual experiences will have to be enhanced via an appropriate and effective use of space, textures, colors, acoustics, and composition. The physical environment can be conceived of as a catalytic agent in the therapeutic process, and it also can suggest and stimulate desired behavior. Environmental manipulation can be either indirect (by modifying the human environment, e.g., by counseling those upon whom the retarded client is dependent) or direct (by modifying the environment per se). In practice, however, most manipulative endeavors end up by being synergetic.

Because the overwhelming majority of retarded individuals reside in the community, recent innovations have been created in needed community adjustments. Institutional milieus are geared toward community placements, and novel foster-home environments have been, and are currently being, pursued energetically. Imaginative vocational habilitation programs are being devised, as well as "halfway" group homes and hostels. Facilities for respite care also are in the works, and a total therapeutic and programmatic functioning is envisioned within the environs of regional mental retardation centers. Hopefully, before too long, the dearth in this area of innovative community placements will exist no longer!

SUMMARY

An attempt was made to clearly delineate the significant critical issues in the sphere of counseling and psychotherapy with the mentally retarded client, and to offer resolutions of these issues in as definitive a fashion as possible. The critical issues were subsumed under the four categories of interaction issues (therapist, client, and familial variables); structural issues (including milieu variables); methodological issues (process and technique variables); and outcome issues. Future trends in the area of psychotherapy with retarded persons also were discussed, and a tabular summarization of the relevant literature was offered. Additional speculative therapeutic modalities were outlined, and several research issues delineated.

REFERENCES

Alvin, J. The response of severely retarded children to music. *American Journal of Mental Deficiency,* 1959, *63,* 988-996.

Appel, E., & Martin, C. H. Group counseling for social adjustment. *American Journal of Mental Deficiency,* 1957, *62,* 517-520.

Ayer, M. J., & Butler, A. J. *Client-counselor communication and interaction in counseling with the mentally retarded.* Final report R.D. 1798-P, Madison: University of Wisconsin, 1969.

Bach, G. R. Dramatic play therapy with adult groups. *Journal of Psychology,*

1950, *29*, 225-246.

Bevan, J. Non-directive activities for the mentally handicapped. *Chicago School Journal,* 1960, *41*, 379-384.

Bialer, I. Psychotherapy and other adjustment techniques with the mentally retarded. In A. A. Baumeister (Ed.), *Mental retardation.* Chicago: Aldine, 1967, pp. 138-180.

Bryer, S. J., & Wagner, R. The didactic value of role-playing for institutionalized retardates. *Group Psychotherapy,* 1963, *16*, 177-181.

Chess, S. Psychiatric treatment of the mentally retarded child with behavior problems. *American Journal of Orthopsychiatry,* 1962, *32*, 863-869.

Cowen, E. L., & Trippe, M. J. Psychotherapy and play techniques with the exceptional child and youth. In W. M. Cruickshank (Ed.), *Psychology of exceptional children and youth* (2nd ed.). Englewood Cliffs, N.J.: Prentice-Hall, 1963, pp. 526-591.

D'Angelo, R. Y. An evaluation of group psychotherapy with institutionalized delinquent girls. *Dissertation Abstracts,* 1962, *23*, 306-307.

Dentler, R. A., & Mackler, B. The socialization of retarded children in an institution. *Journal of Health and Human Behavior,* 1961, *2*, 243-252.

dePalma, N. Group psychotherapy with high grade imbeciles and low grade morons. *Delaware State Medical Journal,* 1956, *28*, 200.

Dichter, A. Psychotherapy for the mentally retarded. *Pathways in Child Guidance* (Board of Education, City of N.Y.), 1962, *4*, 11-12.

Farber, B., & Ryckman, D. B. Effects of severely mentally retarded children on family relationships. *Mental Retardation Abstracts,* 1965, *2*, 1-17.

Fine, R. H., & Dawson, J. C. A therapy program for the mildy retarded adolescent. *American Journal of Mental Deficiency,* 1964, *69*, 23-30.

Friedman, E. Individual therapy with a "defective delinquent." *Journal of Clinical Psychology,* 1961, *17*, 229-232.

Glass, H. L. Psychotherapy with the mentally retarded: A case history. *Training School Bulletin,* 1957, *54*, 32-34.

Goldin, A. *Salt.* New York: Crowell, 1966.

Gorlow, L., Butler, A., Einig, K. G., & Smith, J. A. An appraisal of self-attitudes and behavior following group psychotherapy with retarded young adults. *American Journal of Mental Deficiency,* 1963, *67*, 893-898.

Grossman, H. J. (Ed.) *Manual on terminology and classification in mental retardation: 1973 revision.* Washington, D.C.: American Association on Mental Deficiency, 1973.

Halpern, A. S., Mathiew, P. L., & Butler, A. J. Verbal expressivity as a client variable in counseling the mentally retarded. *Exceptional Children,* 1968, *34*, 693-701.

Heimlich, E. P. Music as a therapy with emotionally disturbed children. *Child Welfare*, 1960, *39*, 7-11.

Heiser, K. Psychotherapy in a residential school for mentally retarded children. *Training School Bulletin*, 1954, *50*, 211-218.

Joseph, H., & Heimlich, E. P. The therapeutic use of music with "treatment resistant" children. *American Journal of Mental Deficiency*, 1959, *64*, 41-19.

Jourard, S. M. *The transparent self.* New York: Van Nostrand Reinhold, 1971.

Kaldeck, R. Group psychotherapy with mentally defective adolescents and adults. *International Journal of Group Psychotherapy*, 1958, *8*, 185-192.

Kaufman, M. E. Group psychotherapy in preparation for the return of mental defectives from institution to community. *Mental Retardation*, 1963, *1*, 276-280.

Knight, D., Ludwig, A. J., Strazzula, M., & Pope, L. The role of varied therapies in the rehabilitation of the retarded child. *American Journal of Mental Deficiency*, 1957, *61*, 508-515.

Leland, H., & Smith, D. Unstructured material in play therapy for emotionally disturbed, brain-damaged, mentally retarded children. *American Journal of Mental Deficiency*, 1962, *66*, 621-628.

Leland, H., Walker, J., & Taboada, A. Group play-therapy with a group of post-nursery mental retardates. *American Journal of Mental Deficiency*, 1959, *63*, 848-851.

London, P. *The modes and morals of psychotherapy.* New York: Holt, Rinehart and Winston, 1964.

Long, W. J. An exploratory study of the use of role playing with severely retarded children. *American Journal of Mental Deficiency*, 1959, *63*, 384-391.

Marcus, I. M. Costume play therapy: The exploration of a method of stimulating imaginative play in older children. *Journal of the American Academy of Child Psychiatry*, 1966, *5*, 441-452.

McDaniel, J. Group action in the rehabilitation of the mentally retarded. *Group Psychotherapy*, 1960, *13*, 5-13.

McDermott, W. H. Art therapy for the severely handicapped. *American Journal of Mental Deficiency*, 1954, *59*, 231-234.

McKinney, J. P., & Keele, T. Effects of increased mothering on the behavior of severely retarded boys. *American Journal of Mental Deficiency*, 1963, *67*, 556-562.

Menolascino, F. J. Emotional disturbances in mentally retarded children. *Archives of General Psychiatry,* 1968, *19,* 456-464.

Miezio, S. Group therapy with mentally retarded adolescents in institutional settings. *International Journal of Group Psychotherapy,* 1967, *17,* 321-327.

Mundy, L. Therapy with physically and mentally handicapped children in a mental deficiency hospital. *Journal of Clinical Psychology,* 1957, *13,* 3-9.

Murphy, M. M. Rhythmical responses of low grade and middle grade mental defectives to music therapy. *Journal of Clinical Psychology,* 1957, *13,* 361-364.

Murphy, M. M. A large scale music therapy program for institutional low grade and middle grade defectives. *American Journal of Mental Deficiency,* 1958, *63,* 268-273.

Pilkey, L., Goldman, M., & Kleinman, B. Psychodrama and empathetic ability in the mentally retarded. *American Journal of Mental Deficiency,* 1961, *65,* 595-605.

Ricker, L. H., Pinkard, C. M., Jr., Gilmore, A. S., & Williams, C. F. *A comparison of three approaches to group counseling involving motion pictures with mentally retarded young adults.* Tampa: MacDonald Training Center Foundation, VRA Project No. RD-989, 1967.

Robertson, M. F. Shadow therapy. *Mental Retardation,* 1964, *2,* 218-223.

Rosen, E. Dance as therapy for the mentally ill. *Teachers College Record,* 1954, *55,* 215-222.

Scheidlinger, S., Eisenberg, M. S., King, S. H., & Ostrower, R. Activity group therapy of a dull boy with severe body ego problems. *International Journal of Group Psychotherapy,* 1962, *12,* 41-55.

Snyder, R., & Sechrest, L. An experimental study of directive group therapy with defective delinquents. *American Journal of Mental Deficiency,* 1959, *64,* 117-123.

Sternlicht, M. Establishing an initial relationship in group psychotherapy with delinquent retarded male adolescents. *American Journal of Mental Deficiency,* 1964, *69,* 39-41.

Sternlicht, M. Psychotherapeutic techniques useful with the mentally retarded: A review and critique. *Psychiatric Quarterly,* 1965, *39,* 84-90.

Sternlicht, M. Psychotherapeutic procedures with the retarded. In N. R. Ellis (Ed.), *International review of research in mental retardation* (Vol. 2). New York: Academic Press, 1966, pp. 279-354.

Sternlicht, M., & Deutsch, M. R. *Personality development and social behavior in the mentally retarded.* Lexington, Mass.: D. C. Heath, 1972.

Sternlicht, M., Siegel, L., & Deutsch, M. R. Evaluation of a remotivation program with institutionalized mentally retarded youngsters. *Training*

School Bulletin, 1971, *68,* 82-86.

Sternlicht, M., & Wanderer, Z. W. Hypnotic susceptibility and mental deficiency. *International Journal of Clinical and Experimental Hypnosis,* 1963, *11,* 104-111.

Stubblebine, J. M. Group psychotherapy with some epileptic mentally deficient adults. *American Journal of Mental Deficiency,* 1957, *61,* 725-730.

Subotnik, L., & Callahan, R. J. A pilot study in short-term play therapy with institutionalized educable mentally retarded boys. *American Journal of Mental Deficiency,* 1959, *63,* 730-735.

Tavris, E. Some notes on group psychotherapy for severe mental defectives. *Delaware State Medical Journal,* 1961, *33,* 301-307.

Tillich, P. *The courage to be.* New Haven: Yale University Press, 1952.

Tyson, F. Music therapy in the rehabilitation of the retarded child. *Newsletter of the Musicians Fund,* 1957, *3,* 1-4.

Vail, D. Mental deficiency: Response to milieu therapy. *American Journal of Psychiatry,* 1956, *113,* 170-173.

Wanderer, Z. W., & Sternlicht, M. Alternative guidance: A psychotherapeutic approach to mental deficiency. *International Mental Health Research Newsletter,* 1964, *7,* 13-15.

Weigl, V. Functional music—A therapeutic tool in working with the mentally retarded. *American Journal of Mental Deficiency,* 1959, *63,* 672-678.

White, B. L. Clinical team treatment of the mentally retarded child and his parents: Group counseling and play observation. *American Journal of Mental Deficiency,* 1959, *6,* 713-723.

Wilcox, G. T., & Guthrie, G. M. Changes in adjustment of institutionalized female defectives following group psychotherapy. *Journal of Clinical Psychology,* 1957, *13,* 9-13.

Luke S. Watson, Jr., is the Assistant Superintendent for Programming at Partlow State School and Hospital in Alabama. He has served on the Psychology Department faculties of Ohio State University and Case Western Reserve University.

Dr. Watson is President of Behavior Modification Technology, Inc., an educational materials publishing and consulting firm, and has conducted a private practice for approximately 7 years. He has served extensively as a consultant in the United States, Canada, the British Isles, and Europe, and has also presented behavior modification workshops at home and abroad.

Dr. Watson has written a number of books and articles on the behavior modification of mentally retarded and autistic individuals. He is currently applying a Clinical Management System approach to the training of the mentally retarded residents at Partlow.

12

Issues in behavior modification of the mentally retarded individual

Luke S. Watson, Jr.

This chapter is concerned with the operant approach to behavior modification of mentally retarded individuals and with the issues which have arisen during the development of that approach. The Behavior Modification Technique consists of a psychotherapeutic or psychoeducational set of procedures that evolved primarily from the animal laboratory. It is a behavioristic-antimentalistic approach. Emphasis is placed on the publicly observable behavior of the client (patient, resident, or pupil), and treatment is directed toward changing the individual's behavior, as opposed to dealing with some inferred underlying "mentalistic" or organic disorder of the "mind" or the central nervous system.

Like laboratory research, behavior modification treatment is a rather precise procedure. The principles used are experimentally testable and have extensive empirical support, both with animal and human subjects (Ayllon & Azrin, 1968; Bijou & Baer, 1967; Gardner, 1971; Honig, 1966; Nawas & Braun, 1970a, 1970b, 1970c; Ullman & Krasner, 1965; Ulrich, Stachnik, & Mabry, 1966, 1970). The behavior to be changed is explicitly identifiable and observable, the results of therapy must be replicable or reproducible, and objective measurement procedures are used. Emphasis also is placed on studying a single individual over long periods.

Based on a deterministic framework, the two main psychological principles upon which the treatment framework is constructed are *reinforcement* and *stimulus* control. The premise is that undesirable or "pathological" behavior often occurs because of the individual's specific reinforcement history, and it continues to occur as a result of certain stimulus conditions usually associated with reinforcement. Thus, "psychopathology" may be seen as either (a) undesirable behavior or behavioral deficits which are the results of specific reinforcement conditions, and/or (b) socially inappropriate behavior (defined in terms of a community's standards of acceptable behavior) which is produced by stimulus conditions. Obviously, certain genetic and nonpsychological environmental factors play an important role in the development of psychopathology in many children labeled as mentally retarded. However, the diagnostic dimensions of these factors play a relatively unimportant role for the behavior modifier. His task is always the same, regardless of the given diagnosis. He must construct a habilitation program that (hopefully) is optimally suited for a client, given the relevant behavioral technology available and the behavior modifier's expertise. The two principles, reinforcement and stimulus control, plus an extensive research literature on their applications with humans, provide the behavior modifier with a relatively simple, straightforward, effective treatment repertoire.

In the 15 or more years since its appearance, the behavior modification approach to different kinds of behavioral disorders has grown rapidly; it also has met with considerable resistance. As with all new disciplines, some members of the "establishment" (e.g., traditional psychologists, psychiatrists, physicians, educators, nurses, administrators) have viewed this movement as a threat to their own particular field of speciality and to society in general. There have been objections to the notion of control of human behavior in any form and to the development of cultures based on principles of behavior modification (Goldiamond, 1969; Rogers & Skinner, 1966; Skinner, 1966). Others criticize it as dehumanizing, mechanical, dictatorial, and as a superficial approach to psychotherapy (Mikulas, 1972). With regard to mentally retarded people per se, not only has this approach been labeled as dehumanizing, but also there have been objections to the use of food or privileges administered on a response contingent basis, and the use of electric shock and physical restraint to eliminate undesirable behavior (Lucero, Vail, & Scherber, 1968). Some of the issues have come from outside the behavior modification movement, while others have come from within. The theoretical, methodological, and ethical issues most relevant to applications of behavior modification procedures to the mentally retarded person constitute the subject matter of this chapter.

THEORETICAL ISSUES

This section is concerned with the following issues: (a) the "Medical Model" versus the "Behavioral Model"; (b) behavior modification as a superficial approach; (c) the question of whether brain-damaged retarded children can learn; and (d) behavior modification as a panacea.

Medical Model versus Behavioral Model

The *Disease* (or *Medical*) *Model* interpretation of "psychopathology" views maladaptive behavior as due to either a "personality disorder" or a central nervous system dysfunction (Szasz, 1969; Ullman & Krasner, 1965). Although this model is concerned with "mental illness," it also is relevant to certain assumptions about mental retardation as a "mental disorder." The focus in this schema is on internal, underlying mental or organic factors which presumably are the *cause* of the observable, maladaptive behavior. Such behavior is supposedly only a sign or symptom of the underlying cause, and therefore is not a legitimate focal point for treatment. This interpretation has been expressed quite clearly by Ullman and Krasner (1965) in their discussion of the psychoanalytic or psychodynamic approach. Within that framework, maladaptive behavior is considered to be merely a symptom of an underlying personality disorder and important only insofar as it leads to the correct diagnosis of the "true," unseen mental cause. For example, emotional feelings that are unacceptable to the individual may cause him psychological pain, and they may be excluded from consciousness through repression. But because these feelings are still active, they may express themselves through certain behavioral patterns, such as unpleasant dreams, obsessional ideas, compulsive behavior, or fears. The psychoanalytic therapist uses the observable behavior (e.g., verbal report of obsessional ideas or compulsive behavior) only as a clue to identify correctly the unacceptable emotional feelings which underlie the personality disorder.

Diagnostic textbooks caution the therapist working within the Medical Model not to deal directly with the observable behavior, since it is merely a symptom produced by the unobservable, underlying causal agent. The therapist is warned that if the deviant behavior is eliminated without removing the underlying cause, it will be replaced by other deviant behavior (i.e., the symptoms will reappear).

This model is often applied by both the medical and the traditional psychological establishment to children who are lagging in their physical and psychological development (for example, children who do not exhibit certain behaviors that are characteristic of a given age group, such as a mute child of 4 years of age) or to children who exhibit severe behavior problems. Concerned parents take such a child to their pediatrician, who in turn may refer him to a pediatric hospital or clinic. There, the child typically receives an extensive physical examination, which usually includes a neurological evaluation and psychological test battery designed to assess his IQ, the integrity of his nervous system, and/or to reveal his "true personality structure." The entire evaluation, which usually consumes much time, is directed toward identifying physiological/neurological or personality factors which may underlie the deviant behavior.

At the conclusion of an extensive examination, the child receives a diagnosis and an IQ score, such as "Mongolism, IQ 35," or "Phenylketonuria, IQ 20," or "Infantile Autism, IQ 42," or "Mental Retardation with Chronic Brain Syndrome, IQ 28." In most cases, the diagnosis is not relevant to a treatment program, assuming one is prescribed. However, the area of deviant *behavior* is almost always totally overlooked, since it does not fit into the disease model of psychopathology. Actually the child may be lagging in his psychological development and may be a severe behavior problem, at least partially, because of unfortunate adventitious contingencies of reinforcement (Bijou, 1966; Ferster, 1961). This factor will be considered in detail later.

The alternative to the Medical Model is the *Behavioral Model,* the model preferred by persons who embrace the behavior modification approach. Here, emphasis is placed on the individual's observable behavior. "Psychopathology" is viewed in terms of behavior that deviates from the norms for a culture (Ullman & Krasner, 1969). All societies have taboos concerning unacceptable behavior. Examples of these taboos in the Western world include excessive violence (e.g., rape), withdrawing money from a bank by force, publicly reporting experiences that others never witness and being agitated about them, and failure to learn as rapidly as others in a given age group while earning an IQ score of 70 or below on an "intelligence" test. Persons exhibiting such behaviors in the Western world have been labeled as "criminal," "psychotic," and "mentally retarded." But as Szasz (1969) pointed out about "mental illness", many behavior problems are not simply the result of some underlying organic or personality factor, but are problems in living within the framework of a society's definitions of acceptable and unacceptable behavior. Although genetic and nongenetic organic factors may in some way be responsible for the initial behavioral deviancy in a child identified as mentally retarded, societal mores or values are responsible for the term "mental retardation" and for the subsequent treatment the child receives by other members of that society. The single social custom that probably has penalized more children in the Western world than any other is the recent tradition that children must participate successfully in the public educational system.

Bijou (1966) conceptualized mental retardation from the standpoint of the Behavioral Model, expressing his basic premise as *"a retarded individual is one who has a limited repertory of behavior shaped by events that constitute his history"* (p. 2). This premise holds that certain crucial behaviors have not developed, partially as a result of biological deficiencies in the individual and partially because of a deficient reinforcement history.

Bijou prefers the term "developmental retardation" to either "mental retardation" or "mental deficiency," and defines it as "observable, objectively defined stimulus-response relationships without recourse to hypothetical mental concepts such as 'defective intelligence' and hypothetical biological abnormalities such as 'clinically inferred brain injury' " (p. 2). Retardation is not seen as a symptom of an underlying mental or neurological disorder. Rather, it is viewed in terms of the individual's reinforcement history. Emphasis is placed on retarded *behavior* rather than on retarded *mentality*.

Within this system, the psychological development of the individual "consists of progressive changes in interactions between the individual, as a total functioning biological system, and the environmental events" (p. 2). The total environment consists of *"effective stimuli* from social and physical events outside the body wall and from biological events inside the organism" (p. 2). The retarded person is viewed as one for whom the rate of "social, physical and biological conditions of development deviates in the direction of slowing down the pace of successive interactional changes" (p. 2). Behavior is acquired at a reduced rate. Thus, "retarded behavior is a function of observable social, physical, and biological conditions all with the status of independent variables" (p. 3).

Bijou illustrated how characteristics of the retarded individual interfere with psychological development. If the person has anatomical or neurophysiological irregularities, his interaction with his environment may be adversely affected. A physically impaired child who can neither walk nor move his head or body will have limited environmental stimulation because he cannot come in contact with as much of his environment or as many people in his environment as a nonaffected individual in a given period of time. Someone who is blind will be deprived of considerable stimulation which ordinarily is received by the sighted individual through the visual modality. A person who is physically unattractive may be avoided by others who find him to be aversive because of his appearance. The same would be true of a child who is not toilet trained, or the child who engages in violent self-destructive behavior, or the child who is chronically negativistic or uncooperative. All these conditions place an individual in a state of relative stimulus deprivation or reduce his opportunities to learn, resulting in a behavioral repertory deficit for that child as compared to the resources of other children in his age group.

Ferster (1965) recommended a new classification system based on the Behavioral Model. He suggested that deviant behavior (e.g., behaviors labeled as symptomatic of infantile autism or mental retardation) can be accounted for most effectively by examining the individual's observable behavior. He argued that the relationship between deviant behavior and the consequences that control it (i.e., reinforcement contingences) is the key to an understanding and treatment of psychopathology. Controlling consequences are usually events in the person's social environment that either generate and maintain deviant behavior at unacceptable high rates ("accelerator" consequences) or that suppress the rate of socially acceptable behavior ("decelerator" consequences).

A child may engage in temper tantrums because each time he has one, his mother or ward attendant gives him an item of food or holds him tenderly. A child in an institution may slap himself on the head continually because head slapping always produces attention from an attendant or some other staff member. They run to him, tell him to stop, and/or place him in restraints—all events which apparently act as reinforcement and thus maintain the behavior (Bucher & Lovaas, 1968). A retarded child may have a very limited verbal repertoire because all attempts to speak are ignored, so that his verbal behavior is constantly undergoing extinction. Ferster's analysis is directed toward identifying the antecedent conditions (i.e., stimulus control) that cause the behavior to occur and the events (i.e. reinforcement) immediately following the behavior which serve to increase, decrease, or maintain the rate at which the behavior is manifested. The methodology used to identify these events is called a *functional analysis of behavior.*

Diagnosis also is carried out by persons who subscribe to the Behavioral Model. However, such diagnosis consists of identifying the behaviors which have caused the client or patient to be labeled as being different from others in his community. If concerned parents bring their child to a behavior therapist, he will attempt to identify all socially important deviant behaviors. If the child is 5 or 6 years old, the therapist will assess his self-help skills, language, social/recreational, and educational behavioral repertoire; and he will attempt to identify all significant socially disruptive behaviors, such as temper tantrums or self-destructive acts. The therapist then will develop a program designed to shape important behaviors which the child does not exhibit, and to eliminate the undesirable behaviors by using a variety of contingent reinforcement procedures. The final objective of the treatment program will be to make the child as much like other children his age as possible.

Let us examine one other crucial assumption of the Medical Model: *symptom substitution.* Is there, in fact, any evidence that attacking the behavior problem (the "symptom") directly and eliminating it only results in another deviant behavior being produced by the "real," underlying, hypothetical personality factor? Evidence to date appears to contradict this traditional concept. Several studies indicate that if treatment of the behavior problem is carried out adequately, there is seldom anything that resembles symptom substitution (Baker, 1969; Hussein, 1964; Lazarus, 1963; Nolan, Mattis, & Holliday, 1970; Paul, 1967; Yates, 1958). As Ullman and Krasner (1965) pointed out, in rare cases where "symptom substitution" has been reported, there are more parsimonious and reasonable explanations that adequately account for the later appearance of maladaptive behavior.

It is extremely difficult to draw any conclusions about the relative effectiveness of the two treatment approaches. Therapeutic methods based on the traditional medical model do not readily lend themselves to experimental analyses, and existing research methodology precludes effective global comparisons of the two approaches. Most current research evaluating behavior modification methodology deals only with one or two principles or procedures at a time, such as contingent reinforcement or "time out" from reinforcement. At this level of research, such principles and procedures appear to be effective. Further research is needed to determine the long-term effects of behavior modification procedures and the extent to which a comprehensive program can remediate more severe behavioral disorders.

Behavior Modification as a Superficial Approach

Recurring criticisms of behavior modification programs are that they are superficial approaches to psychopathology (in that they never deal with *real* personality dynamics) and that they change clients or patients into automatons rather than into normal humans. Such criticisms appear to be partially due to (a) semantic problems, and (b) differences between the basic assumptions or principles found in a behavioristic, anti-intervening variable behavior modification approach, on the one hand, and the pro-intervening variable personality and learning theory approaches, on the other. The operational language of the behavior modifier often alienates the traditional psychotherapist or psychoeducator. It sounds mechanistic and lacks the warm, humanitarian tone that epitomizes the traditional psychotherapist's speech flow. The second problem, that of dramatic differences in the psychological frame of reference, is probably the greatest issue. The operant approach to behavior modification either ignores or dismisses many of the principles that make up the basic framework of many learning and personality systems. Three of the more important incongruities are concerned with intervening variables or hypothetical constructs, the medical model, and the manner in which actual psychotherapy is carried out.

Persons who subscribe to the necessity of considering intervening variables (mentalistic or personality concepts) for formulating a thorough understanding of a person's psychological fabric evaluate all psychological systems in terms of that framework. If, by definition, a psychological system is superficial to the extent that intervening variables are not employed (as is the case in behavior modification), then operant behavior modification systems are labeled superficial by persons embracing that frame of reference.

Traditional psychotherapists are equally shocked because operant behavior modifiers ignore such basic tenets as "symptom substitution." From that standpoint, the operant behavior modification approach if viewed as a ridiculous system.

Traditional clinical psychologists and psychiatrists are "talk therapists." They engage the patient in lengthy exploratory discussion of his problems and feelings, and they focus on various topics, such as historical traumatic experiences or current painful experiences. In contrast, the typical operant behavior modifier sends the patient home to collect data on certain behavior problems, and he plans strategies and assigns "homework" to the patient. Thus, he violates every cardinal rule of the traditional talk therapist. To add insult to injury, the behaviorist accuses the talk therapist of reinforcing the patient's psychopathology by dwelling on it in therapeutic dialogue, thus giving the patient considerable reinforcement for engaging in verbalization about his psychopathology. No wonder the traditional therapist rejects the operant behavior modifier!

In essence, most people interpret other people's theories, beliefs, and philosophies in terms of their own personal, theoretical, moral, religious, and/or philosophical frames of references. When viewed in terms of traditional psychotherapeutic and psychoeducational frames of reference, the operant behavior modification approach does not fare very well.

With regard to the observation that operant behavior modification produces robots, or automatons, this author interprets such a criticism as referring to the behavioral appearances of certain retarded and autistic children who have been in operant behavior modification programs. Clearly, most severely behaviorally disordered children do not look like normal children of their own age, even after 2 or 3 years of intensive behavior modification treatment. Autistic children who have acquired considerable social-recreational skills still are usually lacking in a quality commonly identified as *normal emotional affect.* This lack is expressed in their conversation and in reactions to situations that commonly produce "elation," "excitement," and "warmth" in a normal child's speech and facial-gestural mannerisms. As a result, their behavior does have a robot-like quality. However, this quality is not necessarily a product of behavior modification technology in the sense that the technology produced the behavioral deficit—which, after all, existed before the child entered the program. Rather, it is a result of the failure of the technology to shape normal emotional affect into behavioral components. Behavior modification technology is still in its infancy and has not come to grips with many behavioral deficits or inappropriate behaviors. It is certainly conceivable that as the technology continues to develop, procedures to effectively shape normal emotional affect in such children will be generated.

Another criticism of behavior modification of the mentally retarded child, which falls in the "superficial approach" category, is the statement that behavior modification programs designed for such children are limited to developing self-help skills in a given child and generally ignore such areas as language development, academic achievement, vocational training, and social-recreational skills. Such a statement was relatively accurate 5 to 7 years ago as far as any individual program was concerned. There were programs that dealt with each of these areas individually, but no single program seemed to deal effectively with more than two or three of them at the same time, particularly if clients were severely and profoundly retarded, or if they were psychotic. However, this is not the case today. Our own Community Behavior Modification Project for Children (Watson & Bassinger, 1972, 1974; Watson, in press) is designed to deal with six categories of behavior. These are self-help skills, motor skills, language skills, academic skills, social-recreational skills, and elimination of undesirable behavior. All areas are interrelated and carefully coordinated to provide a comprehensive, effective habilitation program that should eventually allow such children to make a satisfactory adjustment to community life. A summary of the target behaviors identified for the six categories can be found in Table 12.1. Programs have been designed to ensure that each of these target behaviors will be shaped. Effective behavior modification programs at this level of complexity are by no means superficial.

Another behavior modification program that belies the criticism that MR behavior modification programs are superficial is the Mimosa Project at Parsons Training School and Hospital, Kansas (Lent, LeBlanc, & Spradlin, 1970). This project was designed to prepare institutionalized moderately retarded girls to make a satisfactory adjustment to life in the community. Residents in the program were taught high-level self-help skills, such as showering (and getting clean), hair care, nail care, putting on matching clothes and wearing them properly, and ironing and mending clothes. They received training in taking care of their living quarters by activities such as sweeping, dusting, and putting away clothing. They were taught how to talk to and relate with peers, boy friends, bosses, and supervisors; and they were taught a variety of solitary and group recreational activities that were appropriate to life in the community. Residents also received language training and academic training, both of which were aimed at community adjustment. In addition, they learned other skills, such as getting to and from work, walking downtown using sidewalks and observing traffic lights, and selecting items to purchase in clothing or grocery stores and paying for them. Finally, many learned a vocational skill that would enable them to get a job once they were returned to the community. Some of the contingencies that were employed to shape and maintain these skills are summarized in Table 12.2.

Table 12.1

Model Child Schematic

Summary of Training Goals or Target Behaviors Selected for Children in
Children's Behavior Modification Program

Skill	Target Behaviors
Self-Help	
Eating	Can sit at table and eat neatly with spoon or fork (or equivalent to age level).
	Lack of Inappropriate Behavior: Does not jump up from table until meal is completed; does not throw food or eat with his fingers; does not take food from someone else's plate, scream, or cry; does not chew food with mouth open; does not swallow solid food without chewing it; does not pound eating utensils on the table; does not spin plate, drop it, or throw it.
Drinking	Can drink neatly from an appropriate size cup or glass held in one hand (unless younger than age 3).
	Lack of Inappropriate Behavior: Does not pound cup on table, drop it, or throw cup or its contents; does not place fingers or hands in cup or blow bubbles; does not put food, napkins, utensils, clothing, or other objects in cup; does not spin cup; does not spit contents or gargle.
Undressing	Can remove pants, shirt, coat, dress, underpants, undershirt, or other undergarments (with or without buttons, zippers, or snaps), socks and shoes (either with buckles or laces) without assistance or supervision (or equivalent to his age level).
	Lack of Inappropriate Behavior: Does not damage garments when removing them; does not throw them on the floor and leave them.
Dressing	Can put on pants, shirt, coat, dress, or underclothing (with or without buttons, zippers, or snaps), socks and shoes (either with buckles or laces) appropriately without assistance or supervision or equivalent to his age level).
	Lack of Inappropriate Behavior: Does not damage garments when putting them on.

Toileting	Will locomote to toilet when elimination is impending without being cued; removes lower clothing appropriately; sits appropriately (unless male who is urinating); urinates or defecates into toilet bowl; wipes appropriately when elimination is completed without using an excessive amount of paper, deposits paper in toilet, flushes, pulls up underpants and/or pants and washes hands and dries them (or equivalent to his age level).
	Lack of Inappropriate Behavior: Does not play in toilet bowl, nor drink from bowl, nor smear feces, nor urinate on tank or floor or in bathtub; does not stop up toilet with excessive toilet paper or other objects.
Bathing	Can fill tub or turn on shower and adjust water temperature; soaps washcloth and bathes all parts of body, rinses and dries, and allows water to drain from tub (or equivalent to his age level).
	Lack of Inappropriate Behavior: Does not drink bath water, splash excessively, eat soap, suck water from washcloth, urinate or defecate in water, stop up drain with foreign objects, and does not flood the bathroom.
Toothbrushing	Applies appropriate amount of toothpaste to toothbrush; brushes all surfaces appropriately; rinses out mouth and rinses off toothbrush, and returns toothbrush to receptacle (or equivalent to age level).
	Lack of Inappropriate Behavior: Does not squeeze excessive toothpaste onto toothbrush, bite toothpaste tube or damage tube; does not smear toothpaste on sink, mirror, or other inappropriate areas; does not splatter with toothbrush; does not swallow toothpaste; does not gag himself; and does not throw toothbrush.
Motor Coordination Gross Locomotor Development	Can walk down steps one foot per tread; skips, jumps, and runs without inappropriate posture or mannerisms (or equivalent to age level).
Fine Motor Development	Can manipulate small objects with hands and fingers, using thumbs; can place puzzle pieces in formboards, pegs in pegboards, lace shoes, snap, buckle, and tie shoes; can color with crayons and cut with scissors; can throw and catch a ball with two hands (or equivalent to age level).

Table 12.1 (continued)

Skill	Target Behaviors
Absence of Undesirable Behavior	
Elimination of Temper Tantrums	Does not cry, scream, run about, lay on the floor and kick, flail his arms, etc.
Elimination of Destructive Behavior	Does not damage toys, furniture, or other inanimate objects.
Elimination of Self-Abusive Behavior	Does not beat or slap his head with his hands, beat his head against floor, wall, or furniture; does not bite himself, pull out his hair, etc.
Elimination of Abusiveness to Others	Does not hit, bite, or scratch parents, siblings, peers, or staff; nor does he strike them with inanimate objects, spit on them, or pull their hair.
Elimination of Stereotyped or Ritualistic Behavior	Does not rock, sway, or gesture symbolically in a repetitive manner; does not move his fingers in front of his face repetitively; does not twirl or spin objects; does not engage in any other bizarre, repetitive behavior.
Elimination of Smearing Feces	Does not smear feces on himself, others, walls, floors, or furniture.
Elimination of Lack of Eye Contact	Looks at people when they look at him or talk to him or ask him to look at them.
Elimination of Failure to Look at Task	Looks at task he is engaging in, such as completing a puzzle or throwing and catching a ball.

Elimination of Short Attention Span	Can work at a task without interruptions up to 40 minutes.
Elimination of Hyperactivity	Does not constantly run or pace about the house or school.
Elimination of Constantly Getting into Things	Does not strew contents of pantry, kitchen drawers, bathroom cabinets, etc.
Elimination of Uncooperativeness	Does what he is told to do promptly.
Elimination of Lack of Motivation	Active; interested in a variety of tasks and activities; responsive to a variety of edible, manipulatable, and social reinforcements.
Elimination of Eating Non-food Objects	Does not eat string, feces, sticks, rocks, toys, etc.
Elimination of Ignoring Other Children	Looks at children when they are within view; approaches them, talks to them, smiles at them, and plays with them; shows affection for siblings and friends.
Elimination of Ignoring Parents	Looks at parents when they are within view; approaches them, talks to them, smiles at them, and displays affection for them.
Elimination of Ignoring Other Adults	Looks at adults when they are within view; approaches them, talks to them, and smiles at them.
Elimination of Resistance to Change of Routine	Does not cry, scream, or otherwise object when changes occur in daily routine; does not object when furniture, food on plate, or other items are rearranged.

Table 12.1 (continued)

Skill	Target Behaviors
Elimination of Resistance to Being Interrupted at a Task	Does not cry, scream, have a tantrum, or otherwise object when asked to stop a task or activity he is engaging in.
Elimination of Resistance to Being Held or Cuddled	Does not cry, scream, stiffen, or push away when parents, relatives, friends, or siblings attempt to hold or cuddle him.
Elimination of Taking off Clothes Inappropriately	Does not remove clothing in public places or in home other than in bedroom or bathroom or at toileting time, bathtime, or bedtime.
Elimination of Running Away	Does not run away from home or school or from parents in public places.
Elimination of Profane or Hostile Language	Does not express profane or hostile language toward others inappropriately.
Elimination of Misbehaving in Public	Does not refuse to obey in stores or exhibit temper tantrums or behave in other inappropriate ways.
Language Skills Imitates	Models trainer or other children upon command the first time when a novel behavior is introduced (or equivalent to age level).

Responsiveness to Sound	Shows orientation response to a sound that occurs out of line of vision and can discriminate sound (or equivalent to age level).
Receptive Language: Single Words	Responds appropriately to or indicates understanding of approximately 2,500 words (or equivalent to age level).
Receptive Language: Commands	Responds appropriately to approximately 250 commands (or equivalent to age level).
Concepts	Understands prepositional concepts, concepts of time, distance, shape, quantity, location, texture, weight, color, and societal value judgments (or equivalent to age level).
Expressive Language: Single Words	Can say approximately 1,200 words (or equivalent to age level).
Expressive Language: Sentence Complexity Used to Make Demands or Requests	Uses sentences utilizing 6 to 10 words on the average (or equivalent to age level).
Expressive Language: Sentence Complexity Used to Relate Experiences	Uses sentences utilizing 8 to 10 words on the average (or equivalent to age level).
Quality of Articulation	Omits, distorts, or substitutes "r" sounds, "s" sounds, and "z" sounds (or equivalent to age level).
Words Used Appropriately	Uses speech appropriate to situation (or equivalent to age level).

Table 12.1 (continued)

Skill	Target Behaviors
Educational Skills	
Seat Work	Can sit at a table with peers and carry out a *structured* task without interruptions up to 20 minutes and without disturbing neighbors—with limited supervision.
Seat Work	Can sit at a table with peers and carry out a *semistructured* task without interruption up to 20 minutes and without disturbing neighbors—with limited supervision.
Group Tasks	Can interact appropriately with a group of 8 to 10 children in a common task.
Knows His Way Around	Does not get lost going to and from school or from classroom to bathroom, lunchroom, or playground.
Social-Recreational Skills	
Solitary Play	Engages in a variety of *structured* activities appropriately; e.g., works formboard puzzles, plays a solitary lotto game, completes pegboard designs, or swings in a swing up to 30 minutes (or equivalent to age level)—with limited supervision.
Solitary Play	Engages in a variety of *semistructured* activities appropriately; e.g., rocks on a rocking horse, plays with a toy truck, colors in a coloring book, or roller skates up to 45 minutes—with limited supervision (or equivalent to age level).
Solitary Play	Engages in a variety of *unstructured* activities; e.g., plays with a doll, draws a picture, or plays in a sandbox appropriately up to 15 minutes—with limited supervision (or equivalent to age level).
Cooperative Play	Engages in a variety of *structured* activities appropriately; e.g., works puzzles, plays a lotto game, dominoes, swings, or bowls with up to four other children for 25 minutes (or equivalent to age level).

508

Cooperative Play	Engages in a variety of *semistructured* activities appropriately; e.g., teeter-totters, throws and catches a ball, and plays Simon Sez with up to four other children for 35 minutes (or equivalent age level).
Cooperative Play	Engages in a variety of *unstructured* activities appropriately; e.g., plays in a sandbox; plays with a doll; plays house or cowboys and indians with up to four other children for 20 minutes (or equivalent to age level).
Conversation	Engages in dialogue with up to three other children for up to 20 minutes (or equivalent to age level).
Spontaneous Horse Play	Engages in spontaneous horse play for approximately 10 minutes (or equivalent to age level).
Competition	Strives to win at competitive games and appears to enjoy winning; reacts appropriately to losing.
Response to Other Players in Games	Pays attention when another child is taking his turn in a game; smiles, laughs, or makes an appropriate vocal response when another player scores.
Initiative	Initiates conversation and games with other children.

Note. Adapted from "How To Use Behavior Modification with Mentally Retarded and Autistic Children: Programs for Administrators, Parents, and Nurses," by L.S. Watson, Jr. Copyright 1972 by Behavior Modification Technology. Reprinted by permission.

509

Table 12.2

Summary of Ways in Which Residents Could Earn and Lose Points

Reinforcement Categories	Earning Behavior		Costly Behavior	
	Category Breakdown	No. Points Earned	Categories	No. Points Lost
Ironing	Dress	8	Disrespectful attitude toward aide	20
	Full skirt	7	Disrespectful attitude toward peers	5
	Straight skirt	7	Inappropriate verbal behavior	5
	Blouse	6	Disobedient behavior	5
Sewing	Button	5	Neglect of cottage work assignment	10
	Hem of full skirt	7	Failure to complete cottage work assignment satisfactorily	20
	Embroidering	6-8	Stealing	20
	Hem of straight skirt	8-10	Lying	20
	Machine sewing	6-8		
Hair set	Setting hair for resident on immediate floor	5	Tantrum behavior	10
	Setting hair for resident on lower floor	10	Personal effects in disarray (bed drawer, bin, rack, etc.)	15
			Wearing dirty clothes	5
Hair washed		3-5	Wearing other girls' clothing	10
Letter writing	Off campus: to friends and relatives	8	Inappropriate night wear in day hall	5
	On campus: to residents on the lower floor or pen pals in male cottage	10	Sitting on the front steps of the cottage	5
			Turning television volume above the designated mark	10

Errands	For psychiatric aide or demonstration assistant	6-10	Crossing line into aide area or kitchen area	5
Cottage work	Assigned work area	8-10	Sitting in front of the television on the floor	5
Social activities	Cooperative behavior in activities	8-10	Entering demonstration assistant's office without knocking and asking to talk to person desired	10
Personal effects	Neat dressers	3-5	Refusing to take medicine when aide calls	10
	Clothing in bins and dresser drawers clean and neatly folded	3-5	Not cleaning up game or sewing when finished	5
Check station Morning	Beds	4		
	Dresser	4		
	Shoes	2		
	Socks	2		
	Bins	4		
	Teeth	2		
	Hair	4		
Evening	Legs shaved	3		
	Nails manicured	3		
	Hair well groomed	3		
	Dress appropriate	3		
	Shoes polished	3		

Note. From "Designing a Rehabilitative Culture for Moderately Retarded, Adolescent Girls," by J.R. Lent, J. LeBlanc, and J.E. Spradlin, in *Control of Behavior: From Cure to Prevention*, edited by R. Ulrich, T. Stachnik, and J. Mabry. Copyright 1970 by Scott, Foresman & Co. Reprinted by permission.

Can Brain-Damaged Retarded Children Learn?

The concept of brain damage has often been used as an excuse for not habilitating retarded persons who have been so diagnosed. Lindsley (1964) referred to this notion as the "homeopathic" treatment approach. The basic rationalization is that the treatment of a "psychiatric disorder" must be related to the cause. If the disorder was caused by a particular environmental process, then that process had to be involved in treatment of the disorder. Thus, if the disorder was caused by an organic process, then organically oriented treatment methods had to be used to ameliorate the problem. Such a rationalization clearly eliminated serious applications of psychoeducational habilitation techniques to brain-damaged children whose diagnoses included the additional identification of severe retardation or autism.

In point of fact, knowledge about the relationship between brain damage and behavior acquisition is extremely limited. Although it is obvious that certain critical masses of brain damage will interfere markedly with behavior acquisition, it is by no means clear just what this critical mass level is. And even though it is relatively well accepted that certain centers of the brain can prevent effective behavior acquisition if they are destroyed, neurological diagnostic techniques are not sophisticated enough to reliably identify these areas in the living person. In other words, we do not have sufficient knowledge about "brain damage" to justify predicting that children who warrant such a diagnosis are not worth the energy and expense required to provide psychoeducational treatment.

Research in physiological psychology traditionally ignores the influence of careful programming on behavior acquisition in organisms that have had various portions of their brains destroyed. The usual approach with animals is to create a lesion and to evaluate its effects—usually employing discrimination tasks. These evaluations do not involve a task analysis of the organism's behavioral repertoire following surgery, nor does the procedure attempt to systematically regenerate the repertoire up to the point where the organism again has the behavioral qualifications to respond appropriately to the discrimination tasks.

Many pediatricians and psychiatrists only treat brain damage biochemically. Not only has the medical profession been a prime offender with regard to the "brain damage cop-out," but the educational community has also contributed by maintaining that certain groups of neurologically impaired individuals cannot benefit sufficiently from psychoeducational methods to justify the investment.

Children labeled as "brain damaged" are often extremely uncooperative. Many do not even pay attention (give eye contact) to the teacher or to the task at hand. They do not respond to the teacher's instructions, and if the teacher insists on their cooperation, they often respond with violent temper tantrums that invariably intimidate the teacher and cause her to avoid them on future occasions. It is premature to attempt instruction with a child of this type until his cooperation has been developed. The effective psychoeducator begins by shaping eye contact, bringing the child under verbal control, and/or developing sufficient cooperation to enable him to follow instructions. Once these prerequisites are satisfied, the instructor begins teaching a particular task by shaping attention (eye contact) to the task. She also obtains a baseline to determine what other relevant behavioral components are present and missing. Then she introduces the child to a curriculum that is relevant to his own particular behavioral repertory, and begins to build his repertory a step at a time, in the order best suited for him. She moves through the curriculum at a pace that is optimum for that child. Finally, she uses sufficient reinforcement and feedback methods to ensure his cooperation and satisfactory progress through the program. Under these conditions, the teacher will be pleasantly surprised at the progress most "brain-damaged" children can make.

Behavior Modification as a Panacea

Operant behavior modification is an educational technique. As such, it is extremely useful for solving behavior problems that can be remediated through training. Its applicability and effectiveness are limited primarily by the levels of development of relevant behavior modification technology. To the extent that the necessary technology is available, it will be applicable to an enormous number of human problems.

What are some of the factors which currently appear to interfere with the effectiveness of behavior modification programs? One such factor is the integrity of the central nervous system. If an individual is blind, he cannot be shaped or instructed via the visual modality. If he has massive CNS damage, either anatomically or biochemically, a limit is placed on the probability that a person will acquire a given repertory in a specified period of time; and for all practical purposes, it may prevent an individual from learning a given complex skill at all. But as pointed out above, medical technology is not advanced enough to tell us accurately what limitations actually exist in a living person. Therefore, potential can be realized only through training.

Further, the effectiveness of behavior modification technology is clearly limited by reinforcement problems. It is difficult to find sufficient effective reinforcements for some persons, and although schedules of reinforcement increase the effectiveness of weak reinforcements, the technology is not sufficiently developed to allow a behavior modification technologist to operate effectively with all types of persons in their natural environments. Still to be identified are a multitude of reinforcement contingencies that control man in his natural environment.

The effectiveness of a behavior modification program is also limited by the extent to which a person's attention can be maintained in a training program. The technology related to attention span has not been sufficiently developed so as to be usefully applied to all persons with severe behavioral disorders that interfere with attention. Another limitation is the current inability of behavior modifiers to perform a satisfactory talk analysis for a number of complex behavioral disorders and to identify all component behaviors for purposes of programming them in optimum-sized steps.

Failure to communicate effectively with all persons who suffer from various behavioral disorders can likewise limit the applicability of behavior technology. (The term "communication," as used in this context, refers to a special dimension of stimulus control, usually identified as *attention* [Terrace, 1966]. Reports most relevant to this problem are found in a research area labeled "errorless learning.") All these methodological problems must be solved before behavior technology can develop appreciably.

Operant behavior modification technology is in its infancy, being scarcely more than 15 years old. The amount and sophistication of the research that is directly applicable to behavior technology is still quite limited. As both the amount and sophistication level of relevant basic and applied research continue to grow, the applicability of this technology to a greater variety of behavior problems will also increase. This will result in the remediation of a multitude of behavior disorders that previously were considered irreparable because of biochemical and neurological involvement.

The primary reason that behavior technology will never become a panacea is the matter of economics. There will never be available enough funds and enough researchers with sufficiently diversified interests to develop behavior technology with the effectiveness and breadth needed to eliminate the majority of human behavior disorders.

METHODOLOGICAL ISSUES

This section covers three methodological issues: single subject versus group approaches to data evaluation; paraprofessional versus professional practitioners as behavior modifiers; and the use of prosthetics versus the exclusive use of humans as trainers of retarded children.

Single Subject versus Group Approaches

A search of the literature on learning reveals two markedly different views about the correct way to establish the genuineness of data collected in research endeavors (i.e., to identify "true" psychological phenomena). One camp favors the use of group procedures, in which the data of many subjects are analyzed by means of statistical methods. The other view favors the use of single-subject experimental designs that analyze that data from each subject individually, employing a combination of replication procedures, plus the rigorous experimental control of important variables, to establish genuineness. Operant behavior modifiers tend to ally themselves with the latter camp. As Sidman (1960) pointed out, the major issue dividing the two camps revolves around the notion that *variability is an intrinsic property of the behavior of organisms* and that, consequently, one finds a great many fluctuations in the behavior of research subjects.

Historically, the concept of intrinsic variability of behavior evolved from the discovery that human responses to a given stimulus varied *among* several observers viewing the stimulus at the same time and *within* a particular observer over a period of time (Boring, 1950). This discovery later led to a new field of psychology: The Psychology of Individual Differences. In addition, special procedures were developed to deal with this concept, which was identified as a problem that would obscure the psychologist's attempt to identify psychological phenomena. Statistical methods were developed to separate the false effects produced by such variability from genuine psychological effects. One set of statistical procedures was developed to deal with the variability that resulted when a group of subjects responded to a given stimulus. The recorded responses were not the same; rather, they were usually distributed around a central point, such as a mean. Because of this problem, if two groups of subjects were exposed to two different values of some independent variable and a difference was obtained between the averaged group measures, statistical procedures were used to determine whether it could be accepted with confidence as being a true difference or whether it must be rejected as being due only to chance variations of responses that originated from the same parent population.

Another variability problem resulting from general unidentifiable variability intrinsic to or extrinsic to (but influencing) behavior has been dealt with statistically by computing the *standard error*. One assumption is that by increasing the sample size, the effects of such variability will cancel themselves out as the group size increases (assuming such variability is randomly distributed), and thus the probability that the true differences between the values of the independent variable will be revealed will increase.

Sidman (1960) argued that the assumptions upon which these two statistical procedures are based are rather tenuous, and in general that the results obtained from group data that have undergone statistical analyses do not accurately reflect the true behavioral effects produced by a single subject in such an experimental situation. With regard to the concept of distribution characteristics of population parameters, Sidman pointed out that there is very little evidence to support the assumption that any given behavior sample originated from a particular parent population with a specific distribution, a cardinal assumption of parametric statistics. In addition, Type I and Type II errors always create a risk, both for a single experiment and for replicated experiments. There is always the chance that the difference obtained between two averaged values may not be a true difference, even when it has been shown statistically to be a true difference (within certain confidence limits); or, conversely, a difference between two averaged values may be a true difference even though it has been rejected as only a chance effect by a statistical test of significance. With regard to the standard error, Sidman said that increasing the subject sample size for a group does not actually reduce variability. Rather, this is a statistical artifact.

Sidman sees the concept of chance, as used in statistics, as nothing more than a name for uncontrolled variables or as simply ignorance about the variables. He sees science as dedicated to eliminating ignorance about variables, but "statistical evaluation of data against a baseline whose characteristics are determined by unknown variables constitutes acceptance of ignorance. Such baselines in statistics are the presumed population parameters" (1960, p. 162). Sidman submitted that the evaluation of data by means of experimental control (rather than statistical control) is more consistent with the aims of science. He feels that behavioral variability is amenable to control, but not through statistical treatment, which is often "subjective and idiosyncratic to a particular experimenter or a particular laboratory" (p. 162).

Sidman's solution to behavior variability is to use single-subject experimental designs that employ both intersubject and intrasubject replication procedures. The two main requirements for this methodology are (a) stable behavioral baselines, which constitute the basis for evaluating the effects of independent variables on behavior; and (b) reversibility of the behavior under investigation so that intrasubject replication procedures can be employed. The goal of such research is to evaluate the lawful relationships between given variables and behavior—to identify the *order* in the relationships between the environment and behavior.

A unique advantage of the single-subject experimental design for the behavior modifier is that it is highly compatible with Sidman's clinical methodology. He has only to obtain a satisfactory baseline before instituting treatment ('vhich he must do in order to identify his target behaviors), and then collect data on this behavior throughout the course of treatment. Group statistical procedures, on the other hand, require the behavior modifier to dramatically alter the structure of his clinical program in order to meet the assessment requirements of group-statistical methodology. As Browning and Stover (1971) pointed out, operant behavior modification requires an *idiographic* assessment approach if it is to function primarily as a clinical operation. For a highly relevant application of the single-subject design to assessing clinical behavior modification programs, see the discussion by Baer, Wolf, and Risley (1968) on the multiple-baseline design.

Paraprofessional versus Professional Practitioners

Another issue that has recently developed concerns allowing the application of behavior modification procedures by persons who lack formal training in the mental health fields—as opposed to restricting the use of such procedures to professionals trained in mental health areas (e.g., psychologists, psychiatrists, and certain special educators)—even though all concerned may have relevant behavior modification training. Psychiatric aides, teachers, parents (and even children) are currently functioning as behavior technicians in institutional, school, and home settings. Some would argue that such persons do not have sufficient qualifications to permit them to act responsibly as behavior modification practitioners. The main fear here is that without such training as that of a clinical psychologist or psychiatrist, "paraprofessional" persons may cause psychological damage. This issue is particularly relevant, owing to the sudden influx of behavior modification programs that utilize nurse's aides and teachers in institutions (Ayllon & Michael, 1966; Lent, LeBlanc, & Spradlin, 1970; Watson, 1970, 1972; Watson & Bassinger, 1971a; Watson, Gardner, & Sanders, 1971); in schools (Bijou, Birnbrauer, Kidder, & Tague, 1967; O'Leary & Becker, 1970; Osborne, 1970); and in the home (Hawkins, Peterson, Schweid, & Bijou, 1970; Patterson, McNeal, Hawkins, & Phelps, 1970; Watson & Bassinger, 1971b). This is a very important innovation, since use of psychiatric aides, teachers, and parents enables many more retarded children, adolescents, and adults to be trained. It would be inordinately expensive to hire sufficient behavior modification professionals to carry out training now conducted by these paraprofessionals, if the former could be obtained at all in large numbers. Recent research suggests that employing the parent as a therapist may dramatically increase the effectiveness of behavior modification programs for children (Lovaas, Koegel, Simmons, & Stevens, 1973).

However, there is some legitimate basis for the fears expressed by certain professionals. Many of the behavior modification training programs for psychiatric aides, teachers, and parents are very brief; and they pertain primarily to behavior modification methodology. Little attention is given to ethical problems and to the dangers of behavior modification. From this author's standpoint, such persons are to be viewed only as *technicians,* and as such they should conduct behavior modification activities under the supervision of a qualified, responsible, professional. Watson and Bassinger (1970, 1971a, 1971b, 1974) conducted (and are conducting) behavior modification techniques. It is this author's opinion that behavior modification should be conducted by psychiatric aides in institutions only under the supervision of such responsible, qualified people. In addition, it is suggested that institutions develop a policy about acceptable and unacceptable applications of this method. With regard to parents, they should be supervised by a home consultant until they have demonstrated they can utilize the procedures in a responsible manner and until the child's major behavior problems have been eliminated.

Prosthesis versus Human Trainers

In recent years, several articles have appeared proposing the use of prosthetic devices to facilitate adaptation by retarded persons to environments developed for normal individuals. Ellis (1964) recommended the use of certain mechanical devices that compensated for a retarded person's limited discriminative and motor skills in order that he could manage his daily affairs with minimal assistance and supervision. For example, Ellis suggested the use of a single shower-water valve that could be preadjusted for proper temperature control. The resident had to operate only this one valve independently for turning on or turning off the water for his shower, without risking injury from water of too high a temperature. Watson (1968) argued for the use of a prosthetic device that would indicate to an incontinent child when elimination was impending, prompt him to go to the toilet, and reinforce him for eliminating in the toilet. Watson pointed out several advantages of such a procedure over that of technicians serving as toilet trainers of incontinent retarded persons. One of the most comprehensive proposals for employing prosthetic devices was made by Lindsley (1964). His introductory remarks clearly defined the problem for the retarded individual living in an environment developed for "normal" people: "Children are not retarded. Only their *behavior* in average environments is sometimes retarded. We design environments to maintain life, but not to eliminate dignified be-havior" (p. 62).

Lindsley went on to describe some of the useful functions prosthetics can serve for the retarded person. He noted that they can be used to develop discrimination skills and appropriate stimulus control, increase response repertories, and develop responsiveness to normal social contingencies and social reinforcers. He also made the important distinction between two applications of prosthetics; to foster the acquisition of normal behavior and to maintain it. Most persons in the field agree that the acquisition application is an important and necessary one. A number of persons object to the use of prosthetics to maintain a given behavior if it is at all possible to "wean" the client from the prosthesis once he acquires the behavior in question. Such people are opposed to the use of an unnecessary "crutch," particulary if it acts to substitute one form of abnormality for the other.

What are the advantages and disadvantages of a prosthetic device over a human trainer for shaping behavior? A major advantage is that the prosthesis can be designed to arrange optimally important stimulus, response, and reinforcement events so that acquisition of any given behavior is maximized. Toilet training is a case in point. Such training involves conditioning a child to become aware when elimination is impending, to locomote to the toilet itself, remove the appropriate clothing, sit on or stand in front of the toilet, eliminate, wipe if necessary, flush, put the clothing back on, and return to the room and the activity he was engaging in prior to elimination.

Most of these behavioral components can be developed relatively easily by the behavior modification technician, with the exception of one—getting the child to locomote to the toilet without any prompting when elimination is impending. Another behavior component that is sometimes difficult for the technician to shape, particularly on institutional wards, is eliminating in the toilet. However, when a moisture-operated signaling device is attached both in the retardate's underpants and within the toilet bowl, acquisition of the two crucial behavioral components is greatly facilitated (see Figures 12.1 and 12.2. By pairing sphincter sensations with the pants alarm and a verbal cue, "No __(name)__ , go to the toilet," both the pants alarm and sphincter cues become discriminative stimuli for locomoting to the toilet and eliminating. Once elimination occurs, the toilet bowl alarm signals the technician to reinforce the child so that the toilet alarm, the toilet, and the eliminative act acquire conditioned reinforcement properties. After the two appropriate behavioral components are acquired, the prosthetic device can be faded, and the eliminative behavior occurs in a manner identical to that of "normal" humans.

Prostheses used in this manner clearly appear to have an important role in education of the retarded child and are being used widely in toilet-training programs as well as in classrooms to teach sight reading (DuCharme, 1972) and basic mathematical skills to trainable and severely retarded children

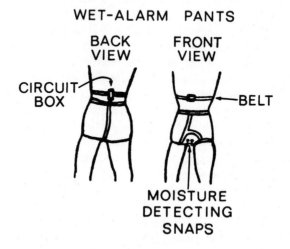

WET-ALARM PANTS

Figure 12.1. The wet-alarm pants are shown as viewed from the back and front of the wearer. The moisture-detecting snaps seen in the front view were two clothing snaps fastened to ordinary men's briefs. Two flexible wires are shown (back view) leading from the snaps to the circuit box. The snaps on the end of the wire were manually removable from the snaps on the clothing. The circuit box was worn on a belt (back view) which was worn "high" on the abdomen. Normal trousers were worn over the special training pants. A tone is sounded by the circuit box when urine or feces mositens the area between the clothing snaps. (Reprinted from "A Method of Toilet Training the Institutionalized Retarded," by N. H. Azrin and R. M. Foxx, *Journal of Applied Behavior Analysis*, 1971, *4*, 88-89. Copyright 1971 by Society for the Experimental Analysis of Behavior, Inc. Used with permission.)

TOILET SIGNAL

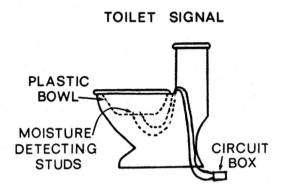

Figure 12.2. The toilet signal arrangement is shown from a side view. The malleable plastic bowl fits into the normal toilet bowl and rests on its top edge. The water level (not shown) of the stool must be below the plastic bowl to avoid shorting of the moisture-detecting studs on the bottom of the plastic bowl, which are designed to be shorted by urine or feces. The dotted lines are the detachable wires that connect the studs to the circuit box which can rest on the floor. The circuit box sounds a tone when moisture shorts the two studs. (Reprinted from "A Method of Toilet Training the Institutionalized Retarded," by N. H. Azrin and R. M. Foxx, *Journal of Applied Behavior Analysis*, 1971, *4*, 88-89. Copyright 1971 by Society for the Experimental Analysis of Behavior, Inc. Used with permission.)

(Reese, 1971). They are also being used to develop complex behavioral repertories and to condition social reinforcers in children with severe behavioral disorders (Watson, 1972).

What types of prosthetic devices have the greatest likelihood of being accepted by the consumer, i.e., by the behavior modifier working in a residential institution, a classroom, a day care center, a mental health clinic, or a home training program? Probably a carefully developed program that involves no complicated or awe-inspiring mechanical devices has the greatest chance of acceptance, particularly if it is inexpensive. Large complicated, exotic, prosthetic devices tend to be aversive to the consumer, particularly if they are expensive and require considerable sophistication to operate. Watson (1968) developed a rather bulky, expensive, very sophisticated and highly effective elimination reinforcement device (see Figure 12.3). Whenever the child eliminated in the toilet, he immediately received conditioned reinforcement (a light and tone) followed by unconditioned reinforcement (candy or a snack item). The device had a variety of safeguards to ensure that only urine and feces would trigger the reinforcement mechanism. It was a highly reliable, splendid device, and could be constructed for approximately $1,500.00, but evidently was aversive to most consumers and, because of lack of interest, it became extinct like the dinosaur.

ETHICAL ISSUES

It seems only appropriate to begin with an ethical issue eloquently delineated by Skinner (1971) in *Beyond Freedom and Dignity*—namely, whether behavior modification is a threat to man's freedom and dignity. Another issue, closely related to the first, may be labeled, "God, the Behavior Modifier," (i.e., he who practices behavior modification is playing God). Other issues, related to recent attacks on behavior modification programs as being dehumanizing, are concerned with the use of certain accelerator and decelerator techniques that have been used in residential institutions.

Freedom, Dignity, and Exploitation

In the following passage, Skinner identified the major issue which makes behavior modification technology unpalatable to many traditional members of the establishment, including writers, scholars, politicians, administrators, academicians, psychiatrists, psychologists, and educators:

The second half of the twentieth century may be remembered for

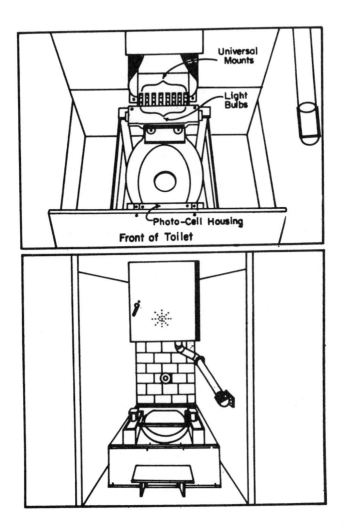

Figure 12.3. Diagram of automated toiletting reinforcement device. The upper drawing shows the interior of the toilet and the photocell trigger. The lower drawing shows the entire device. (Reprinted from "Applications of Behavior-Shaping Devices to Training Severely and Profoundly Mentally Retarded Children in an Institutional Setting," by L. S. Watson, Jr., *Mental Retardation,* 1968, 6(6), 21-23. Copyright 1968 by American Association on Mental Deficiency. Used with permission.)

its solution of a curious problem. Although Western democracy created the conditions responsible for the rise of modern science, it is now evident that it may never fully profit from that achievement. The so-called democratic philosophy of human behavior to which it also gave rise is increasingly in conflict with the application of the methods of science to human affairs. Unless this conflict is somehow resolved, the ultimate goals of democracy may be long deferred. (Skinner, 1966, p. 11)

The basic premise of behavior modification, *determinism,* is in direct conflict with Western democracy's concept of *autonomous man,* a person who controls his own destiny through *free will,* which emanates from his *mind.* Free will allows him to make rational decisions, behave in a responsible, moral or ethical manner, and overcome adversity. It enables him to be the champion of his environment, and to achieve health and happiness. The implication of the principle of determinism for a science of human behavior is that the environment controls man in a manner analogous to the way that bodies moving through space are controlled by gravitational forces. Laws or principles of behavior allow the behavior modification technologist to control man's behavior—within the limits of his technology. If a science of human behavior is correct in its basic premise, autonomous man is a myth.

Skinner (1971) identified two categories of literature that espouse autonomous man: the "literature of freedom" and the "literature of dignity." The literature of freedom is primarily concerned with external aversive control of people (as opposed to self-control), although it also opposes external control in other forms. It states that oppressive, aversive forms of human control should be abolished. It also rejects direct forms of external human control utilizing positive consequences if they are deliberately and systematically employed. The concept of freedom is tied directly to the concept of autonomous man and free will. Operant behavior modification technology opposes this point of view in two ways. It disavows autonomous man by stating that man is controlled by his environment, and it ignores the prohibition against direct control measures by proposing a cultural behavior modification technology that will deliberately and systematically manipulate the environment to generate a "utopian" society of men who are truly "self-actualized."

The literature of dignity opposes operant behavior modification because it deprives man of receiving credit for "heroic accomplishments," such as sending a manned vehicle to the moon and back. The operant behavior technology point of view attributes man's successes to environmental events rather than to free will and determination, the products of autonomous man's mind. The more man's successes are attributed to environmental forces over which he has little or no control, the less he can legitimately receive credit for such accomplishments—in effect, the autonomous man is castrated. As long as man can take a major part of the credit for his accomplishments, autonomous man survives intact, but as more and more credit is given to factors independent of autonomous man, increasingly greater damage occurs to this concept. A science of human behavior and its progeny (operant behavior technology) strikes a death blow to the concept of autonomous man.

The literature of freedom defends primarily against control from aversive consequences, while the literature of dignity is opposed to control through positive consequences. Skinner suggested that the objection to environmentally produced accelerator consequences by the defenders of dignity is due to the emotional side effects resulting from the loss of an important positive reinforcement. Autonomous man loses his "hero" status when viewed through the operant behavior technology prism.

In summary, because the operant behavior technology point of view disavows the concept of autonomous man, threatens his freedom, and undermines his dignity, there are those who are violently opposed to its incorporation into the social science body of knowledge and its application to designing, implementing, and maintaining utopian cultures. Such proposed cultures and their designers are labeled unethical, devious, exploitive, brutal, and inhumane. It is highly unlikely that logical argument and scientific evidence will convince such persons very quickly that the behavior modification approach is acceptable and is even potentially beneficial to society.

Those who support the literature of freedom and dignity actually support the use of aversive and positive consequences to control their fellow man. By opposing a cultural behavior technology and refusing to consider plausible cultural alternatives, they are supporting existing cultural human control procedures such as prisons, fines, and other outmoded primitive cultural control practices. They also support a variety of indirect positive and deferred aversive consequences, but these procedures seem to be acceptable although they were implemented accidentally (as opposed to deliberately, in a systematic fashion based on a master plan for human cultural control). If man is, in fact, controlled by his environment, then the defenders of freedom and dignity are caught in the same trap they accuse behavior technologists of attempting to impose on autonomous man. No matter how they manipulate the environment and its consequences (whether indirectly or accidentally), they are imposing the same kind of control over their fellow man which they are accusing the behavior technologists of imposing. And ignorance, denial, and accidental manipulation of reinforcement contingencies do not make them any less liable.

Skinner proposed that our society will be able to solve a variety of crucial human problems by deliberately applying behavior technology to systematic development of cultures. Such a technology would identify the reinforcement contingencies that control man's behavior, and would design programs to allow him to develop into a happy, capable, productive, talented, and psychologically healthy human being. Such a person could make a sufficient contribution to his culture to maintain it at an optimum level of function, and could give and get an abundance of satisfaction from his life. Man would not lose his individuality, and neither would he lose either freedom or his dignity, since both are myths.

Behavior technology is a natural outgrowth of a science of human behavior. The literature of freedom and dignity represents prescientific concepts of human behavior which are now obsolete, and it should be replaced by newer concepts based on the findings of a science of human behavior. The prescientific concept of autonomous man should give way to the newer, scientifically identified concept of environmental control of human behavior. The field of human behavior is going through the same evolutionary history as once did physics and biology.

Some readers may question the relevance of this issue to behavior modification of the mentally retarded client, particularly of severely and profoundly retarded individuals. The issue is important because of the influence that an antibehavior modification attitude of this type has on the person who is working with the mentally retarded individual, be that person a parent, teacher, psychologist, physician, nurse, or administrator. People who subscribe to that attitude will not be able to countenance a behavior modification program. In fact, to some degree, they probably will attempt to prevent it from being adopted by a particular institution or community. Until objections based on outmoded concepts are eliminated, acceptance of behavior modification programs will be very slow.

God, the Behavior Modifier

There is very little argument today about whether behavior modification works. Anyone who has any familiarity with the relevant literature is convinced that contingent reinforcement techniques provide the therapist, parent, teacher, nurse, and psychiatric aide with a powerful tool for changing human behavior. The disturbing issue that is raised as a result of this realization is this: *If I practice behavior modification, I literally am playing God. I am capable of determining, possibly to a great extent, the destiny of the clients, pupils, or patients placed in my charge.* This is a very sobering realization, since it places an awesome responsibility on the shoulders of the behavior modifier. Of course we have always played God to some extent as parents, therapists, teachers, nurses, and psychiatric aides, but we are never so aware of it as we are when once we begin to use behavior modification techniques *on* or *with* fellow human beings. Heretofore, changes in the behavior of those humans for whom we were responsible could be more easily attributed to accidental events beyond our control. But now, the conscientious, effective behavior modifer is aware that he can make dramatic changes in a fellow human's behavior repertoire, once he is given license to act. And, in the next 10 to 20 years, his effectiveness will be even greater.

Another sobering problem for the behavior modifier is this: *If I am capable of changing behavior in a fellow human, in what directions should I change him? What will I make him to be?* This question is not too disturbing when we are dealing with benign problems with the retarded child, such as behaviors involved in self-help, language, and educational repertoires. However, as we move into the area of social activities, selection of target behaviors becomes more difficult. Should the person be very passive when interacting with other people, or should he be aggressive? If the latter, how aggressive? How should he behave in social-sexual situations? What if he has homosexual tendencies? Should these be eliminated and replaced with a heterosexual social-sexual repertoire? How about social-political attitudes? Should we make him Republican or Democrat, an extreme liberal or a conservative? Should we teach him to be racially prejudiced or to be liberal in his racial attitudes? What if our client resides in a community dominated by persons prejudiced against ethnic minority groups such as Blacks, Jews, and Italians? Should we then teach our client to accept these minority groups? It may cause the client considerable social problems with his boss, friends, and neighbors if they are all prejudiced against such minority groups and he is not. What if our client is destined to live in a community where extreme violence enables a person to adapt and be accepted more readily by members of that community? Do we teach him to be extremely violent? Obviously, questions concerning a suitable repertory or social behavior are not easily answered.

Another basic problem that arises from the previous question is *who* will build the model of human behavior that will guide the behavior modifier as he selects target behaviors for a particular client, patient, or pupil. Should the behavior modifier himself perform this vital function? If so, what will be his basis for selecting these behaviors? Should he use his own personal value system to make the selection, or should he use the value system of the client's parents? Should he involve the retarded client himself? Or, should he use a social-adaptive behavior approach (i.e., identify those behaviors which members of the client's particular community consider as normal) and teach him this behavioral repertoire? What if these behaviors involve extreme violence or prejudice? Or suppose they involve using certain drugs or indulging in sexual promiscuity?

If the behavior modifier himself refuses to accept this responsibility of providing a model, then who will or should? Should a special committee or council be formed in the community to carry out this function? Who should sit on this committee? Who should select these committee members? As the behavior modification technology becomes more advanced, this issue will become more important and will require a solution. There is no simple answer, and any choice will have disadvantages.

Historically, this problem of *who* has been considered under the rubric of values. Rogers and Skinner (1966) debated the issue with regard to selection of values and the role of science in such selection. Rogers argued that value systems lie outside the realm of scientific investigation, but are central to the notion of behavior control. The crucial question for Rogers was: For what purposes or by what power groups will these techniques be used or abused? He felt that value judgments, such as *right, good,* and *appropriate applications of behavior control,* are subjective and cannot be resolved by means of the scientific method. Thus, he did not see research as a solution to the problem of selecting correct values. Skinner countered by stating that value selection was a legitimate subject for scientific analysis. In *Beyond Freedom and Dignity,* Skinner (1971) also considered in depth how many of society's problems could be solved or resolved by using the scientific method to design "good," "healthy," or "ideal" cultures. Designing such cultures involves an extensive analysis of contingencies of reinforcement that exist in social relationships or interactions.

Since the Behavioral Model embraced by practitioners of behavior modification defines criminality, psychosis, neurosis, and mental retardation in terms of social deviance, the main basis the behavior modifier has for selecting appropriate target behaviors is in terms of a culture's explicit and implicit list of acceptable and taboo behaviors (Ullman & Krasner, 1969). The behavior modifier selects target behaviors that will enable his client to be accepted by members of the culture in which he is destined to reside. As Kanfer (1971) pointed out, this same position was taken by the American Psychological Association in its early code of ethics, which Kanfer quoted: " 'The psychologist's ultimate allegiance is to society, and his professional behavior should demonstrate awareness of his social responsibilities. The welfare of the profession and of the individual psychologist [is] clearly subordinate to the welfare of the public.' " (p. 448).

Kanfer identified the bases that exist for selecting target behaviors. There are cultural values, which he calls "metavalues" and there are "personal values," the values of the individual. Problems arise for the individual when there are conflicts between metavalues and his personal values. Kanfer feels that one goal of therapy is to resolve the conflict. He added that when there are no clear-cut social rules that allow the therapist to make a decision about how or whether to bring personal and cultural values to agreement for a given client, the therapist then must rely on his theoretical orientation, his own experiences, and his own value system for selecting target behaviors.

In the future, selection of target behaviors for behavior modification programs probably will be made by the behavior modifier and his supportive staff in collaboration with a Resident or Client Human and Legal Rights Committee appointed to a residential institution or a special educational system. This committee will be made up of key administrative staff assigned to the facility, key clinical staff, certain behavior modification staff, parents, and other relevant "consumers." They probably will employ Wolfensberger's (1972) adaptation of the Scandinavian *Normalization Principle* as a frame of reference for selecting target behaviors. Because of the recent Wyatt versus Stickney landmark court decision (Wexler, 1973), committees of this type will become more frequent. Other articles related to alleged abuses in behavior modification programs also strongly support the development of such committees (Roos, 1974). They would serve an "advocate" or "watch dog" function for persons receiving treatment in behavior modification programs.

Use of Contingent Consequences and Aversive Procedures

Some years ago, Lucero, Vail, and Scherber (1968) published a paper that condemned the use of electric shock, certain "time out" procedures, and making meals and privileges behaviorally contingent in behavior modification programs in institutions for mentally retarded and mentally ill persons in Minnesota. These practices were labeled as "dehumanizing." The authors of the paper were part of a task force that had been formed to investigate the "misuses and abuses" of the behavior modification method in Minnesota state institutions. Their three conclusions and recommendations were as follows:

1. Aversive reinforcement is never to be used in a general program for groups of patients. However, in unusual individual cases in which physical abuse of self or others is otherwise unchangeable, aversive reinforcement methods may be used. They must be administered by a professional, however, and must be cleared with the medical director of the Medical Services Division and with the mental health Medical Policy Committee which has legal responsibility for all treatment and research procedures in the state hospital system.

2.   Deprivation is never to be used. No patient is to be deprived of expected goods and services and ordinary rights, including the free movement of his limbs, that he had before the program started. In addition, deficit rewarding must be avoided; i.e., rewards must not consist of the restoration of objects or privileges that were taken away from the patient or that he should have had to begin with. The ban against deficit rewarding includes the use of tokens to gain or regain such objects or privileges.

3.   Positive reinforcement is the only conditioning technique to be used, with the exception of aversive methods in the approved individual cases noted above (Lucero, Vail, & Scherber, 1968, pp. 53-54).

The task force also recommended that behavior modification programs "must be approved by the Medical Policy Committee and must be administered by thoroughly trained personnel" (p. 53)—no standards were given for staff training—and that all new treatment procedures be reviewed and approved by the same committee. Lucero et al. (1968) pointed out that all recommendations became standard policy for all Minnesota state institutions for mentally retarded and mentally ill people.

The above recommendations have some commendable points as well as some that are devastating to the administration of effective behavior modification programs in residential facilities. Clearly, some board or committee responsible to the state director of institutional programs for mentally ill and mentally retarded persons, or to his commissioners, should be responsible for procedures used in behavior modification programs. Such programs have gone beyond the strictly experimental or special project stage, and it is advantageous for both institutional and central office administrators, as well as for administrators and recipients of behavior modification programs, that uniform, state-wide treatment guidelines be agreed upon and established. Such guidelines should take note of public opinion or "consumer" attitudes regarding humane and/or acceptable treatment of patients or residents. They should include training requirements for staff; and they should determine sources and levels of responsibility that will ensure that programs are carried out as they are intended to be.

Also, they should be developed with full consideration of the techniques required to carry out effective behavior modification programs in institutions. Such a committee would ensure the viability of behavior modification programs in state facilities and would protect program administrators from "witch hunts." In order to ensure that a well-balanced policy is established, such committees should be composed of professionals who hold an enlightened rehabilitation orientation, as well as of those who have a more "custodial" orientation. Such a mixed composition will ensure the development of a balanced set of guidelines by which programs are conducted in a responsible manner to protect patients' or residents' rights, and which are still sufficiently free to operate effectively and to fulfill the habilitation goals for which the programs were created.

Clearly, it would be unwise for each behavior modification administrator to develop his own program independently of anyone else within a state institutional system. This approach invariably meets with resistance from personnel in the institution whose support is required for program success, and it leaves the institution open to a possible scandal—something a number of state institutions already have experienced. Statewide program policy guidelines that are approved by an official such as the state direction of mental health ensure that behavior modification is recognized as a legitimate technique rather than as a stepchild of the institution. This official sanction should assure greater support by central office staff and state administrators.

Should "time out" procedures involving physical restraint, electric shock techniques, and contingent privilege and food procedures be *outlawed* in state institutional behavior modification programs? Absolutely not! For if they were, such programs would become virtually ineffective for a large number of patients and residents who otherwise could benefit enormously from programs that utilize such procedures. Banning such techniques is equivalent to prohibiting medical practitioners from using any procedure that causes the patient pain or discomfort. Such a medical ban would include drugs administered by a hypodermic syringe, anesthesia that produces a nauseating "hangover" or aftereffects, X-rays, metabolism tests, and surgical procedures that require 12-hour food deprivation or involve lengthy, painful recovery periods, and other accepted practices. If such an injudicious prohibition were to be passed by some uninformed governmental committee that regulated medical practice, the entire medical profession would be so restricted that they could not practice as "healers of men" except in a rather superficial manner.

The proper solution is, of course, to *regulate uses* of these procedures rather than eliminate them. Such regulations might specify that all programs be based primarily on positive reinforcement plus careful programming, with primary emphasis on building in new and incompatible behavior (incompatible with undesirable behavior) to develop normal behavior repertories, rather than eliminating bizarre or disruptive behavior using aversive procedures (Goldiamond, 1974). This might be described as the *Alternative I* approach. All programs would begin using this alternative. Then, in the event it became obvious (through a specific troubleshooting procedure to be described later) that this alternative was ineffective with a particular resident, an *Alternative II* approach could be instituted. This might involve the use of contingent meals and privileges. In the event it became obvious that this alternative was not effective (again, after going through the troubleshooting procedure), *Alternative III* might be used. This could consist of time out, Overcorrection Restitution, Positive Practice Restitution, or Quiet Training. If this alternative still was not effective and the problem appeared to be important enough to justify painful peripheral electric shock, then electric shock might be instituted as *Alternative IV.*

These regulations also should specify (a) qualifications of staff working in behavior modification programs, (b) delegation of authority to order the different treatment alternatives, and (c) a specific documentation procedure for recording administration of the different treatment alternatives. A complete hypothetical treatment plan that fits these criteria could read as follows (Watson, 1974):

Sample Human and Legal Rights Committee Behavior Modification Program Proposal

This is a tentative proposal for a behavior modification treatment program at _____. The major goal of the program will be to carry out behavior modification treatment in the most effective manner possible, based on current behavior modification technology, but with full consideration and respect for the human rights and legal rights of residents who will be enrolled in the program. This proposal will be divided into two sections: resident treatment procedure safeguards, and qualifications of staff carrying out behavior modification.

RESIDENT TREATMENT PROCEDURE SAFEGUARDS

The basis for the resident treatment procedure is that the most benign and "comfortable" behavior modification procedures will always be used first. In the event they prove ineffective, more "uncomfortable" and proven procedures will follow. For example, disruptive behavior problems, which are the primary focus of any "uncomfortable" procedure, will be dealt with first by scheduling interesting activities for the resident and using positive or accelerator reinforcement, such as food or praise or toys (i.e., attempting to condition incompatible behavior). In the event that a particular behavior problem of interest does not dissipate as a result of this procedure, then other techniques will be considered, such as contingent privileges, time out from reinforcement or overcorrection.

Hierarchy of Resident Treatment Procedures

It is suggested that the following hierarchy of resident treatment procedures be used.

ALTERNATIVE 1. All resident training programs will be initiated using positive or accelerator reinforcement.

a. New behavior (i.e., desirable behavior that is to be taught) will be shaped using positive reinforcement, such as food (other than meals), praise, toys and games or activities the resident finds enjoyable.

b. Undesirable or disruptive behavior will be dealt with initially by scheduling activities that will potentially interfere with or stop the disruptive behavior. Interesting activities often stop the disruptive behavior. Interesting activities often stop whining and crying (if properly instituted, and if they are reinforced with food, praise, toys, etc.). Extinction (withholding attention by the staff) also will be used at this stage of treatment. However, using meals or privileges on a contingent basis will not be allowed at this stage of treatment.

c. Deviation from this procedure only can be carried out with the approval of the Behavior Modification Program Director and the Human Rights and Legal Rights Committee.

ALTERNATIVE 2. In the event that the data show the resident is not responding to Alternative 1 treatment (requisite data will be considered later in this section), then the use of contingent meals and privileges will be instituted. However, before this procedure can be initiated, a *troubleshooting* technique must first be carried out by treatment staff to assure that the Alternative 1 procedure was applied correctly. The troubleshooting procedure will be outlined at the end of this section.

a. New behavior will be taught using contingent meals and privileges. However, residents will not miss meals. They will only be required to work for them (i.e., carry out steps in training to obtain each bite). Privileges can be withheld if necessary, but this type of contingency (loss of privileges) should not constitute more than 25% of the resident's total habilitation program. At least 75% of the contingencies in the resident's program should involve positive or accelerator reinforcement which the resident *receives.* This qualification should ensure that the resident does not become the victim of a program that consists primarily of loss of privileges, which we deem to be unreasonable and inhumane.

    b. Undesirable or disruptive behavior also will be dealt with through loss of privileges, but not loss of meals. However, this procedure cannot constitute more than 25% of the resident's total habilitation program.

    c. Deviation from this procedure can be carried out only with the permission of the Behavior Modification Program Director and the Human and the Legal Rights Committee.

ALTERNATIVE 3. This alternative deals only with eliminating undesirable or disruptive behavior. Before Alternative 3 can be instituted, the to-be-described troubleshooting technique must first be carried out by treatment staff applying Alternative 2 procedures. Alternative 3 consists of using time out from reinforcement, overcorrection, and positive practice to eliminate disruptive or undesirable behavior, such as temper tantrums, attacking other residents or destruction of property.

    a. *Time out from reinforcement* will be carried out in the following manner: When a resident violates a prohibition previously agreed upon (by treatment staff), the staff person responsible for that client will say, "No!" in a firm voice, using a relatively loud volume (bridging signal), and then place him in "time out." If the resident is confined to a wheelchair (i.e., is nonambulatory), he will be placed in a corner of a room in the wheelchair facing the corner, and a screen that is 5 to 6 feet high will be placed around him to prevent him from seeing out (the essence of time-out). The resident will be left in time-out for 15 minutes—if he is quiet and orderly. If he begins to scream or cry, to tear his clothes or engage in any kind of self-destructive behavior, or tries to get out of his wheelchair, an overcorrection procedure will be instituted. The overcorrection procedure will be used as a backup procedure to minimize staff time (which requires one-to-one involvement). If the client is ambulatory, he will be required to sit in a corner in a chair facing the corner with a screen around him. If he refuses to stay in the chair or is in any other way disruptive (as previously mentioned), overcorrection will be instituted. The resident should not be allowed to leave time-out until he has been quiet and orderly for 15 minutes—unless some unusual or extenuating circumstance requires his removal, such as an acute health hazard.

b. *Overcorrection* should be used only as a backup, unless the Behavior Modification Program Director makes an exception. This is primarily an economy decision, since overcorrection requires considerably more staff involvement than does time-out. Whenever the resident's limbs or body are being forcibly manipulated by staff as part of the overcorrection procedure, extreme caution should be taken to prevent bruising of the resident and ligament damage or any other form of injury. Overcorrection procedures, such as Oral Hygiene Training, should be administered only with a physician's approval to avoid mouth or jaw injury or an allergic reaction.

c. *Positive practice* will be used routinely as part of the overcorrection procedure and also may be used to deal with certain forms of negativism, such as failure to give eye contact. It also may be used to deal with self-injurious behavior. Again, extreme care should be taken not to injure the client in any way if his body and limbs are being forcibly manipulated.

d. Only persons who have been *certified* to exercise time-out, overcorrection, and/or positive practice can administer these procedures.

e. Deviation from this procedure can be carried out only with the approval of the Behavior Modification Program Director and the Human Rights and Legal Rights Committee.

ALTERNATIVE 4. No other treatment procedures can be carried out without prior approval of the Behavior Modification Program Director and the Human Rights and Legal Rights Committee. However, there will be times when exceptions will need to be made to these guidelines, (e.g., when the previously identified procedures prove to be ineffective, and/or when a new, effective, yet undeveloped behavior modification technique becomes available). Therefore, the Human and Legal Rights Committee should expect special requests for special procedures from time to time.

Who Will Order Treatment?

Authority should be delegated to the person who is qualified to order behavior modification treatment. It is suggested that a hierarchy of responsibility be set up for this. For example, an Alternative 1 procedure could be ordered by the Unit Coordinator. Alternatives 2 and 3 probably should be ordered by the Behavior Modification Program Director, and the order should be transmitted through the Unit Coordinator to maintain administrative continuity. Alternative 4 and deviations from any of the above alternatives should be ordered only by the Behavior Modification Program Director, and only after receiving approval from the Human Rights and Legal Rights Committee.

Documentation

The staff person ordering treatment should document this order on a special form set up for the purpose. In addition, the staff person carrying out treatment should also document the treatment very specifically on a similar form, and specify accurately the manner in which the treatment was given and the period of time involved. Each application of the treatment should be recorded as a separate entry. Data procedures taught in Behavior Modification Inservice Training also should be used.

Troubleshooting

Before moving from one treatment alternative to the next (e.g., Alternative 1 to Alternative 2), the following troubleshooting procedure should be carried out:

1. Staff should determine that the recommended treatment procedure was used *every time* it should be used as opposed to less than every time. Prescribed procedures should be used consistently and persistently. Failure to follow such a guideline usually compromises the effectiveness of the technique.

2. Staff should determine that the procedure was used in the *precise manner* that was established for treatment. Deviation from using the procedure as set up often reduces the effectiveness of the procedure.

3. Staff should determine that the reinforcement used with the resident is effective. If the reinforcement has lost its effectiveness due to satiation, or if it never was effective, this could cause the alternative to be ineffective.

4. Staff should determine that the specific training program concerned is suitable for the resident. If the resident either lacks the prerequisite skills or if the steps in the program are too large (or if critical steps have been left out), this could result in a problem, producing lack of effectiveness.

5. In a case where more than one staff person is working with a resident, it should be determined that all staff are using the same procedures with the resident, and that everyone is using the procedure in the manner agreed upon during the staffing of the resident.

Informed Consent

It is recommended that all parents of residents enrolled in Behavior Modification treatment at _____give their signed and witnessed consent *after* being informed of the nature of the program. They should be told (using language they understand) the reason for recommending their son or daughter for this treatment, the advantages of treatment procedure, any disadvantages or undesirable side effects, what might happen if the resident is not enrolled in the program, and other alternative procedures that might be used instead of the Behavior Modification treatment procedure.

QUALIFICATIONS OF STAFF CARRYING OUT BEHAVIOR MODIFICATION

Four different levels of staff will be involved in Behavior Modification treatment programs: the Program Director, the Unit Coordinator, the Mental Health Supervisor, and the Mental Health Technician. It is recommended that these staff have the following qualifications:

1. The Behavior Modification Program Director should have a M.A. degree in a relevant Behavior Modification field, such as psychology or special education, and at least 2 years of Behavior Modification experience in an approved setting (to be determined).

2. The Unit Coordinator of the Behavior Modification Unit should have satisfactorily completed the Behavior Modification Inservice Training Program at _____ and have at least one year's supervised experience in Behavior Modification (with the exception of the first Unit Coordinator), if at all possible.

3. Mental health supervisors should have satisfactorily completed the Behavior Modification Inservice Training Program at _____ and have at least 6 months of supervised experience in Behavior Modification.

4. Mental health technicians should have completed the Behavior Modification Inservice Training Program at _____ .

5. Anyone who has not completed the Inservice Training Program should be classified as a Trainee.

The preceding proposal would be submitted to an institutional Resident Human and Legal Rights Committee for its approval, and perhaps would also have to be approved by a state central office committee, thus giving it the approval of the state mental health director.

A number of writers have commented on the ethics of using aversive procedures or those involving food and privilege deprivation. Baer (1970) pointed out that the question of the use of electric shock is basically a moral one. He indicated that in many cases where electric shock is recommended, we are dealing with human beings whom we (i.e., society) have relegated to institutional life and have "allowed them to be taught their own self-destruction, and confined them to a small hell in consequence. Can we now refuse that they endure a small number of painful episodes over a short span of sessions, hopefully designed to let them live the rest of their lives awake and untied" (pp. 245-246)? His major point is that it is immoral not to rescue a person from the bizarre behavioral pattern that causes him to be repeatedly punished by his caretaker and/or peers through restraint or isolation. Baer added that the question of *how long it will take* to eliminate the problem also is a moral one. As Lovaas (1970) pointed out, self-destructive behavior often can be eliminated in a very brief period of time, using only two or three shocks. By contrast, it ordinarily would take considerably longer to eliminate headbanging by using positive reinforcement alone or positive reinforcement plus a time out from reinforcement procedure; such procedures require greater sophistication on the part of staff than most institutions are capable of providing. Other writers have concurred with Baer's points about the immorality of failing to use aversive procedures to eliminate behavior that causes a patient or resident to be repeatedly punished by his caretakers or peers (Ball, 1970; Bragg & Wagner, 1970; Cahoon, 1970; Miron, 1970).

Baer (1970) also considered the disadvantages of punishment procedures such as electric shock. First, because punishment techniques work so well, the punisher is reinforced by using them. This cultivates a tendency for the behavior modifier to use punishment procedures exclusively, to the detriment of effective, carefully developed programs that utilize positive reinforcement. Since punishment is painful, we still should not use it whenever techniques utilizing positive reinforcement alone are equally effective. Baer also pointed out some of the undesirable side effects of punishment. Persons who utilize aversive procedures exclusively and do not balance them out with techniques involving positive reinforcement will themselves become aversive social discriminative stimuli. The result may well be the destruction or retardation of the development of social behavior in their patients or clients. One way to remedy this problem is to use very limited punishment for undesirable behavior, combined with extensive use of positive reinforcement for desirable behavior.

Finally, application of aversive procedures such as painful electric shock should be considered in light of the undesirable behavior involved. If the behavior problem is a trivial one that simply causes the client to be a nuisance (such as stealing food from someone else's plate), but which does not produce a grave, debilitating social problem for the client, obviously it would be unwise and unethical to use electric shock to eliminate it. This indiscriminate use is particularly undesirable in view of prevailing public opinion and the objections of "establishment" persons and those in the behavior modification arena to use painful electric shock for eliminating behavior problems. As both Wexler (1973) and Goldiamond (1974) pointed out, the result of the Wyatt versus Stickney court decision will necessarily be a profound *deemphasis* on eliminating undesirable behavior by using aversive techniques in behavior modification programs of the future. Rather, there will be a strong *emphasis* on programs that build in normal behavior repertories through positive reinforcement techniques.

Dehumanization

Another issue closely related to (actually overlapping) that of contingent consequences and aversive procedures is the accusation that behavior modification programs are *dehumanizing*. There are two different groups involved in this issue. One group consists of persons outside the behavior modification field, who assert that such programs are, in general, dehumanizing. The other consists of persons both within and outside the field, who feel that specific procedures used in behavior modification programs are dehumanizing—such as making meals, snacks, and beds contingent on behavior, or the use of electric shock to eliminate headbanging.

The first subissue (i.e., behavior modification programs, in general, are dehumanizing) may be primarily due to lack of understanding of the total method or to a dissatisfaction with the behavioristic language used (which has an "antihumanistic" ring to many "humanistic oriented" psychologists and other "humanists"). Such persons complain that the people, patients, clients, or residents in the program are referred to as if they were objects or animals rather than human beings. They complain that the training procedures are too mechanical, that there is no consideration for the person as a human being, and that "will," "love," "warmth," "individual consideration," and other humanistic concerns are totally lacking. This subissue appears to revolve around two factors: (a) behavior modification as a technique for behavior change, and (b) the psychological or behavioral characteristics of the persons who design and implement given programs.

Since *behavior modification* is nothing more than a method for changing behavior, the extent to which a program is humanistic or ahumanistic is a function of the person designing and controlling the program. Even if the program has many humanistic features, it may appear to be dehumanizing to some humanists because of the behavioristic language that is typically based on a task analysis approach and is couched in operational terms. The usual humanistic attack is that people subscribing to the behavior modification approach are unconcerned with a person as an individual, that they disregard his personal psychological needs and desires, and that they are disinterested in developing his opportunity and ability to direct his own destiny and to give and receive love. Although a behavior modification program designer would not hesitate to deal with these target behaviors, once he had translated them into behavioral terms, they probably would not then be recognized or accepted by the typical humanist.

Insofar as the two components of important *psychological characteristics* are concerned, we have made progress in our own Community Behavior Modification Project for Children, where we train parents to be therapists with their own young children who are extremely psychotic and/or severely retarded (Watson, in press). Here, the target behaviors we are concerned with are *giving and receiving affection* and *making decisions*. Children are programmed to give and receive affection appropriately from parents and peers (Watson & Bassinger, 1974). This includes looking at them (eye contact) as they smile, laugh, or make vocal responses that express friendship. It also includes kissing, hugging, and other forms of caresses. The objective of this particular program is to train children to express and receive affection in the same manner as does a normal child. Children are taught to make decisions in educational and social-recreational programs. These decision-making situations begin initially in "free play" activities, where they are taught to make choices as to how they will spend their leisure time. Although, these situations may appear to the casual observer as a far cry from those in which adults make decisions about life, leisure activity choices made by young children hopefully will provide a foundation for making important decisions about life as the child approaches adulthood.

Goldiamond (1966) has pointed out quite clearly the important contribution behavior modification can make for a person who really wants to acquire the freedom to choose what he is going to do during his life span and how he is going to do it (i.e., by exercising his *will*). From a deterministic viewpoint, man's behavior is controlled by the same kinds of events that control a rat in an operant chamber. Certain antecedent events acquire the property of discriminative stimuli that cause specific forms of behavior to occur. Certain consequences associated with stimuli have accelerator or decelerator properties, and they determine how the person will react in the presence of these stimuli. These stimuli and consequences can be internal or external to the person. In a sense, the average person is a prisoner of these stimuli and consequences, since they literally control his behavior. However, if he learns how to manipulate the internal consequences he can acquire sufficient genuine self-control so that he can deliberately externalize the impact of these events.

With regard to the second subissue of the dehumanizing characteristics of certain behavior modification procedures, recent scandals in state institutions for mentally retarded residents indicate that persons responsible for behavior modification programs must consider the "consumer" (the patient, his parents, and the public) when they implement any unusual technique for behavioral control. Both the litigation concerned with Partlow State School, Tuscaloosa, Alabama (Wyatt versus Stickney; see Wexler, 1973), and the investigation at Sunland Training Center *(Miami Herald,* 1972) indicate that behavior modification programs must be kept open to public scrutiny and that their directors be willing to justify any procedure, regardless of its effectiveness, in terms of the community traditions of humanitarian treatment and the taboos regarding such treatment. Typical behavior modification procedures that lead to public criticism include the use of aversive procedures and/or making certain events such as meals, bed, and recreational privileges (see preceding section) contingent upon specific forms of behavior. Any novel or unusual decelerator techniques (unusual in terms of the immediate community's standards of humanitarian treatment, or any procedure that violates a community's taboos about treatment of humans in institutions) will invariably lead to public outcry. For example, the April 5, 1972, edition of the *Miami Herald* ran a rather lengthy article about the behavior modification program at the Sunland Training Center in Miami, Florida. The paper described with considerable distaste the following decelerator procedures:

1. Retarded boys at the Miami Sunland have been compelled to wear women's underwear and eat bars of soap in bizarre treatments for such crimes as fighting or stealing.

2. Others—all teenages in Flagler Cottage—were locked in bare seclusion rooms for as long as 4 hours, beaten by cottage attendants for misbehavior, and forced to masturbate in public.

3. One boy, who had defecated in his pants while in seclusion, was required to hold his soiled underwear under his nose before washing the pants out in the toilet.

The above procedures were used to decelerate fighting, stealing, lying, masturbating, and soiling. However, regardless of their effectiveness, these procedures were seen as a gross violation of the community's standards of appropriate treatment of an institutionalized human being, and in addition the isolation in a seclusion room was a violation of an institutional directive (according to the *Miami Herald*). Such methods are considered bizarre and inhumane by most persons living in the community. Once the consumer becomes aware of these procedures, he invariably also rejects using meals, beds, and privileges contingently, since they are associated with the other unusual decelerator techniques.

The major point to be made here is that specific behavior modification procedures should be selected in terms of both the human and legal rights of the patient or resident, as well as in terms of their effectiveness (see, e.g., Halleck, 1974). Since notions of humanitarianism and legality vary from institution to institution, from community to community, and from state to state, they must be defined in terms of the laws and mores of the legal and social prescriptions of a particular geographical location. If they are not carefully considered when designing and implementing a behavior modification program, its chances of success and acceptance by the consumer and/or by the status quo will be severely jeopardized.

MISCELLANEOUS ISSUES

Are Behavior Modification Programs Economically Feasible?

The statement has often been made about behavior modification programs that although they may be effective, their operational costs are too great to make them practical. Such statements are no longer accurate. The cost of operating behavior modification programs is comparable to that of more conventional types of habilitation programs. The current cost of the Community Behavior Modification Program for Children is $1,000 per child annually (Watson & Bassinger, 1974). For this sum the child is given intensive treatment in the areas of self-help skills, language skills, educational skills, social-recreational skills, and elimination of undesirable behavior (see Table 12.1). The mother, siblings, and children living in the neighborhood serve as behavior modification technicians; and they train the child under the supervision of a home consultant. The home consultant trains the technicians and usually makes one home visit a week to observe the technicians' training, to review their data, and to plan training strategies with them.

We recently proposed a statewide behavior modification training program to teach self-help skills to institutionalized severely and profoundly retarded children for the State of Ohio Division of Mental Retardation (Watson, 1971). Recommended ward staffing attendant/resident ratios were 1:6 to train residents, and 1:8 to maintain their behavior. Shaping self-help skills requires approximately 8 months. After about 2 years, these ratios can be changed to 1:10 or 1:12, as the residents' ability to maintain almost all self-help skills independently increases. These estimates are based on the results of a 4-year Hospital Improvement Project (Watson & Bassinger, 1968, 1969, 1970, 1971a). Staffing ratios of 1:8 are recommended by the Joint Commission on Accreditation of Hospitals (Crosby, 1971) for severely and profoundly retarded individuals and are also the staffing requirements recommended by SCOPE, the procedure used by the Ohio Department of Mental Hygiene to determine ward nurse/resident staffing ratios. In another project (Lent, 1971), once that severely but trainable retarded girls in the Mimosa Project at Parsons (Kansas) Training School and Hospital had acquired all of their self-help skills, only one attendant was required to maintain a ward of 30 girls. As another example of economy, Lindsley (1971) maintained that a teacher can effectively teach as many or more pupils, using his Precision Teaching method, as when using conventional educational procedures.

Although it may take a fairly rich staffing ratio to generate basic behavioral repertoires in severely retarded and psychotic individuals initially, staffing requirements decrease as the clients' repertoires increase, until the ratio of staff to client is substantially less than the requirements recommended by the Joint Commission on Accreditation of Hospitals. Maintaining a child in a community home-training program rather than in a state institution probably saves a state like Ohio about $3,000 a year. The savings to states like Illinois and Wisconsin should be substantially greater.

The conclusion is that behavior modification programs are probably more economical to operate than are more traditional habilitation (albeit not strictly "custodial") programs. Although the initial operating costs may be slightly higher, they are reduced repeatedly as the individual's behavior repertory becomes increasingly greater and more complex, until the costs fall substantially below those of more conventional habilitation programs.

SUMMARY

This chapter concerns issues that have developed in the recent evolution of the operant behavior modification approach with the mentally retarded individual. The issues fall into four categories: theoretical, methodological, ethical, and economic. Theoretical issues involve the Medical Model versus the Behavioral Model, the ·alleged superficiality of the behavior modification approach, the extent to which brain-damaged retarded children can learn, and the applicability of behavior modification to all behavioral disorders. Methodological issues are concerned with single-versus-group approaches to evaluating data, the appropriateness of using paraprofessionals as behavior modifiers, and the applicability of prosthetic devices to behavior modification programs. Ethical issues revolve around the possible threat of the behavior modification approach to man's freedom and dignity, the question of who will build the *model man* as behavior modification continues to expand to other spheres of society, and the appropriateness of certain accelerator and decelerator procedures for client or patients enrolled in behavior modification programs. The issue in the last category is a very practical one: Are behavior modification programs economical enough to be implemented on any wide-scale basis? Our answer is in the affirmative.

The main thrust of this chapter has been to argue the pros and cons of some of these issues, or to identify more clearly the different dimensions of a particular issue. While the reader may not feel that he has been given many neat, clear-cut answers, the author's intention will have been met if the reader has at least been enlightened as to the major problems in the area.

REFERENCES

Ayllon, T., & Azrin, N. *The token economy: A motivational system for therapy and rehabilitation.* New York: Appleton-Century-Crofts, 1968.
Ayllon, T., & Michael, J. The psychiatric nurse as a behavioral engineer. In R. Ulrich, T. Stachnik, and J. Mabry (Eds.), *Control of human behavior.* Glenview, Ill.: Scott, Foresman, 1966, pp. 177-187.

Azrin, N. H., & Foxx, R. M. A method of toilet training the institutionalized retarded. *Journal of Applied Behavior Analysis,* 1971, *4,* 89-99.

Baer, D. M. A case for the selective reinforcement of punishment. In C. Neuringer and J. L. Michael (Eds.), *Behavior modification in clinical psychology.* New York: Appleton-Century-Crofts, 1970, pp. 243-249.

Baer, D. M., Wolf, M. M., & Risley, T. R. Some current dimensions of applied behavior analysis. *Journal of Applied Behavior Analysis,* 1968, *1,* 91-97.

Baker, B. L. Symptom treatment and symptom substitution in enuresis. *Journal of Abnormal Psychology,* 1969, *74,* 42-49.

Ball, T. S. Issues and implications of operant conditioning: The re-establishment of social behavior. In R. Ulrich, T. Stachnik, and J. Mabry (Eds.), *Control of human behavior: From cure to prevention.* Glenview, Ill.: Scott, Foresman, 1970, pp. 353-355.

Bijou, S. W. A functional analysis of retarded development. In N. R. Ellis (Ed.), *International review of research in mental retardation* (Vol. 1). New York: Academic Press, 1966, pp. 1-19.

Bijou, S. W., & Baer, D. M. (Eds.). *Child development: Readings in experimental analysis.* New York: Appleton-Century-Crofts, 1967.

Bijou, S. W., Birnbrauer, J. S., Kidder, J. D., & Tague, C. Programmed instruction as an approach to teaching of reading, writing and arithmetic to retarded children. In S. W. Bijou and D. M. Baer (Eds.), *Child development: Readings in experimental analysis.* New York: Appleton-Century-Crofts, 1967, pp. 309-329.

Boring, E. G. *A history of experimental psychology.* New York: Appleton-Century-Crofts, 1950.

Bragg, R. A., & Wagner, M. K. Issues and implications of operant conditioning: Can deprivation be justified? In R. Ulrich, T. Stachnik, and J. Mabry (Eds.), *Control of human behavior: From cure to prevention.* Glenview, Ill.: Scott, Foresman, 1970, pp. 352-353.

Browning, R. M., & Stover, D. O. *Behavior modification in child treatment.* Chicago: Aldine-Atherton, 1971.

Bucher, B., & Lovaas, O. I. Use of aversive stimulation in behavior modification. In M. R. Jones (Ed.), *Miami symposium on the prediction of behavior, 1967: Aversive stimulation.* Coral Gables, Fla.: University of Miami Press, 1968, pp. 77-145.

Cahoon, D. D. Issues and implications of operant conditioning: Balancing procedures against outcomes. In R. Ulrich, T. Stachnik, and J. Mabry (Eds.), *Control of human behavior: From cure to prevention.* Glenview, Ill.: Scott, Foresman, 1970, pp. 351-352.

Crosby, K. G. *Standards for residential facilities for the mentally retarded.* Chicago: Joint Commission on Accreditation of Hospitals, 1971.

DuCharme, R. W. The use of behavior modification to phase institutional trainable children from individual to group performance. Paper presented at the meeting of the American Association of Mental Deficiency, Minneapolis, May 1972.

Ellis, N. R. Behavioral engineering in mental retardation. Paper presented at the meeting of the American Association on Mental Deficiency, Kansas City, Mo., May 1964.

Ferster, C. B. Positive reinforcement and behavioral deficits of autistic children. *Child Development,* 1961, *32,* 437-456.

Ferster, C. B. Classification of behavioral pathology. In L. Krasner and L. P. Ullman (Eds.), *Research in behavior modification: New developments and implications.* New York: Holt, Rinehart and Winston, 1965, pp. 6-26.

Gardner, W. I. *Behavior modification in mental retardation: The education and rehabilitation of the mentally retarded adolescent and adult.* Chicago: Aldine-Atherton, 1971.

Goldiamond, I. Self-control procedures in personal behavior problems. In R. Ulrich, T. Stachnik, and J. Mabry (Eds.), *Control of human behavior.* Glenview, Ill.: Scott, Foresman, 1966, pp. 115-127.

Goldiamond, I. Justified and unjustified alarm over behavioral control. In O. Milton and R. G. Walker (Eds.), *Behavior disorders: Perspectives and trends.* New York: J. B. Lippincott, 1969, pp. 220-245.

Goldiamond, I. Toward a constructional approach to social problems: Ethical and constitutional issues raised by applied behavior analysis. *Behaviorism,* 1974, *2,* 1-84.

Halleck, S. L. Legal and ethical aspects of behavior control. *American Journal of Psychiatry,* 1974, *131,* 381-385.

Hawkins, R. P., Peterson, R. F., Schweid, E., & Bijou, S. W. Behavior therapy in the home: Amelioration of problem parent-child relations with the parent in a theraputic role. In R. Ulrich, T. Stachnik, and J. Mabry (Eds.), *Control of human behavior: From cure to prevention.* Glenview, Ill.: Scott, Foresman, 1970, pp. 232-237.

Honig, W. K. (Ed.). *Operant behavior: Areas of research and application.* New York: Appleton-Century-Crofts, 1966.

Hussein, A. Behavior therapy using hypnosis. In J. Wolfe, A. Salter, and L. J. Reyna (Eds.), *The conditioning therapies.* New York: Holt, Rinehart and Winston, 1964, pp. 54-61.

Kanfer, F. H. Issues and ethics in behavior manipulation. In E. McGinnies and C. B. Ferster (Eds.), *The reinforcement of social behavior.* Boston: Houghton Mifflin, 1971, pp. 445-450.

Lazurus, A. A. The results of behavior therapy in 126 cases of severe neurosis. *Behaviour Research and Therapy,* 1963, *1,* 69-79.

Lent, J. R. Personal communication, 1971.

Lent, J. R., LeBlanc, J., & Spradlin, J. E. Designing a rehabilitative culture for moderately retarded, adolescent girls. In R. Ulrich, T. Stachnik, and J. Mabry (Eds.), *Control of human behavior: From cure to prevention.* Glenview, Ill.: Scott, Foresman, 1970, pp. 121-135.

Lindsley, O. R. Direct measurement and prosthesis of retarded behavior. *Journal of Education,* 1964, *147,* 62-81.

Lindsley, O. R. Personal communication, 1971.

Lovaas, O. I. Use of aversive stimuli to inhibit self-destructive behavior in retarded/autistic children. Paper presented at the meeting of the Second Congress of the International Association for the Scientific Study of Mental Deficiency. Warsaw, Poland, August-September 1970.

Lovaas, O. I., Koegel, R., Simmons, J. Q., & Stevens, J. Some generalizations and follow-up measures on autistic children in behavior therapy. *Journal of Applied Behavior Analysis,* 1973, *6,* 131-166.

Lucero, J. R., Vail, D. L., & Scherber, J. Regulating operant-conditioning programs. *Hospital and Community Psychiatry,* 1968, *19,* 53-54.

Miami Herald, April 5, 1972, p. 2.

Mikulas, W. L. *Behavior modification: An overview.* New York: Harper & Row, 1972.

Miron, N. B. Issues and implications of operant conditioning: The primary ethical consideration. In R. Ulrich, T. Stachnik, and J. Mabry (Eds.), *Control of human behavior: From cure to prevention.* Glenview, Ill.: Scott, Foresman, 1970, pp. 357-358.

Nawas, M. M., & Braun, S. H. The use of operant techniques for modifying the behavior of the severely and profoundly retarded: Part I. Introduction and initial phase. *Mental Retardation,* 1970, *8*(2), 2-6. (a)

Nawas, M. M., & Braun, S. H. The use of operant techniques for modifying the behavior of the severely and profoundly retarded: Part II. The techniques. *Mental Retardation,* 1970, *8*(3), 18-24. (b)

Nawas, M. M., & Braun, S. H. An overview of behavior modification with the severely and profoundly retarded: Part III. Maintenance of change and epilogue. *Mental Retardation,* 1970, *8*(4), 4-11. (c)

Nolan, J. D., Mattis, P. R., & Holliday, W. C. Long-term effects of behavior therapy: A 12-month follow-up. *Journal of Abnormal Psychology,* 1970, *76,* 88-92.

O'Leary, K. D., & Becker, W. C. Behavior modification of an adjustment class: A token reinforcement program. In R. Ulrich, T. Stachnik, and J. Mabry (Eds.), *Control of human behavior: From cure to prevention.* Glenview, Ill.: Scott, Foresman, 1970, pp. 182-187.

Osborne, J. G. Free-time as a reinforcer in the management of classroom behavior. In R. Ulrich, T. Stachnik, and J. Mabry (Eds.), *Control of human behavior: From cure to prevention.* Glenview, Ill.: Scott, Foresman, 1970, pp. 189-195.

Patterson, G. R., McNeal, S., Hawkins, N., & Phelps, R. Reprogramming the social environment. In R. Ulrich, T. Stachnik, and J. Mabry (Eds.), *Control of human behavior: From cure to prevention.* Glenview, Ill.: Scott, Foresman, 1970, pp. 237-248.

Paul, G. L. Insight vs. desensitization in psychotherapy two years after termination. *Journal of Consulting Psychology,* 1967, *31,* 333-348.

Reese, E. P. *Born to succeed: Behavioral procedures for education.* South Hadley, Mass.: Mount Holyoke College: Author, 1971.

Rogers, C. R., & Skinner, B. F. Some issues concerning the control of human behavior: A symposium. In R. Ulrich, T. Stachnik, and J. Mabry (Eds.), *Control of human behavior.* Glenview, Ill.: Scott, Foresman, 1966, pp. 301-316.

Roos, P., Human rights and behavior modification. *Mental Retardation,* 1974, *12*(3), 3-6.

Sidman, M. *Tactics of scientific research.* New York: Basic Books, 1960.

Skinner, B. F. Freedom and the control of men. In R. Ulrich, T. Stachnik, and J. Mabry (Eds.), *Control of human behavior.* Glenview, Ill.: Scott, Foresman, 1966, pp. 11-20.

Skinner, B. F. *Beyond freedom and dignity.* New York: Alfred A. Knopf, 1971.

Szasz, T. The myth of mental illness. In O. Milton and R. G. Walker (Eds.), *Behavior disorders: Perspective and trends.* New York: J. B. Lippincott, 1969, pp. 17-27.

Terrace, H. S. Stimulus control. In W. K. Honig (Ed.), *Operant behavior: Areas of research and application.* New York: Appleton-Century-Crofts, 1966, pp. 271-344.

Ullman, L. P., & Krasner, L. (Eds.). *Case studies in behavior modification.* New York: Holt, Rinehart and Winston, 1965.

Ullman, L. P., & Krasner, L. *A psychological approach to abnormal behavior.* Englewood Cliffs, N.J.: Prentice-Hall, 1969.

Ulrich, R., Stachnik, T., & Mabry, J. (Eds.). *Control of human behavior.* Glenview, Ill.: Scott, Foresman, 1966.

Ulrich, R., Stachnik, T., & Mabry, J. (Eds.). *Control of human behavior: From cure to prevention.* Glenview, Ill.: Scott, Foresman, 1970.

Watson, L. S. Applications of behavior-shaping devices to training severely and profoundly mentally retarded children in an institutional setting. *Mental Retardation,* 1968, *6*(6), 21-23.

Watson, L. S. Behavior modification of residents and personnel in institutions for the mentally retarded. In A. A. Baumeister and E. C. Butterfield (Eds.), *Residential facilities for the mentally retarded.* Chicago:

Aldine-Atherton, 1970, pp. 199-245.

Watson, L. S. Proposal for behavior modification programs in Ohio institutions for the mentally retarded. Submitted to Ohio Division of Mental Retardation, Columbus, Ohio, 1971. (Unpublished paper)

Watson, L. S. *How to use behavior modification with mentally retarded and autistic children: Programs for administrators, parents, and nurses.* Columbus, Ohio: Behavior Modification Technology, 1972.

Watson, L. S. A blueprint for designing and implementing behavior modification programs for psychotic, mentally retarded and emotionally disturbed children and adults in institutional and community settings. Presented at Sixth Annual Midwestern Behavior Modification/Intensive Practicum Workshop, Chicago, 1974. (Unpublished paper).

Watson, L. S. The home as a therapeutic environment: Training parents to manage problem children. In Bernal, M. E. (Ed.), *Training in behavior modification.* Monterey, Calif.: Brooks/Cole. (In press).

Watson, L. S., & Bassinger, J. F. *Hospital improvement project grant progress report, Columbus State Institute.* Grant No. 51-P-70080-5-01 (-02, 03, 04) formerly No. T-R-20-MR-02119-01 (-02, 03, 04). Washington, D.C.: U.S. Social Rehabilitation Services, Mental Retardation Division, Department of Health, Education and Welfare, 1968, 1969, 1970, and 1971 (a).

Watson, L. S., & Bassinger, J. F. *Community mental retardation facilities staffing grant progress report: Behavior modification community training program.* Grant No. 1-H01-MR-08181-01. Washington, D.C.: U.S. Department of Health, Education and Welfare, 1971. (b).

Watson, L. S., & Bassinger, J. F. *Developmental disabilities act grant progress report: Community behavior modification project for children.* Grant No. 1971-6. Washington, D.C.: U.S. Department of Health, Education and Welfare, 1972.

Watson, L. S., & Bassinger, J. F. Parent training technology: A potential service delivery system. *Mental Retardation,* 1974, *12*(5), 3-10.

Watson, L. S., Gardner, J. M., & Sanders, C. Shaping and maintaining behavior modification skills in staff members in an MR institution: Columbus State Institute behavior modification program. *Mental Retardation,* 1971, *9*(3), 39-42.

Wexler, D. B. Token and taboo: Behavior modification, token economies, and the law. *Behaviorism,* 1973, *1,* 1-24.

Wolfensberger, W. *Normalization.* Toronto: National Institute on Mental Retardation, 1972.

Yates, A. Symptoms and symptom substitution. *Psychological Review,* 1958, *65,* 371-374.

Diane D. Bricker is an Associate Professor of Pediatrics and Educational Psychology at the University of Miami. She is also the Administrator of the Debbie School, the intervention component of the Mailman Center for Child Development, a university affiliated facility located at the University of Miami.

Dr. Bricker received her B.A. degree from Ohio State University (speech and hearing therapy), her M.S. degree from the University of Oregon (special education), and her Ph.D. degee from George Peabody College (special education). Her primary interest has been the development of intervention strategies for the young handicapped and severely impaired child; she is currently directing a major demonstration program for this population at the Mailman Center.

The major focus of Dr. Bricker's research has been on the development of language training procedures for the preverbal child.

William A. Bricker is a professor of special education at Kent State University who received all of his degrees from Ohio State University—his B.S. degree in 1958 (secondary education), his M.A. degree in 1959 (educational psychology), and his Ph.D. degree in 1962 (developmental psychology). Dr. Bricker's primary interests are in the areas of prelinguistic and early linguistic processes of handicapped children that provide a basis for formulating intervention strategies. His research ranges from parent teaching strategies to analyses of infant and toddler learning.

13

Psychological issues in language development in the mentally retarded child

Dianne D. Bricker and William A. Bricker

DELINEATION OF THE ISSUES

Structure and Function of Language

No major dispute exists about the importance of language in defining and structuring human behavior. The acquisition of language by children is the hallmark of normal development, and delay or absence of language is an indicator of developmental problems. In fact, delays or deficiencies in language acquisition are the primary defining characteristic of mental retardation. However, language is a learned form of behavior, so that many delays or deficiencies can be ameliorated through special arrangements of instructional environments, particularly if those arrangements can be provided by parents during a child's early years. As soon as a language delay or deficiency is detected, which can be as early as the 16th month, steps can be taken by the parent to provide special periods of instruction.

However, language is an extremely complex and sensitive form of behavior, and mismanaged instructional routines can produce either more serious delays or distortions in speech which limit intelligibility of the child's utterances. The complexity of language also demands that the instructional programs be focused on generalized forms of behavior rather than on particular utterances that are controlled by a specific set of environmental

This work was supported in part by the Joseph P. Kennedy, Jr., Foundation, and NICHHD Grants No. HD-04510, No. HD-00973, and No. HD-00043 to George Peabody College. We are grateful for the assistance of L. Watson, L. Vincent-Smith, R. Smith, J. Filler, and L. Dennison in the writing of this chapter.

conditions. Consequently, an instructional program that can be used by parents and which will help ameliorate delays and deficiencies in language acquisition must be developed carefully and generated from the full range of our scientific and clinical knowledge about language and language acquisition.

The purpose of this chapter is to present a plausible instructional program for language training of developmentally delayed children and also to include descriptions of the many theories and research investigations that provide this training program with a conceptual and empirical base. The research that has been reviewed and presented in this chapter has been almost exclusively restricted to investigations using moderately to severely retarded children.

Language has been defined by Carroll (1961) as a ".... structured system of arbitrary vocal sounds and sequences of sounds which is used in interpersonal communication and which rather exhaustively catalogs the things, events, and processes of human experience" (p. 332). The ability to use language means more than knowing a specified number of words, phrases, or sentences. "Knowing" a language means a person can understand and generate an infinitely large variety of words, phrases, and sentences in that language. As noted by Chomsky and Miller (1963), normally developing children acquire these competencies rapidly and in the absence of formal instruction. All that appears to be necessary for the development of basic language acquisition is informal exposure to adult language over a relatively short period of about 4 years. This ease of acquisition in combination with flexibility in the use of the learned language indicates to Chomsky, Miller, and most other psychologists that the child is learning something more than a finite set of environmentally controlled responses. The child seems to be learning a set of "generative" rules that have a hierarchical structure that operates in both the comprehension and the production of language.

Some writers, such as Lenneberg (1967) and McNeill (1970), have used Chomsky and Miller's conception of language acquisition to justify the position that language is a biologically evolved and uniquely human capacity. One of the major themes of this chapter will be a partial rejection of this conception of the innate capacity for language because of its implications for the developmentally retarded child and the utility of a structured program to ameliorate such retardation. The assumption of a "language acquisition devise" would seem to indicate that a child who did not learn this complex system quickly and in the absence of formal instruction is not able to do so even under the best instructional conditions. Fortunately, this conception has operated as a challenge rather than as an epitaph for many of those who are investigating language training models to be used with developmentally retarded children.

The development of instructional programs in a complex area of behavior such as language depends on a useful partitioning of the total area into meaningful subareas that can be managed both conceptually and experimentally. In linguistic and psycholinguistic analyses, language has been generally partitioned into the four areas called phonology, morphology, semantics, and syntax. In *phonology,* the unit of analysis is the phoneme, which is the minimal unit of speech that is discriminable in a given language. While differing in the number and the type of phonemes in a given language community, the overall number of phonemes is finite, and can be noted and defined with fewer than 100 phonetic symbols. *Morphology* is defined in terms of the minimal units of speech that "convey" meaning. For example, the word "dog" cannot be divided into a smaller unit and still have meaning. At this level, morphology could be included in the area of semantics except that many morphemes are not words, but rather are letters or sounds attached to words in order to alter meaning. For example, "ed" is added to verbs to change the meaning of the verb from present to past tense in English, and "s" is added to nouns to change the meaning from singular to plural.

Many other examples of such "bound" morphemes exist in English, thus making a distinction between morphology and semantics useful and empirically productive. Morphology overlaps not only semantics but also syntax, especially in the case of bound morphemes. Consequently, in the present chapter, syntax and morphology have been combined into a single section on grammar. *Semantics* covers the concept of meaning or the meaning of concepts (either way seems correct) and remains the most confused of all linguistic areas in both theory and research. Some of the issues which center around semantics will be discussed later in this chapter. Finally, *syntax* (or grammar) deals with the sequence of written or spoken words, as well as morphological changes, which are governed by a set of explicit or implicit rules. The linguist views a grammar as a theory about the structure and organization of those rules.

The three areas of phonology, semantics, and grammar provide the organizational structure of this chapter following a review of the literature on language training programs with retarded children. Each of the three sections begins with a description of the area of language being considered in terms of predominate theories relating to structure of the area, as well as what is being learned and how it is learned by the native speaker of the language. Next, important aspects of the development of behavior in that area are reviewed and summarized. Then descriptive studies that have focused on the behavior of the retarded person in that area are discussed. Finally, the conceptions and data are synthesized with extant intervention studies to build a set of training procedures to ameliorate retarded development in the area. However, the material in each of these sections is restricted to the English language, perhaps more specifically to American English as it is spoken by the majority of people in the United States. This restriction is derived more from the limitations of the writers' knowledge than from the lack of potential relevance of non-English information for an instructional language program for the developmentally retarded child.

Review of Language-Training Literature

A relatively small number of general language-training programs for young moderately to severely retarded children were reported in the literature before 1960 (Blount, 1968). Many programs were possibly in existence, but they were either not reported or the language program was an integral part of the larger ongoing training approach. Before 1960 there was little emphasis on language training with moderately to severely retarded children because the prevailing attitude was one of pessimism. Generally, it was felt that this population of children could develop rudimentary language only, even under the most effective training conditions (Jordan, 1967; Lloyd, 1972; West, Ansberry, & Carr, 1957). Unfortunately, some investigators still advocate this point of view, even in the face of the evidence coming from investigations like the Brooklands experiment (Lyle, 1960), which demonstrates the impact of adequate environments on language behavior. Certainly, moderately to severely retarded individuals have language problems; however, the majority of studies reported in the literature provided at least rudimentary evidence that basic language deficits can be partially ameliorated, given adequate training programs.

Several uncontrolled and relatively short-term intervention studies report improved language functioning in mentally retarded subjects. The earlier studies (Lubman, 1955; Schlanger, 1953; Schneider & Vallon, 1955) utilized traditional speech therapy techniques, while a later program (Bennett, 1969) intervened with ward attendants by reinforcing them for conducting language stimulation activities on their wards.

A number of controlled studies on short-term interventions indicate positive results with a variety of approaches, including traditional speech therapy (Mecham, 1955); language enrichment activities in individual tutoring sessions (Kolstoe, 1958); activities based on the Illinois Test of Psycholinguistic Abilities (ITPA), reported by Bradley, Maurer, and Hundziak (1966) and by Smith (1970); and operant techniques (Barton, 1970; Buddenhagen, 1971; Jeffrey, 1972). Two studies have also reported on the relative effectiveness of different approaches. Thus, Lassers and Low (1960) compared conventional speech therapy with communication-centered speech therapy, and MacCubrey (1971) contrasted operant-type training with general enrichment activities.

Descriptions of long-term language intervention programs with moderately to severely retarded children are rare. Language-training programs are often embedded in general "enrichment" programs for retarded children, and it is often difficult to sort out the specific language-training procedures from the overall approach. For example, 32 institutionalized children in the Brooklands study (Lyle, 1960) were matched on verbal and nonverbal intelligence. Sixteen were then assigned to an experimental project while the remaining 16 subjects were maintained as usual in the institution. The experimental project consisted of "family type" living situations for the children. No formal training or educational procedures were used; instead, the learning experiences were introduced through the children's everyday activities. Evaluation after both 12 and 18 months indicated that the mean improvement in verbal intelligence scores of the experimental group was significantly greater than for the controls. Although this investigation provides little specific information on language-training procedures, it does suggest that family-type living situations can have a positive effect on the verbal behavior of retarded children.

Many institutions and community programs have included language stimulation procedures in their educational curriculum. Unfortunately, the majority of these programs are not data based, nor are they accessible outside the immediate community for which they were developed. However, a group of investigators (Rhodes, Gooch, Siegelman, Behrns, & Metzger, 1969) produced a monograph describing in some detail a language stimulation program undertaken with 10 children with Down's Syndrome over a 2½ year period. These 10 children were institutionalized as infants between the ages of 1 to 4 months. When compared at age 2 with a group of home-reared children with Down's Syndrome, the babies were not grossly different. However, when these two groups were compared at age 5, the home-reared youngsters performed consistently better on the language measures. Consequently, an intensive language stimulation program was begun with the institutionalized children. A language specialist trained the ward personnel, who in turn trained the children through a carefully specified daily training routine. The children were essentially mute at the beginning of the program, but at the end of a 2½ years, most of the subjects had made significant gains on both language and IQ measures.

Another long-term study with a heavy emphasis on language was the Milwaukee Family Rehabilitation Project (Heber & Garber, 1970). A group of 40 pregnant inner-city mothers with IQs of 75 or below were chosen to participate in this investigation. Twenty of the infants of these mothers were assigned to the control group, and the remaining 20 infants to the experimental project. The experimental program was an attempt to prevent sociocultural retardation. The experimental infants entered the training program at 3 months of age, and initially each infant had a special caretaker who had been carefully trained. The authors reported that the educational program had two major emphases—namely, language and cognition. At the end of 42 months, a difference of 33 IQ points existed between the experimental and control groups. Heber and Garber (1970) also stated that, "The most striking difference in the performance of the experimental and control children are reflected in the measures of language performance" (p. 12). These results are impressive, and they demonstrate that early intervention, coupled with an appropriate educational program, can have a significant effect on the language skills of young children.

The Cooperative Language Development Project reported by Dunn and Bruininks (1968) was one of the most ambitious attempts to implement and evaluate a language-training program. The study was designed to examine the effect of the Peabody Language Development Kit (PLDK) with two reading procedures. Although the 1,000 experimental subjects and the 150 control subjects used in this investigation were the mildly retarded classification rather than that of moderate to severe, a discussion of this study seems appropriate because of the overwhelming acceptance of the PLDK by teachers of low-functioning children. The original research was implemented in 1964-1965 with 10 experimental groups and one control group, all in the first grade. During the first year, all experimental subjects received both training with the PLDK and reading training in either traditional orthography (TO) or Initial Teaching Alphabet (ITA). During the second year, 50% of the experimental subjects received training with PLDK; in the third year, only 50% again received PLDK training. Dunn and Bruininks (1968) stated that:

> Overall the PLDK lessons enchanced significantly IQ scores on the 1960 Stanford-Binet Intelligence Scale by the time of posttesting when the experimental phase terminated at the end of the third grade. The significant IQ gains were also retained in follow-up evaluation at the end of the fourth grade; the ITA group with two or three years of PLDK lessons, however, had lost significantly in IQ points from post to follow-up testing. (p. 84)

A second study (Dunn, Neville, Bailey, Pochanart, & Pfost, 1967), using the PLDK paired with three different reading approaches, did not support the facilitating effect of using the PLDK. The lack of significant results in the latter investigation are unfortunate, since sampling problems in the previously cited study call into question the findings of that project. As Dunn and Bruininks (1968) noted, "a bias in selection of the pupils, teachers, and schools in favor of the experimental treatments, as well as the Hawthorne Effect, may have contributed as much or more to the obtaining of positive

Table 13.1

Major Phonemes in English

Consonants

/b/	by	/j/	yes	/n/	no	/ʃ/	she	/v/	vine
/d/	do	/k/	key	/ŋ/	sing	/t/	to	/w/	we
/f/	fine	/l/	lip	/p/	pie	/tʃ/	chew	/ʍ/	which
/g/	go	/ɫ/	ball	/r/	rip	/θ/	thin	/z/	zip
/h/	he	/m/	me	/s/	sip	/ð/	they	/ʒ/	measure

Vowels

/a/	ask	/ɚ/	mother	/ɪ/	bit	/o/	oval
/ɑ/	calm	/ɜ/	burnt	/i/	beet	/ʊ/	cook
/æ/	bat	/ə/	sofa	/ɒ/	cloth	/u/	cool
/e/	vacate	/ɛ/	bet	/ɔ/	jaw	/ʌ/	cut

Diphthongs

/eɪ/	late	/ju/	you	/aʊ/	how
/aɪ/	dine	/oʊ/	soap	/ɔɪ/	boil

results as the PLDK and ITA approaches" (p. 86).

In general, the data generated from both the short-term and long-term language-training programs suggest that some moderately to severely retarded children can benefit from this form of training. However, many of the programs reported in the literature suffer from some basic deficiencies. First, most training programs are not detailed enough for replication; second, measures of language progress are almost as varied as the number of investigations; and third, many of the investigations lack adequate experimental design and controls for assessing the effect of the training program. Fortunately, the more recent investigations being reported in the literature are attempting to eliminate some of these deficiencies.

PHONOLOGY

The phoneme has been generally considered to be a hypothetical unit of speech which affects the meaning of a word or morpheme. It is the minimal unit of speech that has such an effect. For example, if "pin" and "bin" have different meanings, and "buck" and "puck" have different meanings, then the sound differences between these two sets of words (namely, /p/ and /b/) must be phonemes in the language that uses these words. An anthropologist can move into a culture having a language he does not speak and can map the phoneme structure of that culture by first recording the various sounds he hears in the words that are spoken and then varying the sounds in different word contexts in the presence of a native speaker to determine what sound variations make a difference in meaning to the native speaker.

The phoneme spectrum for English has already been mapped. The list in Table 13.1 presents the major phonemes in English and corresponding key words that indicate how the phonemes are translated as sounds in words. The underlined portion of each word indicates the associated sound for the phonemic symbol.

The production of a speech sound (a phone, of which the phoneme is the theoretical counterpart) involves three basic components: the placement of the articulators, the degree or type of interruption of the airstream, and whether the vocal folds are vibrating when the sounds are being produced. The articulators include the tongue, teeth, lips, and velum, each of which is represented in Figure 13.1. Some combination of articulation placement is associated with each sound. The type or manner of interruption of the airstream as a sound is being produced varies greatly from almost none (as in the sound /h/) to a momentary complete blocking (as in /p/). The extent to which the airstream is interrupted is used as the basis for differentiating

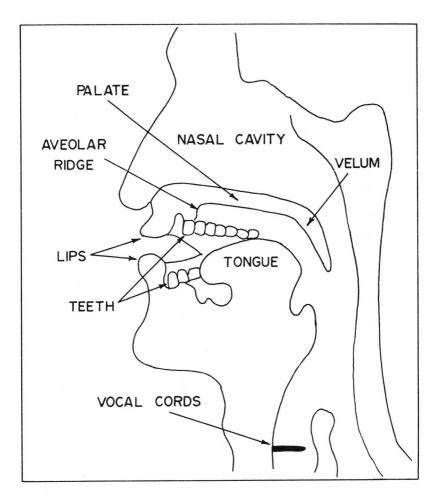

Figure 13.1.   The articulators used to produce speech sounds.

Table 13.2

Classification of English Consonants

Type of articulation	Position of articulation						
	Bilabial	Labiodental	Dental	Alveolar	Palatal	Velar	Glottal
Plosives	p (pie) b (by)[a]			t (to) d (do)[a]		k (key) g (go)[a]	?
Nasals	m (me)[a]			n (no)[a]		ŋ (sing)[a]	
Fricatives	w (we)[a]	f (fine) v (vine)[a]	ϴ (thin) ð (then)[a]	s (sip) z (zip)[a] r (rip)[a]	ʃ (she) ʒ (azure)[a] j (yes)[a]		h (he)
Laterals				l (lip)[a]			

Note. From "Language and Communication" by G. A. Miller. Copyright 1951 by McGraw-Hill. Reprinted by permission of McGraw-Hill Book Co.

[a] Indicates voiced sounds.

vowels from consonants. Vowels are considered to be those voiced sounds that are not interrupted (at least not any more than happens to the /i/ sound in *beet*), while consonants are produced by greater interruptions of the airstream in various ways. These include directing the airstream through the nose (nasal sounds), blocking the sound completely with the tongue, teeth, or lips (plosive sounds), forcing the airstream around the tongue (laterals), or only interrupting the airstream partially (fricatives). A commonly used scheme for representing the articulator placement and the manner of interruption for consonants is contained in Table 13.2. The sounds that are voiced in the process of their production are also noted in the table.

The vowel sounds are classified according to the position of the tongue at the time of each production relative to the position of the tongue in the "neutral" position. The neutral position is defined as that location of the tongue that occurs in the production of /e/ as in bed. In the production of the various vowel sounds, the tongue may be either forward or back from the neutral position, or it may be high (toward the palate) or low. A schematic diagram for representing the various tongue positions for the major vowel sounds is contained in Figure 13.2.

The foregoing description of phonology is the more traditional approach and is useful in developing an instructional sequence in speech sound production. However, the currently dominating theory in phonetics is the *distinctive feature model*. This position was predicated on a theory of successive binary contrasts that was initially formulated by Roman Jakobson (Jakobson, Fant, & Halle, 1963) and subsequently elaborated by Chomsky and Halle (1968), who outlined five major categories of distinctive features. The first class includes those feature distinctions that separate vowels from consonants and voiced sounds from unvoiced sounds. These are called the major "class" features. The second class covers the cavity features and includes the various tongue, lip, and glottis positions that are involved in speech sound production. The third class subsumes manner articulation features and includes definitions for continuants, release features, pressure, and tenseness, as the articulator placement interacts with the emitted airstream in the production of speech sounds. The fourth class, called "source" features, deals with subglottal pressure, vibration of the vocal cords, and the general "noisiness" of the sound being produced. The fifth and final class covers the prosodic features—which include stress contours or sound sequences (in words and phrases), pitch, and length. However, Chomsky and Halle (1968) indicated that little theoretical analysis has been made of this class, and consequently they devoted minimal space to the topic.

For the general purpose of analysis of English speech sounds, the distinctive features can be reduced to those 13 which establish the primary binary distinctions, such as vocalic versus nonvocalic, high versus neutral

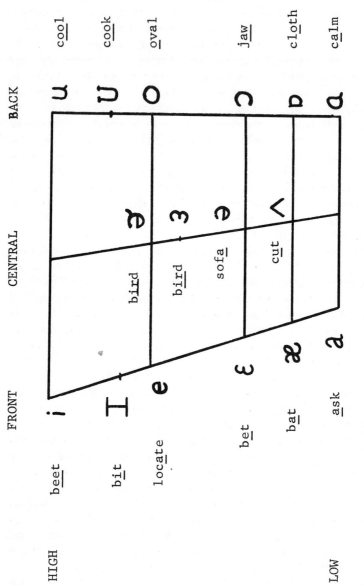

Figure 13.2. Representations of various positions to produce major vowel sounds. (Reprinted from "Language and Communication," by G. A. Miller. Copyright 1951 by McGraw-Hill, Inc. Used with permission of McGraw-Hill Book Co.)

tongue position, and tense versus lax. The names of the 13 features and their basic defining characteristics are given in Table 13.3. In actual analysis, only the first part of the distinction is made, and if that part is present in a given sound, the record is marked plus (+) for that feature. If the alternative aspect is present in the sound (e.g., nonvocalic or neutral), then the feature is marked minus (−) on the record. Sounds may also be unmarked if the pattern of marked features prevents distinctions being made on the remaining features. For example, the consonants (but not the vowels) are marked on conditions of voice (continuant, nasal, and strident), since these features occur only when the airstream is blocked to the extent that defines a consonant. The system used by Chomsky and Halle (1968) for marking sounds is illustrated in Table 13.4 for a representative group of vowels and consonants.

By using Tables 13.3 and 13.4, the reader will be able to identify the way(s) in which one sound is different from another. For example, /t/ and /d/ are marked alike for all features except voice, which means the vocal cords are vibrating in the production of /d/ (which is plus voice), but are not vibrating in the production of /t/ (which is minus voice). This approach has major implications for specifying what is being learned as a child acquires English speech sounds, and for making explicit what must be trained if the child is consistently making errors in the production of a particular sound, either in the context of words or as an imitated response. Such points will be elaborated upon later.

Phonologic Development

The purpose of this section is to describe the sequence in which speech sound production is acquired by the normally developing child. The birth cry is a form of speech sound production and forms the beginning for describing speech sound development. O. C. Irwin and his colleagues have provided the most complete data on phoneme development in the infant (Irwin, 1946, 1947, 1948). Irwin's group acquired data by sitting beside a large number of babies and recording the English speech sounds that they produced on exhaled breaths.

These investigators found that infants do not have the full repertoire at birth and that some sounds are not produced until the typical child is about 12 months of age. The development of the production of consonant sounds between 2 and 30 months of age (according to Irwin, 1947) is shown in Table 13.5 along with data on sound production in adults, according to Voelker (1934). The numbers represent the percentage of all consonant sounds that are in a given speech sound category. Thus, at 2 months of age, over 87% of

Table 13.3

Defining Characteristics of Distinctive Features

Feature	Description
Consonantal	Sound production involves an obstruction in the vocal tract.
Anterior	Sound production involves an obstruction in the vocal tract in front of the palato-alveolar region, that region in which /ʃ/ sound is produced.
Voice	Sound production involves vibration of vocal cords.
Corronal	Tip of tongue is raised from neutral position. "Neutral position" is the position of articulators during production of /e/, as in b<u>e</u>d.
Nasal	Mouth resonator is supplemented by resonation of nasal cavity in production of sound.
High	Body of tongue is raised above neutral position during sound production.
Back	Sound production involves retraction of the body of the tongue from neutral position.
Round	Constriction of lips during sound production.
Low	Body of tongue is lower than neutral position during sound production.
Continuant	No constriction in vocal tract during sound production is extreme enough to block air flow.
Strident	Sound production involves rapid rate of air flow over rough surface at sharp angle, resulting in "noisy" sounds.
Vocalic	No obstruction of vocal tract by articulators during production of sound.
Tense	Sound production involves extreme deviation of articulators from neutral position and great muscular effort.

Table 13.4

System of Marking Distinctive Feature Analysis

	b	d	m	w	h	dʒ	l	a	i	U
Consonantal	⊕ᵃ	+	+	−	−	+	+	−	−	−
Anterior	⊕	+	+	−	−	−	+	−	−	−
Voice	⊕	+	+	−	−	+	+			
Coronal	−	⊕	−	−	−	+	+	−	−	−
Nasal	−	−	⊕	⊕	−	−	−			
High	−	−	−	⊕	−	+	−	+	+	+
Back	−	−	−	⊕	−	−	−	−	−	+
Round	−		−	⊕	−			−	−	+
Low					⊕			+		−
Continuant	−	−	−	−	⊕	−	+	−	−	−
Strident	−	−	−			⊕	+			
Vocalic	−	−	−	−	−	−	⊕	+	+	+
Tense	−		−	−	−	−	−	⊕	−	−

ᵃ⊕ Indicates additional feature.

565

all consonants involve the back consonants /h/ and /ʔ/. The latter is the glottal stop, which is produced by closing the glottis and then releasing it suddenly, making a clicking voiced sound. Interestingly, this sound—which is not produced in English words—drops from the repertoire very quickly. As noted, the adult consonant frequencies in Table 13.5 were taken from Voelker (1934) and represent the terminal state toward which the young child's responses are moving.

While both Irwin's and Voelker's data are old (and both may be criticized), they still represent our best information in the area (cf. Winitz, 1969). Other facts of interest from these data indicate that some sounds (/m/, /d/, and /b/) have a disproportionately high rate of occurrence in comparison with the other sounds and in relation to the adult frequencies of these sounds. The possiblitiy exists that the language community surrounding the child responds most to these particular sounds as they occur in late infancy, owing to their relationship to key words (e.g., mama, daddy, baby, ball). However, this is speculative.

Irwin's data provide an excellent description of speech sound production of children up to 30 months of age. One of the present writers attempted to extend this analysis for children from 3 to 6 years of age, using a different technique (W. Bricker, 1967). Instead of waiting for the spontaneous emission of the various sounds, an imitation procedure was used, and a careful record was made of both correct and incorrect production. The sounds that were missed more frequently were assumed to be more difficult and, in turn, to reflect the developmental progression of speech sound capabilities. The study was then repeated with a group of severely retarded children who ranged in age from 6 to 12 years and whose mean Vineland Social Maturity Scale social quotient was 3.5. The results are contained in Table 13.6, along with the error frequencies from the previous study on normal children (W. Bricker, 1967). The results of the second study indicated that while the retarded children made substantially more errors than the normal subjects, their patterns of error were quite similar. The correlations of data from the retarded population with those of the three normal groups ranged from .80 to .91, with the higher value being between the retarded children and the 3-year old normal children.

The importance of these data is not so much in the description of the overall frequencies as in the specific types of errors the children made. The majority of the errors were substitutions of an incorrect sound for the correct one; for both the normal and the developmentally delayed children, these substitutions formed a definite pattern. Characteristically, the children would emit sounds that differed from the echoic (imitative) stimulus in terms of the position of the articulators and generally not in terms of changing the voicing properties of the sound or the manner of articulation. For example, if /b/ was

Table 13.5

Consonant Phoneme Percentage

Phoneme	Childrens' Age (months)[a]						Adult[b]
	2	6	12	18	24	30	
p	0.10	0.30	1.63	1.27	4.32	4.47	2.41
b	0.19	2.50	9.79	14.95	8.97	7.64	3.18
m	0.21	3.07	6.69	5.43	8.41	7.99	4.47
w	0.07	1.49	3.31	7.02	6.42	3.31	2.99
hw	—	—	0.08	0.04	0.03	0.20	0.60
f	—	0.27	0.37	0.63	1.18	1.79	3.48
v	—	0.16	1.03	0.29	0.52	0.63	2.52
θ	—	0.39	0.85	0.29	0.36	0.14	1.06
ð	—	0.34	0.34	0.36	0.61	1.70	5.13
t	0.17	0.22	4.34	4.61	8.31	11.68	11.66
d	—	2.06	20.58	20.56	15.31	13.98	8.28
n	0.14	0.52	2.65	5.38	9.74	9.49	11.85
s	—	0.20	3.45	3.59	7.42	6.87	7.54
z	—	—	0.56	1.00	0.51	0.41	3.48
ʃ	0.17	0.02	0.37	0.41	0.84	0.82	1.64
ʒ	—	—	0.10	0.11	0.09	—	0.67
l	0.21	0.23	0.96	1.04	2.00	3.37	6.32
r	—	0.15	0.10	1.09	2.67	4.64	10.51
j	—	1.12	1.77	1.95	1.73	1.50	1.89
ç	—	—	0.06	—	—	0.10	—
ŋ	—	0.17	0.33	0.14	0.62	0.48	1.68
k	8.80	4.90	2.12	2.73	4.36	6.98	4.15
g	2.79	7.46	4.15	5.17	2.67	4.05	1.75
x	—	0.10	0.08	0.02	—	—	—
h	44.22	61.93	31.77	20.75	10.93	7.65	2.66
ʔ	42.91	12.41	2.52	1.12	1.90	0.07	—

[a] The data for children came from "Infant Speech: Consonantal Sounds according to Place of Articulation" by O. C. Irwin. *Journal of Speech Disorders*, 1947, *12*, 397-401. Copyright 1947 by American Speech and Hearing Association. Reprinted by permission.
[b] After Voelker (1934).

567

Table 13.6

Table 13.6

Verbal Imitation Error Profiles: Mean Proportion of Sounds Produced in Error

Sounds	MR	Nonretarded Age Groups			Adult
		3 year	4 year	5 year	
p	.36	.15	.15	.07	.02
b	.15	.03	.08	.05	.03
t	.28	.07	.03	.05	.12
d	.16	.07	.08	.03	.08
k	.25	.15	.15	.08	.04
g	.37	.28	.53	.37	.02
f	.47	.35	.28	.20	.03
v	.75	.80	.52	.53	.02
θ	.90	.72	.88	.67	.01
ð	.88	.95	.90	.40	.05
s	.43	.27	.18	.27	.08
z	.68	.64	.43	.38	.03
ʃ	.35	.42	.20	.20	.02
ʒ	.52	.85	.67	.50	.01
tʃ	.50	.55	.27	.12	.02
dʒ	.48	.38	.07	.03	.01
h	.25	.13	.05	.02	.03
m	.18	.07	.07	.02	.04
n	.41	.18	.13	.07	.12
w	.21	.07	.03	.00	.03
l	.53	.53	.15	.12	.06
r	.56	.52	.35	.13	.10

substituted for /d/ by a child, then the response retained voicing and plosive manner of articulation, but it was different in that the child emitted a bilabial sound for a postdental one (or in distinctive feature analysis, changing a + coronal sound for a − coronal one, with all other feature characteristics preserved in the error response).

In the analysis of the errors produced by severely retarded children (W. Bricker & D. Bricker, 1972), 76% of all errors involved a change in the place of articulation, and only 30% of the errors involved a change in voicing. For the nondelayed children (W. Bricker, 1967), these values were 83%, 28%, and 23% for place, manner, and voicing, respectively. Consequently, the major problem in shifting an error response in the direction of correct emission is most frequently one of teaching the child to change the placement of articulators when producing the sound. Training that was focused on variations between labial dental and lingua dental continuants would eliminate some of the most frequent errors made by both normal and developmentally delayed children.

Imitation Training

One of the important aspects of these data is their use in the development of a theoretical model that accounts for generalized verbal imitation. Imitation is a principal component of a systematic language-training program. No other process is as efficient for establishing new verbal responses in a repertoire or maintaining that repertoire while it is brought under other and more meaningful stimulus control. Once the child has generalized verbal imitation, he can be taught to say any word composed of the phonetic units of his language milieu.

According to Ball (1970), imitation has been used in language training since Itard and Seguin, both of whom antedate by many years such investigators as Lovaas (1968) and Baer, Peterson, and Sherman (1967). The general procedures used by these early teachers for establishing the basic imitative repertoire were not greatly different from the methods employed by current investigators. However, the problem remains that there have been few satisfactory explanations of what the child is learning when he acquires "generalized" verbal imitation. Attempts to explain such generalization have varied considerably, especially in their use of mentalistic processes. According to Gewirtz and Stingle (1968), even some of the more behavioristic accounts of imitation resort to nonindexed internal mechanisms or processes. For example, Baer and Sherman (1964) attempted to explain imitation by ascribing to the imitator the (unassessed) ability to discriminate the similarity of his response to that of the model, and they suggested that this similarity has conditioned reinforcement properties. This explanation does encompass the occurrence of imitated responses which have never been specifically reinforced, a condition that is often required in a definition of generalized imitation.

Unfortunately, the discrimination of similarity has the properties of a mentalistic judgment made by the subject, a position to which Gewirtz and Stingle (1968) objected. As an alternative, Gewirtz and Stingle proposed that generalized imitation is a "class of diverse but functionally equivalent behaviors . . . acquired and . . . maintained by extrinsic reinforcement on an intermittent schedule" (1968, p. 379). They went on to state: "Differences in response content of the imitative behavior are thought to play a minimal role as long as the responses are members of the imitative response class as defined functionally by reinforcing agents" (1968, p. 379). This position keeps imitation within the domain of a functional analysis by defining all terms by reference to events that can be observed by two or more people. However, the concept of "functionally equivalent behaviors" needs further clarification.

Functionally equivalent responses are readily observable in an operant conditioning chamber in which a rat presses the lever at a rapid rate, but uses different responses to activate the lever. Several presses may involve the right-front paw, a combination of left-front and left-rear paws, an alternation of left- and right- front, or some other combination involving both the feet and the head. Since each specific movement that has sufficient pressure activates the lever, the different responses are functionally equivalent in producing the same outcome, and are therefore considered to be in the same class of responses. Thus, movements that are topographically different can become a class (an operant) by sharing some property (each depresses the lever until an electrical contact is made), and are maintained as a response class if the shared movement property produces a reinforcing consequence.

An article by Schick indicates that response classes or operants can be defined by:

> properties of several different kinds: properties of having certain effects, properties of occurring in the presence of certain stimuli. In fact, operants can be defined by any property upon which reinforcement can be made contingent. Moreover, operants must be defined only by properties upon which reinforcement can be made contingent. (1971, p. 422)

In imitation, reinforcement is made contingent upon the form properties of the response *in relation to* the form properties of the controlling stimulus, and occurs when the form of the response is topographically similar to the form of the stimulus. Even a single specific imitation would constitute an operant, since repeated occurrences of it would probably vary in the number of similar properties in both the stimulus and the response.

For example, one imitation of "hands on head" might involve a sideward sweep of the two hands to the head, while a second imitation might be a forward swing of the hands and arms. Both responses would probably be reinforced. In this example, the property of similarity upon which the delivery of reinforcement is dependent may only be the terminal state of having both hands pressed firmly somewhere near the top of the head; and variations in arriving at the terminal state would not alter the response dependency. However, if a single imitated response is itself a class, then no discrimination can be made between a single imitation and generalized imitation, using the model of Gewirtz and Stingle (1968), for whom generalized imitation constitutes the class of which a particular imitated movement is a member.

The purpose of this discussion is to propose an alternative conception, based on imitation data, that does not differentiate between particular and generalized forms of imitation, but reduces both to instances of the same process. The alternative model is based on the assumption that both the stimulus and the response in the event of an imitation involve a chain of component parts (properties). When an imitated response is reinforced, the occurrence of each component is made more probable. A recent investigation by Catania (1971) makes this latter assumption plausible. In summarizing his results, Catania stated:

> In descriptions of reinforcement schedules, it is said that a particular response is reinforced and that other responses [that precede it] are unreinforced. In terms of process, however, the present findings make it appropriate to say that all of the responses preceding the one that produces the reinforcer are reinforced; . . . Perhaps it is time to recognize a term (reinforcement) that has long been part of informal usage, and to distinguish operations from processes by saying that when we reinforce the last response of a sequence of responses we strengthen all of the responses in the sequence. (p. 286)

A second assumption is that, as the response-component chain is repeated and reinforced in the presence of the physically similar stimulus component chain, individual components of the stimulus become discriminative in controlling similar components in the response. As other response component chains are brought under control of imitative stimulus component chains, the possibility exists that novel responses will occur imitatively as a consequence of new combinations of previously learned components. However, novel responses would be restricted only to those constructable from previously learned components which are under control of comparable components in the stimulus component chain. This restriction limits the degree and type of generalization and makes implausible an unconstrained generalized imitative repertoire.

The evidence supporting the component structure basis for generalized imitation comes from a variety of sources, varying from anecdotal accounts to systematic experimental analyses. One of the present authors used a component analysis in his investigation of echoic behavior of preschool children (W. Bricker, 1967). An analysis of the imitated responses indicated error responses were like the corresponding stimuli in terms of voicing and manner of articulation (e.g., fricative, nasal, plosive), but they were different (in more than 80% of error instances) from the eliciting stimulus in terms of place of articulation (e.g., bilabial, alveolar, glottal). Thus, neither the consonant-vowel stimulus nor the corresponding responses were unitary events, but were rather sets of components which were related with varying probabilities.

A similar form of the analysis could have been made using the distinctive feature system of Chomsky and Halle (1968). This system construes sounds as bundles of features. Thus, an imitation of a particular sound could preserve some of these features while differing from the stimulus on other features. More importantly, the number of features is many fewer than the sounds generated by combining features; therefore, once a child learns to reproduce each of the features, he should be able to produce all the sounds generated by the various combinations of features. Specific forms of imitation training establishing imitative control of features or properties (read as "components") can then be combined into novel imitative responses without specific training. The component structure will constrain the extent of generalization to those emissions which are combinable from the component imitative repertoire. The component structure model also accounts for observations such as the inability of native speakers of English to imitate specific sounds from another language such as the German umlauts, the French trill-R, or the German palatal fricative (as in I*ch*). The component structure of these sounds is only partially reproduced in English, so that imitations by English speakers will only crudely approximate a well-formed model.

Consequently, even competent adult users of a phonological system cannot imitate certain sounds, a fact that counters both the Baer, Peterson, and Sherman (1967) and the Gewirtz and Stingle (1968) accounts of generalized imitation. Even the evidence presented by Lovaas (1967), indicating that psychotic children learned to imitate three Norwegian words *(tyttebar, appetit, ettemiddag)* without extrinsic reinforcement, is consistent with the component model, since the children did imitate English words containing the phonemes required in the Norwegian words. While the children were not reinforced for imitation of the exact words, they were reinforced for imitating components in the context of other words.

If the component model of imitation is valid, then how can a component be identified? If words and even single speech-sound imitations are composed of components, when are the lower bounds of this successive molecularization reached? The answer does not appear to reside in an analysis of the structure of the responses, but rather is to be derived from systematic variation in the material being taught, followed by probes for generalization effects. Initially, the analysis would be correlational, such as the preliminary work by W. Bricker (1967), described earlier, in which the greater number of speech-sound imitation errors involve the differential placement of the articulators. These correlational findings could then be followed by a series of investigations in which imitation of articulator placement is taught and then the repertoire probed to determine the extent of generalization. This instruction could take place at the level of mouth movements, in the context of speech sounds, or even in the context of words; but in any case, articulator placement training could be evaluated by the generalized responses it produced.

Phonetic Training

The foregoing theory and data provide an adequate basis for phonetic speech or sound training which, because of space limitations, can be described only briefly. For children who are developmentally retarded and who do not imitate either motor movements or sounds, training should begin with imitation of large motor movements, and proceed sequentially to intricate movements of the articulators and then to speech sounds themselves. The success of this sequence of training is dependent upon the skill of the teacher with such procedures as differential reinforcement, defining successive approximations, prompting, fading, extinction, time-out, and shifting stimulus control. Descriptions of these techniques can be found elsewhere (Larsen & Bricker, 1968; Reynolds, 1968; Ulrich, Stachnik, & Mabry, 1966). Prerequisite training may also require the elimination of undesirable behavior that interferes with imitation training. Such behavior would include spitting, hitting, or not attending to the training stimuli. Ullmann and Krasner (1965) provided many useful examples of techniques for eliminating such undesirable responses. The "overcorrection" method used by Foxx and Azrin (1972) may also provide help in this area. In addition, reinforcement control over the child's behavior is assumed as a necessary prerequisite.

Motor imitation training has been described in a number of articles (Baer, Peterson, & Sherman, 1967; W. Bricker & D. Bricker, 1966; Metz, 1965; Risley, 1966) and generally involves a sequence in which the teacher states the command "Do this!" and then presents the motor movement that is to operate as the imitative stimulus. If the child does not immediately imitate the movement, a second person must assist the teacher by physically prompting the child to make the required response which, when maintained for a couple of seconds by the child, is reinforced. On each successive opportunity, the assistant attempts to fade the prompt so that the child is contributing more and more of the required terminal response on a voluntary basis. Once the child spontaneously emits the required movement several times in succession without any prompting, training is shifted to a second response, and the process if repeated. The general finding is that after several such responses have been taught, the child will imitate new motor movements without the prompting which signals the beginning of the generalized process described earlier. However, when the training is shifted to mouth movements such as open mouth, tongue up, tongue on upper teeth, and other articulator movements, prompting may again be needed; a mirror may prove useful during training.

Speech sound training can be combined with mouth movement imitation, or it can be started separately by the use of free operant conditioning techniques. In the latter case, the parents or other caretaker can be instructed to reinforce the child (through praise, edibles, or imitating the child's response) every time a definite terminal or approximate English speech sound is produced. A record of the type and frequency of sounds produced in this way will indicate not only the success of the procedure but also the responses that have a high probability of occurrence. Specific speech sound imitation could then begin with these high probability items. The expectancy from the work of Irwin (1946, 1948), discussed earlier, and from that of Winitz (1969) is that many of these initial sounds will be vowels. In general, training should begin with vowels; and three of these (/a/ as in father, /i/ as in beet, and /u/ as in pool) have special merit in that they operate as three corners of a triangle in terms of the features that define all vowels in English. A child who can imitate these three "extremes" should have relatively little difficulty imitating the remaining vowels.

In training, the teacher might start in a situation where she is imitating the child's responses (as a reinforcing stimulus in free operant conditioning), but then shift by saying "Say_____", with the response just emitted by the child inserted in the blank. Any vocal response should then be reinforced if it occurs within a few seconds of the echoic stimulus, regardless of whether it is correct. This procedure teaches the child to emit a vocal response in the presence of a vocal stimulus and when the command *Say* is given. Only after the child masters this relationship is an attempt made to differentiate the response through successive approximations in the direction of the correct sound. This type of training is continued until the child can emit three or four vowel sounds reliably in a variable order. All vowels need not be trained before consonant training is started.

Consonant training involves approximately the same procedures except that consonant-vowel combinations are generally used as echoic stimuli, since many of the voiced plosives cannot be produced in isolation. The vowels previously learned by the child are the ones that are used in these combinations. The sounds contained in Table 13.7 are listed in probable order of difficulty from the easiest to the hardest, and provide a reasonable starting point for selecting the order in which the sounds can be trained. Consonant-vowel syllables can also be selected in terms of the word combinations that can be made from them. When the child has learned to imitate two or more sounds that can be combined into words, he should be taught to imitate the larger unit before introducing new sounds into training. In this way, an imitated response can be brought under the control of the object class named by the word, and thereby can be used functionally (meaningfully) by the child. As words are learned as imitated responses, they can be combined into phrases and sentences, as indicated in the final section of this chapter.

SEMANTICS

The word "semantics," or "meaning," generates extensive confusion among linguists, psychologists, speech clinicians, and others who are professionally concerned with the nature of language. For example, in a relatively thorough review of experimental investigations of meaning, Creelman (1966) concluded:

> It would appear that we are still a long way from any kind of inclusive theory of meaning. What has emerged with considerable clarity is that the word "meaning" refers to so many different concepts, constructs, functional systems processes, and areas of "experience" that it requires the flexibility of a mountain goat to leap from level to level. (p. 209)

During the past few years little has been added to the literature to make the problem of semantics meaningful. Fortunately, amid the chaos of definitions, a strictly behavioristic and functional account of meaning can be used to

Table 13.7

Ease of Production of English Consonants

Level 1	Level 2	Level 3	Level 4	Level 5
b as in <u>b</u>oy	h as in <u>h</u>at	g as in <u>g</u>o	ʃ (sh) as in <u>sh</u>oe	ʒ as in mea<u>s</u>ure
w as in <u>w</u>ay	n as in <u>n</u>o	s as in <u>s</u>ee	r as in <u>r</u>un	ð (th) as in <u>th</u>at
m as in <u>m</u>an	k as in <u>c</u>at	f as in <u>f</u>at	l as in <u>l</u>amp	ɵ (th) as in <u>th</u>in
t as in <u>t</u>oy	p as in <u>p</u>ipe	dʒ (j) as in <u>j</u>udge	tʃ (ch) as in <u>ch</u>urch	v as in <u>v</u>est
d as in <u>d</u>og			z as in <u>z</u>oo	ŋ as in si<u>ng</u>

Note. Based on data from W. Bricker (1967).

576

good advantage in devising a language-training program, since the approach is empirical and inductive. Consequently, the material that follows is based almost entirely on the interpretations of meaning proposed by Skinner (1957).

A procedure that additionally reduces confusion about meaning involves differentiation between denotative and connotative meaning. Denotative meaning is used in the context of this chapter to refer to the physical properties of events, actions, and objects that define their membership in a class, and the members of this class invoke or control a particular class name. For example, the denotative meaning of "horse" is derived from the observable physical properties that define membership in the class and include (but are not restricted to) four legs, furry coat, two ears, bushy tail, 8 feet in length, and 4 feet in height. The denotative meaning of "cup" includes (but is not restricted to) opaque, cylindrical, has handle, and contains fluid. Thus, denotative meaning involves a specification of the physical attributes of an object that define membership in a particular class of objects.

As indicated by Osgood and others (Osgood, Suci, & Tannenbaum, 1961), the measurement of connotative meaning can be made by setting up a system of polar adjectives, such as good-bad, fast-slow, and strong-weak, and then asking a person to rate terms such as "mother," "school," "snake," "work," "play," and "thinking" on a seven-point scale separating the polar adjectival extremes. The way that a person assigns adjective descriptions to a concept indicates to some extent the kind of personal interaction the rater has had with the objects and events assumed by that concept. While denotative meaning is related to the agreed-upon reference for a word in terms of the attributes of the object class named by the word, connotative meaning is the personal and individualized facet of meaning. Since the emphasis in the present chapter is on aspects of language training that pertain to public rather than personal use of language, only denotative meaning will be considered.

Once word acquisition begins, the growth of vocabulary is usually very rapid. Table 13.8 presents a summary of growth in vocabulary and other linguistic skills in the young child from 12 to 39 months, according to Lenneberg (1966). McNeill (1970) suggested two hypotheses for the acquisition of semantic features in children. *Horizontal acquisition* of semantic features refers to the sequential addition of new meanings for a word already in a child's vocabulary. For example, "fly"—meaning to glide through the sky, in a child's vocabulary—has certain semantic features which will have to be expanded when he encounters a small insect of the same name. *Vertical acquisition* of semantic features refers to simultaneous acquisition of a word and the majority of its semantic features; however, the word and each

Table 13.8
**Summary of Growth of Vocabulary and Other Linguistic Skills
in the Young Child**

Age (months)	Vocabulary and Other Linguistic Skills
12–18	A small number of "words;" follows simple commands and responds to "no."
18–21	From about 20 words at 18 months to about 200 words at 21 months; points to many more objects; comprehends simple questions; forms two-word phrases.
24–27	Vocabulary of 300 to 400 words; has two- to three-word phrases; uses prepositions and pronouns.
30–33	Fastest increase in vocabulary; three- to four-word sentences are common; word order, phrase structure, grammatical agreement, approximate language of surroundings, but many utterances are unlike anything an adult would say.
36–39	Vocabulary of 1,000 words or more; well-formed sentences, using complex grammatical rules, although certain rules have not yet been fully mastered; grammatical mistakes are much less frequent; about 90% comprehensibility.

Note. From "The Natural History of Language," by E. H. Lenneberg, in *The Genesis of Language,* edited by F. Smith and G. A. Miller. Copyright 1966 by M.I.T. Reprinted by permission of M.I.T. Press.

semantic feature which produces differential meaning are responded to independently by the child. Eventually the child consolidates the word and its various meanings into a unified semantic feature.

As McNeill (1970) suggested, either or both of the preceding hypotheses could account for semantic development. A review of earlier literature on the acquisition of meaning may be found in McCarthy (1954); however, the paucity of data then and now allows for little more than speculation. Menyuk (1969) and Reese and Lipsitt (1970) suggested that the acquisition of meaning is a complex process that must depend to a large extent on syntactic and situational contexts, since a word may have not only different referents within a class, but also across several classes.

Semantic development seems to follow a pattern of initially acquiring a single label for objects or events, then generalizing the use of that label to similar but inappropriate stimuli, and finally discriminating the application of the label or concept to only relevant objects or events. According to this pattern, the acquisition of word-environmental object or event association would seem to be the first step in semantic development, both in an expressive and a receptive sense. Initially, a young child relates a specific auditory signal (word) with a specific object(s) or event(s).

For example, "ball" refers to a round object which people often roll or throw. A baby probably learns to attach the label "ball" to a specific object because that specific word is very often elicited from the adult in the presence of that object. Further, when a baby searches in an area where the ball is generally located, the adult may say, "Oh, you want the ball." As these situations multiply, the child learns to associate the auditory signal "ball" not only with the object but also with the various environmental situations in which that word is likely to occur. Consequently, the child begins to expand the semantic features of the word "ball" from his first encounter with the object. When the child walks up to his mother and says, "Ball," his mother may respond by saying, "You want to find the ball so you can play," and may promptly help the child locate the ball. As the child continues to have encounters with ball-like objects as well as the word "ball," the number of semantic features surrounding the ball grows into a concept of "ball-ness." Often little children overgeneralize concepts, so that the child attaches the label "ball" to oranges, circles, potatoes, and the moon. Environmental feedback helps the child begin to restrict the application of a label only to appropriate objects or events and thus to develop conceptual classes.

Relevant Literature

Much of the literature on retardation and semantics concerns vocabulary assessment. Generally, these studies indicate that while mentally retarded subjects produce more verbal behavior than nonretarded subjects of the same mental age, their vocabularies—or the total different number of words produced—are much smaller (Mein & O'Connor, 1960; Wolfensberger, Mein, & O'Connor, 1963). Several investigations report significant correlation between vocabulary size and IQ or MA (Dunn, 1959; Irwin, 1966; Wolfensberger, Mein, & O'Connor, 1963).

A recent study (D. Bricker, Vincent-Smith, & W. Bricker, 1973) compared the performance of retarded and normal toddlers of matched CA on a task of receptive vocabulary. Twenty children were tested on their receptive knowledge of 20 common words. Each word was represented by a small, three-dimensional object. These objects were randomly paired and presented, using a two-choice discrimination situation. On each presentation, the correct object was labeled by the experimenter, and the child's task was to point to the labeled object. Each object was presented three times as the discriminative stimulus (DS) for a total of 60 trials, or three equal segments of 20 trials each. For analysis, the two groups of children were divided into subgroups of older (25 to 30 months) and younger (17 to 20 months) subjects. The overall performance of the older normal children was significantly better than that of the other three groups. Further, the older normal group demonstrated learning across the three segments of the test. The learning curves for the young normal subjects resembled the curves for both the younger and older retarded groups; and all three of these groups showed no learning across the three segments of the test.

Gardner and Gardner (1969) and Premack. (1970) presented some intriguing procedures and exciting results for training chimps to use language systems, which may have applicability to the field of developmental retardation. An approach similar to that of the Gardners was used by D. Bricker (1972) in studying the effects of imitative sign training on the acquisition of word-object associations by low-functioning institutionalized children. Imitative signs were found to facilitate the development of receptive vocabulary in the experimental group. A similar procedure in another study, however, failed to facilitate the acquisition of receptive vocabulary in a group of delayed toddlers (D. Bricker & W. Bricker, 1971). An earlier study by W. Bricker and D. Bricker (1970) compared two structured training procedures employing operant techniques with Hawthorne and do-nothing control conditions. Some of the subjects demonstrated a learning phenomenon during the pretest, which involved repeated presentation of the stimuli and reinforcement for correct responses. The structured training procedures were able to maintain the performance of these experimental subjects from pretest to posttest, while the control subjects showed regression. However, the training conditions were not associated with a substantial change in performance from pretest to posttest.

The fact that the results of the investigations to date are not particularly encouraging is probably a function of doubtful training procedures, lack of appropriate reinforcers, and negative effects of long-term institutionalization, rather than of the inability of retarded children to acquire word meaning. It is hoped that the training approach outlined below will serve as an impetus for investigating appropriate procedures for training semantics in language-deficient children.

Semantic Training

The behavioristic approach to meaning is relatively simple, since it involves a description of the relationship between particular objects and the verbal behavior of the speaker relative to the consequences for speaking provided by the listener. The process is operationalized best for objects, but essentially the same process applies to adjectives, verbs, prepositions, and adverbs.

The environment contains a large array of objects which have names. These objects are members of larger classes of objects that can be labeled in the same way, even though the other objects in the class may differ in important ways such as relative size, texture, and color, and in aspects of form, number, position, and composition. Language training in denotative meaning is a process of bringing the name of a particular class of objects such as cups, babies, horses, or apples under control of those attributes that define membership in the class. The child who is under the control of a sufficient number of these relevant attributes will correctly name members of the class and will use a different name for members of other classes of objects. However, even when using sophisticated attributes of discrimination and stimulus control, errors will result when two classes overlap considerably.

For example, the response "cups" usually occurs in the presence of objects that are opaque, cylindrical, hold liquids, and have a handle; but the response can occur alternately with the response "glasses" in the presence of objects that are opaque cylinders and which hold liquid but do not have handles. The response "mugs" may also overlap the class of stimuli associated with the response "cups" although the former term is generally restricted to examples of opaque cylinders that hold fluids and have handles, but which can contain 10 or more fluid ounces. Fortunately, this is not a large problem in a language community because both the speaker and the listener are under similar stimulus control and tend to make the same shifts in verbal behavior. Skinner (1957) discussed such cases of similar stimulus control and extended his examples to include metaphoric language usage. Problems in denotative meaning can occur when the child's naming responses are under the control of irrelevant attributes.

Consider the case when the speaker uses the name "horsie" in the presence of all four-legged, furry mammals larger than a German Shepherd dog, and the response "doggie" for all smaller animals. If a 3-year-old child classifies animals that way, the listener will respond without question, although with some humor perhaps. However, if a 10-year-old uses the same names in that combination of situations, he may be classifed as deviant. Similarly, if a child calls a pencil "stick," or every grown woman "mama," or couches "chairs," then his behavior indicates a need for corrective training. The correction may take several different forms, dependent upon the nature of the error.

In the cases just cited, there may be two problems. The child may not have a sufficient number of verbal responses (names for the number of discriminations he makes among the objects around him) or he may not have learned to make such discriminations. The former problem can be corrected by using verbal imitation training and then bringing the imitated response under the control of the object attributes, using a fading procedure. The latter problem can be corrected by using a discrimination training procedure in which members of different object classes are responded to differently (e.g., by selecting a member of the named class) and consequently producing differential reinforcement from the listener.

Consider the case of a child who does not name any object and who, when asked to take the dog or to point to the picture of the cat, takes the left object, the green object, or the large object. In such cases, the behavior of the child is under the control of irrelevant attributes rather than under partial control of some relevant components of the objects. Such responses to irrelevant attributes must be extinguished (not reinforced). This is accomplished by prompting the child to respond first to a particular member of a given object class (such as a picture of a small, brown, rough-haired dog) when requested to "Take the dog!" This might be done in the presence of a distracting object (picture) such as a larger, black, smooth-haired horse. If the child is responding to the size of the two figures or pictures, then this shift will detect the problem. Simultaneously it will offer the opportunity to extinguish the tendency to respond to the irrelevant dimension while differentially reinforcing responses to the relevant aspects of form. After criterion is reached for this object, a third size comparison can be used, followed by a fourth and fifth—until the child no longer responds to size as a relevant variable for making a choice. The same variations can be made for color and texture of the dog's fur, until the child is responding only to those aspects of the stimuli that define membership in the class "dog." This procedure can be used for all nounlike object names.

The preceding method can be recycled for training the class of adjective. In the example given above, the teacher could request the child to "Take the brown one!" This could be repeated along with prompting and differential reinforcement until the child took the brown dog five or more consecutive times without an error, at which time, a brown horse would then be contrasted with a black dog. This procedure would be recycled until the child selected the object according to color, regardless of the form, size, position, texture, number, or composition of the objects being compared. Other color contrasts could be made until the child could discriminate a number of color combinations and respond to the named color of the object in each case. The same approach could then be recycled for size ("Take the big one!"), or composition ("Take the wooden one!"). The training of the adjective properties of objects forms the basis of noun phrase expansion. When a person references an object, he can more specifically define the one he means by placing an increasing number of adjectives between the determiner and the lead noun. A child who is trained in the use of adjectives can thereby make more specific demands on his environment. However, he must first discriminate the elementary attributes before he can name the attributes or insert the names in an expanded noun phrase.

Action verbs require a different training paradigm in terms of how the actions are pictured, but it is still appropriate to conceptualize the actions as a set of physical attributes which define membership in a particular action class. Running, hitting, eating, sewing, writing, talking, or jumping are physical events that have a set of attributes, but which have the additional problem that the events are changing very rapidly. Within the space of a few seconds, walking can become running, and eating can change to talking. Consequently, still pictures or immovable object relationships will not provide complete or adequate stimulus situations for action-verb training. Video-tape, motion pictures, and live action are necessary for such training. Given this alteration in the training techniques, however, the procedure remains one of teaching the child to discriminate among the relevant attributes of the movements and subsequently to attach the correct action-naming responses to these discriminated stimuli. Verbal imitation, fading, and differential reinforcement can be used here, as in each of the other aspects of training denotative meaning.

The implications of this sequence of programmed events is that the training leads to a level of discriminated responding equivalent to "having the concept of . . .". If the child can respond to "horse," or "red," or "big" by discriminating the relevant attributes across stimuli, then the child should recognize each example of "horse," and he should differentiate horses from other nonhorse objects. Thus, the child shows he has the concept of "horse." In each case, the child must have been given enough examples of a class so that the necessary and sufficient relevant attributes control membership into a particular object-class. It is impossible to know if a child can classify all appropriate stimuli into a class. However, if the child names 10 horses as "horse," even though they differ in size, color, position, or composition, then it becomes reasonable to infer that the child can correctly name other alterations in the horse configuration.

Such training routines only begin to deal with the complexity of denotative meaning. The area of semantics overlaps phonology and syntax to a considerable degree, which makes the area even more complex. Minimal phonological alterations in an utterance can change the name such that "pin," "bin," and "shin" refer to different object classes. In addition, a blind Venetian is quite different from a Venetian blind. The statement, "The shooting of the hunters was horrible," could mean two different events. However, such complexities define adult language usage and have not been considered in this chapter.

GRAMMAR

The third component of language is grammar, or syntax, which refers to the rules that constitute and describe a language. These rules must allow for the production or "generation" of all grammatically correct sentences, and must differentiate these from all ungrammatical strings of words. Such production is consequently termed a *generative* (transformational) grammar. A grammar must identify the relationship of the various parts of the sentence, such as the subject of the verb and/or the object of the verb. In a generative grammar, the phrase structure can be described using a tree diagram as in Figure 13.3, showing the grammatical relationships among the parts of the sentence. The structure is generated using a set of "rewrite" rules. An arrow is used to specify a rewrite rule that moves the sentence from an ideational thought to a sequence of words.

For example, in Figure 13.3 the sentence, "A girl throws the ball," is rewritten as a noun phrase (NP) plus a verb phrase (VP). This rule is written as S → NP + VP. The list of rules to generate all the transformations in this sentence would be:

S	→ NP + VP
NP	→ Art + N
VP	→ V + NP
Art	→ the, a, etc.
N	→ girl, ball, etc.
V	→ hits, throws, pushes, etc.

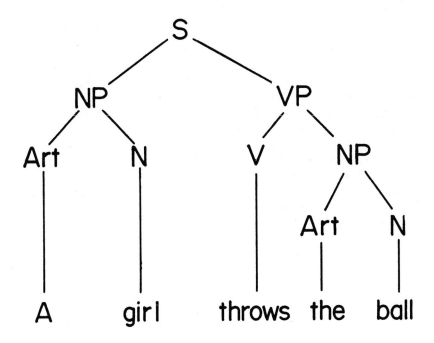

Figure 13.3.   Tree diagram or phrase structure of terminal string "A girl throws the ball."

Rewrite rules can be used to generate a large number of sentences in the English language, but this set of rules is not sufficient to generate all possible sentences in the language. Additional rules or "transformations" are necessary to account for all types of sentence production. Transformational rules specify how the terminal string may be modified to show such variations of a basic sentence as question, passive voice, negation, or past tense. A simplified one-step example of applying the transformational rules which change the sentence from active to passive voice would be:

Art + N + V + Art + N   Art + N + was + V + en + by + Art + N
The girl throws the ball   The ball was thrown   by the girl

A grammar accounts for sentence production through the functioning of three interrelated components: syntactic, semantic, and phonologic. The syntactic component consists of the phrase structure with its transformations. Thus, the syntactic component specifies both the underlying structure and the surface structure for each sentence, with the surface structure being derived from the deep structure by the series of transformations. The tree diagram, or phrase structure, is composed of the kernel sentence, while the surface structure is the utterance heard by the listener; the speaker can move from the deep structure to the surface structure by applying relevant transformational rules, as illustrated in the following example:

Surface Structure   →   The ball was hit by the boy

                                    Transformation
                                    (Passive)

Deep Structure   →   The boy hit the ball

The best support for the rule-forming ability of children comes from a study of their utterances, especially their errors. For example, a child might say, "I hurted my foots," which was probably not a learned response. The child made the error because he had not mastered all the rules governing past tense and plural usage. In the example above, the child probably learned the regular rules but not the exceptions. Berko's insightful study (1958) illustrated how young children grasp such rules. The children had no trouble pointing out that if this "thing" was a "wug," then two of them would be "wugs" and that they were doing something very "wugily." Adults rarely teach children to say "mouses" or "maked" or other frequent responses that children produce by applying rules for a regular form to an irregular grammatical form.

Table 13.9
Grammatical Development

Steps	Response Units	Linguistic Description
Step 1	BA	Phoneme
Step 2	BALL	Morpheme or meaningful unit
Step 3	BALL . . . ROLL	String of morphemes
Step 4	ROLL (verb) BALL (object)	Two-word utterance (topic comment)
Step 5	MAMA (subj.) ROLL (verb) BALL (object)	Expanded by adding subject
Step 6	MAMA (subj.) ROLL (verb) THE (art.) BALL (object)	Expanded by adding modifier
Step 7	MAMA (subj.) ROLLS (verb) THE (art.) BALL (object)	Inflectional ending added
Step 8	MAMA (subj.) ROLLS (verb) THE (art.) BALL (object) TO (ob.) JOHN (prep. phrase)	Expanded by transformation of kernel sentence

Grammatical Development

Once the child has acquired a few single words, he begins stringing words, or morphemes, together. Initially, these words have no relationship, and consequently they are not considered to be syntactical constructions. Lois Bloom (1970) suggested that during this phase the word order is variable, and the words occur with intervening junctures; for example, a child saying, "door . . . open." At approximately 14 to 17 months of age, a toddler begins putting words together and thereby approximates grammatical relations which are the beginning of syntactical development.

Table 13.9 presents our attempt to illustrate how children acquire the response units that terminate in grammatically appropriate sentences. In Step 1 the child acquires a phoneme which he can consistently reproduce, and by Step 2 the child has expanded the phoneme to a meaningful unit of speech, "ball." For the verbal response "ball" to be a meaningful unit, the child must demonstrate that he is consistently labeling a specific environmental object or event. If the child calls mama, books, cars, balls, and swings, "ball" then "ball" cannot be classified as a morpheme. In Step 3 the child is uttering two words, but there is no underlying grammatical relationship between these words. Often the toddler can be observed naming objects in a room rather than attempting to communicate a relationship between objects, event, or activities.

Step 4 is defined by the child putting two words together so that the relationship between the objects, events, or activities is communicated. For example, "roll ball" is emitted by the child as he rolls the ball across the floor. Bloom (1970) called this form of behavior "topic comment." In this instance the topic is the ball and the comment is roll. One has only to listen to a toddler to find many examples of topic-comment behavior such as car (topic) go (comment), baby (topic) up (comment), and mama (topic) shoe (comment). During this step, the child begins using his first syntactic structures. Development appears to proceed from here by adding new grammatical components, which are illustrated in the subsequent steps.

In Step 5 the child begins adding a subject so the verbal sequences produced are some variation of subject-verb-object, such as "daddy go car," "baby sleep bed," or "John sit chair." By Step 6 the child is beginning to add various modifiers, which make his utterances more grammatically correct. During Step 6, a child also develops the ability to use simple transformations such as passive voice, question, and negation. The child has added the use of inflectional endings in Step 7. An analysis of the acquisition of grammatical inflections for verbs suggests the development follows a somewhat orderly progression. The child begins by using some irregular past-tense forms in sentences (e.g., "did"). Next the child begins using regular past tense with familiar verbs (e.g., "played"), and during this stage the child often applies the regular past tense to irregular verbs (e.g., "doed"). Eventually the child learns to apply regular and irregular forms to the appropriate verbs. Step 8 represents the addition of the more sophisticated elements of syntax. Such addition allows for great flexibility and variation in communication for the child who reaches this stage of language development.

The developmental sequence presented in Table 13.9 is a hypothetical representation of how children may acquire complex sentence production. Only future investigations, using young children from a variety of economic and cultural backgrounds, will determine the validity of the content and sequence presented.

Relevant Literature

Research literature on the grammatical development of persons labeled mentally retarded is notably scarce. One of the earliest relevant studies (Mein, 1961) analyzed speech samples of 40 institutionalized, severely subnormal patients in terms of classes of words used and the proportion of words in each class. Four "conversational" interviews and five "picture description" interviews were conducted with each subject. A uniform language sample was taken from each type of interview. Oral and recognition vocabularies were found to differ, the recognition vocabularies (those used to describe pictures) being heavily weighted in favor of nouns and, to some extent, articles. An increase in mental age was associated with a decrease in the percentage of nouns. This was consistent with studies of normal language development from ages 1 to 3 years, a period characterized by a progressive decrease in the percentage of nouns, with a concomitant increase in the proportion of verbs. Mein also compared the performance of children with Down's Syndrome with that of other retarded subjects and found that the former subjects used significantly more nouns in describing pictures, while the latter subjects used significantly more articles.

The grammatical performance of retarded and normal children was compared by Lovell and Dixon (1967), Lyle (1961), and Sampson (1964). The latter investigator analyzed several aspects of the conversation of retarded children, including a summary of the grammatical word classes used. Sampson conducted extensive interviews with 10 severely subnormal children (CA 7 to 13, mean MA = 3.9). When the proportions of word classes found in their speech samples were analyzed and compared to studies of normal children of approximately equal mental ages, a reversal of the noun and verb proportions was found between the two groups, with the retarded children using a larger proportion of nouns and a smaller proportion of verbs. The study also looked at relative proportions of word classes in the total vocabularies of the children and found a balance similar to that reported for normal children. Sampson (1964) suggested that the proportions of word classes in the retarded children's speech samples may have been distorted by their repetitiousness and use of short sentences. In the analysis of speech samples for utterance length, it was found that all the children were capable of using structured two-word utterances that would be characteristic of a normal child's speech around the age of 2 years. The majority of the children managed some five-word sentences, and two of the children produced sentences of 10 to 11 words. The mean length across all subjects was 2.61 words per utterance.

An earlier study by Lyle (1961) used a language test to compare 58 day-school retarded children (mean nonverbal IQ = 36.74) with a group of nonretarded children matched on the basis of nonverbal mental age. A language test was given to all children involving comprehension of familiar names, naming of familiar objects, definitions of words, imitation of speech sounds as contained in simple words, and language complexity (grammatical accuracy and complexity) in describing pictures and answering standard questions about pictures. A significant difference in favor of the normal children was found in language complexity scores. In addition, the retarded children were more delayed, relative to the normal children, on the complexity measure than on any of the other measures taken.

Lovell and Dixon (1967) examined specific grammatical skills in 100 normal children between the ages of 2 and 6 years and in 80 educationally subnormal (ESN) children between the ages of 6 and 7 years. All children were tested with a modified form of the Imitation, Comprehension, and Production Test developed by Fraser, Bellugi, and Brown (1963). The results indicated that for both the normal and retarded children at all ages, correct responses occurred most frequently on the imitation task, followed in difficulty by the comprehension task, with the most errors occurring on the production task. The mean score differences between imitation, comprehension, and production tasks were significant at all age levels. Lovell and Dixon reported that "the overall performance of the 6-year-old ESN pupil is almost exactly the same as that of normal 3-year-olds, while the 7-year-old ESN child responds much as the 4-year-olds" (1967, p. 38). Consequently, the latter study and those of Sampson (1964) and Lyle (1961) all provide some evidence that the retarded child's use of grammar is similar to the performance of a younger normal child, and is not qualitatively different in terms of the developmental sequence or specific content.

The most recent literature has approached the analysis of the grammatical development of retarded subjects from a transformational theoretical viewpoint. For example, Semmel and Dolley (1971) studied comprehension and imitation of sentences in 40 children with Down's Syndrome, ranging from 6 to 14 years of age, with a mean IQ of 34.3. The sentences used were categorized as kernel, negative, passive, and negative-passive transformational types. Comprehension of passive and negative-passive sentences—as measured in a two-choice test situation—was at chance level, while the comprehension of kernel sentences was significantly above chance, and the comprehension of sentences containing the negative transformation was significantly below chance. Those authors suggest that there may have been semantic difficulties with comprehension of negative sentences. In the imitation task, the passive and negative-passive sentences were truncated to roughly equate all sentence types in length. The kernel sentences were correctly imitated significantly more than were the transformed sentences, as would be predicted by transformational theory.

In a related study, Graham and Graham (1971) made a transformational analysis of the speech samples of nine institutionalized retarded males ranging in CA from 10 through 18 years, and in MA from 3½ through 10 years. All sentences in the language sample of each subject were rewritten as a kernel construction, and then a set of transformational rules was derived to recover the surface structure. A deletion error rate was computed for required lexical items omitted in each subject's speech sample. An analysis revealed that use of transformations is related to MA. Those subjects with low MAs had a tendency to produce kernal sentences, while subjects with higher MAs produced sentences with transformations.

The introduction of transformational analysis has led to an interesting debate concerning the innate learning of language. This debate is responsible for producing a series of investigations demonstrating the development of specific generative rules in retarded children as a function of environmental manipulations. Three of these studies were concerned with the acquisition of morphological rules. Guess, Sailor, Rutherford, and Baer (1968) used an experimental behavior analysis design in teaching discriminative use of the plural morpheme to a 10-year-old institutionalized retarded girl. She was trained to emit singular responses to the presentation of a single object and to add the phoneme /s/ or /z/ upon presentation of a pair of like objects. This behavior generalized to the labeling of three like objects using a plural inflection, and the subject also applied the generalized rule to words requiring irregular plurals.

A second study by Guess (1969) used a similar design in training two institutionalized boys with Down's Syndrome in a receptive and an expressive task employing plural morphemes. Receptive comprehension was found to function independently of expressive labeling. When reinforcement contingencies were reversed for the receptive task, but not for the expressive task, the discriminative behavior of the two boys reversed for the receptive task and not for the expressive one. Schumaker and Sherman (1970) reported a similar investigation in which three retarded adolescents were trained to use past and present progressive verb-tense forms appropriately. The experimental procedure employed imitation and differential reinforcement. Each of the subjects was trained using specific verbs, but each was tested with a series of novel or untrained verbs. The data indicated that the subjects learned to apply appropriate generative inflectional rules to untrained verbs as well as to trained verbs. The results of these three investigations support the position that at least limited generative grammatical rules can be acquired by retarded subjects through the manipulation of environmental contingencies.

Although operating within the operant framework, Stremel (1972) developed a more molar language-training program than did the studies of Guess et al. (1968), Guess (1969), and Shumaker and Sherman (1970). Three moderately to severely retarded children were trained sequentially on verb production, subject-verb production, and subject-verb-object production. According to Stremel, the posttest evaluation of the three subjects indicated an increase over their pretest performance in the number of subject-verb-object responses to pictures.

Another orientation was used in a training study conducted by Talkington and Hall (1970). Forty institutionalized subjects with Down's Syndrome were matched and then randomly assigned to either an experimental or control group. All subjects were pretested on language and concepts, the language portion of the test being subdivided into the areas of (a) prepositions, (b) articles, (c) sentences, (d) plurals, (e) shapes, and (f) colors. The experimental group received language instruction using a program called Matrix Games. For an equal amount of time, the subjects in the control group were involved in a music activity. The experimental group showed gains over the control groups in all language areas, but the difference was significant only for the subtest of sentences and for total performance on all language items.

Although the review of the literature presented here is not all-inclusive, it is representative of the information currently available on training procedures and descriptions of grammatical behavior of moderately to severely retarded children. The major conclusions to be drawn from this literature are: (a) The retarded person is clearly deficient in the comprehension and production of appropriate morphological and syntactic constructions; and (b) programmed training procedures have produced systematic and enouragingly positive results. The challenge for the future lies in building more efficient and effective molar training programs for the majority of the low-functioning language-deficient children.

Syntactic Training

A grammar can be thought of as a set of rules which can be used to describe a specific language. Building a program for training grammar is probably the most difficult task of remediating language deficiencies. A generative grammar assumes that the child can apply appropriate syntax or morphologic changes to familiar as well as to novel strings of words. Applying grammatical rules to strings of words is a complex form of behavior because the individual must be able to (a) combine phonological and semantic units of language into an ordered combination of these units, (b) vary these content elements to fit the environmental situation, and (c) rearrange these elements when the environment shifts.

The training program described below for teaching a skeletal grammar to severe language-deficient children is based on a behavioral-linguistic approach described by Lynch and Bricker (1972). The training program is designed to build a rudimentary grammar that will allow a child to express his basic needs and describe simple environmental events. This program is restricted to training kernel sentences and does not attempt to deal with training transformations. A grammatical training program is of limited success unless the child learns to generalize a response to novel but appropriate stimuli. Consequently, this program is concerned with the acquisition of general rulelike responses; therefore, probes are systematically presented during training to ascertain if and when generalization occurs. The application of this training program assumes that the child has the prerequisite skills of both comprehension and production of a core vocabulary. A child should not be expected to sequence words if he cannot produce them in isolation. The words included in the grammar training program must be not only useful, but also those that the child spontaneously produces and receptively understands. A generalized verbal imitation repertoire is also essential for initial training in this program. Since the teacher begins training by providing an echoic model for the child to imitate, a nonimitating child is inappropriate for the program.

The primary goal of a syntax training program is not to develop immutable strings of words but to allow the child to acquire the grammatical rules that provide the organizational system for the generation of a series of sentences appropriate to his language community. This, of course, is an extremely complex and difficult task, and the present training system is only an approximation. However, the behavioral-linguistic approach presented by Lynch and Bricker (1972) holds some promise, since it derives the teaching methodology from the experimental analysis of behavior and the content of the program from the field of linguistics. The training program has been divided into three stages, with the content of each stage generated by linguistic data (Bloom, 1970). These stages are (a) two-word actor-action sequences for expressing simple wants and environmental events such as "baby bye bye" or "dog sleeps"; (b) two-word action-object sequences to express simple environmental happenings such as "hide shoe"; and (c) three-word actor-action-object propositions to express simple kernel sentences such as "boy wants car."

This approach or sequence of steps has at least three deficiencies. First, the three stages are concerned with only the rudimentary form of grammatical production. Second, the sequence and content may not be valid for many children. Finally, the sequence suggests an artificial approach to training language. Resolutions for the first two deficiencies await the acquisition of data that will provide the basis for the development of more comprehensive and appropriate programs. The collection and analysis of this information will take time. The third deficiency can be solved by each language trainer's ability to develop complex verbal skills in the context of meaningful activities rather than as isolated units that have no connection with the remainder of the child's repertoire (W. Bricker & D. Bricker, 1974).

Once the linguistic content has been specified, the training methodology can be outlined. Principles of operant conditioning, such as shaping, differential reinforcing, prompting, and fading are used to shape the appropriate linguistic content into the child's repertoire. Assuming the child is under stimulus control, imitating and producing one-word utterances, a pretest is administered to determine the child's repertoire of three-word utterances, since this is the terminal state of the program. Following assessment, training could follow a sequence such as that outlined below:

> Step 1 The teacher performs an activity that is of interest to the child, such as hiding a ball, and then asks, "What did I do?" The teacher then provides the appropriate echoic model, "hide ball," for the child.
>
> Step 2 The teacher says, while hiding the ball, "What am I doing? Say ." If the child does not respond appropriately, the teacher prompts with the correct response, "hide ball."
>
> Step 3 The teacher begins to fade the echoic model. The teacher performs the activity and asks, "What happened?" If the child does not respond appropriately, the teacher says, "hide___" and waits for the child to reply "ball."
>
> Step 4 The teacher may let the child perform the activity and then ask, "What did you do?" The child should respond, "hide ball."

Notice that the form of the teacher's question changes from time to time rather than using the same eliciting phrase. Also important, in order to maximize the generalizability of the statement for the child, is changing the location of the hiding place, the manner of hiding, and the ball that is being hidden. Once "hide ball" is produced spontaneously, the object hidden should be shifted and the training recycled. The object should continue to be changed and training resumed until the child can spontaneously produce the appropriate action-object sequence on the first trial. Then training on a second verb or action word should be initiated.

A complete and detailed specification of a syntax training program has not been possible in this section. However, an attempt has been made to discuss the theoretical base of such a program, the general content, and the procedures for eliciting that content from a given child.

SUMMARY

The purpose of this chapter has been to present some of the fundamental issues that currently face those who are attempting language training with significantly impaired children. An attempt was made to present and briefly discuss the major component of a language system using a behavioral-linguistic model. The description of phonology, semantics, and syntax suggests that acquisition of these skills follows a relatively predictable hierarchical developmental pattern and, perhaps more importantanly, that these various language components can be taught to children with severe verbal deficits. Finally, with the knowledge that an adequate empirical base for programming language training does not exist, an attempt has been made to sketch out a basic strategy for training the necessary language components of phonetics, semantics, and syntax. The content of the suggested training program has been generated from linguistic, data, while the method of training is based on principles of behavior generated from the experimental analysis of behavior.

REFERENCES

Baer, D. M., Peterson, R. F., & Sherman, J. A. The development of imitation by reinforcing behavioral similarity to a model. *Journal of the Experimental Analysis of Behavior,* 1967, *10,* 405-416.

Baer, D. M., & Sherman, J. A. Reinforcement control of generalized imitation in young children. *Journal of Experimental Child Psychology,* 1964, *1,* 37-49.

Ball, T. Training generalized imitation: Variations on an historical theme. *American Journal of Mental Deficiency,* 1970, *75,* 135-141.

Barton, E. S. Inappropriate speech in a severely retarded child. *Journal of Applied Behavior Analysis*, 1970, *3*, 299-307.

Bennett, F. W. Ward language development program for institutionalized retardates. *Training School Bulletin*, 1969, *66*, 23-31.

Berko, J. The child's learning of English morphology. *Word*, 1958, *14*, 150-177.

Bloom, L. *Language development: Form and function in emerging grammars.* Cambridge, Mass.: The M.I.T. Press, 1970.

Blount, W. R. Language and the more severely retarded: A review. *American Journal of Mental Deficiency*, 1968, *73*, 21-29.

Bradley, B. H., Maurer, R., & Hundziak, M. A study of the effectiveness of milieu therapy and language training for the mentally retarded. *Exceptional Children*, 1966, *33*, 143-150.

Bricker, D. D. Imitative sign training as a facilitator of word-object association with low-functioning children. *American Journal of Mental Deficiency*, 1972, *76*, 509-516.

Bricker, D. D., & Bricker, W. A. Toddler research and intervention project report: Year I. *IMRID Monograph No. 20*, 1971. (Available from George Peabody College, Nashville, Tenn.)

Bricker, D. D., Vincent-Smith, L., & Bricker, W. A. Receptive vocabulary: Performances and selection strategies of delayed and nondelayed toddlers. *American Journal of Mental Deficiency*, 1973, 77, 579-584.

Bricker, W. A. Errors in the echoic behavior of preschool children. *Journal of Speech and Hearing Research*, 1967, *10*, 67-76.

Bricker, W. A., & Bricker, D. D. The use of programmed language training as a means for differential diagnosis and educational remediation among severely retarded children. *Peabody Papers in Human Development*, 1966, *4*(5—entire issue). (Available from George Peabody College, Nashville, Tenn.)

Bricker, W. A., & Bricker, D. D. Development of receptive vocabulary in severely retarded children. *American Journal of Mental Deficiency*, 1970, *74*, 599-607.

Bricker, W. A., & Bricker, D. D. Assessment and modification of verbal imitation with low-functioning retarded children. *Journal of Speech and Hearing Research*, 1972, *15*, 690-698.

Bricker, W. A., & Bricker, D. D. An early language training strategy. In R. Schiefelbusch and L. Lloyd (Eds.), *Language perspectives—Acquisition, retardation, and intervention.* Baltimore: University Park Press, 1974, pp. 429-468.

Buddenhagen, R. G. *Establishing vocal verbalizations in mute mongoloid children.* Champaign, Ill.: Research Press Co., 1971.

Carroll, J. B. Language development in children. In S. Saporta (Ed.),

Psycholinguistics: A book of readings. New York: Holt, Rinehart, and Winston, 1961, pp. 331-345.

Catania, A. C. Reinforcement schedules: The role of responses preceding the one that produces the reinforcer. *Journal of the Experimental Analysis of Behavior,* 1971, *15,* 271-287.

Chomsky, N., & Halle, M. *The sound pattern of English.* New York: Harper & Row, 1968.

Chomsky, N., & Miller, G. A. Introduction to the formal analysis of natural languages. In R. D. Luce, R. R. Bush, and E. Galanter (Eds.), *Handbook of mathematical psychology* (Vol. II). New York Wiley, 1963, pp. 269-321.

Creelman, M. *The experimental investigation of meaning.* New York: Springer, 1966.

Dunn, L. M. *Peabody Picture Vocabulary Test.* Minneapolis: American Guidance Service, 1959.

Dunn, L. M., & Bruininks, R. H. Efficacy of the Peabody language development kits and the initial teaching alphabet with southern disadvantaged children in the primary grades: A follow-up report after the fourth grade. *IMRID Papers and Reports,* 1968, *5*(14—entire issue). (Available from George Peabody College, Nashville, Tenn.)

Dunn, L. M., Neville, D., Bailey, C. F., Pochanart, P., & Pfost, P. The effectiveness of three reading approaches and an oral language stimulation program with disadvantaged children in the primary grades: An interim report after one year of the Cooperative Reading Project. *IMRID Monograph No. 7,* 1967. (Available from George Peabody College, Nashville, Tenn.)

Fraser, C., Bellugi, U., & Brown, R. Control of grammar in imitation, comprehension and production. *Journal of Verbal Learning and Verbal Behavior,* 1963, *2,* 121-135.

Foxx, R. M., & Azrin, N. H. Restitution: A method of eliminating aggressive-disruptive behavior of retarded and brain damaged patients. *Behaviour Research and Therapy,* 1972, *10,* 15-27.

Gardner, R., & Gardner, B. Teaching sign language to a chimpanzee. *Science,* 1969, *165,* 664-672.

Gewirtz, J. L., & Stingle, K. G. Learning of generalized imitation as the basis for identification. *Psychological Review,* 1968, *75,* 374-397.

Graham, J. T., & Graham, L. W. Language behavior of the mentally retarded: Syntactic characteristics. *American Journal of Mental Deficiency,* 1971, *75,* 623-629.

Guess, D. A functional analysis of receptive language and productive speech: Acquisition of plural morpheme. *Journal of Applied Behavior Analysis,* 1969, *2,* 55-64.

Guess, D., Sailor, W., Rutherford, G., & Baer, D. M. An experimental analysis of linguistic development: The productive use of the plural morpheme. *Journal of Applied Behavior Analysis,* 1968, *1,* 297-306.

Heber, R., & Garber, H. *An experiment in the prevention of cultural-familial mental retardation.* Madison, Wis.: Rehabilitation Research and Training Center in Mental Retardation, University of Wisconsin, 1970.

Irwin, O. C. Infant speech: Equations for consonant-vowel ratios. *Journal of Speech Disorders,* 1946, *11,* 177-180.

Irwin, O. C. Infant speech: Consonantal sounds according to place of articulation. *Journal of Speech Disorders,* 1947, *12,* 397-401.

Irwin, O. C. Infant speech: Development of vowel sounds. *Journal of Speech and Hearing Disorders,* 1948, *13,* 34-34.

Irwin, O. C. A comparison of the vocabulary of use and of understanding by mentally retarded children. *Cerebral Palsy Journal,* 1966, *27,* 8-10.

Jakobson, R., Fant, C. G., & Halle, M. *Preliminaries to speech analysis: The distinctive features and their correlates* (2nd ed.). Cambridge, Mass.: The M.I.T. Press, 1963.

Jeffrey, D. B. Increase and maintenance of verbal behavior of a mentally retarded child. *Mental Retardation,* 1972, *10*(2), 35-40.

Jordan, T. E. Language and mental retardation: A review of the literature. In R. L. Schiefelbusch, R. H. Copeland, and J. O. Smith (Eds.), *Language and mental retardation.* New York: Holt, Rinehart and Winston, 1967, pp. 20-38.

Kolstoe, O. P. Language training of low grade mongoloid children. *American Journal of Mental Deficiency,* 1958, *63,* 17-30.

Larsen, L. A., & Bricker, W. A. A manual for parents and teachers of severely and moderately retarded children. *IMRID Papers and Reports,* 1968, *5*(22—entire issue). (Available from George Peabody College, Nashville, Tenn.)

Lassers, L., & Low, G. *A study of the relative effectiveness of different approaches of speech therapy for mentally retarded children: Final report.* Washington, D.C.: U.S. Office of Education, Cooperative Research Program #6904, 1960.

Lenneberg, E. H. The natural history of language. In F. Smith and G. A. Miller (Eds.), *The genesis of language.* Cambridge, Mass.: The M.I.T. Press, 1966, pp. 219-252.

Lenneberg, E. H. *Biological foundations of language.* New York: Wiley, 1967.

Lloyd, L. L. You've come a long way baby, but—. *Mental Retardation,* 1972, *10*(2), 2.

Lovaas, O. I. A behavior therapy approach to the treatment of childhood schizophrenia. In J. P. Hill (Ed.), *Minnesota symposia on child psychology* (Vol. I). Minneapolis: The University of Minnesota Press, 1967, pp. 108-159.

Lovaas, O. I. A program for the establishment of speech in psychotic children. In H. Sloane and B. MacAulay (Eds.), *Operant procedures in remedial speech and language training.* Boston: Houghton Mifflin, 1968, pp. 125-154.

Lovell, K., & Dixon, E. M. The growth of the control of grammar in imitation, comprehension, and production. *Journal of Child Psychology and Psychiatry,* 1967, *8,* 31-39.

Lubman, D. Speech program for severely retarded children. *American Journal of Mental Deficiency,* 1955, *60,* 297-300.

Lyle, J. G. The effect of an institution environment upon the verbal development of imbecile children: III. The Brooklands residential family unit. *Journal of Mental Deficiency Research,* 1960, *4,* 14-23.

Lyle, J. G. Comparison of the language of normal and imbecile children. *Journal of Mental Deficiency Research,* 1961, *5,* 40-51.

Lynch, J., & Bricker, W. A. Linguistic theory and operant procedures. *Mental Retardation,* 1972, *10*(2), 12-16.

MacCubrey, J. Verbal operant conditioning with young institutionalized Down's Syndrome children. *American Journal of Mental Deficiency,* 1971, *75,* 696-701.

McCarthy, D. Language development in children. In L. Carmichael (Ed.), *Manual of child psychology.* New York: Wiley, 1954, pp. 492-630.

McNeill, D. *The acquisition of language: The study of developmental psycholinguistics,* New York: Harper & Row, 1970.

Mecham, M. J. The development and application of procedures for measuring speech improvement in mentally defective children. *American Journal of Mental Deficiency,* 1955, *60, 301-306.*

Mein, R. A study of the oral vocabularies of severely subnormal patients: II. Grammatical analysis of speech samples. *Journal of Mental Deficiency Research,* 1961, *5,* 52-59.

Mein, R., & O'Connor, N. A study of the oral vocabularies of severely subnormal patients. *Journal of Mental Deficiency Research,* 1960, *4,* 130-143.

Menyuk, P. *Sentences children use.* Cambridge, Mass.: The M.I.T. Press, 1969.

Metz, J. R. Conditioning generalized imitation in autistic children. *Journal of Experimental Child Psychology,* 1965, *2,* 389-399.

Miller, G. A. *Language and communication.* New York: McGraw-Hill, 1951.

Osgood, C. E., Suci, G., & Tannenbaum, P. The logic of semantic differentiation. In S. Saporta (Ed.), *Psycholinguistics: A book of readings.* New York: Holt, Rinehart and Winston, 1961, pp. 283-300.

Premack, D. A functional analysis of language. *Journal of the Experimental Analysis of Behavior,* 1970, *14,* 107-125.

Reese H. W., & Lipsitt, L. P. *Experimental child psychology.* New York:

Academic Press, 1970.

Reynolds, G. S. *A primer of operant conditioning.* Glenville, Ill.: Scott, Foresman, 1968.

Rhodes, L., Gooch, B., Siegelman, E. Y., Behrns, C. A., & Metzger, R. A language stimulation and reading program for severely retarded mongoloid children: A descriptive report. *California Mental Health Monograph, No. 11,* 1969.

Risley, T. R. The establishment of verbal behavior in deviant children. Paper presented at the meeting of the American Association on Mental Deficiency, Chicago, Ill., May 1966.

Sampson, O. C. The conversational style of a group of severely subnormal children. *Journal of Mental Subnormality,* 1964, *10,* 89-100.

Schick, K. Operants. *Journal of the Experimental Analysis of Behavior,* 1971, *15,* 413-423.

Schlanger, B. B. Speech therapy results with mentally retarded children in special classes. *Training School Bulletin,* 1953, *50,* 179-186.

Schneider, B., & Vallon, J. The results of a speech therapy program for mentally retarded children. *American Journal of Mental Deficiency,* 1955, *59,* 417-424.

Schumaker, J., & Sherman, J. A. Training generative verb usage by imitation and reinforcement procedures. *Journal of Applied Behavior Analysis,* 1970, *3,* 273-287.

Semmel, M. I., & Dolley, D. G. Comprehension and imitation of sentences by Down's Syndrome children as a function of transformational complexity. *American Journal of Mental Deficiency,* 1971, *75,* 739-745.

Skinner, B. F. *Verbal behavior.* New York: Appleton-Century-Crofts, 1957.

Smith, F., & Miller, G. A. (Eds.) *The genesis of language.* Cambridge, Mass.: The M.I.T. Press, 1966.

Smith, J. O. Group language development for educable mental retardates. In R. L. Jones (Ed.), *New directions in special education.* Boston: Allyn & Bacon, 1970, pp. 154-164.

Stremel, K. Language training. *Mental Retardation,* 1972, *10*(2), 47-49.

Talkington, L. W., & Hall, S. M. Matrix language program with mongoloids. *American Journal of Mental Deficiency,* 1970, *75,* 88-91.

Ullmann, L. P., & Krasner, L. (Eds.) *Case studies in behavior modification.* New York: Holt, Rinehart and Winston, 1965.

Ulrich, R., Stachnik, T., & Mabry, J. (Eds.). *Control of human behavior.* Glenview, Ill: Scott, Foresman, 1966.

Voelker, C. H. Phonetic distribution in formal American pronunciation. *Journal of the Acoustical Society of America,* 1934, *5,* 242-246.

West R., Ansberry, M., & Carr, A. *The rehabilitation of speech* (3rd ed.). New York: Harper & Row, 1957.

Winitz, H. *Articulatory acquisition and behavior.* New York: Appleton-Century-Crofts, 1969.

Wolfensberger, W., Mein, R., & O'Connor, N. A study of the oral vocabularies of severely subnormal patients: III. Core vocabulary, verbosity, and repetitiousness. *Journal of Mental Deficiency Research,* 1963, *7,* 38-45.

Manny Sternlicht and Irv Bialer biographical information: see page 2.

14

Psychological aspects of institutionalization in mental retardation

Manny Sternlicht and Irv Bialer

DELINEATION OF THE ISSUES

The current twin *Zeitgeists* of de-institutionalization and normalization are based, to some extent, upon the genuine concern that institutionalization may have adverse effects on child development and behavior, and (to a considerably larger extent) upon the concept that residential living is at best depersonalizing and at worst dehumanizing to retarded individuals. The latter notion in particular has been fostered (not without some justification) by dedicated workers such as Blatt (1969, 1970, 1973) and Wolfensberger (1969a, 1972). The *Zeitgeist* of de-institutionalization is also served by such "exposés" as that of Braginsky and Braginsky (1971), who hold forth the premise that institutions for mentally retarded people are nothing more than large-scale facilities for the collection of individuals unneeded and discarded by our society. Wolfensberger (1969a) called this phenomenon "warehousing."

Wolfensberger, in one of a series of articles predicting that the "institution," as we know it today, will disappear (1969b) under the combined impact of epidemiological trends (1971a) and new residential service models (1971b), made the point that the features commonly associated with any institution seem to be corollaries of "deindividualization" rather than of those features which emphasize separateness from the community mainstream (1971a). Consequently, Wolfensberger defined the mental retardation institution as:

> A deindividualizing residence in which retarded persons are congregated in numbers distinctly larger than might be found in a

> large family; in which they are highly regimented; in which the
> physical or social environment aims at a low common
> denominator; and in which all or most of the transactions of daily
> life are carried out under one roof, on one campus, or in a largely
> segregated fashion. (1971a, p. 15)

The arguments put forth by the extreme critics of institutionalization of the
mentally retarded individual seem logical, forceful, and persuasive. Also, one
must accept the eventuatlity that residential services, as presently constituted,
will be phased out in favor of new service models such as those discussed by
Wolfensberger (1971b) and by the present authors below. Nor can one ignore
the fact that the bulk of research evidence points to the superiority of home
rearing over that of the institution (Butterfield, 1967).

Nevertheless, as Butterfield (1969) pointed out, more than 200,000
people in this country (of whom nearly half are children) now reside in over
150 public institutions for mentally retarded residents. In addition, there are
at least 31,000 persons on waiting lists, or 2.5 individuals waiting for every
vacancy that arises (Baumeister, 1970). Consequently, the notion that all
present forms of institutional programs are de-individualizing, depersonalizing,
and dehumanizing (i.e., that the *psychological effects* of such residential
programming are all negative) needs to be examined from a pragmatic
standpoint.

In an effort to accumulate data pertinent to such an examination,
Zigler and his colleagues have been engaged in a long series of investigations
and theoretical explorations (see Zigler, 1973). Their work has been guided
by two major assumptions: (a) Different institutions have different effects on
retarded children relegated to their care; and (b) a given institution may
affect children differentially as a function of the personality dynamics of
given children—such dynamics having been determined in large part by the
r⸱sident's pre-institutional history.

In reporting their most recent study, Balla, Butterfield, and Zigler
(1974) reiterated the point that:

> What has perhaps been underemphasized is that insitutionaliza-
> tion may have [some] beneficial effects. . . . Furthermore, the
> condition of institutionalization . . . does not constitute a
> homogeneous psychological variable, but at best refers to the
> demographic status of a child. *More caution is in order before one*
> *can speak of the effects of institutionalization.* Until workers
> discover the particular social-psychological phenomena [which
> determine the behavior and characteristics of the resi-
> dents] . . ., it is difficult to assert that institutionalization will

have some common effect regardless of the particular institution in which the retarded child finds himself. (p. 531; italics added).

In the same vein, Klaber (1969), in discussing the diverse characteristics of the six facilities involved in his study on the differential properties of institutional systems for the retarded resident noted:

> The more detailed our descriptions became, the more different the facilities appeared. The closer we observed the ward routine, the greater the individual quality of the ward experience became evident. The more involved we became in the institutional management, the more untenable became the assumed generality of the institutional experience. (p. 150)

Specifically, with respect to the relationship between the institutional experience and post-institutional adjustment in the community, Heber and Dever (1970, drawing largely on the work of Windle (1962) and of Edgerton (1967), concluded:

> If patients in institutions are to be discharged and adjust successfully, we must devise programs of education and rehabilitation which will facilitate the development of a cognitive structure which is commensurate with the adaptive demands of the world. This world is largely inaccessible to, and beyond the experience of, the institutional resident. The creation of an institutional environment ... in which the retardate is not deprived of all opportunity to exercise responsibility, seems essential to .... adjustment ... after discharge. (p. 413)

The concerns reflected in the discussion to this point encompass the three major classes of psychological issues related to institutionalization in mental retardation with which this chapter is concerned. Since the traditional cycle comprises the three elements of commitment, institutional living, and release, we will organize our subsequent discussion of the current status of the following classes of issues accordingly.

First, such premises as those which posit that institutions for the mentally retarded child merely serve as "warehouses" for storing "discarded" children, or that the community can provide all the needed services—thereby rendering institutions completely unnecessary—connote that the psychological aspects of institutionalization must touch upon that universe of issues covering the need for residential services. Here we must consider the issues as respectively perceived from the viewpoint of the retarded person, his family, and the community.

Next, the expressed concerns regarding the psychological effects of residential programming point to a class of issues which revolve around the phenomenological nature of the institutional experience and its effect on the resident's intellectual, motivational, social, and personal development and behavior.

Finally, we must concern ourselves with issues pertinent to the outcome of institutionalization, or to the resident's eventual discharge back to the community. In this connection, we are particularly interested in those sociopsychological variables that are most closely associated with release from the residential facility, as well as with post-discharge emotional, social, and vocational adjustment.

CURRENT STATUS OF ISSUES

Need for Institutionalization

The retarded individual's point of view. The world we live in is an increasingly competitive and difficult one to negotiate. As a homely example, it has been proposed that a charge be made for dialing telephone information for a number already listed in a phone book. Developmentally disabled persons living among "normals" are penalized in this and in other subtle ways for their disabilities.

Our capitalistic free-enterprise society is increasingly Darwinian. It is geared toward the survival of the fittest in a world where survival is more and more difficult, and where one must be more and more "fit" to survive. All the traditional cliches apply here, such as: "Where there's a will, there's a way," and "pull yourself up by your bootstraps"—as if unlimited opportunity is present in the system, awaiting only the necessary amount of struggle on the part of the individual for the attainment of success.

Yet, mental hygiene professionals are aware of the competition that exists for the high-functioning retarded person, even for those (sheltered) employment opportunities that are available. And once in such a situation, the myriad pressures of life in our increasingly bureaucratic society continue to impinge on the individual.

In any society, public bureaucracies possess characteristics that present their own difficulties to those clients that they are created to serve. Persons of normal intelligence find coping with them a trying burden. "Negotiating the bureaucracy" has become the term used to connote struggling through the red tape with which official bodies preserve themselves. But it is just these public bureaucracies through which developmentally disabled persons most usually receive their health care, their education, their recreation—in short, all social services particularly organized for them.

Consequently, for the retarded child or adult, an institutional setting may conceivably offer the most comfortable milieu in which to negotiate life. There may be great comfort in a lack of competition as a consequence of being with intellectual equals. In addition, an emotionally strained retarded individual may experience institutionalization as a respite and as a comfortable milieu that is much more tolerable than community living. A retarded person with poor self-control may find the established routines and predictable interrelationships in the institution, though rigid, a very welcome relief from the ambiguity and sheer volume of stimuli present in any community setting. In general, for the retarded citizen, organizing and responding to a buzzing confusion of stimuli is a Herculean task, and one which often can result in withdrawal. A limited attention span and difficulty in synthesizing data often results in withdrawal when retarded persons enter an active institituional program after experiencing the simpler milieu of custodial-like ward life.

The controversy here is that it is supremely paternalistic to assume that the retarded individual could not and would not choose to handle the barrage of stimuli that exists in the community, and therefore would prefer the institution. The assumption of "intellectual equals" in the institution also is questionable. Furthermore, as Klaber (1969) found, there is some evidence that "retarded children are happiest when their contact with nonretarded adults is maximized" (p. 184). The field of mental retardation may be one in which consumer participation is most difficult to achieve, but planning *for* people rather than *with* them is a colonialistic philosophy that is more and more a thing of the past.

In those cases where the need on the part of the retarded person for institutionalization must be given primacy, Jaslow, Kime, and Green (1966) set forth in a four-part rubric the criteria for judging that need:

> 1. *Physical handicaps:* to include neuromuscular deteriorating diseases, weight over 35 pounds (in combination with other debilitating conditions), and tube feeding. The degree of nursing care and the difficulty in handling by the parents are the considerations here.
> 2. *Asocial behavior:* but only for children over 8 years. Under the age of 8, the difficult retarded child most probably can be managed at home where two parents are present, with supportive guidance from mental hygiene professionals and admission to part-time, out-of-home, structured programs.

3. *Mental level:* profoundly retarded children under the age of 5 need home care, and institutionalization can result in a self-fulfilling prophecy of inability to respond to stimuli. Severely retarded children under 8 years of age can be cared for in the home where two parents are present.

4. *Single parent or none:* for children over 4 years of age. If the diagnosis is secure at 4 years, and if the single parent has difficulty, then this would serve as a criterion for institutionalization, albeit foster care should be pursued as an alternative under 4 years of age.

This set of criteria is helpful in that if it were applied, it would permit epidemiological studies to be made of the aggregate need of the population at risk of institutionalization. Also, if these criteria could be adhered to, planning programs for the more homogeneous groups that would populate the institutions could be more readily undertaken, and staff could be trained in the special techniques of working with a homogeneous group of retarded persons.

Retarded people with multiple severe physical handicaps need and can respond to a medical or prosthetic environment. Staff and equipment deployed in the care of this group of residents meet their needs with special treatment and with ingenious devices that encourage any degree of independence (regardless of how small) shown in the resident.

In sum, for those residents who genuinely need institutionalization as the optimum arrangement, the need can be acute and often may involve medical considerations. Even in this circumstance, however, the medical diagnosis should be a differential one, subject to updating, and based upon the clear expectation that the functioning of the retarded person will improve following the provision of an optimum medical environment.

The family's point of view. For the family of the retarded child, institutionalization is a resource about which emotions are deep and often mixed. In this extremely emotional situation, families often turn to physicians and mental hygiene professionals for guidance. The need for institutionalization should always be determined in the final analysis by the family—not abdicated to others. Family members are the ones who "must live with it," and they are the ones who are capable of reversing the decision in the future.

But the family that is faced with making a decision is in great distress and must weigh the needs of the retarded child against the needs of the family as a whole; often these needs are rightly seen as incompatible. In many cases, the decision to institutionalize is felt later as a decision to abandon the youngster, with the consequence that guilt arises. The family feels visited by immutable bad fortune and, in our Judeo-Christian society, are all too prone to turn "blame" onto themselves, since humans must believe in an orderly world wherein events are predictable and "effect" follows "cause." A corollary of this orderly universal scheme is that what people get is what they deserve. "As you sow so shall you reap" is a basic tenet of this socio-religio dictum. No wonder that crushing guilt most often accompanies the birth of a "defective" child, and the anguished parent asks: "What have I done to deserve this?" Little wonder that parents of retarded children have not comprised an effective constituency for their offspring until very recently. It was not until the early 1950s, for example, that parents in Minneapolis, Minnesota, formed the first chapter of the National Association for Retarded Children (now called the National Association for Retarded Citizens).

From the family's point of view, several particular considerations influence the need to institutionalize the mentally retarded offspring. One would be the ability of family members to cope with problems that had developed in the past. If the family unit had been able previously to face and overcome major difficulties, to mobilize its resources and to remain intact, it is more likely that the need to institutionalize retarded progeny would not seem acute.

Another factor would be the family's perception of the various available alternatives. If there seem to be few options, or if the available options do not seem to be feasible, the need to institutionalize the child will seem greater. Therefore, the existence of community programs and their perceived availability to the family is an important consideration in this area.

Another variable may be the presence of physical stigmata of retardation, such as in the case of mongolism (Down's Syndrome). Though the mongoloid child may eventually function better than an equally retarded child who looks "normal," his retardation is immediately diagnosable and therefore often leads to an early decision to institutionalize. Although current attitudes are being greatly modified, for many years pediatricians have expressed the opinion that the mongoloid child should be institutionalized immediately after birth (Sternlicht, 1966b).

Other factors influencing the family's decision as to whether or not to institutionalize a retarded youngster are those of birth order, sex, and the extent of the child's deviation from the intelligence level of the parents. If the retarded child is the first-born, there is apprehension that subsequent offspring will imitate the maladaptive behavior of the retarded older child. Especially if the children are the same sex is there likely to be tension. Intellectually oriented parents also often have great difficulty in rearing profoundly retarded children.

The need for institutionalization is very often seen as a solution to antisocial or maladaptive behavior on the part of the retarded offspring. For example, institutionalized retarded children are found to have higher IQs than SQs, as measured on the Vineland Social Maturity Scale (Kershner, 1970). Apparently, when the child's SQ is lower than his IQ, institutionalization is more likely.

When the family makes its appraisal of the need for institutionalization, the child's present social skills, or those which might be developed, are an important determinant in the decision. The family tends to anticipate rejection of their deviant child, not just by the school system but by the other students as well, as a result of his developmental disability. Thus, the needs of the whole family and of the individual child are inextricably combined in the decision to institutionalize the retarded member.

The community's point of view. Attitudes in the community toward the retarded citizen are more than ever in a state of flux. Popular opinion via the media dictates change, and professional convictions are catching up with research findings that indicate community living is not only desirable, but also most feasible, for retarded people. But is this feasible for the community? Many institutionalized individuals are ready for the community, but is the community ready for them? Publicity and planned public education help, but while this is in progress an over-rapid movement toward this single dimension of change can result in disservice to mentally retarded residents. They should not be treated as pawns in a game of politics and publicity— sacrificed in a headlong rush to dismantle the institutions. Nevertheless, at the same time, a lack of readily available (formal) community programs should not be the excuse for continued institutionalization if homes exist and are ready for the placement of such citizens.

The community must be *prepared* to accept developmentally disabled citizens. Yet, young people in general are traditionally neglected by their local communities in our society. How many planned educational, occupational, recreational, and social opportunities exist for the "normal" children now residing in the community? When such opportunities are provided, they are frequently tied in with the acceptance of a social philosophy or message, such as church participation or scouting. They are seldom offered free of charge, just for the taking and enjoying. We must face and accept the notion that our society doesn't nurture our young as much as we say it does. It is against this backdrop of general lack of opportunity for the young that acceptance and provision of community services for retarded youth must be seen as especially lacking.

Should we respect and cherish all offspring, regardless of their development? Do we intervene in the economy to provide adequate social programs for them? These kinds of questions are political because they treat with the distribution of benefits in our society. It would be ignoring political realities if institutions were not viewed as an extension of the political economy. The struggle between the ideologies of individualism and collectivism, and between capitalism and socialism, are represented in the manner in which our society treats all social problems, the developmentally disabled individual among them. At this time, institutionalization of the retarded person has represented the blending (as well as the struggle) of the two philosophies. The collectivity provides the institution as an expression of group concern for disabled individuals. But individualism and the free enterprise system combine to deny the funds for the programs necessary to make residential living a developmentally rewarding and enhancing experience. This concept is, after all, the basis of social welfare. Children belong to everyone, and thus are the legitimate concern of collective society. Families who cannot accept or manage the care of a retarded child have the option of institutionalization open to them, an option made available by a society interested in providing for all its members without stigmatizing or placing blame on the family.

There has been a steady increase in institutional populations in the United States since the first facility was created in 1848, but this increase has been among young children while there has been a general decrease in adolescent and adult residents (Baumeister, 1970). Although improved medical care has served to preserve life in profoundly and severely retarded infants and thus accounts for much of the population increase, another factor is that the more severely retarded young children on institutional waiting lists are admitted while less severely retarded applicants are managed alternatively or remain longer on these same waiting lists.

The need of the retarded person for special care is often eclipsed by the need of the family and community for his or her institutionalization. When designated resources are thus used to meet the family's or the community's needs, fewer resources remain to meet the genuine needs of the retarded individual. For example, when institutions are forced to expand their resources on behalf of residents who have been admitted through lack of appropriate community resources and/or through rejection by the school or the parents, the residential facilities cannot properly serve that group of retarded persons who genuinely need institutional care. The needs of these three groups (the retarded child, the family, and the community) are not necessarily compatible, and indeed we must recognize that they are often in conflict.

Add to these factors the need of institutions to maintain themselves, as well as the need of professionals to fulfill their vocational objectives, and the needs of retarded residents can become all the more submerged. Each factor has its own way of bringing pressure to bear on behalf of the interests of those concerned. Retarded persons are not likely to act effectively or collectively in their own best interests. Their putative advocates are parents who must contend with their own needs, and professionals who tend to take a sacrificing (or compromising) course among what they perceive as the conflicting interests of the retarded citizen, the family, and the community. This is why it is so important that the institutions, and the professionals within them, identify with the retarded resident, even if it dictates the taking of an advocacy role on his behalf.

Another important variable in considering the community's interest in institutionalization is the relative cost of effective and efficient care, and the use of tax funds to achieve such care. Whether tax funds are allocated to local transportation, to schools, to safety, or to care of the mentally retarded person is a political question. But it is of interest to the community that funds committed to the care of the mentally retarded citizen be effectively and efficiently spent in a way which benefits the citizen to the fullest possible extent. Since institutional care tends to be long term and self-perpetuating, it is likely to be much more expensive than foster care and community programming.

When communities see residential care for their mentally retarded populations as a more pressing need than community programming, even though the former is more costly, it is of interest to note that our American democracy has idealized the "average" in many social aspects. For example, public education at all levels is aimed at imparting the same body of knowledge to the broad expanse of American school-aged youth. A broad middle-class exists in this country to an extent that is not true in any other country. Being different has not been a circumstance to be treasured. The rural nature of early American life may have contributed to this ethos, as visibly different children were much more noticeable in the small rural communities. This has changed with increasing urbanization. At the same time, the mass migration to urban centers has been contemporaneous with, and largely responsible for, the scattering of the extended family that might have provided the care necessary for a disabled child who could have gone unnoticed in a rural community.

Nature of the Institutional Experience

Intellectual-cognitive aspects. The available literature is equivocal, to say the least, as to the validity of the sometimes posited notion that there is a general decline in intellectual-cognitive function among retarded individuals following prolonged institutionalization. Thus, the large body of work reviewed by Balla et al. (1974) indicated that while a number of studies report that institutionalized retarded children show a decrement in IQ, as well as in some specific tasks which reflect significant cognitive processes (e.g., language usage, discrimination learning, and formation of learning sets), there is a substantial quantity of literature reporting (a) increases in such cognitive functions as autonomy in problem solving, and (b) either no IQ change or an overall increase in IQ.

In their own investigation (the most comprehensive longitudinal study to date on the multidimensional effects of institutionalization on retarded children) Balla et al. (1974) found that among 103 children from four institutions, there was no overall IQ change after approximately 2.5 years of residence (although given children did show significant increments); however, there was a general increase in MA level. On the basis of their general findings, Balla and his colleagues reiterated the conclusions of many previous studies (Zigler, 1973) which had revealed that institutional effects on intellectual development vary as a function of pre-institutional history of the retarded individual as well as of the particular institutional environment under consideration. They also found that such effects varied with the sex of the subject and with etiology (i.e., "familial" versus "organic") of the retardation.

Other workers (e.g., Collmann & Newlyn, 1958; Sternlicht & Siegel, 1968a) found that differential changes in IQ occur in different age groups. From their data, Sternlicht and Siegel (1968a) concluded that institutionalized children showed a significant decrease over a 4-year period, while adolescent and adult residents exhibited nonsignificant declines in measured intelligence. None of the groups showed any deterioration in cognitive functions as measured by perceptual-motor tasks. Collmann and Newlyn (1958), working in an English residential school, found that after a 1-year period, there was a decline in test-retest IQ for younger children (under CA 11) and a sharp rise in test-retest IQ scores in children over age 13.

Both of these investigations employed a semilongitudinal approach, which allows for making repeated measurements while utilizing different individuals along a given time dimension. This is an imporant consideration in the light of the fact that other workers (Ross, 1971; Sachs & Frisk, 1971; Silverstein, 1969) made the point that incremental-decremental findings regarding intellectual development during institutionalization may depend upon the method used to chart the course of such development as a function of length of institutionalization. Silverstein (1969) called the latter variable "hospital age" (HA).

Silverstein (1969) found that both the cross-sectional and semilongitudinal approaches demonstrated a decline in IQ in residents whose median age at time of admission was 12 2/3 years, and who ranged in HA from 0 to 25 years. However, the former approach showed a 15-point decrement in IQ, while the latter indicated a loss of about 8 IQ points. Silverstein suggested that the greater decrement shown by the cross-sectional method might be explained by the relationship between IQ and the probability of release from the institution: "Patients who are still available for testing 20-30 years after admission are likely to have lower IQs than those who have been released some time prior to that" (1969, p. 127).

In a study which he characterized as "a strictly longitudinal one" (p. 396), Ross (1971) analyzed changes in CA, MA, and IQ among residents whose admission ages ranged from under 4 years to over 30 years and whose mean HA was about 8 years. He concluded that his results agreed better with those obtained by using Silverstein's cross-sectional approach than with the semilongitudinal one. However, after a critical analysis of his data, Ross also concluded that "decrements in IQ in hospitalized mentally retarded children are for the most part spurious. . . . Such IQs are obviously of little value in assessing changes in intellectual level. *MA is a far more meaningful index of patient status*" (p. 397; italics added).

Sachs and Frisk (1971), in what they also characterize as a "longitudinal assessment," investigated IQ changes in child, adolescent, and adult residents at HA levels ranging from 2 to 6 years. They found no evidence of IQ decline, and there were significant increases in IQ at HA levels 3, 4, and 6. These investigators suggested that the relationship between IQ changes and HA is dependent upon specific environmental situations within the institution, and that for the particular facility studied, the obtained IQ increases may have been due to the educational program available to the residents.

The effect of specific environmental situations on intellectual development/behavior of institutional residents has been studied most definitively by the cross-institutional approaches of Balla et al. (1974) and Klaber (1969).

Balla et al. (1974), in what they characterize as "an exploratory attempt," combined a longitudinal approach (test-retest of the same retarded children with a 2.5-year interval) with a cross-institutional comparison (involving four institutions) of the social-psychological phenomena that influence changes in IQ and MA, as well as in a number of social and motivational variables. With particular regard to the intellectual variables, and analyzing their results within the context of the larger body of work (Zigler, 1973), Balla et al. reached the following conclusions:

1. While there was no significant change in IQ across all the institutions, the course of intellectual development in given children appeared to be a function of their history of pre-institutional deprivation and the particular residential facility in which they lived. Thus, in the institution that was the most socially depriving of the four, children with a preinstitutional history of relatively little deprivation showed a decrease in measured IQ. This finding is

in keeping with the considerable body of previous results obtained by these investigators. Interestingly enough, however, the frequently reported converse finding (Rosen, Stallings, Floor, & Nowakiwska, 1968; Zigler, 1973), to the effect that individuals with a history of severe deprivation respond to the relatively less depriving environment of the institution by manifesting increases in IQ scores, was not obtained in this study. Instead, it was found that in a particular institution, children with a history of high deprivation showed an IQ decrease. In any case, the obtained data reinforce the notion that the "negative effects" of institutionalization often can be attributed to the child's pre-institutional experiences of abandonment and neglect.

2. Nevertheless, the finding of a significant general increase in MA level across institutions (along with concomitant changes in social and motivational responsitivity) indicates that children in all institutions involved in the study "showed psychological growth of the type that would be expected of non-retarded children residing in their homes" (Balla et al., 1974, p. 545).

Klaber (1969), in comparing three of the institutions in his study as to intellectual development among residents over a minimal 6-year period, found that there was a general decline in IQ across institutions. However, children residing in the institution which was relatively nondepriving, and which fostered the highest degree of self-sufficiency and social adjustment, showed a "substantial" increase in MA. Subjects in the most depriving institution (which also did little to encourage independence among its residents) showed no change in MA, while the moderately stimulating institution yielded a "moderate" increment in MA.

Consideration of the available literature seems to warrant the conclusions that under certain conditions, and with given retarded populations, institutional living may have facilitating (or at least nondebilitating) effects on intellectual-cognitive development/behavior, and that a negative view in that regard may be overly pessimistic.

Motivational-phenomenological aspects. In another context, Bialer (1970) suggested that the behavioral and situational variables which are critically related to the retarded person's effective behavior in specific situations might be grouped under the rubrics of motivational and phenomenological factors, and that:

> motivational factors refer to those aspects of the person or of the task [or of the situation] which may influence a given individual's performance.... [and] phenomenological factors pertain to the extent to which the retarded person's behavior may be determined ... by his perception of himself and of the world and, ... by the world's perception of him as an individual. (p. 629)

For purposes of the present discussion, we will be concerned with those two variables (motivational and phenomenological) which have been subjected to comparative studies between institutionalized and noninstitutionalized retarded samples. However, where appropriate, differences between retarded and nonretarded individuals, as discrete groups, will be noted for given aspects.

1. *Motivational variables.* Again, Zigler and his colleagues (Zigler, 1973) have contributed the most to our fund of knowledge regarding the motivational factors that differentiate the behavior of institutionalized and noninstitutionalized retarded persons. These investigators have been concerned with the effects of institutionalization upon response to social reinforcement and to success and failure experiences, as well as with a particular aspect of what Bialer (1970) has called the "internal-external dimensions of motivation" (p. 634), namely, inner versus outer directedness in problem solving.

With regard to the role of social reinforcement, Zigler's findings and conclusions proceeded somewhat as follows:

(a) Institutionalized retarded children have a higher motivation to procure contact and approval of adults than do normal children.
(b) Higher motivation for adult interaction (i.e., for social reinforcement in the form of attention and praise) on the part of institutionalized retarded subjects is related to their greater (pre-institutional) social deprivation.
(c) Compared to normal subjects, the relative social deprivation experienced by retarded children, whether institutionalized or not, is responsible for an opposing motivational factor—it makes the retarded children more wary and fearful of adults.
(d) Such a "negative-reaction tendency" may partially account for failure of the institutionalized child on tasks presented by adults—and to a general attenuation in their social effectiveness—over and above the part played by intellectual factors.
(e) Institutionalized retarded children differ among themselves in the extent to which they have experienced pre-institutional deprivation; and there is an interaction between the child's pre-institutional history, his perception of the institution as a depriving environment, and his need for social reinforcement.
(f) Children with a history of relatively little deprivation find the institutional experience more socially depriving and show

increased need for social reinforcement over the course of their residence; the converse holds true for residents with a history of great deprivation.

(g)   The above-noted phenomenon of differential IQ changes following prolonged institutionalization for children with different pre-institutional deprivation experiences reflects these changes in motivation for social interaction (with consequent inhibition or facilitation in production of correct test responses) rather than actual change in "formal cognitive functioning" (Zigler, 1973, p. 303).

(h)   There is an analogous interaction between pre-institutional deprivation and length of institutionalization with regard to the resident's wariness of adults, or his negative-reaction tendency. Thus, children from a relatively highly deprived background apparently become less wary, whereas the wariness of less-deprived children increases over the course of institutionalization.

(i)   All of the above interact with the extent to which given institutions are actually (or are perceived as being) depriving environments for given children.

Zigler's conclusion with respect to the foregoing encapsulates the rationale that all institutions need not be seen as equally depriving environments exerting uniform influences on all retarded children:

> In respect to IQ changes following institutionalization, it would appear that the retarded child's . . . need for social reinforcement, as well as his wariness, compete with the production of correct responses in the testing situation, and [may] result in . . . performance lower than that dictated by the child's intellectual resources. To the extent that the child's need for social reinforcement and his wariness are ameliorated [over the course of institutionalization], one would expect an increase in IQ. . . . *The importance of this work rests upon the fact that such motivationally induced changes in IQ performance would probably be found in respect to a variety of other performance typically utilized to gauge general social competence.* (1973, pp. 306-307; italics added)

The seminal work in the area of the motivational aspects of success and failure among retarded samples has been done by Cromwell and his students (reviewed in Cromwell, 1967). This work proceeded on the assumption that because of a prolonged history of failure (by virtue of their intellectual shortcomings), retarded children would come into new situations with a relatively low generalized expectancy (GE) for success and a much higher GE for failure. One of the major predictions generated by the latter assumption was that, compared to normal children who would respond to failure experiences by increased efforts toward achieving success, retarded subjects would show a failure-avoidance tendency, manifested by decreased efforts. The literature to date (Bialer & Cromwell, 1965; Cromwell, 1967; Zigler, 1973) demonstrates that while normal children, as a group, do respond to failure with success-striving efforts more than do their retarded counterparts, failure may be motivating for retarded individuals under certain conditions—primary among which is the opportunity to succeed in the face of failure.

Zigler and his colleagues (Zigler, 1973) have been virtually unique in their concern with the relationships among institutionalization and success-failure experiences for retarded individuals. Their work argues for the following conclusions: The combination of high failure experience and lowered expectancy for success on the part of retarded children leads them to mistrust the effectiveness of their own intellectual resources on cognitive tasks. This mistrust generates a distinctive problem-solving (i.e., cognitive) style—characterized as "outer directedness"—in which the individual relies on external (environmental) cues as a guide to action in dealing with problems. While outer directedness is not invariably detrimental to performance, and may in certain instances even prove adaptive, extensive reliance on environmental cues may prove excessively distracting from the task at hand, thus reducing the individual's competence. Further, not only are retarded children in general more outer-directed than normal children of the same mental age, but noninstitutionalized retarded individuals are also found to be more outer-directed than their institutionalized peers. Zigler (1973) explained the latter finding as follows:

> The institutionalized retarded live in an environment adjusted to their intellectual shortcomings and should experience less failure than the noninstitutionalized retarded. The noninstitutionalized retarded child must continue to face the complexities and demands of an environment with which he is ill equippped to deal and, as we found, should manifest the greatest sensitivity to external cues. (p. 287) . . . Again, we see that it is not the retardation per se that produces the behavior, but rather the particular experiences to which retarded children are subjected. (p. 292)

Finally, the study of Balla et al. (1974) suggested that the trait of outer directedness among retarded residents may be attenuated over the course of institutionalization. Thus, it was found that, after 2½ years, their subjects, across all institutions surveyed, were less imitative (i.e., made more use of their own cognitive resources in guiding their behavior)—findings generally consistent with previous work on the developmental course of outer directedness. Apparently, this developmental course, toward inner directedness, had not been inhibited by the institutional experience.

2. *Phenomenological variables.* There has been a severe paucity of organized work on the phenomenological factors (i.e., the person's perception of himself and of the world, and the world's perception of him) which discriminate institutionalized from noninstitutionalized retarded persons (Lawrence & Winschel, 1973). Nevertheless, the extant literature presents findings which are in apparent conflict with the historical notion that the self-concept of the institutionalized retarded individual inevitably goes through a process of "mortification" and progressive deterioration. Brief examples follow.

A number of studies investigated the relationship between length of institutionalization and self-concept and found either no association between these variables (Kniss, Butler, Gorlow, & Guthrie, 1962; McAfee & Cleland, 1965) or a small but significant tendency for self-acceptance to improve with length of residence (Gorlow, Butler, & Guthrie, 1963). In a related vein, Cleland, Patton, and Dickerson (1968) found that although there were significant ethnicity and sex interactions, continuously institutionalized retarded individuals showed increments in self-concept ratings over a 4-month period, as opposed to a drop in such ratings among a comparable group in which institutionalization had been interrupted by a summer furlough of that duration.

In a study which related pre-institutional history with effects of institutionalization on self-esteem, Edgerton and Sabagh (1962) pointed out that the pre-hospital experiences of their subjects were typically highly mortifying because of rejection and humiliation at the hands of parents, peers, teachers, neighbors, and strangers. In contrast, institutionalization provided the residents with opportunities for self-aggrandizement and elevated self-esteem because (a) they could compare themselves favorably with more severely retarded residents; (b) they experienced accepting peer relationships which enhanced and sustained a positive self-percept; and (c) they had contacts with staff who encouraged self-esteem.

Rosen, Diggory, and Werlinsky (1966) concluded that residential care fosters optimism and self-confidence among retarded children more than do experiences in school and community. They found that institutionalized children set higher goals and predicted higher performance for themselves, as well as actually producing more than their noninstitutionalized peers. These investigators interpreted their results as being congruent with those of Zigler and his associates, and they summed up this aspect of their findings as follows:

> Institutions for the retarded, . . . provide a set of demands and expectations that differ from those provided by a noninstitutional environment. Protection, encouragement, training, more realistic standards for performance, and more realistic conditions of competition may well serve to heighten optimism and self-evaluation. (Rosen et al., 1966, p. 254)

Social-personal aspects. Sternlicht and Deutsch (1972), in reviewing the literature on the depriving effects of institutionalization, emphasized that there is authoritative backing for the viewpoint that institutionalization, in general, inhibits personal and social development and behavior because of restrictions in both interpersonal relationships with and stimulation by parent-surrogates and peers. Nevertheless, as with all the issues discussed above, a survey of the literature suggests the necessity for reconceptualizing the notions regarding the generally debilitating effects of institutionalization on retarded children. The following examples certainly seem to counteract the concepts that residential placement is both invariably restrictive of personal and social growth, and is inevitably "depersonalizing," "de-individualizing," and "dehumanizing."

In one of the earliest comparative studies of the social behavior of institutionalized and noninstitutionalized retarded children, Capobianco and Cole (1960) found no difference between the groups in social participation, at least as measured by free-play behavior. In the only longitudinal studies that have come to our attention, Mitchell and Smeriglio (1970) found over a 3-year period that institutionalized moderately and severely retarded children receiving a high-saturation teaching program increased in social competence (as measured by the Vineland Social Maturity Scale); and Colwell, Richards, McCarver, and Ellis (1973) found over an average of 7 months that profoundly retarded children in a short-term residence facility made substantial and significant gains in dressing, feeding, and toileting skills.

A number of studies have examined the dynamics of one-to-one interpersonal relationships among institutionalized retarded people, and have found (a) residents can form friendship patterns with various degrees of stability, ranging from relatively unstable friendships (Sternlicht & Siegel, 1968b) to very close and long-enduring relationships (McAndrew & Edgerton, 1966); (b) residents can participate in nonsupervised heterosexual dating activities with consequent internalization of rules for acceptable social behavior (Edgerton & Dingman, 1964); (c) as compared to a noninstitutionalized sample, institutionalized retarded persons show a keen awareness of the utility of the tactic of reciprocity ("If you do something for me, I'll do something for you") among residents (Weiss & Weinstein, 1968); and (d) mentally retarded residents are capable of high levels of cooperative behavior under conditions of free communication (Evans, 1965).

Investigations exploring the dynamics of both informal and formal group relationships in institutions have concluded that (a) residents gravitate toward informal peer groups, which support their members, with consequent enhancement in learning of specific social skils (Forman, 1970) and general socialization (Meile & Burk, 1970); and (b) institutionalization allows for the formation of formal systems of stable social relationships which foster within-group commonality and "one-ness" (Edgerton, 1963).

Finally, there is evidence that institutionalized retarded individuals have the opportunity to exercise some of the rights of all citizens, such as the right to free enterprise (Edgerton, Tarjan, & Dingman, 1961) and the right to vote (Cleland, Swartz, McGaven, & Bell, 1973; Gerard, 1974).

Outcome Issues

As noted earlier, we will be particularly concerned here with those sociopsychological factors—operating within the institution—which have a bearing on getting out of the residential facility (release factors) and with staying out (postdischarge adjustment factors). The relationship between these two sets of variables is extremely important, since administrative decisions to discharge residents back to the community are most frequently made on the basis of a judgment that there is a favorable prognosis for successful post-institutional adjustment. Thus, very often, the "release factors" serve as predictor variables in outcome studies.

Release factors. In his most comprehensive and critical review of the literature concerning the outcome of institutionalization, Windle (1962) noted that, as of that date, there had "not yet been sociological studies of the release processes in institutions for mental subnormals" (p. 111). It is regrettable that at the present writing, there still appears to be no definitive statement as to those factors which are most closely associated with the likelihood of a resident's discharge or placement from the facility. Nevertheless, a number of workers have made some attempt to identify those variables which the institutional staff and the residents themselves consider the most germane with regard to readiness for release.

From his review, Windle (1962) concluded that the resident's "personality," more specifically his emotional stability, is one of the most important criteria in subjective staff evaluations of preparedness for placement. However, the results of a recent "predictive" investigation suggest that it might be job-related emotional stability (as judged during work performance within the institution) which is crucial. Thus, Rosen, Kivitz, Clark, and Floor (1970) found that "of the various behavioral ratings reflecting institutional adjustment, only those dealing with employability were significantly related to criterion variables" (p. 730). This study also indicated that (a) the staff's conclusion as to how well an individual was able to handle a vocational assignment (which also entailed judgment on their part as to his social acumen and ability to engage in interpersonal relationships) was an important aspect of his perceived suitability for discharge; and (b) staff global ratings of potential for discharge were highly correlated with the subject's verbal IQ. Interestingly enough, in a related study, Rosen and Floor (1970) found that the residents themselves perceived work competence as strongly related to both popularity among one's peers and one's chances for discharge. All these findings are in keeping with Windle's (1962) conclusion that work experience in the residential facility is favorable toward success after release.

The above-noted relationship between a resident's IQ and his perceived potential for discharge on the part of the administration also is congruent with the findings emphasized in Windle's (1962) review to the effect that intelligence level is highly related to likelihood of vocational placement in the community. However, in their longitudinal study, Balla et al. (1974) found that a retarded child's chances for discharge into community care (which in most cases did not involve vocational placement) were unrelated to his IQ status. These investigators concluded that, in the case of children, likelihood of discharge from institutionalization is a function of (a) the permanence and stability of their pre-institutional home, (b) the availability of a place for them to go, and (c) their "effectance motivation" (i.e., the extent to which they are motivated to vary their behavior in problem-solving situations in an attempt to manifest competence).

Adjustment factors. Windle's (1962) analysis of pertinent literature pointed out that while IQ was highly related to likelihood of release from institutionalization, it was not an adequate predictor of, nor did it bear any relationship to, postdischarge adjustment. This finding is emphasized in subsequent reviews by Heber and Dever (1970) and by Zigler (1973). The general consensus that the predischarge cognitive status of the retarded individual (given IQ levels roughly between 50 and 75) shows little relationship with his successful adjustment in the community is supported by recent findings of Rosen and his colleagues. Thus, in the above-mentioned study by Rosen, Kivitz, Clark, and Floor (1970), it was found that verbal IQ and academic achievement scores (as measured in residence) were less important correlates of placement success than was perceptual-motor ability. Rosen, Floor, and Baxter (1974) also determined that in a group which had been discharged for about 3 years, there was no increment in IQ or academic achievement, and that there was no relationship between either IQ or academic level and the ability of group members to function effectively in a community setting. Such results seem to offer some support for Zigler's conclusion that "motivational and emotional factors are more important than intellectual abilities in determining the institutionalized individual's prognosis for success in the community" (1973, p. 307).

With regard to personality factors, Windle (1962) concluded that these were not adequate predictors of placement success. However, Zigler (1973) cited evidence that various personal characteristics among residents—such as truthfulness, obedience, attention to details and personal habits, a relative indisposition toward quarrelsomeness, and relatively unaggressive behavior—eventually differentiate the successful from the nonsuccessful individuals.

An early and strongly influential conclusion, to the effect that long institutionalization is inevitably detrimental to later social adjustment, has been subjected to systematic research. All reported findings seem emphatically to refute that conclusion. Reviews by Butterfield (1967), Heber and Dever (1970), Windle (1962), and Zigler (1973) all emphasize that length of institutionaliztion is not necessarily related inversely to outside success or adjustment. In particular, Windle found that length of residence was sometimes unrelated to outcome and sometimes prognostic of success—noting that "a general tendency for long hospitalization to be beneficial is not inconsistent with the . . . prognostic relations of age at . . . discharge. Length of institutionalization and age may act in the same way, toward stabilizing the patient" (1962, p. 109). Butterfield's (1967) review substantiated Windle's conclusions, both with regard to the nondetrimental effects on later social adjustment of long-term institutionalization and to the interaction of length of residence with age. Butterfield pointed out that when the kind of setting into which residents are released is taken into account, we find that (a) older subjects who were placed in family-care settings were more likely to succeed after a longer time in the residential facility; and (b) the longer that individuals were institutionalized prior to being placed in relatively independent vocational situations, the less likely was the necessity for reinstitutionalization.

The most comprehensive and searching analysis of the factors that lead to successful outcome has been that of Edgerton (1967), who pointed out that the most salient feature of the successful community adjustment of his subjects was the extent to which they had the help of "benefactors" in maintaining (a) their self-concept as competent individuals, (b) their ability to cope with the exigencies of community living, and (c) their ability to deny their subnormal intellectual status and "pass" for normal (i.e., in assuming the "cloak of competence"). Edgerton argued that life in even the relatively progressive institution from which his subjects came had not prepared them for community living and that they survived there only because of the availability of supportive figures.

However, in their discussion of the findings of various follow-up studies of both formerly institutionalized retarded adults and graduates of public school special classes, Heber and Dever (1970) noted that both groups of "rehabilitated" retarded individuals exist, for the most part, at the extreme lower end of almost all social and economic indices, and they concluded that "clearly, the recent studies do not suggest that ... special education ... renders most retarded persons capable of an adjustment which we would set as minimally adequate" (p. 405). Also, in a recent study, Rosen, Halenda, Nowakiwska, and Floor (1970) found that employment dissatisfaction among previously institutionalized mentally retarded adults, who were living and working independently in community settings, came from receiving inadequate compensation and from being afforded lowered status positions in the firm.

Consequently, it seems possible to infer that it was not necessarily previous institutionalization per se which was responsible for the plight of Edgerton's sample, and that their adjustment problems probably could be traced in large part to whatever socioeconomic and sociopsychological factors retarded persons, in general, must contend with in the community. This inference does not deny the likelihood that institutional programs are not completely meeting their obligations in training and preparing retarded residents for community employment. Nevertheless, it does seem to deny the notion that institutionalization inevitably puts the former resident at a social and economic disadvantage relative to his noninstitutionalized retarded peers.

ATTEMPTS AT RESOLUTION OF ISSUES

Innovative Forms of Institutionalization

Until relatively recently, institutionalization has been the preferred mode of care for the retarded person. Society's response to mental retardation was seclusion in large, remote institutions. The first such institution was established in Switzerland in 1841 by Johann Guggenbuhl. Organized on a colony principle, Guggenbuhl's institutional regimen consisted of fresh air, good diet, physical exercise, medications, and approaches for developing the senses (Daly & Bellamy, 1969). It was largely the influence of this first effort that, in the 50-year period between 1850 and 1900, led to the construction in the United States of 24 public residential institutions in some 19 states, including New York. At the present time, there are some 167 public and 275 private facilities serving mentally retarded residents in the United States.

One ancient philosopher wrote that the measure of a society's advancement is the manner in which it treats its criminals. Anyone in current times who tours an institution housing mentally retarded people in this country realizes that the measure of this society's advancement is the manner in which it treats its mentally retarded population as well. Among the most vulnerable subgroups in society, restricted by their own intellectual retardation and maladaptive behavior, as well as by the institution that confines them, the retarded residents are unable to affect their own condition. Without power or advocacy in the competitive struggle for rights and resources, they have, until only recently, come out last on both counts. What the large, out-of-sight institutions with their "forgotten" residents have mutely attested to is that, once again, here was an example of a vulnerable group in our society benefiting least from an arrangement that was set up officially to serve them.

Institution programming. The problem of institutionalization of the mentally subnormal individual is one fraught with tremendous emotional controversy. It is relevant to reiterate that for many mild and moderately severely retarded individuals, the institution provides a microcosm of society, a subculture operating at a lower intellectual level than the normal world, but with its own rewards and frustrations. The institutionalized individual is often removed from the frustrating, insecurity-provoking, and anxiety-producing demands of a society which, in essence, makes no provision for him. Since we have become accustomed to judging an individual's overall performance on the basis of what is expected by our own culture, it is important to note (as has been pointed up in our preceding discussion) that those whom we consider to be mentally retarded may function quite successfully when placed in a (prosthetic) societal milieu which they understand and which is often made up of their "equals" and of nonretarded adults dedicated to their positive development.

Institutionalization, then, need not be considered the end of the line, since in many instances it may actually be the beginning of a new and satisfying life for the resident, depending both upon the set of circumstances responsible for the decision to institutionalize and the facility to which he is relegated.

Others have indicated that it serves the routine of the institution better if the retarded resident accepts the concept of his retardation. One takes this to mean that he is to be made aware of his inabilities and failings to the extent that he will have no wish to try anything except to live as unobtrusively as possible in the institution. Otherwise, it is held, in defiance of accepting the concept, he may demonstrate some ability to get attention, even if it is through "acting out" behaviors. But how much better the institution functions on behalf of the resident if it can tolerate some "deviance" from expected routine! A "natural" environment is a desideratum. It is just this kind of flexibility that permits, and indeed stimulates, innovative programming in the institution and fosters normalization.

Innovative approaches have focused on treatment and other programs for emotionally or socially maladjusting residents, vocational training for adolescents, habilitation training for persons newly admitted and for those preparing to leave the institution, as well as on special self-care training, where necessary. Many of the new programs place heavy emphasis on behavior modification procedures, with resultant techniques which are applicable to individuals at various levels of retardation and to the deaf-blind retarded resident as well (Sternlicht & Sullivan, 1975). Insofar as possible, the new programs tend to involve parents, caretakers, or interested correspondents in order to carry out the institution's program of training and to facilitate reinforcing positive behaviors during visits in the home. Implicit in the development of innovative programs in institutions is the carrying out of the normalization principle to the fullest extent possible. Among other things, this means that the normal rhythms of life, rather than the requirements of hospital routine, will govern the daily, weekly, and monthly lives of the residents.

Although emphasis has supposedly always been placed on the welfare of the resident in institutional programming, the very nature of the concept of a "staff-to-patient ratio" implies that there are certain logistical and administrative considerations that are important to the institution, regardless of the client's welfare. With a true concern solely for the benefit and welfare of the resident, a new staffing pattern has emerged, which is known as "post staffing." The main feature of this staffing pattern is that, since the number of personnel required is geared to a specific program designed to enhance the residents' functioning, this number would be variable from program to program. This represents a relatively recent trend in institutional programming, and it is hoped that it will continue.

Also implicit in modern programming in the institution is the philosophy that the resident will be able at some point in the future to return to his home or to another community-based living situation. It is the goal of the institution to prepare him for this eventuality. The current institution is therefore essentially a part of a continuum of services for the retarded individual, which begins and hopefully resumes in the community. Ideally, the institutional stay is designed to remedy those conditions in the retarded individual and/or in his family that retard or impede his healthy progress. This can be accomplished via the application of suitable programmatic efforts. The institution's current programs, when appropriately constructed, are geared toward maximizing the competence of the retarded participants. Programs of appropriate stimulation at all levels of retardation are necessary to evoke and establish mature, adaptive behaviors. The residential center's programming also should play an extremely crucial role in maintaining those residents who have been placed in the community, by supervising the use of and stimulating the creation of adequate and appropriate community resources for serving them. At the same time, it can provide the services of a day-center program to community-based retarded individuals so that the transition to full-time community placement can be most easily facilitated.

The vehicle of resident interaction is another important one in encouraging ego development and the learning of adaptive skills. In addition, there is a need for those mature (nonretarded) adults who are present to interact meaningfully with the resident, since behavior modeling is an important learning device by which retarded individuals advance in their development. Indeed, research indicates that personal adjustment may be maximized under such conditions of contact with nonretarded adults (Klaber, 1969).

Another area of special programming in which a need exists is that presented by the emotionally disturbed retarded person. Emotional or behavioral disturbances represent a formidable problem in institutions for retarded residents. Apparently, a significant factor in determining a child's institutionalization is the degree of willingness and/or ability of the public schools to tolerate disturbing behavior in borderline functioning youngsters. Whatever the etiology of emotional distubance, estimates of its prevalence range between 11% (Koch, Baerwald, McDonald, Fishler, & Rock, 1969) and 16% (Penrose, 1963) of the total institutionalized retarded population.

Obviously, the emotionally disturbed retarded individual requires special programming and therapy. Some emotional distress may be caused and/or exacerbated by the institution itself, and pathology may possibly be acquired as a consequence of prolonged institutionalization. In this instance, community placement or transfer elsewhere, in that order, would be desirable. Curiously, the institution's administrative personnel often consider a resident unsuitable for community placement because of disturbed behavior which may be traced to institutionalization, yet prolongation of residential living may only lead to further disturbances. The resident, in this case, is caught in a double-bind, a Catch-22 dilemma.

Long-term institutionalization should be seen as an arrangement of last resort, and then only for persons whose care requires a prosthetic, possibly medically oriented environment. These individuals are likely to be severely and profoundly retarded, possibly with physical handicaps as well, so that a medical milieu which includes psychoeducational programming, where feasible, is well justified and potentially beneficial. For this group, aids to maximum mobility would be essential. Prosthetic equipment would include supportive chairing, creeping, crawling, and pulling-up devices, with sling crawlers, scoot boards, and tilt tables. Special ramps and specially designed equipment for self-feeding, toileting, hair brushing, and tooth cleaning, all could extend the independent functioning of even the most disabled resident. Programs of this type, however, should not be regarded as essentially custodial in nature, but rather should be planned with a view toward making the resident's adjustment to his institutional living as socially adaptive as possible.

Temporary institutionalization. A recent projection of the estimated need for residential care in 1973 and beyond has suggested that 9% of the mentally retarded population would require institutionalization for a period of less than 1 year, an additional 9% would need to be institutionalized for periods of from 1 to 3 years, and 16% would require long-term institutional maintenance (National Association of Superintendents of Public Residential Facilities, 1972). The indicated long-term stay would be for those critical, high-risk (e.g., low probability of survival) residents who are severely and profoundly retarded as well as physically handicapped, as noted above.

The process of institutionalization is often viewed as a threat by parents of retarded children. It also is often turned to as a "court of last resort," when the parents have utilized all other means to maintain their retarded child in the community, but are no longer able to do so. Whatever the rationale behind this attitude, one way in which it can be dealt with to the benefit of the whole family is through temporary institutionalization. There are distinct times when temporary residential placement becomes a very necessary procedure for the child, and one which can be of immense help. Such short-term placement also can be utilized as an interim procedure or "way station" for troubled, alienated, and maladjusting retarded individuals.

Mentally retarded persons living in the community are taking risks in doing so, for living involves risk for all who live. If we of normal intelligence needed to conduct our daily lives under serious contingencies of "what if" (what if I fall . . . what if I can't . . . what if there's a fire . . . what if I get hurt, and so forth), we might all flee to the protection of an institution.

Again, living in the normal world involves risk; and while retarded people are certainly more prone to danger because of their reduced ability to perceive and to respond, the benefits of living as freely as possible in the world seem worth the risk. However, community living may offer the retarded person more freedom than he himself can tolerate, and therefore an occasional respite from overwhelming community life might be very satisfying. Intermittent residential care, then, is and will continue to be a very real need for those who find that a high degree of freedom is itself intolerable. For others, an occasional and brief retreat to the encompassing protection of a structured institution would be a requisite to permanent, long-term community status. Individuals in the latter category are those who are predominantly dependent, passive, withdrawn, and confused, and whose problems are likely to have been exacerbated by misguided parental actions, or those who may have neurological impairment (Sternlicht & Deutsch, 1971).

But it is also possible that parents may be in need of help to understand and to work patiently with their retarded child. It is the unusual parents who, without some measure of advice and counsel, are able to strike the happy balance between expecting too much and expecting too little of their retarded offspring. Such a child has a larger-than-life impact on the rest of the family, and many factors may militate against his experiencing this happy balance in his home. One study (Kershner, 1970) pointed out that community-based retarded children who receive higher IQ than SQ scores are more likely to become institutionalized, and that thereafter family function improves. A child who has had the interest and indulgence of an accepting family is likely to have a higher SQ than IQ, and he probably will not be viewed as a problem by the family. Thus, it isn't likely he will be placed in a residence, even temporarily. Even such a seemingly neutral factor as birth order can have tremendous influence on the decision to seek institutionalization, temporary or otherwise. If the retarded child is the first-born, he is more likely to be relegated to an institution when younger siblings come to mimic his behavior (Sternlicht, 1966a).

Furthermore, there are times when the parent may be briefly incapacitated and no community resources are immediately available for the retarded child of such an individual, thus necessitating temporary institutionalization. In such cases, the retarded person ought to be housed in a separate building on the institution grounds, rather than co-mingled with other residents. One reason for this procedure is to avoid exposing the community-based child to those physical disorders and infections that may be endemic with any large group of institutionalized persons. Such facilities could be more easily designed with a view toward making easier the child's return to the community. This would be accomplished by providing him with a normalizing routine—toward which the institution as a whole may not yet be geared—and by preventing feelings on the part of the child that he has been "put away."

Alternatives to Institutionalization

It is now widely acknowledged that the costs of institutionalization are very much greater than the costs of community care for retarded people. For instance, costs of caring for retarded individuals in the community in one southern state have been calculated to be *at least* one-third lower than the costs for care in a medical setting (Kaufman, 1971). However, in our previous discussion, we indicated that keeping a retarded child in the community, or the re-integration of the retarded resident into the community, may be much more of a problem for the community than it is for the individuals concerned. As we noted, the problem is the adjustment of the community to the retarded persons in its midst, as evidenced in its reluctance to provide the services that could make it feasible to keep a child in the community or that may make re-integration smooth, efficient, and complete. Sheltered employment opportunities, special education classes, and sociorecreational programs are perhaps the most essential services, but, unfortunately, the development of such programs lags far behind the need (Gordon & Ivey, 1968).

Occupational day programs for adults and occupational training centers for the younger client also are needed for all levels of retardation. However, these are especially necessary for those individuals at a lower level of functioning who are not likely to be given an opportunity for sheltered employment. Such programs can help facilitate social interaction within retarded groups, and between retarded and nonretarded persons, thus promoting the learning of appropriate socially adaptive behavior. Such facilities also serve as self-help and self-care training centers, and they can provide the retarded individual with opportunities to gain a sense of achievement that, for him, otherwise may be very hard to attain. Day centers may become the modal way of delivering needed services to retarded clients. These agencies might be very localized, perhaps even store-front establishments where retarded individuals can participate in day programming which is appropriate to their individual needs. The neighborhood being the "catchment area," the center would attract individuals within a full range of subnormal abilities so that ongoing peer group interaction could occur across levels of retardation, and to some extent, across age levels. While a high degree of skill would be necessary on the part of those supervising the program of the center, there would be opportunity to develop and use many new or innovative teaching and training techniques during the course of the day. Thus, staffs of these centers could be largely made up of paraprofessionals with short-term apprentice-type training, followed by advancement up through the ranks after acquiring further experience.

The alternative of family-care placement also is an extremely viable one, again for individuals demonstrating all degrees of retardation. Success of such placements depend upon factors in the individual, in the placement setting, and in the person with major caretaker responsibility, even as was the case in the original home situation of the retarded person, prior to his institutionalization. Important additional factors are the quality and quantity of support given the foster family by the institution, particularly in terms of encouraging understanding and acceptance of their retarded ward. Especially if the foster family's experience with retardation has been limited, information and counsel needs to be given, and given on a continuing basis, to help the family strike that happy balance between expecting too much or too little from the retarded person in the home. Homemaker services also could be provided, if needed.

Group family care is another very acceptable arrangement, provided sufficient attention is given to the individual needs of each retarded person in the group home and to the harmonious mix of their personalities. The latter variable is especially important because interactions are likely to be extremely intense and highly interdependent.

Another altenative to traditional institutionalization may be that of 5-day boarding schools. Here, the biological or foster parents still retain wardship and total responsibility for the retarded child. During the normal 5-day week, the child would live in a nearby boarding school and participate in a training program (academic or nonacademic) geared to the degree of retarded functioning demonstrated by the child. The child might spend weekends at home. This model would permit families to manage the child in their own homes more easily, as the child would require neither full-time planning by the parents nor permanently separate accommodations in the home. For the child, the benefits would be the opportunity for peer-group learning and social interrelatedness, along with the 2-day-a-week exposure to normal family routines. At the school, the retarded boarder would have privacy as well as his or her own clothing and possessions, including school supplies such as books, paper, crayons, and puzzles. Under such conditions, the retarded child's routine would be approximating the normal "rhythms of life," so important to the normalization principle (Accreditation Council for Facilities for the Mentally Retarded, 1971).

This notion of approximating the normal "rhythms of life" is of primary importance to the general principle of normalization. The rhythms of life have to do with rising from bed at a reasonable hour, one that is relevant to the resident rather than to system convenience. It means eating at established intervals and going to bed at an hour that is in tune with one's bodily needs, rather than at a time that, once again, may be established by the system. It means doing various things on weekends, even as do persons of normal intellect, as well as celebrating special occasions and holidays, and sensing the change of seasons and the normal passage of time. Another appropriate consideration is a program of sex education for community-based retarded individuals. So-called voluntary sterilization and unwanted pregnancies would be replaced by adequate training in the use of contraceptives to avoid unwanted pregnancies. Also, the retarded individuals would be given instruction in the sexual aspects of courtship, and informed about the entire range of social behavior having to do with heterosexual relationships.

Institutionalization may also be circumvented by utilizing existing hotels and motels for group living, with common eating arrangements where necessary, but with the opportunity for independent or paired housekeeping responsibilities, where possible. Appropriate day programming would be crucial to the success of such an arrangement. The location of hotels might be centralized so that day-workshop training or job placement possibilities could be maximized. Risks of long travel would be much reduced in a central city localized setting, although other corresponding risks would have to be acknowledged and the possibility of their occurrence minimized. It is common knowledge that present motels are made deliberately larger than called for by current needs, as an economic expedient against higher construction costs in the future. Therefore, a section of underutilized rooms could be set aside in a local motel for a group of retarded persons, and appropriate day programming could be conducted in the motel's facilities, which also commonly go unused during the day. As an example of such programming, the retarded guests could learn daily housekeeping skills in a setting which offers privacy and a high degree of independence.

Hostels would constitute the next level of supervised community living, with still higher expectations of self-sufficiency for the guest resident. Supervision would be as light-handed as possible, and it would aim toward the complete independence of the retarded guests over a period of time. Hostels can be managed as cooperatively as possible by the residents themselves, with opportunity for each person to learn those everyday tasks that make up independent living. Traveling, sheltered or competitive employment, handling of money, shopping—in short, decision making and the acting upon one's own decisions—would be the focus of training for the retarded residents of a hostel.

To assist in the provision of medical care to community-placed retarded persons with troublesome physical disabilities, a traveling medical clinic service could be established, with the major portion of routine care carried out by a nursing staff, much on the order of a visiting nurse service. This would be especially helpful in the more rural areas where existing medical services may be remote.

For the aged retarded client, community placement is also a currently developing possibility. New data indicate that nearly half of the over-60-year-old group obtain IQs or SQs under 40, and that the mean IQ/SQ score for this group is 39.9 (O'Connor, Justice, & Warren, 1970). Lower-functioning retarded individuals are living longer, necessitating rethinking of the needs of this total group and especially of new ways of meeting those needs, particularly in the sociorecreative sphere. The traditional medical setting for this group of the retarded population allows for a higher probability of wasteful expenditure of facilities in short supply, as well as of restriction in self-help, self-care, and recreational activities among such individuals. Group boarding practices or board-and-care homes may provide the answer for a great many of their number.

FUTURE TRENDS

With increasing tempo, the institution is finding it necessary to coordinate its services with those that are being created in the community, and it will have to function in a specialized manner according to its unique facilities and services.

The trends, therefore, for future development seem clear and unmistakable. The population of the institution will consist more and more of individuals who are profoundly and severely retarded (particularly of young children who meet these criteria), physically disabled, emotionally disturbed and emotionally inadequate, delinquent, homeless, and aged. As a result of this shift in population characteristics, the predominant emphases in the institution will need to be diagnostic, treatment-programming, and therapeutic. Diagnostic services will have to be extended to include those who need short-term observation and eventual referrals to other community agencies. Programmatic and therapeutic services will seek to ameliorate and/or remove those secondary handicaps (physical, psychological, and environmental) which do not permit these individuals to function optimally, as well as to assist them in developing whatever abilities they may have.

Increasingly, the institution also may serve as a laboratory for the exploration of the psychological, biochemical, and neurological roots of mental retardation, and (hopefully) to develop pilot programs in Psychology, Education, Social Service, Physical Therapy, Occupational Therapy, and Recreation for other community services to carry forward. Consultants will be brought in to act as stimulators, and role rotations for staff personnel will be attempted.

Cottage-life departments will seek to provide an appropriate substitute for the parental care so necessary for emotional growth and for the establishment of the philosophy of a therapeutic community, with all workers oriented and dedicated to its purposes, and that philosophy dominating all their activities.

The institution also will move slowly from presently remote, often rural, locations toward major population centers, in order to take full advantage of the needs of residents and parents for each other. And finally, limited services will need to be made available on an ongoing basis for those retarded individuals who may be on institutional waiting lists. In order to meet their objectives, institutions of the future will need to be modifications of existing models or be based on completely new models of design and service.

Modification of Existing Models

One immediate institutional modification which is essential concerns the size of the facility. If the institution is too large, it is quite possible for residents to simply become a statistic within the community. In addition, it becomes nearly impossible for the staff to get to know each retarded resident as an individual member of the (institutional) community, rather than as just another "patient." The concept of "density" also wreaks havoc with effective institutional programming. While there is no generally agreed-upon size that would seem to be most suitable for residential facilities, it would be ideal if institutional capacity could be limited to between 200 and 250 residents, at most. In order to make certain shared services available to such smaller institutions, a number of separate facilities could be ringed about a central Developmental Activities Center, which would then provide appropriate diagnostic/programmatic/therapeutic services for all of the various small institutions bordering it. A certain amount of economy could be effected by making available other centralized services, such as a laundry, bakery, central kitchen, and so forth. In any facility, architectural constraints have to be considered, and therefore building walls, floors, and ceilings should be muffled as much as possible via judicious use of acoustical tile, carpeting, and drapes. Bathroom facilities should be made as inviting as possible, and they should permit individualized privacy as much as is feasible.

Detrimental effects on personality growth result when residents, especially young children, must live 24 hours a day in a medical or quasi-medical setting. In such a surrounding, the primary concern may become the maintenance of an aseptic environment, with training and personal considerations coming second, if at all. The residents may be neat and clean in such a setting, but the living areas are stripped of any homelike furnishings or decorations that could conceivably interfere with the maintenance of this asepsis. The unfortunate aspect of this kind of institutional placement is that the child is seldom able to focus on any one person or to establish the kind of relationship with an adult that could become a vehicle for personality growth or suitable behavior modeling. These negative implications can be overcome through the applications of current principles of normalization, which stress a human, homelike environmental setting.

New Models

An innovative alternative to constricting institutionalization would be cottage or halfway house living for small groups of young retarded adults on the grounds of a facility. The single-level cottages could have five or six double-occupancy bedrooms, a central kitchen-dining area, and a shared living room. The entire cottage would be furnished as a private home might be, with carpeting, comfortable upholstered living room furniture, a fireplace, table linen, and so forth. The dozen or so retarded occupants could share household chores and govern their own cottage life as much as is feasible. Thus, the full range of housekeeping tasks in the cottage—including laundry, mending, cleaning, and cooking—could be done in large part by the residents as training for future, more independent living. The occupants could eventually carry out menu planning and shopping to a large extent, as well as planning cottage group activities and other recreational activities, such as trips.

The advantages of this arrangement would be obvious in the behavior of the residents and their satisfaction with self-governance (Sternlicht, Hammond, & Siegel, 1972). Several adjoining cottages could share in cooperative projects such as gardening and utilizing the particular talents of some of the residents (e.g., appliance repair, sewing). Coed social events across cottages also could be planned and carried out. While the traditional institution strives to keep such social relationships platonic, it is not always successful in doing so; by the same token, a cottage arrangement may conceivably create certain problems. Out-of-wedlock pregnancies do occur among retarded residents, albeit at about one-fifth of the rate they do in the public at large. This translates to 3.15 per thousand among unmarried women between 15 and 44 years of age living in institutions for retarded persons (Wignall & Meredith, 1968). Accordingly, a program of sex education for this group would be indicated, similar in principle to that proposed for the community-based retarded population discussed earlier in this chapter.

If such small residences could be built within the institutional community to accommodate small groups of retarded individuals, then some kind of on-demand transportation system could be made available to these persons (if they are incapable of using public transportation) to assist them in getting to appropriate community activity areas at whatever times are desirable. (In truth, this is a situation that should be available for all institutionalized groups.)

Another new model is that of "building progression" within the institutional complex as an application of behavior-modification techniques. In this proposed arrangement, as residents acquire given adaptive behaviors through behavior modification or behavior-shaping approaches, they progress to a building in which their new level of functioning is expected, and thus ceases to be rewarded. In this new building, another level of functioning is shaped, rewarded, and mastered. At the end of the building progression is the cottage setting, or a program of preparation for an appropriate community placement, depending upon the individual's level of functioning and capability. It is not implied in this model that all residents would advance along a continuum from mastering hand washing to competitive employment, but that (for example) a group of self-care tasks could be mastered, with progression toward one's highest possible level of self-care skills. Mastery of higher-level classes of tasks would be expected and required of higher-functioning residents. This model requires commitment to a full-scale application of behavior modification procedures in all aspects of institutional life.

The application of the principle of a token economy to the management system per se in the institution may provide the base for yet another novel model. This model system, too, requires a complete commitment on the part of the institutional planners and policymakers to behavior modification techniques, a commitment which would include appropriate in-service training for *all* levels of staff. The token economy system is a contingency management arrangement in which individuals receive tokens contingent upon their manifesting appropriate behavior. Inappropriate behavior is either ignored or is punished by removal of tokens. Tokens need to be exchangeable for such primary and secondary reinforcers as candy, favorite foods, and special privileges. That token economies approximate everyday life in the normal population may be an equal point. While this is not a point to be argued here, it seems well enough established that institutionalized persons who have received treatment in a token economy living unit are more likely to be released from the institution, and that, once released, they are more likely to remain in the community (Hunt, Fitzhugh, & Fitzhugh, 1968).

In any modification of present institutional management systems, higher staff-resident ratios, even post-staffing ratios, will not always guarantee that "productive" resident behavior will result. While absenteeism and staff turnover often are tenacious problems for the administration, the amount of chaos created by these difficulties may permit the residents to have more autonomy, whereas a stable complement of attendants often are likely to be overprotective, performing all self-care tasks for residents in the interests of a rigidly organized regimen. The principles of behavior modification should therefore likewise be extended to the staff, by rewarding caretaker personnel on the spot for managing residents habilitatively. Also, achievement of adaptive behavior modification techniques by living unit staff should be made extremely visible, and such achievement should be made obvious to other personnel.

The ideal, of course, is for a full complement of caretaker personnel who will manage residents habilitatively. This ideal requires such personnel to think and behave like behavioral scientists, but without benefit of the broadbased training or the concomitant rewards of prestige, status, or money that attach to the practice of behavioral science. Implicit in the attendant's perception of his position is lack of demonstrated concern on the part of the administration and professional person for the resident in his everyday life. To put someone with the least academic training and least experience in the most direct and influential position with the residents, while the highly trained and highly paid professionals see the resident only briefly and in a professional frame of reference that may or may not be related in any meaningful way to dormitory life, may denote a covert disregard of the resident as a person. Further, as is often the case, when no interpretation of professional findings is made to caretaker personnel, it is easier for them to resist the burden of carrying through recommendations for intervention or planning made by professionals. Therefore, including caretakers in any plan for modification, from the basic planning stages on up, is absolutely necessary, and this implies recognition of the very important role that they play in the development of each resident.

As another new feature, institutions of the future should provide for a resident's advocate—a staff person or volunteer who would have a small client load of a dozen or so residents. This "ombudsman" would plan for the resident's current program of care and for his future placement in the community, coordinating all efforts toward that end. This person also would take an adversary role on behalf of the resident against the institution itself, if necessary, and this advocate would need to be outside, and therefore not threatened by, the existing hierarchical and bureaucratic arrangements that bind the institution together so rigidly that frequently it cannot budge.

SUMMARY

Although logical and persuasive arguments can be made against institutionalization of retarded individuals, the need (and even demand) for such programming continues. Consequently, the concept of residential placement cannot be negated simply by evoking the generalization that all institutions and institutional experiences are de-individualizing, dehumanizing, and counterhabilitative.

Proceeding from the research-supported philosophy that the condition of institutionalization does not constitute a "homogeneous psychological variable," and the conviction that the issue of psychological effects of residential living needs to be examined pragmatically, this chapter has been largely concerned with three major classes of psychological issues pertaining to residential programming for mentally retarded persons: (a) the need for residential services from the respective standpoints of the retarded subject, his family, and the community; (b) the phenomenological nature of the institutional experience and its psycho-social effect on the resident; and (c) sociopsychological variables effecting the resident's discharge back to the community and his consequent adjustment.

The needs of the retarded individual for residential placement were seen as largely revolving around difficulties in coping with the bureaucratic requirements of a modern life and in receiving services in community programs because of profound physical, intellectual, social, or emotional deviance. The family's need to institutionalize a retarded offspring is seen as stemming from such considerations as family stability and intactness, perception of available alternatives, sociopsychological effect of the child on siblings, and especially aggressive and/or maladaptive behavior. With regard to community needs, it was suggested that community interests in maintaining residential facilities were clearly more than economic, since less costly alternatives were not being extensively utilized, and that any practical solution needed to address this issue squarely.

In discussing the intellectual-cognitive, motivational-phenomenological, and social-personal aspects of the institutional experience, it was pointed out that, according to the available literature, (a) under certain conditions, and with given retarded populations, residential living may facilitate (or at least not debilitate) intellectual-cognitive behavior/development, and a negative view concerning this aspect may be too pessimistic; (b) it is possible that the institutional experience may have the effect of reducing the resident's expectancy for failure, enhance his motivational state, and further the utilization of his cognitive resources in problem solving; (c) there is evidence that the resident's self-concept does not inevitably go through a process of mortification and deterioration, and that in certain circumstances his self-esteem may be enhanced in the institution; and (d) residential placement is not invariably restrictive of personal and social growth.

Concerning outcome variables, there are indications that long institutionalization is not necessarily detrimental to later social adjustment and that institutional placement does not inevitably put the former resident at a social and economic disadvantage relative to his noninstitutionalized counterpart.

Attempts at resolving various issues have been described, including innovative forms of institutionalization which would incorporate the principles of individualization, normalization, and preparation for community living. Also discussed were various alternatives to residential care as currently practiced.

As for future trends, it was pointed out that current residential facilities are becoming increasingly populated by more severely and profoundly retarded individuals of all ages as alternatives are developed and implemented for higher functioning persons, both in and out of the institution. It was concluded that the facility of the future—being more responsive to the needs of this changing clientele—will develop innovative staffing patterns along with programs of special benefit to those residents.

REFERENCES

Accreditation Council for Facilities for the Mentally Retarded. *Standards for residential facilities for the mentally retarded.* Chicago: Joint Commission on Accreditation of Hospitals, 1971.

Balla, D. A., Butterfield, E. C., & Zigler, E. Effects of institutionalization on retarded children: A longitudinal cross-institutional investigation. *American Journal of Mental Deficiency,* 1974, *78,* 530-549.

Baumeister, A. A. The American residential institution: Its history and character. In A. A. Baumeister and E. C. Butterfield (Eds.), *Residential facilities for the mentally retarded.* Chicago: Aldine, 1970, pp. 1-28.

Bialer, I. Relationship of mental retardation to emotional disturbance and physical disability. In H. C. Haywood (Ed.), *Social-cultural aspects of mental retardation.* New York: Appleton-Century-Crofts, 1970, pp. 607-660.

Bialer, I., & Cromwell, R. L. Failure as motivation with mentally retarded children. *American Journal of Mental Deficiency,* 1965, *69,* 680-684.

Blatt, B. Purgatory. In R. B. Kugel and W. Wolfensberger (Eds.), *Changing patterns in residential services for the mentally retarded.* Washington, D.C.: President's Committee on Mental Retardation, 1969, pp. 35-49.

Blatt, B. *Exodus from pandemonium: Human abuse and a reformation of public policy.* Boston: Allyn & Bacon, 1970.

Blatt, B. *Souls in extremis: An anthology on victims and victimizers.* Boston: Allyn & Bacon, 1973.

Braginsky, D. D., & Braginsky, B. M. *Hansels and Gretels: Studies of children in institutions for the mentally retarded.* New York: Holt, Rinehart and Winston, 1971.

Butterfield, E. C. The role of environmental factors in the treatment of institutionalized mental retardates. In A. A. Baumeister (Ed.), *Mental retardation: Appraisal, education, and rehabilitation.* Chicago: Aldine, 1967, pp. 120-137.

Butterfield, E. C. Basic facts about public residential facilities for the mentally retarded. In R. B. Kugel and W. Wolfensberger (Eds.), *Changing patterns in residential services for the mentally retarded.* Washington, D.C.: President's Committee on Mental Retardation, 1969, pp. 15-33.

Capobianco, R. J., & Cole, D. A. Social behavior of mentally retarded children. *American Journal of Mental Deficiency,* 1960, *64,* 638-651.

Cleland, C. C., Patton, W. F., & Dickerson, W. L. Sustained versus interrupted institutionalization: II. *American Journal of Mental Deficiency,* 1968, *72,* 815-827.

Cleland, C. C., Swartz, J. D., McGaven, M. L., & Bell, K. F. Voting behavior of institutionalized mentally retarded. *Mental Retardation,* 1973, *11*(4), 31-35.

Collmann, R. D., & Newlyn, D. Changes in Terman-Merrill IQs of mentally retarded children. *American Journal of Mental Deficiency,* 1958, *63,* 307-311.

Colwell, C. N., Richards, E., McCarver, R. B., & Ellis, N. R. Evaluation of self-helf habit training of the profoundly retarded. *Mental Retardation,* 1973, *11*(3), 14-18.

Cromwell, R. L. Success-failure reactions in mentally retarded children. In J. Zubin and G. A. Jervis (Eds.), *Psychopathology of mental development.* New York: Grune & Stratton, 1967, pp. 345-356.

Daly, W. C., & Bellamy, E. E. Historic milestones in mental retardation. *Clinical Pediatrics,* 1969, *8,* 543-547.

Edgerton, R. B. A patient elite: Ethnography in a hospital for the mentally retarded. *American Journal of Mental Deficiency,* 1963, *68,* 372-385.

Edgerton, R. B. *The Cloak of competence: Stigma in the lives of the mentally retarded.* Berkeley: University of California Press, 1967.

Edgerton, R. B., & Dingman, H. F. Good reasons for bad supervision: "Dating" in a hospital for the mentally retarded. *Psychiatric Quarterly Supplement,* 1964, *38,* 221-233.

Edgerton, R. B., & Sabagh, G. From mortification to aggrandizement:

Changing self-concepts in the careers of the mentally retarded. *Psychiatry,* 1962, *25,* 263-272.

Edgerton, R. B., Tarjan, G., & Dingman, H. F. Free enterprise in a captive society. *American Journal of Mental Deficiency,* 1961, *66,* 35-41.

Evans, G. W. Opportunity to communicate and probability of cooperation among mentally retarded children. *American Journal of Mental Deficiency,* 1965, *70,* 276-281.

Forman, M. Social intelligence and the institutionalized adolescent retardate: The influence of the informal social system. *Mental Retardation,* 1970, *8*(2), 12-16.

Gerard, E. O. Exercise of voting rights by the retarded. *Mental Retardation,* 1974, *12*(2), 45-47.

Gordon, L. R., Jr., & Ivey, A. E. Reintegrating institutionalized mental retardates in the community: A descriptive survey. *Community Mental Health Journal,* 1968, *4,* 395-401.

Gorlow, L., Butler, A., & Guthrie, G. M. Correlates of self-attitudes of retardates. *American Journal of Mental Deficiency,* 1963, *67,* 549-555.

Heber, R. F., & Dever, R. B. Research on education and habilitation of the mentally retarded. In H. C. Haywood (Ed.), *Social-cultural aspects of mental retardation.* New York: Appleton-Century-Crofts, 1970, pp. 395-427.

Hunt, J. G., Fitzhugh, L. C., & Fitzhugh, K. B. Teaching "exit-ward" patients appropriate personal appearance by using reinforcement techniques. *American Journal of Mental Deficiency,* 1968, *73,* 41-45.

Jaslow, R. I., Kime, W. L., & Green, M. J. Criteria for admission to institutions for the mentally retarded. *Mental Retardation,* 1966, *4*(4), 2-5.

Kaufman, M. E. Community based alternatives to hospitals for the retarded. Paper presented at the annual meeting of the American Psychological Association, Washington, D.C., September 1971.

Kershner, J. R. Intellectual and social development in relation to family functioning: A longtitudinal comparison of home vs. institutional effects. *American Journal of Mental Deficiency,* 1970, *75,* 276-284.

Klaber, M. M. The retarded and institutions for the retarded—A preliminary research report. In S. B. Sarason and J. Doris, *Psychological problems in mental deficiency* (4th ed.). New York: Harper & Row, 1969, pp. 148-185.

Kniss, J. T., Butler, A., Gorlow, L., & Guthrie, G. M. Ideal self patterns of female retardates. *American Journal of Mental Deficiency,* 1962, *67,* 245-249.

Koch, R., Baerwald, A., McDonald, J., Fishler, K., & Rock, H. The child development traveling clinic project in Southern California. *Mental*

Retardation, 1969, *7*(2), 46-52.

Lawrence, E. A., & Winschel, J. F. Self concept and the retarded: Research and issues. *Exceptional Children,* 1973, *39,* 310-319.

McAfee, R. O., & Cleland, C. C. The discrepancy between self-concept and ideal-self as a measure of psychological adjustment in educable mentally retarded males. *American Journal of Mental Deficiency,* 1965, *70,* 63-68.

McAndrew, C., & Edgerton, R. B. On the possibility of friendship. *American Journal of Mental Deficiency,* 1966, *70,* 612-621.

Meile, R. L., & Burk, H. W. Group relationships among institutional retardates. *American Journal of Mental Deficiency,* 1970, *75,* 268-275.

Mitchell, A. C., & Smeriglio, V. Growth in social competence in institutionalized mentally retarded children. *American Journal of Mental Deficiency,* 1970, *74,* 666-673.

National Association of Superintendents of Public Residential Facilities. *A report of trends in residential services for the mentally retarded.* 1972. (Mimeo)

O'Connor, G., Justice, R. S., & Warren, N. The aged mentally retarded: Institution or community care? *American Journal of Mental Deficiency,* 1970, *75,* 354-360.

Penrose, L. S. *The biology of mental defect* (3rd ed.). London, England: Sidgwick & Jackson, 1963.

Rosen, M., Diggory, J., & Werlinsky, B. E. Goal-setting and expectancy of success in institutionalized and noninstitutionalized mental subnormals. *American Journal of Mental Deficiency,* 1966, *71,* 249-255.

Rosen, M., & Floor, L. The importance attributed to perceived work competence and scholastic achievement by institutionalized retarded persons. *Mental Retardation,* 1970, *8*(5), 33-36.

Rosen, M., Floor, L., & Baxter, D. IQ, academic achievement and community adjustment after discharge from the institution. *Mental Retardation,* 1974, *12*(2), 51-53.

Rosen, M., Halenda, R., Nowakiwska, M., & Floor, L. Employment satisfaction of previously institutionalized mentally subnormal workers. *Mental Retardation,* 1970, *8*(3), 35-40.

Rosen, M., Kivitz, M. S., Clark, G. R., & Floor, L. Prediction of postinstitutional adjustment of mentally retarded adults. *American Journal of Mental Deficiency,* 1970, *74,* 726-734.

Rosen, M., Stallings, L., Floor, L., & Nowakiwska, M. Reliability and stability of Wechsler IQ scores for institutionalized mental subnormals. *American Journal of Mental Deficiency,* 1968, *73,* 218-225.

Ross, R. T. IQ changes in hospitalized mental retardates. *Developmental Psychology,* 1971, *5,* 395-397.

Sachs, L. B., & Frisk, G. C. Longitudinal assessment of the relation between measured intelligence of institutionalized retardates and hospital age. *Developmental Psychology*, 1971, *5*, 541.

Silverstein, A. B. Changes in the measured intelligence of institutionalized retardates as a function of hospital age. *Developmental Psychology*, 1969, *1*, 125-127.

Sternlicht, M. A study of some religious factors as they relate to the institutionalization of retardates. *Psychology*, 1966, *3*(2), 2-3. (a)

Sternlicht, M. *A talk to parents of the mongoloid child.* Staten Island, New York: Staten Island Aid for Retarded Children, 1966. (b)

Sternlicht, M., & Deutsch, M. R. The value of temporary institutionalization in habilitating the mentally retarded. *Mental Retardation*, 1971, *9*(3), 37-38.

Sternlicht, M., & Deutsch, M. R. *Personal development and social behavior in the mentally retarded.* Lexington, Mass.: D.C. Heath, 1972.

Sternlicht, M., Hammond, J., & Siegel, L. Mental retardates prepare for community living. *Hospital and Community Psychiatry*, 1972, *23*(8), 15.

Sternlicht, M., & Siegel, L. Institutional residence and intellectual functioning. *Journal of Mental Deficiency Research*, 1968, *12*, 119-127. (a)

Sternlicht, M., & Siegel, L. Time orientation and friendship patterns of institutionalized retardates. *Journal of Clinical Psychology*, 1968, *24*, 26-27. (b)

Sternlicht, M., & Sullivan, I. *Preparing deaf and blind institutionalized profoundly retarded children for the community.* Staten Island, N.Y.: Willowbrook Developmental Center, 1975.

Weiss, D., & Weinstein, E. Interpersonal tactics among mental retardates. *American Journal of Mental Deficiency*, 1968, *72*, 653-661.

Wignall, C. M., & Meredith, C. E. Illegitimate pregnancies in state institutions. *Archives of General Psychiatry*, 1968, *18*, 580-583.

Windle, C. Prognosis of mental subnormals. *American Journal of Mental Deficiency*, 1962, *66* (Monograph Suppl. 5).

Wolfensberger, W. The origin and nature of our institutional models. In R. B. Kugel and W. Wolfensberger (Eds.), *Changing patterns in residential services for the mentally retarded.* Washington, D.C.: President's Committee on Mental Retardation, 1969, pp. 59-171. (a)

Wolfensberger, W. Twenty predictions about the future of residential services in mental retardation. *Mental Retardation*, 1969, *7*(6), 51-54. (b)

Wolfensberger, W. Will there always be an institution? I: The impact of epidemiological trends. *Mental Retardation*, 1971, *9*(5), 14-20. (a)

Wolfensberger, W. Will there always be an institution? II: The impact of new service models. *Mental Retardation,* 1971, *9*(6), 31-38. (b)

Wolfensberger, W. *The principle of normalization in human services.* Downsview, Canada: National Institute on Mental Retardation, 1972.

Zigler, E. The retarded child as a whole person. In D. K. Routh (Ed.), *The experimental psychology of mental retardation.* Chicago: Aldine, 1973, pp. 231-322.

List of Abbreviations

AA	age acquired
AAMD	American Association on Mental Deficiency
AASF	American Association for the Study of the Feebleminded
ABS	Adaptive Behavior Scale
ABS-PS	Adaptive Behavior Scale (Public School version)
ADL	activities of daily living
ANCOVA	analysis of covariance
APA	American Psychological Association
BI	brain injured
CA	chronological age
CNS	central nervous system
CVC	consonant-vowel-consonant (trigrams)
DSM	Diagnostic and Statistical Manual of Mental Disorders
DNA	deoxyribonucleic acid
DQ	developmental quotient
DSQ	deviation social quotient(s)
ED	extradimensional (shift)
EEG	electrocephalogram
ESN	educationally subnormal children
FAS	free-association strength
GE	generalized expectancy
G-G	Gerjuoy-Gerjuoy
GPU	alpha-*d*-galactose-1-phosphate uridyl tranferase
HA	hospital age (length of institutionalization)
HEW	Health, Education, and Welfare
HGPRT	hypoxanthine-quanine phosphoribosyl tranferase

ID	intradimensional (shift)
IQ	intelligence quotient
ITA	initial teaching alphabet
ITM	inductive-teaching method
K-S	Kolmogorov-Smirnov test
K-R	Kent-Rosanoff
LDCA	learning disability curriculum approach
MA	mental age
MR	mental retardation
mRNA	messenger RNA
NAS	National Academy of Sciences
NBI	nonbrain-injured
P-A	paired associates
P-J	Palmero-Jenkins
PKU	Phenylketonuria
PLDK	Peabody Language Development Kit
RNA	ribonucleic acid
SD	standard deviation
SES	socioeconomic status
SLC	social learning curriculum
SOI	structure of intellect (model)
SQ	social quotient
TACL	training adults for community living
T-L	Thorndike-Lorge
TO	traditional orthography
tRNA	transfer RNA
UAF	university affiliated facility
VSMS	Vineland Social Maturity Scale
WISC	Wechsler Intelligence Scale for Children

Author Index

Subject Index

NT